WILDERNESS

EARTH'S LAST WILD PLACES

PATRICIO ROBLES GIL

EDITOR

RUSSELL A. MITTERMEIER
CRISTINA GOETTSCH MITTERMEIER
JOHN PILGRIM
GUSTAVO FONSECA
WILLIAM R. KONSTANT
THOMAS BROOKS

GORDON MOORE

FOREWORD

CEMEX

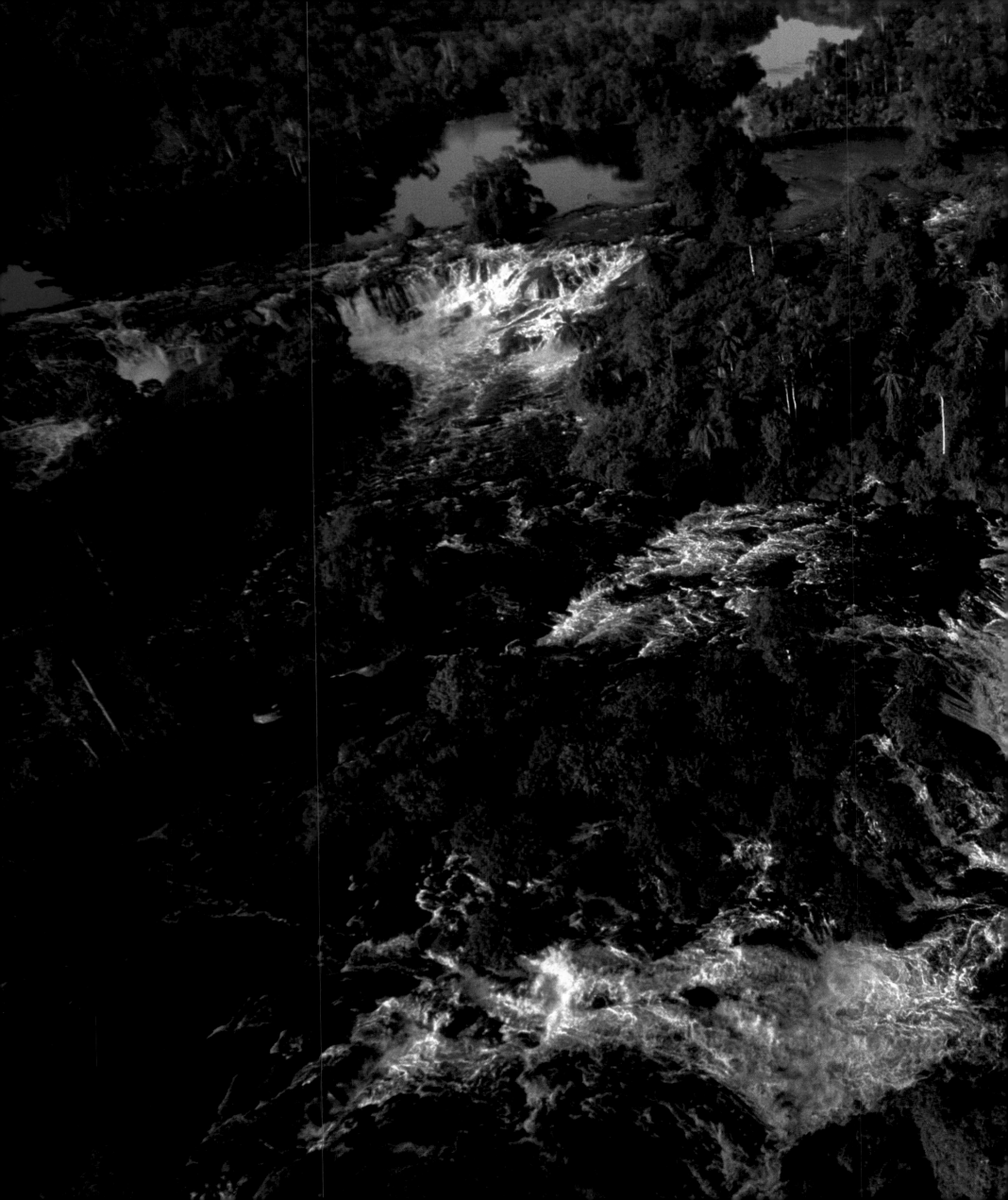

For centuries, humans have referred to primordial nature, to the territories that have eluded their domination, with words such as wild, untamed, virgin, and pristine. Yet these words may not be the most appropriate for describing the vocation of life on Earth and the wide variety of life-forms that inhabit it.

Today that which is wild and fundamental in nature regains its essence, exemplified by the jaguar's gaze. It is that which can not be named because it goes beyond the grasp of humans and their language. It is the longing for original plenitude that echoes in us when we have been touched by its indescribable beauty.

Despite the critical expansion of human activities, there are millions of square kilometers of remote and inaccessible wild lands that have resisted human conquest. Now, keeping them undisturbed will be humanity's greatest victory.

In life on our planet, many generations have come before us and many more will come after. But our generation, precisely, is responsible today for ensuring the future of all the great wilderness areas that still exist, and which CEMEX is proud to present in this book.

CEMEX is a company that has an intimate relationship with certain natural resources. Thus, it has made a commitment to conserve biodiversity. A decade of producing books that make known this planet's natural riches has enabled us to attest to the power of communication in promoting a culture geared to the environment.

We have made great efforts to see to it that our books highlight the most up-to-date conservation strategies; on occasion, our books have disseminated them for the first time. These strategies are currently part of the international environmental agenda and have become obligatory reference points not only for conservationist organizations, but also for government officials and agencies, since they influence their decision-making and create an awareness on the part of society regarding the importance of biodiversity. For the conservationist organizations with which we work, the books we have published have been an excellent vehicle for promoting their conservation strategies. In addition, these volumes have strengthened their negotiating capabilities and have served as effective tools for fund-raising.

The work done by Agrupación Sierra Madre has been crucial during this time, not only as our editor, but also because it has defined proposals for these different projects, given us advice, coordinated the campaigns for presenting these books, and served as a liaison with other organizations.

Conservation International is another organization with which we have had the honor to work. The three priority conservation strategies it has established have been the topics of the books we have been publishing in this series: *Megadiversity* in 1997 and *Hotspots*, which disseminated this concept in 1999. *Wilderness*, the book we are now presenting, completes this trilogy.

Since 1998, Conservation International has been working on the concept of wilderness areas. At first this only included the three major tropical regions —Amazonia, the Congo, and the island of New Guinea. Nevertheless, while this book was being prepared, it was suggested to CI that other ecosystems be discussed such as deserts, wetlands, and polar regions... and a total of 37 regions was selected for this volume.

Three fundamental criteria define wilderness areas: size, state of conservation, and human presence. An important element are the human groups that have lived in these regions for millennia, coexisting with nature. The cultures of those groups depend on the conservation of these areas as their only possibility for survival. Many are the reasons justifying the permanence of Earth's major wilderness areas. It would suffice just to consider that over 90% of its terrestrial biodiversity can be found there. There is a wide range of arguments insisting on their importance, going from economic reasons to ethical and aesthetic ones. At the very center of all of these is human well-being.

At CEMEX we are aware of the responsibility we are assuming to help preserve the planet's biodiversity. That is why we have decided to take another step forward by launching the El Carmen Project, purchasing a tract of 55 000 hectares in the heart of the Chihuahuan Desert. This area includes part of the Sierra de Maderas del Carmen within what have come to be called the "sky-islands." This project entails a greater commitment and, at the same time, a big challenge.

It was a source of great satisfaction to discover that, as a result of the research conducted for this book, it was determined that the deserts of North America —where El Carmen is located— constitute one of the five most important wilderness areas in the world. We have pledged to make a long-term effort to ensure the continuity of biological riches, not only those of El Carmen but also of an entire ecoregion that goes beyond the Mexican-U.S. border. There we hope to contribute to greater coordination between government agencies and civil organizations in these two countries, as well as between their rural communities and ranchers, so as to facilitate the joint work done in this area.

We feel that the need to safeguard our planet's natural territories is most evident; but it is also obvious to us that no action will bear fruit if we fail to set up alliances and unite different efforts. Therefore, it is an honor for us to present, in the introduction of this book, a description of a large number of organizations that work in favor of major wilderness areas from day to day, as a way of demonstrating our recognition of those efforts.

Nature has always held all the answers. It is about time to ask the right questions. We sincerely hope that the readers of this book will find that secret word which names the purest spirit of wilderness.

CEMEX

Wilderness gives a unique and humbling insight into our place in nature. Our world's population of six billion people, all together, represents but one species among perhaps 100 million. In my daily life, I, like a growing proportion of these billions of people, am cocooned by modern human society —offices, highways, malls, cars, e-mail. It is worryingly hard to comprehend that we share our planet with such a wealth of wild species. Only in those regions of the world that persist in a largely natural state —wilderness areas— can we still understand the true magnitude of biodiversity.

Why is this variety of life so important to us? Four reasons stand out. Most immediate is that biodiversity is enormously valuable economically. The planet's biosphere has been valued at \$33 trillion annually —twice the entire global economy. Second, biodiversity is a safety net, buffering us from natural shocks. For example, the world's forests hold 1 146 billion tons of carbon dioxide, nearly as much as is contained in the atmosphere, which if released would fatally disrupt the global climate. Third, biodiversity represents the world's greatest medicine cabinet and chemical laboratory rolled into one. More than 40% of all medicines sold in the U.S.A. are derived directly from plant and animal species; who knows how many cures for cancer, AIDS, and other modern ills remain to be discovered. Finally, the moral and spiritual value of biodiversity is enormous, originating from what E.O. Wilson has called our love of life —*biophilia*— and permeating all world cultures and religions.

Yet this biodiversity, so crucial to the quality of life and even the survival of humankind, is under increasing threat. The last few hundred years of accelerating human population growth and economic development have destroyed the natural habitats of most of the temperate world in the United States, Europe, Russia, and China. Terrifyingly, the focus of destruction has now shifted to the megadiverse tropical hotspots, 25 regions which all together hold more than half of the planet's species. Already, nearly 90% of the natural habitat of the hotspots has been lost; their fantastic biodiversity is now facing its last stand in a mere 1.4% of the world's land area. Only in the wilderness areas does biodiversity still reign supreme. These areas are not only the last places where we can find biological diversity in a pristine state, but also the only remaining lands where indigenous people, representing the world's cultural diversity, maintain at least some semblance of their traditional life-styles in the midst of our increasingly globalized twenty-first-century planet.

This book documents these spectacular wildernesses. Three stand out as by far the most important. Greatest is the renowned rainforest region of Amazonia, holding an incredible 30 000 plant species found nowhere else (that is, 10% of all of the world's species). The two other surviving rainforest expanses —the Congo Forests of Central Africa, and the island of New Guinea— come close behind. This book, however, has revealed that several other, less familiar, wildernesses are also astonishingly biodiverse. Consider, for example, the deserts of northern Mexico and the southwestern U.S. and the Miombo-Mopane woodlands of southern Africa; both of these hold thousands of plant species found nowhere else. Between them, these five wildernesses hold no less than a sixth of all vascular plant species as endemics in a mere 6% of the planet's land. Add to these the hotspots, and we find that at least 61.5% of all vascular plants and 43.2% of all non-fish vertebrates are endemic to only 7.5% of the land surface of this planet. Many more widespread species also occur, and so in total these areas probably represent at least three quarters of terrestrial biodiversity: a remarkable conservation bargain.

In contrast to this biodiversity bargain, most of the other wilderness areas are not particularly diverse. In fact, adding the other 29 wilderness areas in this book to these totals takes us up to more than 54% of Earth's land surface, but only adds a tiny 1.6% of the world's plants and 2.3% of the non-fish vertebrates as endemics. However, these drylands and coldlands have other important values. Apart from anything else, they are crucial in the maintenance of regional ecosystem processes (such as water cycles) and even global ones (for example, carbon sequestration). Maybe most importantly, however, these are the last places on Earth where nature functions fully, free from the influence and impact of modern humankind.

One of the most exciting findings of this study is that 19 of these wilderness areas have human population densities at or less than 1 inhabitant/km^2. Together, the intact portions of these cover an astonishing 57 million km^2, or nearly 40% of the planet's land area, yet have within them less than 43 million people. This is only 0.7% of the world population —roughly equivalent to that of three of the world's larger cities— in an area about the size of the world's six largest countries (Russia, Canada, China, United States, Brazil, and Australia) combined! In other words, a very large portion of planet Earth is still intact, and maintaining it that way should not require great sacrifices —just common sense and a thoughtful approach to development. These are the last places on Earth we can visit and thus understand our origins as a species and see what the world looked like to our ancestors, and also the only places where tribal people can truly retain the option to live as their forebearers have done for millennia. The intrinsic, spiritual, and cultural values of wilderness areas are higher than they have ever been, and will only continue to grow as they themselves become ever more scarce.

We at Conservation International have always taken a two-pronged strategy to the preservation of our planet's biodiversity. Much of our approach involves conservation in the hotspots, fighting to save their threatened species and remnant habitats for current and future generations. Meanwhile, though, we have always recognized that conservation strategy should involve more than reactive fire-fighting. Thus, we have also set the remaining high-biodiversity wilderness areas as conservation targets, and strive to protect these vast areas for the global good. While Conservation International's prime interest in such proactive conservation will always be in the species-rich major tropical wilderness areas (such as Amazonia, the Congo, and New Guinea), in this book we also salute the outstanding work under way by a whole suite of other individuals, organizations, and governments to protect natural habitats wherever they survive. We also salute CEMEX, the publisher of this book and many others, for its vision and commitment to biodiversity conservation, both in Mexico and internationally. We are confident that such global solidarity will ensure the preservation of the Earth's last wild places, to the enrichment of all of our lives.

PETER A. SELIGMANN
Chairman of the Board and CEO
Conservation International

Today, we face a world with unprecedented environmental problems. Driven by rapid population growth and rising resource consumption, humans are transforming the planet fundamentally —whether through massive urbanization, forest destruction, escalating greenhouse gas emissions, or freshwater depletion. The decisions we make about the energy we use, the goods we produce, the food we eat, or the number of children we bear now have implications that extend well beyond our homes, our communities, and even our countries. This has led to a global call for "sustainable development," often defined as a way of living that protects the quality of life for future generations. Achieving sustainable development is arguably the defining challenge of the new millennium.

Unfortunately, the shifting interpretation of sustainable development is progressively marginalizing the role of conservation, with the implication that protecting natural areas is peripheral to or even at odds with sustainable development goals. This book serves as a powerful counterpoint —reminding us of the essential value of wild places and of their critical link to a bright future for humankind.

It is difficult to overstate the biological importance of wilderness areas. On a meaningful scale, they provide ecosystem services such as watershed protection and carbon storage, preserve tremendous reservoirs of biological diversity, and maintain intact assemblages of animals and plants with the ecological processes that link them. Wilderness areas have significant non-biological attributes as well. They are the only remaining places where traditional tribal people have a hope of maintaining their customary life-styles. They offer growing economic value as recreation destinations for an increasingly urbanized world. They have significant spiritual importance, fulfilling our need for what Henry David Thoreau called the "tonic of wildness."

Contrary to popular perception, wilderness areas are not glass houses isolated from modern civilization. Though rarely appreciated, the benefits they provide –biological, cultural, economic, and spiritual— affect every human being on Earth. Conversely, human activities at all levels are having tremendous impacts on them. Climate change, ozone layer depletion, and the spread of toxic chemicals are disturbing even the most remote places, from the Arctic tundra to the Amazonian rainforest. At the same time, local actions like artisanal mining, fuelwood collection, and agricultural encroachment are chipping away at their edges, steadily turning large blocks of intact nature into fragmented landscapes. Despite these pressures, this book reveals that wilderness maintains a foothold in many regions across the planet. In cataloguing Earth's last wild places, it presents as never before the values that these areas sustain while underscoring what we stand to lose should they disappear. After reading these pages, it should be obvious that losing wilderness is simply not an option —that a world without large, unspoiled natural areas is unacceptable and fundamentally inconsistent with the principles of sustainable development.

Success in conserving wilderness will require bold vision and hard choices. Perhaps most important, we must better understand the services that these places provide and then find innovative ways of valuing those services so that they reward conservation efforts, especially those by people living in closest proximity to the areas we are trying to protect. Some economic analyses suggest that worldwide, the value of ecosystem services —such as carbon sequestration, watershed protection, etc.— runs into the trillions of dollars. Yet these contributions are not included in decisions regarding land use in any meaningful way. The millions of people who benefit from them essentially get a free ride, while the local communities that often have the greatest say in maintaining them have little or no economic incentive to do so.

Quantifying the value of intact natural systems is an important step toward changing the common perception that resource exploitation is the only alternative for economic development. Only then can a long-term perspective compete with the short-term benefits derived from destruction of the resource. Wilderness will never endure over the long term if conservation efforts focus on making such utilization "less bad" rather than on eliminating it altogether from our most precious remaining areas.

Of course, the picture is far more complicated than even just this. To effectively conserve wilderness requires transforming private-sector attitudes and practices, improving government policies, and better educating the population about the importance of conservation and the actions they can take in this regard.

There is reason to be hopeful. Attitudes are changing in terms of the need to conserve what remains, at grassroots, corporate, and governmental levels. One example of corporate commitment is that of CEMEX, the sponsor of this book. CEMEX has produced a total of 10 books of this kind since 1993, it has supported many conservation projects in Mexico, and it even has its own private reserve, the magnificent El Carmen Project, which is adjacent to the world-renowned Big Bend National Park in Texas. Other major new financial tools are becoming available as well. Conservation International's new Global Conservation Fund places immediate economic value on protecting wilderness by providing resources to create national parks and establish sustainable funding flows to benefit local communities. The Critical Ecosystems Partnership Fund —a $100-million alliance between The World Bank, the Global Environment Facility, the MacArthur Foundation, and Conservation International— has recently been established to target resources at the "biodiversity hotspots," Earth's most threatened reservoirs of life. The UN Foundation, established by businessman and philanthropist R.E. (Ted) Turner, has established the protection of World Natural Heritage sites as a top priority and is committing significant resources to them. Ford Motor Company has partnered with CI to create the Center for Environmental Leadership in Business in an effort to encourage some of the world's most influential companies to become better environmental citizens.

These initiatives and others like them are starting to make wilderness conservation a more viable option for countries and communities around the world. Perhaps the most encouraging example comes from Suriname, where the government rejected a future of industrial-scale logging and chose instead to create the Central Suriname Nature Reserve, at 1.6 million ha one of the largest protected tracts of truly pristine tropical wilderness in the world. CI, the UN Foundation, the Global Environment Facility, the United Nations Development Programme (UNDP), and other partners worked together to establish a trust fund for the reserve that will provide sustainable funding to ensure its effective management and to provide for local communities. Further efforts are under way to encourage ecotourism and to capture other benefits from Suriname's bold conservation action. Our challenge must be to make Suriname's example the opening chapter in a large volume of successes in protecting Earth's last great wild places.

GORDON MOORE
Co-Founder and Chairman Emeritus,
Intel Corporation

EARTH'S LAST

PACIFIC NORTHWEST

THE NORTHERN ROCKY
MOUNTAINS

THE COLORADO
PLATEAU

THE MOJAVE
DESERT

THE SONORAN
AND BAJA CALIFORNIAN
DESERTS

THE GREATER
CHIHUAHUAN DESERT

THE APPALACHIANS

THE BOREAL
FORESTS

EUROPEAN
MOUNTAINS

THE LLANOS

AMAZONIA

THE SAHARA / SAHEL

THE ARCTIC TUNDRA

THE CAATIINGA

THE CONGO
FORESTS OF
CENTRAL AFRIC

COASTAL DESERTS
OF PERU AND CHILE

THE CHACO

THE PANTANAL

THE NAMIB
DESERT

BAÑADOS DEL ESTE

MAGELLANIC
SUBPOLAR RAINFORESTS

PATAGONIA

WILD PLACES

ASIAN DESERTS

ARABIAN DESERTS

THE SUDD

THE SUNDARBANS

THE SERENGETI

NEW GUINEA

ARNHEM LAND

KIMBERLEY

CAPE YORK

MIOMBO-MOPANE
WOODLANDS
AND GRASSLANDS

THE OKAVANGO

THE KALAHARI
DESERT

AUSTRALIAN DESERTS

TASMANIA

ANTARCTICA

dawn of the twentieth century, fully half are no longer being taught to schoolchildren, which means that they are effectively dead. Furthermore, linguists estimate that within another century the linguistic diversity of the world may be down to as little as 300 languages, or only 5% of what existed in 1900 (Davis 2002). Speakers of a number of those that have survived are going back to their roots and trying to save or recover centuries-old traditions. These traditions are strongly linked to the natural world, and are extremely difficult, if not impossible, to maintain in heavily-impacted ecosystems like the hotspots. In contrast, it is still possible in the largely-intact wilderness areas. Indeed, we believe that the wilderness areas are critical to maintaining human cultural and linguistic diversity for the future.

Of course, we are not advocating that indigenous people freeze their cultures in a utopian, Stone Age paradise. Rather, we believe that they should have the option of maintaining their cultural heritage, while at the same time integrating what is of value from the modern world. Given that many of these cultures have always lived at very low densities in vast natural areas, many of their traditions are strongly linked to the maintenance of large tracts of intact habitat. Indeed, these indigenous cultures are actually "wilderness dependent," with social customs, values, religions, daily sustenance, and language wholly derived from a milieu of wild nature —without the wilderness, they perish. Maintaining life-styles of this kind requires that large reserves or conservation management areas be set aside, and the wilderness areas are usually the only places where this is still possible. Striking examples of such reserves exist in the far north (e.g., Alaska, northern Canada, Greenland), in Amazonia (especially Colombia and Brazil), and in the wilderness areas of Australia (e.g., the Australian Deserts, Cape York, Arnhem Land, and the Kimberley), where groups of a few thousand people live in demarcated indigenous territories millions or even tens of millions of hectares in size.

Wilderness areas also have economic value through *recreational use*. On an increasingly overcrowded planet, people in growing numbers are seeking a "wilderness experience." This can include ecotourism, nature tourism, or adventure tourism, getting out into nature to camp, raft, canoe, hike, observe wildlife, and just "get away from it all," escaping the pressures of modern urban society if only for a short while. Furthermore, they are willing to pay a premium to do so, opening many opportunities to generate foreign exchange for developing countries that have managed to maintain wilderness areas.

Closely associated with recreational use are the *aesthetic and spiritual values* of wilderness, the psychological need to feel connected with nature, and to reestablish one's roots. Most, perhaps all, of the world's religions have a strong empathy with the natural world. This ranges from the pantheistic religions of the East that see nature as part of God, to the Judeo-Christian tradition that sees Creation as displaying the glory and wonder of God, to animistic religions that see the natural world as inhabited by many different spirits. Furthermore, as people become increasingly affluent, the first thing they do is try to reestablish some link with nature, buying a house in the country, taking long trips to wild areas, and the like. To be sure, such "escape" can to a limited extent be achieved even in the smallest natural area. But it reaches its full potential in large areas that are still pristine. This, of course, opens the question of potential conflict between "use" and maintaining the pristine condition of such areas. However, there are many examples of intelligent zoning that makes this not only possible, but highly desirable.

Finally, we believe that maintaining wilderness is one of the most critical *moral imperatives* for human society and culture, and a real test for us as a species. We need to change our personal and societal value systems to place the same importance on the natural world that we do on our own creations, our art, our music, our literature, our languages, our history, even our sports teams and entertainment industries that occupy so much of our attention. The species and ecosystems surrounding us are as much a part of us and our culture as are the things that we have made with our own hands, and their loss would result in a greatly-impoverished world. We would all be horrified if someone burned down the Louvre in Paris or the Metropolitan Museum in New York, or if someone blew up the Pyramids or the Taj Mahal, or even Yankee Stadium, the SuperDome, or the Maracana. In contrast, hardly anyone notices when a forest in Madagascar or the Philippines is chopped down, when an area the size of an American state burns in Amazonia or Indonesia, or when a magnificent bird like Spix's macaw (*Cyanopsitta spixii*) from the Brazilian Caatinga disappears from the wild. Nonetheless, these things happen every year, and represent an irreplaceable loss to human society.

We are not talking about a major overhaul of our value systems, just an incremental change that opens our hearts and minds and makes us realize what a special place planet Earth really is. This might seem far-fetched, but if the adherents of the world's major religions would all follow what their faiths actually teach about the natural world, then the world would be a very different place. In other words, we should conserve wilderness, hotspots, and the full range of other living creatures with which we are so fortunate to share our planet *because, first and foremost, it is good for us, but also because ultimately it is the right thing to do and the only appropriate behavior for civilized twenty-first-century society*.

The Wilderness Concept

Any discussion of wilderness must look at the historical context and acknowledge the many facets and the range of meanings associated with the term. Indeed, the word "wilderness" has deep historical roots, and far-reaching and sometimes controversial implications. Given the many implications of the term and the often visceral reactions it provokes, we believe that it is important to provide a broad view of wilderness conservation and at least begin to take into account the wider sociopolitical context. The discussion that follows therefore summarizes some of the key nonbiological aspects of wilderness, and examines how these many aspects have been integrated in an applied context, i.e., by means of the various legal definitions of wilderness in use throughout the world.

A logical starting point for an inquiry into the meaning of any word is its etymology. As detailed by Roderick Frazier Nash in his classic work *Wilderness and the American Mind* (1967), the word "wilderness" is derived from Teutonic and Norse languages. The word originally comes from "will," which was used in particular to designate something "self-willed" or, more broadly, something that is not easily controlled. "Willed" became wild, referring to a confused or uncontrolled state, and wild was in turn combined with "deor" meaning "animal." Thus, the three components of the word are "wild," "deor," and "ness," which together refer to "a place of wild animals" and, by extension, to a place that humans do not control.

In practical terms, a place that humans do not control is also land that has not been, or can not be, cultivated, which explains the biblical use of the term to describe the desert in the Middle East. It also explains its current definition in the *Concise Oxford English Dictionary* (1999) as "an uncultivated, uninhabited, and inhospitable region." The *Cambridge International Dictionary of English* (1995) further defines "wilderness" as "an area of land that has not been cultivated or had towns and roads built on it, especially because it is difficult to live on it as a result of its extremely cold or hot weather or bad earth." The term's historical roots therefore suggest an absence of agriculture and civilization and, more generally, an environment without discernible human presence.

As Nash (1967) further relates, land that is beyond human control is potentially hostile and consequently inspires an element of fear. Hence the term "bewildered," i.e., the feeling of disorientation and fear one feels when in a wilderness environment, and the term "panic," i.e., the fear of encountering Pan, the Arcadian satyr in Greek mythology who inhabits wild lands. Thus, the earliest associations with the term wilderness in a Western context were negative. Wilderness was uncontrollable, uncultivated, mostly empty, except for demons and monsters and, in the final analysis, frightening.

It was not until the eighteenth and nineteenth centuries, when new scientific understanding suggested that Nature was orderly, and subject to laws that could be ascertained through scientific reasoning, that perceptions began to shift. Anticipating the Romantic movement, Rousseau wrote in *L'homme primitif, Emile,* and other works that Nature provided true freedom, and praised the nobility of the self-sufficient savage; after a trip to Tahiti, Diderot noted the virtues of escaping the artificial confines of civilization for more expansive and inspirational natural horizons.

The wilderness movement gathered momentum throughout the nineteenth century, becoming a full-blown source of inspiration to Romantic and Transcendentalist writers, from Wordsworth, Shelley, and Byron to Thoreau, Whitman, and Emerson. Writers of popular fiction also figured prominently, from James Fenimore Cooper to Jules Verne and Edgar Rice Burroughs. Wilderness became virtuous, a pure alternative to the decadence of civilization, a sanctuary from social ills and corruption, in essence a vast natural cathedral inspiring sublime thoughts. As wilderness increased in popularity, some noticed that it was also decreasing in supply. Romantic rhetoric turned to political action, and a wilderness conservation movement began to take shape, first in the United States, with Muir and Audubon, and later elsewhere.

Charles Darwin, Alfred Russell Wallace, Henry Walter Bates, Prince Maximilian zu Wied-Neuwied, and a host of other explorer-naturalists of the nineteenth century also began to point out the abundance and luxuriance of nature in the tropical regions of the world —adding considerably to the romantic appeal of jungles and other tropical systems. Alfred Bierstadt, Frederic Edwin Church, and others from the Hudson River school of landscape painters also captured the essence of the American wilderness and, to a lesser extent, that of Central and South America, in their magnificent paintings, contributing still further to the positive perception of wilderness.

In the early part of the twentieth century, a handful of science-fiction writers, most notably Edgar Rice Burroughs, further romanticized wilderness through the exploits of Tarzan in the jungles of Africa, David Innes in Pellucidar, the prehistoric world at the Earth's core, Apache Indians in the American West, and a host of other characters. The strong focus on jungles by writers like Burroughs, combined with the writings of the nineteenth-century explorer-naturalists, also served to broaden the geographic scope of the wilderness concept.

In spite of the radical shift in the perception of wilderness beginning in the eighteenth century, the concept continues to generate a fair degree of controversy. For some, very simply, wilderness never became a good thing. Echoing the old dichotomy between farmed land under human control, and wilderness that is not, many farmers and ranchers (e.g., in the western United States) still view wilderness and wild animals as a threat to their livelihoods. More broadly, some view wilderness as anti-progress, and criticize advocates of wilderness as suffering from a kind of retrograde, Luddite impulse that leads them to favor animals and wild places over human needs.

For others, objections to the term are based on its colonial associations. Early colonists described North America and Australia as wilderness, suggesting they were empty of human habitation and, as a result, discounting or ignoring the major indigenous populations living in these vast territories. Describing the land as an empty wilderness conveniently made it *terra nullius*, which consequently establishes a moral imperative to

On pp. 26-27, moose (Alces alces) in Denali National Park, Alaska, U.S.A. during the change of seasons.
© Thomas D. Mangelsen

take over those lands and, worse still, empty them of their inhabitants. Given these colonial connotations, some critics argue that the word itself should not be used, even if they agree that protection of large, pristine areas is necessary, justifiable, and ultimately achievable.

More broadly, though along the same lines as the neocolonial argument above, the concept is criticized as a primarily Western construct that is inconsistent with other cultures and beliefs. The notion that wilderness should be wild and empty and separate from humans, is criticized on the grounds that wilderness not only wasn't empty when it was first "discovered" by Westerners but, to the indigenous populations living in it, it wasn't wild or separate either. Finally, a mix of the arguments above has been articulated against proposals for wilderness conservation in developing countries. Wilderness conservation is branded as a form of neocolonialism, both as an American ideological export unsuited to political and economic realities in other countries and, more concretely, as an attempt to control large areas of land and their indigenous inhabitants.

We disagree with these interpretations of wilderness, and strongly believe that wilderness protection is neither anti-development nor neocolonialist, and that it in no way disrespects the rights and traditions of indigenous people. In fact, we would argue quite strongly that *wilderness protection is very much in the interest of those countries that still possess wilderness, that protection of wilderness is their best long-term economic alternative, and that it is not only entirely consistent with protection of indigenous cultures, it is perhaps their most important tool in achieving recognition of their territorial and legal rights.*

Nonetheless, whether or not one agrees with the criticisms above, it is important to acknowledge them. The range of objections highlights the fact that there are so many views regarding what wilderness is or should be. Indeed, the term causes such a variety of reactions because it means many different things to different people. Consequently, developing a specific, nonbiological definition of the term is not easy.

However, we hasten to point out that this problem is mainly one for English-speaking countries, where the term has had significant use. When one begins to look at Spanish-, Portuguese-, and French-speaking countries, i.e., most of Central and South America and a significant portion of Africa, the term has much less baggage simply because it does not translate well. As Nash points out, "Áreas Salvajes" (Sp.), "Areas Selvagens" (Port.), "Aires Sauvages (Fr.)", or simply "Deserts" (one French translation), quite simply don't carry the same implications as the English "Wilderness" or the German "Wildnis." Others, such as Sertão (Port.), Mata (Port.), and Selva (Sp.), generate some sense of a frontier to be conquered, but again carry neither the same baggage nor the positive connotations that are associated with "Wilderness" in English. Consequently, introduction of a "wilderness concept" in these countries is less emotion-laden than it might be in some of the English-speaking countries.

As Nash argues, one difficulty with establishing a definition for wilderness is that most people think of wilderness as a quality or a value, rather than as something that can be fixed precisely. Thus, even though most people share a general understanding of the term, employing it to refer to a large, remote, and undisturbed natural area, the majority of them would have difficulty explaining exactly how large, how remote, and how undisturbed an area must be to qualify as wilderness. Most people would place an area somewhere on a wilderness spectrum or continuum, using a range of determinants such as size and existence of human infrastructure to guide them. The result is a subjective judgment rather than a scientific classification.

Another reason why pinpointing a definition for wilderness is difficult is that the term is usually defined in relation to the set of objectives that wilderness protection is meant to achieve. Since there are many nonbiological wilderness objectives, ranging from the social to the political to the economic, and even the aesthetic and the spiritual, there is an almost limitless potential for variation in definitions.

Legal and Other Definitions of Wilderness

The many variations in wilderness definitions are perhaps most easily seen in the legal context, where legislative definitions reflect the biases of the drafters towards particular wilderness functions, and the delicate political balancing act that has to be achieved between conservation and other socioeconomic and political priorities. Given that wilderness remains a primarily Anglo-Saxon concept (though it seems to be taking root legally in non-English-speaking European countries as well), wilderness exists as a legislative land-use classification mainly in the United States and Commonwealth countries. We review some of these definitions of wilderness below.

The first mention of the wilderness concept in a regulatory context was in 1929, in Regulation L-20 of the U.S. Department of Agriculture's *National Forest Manual*. This required creation of "… a supplemental series of areas… to be known as primitive areas, and within which will be maintained primitive conditions of environment, transportation, habitation, and subsistence, with a view to conserving the value of such areas for purposes of public education and recreation."

However, the most famous wilderness definition of all is that contained in the Wilderness Act of 1964 in the United States, which set forth the standard for protection of wilderness on federal lands. This statute is not only the first legislative articulation of the wilderness concept, it is also by far the most lyrical. The Act defines wilderness in Section 2 (c) as the following:

"A wilderness, in contrast with those areas where man and his own works dominate the landscape, is hereby recognized as an area where the Earth and its community of life are untrammeled by man, where man himself is a visitor who does not remain. An area of wilderness is further defined to mean in this Act an area of undeveloped Federal land retaining its primeval character and influence, without permanent improvements or human habitation, which is protected and managed so as to preserve its natural conditions and which (1) generally appears to have been affected primarily by the forces of nature, with the imprint of man's work substantially unnoticeable; (2) has outstanding opportunities for solitude or a primitive and unconfined type of recreation; (3) has at least five thousand acres of land or is of sufficient size as to make practicable its preservation and use in an unimpaired condition; and (4) may also contain ecological, geological, or other features of scientific, educational, scenic, or historical value."

This definition has been much commented upon, so we will only briefly point out the many layers included in this short paragraph. The definition first focuses on biological criteria, defining wilderness as land that is unaffected by man, and where natural rather than human processes dominate the landscape. The definition then requires that the land offer potential for solitude and recreation, which is clearly a social rather than a biological criterion. It then proposes a somewhat arbitrary 5 000-acre (2 000-ha) threshold for a wilderness area, while at the same time calling for areas of whatever size necessary to ensure preservation of the land in an unimpaired condition, which suggests an area very much larger than 2 000 ha. Finally, the definition articulates several more social objectives: research and education, aesthetic value, and historical importance. The terminology is somewhat ambiguous (e.g., what is a "permanent improvement" and what does "primeval" mean in a wilderness context?), but on balance, the Wilderness Act opens with a definition that has a strong biological slant.

Section 4 further reinforces Section 2, banning roads, motorized vehicles, and commercial enterprises in wilderness areas, but also makes a number of compromises and softens many of the restrictions enumerated in the definition: use of motor boats or aircrafts is tolerated in a wilderness area if the use of those vehicles was established prior to the wilderness designation; mining exploration in wilderness areas is permitted, and mining leases in effect at the time the Act was passed were "grandfathered" in; grazing rights established prior to the passage of the Act are also allowed to continue. Finally, the President is also given the authority to prospect for water resources, establish and maintain reservoirs, water conservation works, power projects, transmission lines, "and other facilities needed in the public interest."

Despite the compromises struck in Section 4, the Wilderness Act was nonetheless viewed as having set too high a standard, in particular for many forests in eastern states that were not quite pristine enough to be deemed wilderness worthy. To ensure that western states did not monopolize the designation, Congress therefore passed the Eastern Wilderness Act of 1975, establishing 15 eastern forests as wilderness, and calling for review of 17 others for possible wilderness designation. In the Act, Congress noted the urgent need to protect additional lands in the "more populous" eastern United States, where a "growing and more mobile population" and "large-scale industrial and economic growth" were threatening the wilderness character of the lands being designated. The Act cited the need to protect not just the wilderness character of the land but, in particular, the "specific values of solitude, physical and mental challenge, scientific study, inspiration, and primitive recreation for the benefit of all the American people of present and future generations."

Although the Wilderness Act of 1964, like the 1975 Act, mentioned recreation as an objective, the other elements of the definition were mainly biological. Whether the lands were used for recreation was important, but ultimately not the fundamental issue. The key seemed to be that the lands were in pristine condition. If there was another social function of the wilderness designation, besides recreation, it was in providing satisfaction that the lands were protected in an "untrammeled" state, and that their intrinsic value as wilderness was secure. But the emphasis of the definition was clearly on pristine land.

In the 1975 Act, however, wilderness is explicitly intended to serve a much broader range of social functions, e.g., as a sanctuary from a sprawling urban eastern seaboard and as a reserve for future generations, and there is no mention of the criteria in the 1964 Act. This departure from a stricter biological standard is important because it is the path that most other legal definitions of wilderness have also followed.

Indeed, all legislative definitions include a range of social and biological determinants. The mix of factors, of course, varies from country to country, and between provinces or states within countries, but the factors can be summarized relatively easily. They are grouped in the paragraph below, based on a survey of national and provincial wilderness definitions in use in Australia, Canada, New Zealand, South Africa, Finland, and the United States.

Biological criteria include land that is *not substantially modified* (Canada, national and provincial legislation, Finland, United States), *capable of restoration* (New South Wales, Finland, United States), *of sufficient size to maintain its wilderness quality* (New South Wales, British Columbia, Newfoundland, Finland, United States), *unaffected by exotic species* (South Australia, British Columbia, Victoria), *able to evolve without significant human interference and to maintain natural processes* (Queensland, British Columbia, Newfoundland, Finland), or *land that can be restored to a pre-European settlement condition* (South Australia, British Columbia).

Although comparing the definitions in each jurisdiction in detail is not necessary, some commentary is

On p. 31, bonobo family
(Pan paniscus) *at the edge of
a forest, Wamba, Zaire.*
© **Frans Lanting**

On pp. 32-33, Atlantic puffins
(Fratercula artica)*, Iceland.*
© **Patricio Robles Gil** /*Sierra Madre*

TABLE 1. The 37 wilderness areas covered in this book, organized by major biome. Included here are data on total area (km²), percent remaining intact, area protected, percent protected, total human population, population minus urban areas ("wilderness population"), and "wilderness population density" in inhabitants/km².

Category	Wilderness	Total area (km²)	Percentage intact	Area protected (km²)	Percentage protected	Total population	Population minus urban areas	Wilderness population density (inhabitants/km²)
TR	Amazonia	6 683 926	80	557 230	8.3	21 430 115	7 355 126	1.1
TR	Congo	1 725 221	70	140 000	8.1	16 000 000	10 000 000	5.8
TR	New Guinea	828 818	70	94 720	11	6 000 000	4 197 200	5.1
		9 237 965		**791 950**		**43 430 115**	**21 552 326**	
TW/S	Chaco	996 600	70	74 800	7.5	2 810 000	648 693	0.65
TW/S	Caatinga	735 000	70	35 063	4.8	26 696 000	8 305 500	11
TW/S	Miombo/Mopane	1 160 000	90	422 000	36	5 780 000	3 757 000	3.2
TW/S	Serengeti	71 626	70	30 876	43	500 000	480 000	6.7
TW/S	Cape York	121 000	99	15 576	13	12 130	588	0.0050
TW/S	Arnhem Land	137 000	99	25 008	18	15 600	10 600	0.077
TW/S	Kimberley	327 239	95	21 500	6.6	33 000	13 000	0.040
		3 548 465		**624 823**		**35 846 730**	**13 215 381**	
WL	Pantanal	210 000	80	5 669	2.7	1 125 200	81 200	0.38
WL	Llanos	451 474	80	66 473	15	4 444 243	1 065 956	2.4
WL	Bañados del Este	38 500	81	1 083	2.8	200 000	40 000	1.0
WL	Sundarbans	10 000	80	3 133	31	3 000	3 000	0.30
WL	Sudd	179 700	85	10 800	6.0	2 300 000	1 999 000	11
WL	Okavango	16 000	75	4 871	30	59 000	59 000	3.7
		905 674		**92 029**		**8 131 443**	**3 248 156**	
D	North American Deserts	1 416 134	75	320 255	23	15 348 342	4 509 403	3.2
D	Sonora/Baja	324 300	80	86 000	27	2 719 000	1 100 000	3.4
D	Chihuahuan	634 800	70	15 593	2.4	9 288 006	2 306 000	3.6
D	Mojave	130 634	75	44 418	34	1 351 434	490 000	3.8
D	Colorado Plateau	326 400	80	174 244	53	1 989 902	613 403	1.9
D	Coastal Deserts-Peru/Chile	290 032	80	2 284	0.78	14 450 000	2 000 000	6.9
D	Sahara/Sahel	10 970 051	80	380 707	3.5	69 590 712	43 250 045	4.0
	(Sahara only)	(7 780 544)	(85)	(217 167)	(2.8)	(35 187 620)	(10 273 595)	(1.3)
D	Kalahari Desert	588 100	80	90 691	15	1 330 700	419 900	0.71
D	Namib Desert	126 600	95	89 078	70	92 000	6 000	0.047
D	Arabian Deserts	3 250 000	90	270 000	8.3	47 000 000	15 000 000	4.6
D	Central Asian Deserts	5 943 000	80	164 132	2.8	9 000 000	5 500 000	0.93
D	Australian Deserts	3 572 209	90	334 850	9.4	400 000	285 000	0.080
		26 156 126		**1 651 997**		**157 211 754**	**70 970 348**	
TF	Northern Rocky Mountains	570 500	70	97 000	17	1 574 986	1 035 174	1.8
TF	Pacific Northwest	315 000	80	152 000	48	770 000	597 095	1.9
TF	Appalachians	249 000	60	53 000	21	22 000 000	12 450 000	50
TF	Magellanic Forests	147 200	95	105 884	72	253 264	34 501	0.23
TF	European Mountains	372 500	16	59 456	16	8 600 000	2 800 000	7.5
TF	Tasmanian WHWA	13 800	90	13 800	100	8	8	0.000058
		1 668 000		**481 140**		**33 198 258**	**16 916 778**	
HL	Patagonia	550 400	70	22 733	4.1	800 000	200 000	0.36
HL	Boreal Forests	16 179 500	80	614 000	3.8	30 337 925	15 438 546	0.95
HL	Arctic Tundra	8 850 000	90	1 732 500	20	4 288 613	2 385 713	0.27
HL	Antarctica	13 900 000	99	3 484	0.025	1 000	1 000	0.000072
		39 479 900		**2 372 717**		**35 427 538**	**18 025 259**	
	TOTAL	**80 996 130**	**84**	**6 014 656**		**313 245 838**	**143 928 248**	

TR = Tropical Rainforest   TW/S = Tropical Woodland and Savanna   WL = Wetland   D = Desert   TF = Temperate Forest   HL = High Latitude

nonetheless in order. The first critical point is the size of the wilderness area. Some statutes include requirements that would suggest a significant land set-aside. For example, the Queensland Nature Conservation Act, 1992 s. 24, states that the wilderness area must be of sufficient size to "evolve in the absence of significant human interference." Section 6 of the New South Wales Wilderness Act of 1987 requires that the area of land be "of a sufficient size" to ensure that "the area is, together with its plant and animal communities, in a state that has not been substantially modified by humans and their works, or is capable of being restored to such a state."

However, other statutes in Canada, South Africa, New Zealand, and the United States (given that the minimum unit is so small) do not have size requirements. This produces a wide variation in the resulting areas. In New Zealand, for example, the smallest wilderness area is 18 009 ha (Pembroke in the Fiordland National Park), while the largest is 124 753 ha (Glaisnock, also in Fiordland National Park). In the United States, one historic act of Congress, the 1980 Alaska National Interest Lands Conservation Act, created eight new units totaling 13 346 751 ha —an area larger than New York State. On the other hand, Jack Turner notes with dismay in *The Great New Wilderness Debate* (1998) that one third of the wilderness areas in the U.S. are less than 4 047 ha, which makes them smaller than Disney World (10 927 ha). Thus, legal definitions of wilderness produce widely varying results in terms of size of the area protected.

The second point is that wilderness areas in different countries, or even within countries, often have different levels of administrative and/or legislative status or protection, making it somewhat difficult to compare areas with a wilderness designation across political jurisdictions. Under Finland's Wilderness Act, for example, forestry is permitted in specified zones within wilderness areas, though only on an area amounting to less than 5% of the wilderness land base, and some resource use is also allowed in the United States (see above). In Alberta, on the other hand, the Wilderness Areas, Ecological Reserves, and Natural Areas Act of 1981 places wilderness areas completely off limits, even for recreation. In the United States, federal legislation drives wilderness legislation, arguably providing a greater degree of legislative uniformity than in Australia or Canada; on the other hand, wilderness areas are managed by three different Agencies in two different Departments, the Bureau of Lands Management and the National Park Service in the Department of the Interior and the Forest Service in the Department of Agriculture, each applying varying interpretations of what qualifies as wilderness.

In an effort to distinguish between these different levels of protection, and to provide some degree of standardization, the WILD Foundation has established a classification system for wilderness areas. Class 1 designates areas benefiting from full legislative protection, either from national legislation or from state or provincial legislation, essentially amounting to Category 1b in the IUCN protected area classification system. Class 2 designates those areas that are zoned as wilderness though without full legislative protection (e.g., designated via municipal act, or tribal authority, or ministerial authority). Class 3 refers to areas protected by administrative designation within a conservation or natural resource management program (e.g. the Waterberg Wilderness in Namibia or the Palanan Wilderness in the Philippines).

The third point is that given the balancing of factors necessary to determine whether an area qualifies as wilderness and the fact that the ultimate decision on wilderness designation is often awarded to individual politicians, the predominant factors in determining whether any given area is or is not wilderness may not be biological. Thus, there is a clear need for some standardization in the definition of wilderness.

In an attempt to fill this void, IUCN—The World Conservation Union proposed a definition in its "Framework for Protected Areas." The IUCN's definition states that a wilderness area is a:

Large area of unmodified or slightly modified land and/or sea, retaining its natural character and influence, which is protected and managed so as to preserve its natural condition.

In terms of its IUCN classification, wilderness areas fall just after strict scientific reserves, making them Category 1b in the IUCN classification system. The management objectives are:

- *To ensure the enjoyment by future generations of areas largely undisturbed by human action;*
- *To maintain essential natural attributes and qualities, long term;*
- *To provide appropriate public access to best serve the physical and spiritual well-being of visitors while maintaining wilderness; and*
- *To enable indigenous communities to continue living at low density and in balance with available resources to maintain their life-style.*

This definition is a very useful one, and incorporates many of the elements that we consider important. It is also significant in that it recognizes that wilderness areas are not always 100% pristine. However, like the legal definitions discussed here, it focuses on wilderness in the context of protected areas. Our definition, discussed in more detail below, attempts to take the concept to the next level, looking at wilderness in a much broader context.

It is also important to mention the *Frontier Forests* concept developed by the World Resources Institute (Bryant et al. 1997). Although it does not use the term "wilderness" and focuses only on forests, the Frontier Forest definition goes beyond protected areas and presents a vision of intact forests that shares much with our broader definition for wilderness areas in general. Frontier Forests are defined as:

*On pp. 36-37, South American tapir (*Tapirus terrestris*) crossing Tambopata River, southeast Peru.*
© **Kevin Schafer**

TABLE 2. Biodiversity data on the 37 wilderness areas covered in this book, including vascular plant richness and endemism, bird richness and endemism, mammal richness and endemism, reptile richness and endemism, amphibian richness and endemism, and total non-fish vertebrate richness and endemism.

	Vascular plant species			Bird species			Mammal species			Reptile species			Amphibian species			Non-fish vertebrates		
	R	E	%	R	E	%	R	E	%	R	E	%	R	E	%	R	E	%
Amazonia	40 000	30 000	75.0	1 294	260	20.1	427	173	40.5	378	216	57.1	427	364	85.2	2 526	1 013	40.1
Congo	9 750	3 300	33.8	708	10	1.4	270	39	14.4	142	15	10.6	139	28	20.1	1 259	92	7.3
New Guinea	17 000	10 200	60.0	650	334	51.4	233	146	62.7	275	159	57.8	237	215	90.7	1 395	854	61.2
	43 500			**604**			**358**			**390**			**607**			**1 959**		
Chaco	2 000	90	4.5	500	7	1.4	150	12	8.0	117	17	14.5	60	8	13.3	827	44	5.3
Caatinga	1 200	360	30.0	320	8	2.5	148	2	1.4	96	24	25.0	44	0	0.0	608	34	5.6
Miombo/Mopane	8 500	4 600	54.1	938	54	5.8	336	14	4.2	300	68	22.7	138	33	23.9	1 712	169	9.9
Serengeti	1 200	20	1.7	552	1	0.2	186	0	0.0	87	1	1.1	22	0	0.0	847	2	0.2
Cape York	2 400	264	11.0	339	0	0.0	210	4	1.9	127	18	14.2	34	5	14.7	710	27	3.8
Arnhem Land	2 682	100	3.7	293	3	1.0	66	5	7.6	136	13	9.6	26	1	3.8	521	22	4.2
Kimberley	1 977	230	11.6	308	1	0.3	74	4	5.4	183	35	19.1	38	9	23.7	603	49	8.1
	5 664			**74**			**41**			**176**			**56**			**347**		
Pantanal	3 500	0	0.0	423	0	0.0	124	0	0.0	177	0	0.0	41	0	0.0	765	0	0.0
Llanos	3 424	40	1.2	475	1	0.2	198	3	1.5	107	1	0.9	48	6	12.5	828	11	1.3
Bañados del Este	1 300	5	0.4	311	0	0.0	79	0	0.0	33	0	0.0	31	0	0.0	454	0	0.0
Sundarbans	334	0	0.0	174	0	0.0	54	0	0.0	14	0	0.0	3	0	0.0	245	0	0.0
Sudd	1 200	1	0.1	419	0	0.0	91	1	1.1	24	1	4.2	7	0	0.0	541	2	0.4
Okavango	>1 000	0	0.0	450	0	0.0	128	0	0.0	89	1	1.1	36	0	0.0	703	1	0.1
	46			**1**			**4**			**3**			**6**			**14**		
North American Deserts	5 740	>3 240	56.4	>239	>4	1.7	>197	>32	16.2	>225	>93	41.3	>53	>7	13.2	>714	>136	19.0
(Sonora/Baja)	3 300	1 650	50.0	206	4	1.9	108	19	17.6	148	67	45.3	16	2	12.5	478	92	19.2
(Chihuahuan)	3 500	1 000	28.6	235	0	0.0	176	11	6.3	156	24	15.4	46	0	0.0	613	35	5.7
(Mojave)	1 556	389	25.0	230	0	0.0	71	2	2.8	45	2	4.4	14	5	35.7	360	9	2.5
(Colorado Plateau)	2 556	201	7.9	222	0	0.0	107	0	0.0	61	0	0.0	11	0	0.0	401	0	0.0
Coastal Deserts-Peru/Chile	1 379	400	29.0	184	2	1.1	48	6	12.5	52	32	61.5	3	2	66.7	287	42	14.6
Sahara/Sahel	1 660	228	13.7	660	5	0.8	221	35	15.8	126	8	6.3	20	2	10.0	1 027	50	4.9
(Sahara only)	(1 600)	(188)	(11.8)	(360)	(0)	(0.0)	(124)	(14)	(11.3)	(82)	(7)	(8.5)	(12)	(0)	(0.0)	(578)	(21)	(3.6)
Kalahari Desert	500	0	0.0	338	0	0.0	101	0	0.0	88	1	1.1	15	0	0.0	542	1	0.2
Namib Desert	1 200	80	6.7	262	3	1.1	68	2	2.9	74	17	23.0	19	0	0.0	423	22	5.2
Arabian Deserts	3 300	340	10.3	213	2	0.9	102	10	9.8	108	52	48.1	8	4	50.0	431	68	15.8
Central Asian Deserts	2 500	750	30.0	90	6	6.7	82	27	32.9	100	20	20.0	6	0	0.0	278	53	19.1
Australian Deserts	3 000	150	5.0	346	3	0.9	98	14	14.3	340	83	24.4	34	5	14.7	818	105	12.8
	5 188			**25**			**126**			**306**			**20**			**477**		
Northern Rocky Mountains	1 414	22	1.6	264	0	0.0	92	1	1.1	14	0	0.0	14	2	14.3	384	3	0.8
Pacific Northwest	1 088	7	0.6	227	0	0.0	80	3	3.8	8	0	0.0	10	0	0.0	325	3	0.9
Appalachians	3 000	100	3.3	255	0	0.0	78	0	0.0	58	0	0.0	76	21	27.6	467	21	4.5
Magellanic Forests	450	35	7.8	121	0	0.0	43	2	4.7	2	1	50.0	11	2	18.2	177	5	2.8
European Mountains	5 000	>1 000	20.0	317	1	0.3	109	3	2.8	44	2	4.5	36	3	8.3	506	9	1.8
Tasmanian WHWA	924	62	6.7	121	0	0.0	32	2	6.3	13	2	15.4	7	1	14.3	173	5	2.9
	1 226			**1**			**11**			**5**			**29**			**46**		
Patagonia	1 221	296	24.2	211	10	4.7	61	4	6.6	47	19	40.4	12	5	41.7	331	38	11.5
Boreal Forests	2 000	200	10.0	650	0	0.0	196	0	0.0	16	0	0.0	36	0	0.0	898	0	0.0
Arctic Tundra	1 125	100	8.9	379	1	0.3	115	10	8.7	3	0	0.0	10	0	0.0	507	11	2.2
Antarctica	60	0	0.0	49	1	2.0	6	0	0.0	0	0	0.0	0	0	0.0	55	1	1.8
	596			**12**			**14**			**19**			**5**			**50**		
TOTAL	**56 220**			**717**			**554**			**899**			**723**			**2 893**		

R = Richness   E = Endemism   % = Percentage of endemism

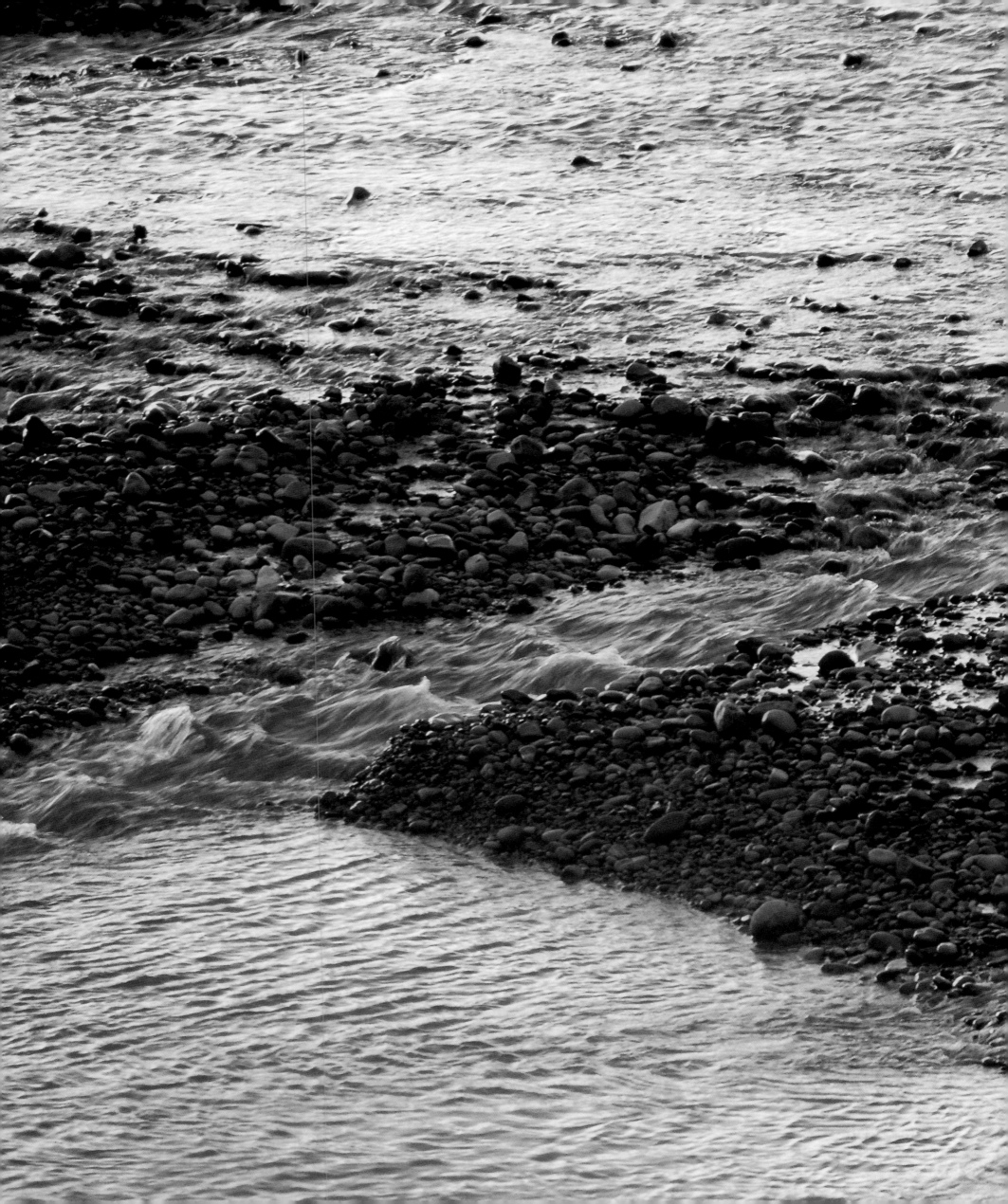

TABLE 3. Wilderness areas with human population densities at or below 1 inhabitant/km².

Wilderness	Total area (km²)	Percentage intact	Area intact	Total population	Population minus urban areas	Population density (inhab./km²)
Amazonia	6 683 926	80	5 347 141	21 430 115	7 355 126	1.1
Chaco	996 600	70	697 620	2 810 000	648 693	0.65
Cape York	121 000	99	119 790	12 130	588	0.0050
Arnhem Land	137 000	99	135 630	15 600	10 600	0.077
Kimberley	327 239	95	310 877	33 000	13 000	0.040
Patagonia	550 400	70	385 280	800 000	200 000	0.36
Pantanal	210 000	80	168 000	1 125 200	81 200	0.38
Bañados del Este	38 500	81	31 185	200 000	40 000	1.0
Sundarbans	10 000	80	8 000	3 000	3 000	0.30
Sahara Desert	7 780 544	85	6 613 462	35 187 620	10 273 595	1.3
Kalahari Desert	588 100	80	470 480	1 330 700	419 900	0.71
Namib Desert	126 600	95	120 270	92 000	6 000	0.047
Central Asian Deserts	5 943 000	80	4 754 400	9 000 000	5 500 000	0.93
Australian Deserts	3 572 209	90	3 214 988	400 000	285 000	0.080
Boreal Forests	16 179 500	80	12 943 600	30 337 925	15 438 546	0.95
Magellanic Forests	147 200	95	139 840	253 264	34 501	0.23
Tasmanian WHWA	13 800	90	12 420	8	8	0.000058
Arctic Tundra	8 850 000	90	7 965 000	4 288 613	2 385 713	0.27
Antarctica	13 900 000	99	13 761 000	1 000	1 000	0.000072
TOTAL	**66 175 618**	**86**	**57 198 983**	**107 320 175**	**42 696 470**	**0.65**

* Amazonia and the Sahara Desert are also included here, even though their population densities, 1.1 and 1.3 inhabitants/km², respectively, are slightly above 1 inhabitant/km².

(>1 500 endemic vascular plants) was the first consideration. This difference recognizes the multiple values of wilderness, and their great importance in other aspects of global environmental health and integrity.

Results of This Study

The current study began by doing a global scan of possible wilderness areas based on the first three criteria mentioned above. A total of 37 areas were selected for further analysis, and fell within nine major biome types: Tropical Rainforests (3), Tropical Woodlands and Savannas (7), Wetlands (6), Deserts (11), Temperate Grasslands (1), Temperate Forests (6), Boreal Forests (1), Arctic Tundra (1), and Antarctica (1). The most important data from this study are presented in Tables 1 and 2, and each region is discussed in detail in the chapters that follow. Tables 3 and 4 provide additional analysis. Table 5 gives global totals for vascular plant, bird, mammal, reptile, and amphibian diversity.

Table 1 presents the wilderness areas by major biome type and summarizes information on size, intactness, area protected, total human population, population outside urban areas, and population density. Size was measured as accurately as possible and, in many cases, made use of work already done by World Wildlife Fund (WWF) in their excellent global ecoregional analysis. Intactness was usually based on the opinion of regional specialists. Area protected was calculated using a variety of information (e.g., Environment Australia 2002a; Castillo and García 2000; Ricardo and Capobianco 2001). Although each chapter provides information on forest

reserves, sustainable use reserves, indigenous lands, and a host of other categories, the data presented in this table include only the strictest forms of protection (IUCN Categories I-IV, including Scientific Reserves/Strict Nature Reserves (I), National Parks/Provincial Parks (II), Natural Monuments/Natural Landmarks, and Nature Conservation Reserves (III), Managed Nature Reserves/Wildlife Sanctuaries (IV)). Human population density for wilderness was calculated by taking the total human population for the region, subtracting the population of cities and towns (if any), and then calculating population density for the resulting rural or "wilderness area population."

Table 2 provides data on diversity and endemism for vascular plants, birds, mammals, reptiles, and amphibians. This information is based on the latest references and on the opinion of experts working in these different regions. Fish and invertebrate data are included in the chapters whenever available; however, since information on these groups was not available for all areas, they have not been included in this table.

Looking at the information presented in Table 1, we see that the wilderness areas described in this book originally covered nearly 81 million km², a huge 54.4% of the land surface of the planet. Of this, about 84%, 68 million km² —around 46% of Earth's land surface— remains largely intact.

Our results also indicate that the human population in these areas is extremely low. Total population of the 37 wilderness areas is estimated at 313 million people, or about 5.2% of the global total (about 6 billion). Urban areas occupy only a tiny portion of this land area and are in the parts of each wilderness that are no longer

On the opposite page, Mount Hagen Highlands Show performer, Papua New Guinea.
© **Cristina Mittermeier**

intact; if the population of these areas is removed from the total, the figure drops to 144 million —a mere 2.4% of Earth's population in nearly half of its land area.

If we look at those wilderness areas that have <1 inhabitant/km² , the results are even more striking (Table 3). If Amazonia (1.1/km²) and the Sahara Desert portion (1.3/km²) of the Sahara/Sahel region are included, we find that all or part of 19 wilderness areas fall into this category. Together, they cover an amazing 66.2 million km², representing 82% of the wilderness areas described in this book and 44.5% of Earth's land surface as a whole. Looking only at the 86% that remains intact, this becomes 57.2 million km², or 38.5% of Earth's land surface. In this vast area, there are only about 42.7 million people, or 0.7% of Earth's human population. *This translates to a human population roughly equivalent to that of three large cities (e.g., New York, Mexico City, and São Paulo) in a land area about the same as that of the world's six largest countries (Russia, Canada, China, United States, Brazil, and Australia) combined —or about six times the size of the United States (including Alaska)!* This does not even take into consideration largely or entirely pristine "mini-wildernesses" within larger wilderness areas that have >1 inhabitant/km² (e.g., the 5 million-ha Selous Game Reserve in the Miombo-Mopane Woodlands, large areas of the Congo and New Guinea, etc.), which would make a significant contribution to the total land area, while adding almost nothing to the human population number.

Size Range of Wilderness Areas

As indicated in Table 1, wilderness areas identified in this study range in size four orders of magnitude from 10 000 km² (1 million ha) to almost 16 million km² (1.6 billion ha). Twenty-five of these range from 10 000-735 000 km², the upper end being about the size of the largest American state (Texas, 691 020 km²), exclusive of Alaska. This is also a range comparable to what remains intact in the 25 hotspots (5 200-356 634 km², Mittermeier et al. 1999). These small to medium-sized wilderness areas include a great mix of biome types and sociopolitical situations. Several are intact areas within highly-developed, densely-populated regions, the best examples being the European Mountains and the Appalachians, which exist as islands in some of the most densely-populated parts of our planet. Other smaller wilderness areas —often partly or entirely within national parks or other protected areas (e.g., Serengeti, Sundarbans)— are in less-developed but still heavily-populated areas and are surrounded by more degraded lands. Still others are largely pristine, far from developed areas, and very low in human population (e.g., Kimberley, Cape York, Arnhem Land, Magellanic Subpolar Forests). Many of these smaller areas are of great national and regional significance because they are relatively large in the context of the country in which they occur, because they are the only represen-

tation of a major biome in a particular country, or because they have great symbolic value and truly "represent" wilderness to the people of that country. Still others have taken on symbolic value at the global level because of their role in the wilderness movement —having sometimes played key roles in defining national wilderness policies or because of their high international name recognition (e.g., the Northern Rockies, the park lands of the Colorado Plateau, the Serengeti, the Tasmanian World Heritage Wilderness Area).

In a number of cases, these smaller wilderness areas have been given international recognition as World Heritage Sites, either in part (Northern Rocky Mountains, Colorado Plateau, Arnhem Land, Sundarbans, Kruger National Park in South Africa) or in their entirety (e.g., the Tasmanian World Heritage Wilderness Area).

Many of the world's most important wetlands are also included here, such as the Pantanal, the Sudd, the Okavango, the Llanos, and the Sundarbans. These areas tend to be low in endemism and moderate in diversity, but often support very high animal biomass and are tremendously important for migratory species.

It is also important to note that we have included in our analyses several areas that do not meet our criterion for population density (European Mountains, Appalachians, Sudd, Serengeti, Caatinga, the Coastal Deserts of Peru and Chile) and two (European Mountains, Appalachians) that also fail to make the cutoff for intactness. We have chosen to include these areas nonetheless because they have wilderness significance for a variety of other reasons. The Appalachians and the European Mountains are symbolically very important as wilderness enclaves in the eastern U.S. and Europe, and have tremendous recreational, aesthetic, and spiritual value to these highly-developed areas. The Serengeti, though not in a developed country, has great global symbolic value as one of the last great strongholds for the Pleistocene megafauna of Africa. The Sudd, the Caatinga, and the Coastal Deserts of Peru and Chile, though they have larger rural populations than other wilderness areas, nonetheless have within them very significant natural areas that are intact and nearly pristine.

An additional 11 wilderness areas fall into the *mega-wilderness* category and are 1 000 000 km² or more in extent, with the largest being Antarctica at 13.9 million km² and the Boreal Forests at 16.2 km² (the Chaco is also included here, although it is just under 1 million km²). These occupy a substantial portion of the land surface of our planet, most of them are still 80%-90% intact, and most have low human population densities. In addition, they provide a host of ecosystem services and thus are critically important to the ecological health and integrity of our planet. However, their terrestrial and freshwater biodiversity is not comparable to that of the much smaller hotspots or the high-biodiversity wilderness areas discussed below, and extinction risk is generally low as well. Among the most significant of these are Antarctica, the Arctic Tundra, the Boreal Forests, the Australian Deserts, the Sahara, and the Central Asian Deserts.

On the opposite page, Yanomami woman grating manioc to get flour. Amazon rainforest, Brazil.
© Victor Englebert

TABLE 4. **High-biodiversity wilderness areas with more than 1 500 endemic vascular plant species. The four North American Deserts covered in individual chapters in this book (Sonoran/Baja Californian, Chihuahuan, Mojave, and Colorado Plateau) are combined as a single unit for purposes of this analysis (see text for explanation). The same is true of the Miombo/Mopane Woodlands and Savannas of Southern Africa and the Okavango, which are also treated as individual chapters, but are combined as single unit for purposes of this analysis.**

	Amazonia	Congo	New Guinea	Miombo/Mopane and Okavango	N. Am. Deserts	Total
Total area (km^2)	6 683 926	1 725 221	828 818	1 176 000	1 416 134	**11 830 099**
Percentage intact	80	70	70	90	75	**78**
Area protected (km^2)	557 230	140 000	94 720	426 871	320 255	**1 539 076**
Percentage protected	8	8	11	36	13	**13**
Population minus urban areas	7 355 126	10 000 000	4 197 200	3 816 000	4 509 403	**29 877 729**
Population density (inhab./km^2)	1.1	5.8	5.1	3.2	3.6	**2.5**
Plant species richness	40 000	9 750	17 000	8 500	5 740	**>70 990**
Plant species endemism	30 000	3 300	10 200	4 600	>3 240	**>51 340**
Bird species richness	1 294	708	650	938	>239	**>1 696**
Bird species endemism	260	10	334	54	>4	**>662**
Mammal species richness	427	270	233	336	>197	**>726**
Mammal species endemism	173	39	146	14	>32	**>404**
Reptile species richness	378	142	275	301	>225	**>784**
Reptile species endemism	216	15	159	69	>93	**>552**
Amphibian species richness	427	139	237	138	>53	**>758**
Amphibian species endemism	364	28	215	33	7	**>647**
Endemic vertebrate species	1 013	92	854	170	136	**>2 265**

High-Biodiversity Wilderness Areas

Finally, we have a handful of wilderness areas that are both large (>750 000 km^2) *and* rich in biodiversity, with levels of endemism (>1 500 endemic plants) comparable to or even exceeding those of the richest and most diverse hotspots —and also being much larger. Not surprisingly, these are few and far between. The most obvious are the three *major tropical rainforest wilderness areas*, Amazonia, the Congo Forests of Central Africa, and the island of New Guinea —places that Conservation International and other international conservation organizations have recognized as global priorities for over a decade.

However, this study has also revealed several surprises. One of these is the Miombo-Mopane Woodlands and Grasslands of Southern Africa, which have very high levels of diversity and endemism in both plants and vertebrates. In this complex, we also include the Okavango Delta. Although it is treated as a separate chapter in this book because of its importance as a major global wetland, it is in reality a subcomponent of the Miombo-Mopane region. The other is the complex of North American Deserts (Sonoran/Baja Californian, Chihuahuan, Mojave, Colorado Plateau) that are located in northern Mexico and adjacent portions of the southwestern U.S. This is by far the richest and most diverse desert region on Earth, and it is particularly high in plant diversity and endemism. Although each of these North American deserts is presented here as an individual chapter because of its great importance, we combine their biodiversity data to make them comparable to the other large desert regions (Australian Deserts, Central Asian Deserts, Arabian Deserts, Sahara/Sahel) covered in this book (Table 4). The Old World desert regions are three to seven times larger than their North American counterparts, but are not nearly as rich in biodiversity.

Combined, these high-biodiversity wilderness areas cover an area of 11 830 099 km^2, of which approximately 8 980 744 km^2 (76%) remains intact. This represents about 6.0% of the land surface of the planet. In this relatively small portion of planet Earth, we have as endemics at least 51 340 vascular plant species, or 17.1% of the global total, and 2 265 non-fish vertebrate species, or 8.2% of the global total. Individual vertebrate groups vary from 6.8% to 12.9% of global endemism, with reptiles at 552 endemic species (6.9% of the global total), birds at 662 species (6.8% of the total), mammals at 404 species (8.4%) and amphibians at 647 species (12.9% of the global total) (Tables 4, 5). This represents a large contribution to global biodiversity and highlights these areas as focal points for biodiversity conservation. By contrast, all the other wilderness areas discussed in this book account for only 4 880 endemic plant species (1.6% of the global total) and 628 non-fish vertebrate species (2.3% of the global total) in 69.2 million km^2, an area nearly six times larger.

These numbers also highlight the great importance of the hotspots, as already outlined in the second book in this series (Mittermeier et al. 1999) and other papers (e.g., Myers et al. 2000). Although what remains of the hotspots only accounts for 1.4% of the planet's land surface, or 23.6% of what remains in the five high-biodiversity wilderness areas, the hotspots have 81 809 more endemic plant species and 7 380 more endemic vertebrates —once again emphasizing their critical role in global biodiversity conservation.

Combining what is found in the hotspots (133 149 endemic plants, 9 645 endemic vertebrates) with what occurs in the five high-biodiversity wilderness areas, we can account for at least 184 489 endemic vascular plant species and 11 910 endemic vertebrate species. This translates to 61.5% of all vascular plants and 43.2% of all non-fish vertebrates endemic to just 7.5% of the land surface of the planet. Clearly, *if the objective is to stem the tide of extinction and have maximum impact on biodiversity conservation at a global level, we must have a two-pronged strategy that focuses simultaneously on the hotspots and on these rich high-biodiversity wilderness areas.*

Protected Areas in Wilderness

Table 1 also summarizes protected area coverage in the wilderness areas. Although several of the smaller areas fall largely or entirely within parks and reserves, total protected area coverage is relatively low. Of the 80 996 130 km² covered by the 37 wilderness areas described here, only 6 014 656 million km², or 7.4%, is in protected areas falling under IUCN categories I-IV. Coverage varies enormously, from minimal (e.g., Antarctica, 0.025%) to total (Tasmanian World Heritage Wilderness Area, 100%), but is inadequate at a global level. Although many of these areas are under no immediate threat, others are increasingly so —especially in the tropical rainforests and the boreal forests. This means that immediate action of the kind being carried out by CI's Global Conservation Fund is urgently required.

Final Thoughts

The value of wilderness areas in conserving global biodiversity is clear. However, their value in providing essential ecosystem services and maintaining the ecological health of our planet, though intuitively obvious to many, remains to be documented in a way that is convincing to global leaders and decision-makers and to the public at large. Nonetheless, we believe that maintenance of these areas in their current condition should be a fundamental component of any attempts to sustainably develop and manage planet Earth for the future. If these wilderness areas occupy more than half of Earth's land surface, yet have only about 2.4% of its human population, it should be possible to maintain them largely intact without deprivation to global society.

Furthermore, if one focuses on those 19 areas that occupy 38.5% of the land surface yet have within them only the population of three large cities (or 0.7% of Earth's population), this point becomes even clearer. Many of these areas are largely uninhabitable or can support only very low human populations; others could conceivably support larger numbers, but only through costly inputs and drastic modification of the environment. At the same time, these areas are the largest and most important providers of ecosystem services in the terrestrial realm, and are fundamental to maintaining our planet's long-term health and stability.

The bottom line is that maintaining much of the world's wilderness intact would not require major sacrifices by human society. Quite the contrary, doing so is critically important to our future well-being. Furthermore, it is not at all in conflict with the commonly-held global

TABLE 5. Global totals for vascular plants, birds, mammals, reptiles, amphibians, and non-fish vertebrates.

	Global total	
Plants	300 000	Prance et al. 2000
Birds	9 785	Clements 2000
Mammals	4 809	Nowak 1999
Reptiles	8 002	Uetz et al. 2002
Amphibians	5 000	Glaw and Köhler 1998
Total non-fish vertebrates	**27 596**	

objective of poverty alleviation, but rather should be seen as a basic element in this noble effort. The exploitation of wilderness is often detrimental to economic development overall in that it diverts scarce resources away from more economically-promising regions. However, even where some kind of wilderness development must proceed, society should give much more thoughtful consideration as to how these wilderness areas are treated. This should include careful placement of extractive industries, implementation of best practices of the highest quality, exclusion of large areas from permanently-destructive activities (e.g., logging) that benefit only a very few, and much more emphasis on protection —not as an esoteric exercise, but as one of the best investments we can ever make in our own future.

What is needed now is a new vision of the value of natural systems, as providers of immensely valuable ecosystem services, such as pollination, watershed maintenance, and carbon sequestration —which are best measured in the trillions of dollars–, as critical elements in the global effort to prevent extinction, and as long-term sources of truly sustainable income through ecotourism, research, direct payments for conservation, and protection activities themselves. All of these, especially the last three, have been grossly undervalued in the past, but are finally coming into their own. We hope that this book, by identifying and highlighting the wide range of wilderness areas that planet Earth fortunately still possesses, can move us along in this positive new direction.

RUSSELL A. MITTERMEIER   ROBERT WALLER
CYRIL KORMOS   PATRICIO ROBLES GIL
CRISTINA G. MITTERMEIER   ADRIAN FORSYTH
JOHN PILGRIM   JIM CANNON
THOMAS BROOKS   JORGEN THOMSEN
WILLIAM R. KONSTANT   GLENN PRICKETT
GUSTAVO FONSECA   MICHAEL TOTTEN
NICHOLAS LAPHAM   SONAL PANDYA
VANCE G. MARTIN   MOHAMED BAKARR
CLAUDE GASCON   RODERIC B. MAST
SIMON STUART   RICHARD RICE
ANTHONY B. RYLANDS   STEPHEN D. NASH
MARIANNE GUERIN-MCMANUS   IAN BOWLES

A number of organizations throughout the world have made wilderness protection their primary objective. In the United States, where the wilderness conservation movement originated and where it is strongest, the leader was the Sierra Club. Founded in 1892, the Sierra Club led early efforts to protect and expand national parks such as Yosemite and Yellowstone, and has continued to play a key role in wilderness protection initiatives in Alaska and the Western United States. In 1993 the Sierra Club launched the Wildlands Campaign, which seeks to protect 100 million acres (40 million ha) by 2003, giving the organization an even more explicit wilderness goal. The Wildlands Campaign targets six priority areas: the Arctic region, as well as the Tongass and Chugach forests in Alaska, the Northern Rockies, the Maine Woods, the Everglades, the Utah Wilderness, and the Sierra Nevada and Sequoia National Forests.

The Wilderness Society was founded in 1935 with the express purpose of saving "from invasion…that extremely minor fraction of outdoor America which yet remains free from mechanical sights and sounds and smells." Among the group's most significant accomplishments is its legislative advocacy work, beginning in the mid-1950s and culminating in the passage of the Wilderness Act of 1964. Like the Sierra Club, The Wilderness Society also played a central role in protecting large portions of Alaska via the Alaska National Interest Lands Conservation Act, and was also at the forefront of the coalition of environmental groups that lobbied the Clinton administration in favor of new wilderness area designations in Utah and California.

Two other organizations, the Natural Resources Defense Council (NRDC) and the Earth Justice Legal Defense Fund (EJLDF, formerly the Sierra Club Legal Defense Fund) deserve mention for the critical roles they played in pioneering new legal doctrines in the courts, both to prevent national treasures from being developed and to ensure that environmental protections are enforced effectively. Although many other organizations, including the Sierra Club and The Wilderness Society, have also used the courts to great effect, NRDC and EJLDF have focused their strategies almost entirely on litigation and their attorneys have played an essential role in developing a substantial and critical body of environmental precedent in state and federal courts.

In addition to the role played by federal land management agencies in managing federal wilderness areas in the United States, the U.S. Forest Service also administers the Aldo Leopold Wilderness Research Institute at the U.S. Forest Service Rocky Mountain Research Station in Montana. The Institute operates under an agreement between the U.S. Forest Service (USFS), the U.S. Geological Survey (USGS), the Bureau of Land Management (BLM), the U.S. Fish and Wildlife Service (USFWS), and the National Park Service (NPS). Established in 1993, the Institute's research agenda focuses primarily on wildlife health in wilderness areas, as well as understanding the effects of recreation, fire, and non-native species on wilderness. These same agencies, with the exception of the USGS, administer the Arthur Carhart National Wilderness Training Center at the University of Montana for training federal land managers responsible for wilderness areas. Also at the University of Montana is the School of Forestry's Wilderness Institute, established in 1974 to study wildlands allocation and management. The Wilderness Institute holds an international seminar cosponsored with the USFS and several other universities, to provide international training. In addition, the institute administers the Wilderness Information Network, and sponsors a number of international wilderness management projects.

The organization that has perhaps the most macro-scale approach to wilderness conservation in the U.S. is the Wildlands Project, which has articulated a long-term vision that would result in the setting aside of approximately half of the North American continent for biodiversity conservation. The Wildland Project's strategy is based on a system of core-protected areas of significant size (up to 25 million hectares) that would be linked together via conservation corridors in which only biodiversity-friendly activities would be permitted. The resulting network would allow for protection of the full range of ecosystems in North America and lead to restoration of large predators, such as bears and wolves, to their original ranges.

A number of regional organizations have adopted the corridor approach at a smaller scale. The Northwest Ecosystem Alliance, for example, focuses on maintaining a Cascades corridor, while American Wildlands works in the Northern Rockies. American Wildland's *Corridors of Life Project* is designed to work in those places with the greatest potential to ensure wildlife movement and genetic exchange in the Northern Rocky Mountains.

Another U.S.-based group that has had an important

On the opposite page,
Tepui Mountains, southeastern
Venezuela.
© **Patricio Robles Gil**/*Sierra Madre*

impact on wilderness protection, both domestically and abroad, is The Nature Conservancy. Founded in 1952, The Nature Conservancy (TNC) has protected close to 90 million acres of land (> 36 million ha), marine, and freshwater systems worldwide. TNC recently launched a campaign entitled "The Last Great Places" to raise $1 billion for 200 critical areas. Due to end in 2003, the campaign to date has raised almost $900 million, and has already made possible protection of the pristine Palmyra Atoll in the South Pacific and expansion of the Noel Kempff Mercado National Park in Bolivia by 2.2 million acres (890 340 ha).

The World Wildlife Fund (WWF, known outside the U.S. as the World Wide Fund for Nature) has also played a major role in wilderness protection over the past four decades. Its global support for conservation has led to the establishment of more than 500 parks and reserves, many of them in wilderness areas and including some of great global importance, such as the Congo's new Sangha River Tri-National Protected Area and Amazonia's Manu National Park. Over the past five years, WWF has focused its conservation actions on the Global 200 ecoregions —a collection of Earth's most outstanding and diverse terrestrial, freshwater, and marine habitats. WWF's Ecoregional Conservation Program aims to conserve the broadest variety of the world's habitats in order to protect the greatest species diversity. Many of WWF's Global 200 sites are featured in this book, including the rainforests of New Guinea, the Serengeti plains, the Sudd wetlands, the Namib desert, the Patagonian steppe, the Sundarbans mangroves, and the boreal forests of the Russian Far East. Furthermore, we used their ecoregions extensively in defining the wilderness areas that we recognize in this book.

At an international scale, the organization that perhaps has done the most to promote the concept of wilderness in recent years is the California-based WILD Foundation, headed by Vance G. Martin. The WILD Foundation provides funding for a number of different mechanisms to further wilderness conservation. These include the very important World Wilderness Congress, which is held every three to five years, and support for field projects and various NGO communication networks. The World Wilderness Congresses, the most recent of which was held in South Africa in November, 2001, have had a significant catalytic effect, helping to create new organizations with a wilderness focus. Among the organizations whose creation the WILD Foundation helped facilitate are The World Wilderness Trust in India, Wilderness Associazione in Italy, The Wilderness Action Group of Southern Africa, and The Wilderness Foundation based in South Africa. The World Wilderness Congresses have also had the important effect of prompting organizations such as the IUCN to take a more systematic approach to defining wilderness. In addition, the WILD Foundation supports conservation projects, ranging from species protection work to large-scale transboundary protection initiatives. Finally, The WILD Foundation produces the *International Journal of Wilderness*, which appears three times a year, and a variety of books on wilderness management and related topics.

The country with the most established wilderness movement outside of the United States is Australia –not surprising, since Australia has one of the largest portions of its land area (4 171 248 km^2, or 54%) in what we consider wilderness. Wilderness protection efforts in Australia in many ways mirror the evolution of the process in the U.S. The movement has comparably early roots, dating back to the formation of the National Parks and Primitive Areas Council in 1932 (the term "primitive" having been borrowed from U.S. Forest Service Regulation L-20, which designated primitive areas in National Forests in 1929). This led to the gazetting of the Tallowa Primitive Reserve in New South Wales in 1934, which is now Morton National Park. One important difference between the Australian and American wilderness organizations is that the Australian NGOs have relatively low levels of funding compared to their American counterparts. On the other hand, as indicated in a 1996 study by the Australian Heritage Commission, Australian groups benefit from a very broad base of public support.

Providing further momentum to wilderness conservation in Australia is the Australian Heritage Commission's National Wilderness Inventory conducted in 1986 (in conjunction with the University of Adelaide, the Environmental Resources Information Network, and state and territory governments) to assess the extent of Australia's wild lands. This inventory, completed in 1994, has provided a guide both for NGOs and for government in mapping a conservation strategy, and has generated a more integrated vision than the wilderness assessments conducted by federal land management agencies in the United States.

The largest Australian NGO dedicated to wilderness conservation is the Wilderness Society, formed in 1976 with the goals of protecting Tasmania's Franklin River and expanding the Southwest National Park (see Tasmania chapter). Since then, it has led the way in protecting over 7 million ha throughout the country, as well as advocating marine protection for the Great Barrier Reef and the Great Australian Bight. The Wilderness Society, now a national organization headquartered in Canberra (ACT) with offices throughout the country, has also been effective in pushing for wilderness legislation, which has now been enacted in most of Australia's states and territories. Inspired by the Wildlands Project in the United States, The Wilderness Society has also launched a WildCountry campaign, which provides a 50-year vision for wilderness corridors

On the opposite page, "The Pinnacles," aerial view. The limestone pillars were formed underground by vertical seepage; the dissolved lime cemented and shifting sand dunes exposed pillars in the past 200 years, Namburg National Park, Western Australia.
© **Jean-Paul Ferrero**/*Auscape*

AMAZONIA

The vast Amazonian region is the ultimate biodiversity-rich major tropical wilderness area. It is one of the largest mega-wildernesses overall, and in terms of forested regions is exceeded only by the vast boreal forests of Russia, Canada, and Alaska that span two continents. However, in terms of biodiversity, there is no other wilderness area that comes close. Amazonia simply exceeds all other regions described in this book in all categories for which comparative information is available, including vascular plants, birds, mammals, reptiles, amphibians, and freshwater fish. When combined with the comparably spectacular Tropical Andes Hotspot immediately adjacent and connected to Amazonia at its western edge, the sum total of biodiversity in these two regions makes northern South America the richest region on Earth for terrestrial and freshwater biodiversity. Furthermore, although parts of the region have been heavily impacted over the past three decades, most notably at its southern fringes in Brazil where the agricultural frontier is rapidly advancing northward, the vast majority of Amazonia is still intact and still offers opportunities for large-scale biodiversity conservation that simply no longer exist in other parts of the world.

Definitions of the extent of Amazonia vary widely. Many define it in terms of the extent of the continuous tropical forest (accepting enclaves of non-forest formations such as savannas) or base it on distributions of certain key groups of animals or plants, while others describe it using a combination of climatic and physiographic features. Meggers (1971, 1973), for example, defines it by physical and climatic features, calling it: "that portion of South America east of the Andes that lies below 1 500 m in elevation, where rain falls on 130 or more days per year, where relative humidity normally exceeds 80%, and where annual average temperature variations do not exceed 3°C. These characteristics prevail over most of the Amazon drainage, with the exception of the headwaters of the longer tributaries, and extend over the Guianas to the mouth of the Orinoco. Vegetation consists of tropical rainforest broken by small enclaves of savanna where the soil is too porous to retain moisture during the dry months" (Meggers 1973).

Brazilian botanists Ducke and Black (1953) defined Amazonia on the basis of the distribution of the genus *Hevea*, the economically-important rubber trees.

Mammalogists Cabrera and Yepes (1940) define Amazonia ("Distrito Amazônico" in their terminology) by the presence of some characteristic mammal species, such as the marsupial *Marmosa noctivaga* and certain rodents *(Sciurillus pusillus, Dactilomys* spp., *Mesomys* spp)*. Fittkau (1971, 1974) equates Amazonia with the zoogeographical province Hylaea of the Neotropical Guiana-Brazilian subregion, and includes in it the entire tropical forest region and its enclaves, as well as the transitional regions between forest and other drier areas to the north and south.

These definitions all refer to roughly the same area, the main differences being in where the northwestern and southern boundaries are placed. The southern boundary is especially difficult to determine because of an extensive system of interdigitating peninsulas of savanna and forest located roughly between 48° and 62°W (Hueck 1972), and today is complicated still further by the large-scale conversion and degradation that is taking place in this region in particular.

For the purposes of this book and our vision of the world's wilderness areas, we define Amazonia as the full extent of the *Hylaea* (a term of Greek origin that refers to "a rainy wooded area," and was first used by Humboldt to refer to the Amazon forest; Stone 1985), that vast region of tropical rainforest of northern

South America, including the forests of great drainage basins of the Rio Amazonas and its tributaries, the forests of the southern (in Venezuela) and southwestern (in Colombia) tributaries of the Río Orinoco, and the forests of the Guianas, the rivers of which drain into the Atlantic. The region is bordered on the west by the foothills of the Andes up to 500 m (above which begins the Tropical Andes Hotspot), on the east and northeast by the Atlantic, on the northwest by a transition zone between forest and the *Llanos* of Colombia and Venezuela, which in Venezuela at least is clearly demarcated by the mainstream of the Orinoco, and to the south by an extensive transition zone between rainforest and the Cerrado formations of central Brazil and other dry forest formations of Bolivia. The Atlantic forest region of eastern Brazil is separated from Amazonia by the Cerrado (sclerophytic savanna and savanna forest) of central Brazil and the Caatinga (tropical xerophytic and deciduous thorn scrub) of northeastern Brazil, and is not part of Amazonia. Included within the boundaries of Amazonia are a number of natural non-forest formations, including terra firme and inundated savannas, scrub vegetation in inundated areas and on white sand soils, coastal scrub (*restinga*), and subalpine vegetation on rock outcrops (Rizzini et al. 1988) and, along its northeastern edges, a series of coastal wetlands, swamplands, and mangroves.

This definition corresponds most closely to that of Ducke and Black (1953) and Hueck (1972), but includes the Orinoco Delta, which is left out of several other definitions, along with the large forested area south of the Río Orinoco referred to as the Pantepui region. The Pantepui includes the major peaks and sandstone table mountains (*tepuis*) of the Guayana Highlands, that occur mainly in Venezuela but also extend into the Pakaraima and Parima mountain ranges in Guyana and Brazil and with outliers in Suriname (the Tafelberg), Brazil (the 3 045-m Pico da Neblina and the 2 992-m Pico 31 de Março), and to the west, where the Serranías of Chiribiquete and La Macarena are considered "Colombian *tepuyes*." These mountains, including Monte Roraima, Auyan Tepui, and many others, together with vast savanna areas such as the Gran Sabana (35 000 km² of the Río Caroni Basin at the base of the eastern Venezuelan tepuis), lowland montane forests, cloud forests, and subalpine herbaceous vegetation on rock outcrops, provide for one of the most spectacular landscapes on Earth.

Interpretations of the extent of Amazonia vary considerably, and range from 6 million to more than 7 million km² (for example, Cabrera and Yepes 1940; Fittkau 1971, 1974; Pires 1974). There is also the official, political and legal definition of Amazonia in Brazil (*Amazônia Legal*), which covers 4 975 527 km² but includes in it 730 000 km² of the Cerrado and the Pantanal to the south and is therefore considerably larger than the 4 245 278 km² that we consider Brazilian Amazonia.

For purposes of this analysis, we define the extent of Amazonia using ecoregions defined by the World Wildlife Fund —a total of 34 in all. Of these, 17 are trop-ical moist broadleaf forests, mostly delimited by the larger rivers due to their importance as boundaries to species ranges (Ayres and Clutton-Brock 1992; Hershkovitz 1977, 1983); five are white-water flooded forest (*várzea*) regions; one is white sand forest (*campinarana*) in the Rio Negro region; two are coastal swamp forests; four are coastal mangrove formations at the northern and eastern fringes of Amazonia; two are major savanna enclaves within the Hylaea; one is in the *tepui* (sandstone table mountain) region of the Guayana Highlands of southern Venezuela; and two are in transitional tropical dry forests.

Starting in the north at the Delta of the Orinoco and proceeding clockwise through the region, the 34 ecoregions in what we are calling Amazonia are as follows: Orinoco Delta Swamp Forests (NT0147) (28 147 km²); Orinoco Wetlands (NT0906) (6 014 km²); Guayanan Highlands Moist Forests (NT0124) (337 587 km²); Tepuis (NA0169) (48 845 km²); Guyanan Savanna (NT0707) (104 355 km²); Guianan Moist Forests (NT0125) (512 889 km²); Uatumã-Trombetas Moist Forests (NT0173) (473 118 km²); Marajó Várzea (NT0138) (88 707 km²); Gurupá Várzea (NT0126) (9 926 km²); Tocantins-Araguaia-Maranhão Moist Forests (NT0170) (193 637 km²); Pará Mangroves (NT1427) (4 413 km²); Maranhão Babaçu Forests (NT0139) (142 270 km²); Xingú-Tocantins-Araguaia Moist Forests (NT0180) (266 241 km²); Tapajós-Xingú Moist Forests (NT0168) (336 576 km²); Madeira-Tapajós Moist Forests (NT0135) (719 692 km²); Purus-Madeira Moist Forests (NT0157) (174 016 km²); Monte Alegre Várzea (NT0141) (66 803 km²); Purus Várzea (NT0156) (177 550 km²); Juruá-Purus Moist Forests (NT0133) (242 563 km²); Southwest Amazon Moist Forests (NT0166) (749 749 km²); Beni Savanna (NT0702) (126 066 km²); Ucayali Moist Forests (NT0174) (114 937 km²); Iquitos Várzea (NT0128) (115 037 km²); Napo Moist Forests (NT0142) (251 729 km²); Solimões-Japurá Moist Forests (NT0163) (167 659 km²); Caquetá Moist Forests (NT0107) (184 193 km²); Japurá-Solimões-Negro Moist Forests (NT0132) (269 665 km²); Negro-Branco Moist Forests (NT0143) (212 857 km²); Rio Negro Campinarana (NT0158) (80 864 km²); Amapá Mangroves (NT1402) (1 562 km²); Guianan Mangroves (NT1411) (14 570 km²); Paramaribo/Guianan Freshwater Swamp Forests (NT0149) (7 724 km²); Maranhão Mangroves (NT1419) (11 309 km²), and an additional transitional area in the far south, the Mato Grosso Tropical Dry Forests (NT0140) (414 007 km²). Together, these areas cover a total of 6 241 270 km², and with the transitional area of Mato Grosso dry forest, the total comes to 6 655 277 km². In addition, there is a total of 14 226 km² of shared riverine areas and other portions of the region not readily attributable to any one country or ecoregion. Using GIS coverage of these ecoregions and rivers and accurate atlas data on the three countries of the Guianas, Amazonia as defined here covers 6 683 926 km².

Amazonia is shared by a total of nine countries. Based on these ecoregions, Brazil has by far the largest area, with 4 245 278 km², or 63.7%. Peru is next with 661 331

Above, black uakari monkey (Cacajao melanocephalus) from the Rio Negro region of Brazilian Amazonia. The uakaris are the only short-tailed monkeys in the Neotropics.
© **Erwin & Peggy Bauer**/*Auscape*

On the opposite page, white uakari monkey (Cacajao calvus calvus) from the Mamiraua Sustainable Development Reserve, state of Amazonas, Brazil. This unusual monkey is restricted to a relatively small area among the Rio Solimões, the Rio Japurá and the Rio Auati-Paraná.
© **Luiz Claudio Marigo**

tee, *Trichechus inunguis*, and the pink Amazon River dolphin, *Inia geoffrensis*.

Many of the mammal groups are currently undergoing systematic revisions, their distributions are poorly known, and many new species are being described. It is possible to predict that more precise information on distributions based on regional analyses will increase the number of mammal species to nearly 500. For example, the Fundación Puerto Rastrojo (2001) in Colombia documents 408 species and 483 taxa just for Colombian Amazonia, although this may include some areas within our Tropical Andes Hotspot. Silva et al. (2001) listed 331 mammal species and Fonseca et al. (1999), 350 for Brazilian Amazonia alone.

Of the 1 294 species of birds that regularly occur in Amazonia, 260 (20%) can be considered endemic (CI, unpublished data). The rich diversity of birds in Amazonia is not evenly distributed, with higher species richness in the wetter regions towards the west. Typical Amazonian groups include the tinamous, the ovenbirds (Furnariidae; 87 species, 20 endemic), the antbirds (122 species, 53 endemic), and the tanagers (71 species, 12 endemic), with the largest contribution to species richness being made up by the multitude of flycatchers (172 species, 25 endemic).

Reptiles are represented by at least 378 species, most of them lizards (138 species) and snakes (196 species), but also including 21 turtles, 5 crocodilians, and 18 amphisbaenids (R.C. Vogt, pers. comm., 2001; M. Rodrigues, pers. comm., 2001). Of these, at least 216 are endemic, including 111 lizards, 82 snakes, seven turtles, three crocodilians, and 13 amphisbaenids.

Amphibian diversity is currently estimated at 427 species, of which 364 are endemic. This includes 406 frogs, 348 of them endemic, 19 caecilians (Gymnophonia), of which 16 are endemic, and two non-endemic salamanders (*Bolitoglossa altamazonica, B. peruviana*). Although only these two salamander species are officially recorded from the region, it is highly likely that additional species will be discovered in the future. As in many other parts of the tropical world, many new amphibian species are likely to be discovered in Amazonia as more research is conducted —meaning that the above numbers are almost certain to increase dramatically.

The size of the basin, the enormous complexity and variety of aquatic ecosystems, and especially the vast areas of inundated forest contribute to the Amazon having the richest freshwater fish fauna in the world (Junk 1983; Junk and Furch 1985; Junk et al. 1989). Roughly 3 000 species have been described, but estimates of total diversity range as high as 9 000; the described species alone represent 27-30% of the world's known freshwater fish fauna (Goulding 1980; Menezes 1996; B. Chernoff, pers. comm., 2002). The recognition of three principal river types, white-water, black-water, and clear-water, by Alfred Russel Wallace (1853a, 1853b), is still a useful classification, and corresponds well not only to their chemical properties, but also to their biology and productivity. The biological communities differ between the larger rivers and also the affluents of each (Goulding et al. 1988). The differences in chemical properties and biological communities of even the creeks (known in Brazil as *igarapés*) are at least as large as between the major rivers. Waterfalls and cataracts are environments for specialists, and the fish fauna of creeks with rapids is quite different from that of slow-running streams in the lowlands. Other aquatic ecosystems include closed shallow lakes, common in the savannas of Roraima, open shallow fluvial lakes such as the numerous oxbow lakes or *cochas* of the white-water rivers (Salo et al. 1986), some few deep closed lakes in the iron-rich soils of the savannas (*cangas*) of Carajás, Pará and the Morro dos Seis Lagos in the northwest of the basin near Pico da Neblina, and floodplains, swamps, and brackish coastal waters. Human-made aquatic environments include fishponds, rice paddies and artificial pools, and wastewater arising from road construction. On a grand scale, there are also the huge human-made lakes resulting from hydroelectric dams such as Tucuruí on the Rio Tocantins, Samuel on the Rio Ji-Paraná, and Balbina on the Rio Uatumã in Brazilian Amazonia, Guri in Venezuela, and Brokopondo in Suriname.

There are also a number of marine groups that have adapted to fresh water in this region. They include at least 50 species in 14 families, noteworthy among them being the bull shark (*Carcharinus leucas*), occurring upriver as far as Manaus; the freshwater stingrays (Potamotrygonidae), commonly found along sandy shallows of rivers such as the Rio Tapajós and even in far flung streams up the farthest tributaries of the Rio Negro; herrings (Clupeidae); mullets (Mugilidae); and anchovies (Engraulidae).

Invertebrates are also incredibly diverse in Amazonia, but the vast majority remains undescribed by science. For example, only 250 millipede species (Diplopoda) have been described, but it is possible to estimate that 5 000-7 000 species exist in the basin (Adis and Harvey 2000). Likewise, about 1 000 spiders have been described in the Amazon, but projections indicate a true number of at least 4 000-8 000; 472 species have been collected from a single terra firme site of 15 km² in the Ducke Forest Reserve, to the north of Manaus (Overal 2001). Butterflies and bees are better known, and the Amazonian faunas of each represent large percentages of global totals. Brazilian Amazonia's 1 800 butterfly species account for 24% of the world total of about 7 500, and its 2 500-3 000 bee species are between 8 and 10% of the world total for that group (Overal, *op. cit.*). A single locality in Tambopata, Peru supports 1 437 species of butterfly, double the total for the entire North American continent (Foster et al. 1994). Another locality in Peru, the Río Amigos Biological Station in Madre de Dios, has a dung beetle fauna (Coleoptera: Scarabidae: Scarabaeinae) of 136 species, two to three times the alpha richness of dung beetle communities in moist forest areas in Central America and the Old World tropics (A. Forsyth, unpublished data).

Particularly high arthropod diversity is found in tree

canopies and, due to their very low vagility, species are frequently documented from only single forest types and even single trees. Erwin (1983) surveyed canopy beetles in four different forest types near Manaus: white-water flooded forest, black-water flooded forest, mixed (black and white) flooded forest, and terra firme

distinct diversity gradient from east to west, with species richness being highest close to the Andes (Gentry 1988), a characteristic that is shared with many animal species as well (Brown 1999). Gentry (1988) attributes this to richer soils, higher rainfall, and less seasonality in the climates of the upper Amazon (Junk

dated forest *igapó* (Prance 1979). Seasonal *várzea*, as its name suggests, is inundated for varying periods each year. It has an uneven and broken canopy, and lower tree species diversity than terra firme forest. Comparing it to *igapó* forest, the trees are more deciduous, the density of trees is higher, and it has fewer epiphytes (the orchids and bromeliads of the *igapó* are exceptional). The two formations share very few plant species, one of the reasons being the nutrient-rich substrate of the *várzea* (renewed at each flood) contrasting with the extremely nutrient-poor sandy soils of the *igapó*. The seasonal *igapó* has a more even and closed canopy, a lower diversity of tree species than *várzea*, and leaves are typically smaller and scleromorphic. Permanently-flooded *várzea* and *igapó* occur along watercourses throughout the basin. They are swamps and often take the form of palm forests dominated by *Mauritia* or *Euterpe*. The fifth form of flooded forest is tidal *várzea*, similar to seasonal *várzea*, but inundated twice a day along the banks of the Amazon and the lower parts of its tributaries up to 100 km from the delta. Floodplain forests are again similar to *várzea*, but inundated only at times of irregular and very heavy rainfall. Lastly there are the mangrove forests of the Atlantic coast, and particularly the deltas of Amazon and the Orinoco, but also along the coasts of the Guianas, and the states of Amapá and Maranhão in Brazil.

Terra firme or dryland rainforests are not affected by seasonal fluctuations in river level. They make up about 51% of the Amazonian forest (Pires 1974; Prance 2001). Even the youngest soils of the terra firme date back to the Tertiary, and the soils of the Guayana and Brazilian Shields, where much of this forest occurs, are among the oldest geological formations on Earth. The soils of the terra firme have therefore been exposed to millions of years of leaching and are generally poor. Most of their nutrients are locked up in the living plants, and these plants are unsurpassed in their ability to capture and store nutrients from the air and from whatever decaying organic matter may be available. On top of this, plants have evolved many chemical defenses, poisonous compounds, to protect against nutrient loss to herbivorous animals in this low primary productivity habitat (Janzen 1974). In general, these forests occur in areas where seasonality is marked and where annual rainfall does not exceed 2 000 mm. Biomass and species diversity are very high, the canopy is closed, understories are sparse, and the number of lianas is limited. Two types have been distinguished. Lowland forests occur on Tertiary sediments at altitudes below 250 m, with a closed canopy of around 30 m and emergents reaching 50 m. Hill forests replace lowland forests above 250 m. They are less uniform, generally lower in diversity, and have a more open canopy and different species composition.

In addition to the *várzea*, *igapó*, and terra firme forests, there are a number of other forest and non-forest formations. Three of these are in transitional areas. Semi-deciduous forests occur mainly along the southern border of Amazonia, but are also common along the more seasonal drier belt running southeast to northwest through the lower Rio Madeira. Babassu palm (*Attalea speciosa*) forests occur along the southeastern border of Amazonia, in the states of Tocantins, Pará, and Maranhão. Babassu is fire-resistant, which probably accounts for its abundance in the transition zone with savanna, and makes it likely that the extent of this forest type has probably increased, both historically and recently, due to forest burning by Indians and colonists.

The western portion of Amazonia also has the largest expanse of bamboo-dominated vegetation in the world. The stands of *Guadua* spp. and *Merostachys* spp. bamboo in the states of Acre and Rondonia in Brazil and the departments of Madre de Dios and Ucayali in Peru cover some 180 000 km², an area about the size of Great Britain, and also extend into Bolivia. These forests are a transitional open forest formation, characterized by predominance of a number of bamboo species. The bamboo forms a dense understory, but also reaches up to 30 m in height, often above the canopy, and is easily recognizable in aerial photographs. These forests harbor many bamboo-specialist endemic birds, rodents, and insects, and are even a major habitat for a monotypic primate genus, the unusual Goeldi's monkey, *Callimico goeldii*.

Liana forest is another open forest formation, dense in lianas and woody vines, but poor in epiphytes and low in overall species diversity. It occurs mainly in southern Pará and northern Mato Grosso, especially between the upper Rios Xingu, Tapajós, and Tocantins, and also in the interior of the Guianas.

Mangrove forests, subject to saltwater inundation, occur along a narrow belt of the coastal area of the Guianas, and Amapá and Maranhão States in Brazil, and around the deltas of the Orinoco and Amazon. They are species-poor and quite uniform, dominated by the red mangrove (*Rhizophora mangle)* in the saltiest water, and *R. racemosa* in more brackish waters. The black mangrove, *Avicennia nitida,* is also abundant.

Montane forests within Amazonia are those occurring above 700 m altitude, mainly around the northern and southern fringes of the basin. These forests are further subdivided into lower montane (700-1 000 m) and upper montane rainforest or cloud forest above 1 000 m. Upper montane forests are humid elfin forests, with a distinct flora, highly dependent on soil type, and abundant in epiphytic bromeliads and lichens. At the highest altitudes (above 1 600-1 800 m), especially on the tepuis of the Guayana Highlands, these forests give way to low, shrubby subalpine vegetation on rocky outcrops, either of sandstone or granite (the inselbergs). The flora of these outcrop communities has adapted to extreme seasonal drought, and is composed of complex and variable communities of herbaceous plants, many of them endemic, especially in the sandstone massifs of the eastern part of the Pantepui. Auyán-Tepui and the Chimantá massifs form extensive upland plains, each covering more than 600 km², with rivers, valleys, and abysses. Vegetation varies from herbaceous meadows and rocky

On the opposite page, Weddel's saddleback tamarins (Saguinus fuscicollis weddelli), *Tambopata, Peru.*

Above, night monkeys (Aotus nigriceps) *in the Tambopata area. Aotus is the only nocturnal primate genus in South America.*
Both photos: © **Günter Ziesler**

outcrops to thickets, shrubby vegetation, and stunted but full-blown forests dominated by the tree *Bonnetia roraimae* (Theaceae), endemic to the region and characterized by its thick, reddish foliage. Much of the flora of the tepuis and especially these massifs is endemic. Many of the fishes and frogs are also endemic. These include the extraordinary loricariid mailed catfish (*Neblinichthys pilosus*), a new genus described from the base of the Pico da Neblina (Ferraris et al. 1986), and the endemic frog genus *Oreophrynella*. In addition, there are a number of endemic birds, including 36 restricted-range species with multiple endemics in the genera *Campylopterus*, *Phylloscartes*, *Diglossa*, and *Myioborus* (Stattersfield et al. 1998).

Non-forest formations include terra firme savannas (*campos*), inundated savannas or *campos de várzea*, scrub vegetation on white sand soils (*campinas* or *caatinga baixa*), *campina rupestre* (subalpine vegetation on sandstone rock outcrops), and coastal *restinga*. Amazonian terra firme savannas, often containing gallery forest and semideciduous forest patches, are scattered throughout the region, but are especially widespread in coastal Amapá in Brazil and French Guiana, in southern Pará (Cachimbo-Cururú), in the upper Rio Madeira, in the Pantepui region (Roraima-Rupununi and Gran Sabana), in southern Suriname (Sipalwini), and on the eastern part of Marajó Island in the Amazon estuary. White-sand savanna patches are common in the basins of the Rios Orinoco and Negro, and have a specialized flora related to that of the mountaintops of the Guayana Highlands, but each with well-defined and differing plant communities and a high degree of endemism (Huber 1989). Inundated savannas are periodically-flooded grasslands which occur irregularly along all the white-water rivers.

Nutrient-deficient white sand soils, widespread in the drainages of the Rios Orinoco, Casiquiare, and Negro, give rise to highly-distinct scleromorphic scrub (*campina*, *caatinga baixa*, also known as *bana* in Venezuela) and high forest (*campinarana* or *caatinga alta*). There are also white sand forests in the Guianas, where they are called *wallaba* forest in Guyana and savanna forest in Suriname. In the Guianas, they are found mainly in an east-west white sand belt immediately to the north of the Guayana Shield and known in Suriname as the Zanderij Formation. These white sand forests are quite different from all other Amazonian forests and similar to the heath forests in Southeast Asia, but have no equivalent in Africa. *Campinas* have low, tortuous bushy trees up to 7-8 m in height, and are rich in epiphytes, lichens, and mosses. They often occur as very small, isolated patches on elevated domes of white sand in the middle of the forest. The *caatinga alta*, up to 20 m in height, is widespread along the upper Rio Negro. The name of this forest refers to the fact that the understory is light as a result of the typically thin trunks and small, scleromorphic leaves; the forest has a low density of trees (60-70 per ha), the majority of them occurring only in these forests.

Flagship Species

Amazonia has many flagship species, but the primates, all of them monkeys in this part of the world, are clearly the most important group. This region has the greatest concentration of primate diversity anywhere on Earth, with no less than 15 genera, 81 species, and 134 taxa. Of these, one entire family (Pitheciidae), three genera (20%), 69 species (85%), and 122 (91%) taxa are endemic. These range in size from the tiny pygmy marmoset (*Cebuella pygmaea*) and the recently-described dwarf marmoset (*Mico humilis*), which weigh 120 g and 150 g respectively, all the way up to the spider monkeys (*Ateles* spp.) and woolly monkeys (*Lagothrix* spp.), which can exceed 10 kg. The three genera of the endemic family Pitheciidae, *Pithecia*, *Cacajao*, and *Chiropotes*, are uniquely Amazonian. The shy, secretive sakis (*Pithecia* spp.) are characterized by their long, thickly-haired tail and fluffy fur. They live in small family groups in a variety of forest types, feeding mainly on fruits and seeds. The bearded sakis of the genus *Chiropotes* also have thick tails which, like those of the sakis, are sometimes cut off by local people to be used as dusters. Bearded sakis differ from sakis, however, in their long beards and the distinctive bumps on top of their heads, indicative of the strong jaw muscles that they use to crack open the hardest of nuts. Classic seed predators, they feed on the seeds of unripe fruits and move about in large groups. The uakaris (*Cacajao* spp.) are the only short-tailed South American monkeys and are characterized by their bald red or black faces and their long, shaggy red, white, or black fur. Although they too use a variety of habitats, they are best known as denizens of the flooded forests, often being the most abundant monkey species in certain small tributary rivers (e.g., in the Rio Negro region).

The marmosets (*Cebuella*, *Mico*) and tamarins (*Saguinus*) are also especially noteworthy. Small, squirrel-sized monkeys, they come in an enormous variety of colors and facial hair patterns, being adorned with ear tufts, mustaches of different sizes and shapes, and sometimes bald faces. All but one species give birth to twins, in contrast to other Neotropical monkeys, and male care of infants is a characteristic feature. In all, there are four genera and at least 48 taxa in Amazonia, with new species being discovered almost every year. One species, the distinctive Goeldi's monkey (*Callimico goeldii*), a small, shiny black species that remains very poorly known, appears to be specialized on bamboo forest habitats in upper Amazonia.

Two other excellent mammal flagships for the region are the giant otter (*Pteronura brasiliensis*) and the Amazonian manatee (*Trichechus inunguis*), both of which were driven to near extinction by commercial hunting in the 1960s and 1970s. The giant otter is the longest otter in the world and compares in weight to the sea otter of the Pacific coast of North America. A magnificent animal, it is diurnal and travels in family groups throughout the smaller rivers, streams, and oxbows of

On the opposite page, morpho butterfly at rest, Manu National Park, Peru. When flying, this butterfly displays its electric blue upper-wing surfaces.
© **Patricio Robles Gil**/*Sierra Madre*

Above, juvenile dwarf caiman (Paleosuchus palpebrosus), *Kaw River, French Guiana.*
© **Russell Mittermeier**

Amazonia. Its loud, distinctive calls can be heard from a long distance and, where not persecuted, it can easily be observed as its swims, plays, and hunts in the water and on the riverbanks. It was heavily hunted for its pelt, which was as valuable as that of a jaguar, resulting in its extermination from many areas. However, with increased protection, it now appears to be making a comeback in some areas, and can be observed in places like Manu National Park and Bahuaja-Sonene National Park in Peru and at various sites in Suriname and Guyana.

The Amazonian manatee is endemic to Amazonia and smaller than its Caribbean and West African relatives. Once a very widespread species, it has been heavily hunted for its meat and oil for centuries. Now protected throughout its range, it too seems to be making a comeback and can be found in a number of protected areas, especially in Brazilian Amazonia.

Among the birds, the best flagships are unquestionably the psittacines, including the parrots, macaws, parakeets, conures, and their relatives. In all, there are at least 57 species in Amazonia, of which 20 are endemic. One of the most spectacular is the Endangered golden parakeet (*Guarouba guarouba*), whose yellow and green colors are the same as those on the Brazilian flag. Indeed, one Brazilian conservation organization, FUNATURA, has adopted this species as its logo. Macaws are also well-represented, with 10 species in all, including the largest and arguably the most spectacular, the hyacinth macaw (*Anodorhynchus hyacinthinus*), and also the blue-and-yellow macaw (*Ara ararauna*), the red-and-green macaw (*A. chloroptera*), the scarlet macaw (*A. macao*), and the blue-throated macaw (*A. glaucogularis*), a Critically Endangered endemic that is found only in Santa Cruz, Bolivia and was unknown in the wild until 1992. Macaws and parrots also provide Amazonia with one of its most spectacular wildlife phenomena, the amazing *collpas*, or mineral "licks" in Peruvian Amazonia. These are riverbanks that have been exposed by natural erosion where enormous mixed flocks of parrots and macaws gather en masse every morning to feed on clay. Such behavior takes place only in very restricted areas, although there are many riverbanks that superficially seem indistinguishable from those that are intensively used. As many as 15 different species will congregate on these *collpas* every morning, with different combinations of species descending at different times, in what appears to be a predetermined order. The exact reason (or reasons) for such feeding remains uncertain. It may be that these clays provide critical trace elements or that they assist in the detoxification and digestion of plant toxins in the many seeds eaten by macaws and parrots —or some combination of the two. The largest and most impressive *collpas* appear to be in Manu National Park and the Bahuaja-Sonene National Park in Peru, where tourists can readily observe them.

Other spectacular Amazonian bird groups are the hummingbirds with 71 species and the cotingas with 26 species. The cotingas include some of the most peculiar of Amazonian birds, such as fruitcrows, the Amazonian umbrellabird (*Cephalopterus ornatus*), the capuchinbird (*Perissocephalus tricolor*), the bellbirds, and the Guianan cock-of-the-rock (*Rupicola rupicola*). The cotingas also include the screaming piha (*Lipaugus vociferans*), a dull gray bird that lives high in the canopy; rarely seen, its piercing, drawn out, *wheet-weee-oooh* call is one of the most characteristic sounds of the Amazonian forest.

The reptiles also include a number of important flagship species. The anaconda (*Eunectes murinus*) is the heaviest snake in the world and competes with the reticulate python of Southeast Asia for the title of longer. A much-feared species, this semiaquatic giant can be quite dangerous and still occasionally kills and eats humans, usually fishermen who are captured unaware at the river's edge. Although reports of its size are often exaggerated, it can certainly reach 8 m and possibly much more.

Turtles are especially diverse in the many rivers and lakes of the region, with Amazonia as a whole ranking as one of the top five regions on Earth for turtle diversity. In all, there are 21 species, of which seven are endemic. These include six members of the Family Pelomedusidae, Subfamily Podocneminae, among which is the giant Amazon river turtle, *Podocnemis expansa*, which can reach 80 cm and 33 kg and is one of the world's largest freshwater chelonians. Known as *tartaruga* in Brazil and *arrau* in Venezuela, this impressive animal once occurred over much of the Amazon and Orinoco drainages below the large rapids, and reached incredible densities. A social nester, it hauls out on sand beaches in large numbers, making it easy prey for humans. Not surprisingly, given its size, visibility, and high productivity in terms of eggs, it has been exploited for centuries by Indians and later by colonists. Alexander von Humboldt observed the Orinoco nesting beaches and the wholesale destruction of eggs during his historical voyage at the end of the eighteenth century and the first few years of the nineteenth century. He calculated that some 5 000 jars of oil were harvested annually at just three of the major Orinoco nesting beaches. Assuming that a jar contained 25 bottles of oil, each bottle being the production of 200 eggs, and allowing for wastage, he calculated that some 33 million eggs had been harvested to fill those 5 000 jars at just three of the major beaches (Humboldt and Bonpland 1811-1812). The British naturalist Henry Walter Bates made similar observations between 1848 and 1859 in Brazilian Amazonia, especially in the vicinity of Tefé on the Rio Solimões (the Brazilian name for the Rio Amazonas between Manaus and the Colombian border). Well over a century later, Mittermeier in 1973 was unable to find any *Podocnemis expansa* in the vicinity of Tefé. However, two of the smaller species, *P. unifilis* and *P. sextuberculata*, could still be found —and were also being overexploited (Mittermeier 1975, 1978). Not surprisingly, this species has disappeared in many parts of its range, and it is still exploited for a black market trade. Fortunately, however, most of the major nesting beach-

Above, spectacular fringed leaf frog (Agalychnis craspedopus) *from Cocha Cashu, Manu National Park, Peruvian Amazonia.*
© **Russell Mittermeier**

On the opposite page, "Terra-firme" rainforest, Serra das Carajás, southern Pará State, Brazilian Amazonia.
© **Luiz Claudio Marigo**

es in Brazil and Venezuela are now protected, making it unlikely that the species, though greatly depleted relative to its original abundance, will go extinct.

There are also at least seven species of Chelidae, with several new species awaiting description. These include the bizarre mata mata (*Chelus fimbriatus*), with its broad, flat head, tiny, anteriorly-situated eyes, long snorkel-like snout, fleshy filaments on the ventral side of its head, and long, thick, fleshy neck that folds laterally under the shell. The shell is also flattened and very rough, with three knobby, tuberculate keels.

Crocodilians also reach their greatest diversity in Amazonia, with five species in four genera (*Caiman crocodylus, Melanosuchus niger, Paleosuchus trigonatus, P. palpebrosus, Crocodylus intermedius*), about one fifth of all the world's crocodilian taxa. Three of these, the two *Paleosuchus* and *Melanosuchus,* are endemic, as is a distinctive subspecies of the spectacled caiman, *Caiman crocodilus apaporiensis,* from the upper reaches of the Río Apaporis in Colombian Amazonia (Medem 1955). The black caiman (*Melanosuchus niger*) is one of the largest reptiles on Earth, and reaches at least 6 m and perhaps as much as 7-8 m in length. Heavily hunted for its skin and meat, it too declined severely in the 1960s and 1970s. Now, however, it appears to be making a comeback in many areas.

The amphibians also include some flagship species, especially members of the brilliantly-colored but highly toxic poison-dart frogs (Dendrobatidae). The best Amazonian example of these is the striking *okopipi,* or blue poison-dart frog (*Dendrobates azureus*) from southern Suriname. This large (38-45 mm), striking dendrobatid has a light blue body and is covered with a reticulate pattern of large and small round black spots set off against darker blue limbs. Though not the most brightly-colored member of its family, it is surely one of the most beautiful. It was first described in 1969, and is found only in a few small forest islands in the middle of the Sipaliwini Savanna in extreme southern Suriname. Indeed, its tiny range seems to be concentrated on the Vier Gebroeders Mountain, a series of outcrops 554 m above sea level and about 300 m above the surrounding savanna. Although its range is right on the Brazilian border, it has never been recorded from Brazilian territory and appears to be endemic to Suriname (Hoogmoed 1969; Walls 1994). Fortunately, it breeds well in captivity and is now commonly seen in zoos in the U.S. and Europe. Its image is used in dozens of different toys, stickers, posters, and T-shirts sold in gift shops around the world —rather amazing for a species with a range no larger than a few city blocks. On top of this, it has become one of the principal biodiversity flagships for Suriname, rather like a "mini-giant panda" for that country.

Fish are also important flagship species in Amazonia, especially the fruit-eating species of the flooded forests. Indeed, the immense areas of flooded forest have resulted in an extraordinary radiation of fruit-eating fishes among the 11 characin families found in Amazonia and also in the other major Amazonian fish group, the cat-

Margay (Leopardus wiedii), *an agile hunter of the Amazonian forest.*
© **Günter Ziesler**

fishes or siluroids. The characins (Characidae) include the pacu, the tambaqui, the piranha, and the tetra and are the single most diverse group, with more than 1 200 species. The tambaqui (*Colossoma macropomum*) reaches up to 30 kg in weight and is one of the most prized by fishermen. It enters the forests when they flood and feeds on fallen fruits, especially of rubber trees (*seringa verdadeira, Hevea brasiliensis,* and *seringa barriguda, H. spruceana*). It crushes the hard, dehiscent, capsular fruits with its molar-like teeth, strong enough to even deal with palm fruits such as those of the *jauari* (*Astrocaryum jauari*), *açaí* (*Euterpe* spp.), and *marajá* (*Bactris* spp.).

The characins and siluroids together make up about 80% of the Amazonian fish fauna. Some of the most spectacular are the larger carnivorous catfishes, such as the *piraíba* (*Brachyplatystoma filamentosum*), which can reach 2.8 m and over 140 kg, and the colorful *pirarara* (*Phractocephalus hemiliopterus).* These are extremely important commercially, with catfish in general sustaining the widespread fisheries of the lower Amazon. Migrations of some Amazonian catfish are the longest freshwater migrations in the world. Many species travel from the Amazon estuary to the foothills of the Andes, where spawning takes place, after which the resultant fry return back to the estuary —a 10 000-km route (Barthem and Goulding 1997).

Other notable Amazonian species include the *pirarucú* (*Arapaima gigas*), a member of the ancient bony-tongue family Osteoglossidae. One of the largest freshwater fish in the world, it can reach a length of 4.5 m, although averaging 2-2.4 m and 90 kg in weight, and is a very important commercial species. There is also the famous electric eel or *poraque,* not actually an eel but a member of the family Electrophoridae, and one of a group called the gymnotoids, all of which share electrogenic and electrosensory organs.

Human Cultures

In striking contrast to the Congo, where humans have existed since the dawn of our species, humans are a relatively recent arrival in Amazonia. Early theories placed human arrival in the New World at 12 000-15 000 years ago, when the Bering Strait was frozen and traversable on foot from Siberia. Now, however, it appears that humans arrived in a variety of different ways, and that they did so much earlier, going back at least 40 000 years and perhaps even earlier than that. Indeed, the oldest dated site is now thought to be as early as 47 000 years, meaning that people were probably there 50 000 or more years ago. When and how people actually arrived in Amazonia remains uncertain, but some probably came via Central America, whereas others may have island-hopped through the Caribbean. In any case, there was almost certainly no single arrival, but rather a series of successive waves over the course of tens of thousands of years.

By the time the first Europeans arrived in Amazonia,

the indigenous population probably numbered between three and five million, with large populations settled along the mainstream of the Amazon and some of its bigger tributaries and much smaller, nomadic or semi-nomadic groups in the interfluvial areas. Indeed, the rich nutrients of the *várzea* supported quite large populations and cultures, which were encountered by the first Portuguese descending the Amazon in the early 1500s.

Unfortunately, contact with Europeans was disastrous for the indigenous people of Amazonia. After most of the accessible groups along the big rivers had been decimated, missionaries sought out those living in more remote areas, bringing them into *reduções* in "civilized" areas, where disease inevitably wiped out contingent after contingent. How many died in the first four centuries is impossible to determine. However, in the twentieth century it is estimated that some 80 tribes disappeared in Brazil alone between 1900 and 1957. How many more have disappeared since then, during the building of the Trans-Amazonian and other major infrastructure development projects, will probably never be known.

In Brazil, there now remain 206 documented groups. The vast majority of these, 170 tribes, are in Amazonia, where the indigenous population *in reserves* numbers about 180 000. Of these, about one third have a population of less than 200 individuals, a quarter number 201-500, and a little more than a third number between 500 and 5 000. Two Amazonian groups, the Sateré-Mawé in central Amazonia and the Yanomami on the Brazil-Venezuela border, number between 5 000 and 10 000, with the Yanomami having at least as many on the Venezuelan side. The famous Kayapó of southern Amazonia are in the same range, numbering only about 6 000. The Macuxi (also known as Machushi on the Guyana side), the Guajajara, the Terena, the Kaingang, and the Ticuna all number between 10 000 and 30 000, and are the largest groups. In addition to the known groups, there may be as many as 50 uncontacted groups (Ricardo 2001a), although the Indian Agency, FUNAI, recognizes only 12.

In all, the population of Brazilian Amazonia is about 15 168 145, of which 10 304 832 live in urban areas and towns. The rural population is only 4 863 313 (2000 census), for a wilderness population density of 1.1 inhabitants/km².

In Peru, there are 42 ethnic groups belonging to 12 language families, and their population in Amazonia is about 200 000 individuals. Many of these consist of a few hundred individuals teetering on the brink of extinction. Others such as the Aguaruna and Machiguenga number in the tens of thousands. There are also 12-14 uncontacted indigenous tribes mainly along the border with Brazil in the headwaters of the Rios Purus, Piedras, Tahuamanu, Los Amigos, Chandler, and related drainages. These groups are at great risk from incursions by illegal mahogany loggers. Overall, the human population of Peruvian Amazonia is estimated at 1 270 515 individuals, of which 60% lives in urban areas (INEI

1996). This gives a rural population of 508 206, or about 0.8 inhabitant/km².

Colombian Amazonia is inhabited by some 60 different indigenous groups. Among the best-known are the Witoto, the Tukuna, the Yucuna, the Macuna, and the recently-discovered Nukak. Overall, the population of Colombian Amazonia is about 643 147, of which 262 839 live in urban areas. The rural population is 380 308, for a population density of 0.8 inhabitant/km².

In Venezuela, there are about 31 indigenous groups, the vast majority occurring in Amazonia, where the total indigenous population is estimated at about 250 000. Among the most notable are the Ye'kwana (or Makiritare) in the states of Amazonas and Bolívar, the Yanomami in the State of Amazonas on the Brazil border, the Sanema in the Rio Caura region, the Piaroa also in Amazonas State, the Panare (or Enyehpah) and the Hoti just south of the Orinoco in the State of Bolívar, the Pemon living in the region of the Gran Sabana and on the Guyana border, and the Warao at the mouth of the Orinoco. The total human population of the Amazonian portion of Venezuela (including the states of Amazonas, Bolívar, and Delta Amacuro) in 2000 was 1 535 175, of which 83.4% lived in urban areas (OCEI 2000). The rural population was only 254 839, for an overall population density of 0.6 inhabitant/km². However, the State of Amazonas (180 000 km²) in the far south has only 54 851 people living in rural areas, for a population density of just 0.3 inhabitant/km² —comparable to that of the interior of Suriname and French Guiana.

In Bolivia, there are 20 indigenous groups living in Amazonia, with a total indigenous population of only 65 575 people living in 816 different villages. The largest group is the Moxeño, with nearly 20 000 people. Ten other groups, including the Guarayo, the Movima, the Itonama, the Tacana, the Reyesano, the Yuracaré, the Juaquiniano, the Loseten, and the Loretano number between 1 000 and 7 500. The remaining nine groups have only between 100 and 800 per tribe, and include the Yaminahua, the Sirionó, the Ese-Ejja, the Chama, the Maré, the Yuqui, the Canichana, the Baure, and the Chácobo. The total human population in Bolivian Amazonia as of 2000 is estimated at 1 080 032, of which 520 528 live in urban areas. The rural population is 559 504, for a human population density of 1.6 inhabitants/km².

In Ecuador, there are five main groups living in the Amazonian portion of the country, and they total 75 300 individuals. By far the largest group is the Kichwa, which total 70 000 and also extend up into the Andes. Other groups include the Achuar and Shuar (better known to the outside world as the Jivaro, and numbering about 2 000), the hunter-gatherer Huaorani (or Auca, also about 2 000), the Cofán (or Kofán, and also calling themselves A'i; only about 500), and the Siona-Secoya (800). The Huaorani, the Cofán, and the Achuar/Shuar are all blowgun hunters, some of them still actively using this rapidly-disappearing weapon and each making different dart poisons, with the Huaorani

Silky anteater
(Cyclopes didactylus) *waking up. This tiny relative of the giant anteater and the tamandua is rarely seen.*
© **Günter Ziesler**

also making the only flat blowgun in the world. The total population of Amazonian Ecuador is 372 101, of which 141 145 live in urban areas. The rural population is 230 956, for a population density of 3.3 inhabitants/km².

Guyana is the largest of the three Guianas in size and population and, like the other two, is included in its entirety within Amazonia as we define it. Its human population is only 781 000 in a land area of 214 969 km². The urban population is about 298 000 (38.2%), so the rural population is about 483 000 —for an overall wilderness population density of 2.2 inhabitants/km² for the country as a whole. However, most of the population (*ca*. 80%), both urban and rural, lives along the coast in a narrow band that occupies no more than 10% of the country. This means that the population density in the interior is only about 0.8 inhabitant/km². The principal ethnic groups in the country are East Indians from India (49%), Afro-Guyanese of African origin (36%), Chinese, Portuguese, and Europeans (1%), people of mixed origin (8%), and Amerindians. In all, there are nine Amerindian groups totaling 46 000 people, or approximately 6% of the total population. They include the Arawak, the Wapishana, the Warao, the Carib, the Akawaio, the Arekuna, the Makushi, the Patamona, and the Wai-Wai, the last five belonging to the widespread Carib language group. The Awawak and the Carib live mainly along the coast, as do the Warao, while the others are in the interior.

Suriname is the second of the Guianas in size and population, with approximately 423 000 people (1997) in a land area of 163 820 km². About 85% of the population lives along the coast, with 70% living in a radius of just 30 km of the capital city of Paramaribo. Only about 60 000 live in the interior. Population density for the country as a whole is quite low at 2.6 inhabitants/km², and in the interior it is under 0.4 inhabitant/km², an interior density surpassed only by French Guiana. However, in nearly 50% of the country, especially along the entire southern border with Brazil, in the southwest, and in the region of the Central Suriname Nature Reserve that occupies 10% of the country (see below), the human population is extremely low, usually less than 0.05 inhabitant/km². Not surprisingly, Suriname has some of the most pristine forests left in the tropics, and more than 85% of them still intact.

Suriname is unusual in that it not only has several different Amerindian groups, but also a very interesting population of African origin, known as the Bushnegroes or Maroons. The Bushnegroes are the descendants of runaway slaves that escaped from the Dutch and English plantations along the coast and established themselves in the interior of the country in the 1600s and 1700s. Divided into six tribes, they now number about 45 000-50 000 people, or around 10%-12% of the total population and are the only people of African origin living in the Diaspora that still lead a largely traditional West African life-style. The two largest groups are the Saramaccaner (or Saamaka) and the Aucaner (also known as

Djuka, Ndjuka or Ndyuka), each with 15 000-20 000. The Paramaccaner (Paramaka), the Matawai, and the Aluku (or Boni) are smaller, numbering in the low thousands, while only a few hundred Kwinti survive. The Aluku now live mainly in French Guiana, although their chief still resides in Suriname.

Amerindian groups include the Arawak (Arowak, or Lokonon) and the Caribs (or Kalinha) along the coast, the Trio or Tareno (known as Tirio in Brazil) in the extreme south and southwest, the Wayana in the southeast on the border with French Guiana and Brazil, and the hunter-gatherer Akurio, numbering only a few dozen and associated mainly with the Trio.

The Trio are divided into a number of subgroups, including the Okomojana, the Katujana, the Kasujana, the Mawajana, the Tunejana, and Sikijana, all of which use Trio as their language. Families of Wai-wai from Guyana and other groups from Brazil are also encountered in southern Suriname, especially in the large Trio village of Kwamalasemutu, and take up temporary or permanent residence there. These people have very small human populations and occupy extensive and still largely pristine areas. The Trios, for example, live in just three main villages, Kwamalasemutu and Tepoe in Suriname and Pouso Tirio in Brazil and number only about 3 000-4 000, of which about 2 400 are in the two Suriname villages, 400 in Tepoe and 2 000 in Kwamalasemutu. Nonetheless, they make use of an area of nearly 4 million ha in Suriname alone. In all, the Amerindian people of Suriname number about 12 600 (3%), of which the majority are Arawaks and Caribs living in the coastal region (UNDP 1998).

The largest ethnic group in Suriname is that of the Hindustanis, descendants of people from India who came over as indentured servants at the end of the nineteenth century. They account for 35% of the population. The next largest group is the Creoles (32%), people of African origin but distinct from the Bushnegroes and living along the coast. Suriname is also unusual in that it has a large population of people from Java (15%), who came as migrants to work the sugar plantations after the immigrants from India. There is also a much smaller group of Chinese origin (2%), who came as contract laborers before the Indians or the Javanese. Finally, there are very small but long-standing populations of Europeans and other origins that account for an additional 3%, including people from the Netherlands who have lived in Suriname for centuries and old Jewish communities that date back to the plantation days (Chin and Buddingh 1987).

French Guiana is an overseas department of France, and is also included in its entirety within our definition of Amazonia. It has a very low human population of only 157 000, for an overall population density of only 1.7 inhabitants/km² for the entire department, including urban areas along the coast. However, less than 10% of the population (15 000) lives in the interior, where the population density is less than 0.2 inhabitant/km² —the lowest anywhere in Amazonia.

Above, pygmy marmoset
(Cebuella pygmaea),
the world's smallest monkey
species and the most widespread in
upper Amazonia. This one is
in Amacayacu National Park
in Colombia.

On the opposite page,
squirrel monkey
(Saimiri sciureus), *Colombia.*
Both photos:
© **Patricio Robles Gil**/*Sierra Madre*

factor in making this region a biodiversity hotspot. More recently, this crop has been moving into southwestern Amazonia and even into central Amazonia in *Cerrado* enclaves. Between 1997 and 2000, annual soybean production in the State of Rondônia alone increased from 4.5 to 45 thousand tons a year (Veríssimo et al. 2001). These patches of *Cerrado* habitat are remnants of the last glacial period and, in biodiversity terms, are often more important than equivalent-sized areas of tropical forest because of their high diversity and endemism. Oil-palm plantations are cropping up in some regions as well (notably in eastern Amazonia) and could represent another major agricultural threat in the coming decades —especially when one looks at the enormous impact that they have had in places such as Sumatra and elsewhere in southeast Asia.

Another threat is posed by drug crops, especially in Colombian Amazonia where they have been responsible for the destruction and/or deterioration of more than 400 000 ha of pristine forest (United States Embassy, Colombia 2002). Since the early 1990s, the Putumayo and Caquetá Departments of Colombia have been the core area of this raging illegal activity, with the result that some 101 250 ha have been destroyed. More recently, this has also spread to large forested areas in the Guaviare, Vaupés, and Vichada Departments. This activity impacts biodiversity directly through forest clearing and subsequent loss of soil fertility, and indirectly through the pervasive and indiscriminate use of large amounts of chemical substances for drug processing. Thousands of gallons of sulphuric acid, ammoniac, gasoline, and toluene are discharged every year into rivers and streams by cocaine-processing laboratories operating in very remote areas of the region, poisoning aquatic habitats and posing potential health threats to many peasant and indigenous populations. The magnitude of the many destructive facets of illegal crops has been widely recognized by the Colombian government, and aerial herbicide spraying has been implemented to destroy about 30 000 ha of cocaine plantations, especially in Caquetá and Putumayo. However, this too poses threats. Although the glyphosate products used in spraying are supposed to destroy only coca plants, this chemical is nonselective and also impacts other plants and animals and even local human populations (Castrillón Márquez 2000; Hansen 2002).

Although human population density has been and continues to be low in most of Amazonia, patterns and policies of human settlement have represented one of the main threats to the forest. For example, in the 1970s, massive government incentives resulted in the migration of large numbers of people to the recently-constructed Trans-Amazonian Highway in Brazil, and many of the communities that resulted have now become small cities. In areas where human settlement has occurred, large areas of forest have been cut down. These include parts of eastern Brazilian Amazonia, and areas around large cities like Manaus and Belém. Fortunately, the Brazilian government has suspended its policy to settle families on forested lands in the Amazon, now favoring recuperation of deforested lands for human settlement.

Governmental forest protection policies have long been a controversial issue in Amazonia as well. Brazilian law requires that at least 50% (and in some cases 80%) of privately-held forested land remain as standing forest. However, the flip side of this regulation is that up to 50% of forest can be converted on private properties for "productive" uses. This legislation results in a very fragmented landscape, in which each landowner creates small patches of forest in places where continuous forest once existed.

Historically, fire has not been a major factor in the dynamics of the Amazon forest. Isolated fires did occur, and were sometimes large-scale, but they only took place every few thousand years during severe El Niño events. Furthermore, there is relatively little evidence of past human use of fire as a tool for land clearing. Recently, however, for a variety of reasons, fire has become a very serious threat to many parts of Amazonia. First, the increased incidence of El Niño events imposes water stress on large areas, with rainfall during these years dropping to below 50% its annual average. This change in the hydrological pattern of the Amazon is exacerbated by local and regional deforestation (due to logging, agriculture or cattle ranching), which significantly reduces the amount of evapotranspiration and thus the amount of water vapor in the atmosphere that ordinarily fuels cloud formation and precipitation. Selective logging also increases the susceptibility of forests to fire, by "punching" holes in intact forests and allowing them to dry up and increase their fuel load. Nepstad et al. (1999) estimated that logging crews damage 10 000-15 000 km² of forest each year, that the area of forest that burned in 1998 was equivalent to the area that was deforested, and that an area 10 times larger than that was susceptible to forest fires because of the combined effects of the factors listed above. Moreover, forests that are burned once become much more prone to repeated fires, with the end result being a trend toward more open formations such as grasslands. Forest fires obviously have very serious impacts on the region's biodiversity. Direct mortality is high, and the indirect effects of altering the forest dynamics and decreasing fruit and insect abundance also create great stress.

Amazonia has large reserves of many minerals including iron (the largest high-grade deposits on the planet), copper, lead, gold, tin, manganese, kaolin, bauxite (15% of the world's deposits), nickel, and silver. Deposits of these, along with less-known but increasingly precious minerals such as niobium-tantalum and titanium, occur throughout the basin. Bauxite (aluminum) mining is a major activity in northern Suriname, and on the upper Rio Trombetas and the Carajás region of southern Pará in Brazil. Industrial mining in itself has limited direct effects on the forest, being restricted to relatively small areas. However, serious and widespread indirect effects include pollution from

Above, mother and infant brown-throated three-toed sloth (Bradypus variegatus), *Brazil.*
© **Pete Oxford**/*Nature Picture Library*

On the opposite page, harpy eagle (Harpia harpyja) *and chick on nest, Peruvian Amazonia. One of the world's largest and most impressive raptors, this species does well in intact forest areas.*
© **Tui De Roy**/*Auscape*

by-products (such as arsenic in the extraction of manganese), tailings, and the siltation of the rivers, and development of major infrastructure such as roads, cattle ranches, dams, electricity lines, and railways to service these activities.

The Carajás region in the eastern Brazilian Amazonia covers an area considered one of the most important metallogenetic anomalies of the Earth's crust, comparable with the Abitibi Belt in Canada and the Witwatersrand in South Africa (Santos 1983). With massive deposits of many of the minerals listed above, the Grande Carajás Program covers an area of 895 265 km², corresponding to 10.6% of Brazil. The destruction of forests and rivers in the region has been extraordinarily rapid and widespread. Forests have been logged and cut to supply charcoal for pig-iron smelting factories, enormous areas of eucalyptus plantations have replaced them, and there are ever-expanding networks of roads, cattle ranches, and railroads. The demand for electricity, especially important for processing bauxite, stimulates the construction of dams which destroy still more forest through large-scale flooding.

Petroleum and natural gas are now being exploited in a number of areas of Amazonia, notably in the Napo Basin in Ecuador, in lowland Colombia, in the Marañon Basin in Peru, and along the Rios Juruá and Urucú in Brazil. As with mining, the actual area impacted by oil extraction and pipeline construction may be small, but the infrastructure needed to support them requires the construction of roads, which inevitably open remote areas to loggers, miners, ranchers, and colonists. Spillage from pipelines remains an ever-present threat as well. In Ecuador, where petroleum exploration is taking hold in Amazonia, a proposed pipeline to take crude oil to the Pacific Coast for export to the United States would impact such important protected areas as Yasuní National Park, Cuyabeno Wildlife Reserve, the Limoncocha and Pañacocha Biological Reserves, and a host of indigenous communities as well.

Perhaps the most devastating mining activity is that associated with the extraction of gold over the entire extent of Amazonia. Gold is mostly in alluvial form, which means that it has to be precipitated out of river sediments using mercury. This activity is performed mainly by placer miners, known in Brazil as *garimpeiros*, and is widespread throughout the region. Since mercury can be found in large quantities and is cheap, there is no effort to recycle it in the extraction process. The result is that this heavy metal accumulates in the aquatic food chain and represents a serious health issue for people and wildlife dependent on fish as a source of food. The physical impacts of gold mining are also a major concern. Miners often use high-powered hoses to blast away riverbanks, resulting in the enormous siltation of smaller rivers and streams. In larger rivers such as the Madeira and Tapajós, the riverbed is constantly turned over with massive suction pumps set up on fleets of anchored rafts. Siltation seriously changes the chemistry of small and medium-sized rivers, resulting in the

loss of many wildlife species downstream. New "gold finds" can result in migration of tens or even hundreds of thousands of people to previously uninhabited areas. Perhaps the best example is the gold rush of Serra Pelada in southern Pará State, Brazil, which took place in the early 1980s and attracted much international attention. Approximately four tons of gold were extracted in the first seven months after its discovery, and where once there was a mountain there is now nothing more than a huge hole in the ground (Santos 1983).

The Amazon has long been regarded as an area with a vast hydroelectric potential because of the massive scale of the main river and its tributaries. Energy demand is industrial rather than domestic. The Tucuruí Dam on the Rio Tocantins was constructed for the Grande Carajás Program to fuel energy-hungry aluminum plants. Completed in 1984, it was the first major dam in Brazilian Amazonia, flooding 287 500 ha. The Balbina Dam on the Rio Uatumã, near Manaus, closed its floodgates in 1987, inundating an area of 238 000 ha (Fearnside 1989). Demand for electricity for the bauxite industry also led to the construction of the Brokopondo Dam in Suriname in 1964, flooding an area of 160 000 ha of pristine forest, displacing 28 Saamaka and six Ndyuka Bushnegro villages, and creating a huge, 135 000-ha lake officially known as W.J. Van Blommestein Meer. Plans for additional dams in Suriname have been on the books for the past 20 years, and some may again be ready for implementation. The impacts of dams such as these are enormous, diverse, and little understood, but there are disastrous consequences for aquatic and terrestrial biodiversity. Vast areas of forest are permanently destroyed through flooding, fish migration patterns are altered, and water quality, aquatic habitats, and fish diversity downstream are modified in many different ways.

Given the relatively low elevation differences in most of lowland Amazonia, the area that needs to be flooded to justify significant power benefits is really huge. This creates serious short-term problems of silting and clogging of turbines. Also, due to the decomposition of trees flooded by the reservoirs, the release of greenhouse gases has been a serious environmental concern (Fearnside 1995). The Tucuruí Dam, the largest ever built in a tropical rainforest, emits the same amount of greenhouse gases annually as that emitted by cars and industries in the city of São Paulo, one of the largest on Earth. Finally, although relocation of fauna has accompanied the reservoir projects, this is nothing more than window-dressing and, unfortunately, most of the relocated fauna dies. Fish diversity was reduced by 50% following the construction of the Tucuruí Dam and areas of forest the size of a small American state were destroyed outright or severely modified (Araújo-Lima et al. 1998).

As a result of the significant environmental and social costs, no large-scale hydroelectric development has been undertaken in Brazilian Amazonia in the last 15 years. In 1999, however, the Brazilian Government

On the opposite page, the emerald tree boa (Corallus caninus), *an arboreal predator of Amazonia and one of the world's most attractive snakes.*
© **David Northcott**/*DRK Photo*

Above, tiger-striped leaf frog (Phyllomedusa tomopterna), *one of a great variety of tree frogs found in the Amazonian forest.*
© **Michael Fogden**/*DRK Photo*

released new plans to construct a cascade of six large dams on the Rio Tocantins, turning the river into a chain of great lakes. Two large dams are also planned for the Rio Araguaia (Marabá and Santa Isabel), and a further two on the Rio Xingú, at Altamira and Belo Monte. Plans and financing for the Xingú dams were abandoned in 1988 in the face of major protests from the indigenous communities of the region. The proposed Altamira dam, then called Babaquara, became infamous because its construction would have flooded a record 600 000 ha of forest, more than Balbina and Tucuruí combined.

Hunting of wildlife for subsistence purposes and for commercial markets is another threat to the wildlife of the region (e.g., Mittermeier 1977; Ayres and Ayres 1979; Robinson and Redford 1991a and 1991b; Ayres et al. 1991; Mittermeier 1991). In the past, commercial hunting of species such as the black caiman (*Melanosuchus niger*), jaguar (*Panthera onca*), giant river otter (*Pteronura brasiliensis*), and a number of river turtles (*Podocnemis* spp.) had profound effects on populations —to the point of driving them to local extinction in some areas. Such hunting, however, has decreased over the past decade, and some species such as the black caiman have made impressive comebacks in some rivers (e.g., the Rio Madeira). Subsistence hunting, on the other hand, is still pervasive, and is probably increasing with the growth of new agricultural settlements and extractive reserves. Although its impact is still less than that of bushmeat hunting in Africa, China, and Southeast Asia, it should not be underrated. Indeed, studies indicate that between 9.6 and 23.5 million reptiles, birds, and mammals are consumed each year by the rural population in Brazilian Amazonia, corresponding to approximately 36 400 to 89 000 tons of edible bushmeat (Peres 2000b).

Subsistence and commercial fishing are also pervasive throughout Amazonia, and represent a good portion of the livelihood of local inhabitants. The floodplains of white-water rivers, although only representing 4% of the region, provided for most of the protein needs of Amazonian inhabitants in the past (Smith et al. 1995). Commercial fishing, estimated by Bayley and Petrere (1989) to exceed 200 000 tons a year, on the other hand, can have devastating effects in certain regions where large boats exploit fish for sale in the larger cities of Amazonia.

The ornamental fish trade took hold in the Amazon in 1959, and is still very active throughout the region. In the Brazilian Amazon, it generates more than $2 million a year and is especially concentrated in the Rio Negro and its tributaries (Chao 1993). In a peak year (1979), 20 million ornamental fish were exported from Manaus, and annual exports during the 1980s averaged 17 million (Barthem et al. 1995). It is to be expected that the impacts on local and even regional populations of the small loricariid and callichthyid fishes targeted for this trade are considerable, but they have never been evaluated.

White-plumed antbird (Pithys albifrons) *from Colombia. An ant army follower, it is rarely seen other than near ant swarms.*
© **Doug Wechsler**/*VIREO*

Conservation

Much time has been dedicated to establishing conservation priorities for Amazonia over the past 12 years, most of them in the form of workshops in which experts have reviewed the biodiversity of the region and attempted to establish biogeographical frameworks for field-based conservation action. The first ever was held in Manaus in 1990, and was officially entitled "Priority Areas for Conservation in Amazonia," although it is much better known simply as "Workshop-90." Organized by Conservation International, the New York Botanical Garden, the National Institute for Amazon Research (INPA), and the Brazilian government's environmental agency, IBAMA, it focused heavily on expert opinion and introduced for the first time a very effective methodology that has driven priority-setting ever since. A total of 94 priority areas were identified and mapped for the Amazon Basin and the Guayana Shield through an analysis of plants, vegetation types, mammals, birds, reptiles, amphibians, fishes, insects, geomorphology, and protected areas (Collar 1990; Conservation International 1991; Rylands 1990b).

A second similar, but more broad-scale, analysis was carried out for all of Latin America and the Caribbean in a 1994 workshop in Miami, organized through the Biodiversity Support Program (1995) and with major input from Conservation International, the World Wildlife Fund, and the Wildlife Conservation Society. Using a similar approach to "Workshop-90," priority rankings were established within seven major habitat types for the region. Those identified and prioritized for Amazonia were: Tropical Moist Lowland Forest (Northeast Amazonia, Southeast Amazonia, and the upper Amazon), Tropical Moist Montane Forest (Guayana Montane), Herbaceous Lowland Grasslands (Amazonian Savannas), and Herbaceous Montane Grasslands (Pantepui).

Building on the Miami Workshop of 1994, the World Wildlife Fund carried out an extensive biogeographical assessment of Latin America and the Caribbean, using as key parameters conservation status (Critically Endangered, Endangered, Vulnerable, Relatively Stable, and Relatively Intact) and biological distinctiveness (parameters include estimates of species richness, endemism, and ecosystem diversity with special consideration given to cases of rarity in their representation of the major habitat type, and unusual evolutionary or ecological phenomena). The result was a division of Latin America and the Caribbean into five major terrestrial ecosystems, 11 major habitat types, and 191 areas which they refer to as ecoregions —defined as "geographically distinct assemblages of natural communities that share a large majority of their species, ecological dynamics, and similar environmental conditions and whose ecological interactions are critical for their long-term persistence."

As a follow-up to this, World Wildlife Fund is carrying out for Brazilian Amazonia detailed analyses of the vegetation types and the numbers, extent, and type of parks, reserves, and indigenous reserves in each ecoregion in order to identify where protected areas are lacking or insufficient (Ferreira et al. 2001).

The ecoregion concept of analysis has also been applied to freshwater ecosystems of Latin America and the Caribbean (Olson et al. 1998). Eleven ecoregions were considered as globally outstanding in terms of their biological distinctiveness, five of them Amazonian: the western arc of the Rio Amazonas, the southern Orinoco, the Rio Negro, the Guiana watershed, and the Várzea flooded forests. All were considered Vulnerable except for the Guiana watershed, which is Relatively Intact. Regionally outstanding ecoregions include the Amazon and Orinoco Deltas (both considered Relatively Stable), the northern Amazon Shield tributaries (Relatively Stable), the western Amazon lowlands (Relatively Intact), the Central Brazilian Shield tributaries (Vulnerable), and the Rio Tocantins-Araguaia (Vulnerable).

In 1999, the Brazilian Ministry of the Environment, through the National Program for Biological Diversity (PRONABIO), held a major workshop in Macapá, in the State of Amapá, in which more than 200 people and numerous nongovernmental organizations set priorities for biodiversity conservation throughout *Amazônia Legal,* the political definition of Amazonia within Brazil (Veríssimo et al. 2001). Whereas Workshop-90 considered only biological information, geomorphology, and protected areas, this workshop also took into account socioeconomy, indigenous reserves, deforestation, population data, fire risk, development projects, and emerging economic activities such as ecotourism, forest management, reforestation, and extractivism. By a complex process of integration, a final map outlined 385 priority areas, all of which were characterized and detailed in terms of the need for action in the creation of protected areas (strict protection and sustainable use), indigenous areas, restoration and the use of already degraded areas, economic activities, development projects, and scientific research.

As in all other wilderness areas, we believe that protected areas hold the key to maintaining the biodiversity of Amazonia —with particular emphasis being placed on the highest categories of protection, notably national parks, biological reserves, nature reserves, wildlife sanctuaries, and their equivalent (IUCN Categories I-IV). In this section, we review the protected area situation of each of the nine countries that share Amazonia, focusing on the full range of categories, including traditional federal park and reserve networks, state reserves, privately-protected areas and, where they exist, indigenous lands that also have great significance for biodiversity conservation.

With by far the largest portion of Amazonia, Brazil also has the most extensive protected area network. However, this is a recent phenomenon that has only been developed over the past three decades. Until 1974, there was only one protected area in Brazilian Amazonia, Araguaia National Park, covering part of the fluvial island of Bananal in the Rio Araguaia. In that year, in part as a response to concerns over the construction of the Trans-Amazonian and Cuiabá-Santarém Highways, the Brazilian government created a second protected area, Amazonia National Park (994 000 ha) on the east bank of the Rio Tapajós.

This got the ball rolling and led to a detailed plan, completed in 1976, for the establishment of an extensive system of parks for the region (Wetterberg et al. 1976). This plan, led by Maria Tereza Jorge Pádua (then the Director of National Parks and Equivalent Reserves in the Brazilian Forestry Development Institute - IBDF), was truly remarkable in that it represented the first-ever effort to base the creation of a protected area network on biogeographic principles —including the representation of vegetation types (Pires 1974), phytogeographic regions (Prance 1973), and the protection of areas within 30 Pleistocene forest refugia that were just beginning to be identified at the time (Haffer 1969; Brown 1975, 1987; Prance 1973, 1977). This outstanding program led to the creation of a series of large parks and reserves in the period from 1979 to 1982. Notable among them were two very large national parks, Pico da Neblina (2 200 000 ha), protecting white-sand forests, the Morro dos Seis Lagos, and the highest mountain in Brazil, and Jaú (2 272 000 ha), covering a large area of black-water *igapó* forests, terra firme forest, and white-sand scrub (*campina*) in the interfluvium between the Rios Japurá and Negro, west of Manaus. The Pico da Neblina National Park is continuous with the Serranía La Neblina and Parima-Tapirapecó National Parks in Venezuela, and together they cover an enormous area of 3 594 200 ha. Jaú is one of only three Amazonian parks to protect an entire watershed, the Pacaya-Samiria in Peru and the Central Suriname Nature Reserve in Suriname being the other two.

Three further parks created as a result of the proposals of Wetterberg et al. (1976) were Pacáas Novos, a mountain range of savanna and forest in southern Rondônia, protecting a number of tributary headwaters feeding the Rios Madeira and Mamoré-Guaporé; Serra do Divisor on the upper Rio Juruá, on the border with Peru; and Cabo Orange on the border with French Guiana in Amapá, which protects mosaics of seasonally-flooded savanna, lowland terra firme rainforest, coastal scrub, mangroves, gallery forests, and beaches. Monte Roraima National Park was created in 1989; part of the Pacaraima mountain range, it protects the Brazilian side of this sandstone tepui of 2 875 m where Guyana, Venezuela, and Brazil meet. Two further parks were decreed in 1998 in the State of Roraima, Virua National Park and Serra da Mocidade National Park, and the most recent, Serra da Cotia, was created in Rondônia in 2001. In all, the 11 National Parks cover an area of 8 994 695 ha.

Biological reserves created as a result of the Wetterberg et al. (1976) proposal included Lago Piratuba, protecting the Amapá savanna on the Rio Araguari; Rio Trombetas, important for the protection of turtle-nesting beaches; Jarú in northeastern Rondônia; and Guaporé,

91

Above, a bromeliad from Peru.
© **Günter Ziesler**

On the opposite page, Angel Falls, the world's highest waterfall, Auyán-Tepui, Venezuela.
© **Patricio Robles Gil**/*Sierra Madre*

On pp. 94-95, the Amazon river dolphin (Inia geoffrensis), *one of two Amazonian dolphin species. This animal is endemic to the region, and easily seen in the drainage basin of the Rio Amazonas.*
© **Andrea Florence**/*ARDEA LONDON*

with flooded savannas and forests on the Rio Guaporé in southern Rondônia. Two further reserves were created in the context of regional development projects —Tapirapé in southern Pará (the Grande Carajás Program), and Uatumã, north of the Rio Amazonas (the Balbina hydroelectric dam). The Gurupi Biological Reserve was created in 1988 in order to protect species restricted to eastern Amazonia, east of the Rio Tocantins, such as the endangered black-bearded saki monkey (*Chiropotes satanas satanas*) and the golden parakeet. Brazilian ornithologists Oren and Novaes (1986), who proposed its creation in 1986, recorded a further 21 threatened bird species restricted to the region which at that time had no protected areas at all. This is the most threatened of any of the Amazonian parks, and unfortunately has been largely destroyed by illegal logging. Lastly, Abufari is one of the most important protected areas for Central Amazonia, traversing the Rio Purus, covering an important sample of *várzea* forests, protecting turtle-nesting beaches, and harboring a number of primates not occurring in other Amazonian parks, such as the buffy saki monkey (*Pithecia albicans*). Together, these eight Biological Reserves total 2 940 800 ha.

In 1981, the then Ministry for the Environment (SEMA), led by Paulo Nogueira Neto, initiated the creation of a series of Ecological Stations, the aim of which was to protect representative samples of all the different Brazilian ecosystems (Nogueira Neto and Carvalho 1979; Nogueira Neto 1991). This resulted in a number of other valuable areas being protected in Amazonia, and provided an important complement to the national park and reserve system. These include the Anavilhanas Archipelago, a remarkable complex of islands created just upstream of the mouth of the Rio Negro through an unusual process of sedimentation of alluvial silt, mostly kaolinite, entering from the Rio Branco (Goulding et al. 1988). Unlike other fluvial islands in Amazonia, these are very elongated, have steep banks, and seasonally deep lake-like water bodies in their centers. With Jaú National Park, the Anavilhanas Ecological Station is significant in its protection of representative areas of black-water flooded forest or *igapó*. The Jutaí-Solimões Ecological Station in the upper Amazon protects wide expanses of *burití* (*Mauritia flexuosa*) palm swamp, and the remarkable red uakari monkey (*Cacajao calvus rubicundus*). The Rio Acre Ecological Station, on the border with Bolivia, is very remote and inaccessible and especially significant for its protection of a number of species, especially primates, found in no other protected areas. The Roraima savannas are protected in three Ecological Stations, Niquiá and Caracaraí near the Rio Branco, and the large fluvial island of Maracá on the Rio Uraricoera, which combines savanna and humid forest. Maracá is the best studied of any of the Brazilian Amazonian protected areas as a result of a two-year expedition carried out by the National Institute for Amazon Research (INPA) and the Royal Geographical Society in 1987-1988 (Milliken and Ratter 1998). Savanna and mangrove swamps are also protect-

ed in the Maracá-Jipioca Ecological Station, islands off the coast of Amapá with important nesting sites and roosts of the scarlet ibis (*Eudocimus ruber*), the greater flamingo (*Phoenicoptera ruber*), and many other aquatic birds. In all, the 14 Ecological Stations in Brazilian Amazonia total 3 191 688 ha.

There are now also a significant number of protected areas which allow for sustainable exploitation. The two main types are the so-called Extractive Reserves (*Reservas Extrativistas*) and National Forests (*Florestas Nacionais* - FLONAS). Extractive Reserves were set up to guarantee the livelihoods of rubber-tappers (*seringueiros*), Brazil nut gatherers (*castanheiros*), and riverside dwellers (*ribeirinhos*), who depend on the forest and have a direct stake in its conservation. Of interest is that this category of protected area arose from a well-organized grassroots movement of rubber-tappers in the State of Acre towards the end of the 1970s, all of them suffering from wholesale expulsion and widespread conversion of forests to pasture by big landowners (Alegretti 1990). By 2001, 16 Federal Extractive Reserves covering 3 323 179 ha had been established in Brazilian Amazonia (Ricardo and Capobianco 2001).

National Forests are created specifically for silviculture and the elusive and unachievable goal of sustainable logging. To date, scientific programs and silvicultural projects have been set up in only two of these, the 600 000-ha Tapajós National Forest on the east bank of the Rio Tapajós and the Caxiuanã National Forest Reserve east of the lower Rio Xingú, where the Goeldi Museum has a permanent research base. There are currently 35 National Forests in Brazilian Amazon, covering 16 334 987 ha. Although not protected areas in the true sense, they do provide some level of deterrent to illegal logging, which is rampant in some parts of Amazonia.

The Federal protected area system also includes Environmental Protection Areas (APAs; three totaling 4 39 726 ha), where environmentally prejudicial activities are prohibited, and three Areas of Relevant Ecological Interest totalling 20 864 ha. They include the reserves of the long-term research project on forest fragmentation, the "Biological Dynamics of Forest Fragments Project" (3 288 ha), which began in 1979 and is run by the National Institute for Amazon Research (INPA), Manaus, in collaboration first with the World Wildlife Fund and now with the Smithsonian Institution, Washington, D.C. (Bierregaard et al. 2001).

All these 90 Federal protected areas are now administered by the Brazilian Institute for the Environment and Renewable Natural Resources (IBAMA). They number 90 in all and cover 35 245 919 ha, or 8.3% of the area of Brazilian Amazonia.

Paralleling these, and also making an important contribution to conservation in Brazilian Amazonia, are equivalent state systems that have been developed by the nine State Environmental Departments. Although they are recent (mostly set up in the late 1980s and 1990s), they now form a significant portion of the pro-

tected area network of Brazilian Amazonia, totaling 77 and covering 28 632 440 ha, or 6.7% of Brazilian Amazonia. Thirty-four (5 353 951 ha) are strictly protected, and 43 (23 278 489 ha) allow for varying degrees and types of exploitation. The latter include 20 State Extractive Reserves covering 3 783 943 ha, 19 State Environmental Protection Areas (APAs) totaling 15 156 103 ha, one State Forest covering 57 629 ha, and three Sustainable Development Reserves covering 4 280 814 ha.

The Sustainable Development Reserve is worthy of special mention. The first of these, Mamirauá, was decreed an ecological station in 1990, but was converted into a Sustainable Development Reserve in 1996. It is the largest protected area for white-water inundated forest, stretching over 1 124 000 ha between the Rios Japurá and Solimões to the Rio Auatí-Paraná and covering the entire known range of the white uakari monkey, *Cacajao calvus calvus*. This animal was studied in the 1980s by José Márcio Ayres, who first proposed the creation of the larger reserve, finally bringing to fruition a much earlier recommendation by Mittermeier (1973) to protect both, "the entire fluvial island formed by the Rio Japurá, the Rio Solimões, and the Auatí-Paraná" and especially "the Rio Panauá," all now subsumed within Mamirauá. Mamirauá has been an extraordinarily successful model in which local fishing communities, dependent on the flooded forests, have participated in and benefited from the management of the reserve. They have collaborated with long-term research programs and surveys of key species, with anthropological studies, and with programs for nutrition, education, and health (Ayres et al. 1995; SCM, CNPQ/MCT, and IPAAM 1996).

The Amana Sustainable Development Reserve was created one year later, in 1997. Its 2 350 000 ha connects the Mamirauá Reserve to the Jau National Park. The Jau National Park, in turn, is connected to the Rio Negro State Environmental Protection Area, the Rio Negro State Ecological Station, and the Anavilhanas Ecological Station. Together, this series of protected areas covers 7 477 133 ha, from the Japurá-Solimões interfluvium east as far as the left bank of the lower Rio Negro, and represents the largest single continuum of protected tropical rainforest anywhere on Earth. The creation of the Amana reserve was a response to the proposition of the Parks and Reserves component of the G-7 Pilot Program for Brazilian Tropical Forest to create large-scale biological corridors.

Looking at these different categories of protected areas, we find that 36 federal protected areas (11 national parks, 8 biological reserves, 14 ecological stations, and three areas of relevant ecological interest) and 34 state strictly-protected areas fall under the categories of strictest protection (IUCN Categories I-IV). These cover a total area of 20 501 798 ha, or 4.8% of the region as defined.

In addition to these, there are another 97 areas destined for various kinds of sustainable use, including 54 federal reserves (including federal APAs, forest re-

serves, and federal extractive reserves) and 43 state reserves (including state APAs, state forests, state extractive reserves, and sustainable development reserves). These are not primarily intended for biodiversity conservation and do not provide strict protection, but rather allow for more controlled use of certain resources (e.g., timber, Brazil nuts, rubber, other forest products) and require the permanence of forest over large areas. These total 43 376 381 ha, or 10.2% of Brazilian Amazonia. Although these are not mainly intended for biodiversity protection, they can play important roles.

Finally, there are 397 Indigenous Reserves and Areas, which account for 103 396 964 ha, or 24.4% of Brazilian Amazonia as we define it (Rylands 1990a, 1991; Ricardo 2001a). It is estimated that 180 000 Indians live in these indigenous areas, which come under the jurisdiction and administration of the National Indian Foundation (FUNAI). An additional 80 indigenous areas have still to be formally recognized by FUNAI, while 234 have been formally approved but are still in varying states of delimitation, demarcation, and gazetting.

The extent of these indigenous reserves points to their overwhelming importance in terms of the conservation of the forest (Posey 1983; Zimmerman et al. 2001). Although not generally considered to be conservation areas, indigenous people in these areas are often very successful in preventing the destruction of forests, and many are requesting to develop management plans and strategies for sustainable use of forest products. One of the most important of these areas is the Kayapó Indigenous Reserve in southern Pará. The Kayapó Indian nation has achieved, both in law and in practice, the control of 13 million ha of forest and Cerrado, and they have been successful in excluding ranching, colonization, and even hydroelectric schemes. Myriads of roads end at the borders of the reserve, and its forests maintain healthy populations even of game species such as peccaries, tapirs, and deer (Zimmerman et al. 2001). Conservation International, through its Global Conservation Fund and its Brazil Program, is now helping the Kayapo monitor and protect their lands through establishment and maintenance of guard posts in the most vulnerable areas.

Combined, the federal and state protected areas and sustainable development reserves and the demarcated indigenous reserves total 167 275 143 ha, or 39.4% of Brazilian Amazonia as we define it. However, this total is an overestimate of what is actually set aside because of a major problem of overlap —mainly between parks and reserves and indigenous reserves on the one hand, and forest reserves and indigenous reserves on the other (Ricardo 2001b). To give an idea of the scale of this problem, Ricardo and Capobianco (2001) calculate that the sum of all federal and state protected areas, including those strictly-protected and those destined for sustainable use, is 64 586 259 ha or 12.9% of *Amazônia Legal* (not to be confused with our biological definition of Brazilian Amazonia). However, if one takes into account the overlap among them and with indigenous

Above, blue-and-yellow macaw (Ara ararauna) *pair interacting on top of broken palm-tree trunk.*
© **Theo Allofs**

On the opposite page, a pair of hoatzins (Opisthocomus hoazin), *Manu National Park, Peru.*
© **Patricio Robles Gil**/*Sierra Madre*

reserves, this falls to an actual protected area of about 8.5% of Legal Amazonia, a difference of 34.1%. This means that the total land area protected could be considerably closer to 25%-26% than to the 39.4% indicated above, but it is impossible to define this precisely at this time.

A major financing initiative to promote the protection of Brazil's tropical forests (including the Atlantic forest) was set up through a German initiative at the G-7 Summit meeting in July of 1990, and approved by the Brazilian government just prior to the 1992 Earth Summit in Rio de Janeiro. One of the major components of this "Pilot Program to Conserve the Brazilian Rain Forest (PPG-7)" was dedicated to improving the management of protected areas, including extractive reserves, indigenous lands, and national forests (Kohlhepp 2001). The aim of the Indigenous Lands Project was to promote the integrity of these reserves and the conservation of their resources by completing the necessary legislation, demarcation, and registration. In addition, another major concept, this one to emerge from the Parks and Reserves Project, was the macro-level, regional approach to establishing very large "biological corridors" that link key protected areas in broader landscape. A detailed analysis considering a variety of biogeographic parameters as well as protected areas already in place resulted in the selection of five major corridors in Brazilian Amazonia: the Central Corridor, extending from the west of the Rio Japurá to the east of the Rio Negro in the State of Amazonas; the Northern Corridor, from the Colombian border along the Venezuelan frontier in the states of Amazonas and Roraima; the Western Corridor, extending through the states of Acre and Rondônia along the Bolivian and Peruvian frontier; the Southern Corridor, stretching from west of the Rio Tapajós to the Rio Gurupi in southern Pará; and the Ecotone Corridor, along the southern arc of the Amazonia, the region most threatened by the northward progression of the agricultural frontier (Ayres et al. 1997).

The mere announcement of this project resulted in the creation of the Amana State Sustainable Development Reserve, which now links the Mamirauá State Sustainable Development Reserve and the Jau National Park, consolidating a very large part of the Central Corridor. The Brazilian Government has also been making considerable progress in the consolidation of the Southern Corridor, most particularly at its eastern half along the Rio Guaporé, and working towards the creation of trans-frontier parks with Bolivia.

The biological corridor concept was also adopted by Conservation International as a major strategic vision for all the regions in which it works, and has now been applied to the Andean countries, the Guianas, and many other parts of the tropical world (Ayres et al., *op. cit.*; Conservation International 2000c). This concept is consistent with the enormous opportunities that still exist to protect vast areas of Amazonia —something that simply is no longer possible at a comparable scale in other rainforest areas.

Peru has within its borders the second largest portion of Amazonia after Brazil. Within this area are a total of six national parks (Manu National Park, 1 532 806 ha; Bahuaja-Sonene National Park, 1 091 416 ha; Yanachaga-Chemillén National Park, 122 000 ha; Cordillera Azul National Park, 1 353 191 ha; Rio Abiseo National Park, 274 500 ha; Tingo Maria National Park, 18 000 ha), and two national reserves (Pacaya-Samiria National Reserve, 2 080 000 ha; Tambopata National Reserve, 274 690 ha), together totaling 6 746 603 ha, or 10.2% of Peruvian Amazonia.

To these should be added a further seven reserved zones, or *zonas reservadas* (Santiago-Comaina, 1 642 567 ha; Gueppi, 625 971 ha; Allpahuayo-Mishana, 57 667 ha; Apurimac, 1 669 200 ha; Alto Purus, 2 724 264 ha; Manu, 257 000 ha; and Amarakaeri, 419 139 ha) totaling 7 395 808 ha. The reserved zone category is very important because it represents a step prior to national park creation, with many of the current national parks having first passed through a reserved zone stage. Some are close or directly adjacent to existing parks (e.g., Manu) and are thus critical elements in corridor establishment; others (e.g., Purus) are quite large and would represent major additions to the national park network. On top of these, there are also two communal reserves, or *reservas comunales* (El Sira, 616 404 ha; Yanesha, 34 745 ha) and one protected forest, or *bosque de protección* (San Matías-San Carlos, 145 818 ha). Together, these three categories account for 8 192 775 ha, or 12.4% of Peruvian Amazonia.

In terms of indigenous lands, Peru recognizes "indigenous communities" (*comunidades indígenas*) belonging to 42 groups in Peruvian Amazonia. The total titled land area occupied by these communities is 7 379 942 ha, with an additional 344 887 ha reserved in a special category for the Nahua and Kugapakori tribes. Together, these lands cover 7 724 829 ha, or 11.7% of Peruvian Amazonia as defined here.

Combining all these different categories of protection, we arrive at 22 664 207 ha or 34.3% of the region under some designation. Obviously, these areas do not receive equal protection, with the national parks and national reserves receiving the most attention, but they are an important start.

Two of the national parks stand out as being globally important. The first is Manu, which was established in 1973, was recognized as a World Heritage Site in 1987, and became the core area of a Biosphere Reserve in 1997. It is considered by many to be the single richest protected area on Earth in terms of biodiversity, and has an enormous altitudinal range from 200 m in the Amazonian lowlands up the foothills and slopes of the Andes to 4 000 m. Its bird diversity approaches 1 000 species —200 more than all of the United States and Canada combined—, and other groups are comparably diverse. Wildlife is not just diverse but also abundant, making for excellent wildlife-viewing. Indeed, one of the authors (RAM) considers Manu to be the single best site in the world for observing rainforest species.

Campa Indian hunter from the Gran Pajonal area of Peruvian Amazonia.
© **Victor Englebert**

A number of interesting indigenous groups live in small communities in the vicinity of the park, including Matsiguenka, Arahuaca, Yine, Amarakaeri, Huachipaeri, Mashco-Piro, and Nahua, some of them still uncontacted. The second important national park is Bahuaja-Sonene, sometimes still referred to by its earlier name, Tambopata-Candamo. Established in 1996 and expanded to its current size in 2000, it is the result of a complex and lengthy series of negotiations involving Peruvian authorities, local indigenous and campesino communities, Mobil Oil, and Conservation International —a fascinating story that has already been documented in one major book (MacQuarrie 2001). In addition to protecting rainforest, it also includes Pampas del Heath, the only humid tropical wetland system in Peru with non-rainforest species like the marsh deer (*Blastoceros dichotomus*) and the maned wolf (*Chrysocyon brachyurus*). It is immediately adjacent to Madidi National Park in Bolivia and forms the core area of the critically important, trans-frontier Vilcabamba-Amboro Corridor that has been the major focus for Conservation International in this region for more than a decade.

Peru is also experimenting with a number of interesting new conservation mechanisms. In 2001, following passage of a new Forestry Law, the government of Peru awarded the first permanently-renewable large conservation concession to the Amazon Conservation Association, an environmental NGO. This 136 000-ha concession in the Los Amigos watershed protects a rich mixture of wetland, riparian, and terra firme habitats in the biological corridor between Manu National Park and Bahuaja-Sonene National Park, and harbors many plant communities and wildlife not otherwise represented in the Peruvian national park system. The watershed also has the highest known density of clay-lick *collpas* in the world. This conservation concession mechanism allows NGOs to play a role in the management and conservation of vast amounts of state-owned land in Peruvian Amazonia, and in the future may significantly complement the government's protected area system and help to distribute the responsibility for biodiversity management to civil society.

In the Colombian portion of Amazonia, there are eight national parks (Serranía de La Macarena National Park, Amacayacu National Park, Cordillera de los Picachos National Park, La Paya National Park, Serranía de Chiribiquete National Park, Cahuinari National Park, Tinigua National Park, and the recently-created Alto Fragua-Indiwasi National Park) and two national natural reserves (Puinawai and Nukak) that together total 5 882 280 ha, or 13.1% of the region (Colombia, INDERENA 1989).

Of these, three stand out as being particularly important. Serranía de Chiribiquete National Park, at 1 280 000 ha, is the largest in the country. It is situated on the Colombian portion of the Guayana Shield in an area characterized by tepui formations similar to those in southern Venezuela. This was once the tribal land of the Karijona tribe, now extinct, who left behind many rock paintings on the vertical walls of the tepuis. The flora is a mix of rainforest formations in the lowlands and shrubby formations on the tepuis.

Created as a biological reserve in 1948, Serranía de La Macarena National Park (1 131 350 ha) was the first protected area in the country. It is continuous with Tinigua National Park and Cordillera de Los Picachos National Park extending up the eastern slopes of the Cordillera, and together they cover 1 619 225 ha. La Macarena is considered one of the most important wildlife refuges in the country, in part because of its isolation from the rest of the Andes and its sedimentary origin. Its flora and fauna is a very diverse mix of Guayanan (e.g., *Vellozia macarenensis*), Andean (spectacled bear, *Tremarctos ornatus*), Orinocoan, and typical Amazonian species. It has also been the site of some of the longest-running primate field studies in South America, mainly by teams of Japanese researchers (Nishimura et al. 1995).

In contrast to the other two rather unique national parks, Amacayacu (293 500 ha) is typical lowland Amazonian, consisting mainly of rainforest and a number of other formations, among them *Mauritia flexuosa* palm forests, locally known as *morichales*. It is rich in wildlife, with at least 500 bird species and 150 mammals, including 12 monkey species.

The protected area network is complemented by an extensive system of indigenous reserves or *resguardos indígenas*, totaling 210 in all. These cover 13 000 000 ha, or 28.9% of Colombian Amazonia, and constitute what is probably the most representative network of indigenous lands in all of Amazonia.

Combining the protected area network and the indigenous reserve network, we find that a total of 18 882 280 ha, or 41.9% of Colombian Amazonia is under some designation.

The Venezuelan portion of Amazonia is located south of the Orinoco in the Guayana Highlands. The entire region falls within the borders of three states, Amazonas, Bolívar, and Delta Amacuro, all of which have large protected areas. In all, there are seven national parks totaling 9 040 000 ha and three national monuments covering 1 069 865 ha, for a total of 10 109 865 ha, or 24.2% of the Amazonian portion of Venezuela.

In addition to these, there are also two Biosphere Reserves, the 8 400 000-ha Alto Orinoco Biosphere Reserve and the 1 125 000-ha Delta del Orinoco Biosphere Reserve, which cover a further 9 525 000 ha, or 22.7% of the region.

Finally, there are three forest reserves totaling 9 552 100 ha; three Forest Lots covering 796 596 ha; and one Protected Zone covering 7 262 358 ha, for an additional 17 611 054 ha, or 42.1% of the region.

In contrast to most other Amazonian countries, Venezuela has no formally designated indigenous lands.

Canaima was the first to be decreed in 1962, and is one of the largest, covering 3 000 000 ha in the heart of the Gran Sabana in Bolívar State, with significant areas of forest in its eastern part and including the enormous Auyán-Tepui and the spectacular Chimanta-Tepui. Au-

Huaorani Indian hunting with blowgun in the Yasuni area of Ecuador. The Huaorani make the world's only "flat" blowgun.
© **Jim Clare**/*Nature Picture Library*

yán-Tepui has a surface area of 70 000 ha and numerous spectacular waterfalls, including Kukenán Falls and the world-renowned Angel Falls, the highest waterfall on Earth with a drop of more than 1 000 m. Although the entire tepui region is visually breathtaking, it is fair to say that Canaima, with its combination of vast open savannas, forest-covered table mountains, pristine rivers, and unbelievable waterfalls, simply has some of the most impressive landscapes on Earth.

A number of other important parks were all decreed in 1978. Yapacana National Park (320 000 ha) is at the confluence of the Ríos Orinoco and Ventuari and protects the Cerro Yapacana, a tepui formation 1 345 m high. It includes important areas of high forest, white-sand forests, and terra firme savanna. Duida-Marahuaca National Park (210 000 ha) includes the Cerro Duida (2 580 m) and Cerro Marahuaca tepuis. Serranía La Neblina National Park (1 360 000 ha) protects the northern slopes of the highest mountain east of the Andes (3 014 m) and is contiguous with Pico da Neblina National Park in Brazil. It is known for its deep valleys, such as the Grand Canyon of the Rio Baría, a tributary of the Rio Casiquiare. Jauá-Sarisariñama (330 000 ha) protects the headwaters of a number of important tributaries of the Rio Caura and three important tepui formations. In addition, it is famous for its unique and amazing *simas de colapso,* round vertical holes up to 352 m wide at top, 500 m at the base, and 350 m deep: gigantic pits where the central core of sandstone has collapsed leaving enormous forest-covered sinkholes. Parima-Tapirapecó National Park is a huge park covering 3 500 000 ha. Decreed in 1991, it too is contiguous with Pico da Neblina in Brazil. All five of these parks are in Amazonas State. One additional park, the Mariusa, is located in Delta Amacuro, and covers 320 000 ha.

The Pantepui Natural Monument covers 1 069 820 ha and is spread over Amazonas and Bolívar States, protecting all the tepuis not already in one of the national parks. Two other tiny natural monuments, Cerro Autana (30 ha) and Piedra de El Cocuy (15 ha), are both in Amazonas State.

One of the forest reserves, the Caura, is also noteworthy. It encompasses the basin of the Rio Caura, one of the largest and most pristine in Venezuela, and covers 5 134 000 ha. Unfortunately, being a forest reserve, it is potentially vulnerable to timber exploitation and the lower portion of the basin is at risk from colonization and an expanding agricultural frontier. To ensure that the region's biodiversity and its indigenous people (Ye'kwana and Sanema) are protected, Conservation International is working with the Venezuelan government, the oil company BITOR (PDVSA), and three Venezuelan conservation NGOs, PROVITA, Audubon de Venezuela, and ACOANA, to create a series of protected areas and eventually a biosphere reserve in the Caura.

The Amazonian portion of Bolivia has two national parks (Noel Kempff Mercado, 1 523 446 ha; Tunari, 300 000 ha), one combined national park and wildlife refuge (Carrasco National Park and Cavernas de Repe-

chon Wildlife Refuge, 622 600 ha), one combined national park and indigenous territory (Isiboro-Sécure, 1 200 000 ha), three combined national parks and "natural areas of integrated management" (Madidi, 1 895 750 ha; Amboró, 637 600 ha; Cotapata, 40 000 ha), one "natural area of integrated management" (Apolobamba, 483 744 ha), one national reserve (Amazonica Manuripi, 768 000 ha), one biosphere reserve (Estación Biológica del Beni, 135 000 ha), and one combined biosphere reserve and indigenous territory (Pilón Lajas, 400 000 ha). Together, these total 8 006 140 ha, or 22.5% of the region as defined here.

Indigenous areas in Bolivia are referred to as "community lands," and they fall into two categories, *tierras comunitarias de origen de decreto supremo* and *tierras comunitarias de origen inmovilizadas.* In all, there are eight of the former and 13 of the latter, and they cover an area of 8 548 800 ha, or 24.0% of Bolivian Amazonia.

In addition, there are 12 forest reserves of various different categories and two watershed protection areas that together total 10 476 600 ha, or 29.5% of Bolivian Amazonia. However, as with other forest reserves, these are intended for timber exploitation and not biodiversity protection.

Combining all designated areas, including forest reserves, we arrive at a total of 27 031 540 ha or 76% of Bolivian Amazonia as defined here.

The most important protected area in Bolivia is without a doubt Madidi National Park, which was established in 1995. In large part, the movement to protect this area resulted from the first ever RAP (Rapid Assessment Program) Expedition carried out by Conservation International in 1990. This expedition, led by the late ornithologist Ted Parker, stimulated enormous interest in Madidi, both within the country and internationally. Beginning in 1992, Charles Munn of the Wildlife Conservation Society and Rosa María Ruiz of the Bolivian NGO Eco-Bolivia also began to focus attention on Madidi, and Ruiz was contracted by the government's Institute of Ecology to help delimit the park's boundaries. This, together with continuing involvement by Conservation International's Bolivia Program, finally led to the creation in 1995 of the 1 895 750-ha Madidi National Park and associated Integrated Natural Management Area by then President Gonzalo Sánchez de Lozada.

Like Manu and Bahuaja-Sonene in Peru, Madidi National Park covers an enormous altitudinal range and harbors one of the highest levels of biodiversity of any protected area on Earth. Among its many superlatives, this park is thought to harbor 1 100 bird species which, if confirmed, would be the highest for any protected area on Earth. In Bolivia, it is contiguous with Pilón Lajas, Manuripi Heath, and Apolobamba, and it borders the equally spectacular Bahuaja-Sonene National Park on the Peruvian side. Together, these protected areas form the core of the Vilcabamba-Amboro Corridor, a 4 420 300-ha area that is the focal point of Conservation International's work in these two countries.

Above, Yanomami Indian girl in southern Venezuela. The Yanomami live on the Brazil-Venezuela border and constitute one of the largest indigenous groups in Amazonia.
© **Victor Englebert**

On the opposite page, Kayapó Indian from the Rio Xingú region of southern Brazilian Amazonia. The lip disc was much used in the past, but is now disappearing in the younger generation.
© **Art Wolfe**

million ha in the interior of the country (Sizer and Rice 1995). Making the reserve a reality required a major commitment on the part of then President Jules Wij-

forest reserves and other categories eventually slated for utilization), we find that 55 723 047 ha, or 8.3%, of Amazonia as defined here is already protected —at least

In the Amazonian portion of Ecuador, there are two national parks, Yasuní (982 000 ha) and Sumaco Napo-Galeras (205 249 ha, of which about 20%, or 41 050 ha, is in the foothills of the Andes below 500 m and the caiman, and also have 60% of the bird species recorded from Guyana. Conservation International Guyana, the lead agency for the three-part consultation process for this proposed park, has completed Phase One in which the government of Guyana ensured that the indigenous

on paper. This represents a very significant land area a third again as large as California and almost the size of Texas. Nonetheless, given the many threats that the region faces, it is certainly not enough. When one adds to this the fact that no single park or reserve in the region is currently protected to the full extent required, the challenge becomes even greater.

Indigenous lands also play a key role. Although they have different names in seven of the nine countries that share Amazonia (and are still entirely lacking in two), they cover a combined area of 138 046 995 ha, or 20.7% of Amazonia as defined here —an area a little smaller than the State of Alaska. This is an area two-and-a-half times what is covered in parks and reserves, and therefore represents a very significant piece of the overall biodiversity conservation effort.

Finally, we have the areas destined for various forms of controlled utilization but, in theory at least, providing some level of protection to the forest. These cover a further 89 536 910 ha, or 13.4% of Amazonia. The protection that they provide is far less than that in strict parks and nature reserves, or even indigenous reserves. Nonetheless, they have some potential for biodiversity conservation —and some can be or already are in the process of being converted to stricter categories of protection (e.g., the Caura Forest Reserve in Venezuela).

In all, these many different categories cover a total of 283 306 952 ha, or 42.4% of Amazonia as a whole. Even taking into account the overlap that exists among some of these categories in countries like Brazil, there is no doubt that a large portion of Amazonia —at least one third— is already under some designation.

Although many different protected areas, reserves, and indigenous territories of different kinds already exist —at least on paper— there is certainly no reason to be complacent. The great challenges that now lie before us in this most important of all wilderness areas are, first and foremost, to *ensure that existing areas are effectively managed and funded in perpetuity.* Also of great importance is the need to *convert many of the areas currently destined for use into strictly-protected parks and reserves,* a process that is already under way in some countries. Next is the need to *establish new parks and reserves* in areas not yet under any designation, and thus vulnerable to the most destructive forms of exploitation. *Creation of many additional indigenous lands* is also a priority and an urgent need, as indicated by the fact that several hundred have been identified as requiring such protection. Finally, we have the need to *create megacorridors linking protected areas* —to ensure maximum ecological and evolutionary continuity and continued delivery of globally-important ecosystem services for the region and the world. Indeed, if all the current protected areas were adequately protected but everything around them were to be lost, it is unlikely that even such large areas would survive in the face of the drastic regional climate changes that would result.

Fortunately, this is a region where enormous opportunities still exist and where conservation can be achieved at a scale far beyond what is possible in most other biodiversity-rich areas. Now is the time to make it happen, and to ensure that the magnificent biological exuberance of Amazonia, its great diversity of indigenous peoples, and the many essential services it provides for the entire planet are maintained into the future.

ANTHONY B. RYLANDS
RUSSELL A. MITTERMEIER
JOHN PILGRIM
CLAUDE GASCON
GUSTAVO FONSECA
JOSE MARIA CARDOSO DA SILVA
CRISTINA G. MITTERMEIER
THOMAS BROOKS
JOSÉ VICENTE RODRÍGUEZ
JOE SINGH
WIM UDENHOUT
LISA FAMOLARE
NEVILLE WALDRON
STANLEY MALONE
VÍCTOR HUGO INCHAUSTY
CARLOS PONCE DEL PRADO
ROBERTO ROCA
ROBERTO CAVALCANTI
FABIO ARJONA
FAUSTO LÓPEZ
CHARLES HUTCHINSON
MARC G.M. VAN ROOSMALEN
JOSÉ MÁRCIO AYRES
ADRIAN FORSYTH
IAN BOWLES
CYRIL KORMOS
ADAM MEKLER
ROBERT WALLER
ERWIN PALACIOS
FREDDY MIRANDA
ANA LIZ FLORES
LUIS DÁVALOS
REGGY NELSON
ANNETTE TJON SIE FAT
JENNY CHUN
THOMAS AKRE
JOSÉ VICENTE RUEDA

Above, Trio Indian boy with bow and arrow, Kwamalasemutu village, Sipaliwini River, southern Suriname.

On the opposite page, Kwamalasemutu Indian village, Sipaliwini River, southern Suriname. Kwamalasemutu is one of the three main villages of the Trio Indians who live on the Suriname-Brazil border in one of the most remote and least impacted portions of Amazonia.
Both photos:
*© **Russell Mittermeier***

THE CONGO FORESTS OF CENTRAL AFRICA

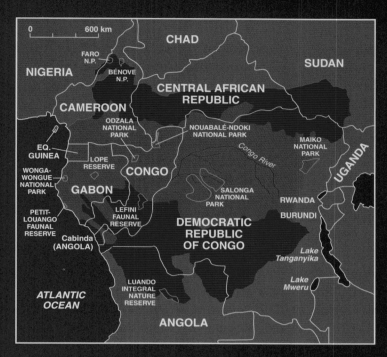

The Congo Forests of Central Africa are the second largest block of tropical rainforest left on Earth. Including part or all of seven countries (Democratic Republic of Congo, Republic of Congo, Gabon, Cameroon, Central African Republic, Equatorial Guinea, and the tiny Cabinda enclave of Angola), the core forest zone covers some 1 725 221 km², and globally is surpassed only by Amazonia. The majority of this region, a total of 1 011 400 km², or 58.6%, lies within the Democratic Republic of Congo. The Republic of the Congo, Gabon, and Cameroon all have similar-sized portions, with 233 098 km² (13.5%), 220 671 km² (12.8%), and 168 018 km² (9.7%), respectively. Smaller portions lie within the Central African Republic (64 735 km²; 3.8%), mainland Equatorial Guinea (24 931 km²; 1.4%), and the Cabinda enclave of Angola at the mouth of the Congo River (2 368 km²; 0.1%) (WCMC 2002).

As we define it here, the core region of Congolian Forest is bordered on the west by the Atlantic, and extends from the Sanaga River, which cuts across the center of Cameroon, south through southern Cameroon, the mainland portion of Equatorial Guinea, Gabon, the Republic of Congo, the tiny Cabinda enclave of Angola, and the westernmost extension of the Democratic Republic of Congo. It includes all of mainland Equatorial Guinea, plus much of Gabon and the Republic of Congo, and the southernmost rainforest portion of the Central African Republic. Moving east, it covers a large proportion of the Democratic Republic of Congo, both north and south of the Congo River through the Ituri Forest and extending as far as the mountains of the Albertine Rift. However, the threatened forests of the Albertine Rift are considered a distinct new hotspot and are not part of the wilderness area discussed here. Furthermore, the islands of Bioko and Annobon (which are politically part of Equatorial Guinea) and the independent nation of São Tomé

and Príncipe are also considered part of the Guinean Forests of West Africa Hotspot, and are not included in this wilderness area (Mittermeier et al. 1999; Myers et al. 2000).

Our definition of the core Congolian Forest portion of this region encompasses almost all of six WWF ecoregions, including the Atlantic Equatorial Coastal Forests (AT0102) (189 665 km²); the Central Congolian Lowland Forests (AT0104) (414 758 km²); the Northeastern Congolian Lowland Forests (AT0124) (533 473 km²); the Northwestern Congolian Lowland Forests (AT0126) (434 148 km²); the Western Congolian Swamp Forests (AT0129) (128 643 km²); and the Eastern Congolian Swamp Forests (AT0110) (92 736 km²) —a total area of 1 793 423 km² (Olson et al. 2001). However, it does not include their Cameroonian Highlands Forests, Cross-Sanaga-Bioko Coastal Forests, Mount Cameroon and Bioko Montane Forests or their São Tomé and Príncipe Moist Lowland Forests, all of which are included in our Guinean Forests of West Africa Hotspot, nor does it include their Albertine Rift Montane Forests, which we also consider a hotspot. Given that ecoregion areas in the Albertine Rift and Guinean Forests hotspots have been excluded, the total area of core forest considered here is 1 725 221 km².

However, for purposes of this analysis, we are also considering as wilderness a large transitional savanna-forest mosaic region located both north and south of the core forest block. This area is nearly as extensive as the main rainforest block itself, and

▮ Transitional zones
▮ Rainforest zone

On the opposite page, Mbeli Bai, Nouabalé-Ndoki National Park, Republic of Congo. Bais are unusual natural clearings in the forest that attract many rainforest species such as gorillas, elephants, sitatunga, bushpigs, and forest buffalo. They provide excellent wildlife viewing opportunities for species that are otherwise very difficult to observe.
*© **Michael K. Nichols**/National Geographic Image Collection*

taining an unbroken tract of forest in protected areas of various kinds, including conservation concessions, throughout this vast region.

Biodiversity

The Congo Forests are rich in biodiversity and rank among the top four wilderness areas on Earth in this category. However, they are not as rich as the rainforests of Amazonia and New Guinea and, surprisingly, are matched or exceeded in several categories by the Miombo-Mopane Woodlands and Grasslands to the south.

Vascular plant diversity is estimated at up to 12 000 species for the Guineo-Congolian Center of Endemism as a whole, which includes the forests of West Africa (Davis et al. 1994). Of these, at least 2 250 species are endemic to the Guinean Forests of West Africa Hotspot (Mittermeier et al. 1999; Myers et al. 2000), meaning that the Congo Forests, as defined here, have at least 9 750 species. Endemism is harder to calculate, but the total is at least the sum of the national plant endemism totals for the countries enclosed in these wilderness areas, namely Gabon (1 573 endemic species), the Republic of Congo (1 200 endemic species), and mainland Equatorial Guinea (17 endemic species). Although significant portions of the Democratic Republic of Congo (1 200 endemics), Cameroon (156 endemics), and Central African Republic (100 endemics) also fall into this wilderness area, many of the endemics in the Democratic Republic of Congo are concentrated around the new Albertine Rift Hotspot, while a large portion of those in Cameroon are in the highlands that we consider part of the Guinean Forests of West Africa Hotspot and consequently are excluded from our totals here. As a result, we estimate that endemism for this core Congo Forest wilderness is at least 2 800 species, with a reasonable estimate being about 3 300 species and an upper limit of about 4 000 endemics. The estimate of 3 300 would represent a level of endemism of 34%, slightly higher than that of the Guinean Forests of West Africa Hotspot.

Bird diversity is 708 species, of which 10 are endemic; mammals are represented by 270 species, with 39 endemics; reptiles by 142 species, 15 of them endemic; and amphibians by 139 species, of which 28 are endemic (WWF, in prep.; A. Rylands, in. litt.).

If one adds the transitional savanna-forest mosaics to the north and south, these totals increase to 939 birds (17 endemic); 393 mammals (56 endemic); 226 reptiles (25 endemic); and 189 amphibians (46 endemic) (A. Rylands, pers. comm., 2002; CI unpublished data; WWF, in prep.).

Certain groups are especially diverse in these forests. Primates, for example, reach very high levels of diversity here, with at least 17 genera, 43 species, and 68 taxa, of which at least 40 taxa (59%) are endemic (A. Rylands, in litt., 2002) —numbers that are exceeded only by the much more extensive forests of Amazonia. Also remarkable is that this high total diversity is main-

tained at the site level. A number of African forest sites have 13-15 primate species, with the record being 16 in a single study area, the Edoro Field Station in the central Ituri Forest of the Democratic Republic of Congo.

Given that this region has within it the mighty Congo River, the world's third largest river in terms of volume (after the Amazon and the Rio Negro), freshwater diversity is also high. The Congo Basin alone has at least 686 species (Teugels and Guégan 1994), of which at least 548 are endemic (Groombridge and Jenkins 1998). The Democratic Republic of Congo has 962 species, but this number probably includes the Great Lakes to the east, which are not part of this wilderness area (McAllister et al. 1997). On the other hand, these numbers do not include the drainage basin of the Ogooué and other large rivers that exist in this region but are not part of the Congo drainage itself. A conservative estimate would be that there are at least 800-1 000 freshwater fish species in the wilderness area as we define it; in any case, these numbers are likely to increase dramatically as more research is conducted.

Looking at major vegetation types, very few studies have mapped the vegetation of the whole Central African region. White (1983) compiled the existing national maps and relied on the opinion of local experts to produce a vegetation map for the entire continent. More recently, l'Institut de la Carte Internationale de la Végétation (ICIV) produced a vegetation map based on existing national maps completed by the interpretation of Landsat images. Additionally, the TREES vegetation map of Africa focuses on the Guineo-Congolian ecological domain. It was prepared on the basis of satellite data and proposes a classification based on spectral characteristics of the vegetation formations (Mayaux et al. 1999). Based on these references, three major forest types and a number of others of smaller distribution can be identified from the dense moist forest of the Guineo-Congolian Domain, the principal ones being *evergreen tropical forest, semideciduous tropical forest,* and *swamp forest* (Mayaux et al., *op. cit.*).

Evergreen tropical forest canopy composition varies, from highly-diverse mixed forests, to forests dominated by one or more tree species. In the east, dominant species are often members of the Caesalpinaceae, including *Julbernardia seretii* and *Cynometra alexandri*. Particularly noteworthy from Central Cameroon and Congo east to the Albertine Rift, are the monodominant forests where a single species, *Gilbertiodendron dewevrei*, represents from 60% to over 80% of the canopy over areas from several hectares to more than hundreds of square kilometers (Hart et al. 1996).

Another distinctive formation is the open canopied forest with thick herbaceous understory that occurs in many areas across the entire region, particularly in the west. In the Odzala National Park in the Republic of Congo and the Minkebé and Lopé Reserves in Gabon, the understory is dense and largely dominated by Marantaceae and Zingiberaceae (Dowsett-Lemaire 1995; White and Abernethy 1997). This dense ground vegetation

On the opposite page, naive forest chimpanzees (Pan troglodytes) *that have never before encountered humans. This photo was taken in the Goualougo Triangle.*

Above, moustached guenon (Cercopithecus cephus)*, one of a large group of African forest monkeys that reach their highest levels of diversity in the Congo Forests.*
Both photos:
© **Michael K. Nichols**/*National Geographic Image Collection*

that grows up to more than 2 m high appears after savanna has been colonized by trees and disappears as the forest becomes mature. Marantaceae forest is an important source of food for large mammals such as forest elephant, western lowland gorilla, and chimpanzee, and supports high animal densities.

Semideciduous tropical forest is the climax forest ecosystem of the periphery of the Congo Basin. The canopy is lower and contains up to 70% deciduous species, mixed with evergreen forest. The canopy reaches 30 to 40 m, with a few emergents reaching 60 m, and allows the development of a shrub stratum. Tree species diversity is high, with legumes being particularly common (e.g., *Afzelia bipindensis*, *Anthonotha ferruginea*, *Piptadeniastrum africanum*). In the Republic of Congo, this type of forest, found mostly in the Mayombe and the Massif du Chaillu, is extremely biologically rich and very important economically because it contains timber species such as *Aucoumea klaineana*, *Staudtia gabonensis*, *Entandrophragma utile*, and *Nauclea diderrichii*.

Swamp forest is located along rivers and is dependent on frequent floods and the presence of soils with insufficient drainage. Differences in flooding cycles and soil drainage conditions induce a gradient from riparian forest and periodically-inundated forest to permanently-inundated forest (Evrard 1968). As a result of the extensive hydrographic network, swamp forests cover large areas in the central part of the Congo Basin. This type of forest is characterized by the presence of species such as *Raphia* spp., *Entandrophragma palustre*, *Uapaca heudelotii*, *Alstonia congensis*, and the canopy reaches 25-30 m, with emergents.

In addition to these three main forest types, mangrove, a forest formation associated with marine alluvium, is also found in Central Africa, mostly in Cameroon, Equatorial Guinea, and Gabon, but also in the Republic of Congo. It covers about 33 600 km² (Mayaux et al., *op. cit.*). Mangrove in Central Africa is largely dominated by *Rhizophora racemosa* reaching 25 m in height. Other species include *R. harrisonii* and *R. mangle* (Sayer et al. 1992).

Other vegetation types found in Central Africa include the forest/savanna mosaic, which includes elements from the forest and the savannah, and covers about 30 000 km² (Mayaux et al., *op. cit.*). These savanna mosaics end abruptly in the northern part of the Congo Basin and are more gradually integrated in the Miombo Woodland in the southern part of the Congo Basin. The existence of savanna patches in the forest domain is related to the presence of poor (sandy or lateritic) soils, or the past or current presence of human activity. In this last case, fire is a major factor in allowing the persistence of savanna patches within the forest (White 1995). Some of these savanna patches have been well studied, such as the ones found in the Lopé Reserve in Gabon (White, *op. cit.*), or in the Odzala National Park in the Republic of Congo.

Swamp grassland is a type of vegetation that is found where flooding precludes the presence of trees, general-

ly at the edge of inundated or partially-inundated forests, and covers about 10 000 km² (Mayaux et al., *op. cit.*).

Inselberg outcrops, made of gneiss and granite, emerge from the forest in Equatorial Guinea and Gabon, northeast of the Monts de Cristal, as well as in southwestern Gabon near the Gamba Reserve Complex, and northern Gabon in the Minkébé Reserve (Reitsma et al. 1992). They vary from 100 m to 1 000 m in height. The vegetation of the inselbergs found in Equatorial Guinea is typified by the presence of *Podocarpus latifolius* and *Olea capensis*, that are otherwise found sparsely in the Afro-montane biogeographical region (Parmentier and Maley 2001). Edaphic and microclimatic factors favored the emergence of strictly endemic plant species, such as *Impatiens floretii*, unique to this particular geological formation (Reitsma et al., *op. cit.*). Inselbergs in the Ituri region are particularly distinctive, with flortistic affinities linking them to east Africa, and containing a number of endemics, notably a giant cycad, *Encephalartos ituriensis*.

The Central Africa humid forest is inhabited by a large rural population, more than 80% of which uses some slash-and-burn cultivation. As a result, secondary forest is a major forest type in Central Africa, located mostly along roads and often characterized by a mono-specific formation of *Musanga cecropioides*, a very fast-growing heliophyte pioneer species. This covers about 230 000 km² (Mayaux et al., *op. cit.*).

Flagship Species

Although more difficult to see than wildlife in the plains of eastern or southern Africa, many creatures in the forests of Central Africa are spectacular and unique. Indeed, the forests of Central Africa are home to a number of striking flagship species that have captured the imagination of the world since the last century. Foremost among these are the primates, and especially the three species of great apes, the okapi, the forest elephant, the Congo peacock, the goliath frog, and several others.

Primate diversity in this region ranks among the highest in the world, with 17 genera, 43 species, and 68 taxa in all, at least 40 of which are endemic. The three great apes are probably the most outstanding flagships for these forests, and include the western lowland gorilla (*Gorilla gorilla gorilla*), the Central African chimpanzee (*Pan troglodytes troglodytes*), and the bonobo (*P. paniscus*). The bonobo is our closest living relative, sharing more than 98% of our DNA, and therefore of great scientific interest; indeed, it is more closely related to us than to gorillas. Endemic to the Democratic Republic of Congo, this unique species is found between the Congo and Kasai Rivers, sparsely occupying an area of about 840 000 km². Although little information on its current status is available, its population is estimated at between 5 000 and 20 000 individuals, and it is threatened by commercial logging, other forms of habitat destruction, and hunting for the bushmeat trade. The

West African dwarf crocodile (Osteolaemus tetraspis), Petit-Loango Reserve, Gabon. This small crocodile species is widespread in the forests of Central and West Africa, and occupies a niche very similar to the small forest caimans (Paleosuchus spp.) of Amazonia.
© **Michael K. Nichols**/*National Geographic Image Collection*

species is found within Salonga National Park, but more protected areas are needed within its range if it is to have some hope of surviving. An Action Plan for this species was developed in 1995, and a new one is now in preparation, with a number of international and local conservation groups working together to ensure the survival of this very special animal.

The gorilla is the largest living primate, and the western lowland gorilla that occurs in this region has by far the largest remaining population —perhaps exceeding 100 000. Nonetheless, populations are in decline due to habitat destruction and especially bushmeat hunting.

Finally, the region is also home to the largest remaining populations of the chimpanzee, since the Central African subspecies, *Pan troglodytes troglodytes,* has by far the most extensive range. Although not immediately endangered with extinction, it, like the lowland gorilla, is also a target of bushmeat hunters. Not only does hunting of these apes threaten their existence, it also represents a grave human health threat —as more and more evidence becomes available on the link between deadly Ebola outbreaks and the consumption of ape meat.

Yet another primate flagship and a species that is indicative of how little we know of the forests is the sun-tailed guenon (*Cercopithecus solatus*) from central Gabon. Unknown to science until 1984 (Harrison 1988), it was first discovered in the Forêt des Abeilles and has a very limited distribution, being largely restricted to an area enclosed by the Ogooué, Lolo, Bouenguidi, and Offoué Rivers and extending a short distance to the west of the Offoué —for a total range of only about 7 000 km² (Oates 1996).

Along with the bonobo, the other great flagship of the Congo Forests is the okapi (*Okapia johnstoni*), a strikingly beautiful relative of the giraffe that again is endemic to the Democratic Republic of Congo, and is found only in the northeastern forests of that country. Sometimes called the "forest giraffe" and unknown to science until 1901, the okapi is the giraffe's closest living relative. Though not as large as a giraffe, this magnificent animal stands about 1.5 m at the shoulder and is about the size of a large horse. With its deep purplish, reddish or blackish brown coat, and alternating black and white stripes on the hind and forelegs, this secretive forest dweller is unquestionably one of the Congo's and indeed Africa's most extraordinary mammals.

The forest elephant (*Loxodonta cyclotis*) also lives in these forests. With a smaller body, tusks that point down instead of forward, and with hindquarters level with its withers, the forest elephant is quite different from its savanna cousin (*L. africana*). Indeed, after having long been considered only a subspecies, it has now finally been recognized as a distinct species. More difficult to study than savanna elephants due to its dense forest habitat, the forest elephant has remained poorly known for a long time, with most information about it being learned from dung, tracks or feeding remains.

The aquatic genet (*Osbornictus piscivora*) is another interesting mammal endemic to the eastern forests of the Democratic Republic of Congo, which for most of the twentieth century was known only from a skin in the British Museum. It is an adept fisherman in forest streams and uses an interesting technique of tapping the surface of the water with its paw and then dipping the tips of its whiskers under the surface. Presumably this is a strategy for attracting the fish and then detecting their presence.

These forests are also home to a magnificent array of birds. One of the most familiar is the magnificent Congo peacock (*Afropavo congensis*), which has a wide but very patchy range across eastern and central Democratic Republic of Congo, and appears to be nowhere common (Hart and Upoki 1997). This secretive and quiet bird eluded science until 1936, when it was first described by ornithologist James Chapin from a stuffed museum specimen collected years earlier. The Congo peacock is the only member of the largely Asian pheasant family living in Africa.

There are also some impressive amphibians in the Congo forests, of which the goliath frog (*Conraua goliath*) is clearly the most spectacular. The world's largest frog, sometimes measuring more than 60 cm when its back legs are extended and weighing as much as 2 kg, it is a denizen of fast-flowing rivers and streams in Cameroon and Equatorial Guinea. The goliath frog doesn't make any sounds since it lacks a vocal sac. First identified in 1906, it is sometimes captured for the pet trade, bringing as much as $3 000 from private collectors. On top of this, it is hunted locally as a source of food.

In terms of plants, perhaps the best-known species is *okoumé* (*Aucoumea klaineana*), the most important timber species in the region. Found only in southern Gabon and just across the border into Equatorial Guinea, Congo, and Cameroon, it historically made up about 90% of the timber exports from Gabon —still accounting for more than half today. Used mainly for plywood, it even provides the paper from which Gabon's postage stamps are made and appears on Gabon's coat of arms. Okoumé is also unusual in that individuals close to one another are often joined below ground in order to exchange nutrients. Okoumé trees leak a clear, sticky resin that eventually solidifies into a hard, white substance that is highly flammable and aromatic. This resin has often been used to burn as a light source, and is sometimes put into water to add a perfumed flavor (White and Abernethy 1997).

From the cathedral-like forests with tremendous towering trees measuring up to 65 m to the dense undergrowth of Marantaceae bush, the Congo forests are among the most spectacular in the entire world. From the fresh scent of giant wild ginger (*Aframomum giganteum*), bent and twisted into the formation of a gorilla nest, to the moabi (*Baillonella toxisperma*) seedlings spouting from an old pile of elephant dung, a walk in this wonderful forest reveals the intricate relationship between plants and animals within this ecosystem.

Above, red river hog (Potamochoerus porcus) in the Petit-Loango, Gabon. A widespread species found throughout the forests of Central and West Africa.

On pp. 116-117, slender-snouted crocodile (Crocodylus cataphractus) in Odzala National Park, Republic of Congo. One of three African crocodile species, this animal is found mainly in forest rivers in Central and West Africa, and is easily distinguished from the widespread Nile crocodile by its much narrower snout.
Both photos:
© **Michael K. Nichols**/*National Geographic Image Collection*

115

what higher population of 29.7 million (CIESIN 1995), of which about 13 million live outside urban areas —for a population density of 7.8 inhabitants/km² (The World Gazetteer 2002).

Threats

Commercial exploitation of natural resources has been present in Central Africa for centuries. In the late nineteenth century, one of the main driving factors behind European exploration and colonization was the exploitation of the interior for ivory and rubber. Millions of Congolese were killed during this period when agents of Leopold II forced production quotas on the local population of the region. This period was followed in the early 1900s by the introduction of foreign-owned logging operations, and coffee, rubber, and oil-palm plantations.

Today, the wholesale extraction of the region's natural resources continues and efforts to gain access to rich natural and mineral resources seems to be a principal motivation for the past or present involvement of several countries in a civil war that has greatly destabilized the region. At least six of the Democratic Republic of Congo's nine neighbors are now heavily involved in the fighting. This unrest is a vicious cycle and one of the single most significant underlying threats to biodiversity in the region. For example, this country, which covers almost 60% of the core of the Central African Wilderness Area, suffered from more than 30 years of mismanagement and saw a collapse of its institutions. Tropical hardwoods are currently pouring out of the forests of the eastern part of the Democratic Republic of Congo, through Uganda and Rwanda, and a massive increase in mining, in particular for Coltan, is having a disastrous impact on wildlife through the wholesale slaughter of wildlife for the bushmeat and ivory trades. In the mineral-rich Shaba and Kasai Provinces, in the south of the country, the scramble for riches is undoubtedly also having a major negative impact on an already-impoverished wildlife.

Furthermore, high-level political and military authorities are regularly involved in illegal logging, the bushmeat trade, and elephant poaching for the illegal ivory trade across the entire region, and the complicity —sometimes overt— of government officials in poaching and bushmeat makes applying wildlife laws even more difficult. In the context of this economic collapse and breakdown of law and order which characterizes much of Central Africa, it is not surprising that wildlife is suffering. At such times of hardship, wildlife offers both an immediate source of sustenance and a source of ready cash.

The most direct threats to biodiversity in the region are the conversion of land for agriculture and exploitation of natural resources. Although considered a long-term threat, habitat loss as a result of forest conversion for agriculture is expected to have severe impacts on biodiversity if population growth rates hold and agricultural practices do not change. Studies indicate that

the current population needs approximately 20 million ha of land, or 11% of the forests of Central Africa, for sustainable cultivation. With population growing at roughly 2%-3% per year, it is estimated that the extent of deforestation by forest farmers is likely to double by 2025 and increase fourfold by 2050 (Toham 2001). In the Central African Republic, it is estimated that almost all of the forests could be converted to agricultural land by 2025 (Toham, *op. cit.*).

An even more immediate threat to the Congo forests of Central Africa is industrial-scale logging, which began in Central Africa with European colonization at the end of the nineteenth century, but has intensified in the last 100 years as a result of road and railroad construction to the interior of the region. At the time of colonization, timber was felled along the coast, after which logging spread inland along major rivers so that logs could be floated down to ports and exported. As the supply of quality trees diminished and the demand for timber grew, logging companies advanced ever deeper into the forest interior.

Today, the ability of humans to push a modern, mechanized, way of life into the deepest reaches of the African wilderness is transforming the Central African landscape by orders of magnitude. In fact, in Central Africa, with the exception of the Democratic Republic of Congo, almost all land outside national parks has been either zoned for logging or already issued as logging concessions, and in many countries logging has become a mainstay of national economies. For example, in 1998, timber generated 28% of all non-petroleum export revenue in Cameroon, and in the period 1997-1998 it brought in $60 million and $30 million in taxes in Cameroon and Gabon, respectively. Logging in the latter two countries is now one of the largest employers (CARPE 2001).

As in many parts of the world, logging in Central Africa is very selective due to high operational costs, poor infrastructure, and the demand for particular species. Loggers focus on only a few valuable species. For example, in Gabon, a single species, okoumé (*Aucoumea kleineana*), accounts for more than half of all log exports. The largest individuals of the best-quality trees are also harvested first, in effect reducing the commercial value of the remaining forest and altering its species and size-class composition.

The rate of exploitation of the forest is completely unsustainable; in other words, forests are cut faster than they grow and wildlife is hunted faster than it can reproduce. The damage to the ecosystem caused by logging is considerable. Erosion is excessive in areas with steep slopes and stream flow becomes more erratic. Some studies indicate that massive deforestation could also result in rainfall decreasing by as much as 50%. This would bring rainfall down to a level comparable to that of many of the savanna regions of Africa (CARPE, *op. cit.*).

Since commercial tree species are scattered in low density throughout the forest, loggers construct numerous survey trails and roads to find trees. In effect, this

Above, a woodland kingfisher (Halcyon senegalensis).

On the opposite page, close-up of an African forest elephant (Loxodonta cyclotis) hidden in the foliage, Dzanga Bai, Central African Republic.
Both photos:
© **Michael K. Nichols**/*National Geographic Image Collection*

Above, serrated hinge-back tortoise (Kinixys erosa) from the area near Bomassa, Republic of Congo. This species eats mushrooms and other plant material on the forest floor, and is itself eaten by the pygmies and other local people.

On the opposite page, rhinoceros viper (Bitis nasicornis) in the Petit-Loango Reserve, Gabon. This strikingly beautiful species is venomous, but not particularly aggressive.
Both photos:
© **Michael K. Nichols**/*National Geographic Image Collection*

heavily fragments the forest and opens it up to hunters. Logging generally occurs in stages, with the initial forays into the forest for surveys being far less damaging to the wildlife than what follows. First, loggers enter a pristine area to inventory wood resources and to determine access routes for mechanized logging. This initial inventory is followed by the entry of teams numbering in the hundreds who cut a dense pattern of transects. When loggers first enter an area, they are armed with shotguns, snares, and high-powered rifles to hunt game. Although they impact wildlife, it is usually still abundant. Once there is a dense grid pattern of trails and greater access to the interior of the wilderness, however, these teams not only hunt and consume wildlife themselves, they also export large quantities —decimating or eliminating entire populations of gorillas, chimpanzees, monkeys, duikers, pigs, and leopards, and causing elephants to move to other areas. By the time trees are being marked in each block, there are few animals that have not been killed, injured or had some contact with humans. Commercial hunters are generally present as well, and export meat to the roadheads. Following these initial surveys, a road team comes in with bulldozers to cut primary access roads, most of which require clear-cutting. Once roads are graded, areas deep inside the wilderness that once took weeks to reach can be accessed in an hour or two. More teams of loggers are sent into the forest, this time with chain saws. At this point, the canopy is broken, most of the giant trees are gone, and most of the fauna of the area has been hunted out. The vast network of roads that allows loggers to exploit rich areas and get their products to market rapidly also provides access for commercial hunters. Even in places where loggers have left the forest cover relatively intact, we find forests with no animals in them, a phenomenon that has become commonly known as the "empty forest syndrome."

Further, camps along the roads that start out as housing for loggers eventually become small towns where people settle for the employment and social services that the logging operation provides. Once an area has been logged, however, and the company has moved to another area, people remain and continue to exert pressure on the surrounding environment by hunting and growing crops. These pressures continue long after a logging company has moved on.

Thus, logging companies not only increase demand for meat by hiring a large workforce, they also greatly facilitate workers' entry into the commercial trade. This same scenario played itself out in West Africa in the 1950s and 1960s, and contributed to the regional decline in wildlife populations evident in West African forests today. We believe that this type of uncontrolled bushmeat trade has become the most immediate threat to the future of wildlife in the Central African wilderness in the next five to fifteen years.

Market studies indicate that bushmeat, not the meat of domesticated animals, now constitutes the primary source of meat for most residents of the Congo Basin,

and that bushmeat consumed in forest and urban areas throughout the region may exceed 1 million metric tons per year, the equivalent of almost 4 million cattle (Toham, *op. cit.*). Bushmeat is commonly defined as all wildlife and meat derived from the forest, including threatened or endangered species. The most commonly-hunted groups in the Congo forests are duikers, pigs, primates, and rodents. Duikers are certainly the most heavily hunted in terms of numbers and biomass and, although estimates vary considerably, studies indicate that the rate of consumption is unsustainable (Toham, *op. cit.*). Apes are hunted opportunistically and tend to constitute the "bycatch" of hunters seeking the more abundant and lucrative duikers.

Why people consume bushmeat is controversial, and the reasons vary between rural and urban areas. In rural areas, evidence suggests that bushmeat is either the only source of animal protein available or the least expensive. In urban areas, however, bushmeat, including apes, is often viewed as a luxury item for which consumers are willing to pay a price premium. Studies indicate that meat consumption may increase by 3% or more per year as human populations continue to grow and household incomes increase. With such demand, it is likely that many species in proximal forest areas will be driven to extinction (Toham, *op. cit.*).

The precarious economic situation and the inability of government institutions to apply their own wildlife laws are key factors contributing to the seriousness of the problem in Central Africa. Ongoing efforts to enforce laws prohibiting commercial trade in bushmeat, and encouraging logging companies to ban commercial hunting for bushmeat on their concessions, can help in the short term. Over the longer term solutions to the bushmeat crisis must include measures to increase alternatives and competitively-priced sources of protein.

Another major threat to the Congo forests is mining, mostly for gold and diamonds, but increasingly in the Democratic Republic of Congo for a mineral ore called Coltan, used in the manufacture of electronic equipment. A report from the UN Security Council published in April 2001 found that the illegal and systematic exploitation of the Democratic Republic of Congo's minerals, including Coltan, by top Rwandan and Ugandan military and political officials was perpetuating the civil war. In addition, illegal mining of Coltan is having devastating effects on wildlife. According to a report released in May 2001, roughly 10 000 miners overran Kahuzi-Biega National Park in DRC. Before the civil war, this park had an estimated 8 000 eastern lowland gorillas, but because miners are hunting gorillas for bushmeat, this number has been reduced to fewer than 1 000. Other environmental impacts of Coltan mining include forest clearing to build mining camps, pollution of streams, and ecological changes due to the loss of keystone species such as elephants and apes.

In fact, illegal Coltan mining was already a problem in national parks before the current war, but the surge in prices over the last decade led to a major rush on

Lobéké National Park of Cameroon (217 000 ha). In another landmark decision in May 2001, the Government of the Republic of Congo revoked 1.1 million ha earmarked for logging when it signed a decree expanding Odzala National Park over fivefold, from 250 000 ha to 1.36 million ha. The park was originally created in 1935 but it was only in 1992, with the intervention of the EC-funded ECOFAC program, that the area started to receive proper protection. These two parks, Nouabalé-Ndoki and Odzala, are the two most important protected areas in the core of the wilderness area. Together, they cover 1.7 million ha or 7.3% of the core forest zone that lies in the Republic of Congo.

What sets this whole area of northern Congo, the southwest Central African Republic, and southeast Cameroon apart from the rest of the central African wilderness area is the existence of hundreds of forest clearings, called *bais*, which attract high concentrations of large mammals, including gorillas, elephants, buffalos, and bongos. Odzala's gorilla population is particularly high and is estimated to be more than 5 gorillas per km². For example, over 30 different gorilla families have been recorded visiting a single *bai* in the north of the park. The importance of this vast complex of protected areas straddling Congo, Cameroon, and the Central African Republic has been recognized by the international conservation community, which is reflected in the support that these areas have received over the past decade, particularly from WWF (Dzanga-Sangha, Lobéké), WCS (Nouabalé-Ndoki), ECOFAC (Odzala), and, more recently, Conservation International (Odzala).

In Cameroon, in addition to Lobéké, two other important new forest protected areas, Boumba Bek and Nki totalling some 600 000 ha, have also been created recently and are currently receiving support from WWF. The Dja Reserve, covering 526 000 ha, was established in 1950 and a "reserve de faune et de chasse" was changed to a "reserve de faune" under the National Forestry Act of 1973, and was then declared a World Heritage Site in 1987. It is the only World Heritage Site in the Congo forest outside the Democratic Republic of Congo, and has been managed with support from ECOFAC since 1992. The pressures on this reserve are intense, as it is almost entirely surrounded by logging concessions and the human population living around the reserve is significantly higher than for other forest protected areas in Cameroon. In 2001, an interesting opportunity for conservation arose when the government of Cameroon revoked nine logging concessions, totalling roughly 830 000 ha, in the Ngoïla-Mintoum region to the southeast of the Dja Reserve. This forest forms a corridor between the Dja and Nki Reserves in Cameroon and the Minkébé Reserve in Gabon, and represents a critical element of a trans-frontier conservation initiative being developed by WWF, ECOFAC, and CI. In all, Cameroon has a total of 2.7 million ha of protected areas in the wilderness area, which represents 16% of the core forest zone that lies in Cameroon.

Gabon currently has no National Parks, but all of its protected forests —the Lopé Reserve (490 000 ha), the Gamba Complex (1 132 000 ha), Minkébé (600 000 ha), Ipassa (10 000 ha), and Wonga-Wongue (496 700 ha)— have been proposed for upgrading. Together, they now total 2.7 million ha or 12% of the country's core forest zone. There are no reserves in Gabon's transitional forest. The Lopé Reserve has received management support from ECOFAC since 1992, while WWF provides support for the management of Minkébé and Gamba. The Gamba complex, which borders the Atlantic Ocean, is undoubtedly one of the most important protected areas of the Congo Wilderness Area because of its diversity of habitats. One of the extraordinary spectacles of this reserve is to see forest elephants, hippos, and buffalo on the beaches and even in the sea. Even gorillas and chimpanzees have occasionally been seen on the beaches. Manatees (*Trichechus senegalensis*) are found in the lagoons, and the beaches are also important nesting areas for at least four species of marine turtles.

In June 2000, Gabon's wildlife department (*Direction de la Faune et de la Chasse* - DFC), with the collaboration of WWF and WCS, embarked on a process of identifying and evaluating a potential network of protected areas. The aim of the project is to create 15 strategically-located National Parks, covering at least 10% of the country and including at least part of most of the existing reserves.

Among the potential new National Parks is an area in central Gabon, the proposed Langoué-Ivindo National Park totalling some 300 000 ha. The area was identified as a priority during the recent "megatransect" across Central Africa by J. Michael Fay of WCS. What makes the area so unique is the presence of naïve gorillas and large-tusked forest elephants, indicating that humans have not yet impacted the area. In an effort to protect Langoué, WCS has put in place a research program and, in partnership with CI, has begun negotiating with the Government of Gabon to revoke several overlapping logging concessions and to create this new area as quickly as possible.

Equatorial Guinea has a network of 13 protected areas (10 on the mainland) covering 591 000 ha, or 21% of the country, although those on Bioko and Annobon Islands are considered part of the West African Hotspot. Those on the mainland cover 484 000 ha, or 17% of the country. To date only one protected area, Monte Alen National Park (150 000 ha), is being actively managed, with support from ECOFAC. This park was recently extended, linking it with the Rio Muni Nature Reserve to the south and giving it a combined area of 260 000 ha under protection. By linking Monte Alen to Rio Muni, several important contiguous habitat types are protected including mid-altitude montane forest, lowland forest, and an important area of mangrove forest.

By far the greatest number and the most extensive coverage of protected areas in Central Africa is in the Democratic Republic of Congo, which has within its borders five of Central Africa's six World Heritage Sites: Virunga National Park (790 000 ha), Garamba National Park

Above, female African pied hornbill (Tockus fasciatus), *Bomassa, Republic of Congo.*

On the opposite page, forest elephants (Loxodonta cyclotis) *in the Dzanga Bai, Dzanga-Ndoki National Park, Central African Republic. Long considered a subspecies of the savanna elephant* (Loxodonta africana), *the forest elephant is now recognized as a distinct species.*
Both photos:
© **Michael K. Nichols**/*National Geographic Image Collection*

(492 000 ha), Kahuzi-Biega National Park (600 000 ha), Salonga National Park (3 656 000 ha), and Okapi Faunal Reserve (1 372 625 ha). In addition to these World Heritage Sites, the Democratic Republic of Congo has another three National Parks: Maïko (1 083 000 ha), Upemba (1 173 000 ha), and Kundelungu (760 000 ha). Together, all of these areas cover 9.9 million hectares, or 4% of the country.

However, two of the DRC's national parks, Virunga and Kahuzi-Biega in the east, are in the new Albertine Rift Hotspot and therefore fall outside of the Congo Wilderness Area as we define it. In the core area of the Congo forest zone that falls within the borders of the Democratic Republic of Congo, there are two national parks —Maïko (1 083 000 ha) and Salonga (3 656 000 ha)— and the Okapi Faunal Reserve. These three areas provide coverage of 6.1 million ha, or 6% of the DRC's 101 million ha of the Congo wilderness area. Of the remaining national parks, Garamba National Park and the Bili-Uere Reserve are found in the savanna-forest transition zone, while Upemba and Kundelungu National Parks and the Lukuru/Lukenie and Luama Reserves are in the southern ecotone.

Despite the current war, Garamba National Park is still being actively managed —thanks to long-term support provided by the Frankfurt Zoological Society and the International Rhino Fund. Garamba is a particularly important park since it holds the last remaining population (some 30 individuals) of the northern white rhino (*Ceratotherium simum cottoni*). It is also of great historical interest, since it was there that the Belgians, in the early 1900s, successfully demonstrated that the African elephant could be domesticated. At one stage in the 1920s, at least 200 working elephants existed at Gangala na Bodio, which became part of the park when it was created in 1935. Today, it is still possible for park visitors to experience the remarkable sensation of observing white rhinos and herds of wild elephant and buffalo while perched on the back of an African elephant.

Of the DRC's forest protected areas, the Okapi Reserve is particularly important because it is home to several species endemic to the country, including the okapi, the Congo peacock, and the aquatic genet. It also has a higher diversity of primate species than any other protected area in the DRC, and one of the highest densities on Earth. Sixteen species of primates are known to occur in this reserve, 13 of them diurnal. Since the nocturnal species remain poorly known, even this striking total could increase. The Wildlife Conservation Society was instrumental in setting up the Okapi Wildlife Reserve in 1992, and has been the leader in protection and exploration of this area since 1985.

Salonga National Park, which covers 3 656 000 ha, is the largest protected area in central Africa, and one of the largest rainforest national parks in the world. It was given national park status in 1970 and was later declared a World Heritage Site in 1984. What makes Salonga so important is the fact that it is the only federally-protected portion of the habitat of the bonobo, although the core area of the bonobo's range probably lies outside current park boundaries. It is probably also an important refuge for forest elephants in the Congo Basin. Despite its importance, however, there is very little official management of the park, and large-scale poaching, facilitated by the network of large rivers that provide easy access deep into the park, is a serious threat. As the park currently falls on the dividing line between government-held and rebel-held territories, most of it is effectively off limits. Efforts are currently under way to survey the habitat of the bonobos, mainly by the Zoological Society of Milwaukee and WWF.

In addition, because bonobos are well known for their peaceful, cooperative society and have traditionally been protected by certain groups of indigenous people, there are several proposals under way for creating new national parks for them in the Democratic Republic of Congo. Some of these are at a very large and significant scale. The hope is that bonobos can be used as a symbol of peace in the war-weary Democratic Republic of Congo.

Of all the forest protected areas in the Democratic Republic of Congo, Maïko National Park is probably the most species-rich, and one of the least known. The first exploration of this park was undertaken by WCS between 1989 and 1992, and revealed important populations of eastern lowland gorilla, okapi, chimpanzee, elephant, and Congo peacock (Hart and Sikubwabo 1994; Hart and Hall 1996). On the botanical side, isolated massifs of low mountains scattered throughout the park have a distinctive flora yet to be explored.

The Central African Republic has a network of 16 protected areas covering some 7.6 million ha or about 12% of the total area of the country (Ngatoua 2002), although all but two of these protected areas are outside the core forest wilderness area. The two areas in the core forest zone, the Dzanga-Sangha Special Dense Forest Reserve (335 900 ha) and the Dzanga-Ndoki National Park (122 000 ha), total 457 900 ha, or 7% of the core forest zone that lies in Central African Republic. Situated in the southwest part of the country, these two areas protect healthy populations of forest species, including forest elephant, bongo, and western lowland gorilla. A key feature of these two areas is the presence of many forest clearings or *bais*, including the famous Bayanga *bai*, where a long-term study conducted by Andrea Turkalo has estimated that 3 200 different individual elephants use the *bai* (Turkalo and Fay 2001).

Currently, there is no up-to-date, complete dataset to accurately calculate the total protected area coverage for the Congo Forest Wilderness as defined here. However, based on preliminary work undertaken by the Association pour le Developpement de l'Information Environnementale of Gabon and World Resources Institute's Global Forest Watch, we estimate parks and reserves in this region cover roughly 23.8 million ha, or roughly 7% of the combined core wilderness area and transitional zone (3 390 428 km²) of the region. Of these, roughly 14 million hectares are within the core forest area as we define it. This represents 8.1% of the core

On the opposite page, African forest buffalo (Syncerus caffer nanus) walking along a stream. Like many other large mammals of the Congo forest, this animal has been heavily impacted by the bushmeat trade.

Above, an unidentified and possibly still undescribed species of forest floor beetle photographed deep in the Ndoki Forest, Republic of Congo. Both photos:
© **Michael K. Nichols**/*National Geographic Image Collection*

131

wilderness area (172 522 000 ha) –a good start to be sure, but much more still needs to be done.

Despite all of these efforts at creating protected areas in Central Africa, more than 90% of Central Africa's wildlife is outside protected areas, and most of that is within logging concessions. This means that over the short term we have to negotiate and work with these companies to minimize the impacts of logging activities but, over the medium to long term, these nineteenth-century practices need to be replaced by protection at a scale far beyond what has taken place in the past. This will require far greater investment from the conservation community than ever before, but it is certainly feasible.

The last five years have seen a very significant shift in the attitude of logging companies towards wildlife conservation, and several companies are now collaborating with conservation projects to help them manage the wildlife in their concessions (CIB with WCS in Congo; Leroy-Gabon with ECOFAC, and Bordamur and SHM with WWF in Gabon; IFB with ECOFAC in CAR). This change in attitude has been brought about by a combination of factors, including new forestry legislation that now requires logging companies to develop proper management plans; commercial considerations, particularly the need to obtain certifications which are becoming increasingly important for companies that sell their timber in European markets; and international pressure, particularly on the bushmeat issue.

Such collaboration can lead to positive conservation impacts because in many parts of Central Africa the intensity of logging does not approach that seen in Indonesia, where wholesale conversion of the forests has occurred. Specifically, in Central Africa, where perhaps only one to three trees per hectare are removed and damage to the forest structure is relatively light, healthy wildlife populations are able to survive *provided that* illegal hunting for the bushmeat trade can be prevented. Additionally, as logging companies generally have far greater financial resources than conservation organizations and are able to control access to their concessions, they have the potential to make a very significant contribution to biodiversity conservation in Central Africa.

Nonetheless, many people in the conservation community remain very sceptical that these logging companies are sincere in their stated commitment to reduce the impacts of their activities. Ultimately, they are out for the bottom line, and any conservation activities that substantially cut into that will be given minimal attention or nothing more than lip service. Even if a few companies are truly sincere, the majority of those working at an international level in tropical countries are not, and they will continue to be a problem for conservation until the full-scale shift to fully protecting these unique resources is finally made. The faster this can be done and the faster the nineteenth-century colonial practice of logging tropical rainforests can be eliminated forever, the better it will be for the people and the wildlife of Central Africa.

Of particular concern is the growing number of national and international operations now moving into the logging sector in the Democratic Republic of Congo and especially in the species-rich forests of the east, where proper management of concessions is all but nonexistent.

In the final analysis, maintenance of biodiversity and the wilderness characters of the Congo Forests of Central Africa will require major international attention and commitment. Political and economic instability in the countries of Central Africa are unlikely to improve in the short to medium term, and it is therefore absolutely essential that these countries continue not only to receive support from the donor community and NGOs, but to receive it at a much higher level than ever before.

Strengthening capacities through training of conservation biologists and wildlife managers will be vital, as will be continued direct support to protected areas since management costs are such that governments will simply be unable to commit the necessary financial resources to them in the foreseeable future. The absence of specialized protected area management structures everywhere except the Democratic Republic of Congo (and even there they are weak) is undoubtedly another key institutional issue that needs to be addressed if protected areas are to serve as effective conservation tools in the future. Over the years, the Democratic Republic of Congo's National Parks Institute (ICCN) has demonstrated the strengths of a semiautonomous protected area structure, including the ability to attract donor support. Other countries in Central Africa, including Equatorial Guinea, Republic of Congo, and Gabon, are now considering moving in this direction.

Despite the precarious economic and political situations of most of the central African countries, there is nevertheless cause for optimism. Vast tracts of forest still remain relatively intact, which means that it is not too late to achieve significant conservation goals. Central Africa is not facing the kind of irreversible situation resulting from wholesale forest destruction that has occurred in Southeast Asia. As international attention is increasingly focused on this globally-important wilderness area, conservationists must seize the occasion to leverage the very significant resources that are going to be required to secure the long-term future of Central Africa's forests and their rich wildlife heritage.

CONRAD AVELING
J. MICHAEL FAY
REBECCA HAM
OLIVIER LANGRAND
CHERI SUGAL
LEE WHITE
JOHN A. HART
JOHN PILGRIM
RUSSELL A. MITTERMEIER

Above, Bambendjelle pygmy women with traditional body paint and ornaments.

On the opposite page, Bambendjelle pygmy women resting after a day of net hunting, near Makao village, northern Republic of Congo. All they were able to capture was a small monitor lizard, but they did gather many nuts and roots during their day's work.
Both photos:
*© **Michael K. Nichols**/National Geographic Image Collection*

NEW GUINEA

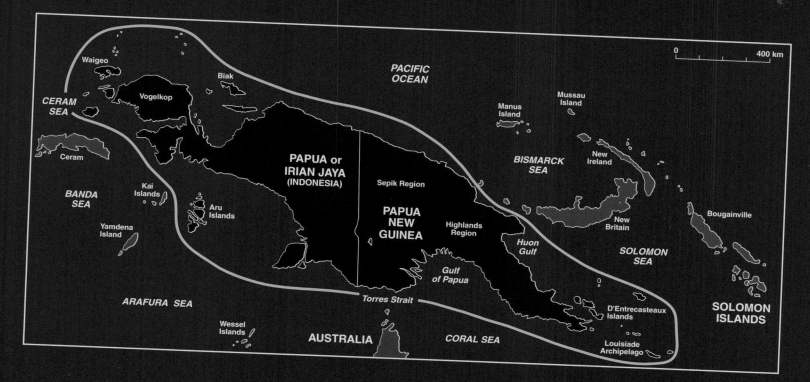

Situated to the north of Australia, the amazing island of New Guinea is the world's largest tropical island, considerably larger than either Borneo or Madagascar, and dwarfing Sumatra and Sri Lanka. Only ice-bound Greenland is larger. It is also the highest island, topped by the only tropical alpine glaciers between the Himalayas and the Andes (Gressitt 1982). The tropical humid forests of New Guinea constitute the largest remaining wilderness in the Asia/Pacific region. New Guinea has a land area of 828 818 km², and is 2 400 km long and 720 km wide at its widest point (Pieters 1982). The eastern half of the island constitutes the "mainland" of the country of Papua New Guinea; the western half is the easternmost province of Indonesia, formerly Irian Jaya and now called Papua. This entire great island lies in the southern hemisphere, from the equator to about latitude 10° South.

The island of New Guinea sits at the hub of the insular Southwest Pacific. To the west are the fringing Raja Ampat Islands, and still further to the west lie Halmahera and the rest of the Moluccas, which belong to Indonesia. To the south is the nearby Cape York Peninsula of northernmost Queensland, Australia. To the southeast lie the D'Entrecasteaux, Trobriand, and Louisiade Islands, politically part of Papua New Guinea. Due east across the Solomon Sea lies the Solomon Island Chain, with northernmost Buka and Bougainville being part of Papua New Guinea and the remainder constituting an independent nation, the Solomon Islands. Just northeast lie New Britain, New Ireland, and New Hanover of the

Bismarck Archipelago, and due north is the open South Pacific and the Bismarck Sea on New Guinea's eastern side. Here, we consider the major tropical wilderness area to comprise the main island of New Guinea and associated islands such as the Raja Ampat group, Aru, and the D'Entrecasteaux and Louisiade Islands. The nearby islands of New Britain, New Ireland, the Admiralty Islands, the Solomons, and Vanuatu further to the south are considered a new biodiversity hotspot, the Melanesian Islands Hotspot. This area will be covered in a future book focused on a series of new hotspots.

The shallow Arafura Sea and Torres Strait separate New Guinea from Australia. In fact, New Guinea and Australia lie atop a single tectonic plate that is slowly plowing northward into the Pacific Plate. At the front of this moving plate, New Guinea is suffering remarkable compression and mountain uplift all along the contact zone. New Guinea's northern margin today is a melange of more than thirty tectonostratigraphic terranes —former oceanic and continental fragments that have accreted to the main body of the island as it has been pushed northward at the prow of the Australian Plate (Pigram and Davies 1987). By contrast, Australia is typified by little relief or tectonic activity. Also by way of contrast, New Guinea is tropical and humid, whereas Australia is temperate/subtropical and mainly arid.

The youthful topography of New Guinea is evident from its ungraded rivers, numerous waterfalls, narrow V-shaped valleys, frequent land slippage, and harsh physiography. This rugged topography is in

—— Wilderness Area boundary

On the opposite page, limestone pinnacles, Mt. Kajande area near Tari, Southern Highlands, Papua New Guinea.
© Jean-Paul Ferrero/Auscape

still an impressive creature, with several remarkable features. First, it is active mainly at dusk and at night. Its large facial disks probably aid in seeing in low light. Its strange, gulping notes resonate through the night forest. Typically, two birds call back and forth for a considerable time. The bird is remarkably terrestrial, using its long legs to chase down its prey, mainly wallabies and giant rats. It also clambers around adeptly on trees, and reaches into tree cavities to capture denning possums.

loid (homobatrachotoxin) that is identical to the poison in South America's most toxic poison-dart frogs. It seems the bird uses the poison to ward off predators such as snakes, and also against ectoparasites such as lice, ticks, and fleas.

Twelve bowerbird species inhabit New Guinea. Famous for the ability of the male to construct an elaborate mating structure or "bower," these polygynous for-places interrupted by extensive intermontane valleys (e.g., Wahgi, Balim, Tari), most of which drain south-

Earth, exceeded only by the Amazonian and Congolian Forest blocks, covered in other chapters of this book.

the New Guinea rainforests are most typically lacking in strong species dominance. For instance, the diptero-carps, so important for timber in Southeast Asia, are rela-tively species-poor in New Guinea and dominate only selected forests where large-scale disturbance has occurred.

Across New Guinea, these forests include many species of mahogany (Meliaceae), laurel (Lauraceae), fig (Mora-ceae), eucalypt relatives (Myrtaceae), and nutmeg (Myris-

This moss forest is physiognomically very distinctive, although it is difficult to characterize taxonomically. The forest is still relatively species-rich, with oaks, Antarctic beeches, and podocarps, but is most distinc-tive in its profusion of epiphytic plants: orchids, ferns, bryophytes, rhododendrons, and other ericoids. This must be the favorite forest type of many visiting natu-ralists, and has been called a "Papuan wonderland" (Hides 1936). At the higher elevations, the profusion of moss is almost hard to believe. Even the floor of the for-

type specimen. An undescribed form of *D. goodfellowi* has also been reported recently from the Foya Moun-tains of Papua.

Unfortunately, unlike the birds of paradise, the tree kangaroos represent the most endangered group of mam-mals on the island. All the New Guinean species are heav-ily hunted for food and for their skins, and have been largely extirpated from areas inhabited by people. Not surprisingly, they are extremely difficult to observe in the wild, and are only seen as pets in villages or as skins adorning dancers in a sing-sing. Indeed, Tim Flannery considers two of them to be among the most critically endangered of all mammals, the *tenkile,* or nominate subspecies of Mrs. Scott's tree kangaroo (*Dendrolagus scottae*), described in 1990, and the golden-mantled tree kangaroo or *weiman* (*Dendrolagus goodfellowi pulcher-rimus*), described in 1993 (Flannery et al. 1996). The *tenkile* now occurs in an area of about 40 km^2 lying just east and west of Mt. Somoro in the Torricelli Mountains. The one place where it used to be protected by power-ful spirits, a mountain summit called Sweipini, has lost its sacred status. The golden-mantled tree kangaroo, which occurs at the extreme eastern end of the Torri-celli Mountains in the vicinity of Sibilanga and possibly Weigin villages, may have a remaining range as small as 20 km^2. Several of the other species, though somewhat more widespread, may be headed in the same direction. Clearly, more attention to the conservation of these ani-mals is urgently needed. Conservation International, in collaboration with several American zoos, has produced a poster depicting all known tree kangaroos in both the Tok Pisin and Bahasa Indonesia languages, and has iden-tified them as a target group for threatened species con-servation in Melanesia. In addition, a tree-kangaroo conservation group, the Tenkile Conservation Alliance, has been established in Papua New Guinea and initial-ly is focusing its efforts on conservation of the *tenkile.*

Other striking New Guinean mammals are the echid-nas which, along with Australia's platypus, are the only egg-laying mammals in the world and the only mem-bers of the Subclass Protheria and the Order Monotrema-ta. One of the two genera and three of the four known species are confined to New Guinea. Although "primi-tive" in certain respects, these slow-moving and retiring creatures are remarkable for their large brains, high intelligence, and ability to live 50 years or more. Look-ing much like a large hedgehog, the echidnas are spiny, long-beaked insect-eaters that specialize on unearthing prey underground. When disturbed, the short-beaked echidna curls into a ball and can bury itself very quick-ly in soft earth. Although widespread and fairly common in Australia, echidnas are uncommon and difficult to observe in New Guinea because of hunting pressure. The endemic long-beaked echidna (*Zaglossus bruijnii*), which is twice as large as the short-beaked echidna and cer-tainly one of the most appealing and bizarre animals on Earth, is unfortunately endangered because of hunting.

Some endearing New Guinean mammals are the trioks and gliders. These small, squirrel-like marsupials

in the family Petauridae are tree-dwellers, with soft fur and, in several instances, boldly-patterned black-and-white pelage.

New Guinea's 11 species of possums (also known as cuscuses or phalangers) are an important component of the forest biota, usually being among the most numer-ous mammals. Consuming leaves, fruits, and seeds, these possums in some ways seem to approach the Neotropical sloths in looks and sluggish behavior. In spite of being heavily hunted for the stewpot, most species remain common.

New Guinea also has eight species of giant rats [East-ern white-eared giant rat (*Hyomys goliath*), rock-dwelling giant rat (*Xenuromys barbatus*), Western white-eared giant rat (*Hyomys dammermani*), giant naked-tailed rat (*Uromys anak*), giant white-tailed rat (*Uromys caudi-maculatus*), rock-dwelling giant rat (*Xenuromys barba-tus*), Emma's giant rat (*Uromys emmae*), and Biak giant rat (*Uromys boeadii*)], some of which can reach 2 kg in weight. These are the most spectacular of New Guinea's wide range of murid rodents, and are a favored prey of the New Guinea eagle.

A total of 80 species of bats inhabit New Guinea, of which 27 species are flying foxes of the family Pteropo-didae. These represent another important flagship group, and can reach considerable size, the largest having wingspans approaching 1.5 m (Bonaccorso 1998). As with the birds of paradise, they are keystone seed dispersers. Several species are also quite visible, and can be seen roosting in the hundreds or even thousands in the mid-dle of several of Papua New Guinea's larger towns like Madang and Lae, a spectacle of great appeal to visiting tourists.

The story of Mrs. Bulmer's fruit bat (*Aproteles bul-merae*) is worth recounting. Bones of this species were collected in subfossil cave deposits by Susan Bulmer in Highland Papua New Guinea in the 1960s. Described in 1972 by James Menzies as a recently-extinct species, a living population was discovered by David Hyndman in 1975. More recently, studies of the species by Tim Flan-nery indicate this may be New Guinea's rarest fruit bat, and it has been classified as Critically Endangered by the IUCN's Species Survival Commission. Thus, what sci-entists originally described as extinct may once again join the list of recently lost.

The herpetofauna of New Guinea is rich but poorly known. Of the 275 reptile species, 182 are lizards, 81 are snakes, 10 are turtles, and two are crocodiles. All of New Guinea's 237 amphibians are frogs, there being no sala-manders or caecilians on the island. As indicated earlier, these numbers are likely to increase as more research is conducted. This is especially true of the frogs, whose numbers are sure to rise dramatically. Indeed, a recent Conservation International Rapid Assessment Program (RAP) expedition increased the known frog fauna of Irian Jaya by nearly 30% in just 16 days (Richards et al. 2000).

The reptiles include a number of globally noteworthy flagship species. Two of the island's snakes are espe-cially remarkable. The highland-dwelling Boelen's python

Above, long-beaked echidna (Zaglossus bruijni), an Endangered endemic that is also the largest of the living monotremes, or egg-laying mammals.
© **Jean-Paul Ferrero**/*ARDEA LONDON*

On the opposite page, palm cockatoo (Probosciger aterrimus), a spectacular flagship species of the New Guinea forests, Papua, Indonesia.
© **Konrad Wothe**

On pp. 144-145, the Kikori Delta, Gulf Coast region, Papua New Guinea.
© **Gerry Ellis**/*Minden Pictures*

142

pigeons and certain genera of these trees. No systematic botanist has had the courage to revise this important Malesian rainforest family, which is species-rich and difficult to identify.

Nutmegs and mahoganies are other important New Guinean rainforest families (Myristicaceae and Meliaceae). Widespread and species-rich, these families are found in every forest from sea level to at least 1 500 m

Guinea and immediately adjacent islands, about 850 in Papua New Guinea and 250 in Papua on the Indonesian side. This represents about one in six languages that were spoken by the human race at the beginning of the twentieth century; however, because of continuing extinction of languages, it now represents about *one in every three languages still spoken*. This is so in spite of the fact that the area of the island of New Guinea, a

147

(*Morelia boeleni*) is a large and little-known constrictor found in mossy forests. Reaching more than 3 m in length, it is a striking creature: blue-black dorsally, with cream patterning and underside. The even more spectacular green tree python (*Morelia viridis*) is an amazing ecological counterpart to the unrelated but morphologically very similar emerald tree boa (*Corallus caninus*) of South America. Both are arboreal species that feed mainly on birds, and both are renowned for their nasty dispositions.

base of a tree buttress to enhance sound transmission, are one of the remarkable sounds of the night in New Guinea's lowland rainforest. This colossal "call" belies the small size and retiring habits of this little creature.

New Guinea is also a paradise for insects. However, given the richness, the diversity, and the difficulty of survey, it would be hard to make an estimate of just how many insects inhabit the island —at least several hundred thousand, only a fraction of which have been described (Miller et al. 1994). Most are tiny and cryptic,

little more than twice the size of California, is only about 0.5% of the land surface of planet Earth, while its human population of six million represents only about 0.1% of the people on the planet. In other words, we have in this region a concentration of human diversity that is truly extraordinary and, like its biodiversity, very much worth conserving.

On top of this, not only do these languages and cultures still exist, but most of them are still intact as vibrant, functioning entities and not mere remnants of what once existed —unfortunately, the case in many other culturally rich parts of the world, where tribal cultures are in serious decline. Furthermore, 97% of the land, on the Papua New Guinea side at least, is still in the hands of the traditional landowners, again a situation that is largely unique in today's world. An apt comparison would be the United States at the beginning of the nineteenth century, when much of the land was occupied and still under the control of the native Amerindians.

This is not to say that New Guinean societies have not changed considerably over the last century. A good part of this is attributable to religion and war. In all or virtually all, much of their original belief system has been replaced by some form of Christianity. Most of the chronic tribal fighting has been eradicated or suppressed, mainly by missionary work. These are just two of many adaptations they have had to make to accommodate the arrival of Western civilization. The richness, diversity, and wonderful intensity of New Guinea's cultures are best captured by photographs, as we have tried to do on the pages of this chapter, but a few of the cultures are particularly worthy of mention.

The region of New Guinea that best symbolizes the uniqueness of the island's human cultures is the Highlands. The Highlands region of New Guinea was among the last large land areas on Earth to be explored. When German explorers penetrated the Sepik River in the late nineteenth century, they saw high mountains to the south, and a German survey team encountered Eastern Highlanders in 1914. Later, in 1927, the explorers Karius and Champion came across Western Highlanders while crossing from the Fly River to the Sepik River. However, it was not until the early 1930s that the gold-prospecting Leahy brothers put the cultures of the large valleys like the Wahgi, the Asaro, and the Tari on the map. They found a succession of wide, well-populated upland valleys separated by mountain barriers; sometimes they included large ceremonial areas that looked like parks. Each valley had entirely different tribes with different costume and dress, and they decorated themselves in the most amazing ways imaginable, with feathers of birds of paradise, parrots, and cassowaries among others, as well as dogs' teeth and shells traded from the coast. The languages of these people are also very distinctive and fall into a loose group usually described as Papuan or non-Austronesian languages. Not only are these languages mutually unintelligible, they are so different from one another that it is not clear whether

they are distant relatives in a single language family or belong to completely distinct language families.

We find a similar Highlands society in Papua, in the Grand Valley of the Balim. This, too, was not discovered by the West until Richard Archbold overflew the valley in his great Third Archbold Expedition to the Snow Mountains in the late 1930s. His team, led by Dutch military officer Captain C.G.J. Teerink, traversed the valley on foot to establish staging camps at the base of Mt. Trikora and Lake Habbema. The Balim is New Guinea's largest mid-montane valley and its most populous, being occupied by the Dani people. The Dani are much like their mountain brothers to the east in Papua New Guinea —aggressive, war-loving, and robust. Although tribal fighting has been suppressed by the Indonesian Government, the Dani maintain many of their traditions (Muller 1997). These are most evident in their dress. Men in the villages continue to wear little more than a penis gourd, whereas the women wear only a tiny grass skirt. The Dani were made famous in the 1960s by Robert Gardner's documentary *Dead Birds,* a film for which Michael Rockefeller served as sound man before disappearing among the Asmat on the southeastern coast of Papua (Machlin 1972).

As a spectacle of Highlands culture, the Highland Shows, held annually in Mt. Hagen and Goroka in Papua New Guinea, provide a showcase for Highlanders of different cultures; as many as 60 000 dancers from widely-separated parts of the region participate in these shows every year. A recent one, held in Mt. Hagen in August, 2001, featured more than 2 000 performers from 83 different cultural groups, with more than 30 000 Highlanders and 300 tourists as spectators. Considered by many to be "the greatest cultural spectacle left on Earth," these yearly shows are a must for anyone interested in human cultural diversity.

Among the noteworthy cultures of the Highlands are the Huli of the Tari Valley, best known for their marvelous wigs made from their own hair and elaborately decorated with feathers and flowers; the neighboring Mendi; the Enga; the Melpa-speaking people of the western Wahgi and Baiyer Valleys; the Asaro people with their world famous mudmen; and the Kukukuku, long known as ferocious warriors. They are all established agriculturists, growing taro, sweet potatoes, and yams in neatly-organized farming plots, and having pigs as the principal sign of wealth. Although there has been a great deal of change in this area with the arrival of missionaries, increasing influence of Western technology, and some out-migration to the larger coastal cities like Port Moresby, Jayapura, and Lae, there is much that is still traditional in Highlands New Guinea.

The Asmat live in the tidal swamp forests of the southern coast of Papua, east of Lorentz National Park and centered on the administrative center of Agats (Muller 1997). They inhabit the great muddy deltaic rivers that drain southward from the massive wall of the Jayawijaya Range. Known to be great canoe-faring headhunters, the Asmat today are most famous for their

On the opposite page, great woodswallow (Artamus maximus), *Tari, Papua New Guinea.*
© **Patricio Robles Gil**/*Sierra Madre*

Above, the strikingly beautiful green tree python (Morelia viridis) *is one of New Guinea's best-known reptile flagships.*
© **Günter Ziesler**

149

wood carvings, which are in demand around the world by collectors of traditional art. Their villages are mainly constructed on stilts because the rivers flood annually and because of seasonal tidal surges. This low country is much like that of the Sepik in Papua New Guinea, but is even lower, more flood-prone, and less developed.

The Sepik River drains a massive lowland forest basin in the northern watershed of Papua New Guinea. The inhabitants of this incredible region speak nearly two hundred languages, making it the linguistically most diverse region in the country. Traditionally headhunters, the Sepik people use the sago palm as their staple food, and are renowned as some of the greatest woodcarvers in the world. Every village has its own distinctive wood-carving tradition, and some of these art forms are well known and much sought after in international markets. These wood carvings are still used for traditional purposes, as is the case with some of the crocodile cultures of the Karawari region (e.g., the Yokoim-speaking people of the Konmai and Karawari Rivers), and increasingly to attend to a growing tourist market. Another characteristic of the Sepik cultures is the *haus tambaran* or men's spirit house, a magnificent structure that is the center of village activity. These are such a dominant feature of Papua New Guinea culture that the National Parliament Building in the capital of Port Moresby is patterned after and decorated like a *haus tambaran*.

Among the singular cultures of the Sepik are the Iatmul, the Abelam, the Sawo, with their elaborate yam ceremonies, the Arambak speakers and their unusual *yip-won* spirit hooks, the Blackwater Lakes people, the Yuat River people, and the Murik Lakes people at the mouth of the Sepik.

Off the eastern tip of the main island of New Guinea, in Milne Bay Province, are a number of interesting islands and cultures, the best known of which are the Trobriands. The Trobriand Islanders became internationally famous through the detailed studies done by the Polish anthropologist Bronislaw Malinowski during the First World War. He described their complex ceremonial exchange, the Kula Ring, their sexual practices, and a number of other cultural features in a study that is now part of classical anthropological literature. The Trobriand Islanders also have a system of hereditary chiefs, like the cultures of Polynesia and unlike much of the rest of Melanesia, whose social systems tend to be more egalitarian, with headmen gaining status through personal influence and meritorious acts.

In all, the human population of the island of New Guinea is just over six million, with 3.8 million on the Papua New Guinea side and 2.2 million on the Indonesian side. A great number of people are concentrated in the larger cities and towns like Port Moresby, Lae, Madang, Jayapura, Sorong, Biak, Manokwari, and a handful of others, as well as in the fertile valleys of the Highlands below an elevation of 2 400 m, the limit above which sweet potato can not grow. Together, these larger centers have approximately 800 000 people or

about 14% of the population, to which should be added the roughly 1 million people inhabiting the Highlands valleys on both the Papua New Guinea and Papua sides of the island. This represents a total of about 1.8 million people, or 30% of the population of New Guinea. As a whole, the population density of New Guinea is about 7.2 inhabitants/km^2. If one factors out the 1.8 million in the major population centers, this drops to 5 inhabitants/km^2, and in many parts of the island it is far lower than that (e.g., Western Province).

Threats

Threats to biodiversity in New Guinea are similar to those in most other parts of the tropical world, with the proviso that the island is still fortunate to have the majority of its resources intact, i.e., forests, waters, and fisheries. Obvious short-term threats include industrial logging, unplanned development, mining, and the like. Longer-term threats would include population growth and its various impacts (although this is much less of a problem than in most other parts of the tropics), forest conversion for large-scale monoculture agriculture (especially oil palm), climate change, industrial megaprojects, and exotic species introductions.

At this time, timber and minerals are the major land resources, with non-timber forest products and ecosystem use values like watershed protection not yet competitive or even appropriately measured (see Sekhran and Miller 1994). The idea of trying to harvest timber on a more sustainable, smaller scale has been tested in Papua New Guinea, especially through the use of portable "walkabout" sawmills, but the effectiveness of this approach has yet to be proven. New Guinea, unfortunately, has been one of the major targets of Asian predatory logging companies since the 1980s, as part of a global push by these companies to co-opt much of the world's remaining primary forest and lock it away in large-scale concessions. In spite of their protestations to the contrary, logging carried out by these companies is not sustainable: it involves large-scale underreporting and outright cheating, and certainly does not benefit local people in any meaningful way, except for a few individuals that might be bribed to sign over tracts of their communal land. Much damage is done to residual tree stands below harvestable size, and much of the logging is being conducted in areas where social and physical impacts on communities and watersheds can be severe. In general, commercial logging in New Guinea's forests has received little or no environmental management, is carried out with no consideration whatsoever for impacts on biodiversity, and employs methods that cause great ecosystem degradation. This kind of exploitation is very much like that which took place in the colonial period of the nineteenth and early twentieth century. It takes advantage of, and provides virtually no benefit to, local communities and the country as a whole, and has no place in the twenty-first century.

Above, Raggiana bird of paradise (Paradisaea raggiana), *the best-known of the birds of paradise and also a national symbol.*
© **Bruce Beehler**

On the opposite page, male Vogelkop bowerbird (Amblyornis inornatus) *in his elaborate bower, Arfak Mountains, Papua, Indonesia.*
© **Konrad Wothe**

Land clearance for subsistence gardening is sometimes considered to be the main cause of forest loss in New Guinea, a claim that is often made in defense of commercial logging. Recent estimates indicate that several hundred thousand hectares are in fact cleared annually for gardens, but it is likely that a large portion of such clearing is secondary forest that has regenerated from earlier gardening. In areas of relatively low human population density, as is the case in much of New Guinea, such slash-and-burn agriculture seems to be environmentally sustainable. These small plots regenerate quickly back to natural forest, and can be exploited once again after a few decades of fallow.

Large-scale commercial agriculture also exists, with the major export crops being coffee, oil palm, cocoa, copra, tea, and rubber. Large-scale operations of this kind are still relatively few compared to most other parts of the world, but they are on the increase and should be watched. Oil-palm cultivation is especially serious, since it involves total clear-cutting and has even more long-term impact than logging. Often, especially in some of the other Melanesian islands (e.g., New Britain), it follows on the heels of logging, with the valuable trees being extracted first and the rest then being clear-cut for plantations. In order to see what could happen to New Guinea, one need only look a short distance to the west and observe what has already taken place in Sumatra.

New Guinea also has large stocks of valuable oil, gas, and minerals, and their extraction, especially copper and gold, has caused environmental problems, above all in fragile wetland and catchment areas. The Fly River system has been particularly affected by the giant Ok Tedi mine, as have the watersheds of the rivers draining the huge Freeport mine above Timika in Papua. By contrast, the Lake Kutubu oil field has been developed in collaboration with a team from the World Wide Fund for Nature, and has apparently avoided major environmental damage.

Threats to the marine fisheries that surround New Guinea are growing. These tend to be the same that impact fisheries in other parts of the tropical world, and include overfishing, pollution, coral-reef mining, dynamite fishing, and cyanide fishing. Aside from these direct impacts, uncontrolled logging, clearing for agriculture, and mangrove cutting can result in increased siltation on reefs, sea-grass beds and mangroves, with very negative results. Although New Guinea is still fortunate in that these problems have not yet reached levels like those in the Philippines, it is likely that pressures will increase considerably over the next few decades, especially as the resources of most other nations in the Asia-Pacific region continue to decline. Now is the time for Papua New Guinea and Papua to enact measures to ensure that their globally-important marine resources are maintained, both for conservation purposes and for long-term sustainable utilization by local people.

Road building is also a problem, and a case developing in Papua at this time merits special attention. The provincial government has engaged one or more Korean logging companies to construct a national highway system in Papua, payment being free access to timber resources within five kilometers to either side of the road being constructed. Details of the agreement are not currently known, but it appears the companies are permitted to have considerable say over where roads are sited, presumably to ensure they pass through areas with suitable timber resources. This agreement could wreak havoc in a number of lowland forest areas, particularly in the Mamberamo watershed.

Fire has also been identified as a potential threat to New Guinea, especially in the wake of the forest fires that raged through Indonesia and Papua New Guinea during the great El Niño drought of 1997-1998. That said, fires are a part of the Southern Oscillation drought cycle, and have periodically burned large areas of New Guinea in the past, aided by the fire-loving tendencies of the local populace (Johns 1986). Certain fire impacts need to be closely monitored, especially in association with industrial logging and habitat conversion, but at the moment fire is only a minor threat to biodiversity in New Guinea.

Hunting, on the other hand, is a major concern, and has impacted the fauna of New Guinea in many ways. It is probable that the extirpation of the New Guinea megafauna (the thylacine, large wallabies, giant cassowaries, and diprotodonts) in the last 10 000 years could be a product of human hunting. Current hunting impacts are obvious to any naturalist who has compared forest wildlife populations in New Guinea and northern Queensland. In the latter, where hunting is absent, large birds and mammals (e.g., tree kangaroos, cuscuses) are present in considerable numbers and easy to observe. By contrast, in the New Guinea forest, large-mammal populations are much lower and much more difficult to spot. One must assume that chronic hunting with both traditional methods and now with firearms has made certain restricted populations vulnerable to extinction. The two endangered populations of tree kangaroos in the Torricelli Range of Papua New Guinea serve as a case in point. On the other hand, densities of most bird species are still very high, with the exception of some of the largest and most heavily-hunted species like the crowned-pigeons and the cassowaries, and visibility is excellent —making the country a bird-watchers' paradise. This is especially true compared to many parts of Asia (e.g., China), where birds of all sizes are exploited for food and the live-animal trade.

The live-animal trade has been an important part of the black market in Papua for decades, admittedly associated with the presence of the military. The main focus of the trade is parrots (especially lories and cockatoos), but also includes other wildlife (e.g., birds of paradise). It is unclear how serious the impact is upon the target populations, but it is worthy of additional scrutiny. It is hoped that with the establishment of special autonomy for Papua (granted in December 2001), this trade may be substantially reduced.

Over the medium to long term, the advent of local decision-making in Papua New Guinea and Papua may

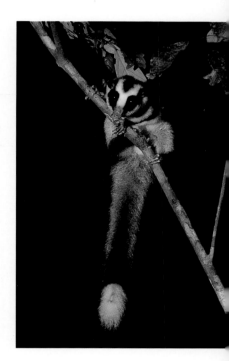

On the opposite page, Blyth's hornbill (Aceros plicatus)*, the only hornbill species on New Guinea and widespread on the island.*
© **Patricio Robles Gil**/*Sierra Madre*

Above, striped possum (Dactylopsila trivirgata)*, one of a great variety of marsupial species on New Guinea.*
© **D. Parer & E. Parer-Cook**/*Auscape*

153

have negative impacts on biodiversity —or it may provide some amazing new opportunities. If planning and development decision-making is conducted at the provincial or local level, it may be that national and global environmental considerations are ignored in favor of short-term local economic interests. This is a common phenomenon in the U.S., and can be seen in stark fashion in the development of the Adirondack region of New York and in the Arid West over the last two decades (witness the inappropriately-named "Wise Use" movement). The goal of conserving large blocks of habitat can be hindered by planning only at the local scale. On the other hand, this decentralization of power and decision-making may provide previously unavailable openings to work on biodiversity conservation activities with those local stakeholders that have the most to gain, and the most to lose if conservation measures are not effective. Properly designed, such conservation programs could be much stronger than those imposed by centralized federal governments.

Grandiose megaprojects are much more common in Papua on the Indonesian side than in Papua New Guinea, and are the outcome of ambitious planning groups. The Mamberamo Mega-Development Project, envisioned by then-Minister for Industry Habibie, is just one of these ill-conceived schemes. This great Mamberamo Project proposes to dam and flood much of the Mamberamo watershed in order to create gigawatts of electricity that would power a series of large-scale industrial development operations in the development zone in northern Papua. This plan is on the back burner at this point because of the echoes of the economic crisis that struck the region in 1997, but it could come to life once again if one or more Western investors demonstrate interest.

As indicated above, oil palm may be the next great threat to the island of New Guinea. Already proven to be a money winner in Papua New Guinea, there is now a push to expand oil-palm development in both eastern and western New Guinea. Oil-palm monoculture has the potential to cause substantially more damage to New Guinea's rainforests than industrial logging, mainly because the logging is selective, whereas the oil-palm operation mandates wholesale clearing of forest, with the result being total loss of local biodiversity. Oil-palm cultivation also has a range of negative social and cultural impacts, and is highly inappropriate for sustainable development in any forested area on the island. Furthermore, the quantity and kind of labor needed to create and maintain oil-palm estates will cause serious social dislocation, especially among traditional, conservative Melanesian societies.

Islands like New Guinea are also vulnerable to invasive exotic species. Witness the devastation wrought by exotic species in Australia, New Zealand, Guam, and Hawaii. New Guinea may be no exception, although the impacts have not yet been as strong as in these other island systems. Today New Guinea is home to a wide range of exotic plants, as well as a few vertebrates about which we should be concerned. These include common mynas (*Acridotheres tristis*), house and tree sparrows (*Passer domesticus, Passer montanus*), rusa deer (*Cervus timorensis*), and crab-eating macaques (*Macaca fascicularis*). The macaque is perhaps the great source for concern. This highly-adaptable, widespread species has a large natural range on mainland Southeast Asia, the Philippines, Malaysia, and Indonesia as far east as Halmahera. It has also been introduced to a number of places, notably Mauritius, where it has had a devastating impact on native bird species. A small but persistent population currently inhabits an area of northeastern Papua near the border with Papua New Guinea. Although it seems to be limited in distribution at this time, it could cause very serious damage to native bird, mammal, reptile, and amphibian populations if it begins to spread, especially since many of these have evolved in environments with very few opportunistic and adaptable predators like this monkey. It is imperative that authorities on both sides of the border address the macaque issue before it gets out of control.

Climate change threatens islands, local coastal zones, and sensitive habitats. The rapid melting of the Highland glaciers makes clear that the local climate in New Guinea is warming. The nature of future impacts is difficult to anticipate, but could be extensive.

Human population growth is a major underlying threat that looms on the horizon. With low population, subsistence agriculture and local forest and coastal resource extraction is sustainable. With higher population density, sustainability disappears. The demographics of population growth may well determine the level of impact. If rural youth abandon the villages for the cities, urban intensification will concentrate the impacts and backcountry ecosystems may survive. On the other hand, secondary effects, such as loss of traditions and abandonment of subsistence systems, may pave the way to large-scale habitat conversion by foreign economic interests. However, once again, New Guinea as a whole still has time to address this issue, in striking comparison to most of the rest of the Asia-Pacific where the crisis is already upon us.

Conservation

Conservation on the island of New Guinea is a tale of two very different government systems. In the west, in Papua, the nature conservation mandate has focused on the creation of a national system of protected areas. In the east, in Papua New Guinea, the realities of local land tenure have made the establishment of national protected areas difficult and the story is more one of community-based activities at a small scale. Indeed, in Papua New Guinea, there is no significant network of national protected areas. With regard to species conservation, both Papua New Guinea and Papua have followed a CITES-mandated legislative approach, banning the export of protected species, but permitting their harvest at the local level.

Above, short-tailed spotted cuscus (Spilocuscus maculatus), *a large, common species on New Guinea.*

On the opposite page, Victoria crowned-pigeon (Goura victoria), *another of New Guinea's spectacular flagship bird species. Both photos:*
© **Patricio Robles Gil**/*Sierra Madre*

Above, man from the lower Karawari River region, East Sepik Province, Papua New Guinea.

On the opposite page, girl with elaborate cowry shell headband and cowry and kina shell necklace, Karawari River region, East Sepik Province, Papua New Guinea.
Both photos:
© **Patricio Robles Gil**/*Sierra Madre*

On pp. 158-159, masked dancers, Asmat people, Sjuru, Papua, Indonesia.
© **François Gohier**/*Auscape*

Papua New Guinea poses many challenges in terms of Western-style conservation through national parks and reserves. Since more than 97% of the land is still in the hands of traditional landowners, and not held by the State, protected area establishment, which has worked so well in the West and also in tropical countries where land is largely in the hands of the government, is not appropriate. Only five National Parks covering just 8 238 ha or 0.02% of Papua New Guinea's land area currently exist. In addition to these, there are five Sanctuaries for breeding of and research on indigenous wildlife, three Provincial Parks near urban areas, three Protected Areas where hunting of wildlife is permitted except for certain specified protected species, three Nature Reserves protecting specific ecosystem types, two Historic Sites, and several National Walking Tracks. Many of these existing areas are very small (under 100 ha) and unlikely to have long-term conservation significance.

Currently, the most appropriate conservation area category for Papua New Guinea is the Wildlife Management Area (WMA) which, in fact, mandates little more than local species- and habitat-management under the aegis of a blanket national government approval. Not strictly protected areas, 20 of these WMAs exist and cover 946 764 ha or 2.0% of the country's land area (with one additional marine WMA, Maza, covering 184 230 ha). As an indication of how important these could be in the future, an additional 120 areas have been proposed in the WMA category. However, in spite of this, only two new ones, Crater Mountain at 270 000 ha and Lake Kutubu at 24 000 ha, have been added recently, and these because of heavy lobbying from nongovernmental organizations. Clearly, much more needs to be done to promote habitat conservation in Papua New Guinea.

Combining what is covered in terrestrial parks, reserves, sanctuaries, and wildlife management areas, we have a total of 972 013 ha of the Papua New Guinea part of the island covered in protected areas of one kind or another.

By contrast, in Papua, a large nationally-mandated network of reserves, sanctuaries, and parks has been gazetted, although this has not been matched by significant management and investment on behalf of these designated reserves. At this time, there are 55 national marine and terrestrial reserves covering a total of 10.1 million ha (Supriatna 1999) in Papua. Of this, 8.5 million ha is terrestrial and 1.6 million ha is marine. This includes the 1.1-million-ha Lorentz National Park, the largest protected area in the Pacific. A major question we face today is the future of these nationally-mandated reserves under a regime of decentralization and local decision-making in Indonesia. In many instances, local landowners are not even aware that the land they traditionally claim is nationally gazetted as a protected area. This poses a significant challenge to conservationists who are working to conserve habitat on the ground in a decentralized Papua in the twenty-first century.

Together, the terrestrial protected area networks

(including Wildlife Management Areas on the Papua New Guinea side) cover a total of 9 472 013 ha, or roughly 11.4 % of the entire island.

It is safe to say that there is a lack of appropriate and robust legislation for either habitat conservation or species conservation in Papua New Guinea and Papua. Both require new conservation-areas legislation that will balance local needs and local decision-making with global biodiversity priorities. Probably, provincial reserves, sustainable development reserves, and/or watershed protection reserves, as well as locally-managed forest lands will have to be included in the landscape-scale protection schemes designed for New Guinea in the coming decades.

Although progress with legislation lags, New Guinea has benefited from considerable conservation planning and biodiversity priority-setting over the last decade. The *Papua New Guinea Conservation Needs Assessment* (Alcorn 1993), a collaboration between government, international scientists, and environmental NGOs which follows a methodology pioneered by Conservation International, produced a biodiversity priorities map and a detailed species and habitat analysis that has since guided the field activities of both the government and conservation NGOs. This was followed by the UNDP-sponsored *Papua New Guinea Country Study on Biodiversity* (Sekhran and Miller 1994), which sought to provide a synthesis of the economic, social, biological, and cultural values of native biodiversity in a manner that would influence decision-makers. With these two publications, Papua New Guinea can claim to be one of the best-analyzed small nations in terms of its native biodiversity wealth.

Papua benefited from a *Biodiversity Conservation Priority-Setting Workshop* in 1997 (Supriatna 1999), which included a priorities map, a report, and a CD with the raw biodiversity analysis data. This process, again developed and coordinated by Conservation International, included a wide range of NGOs, scientists, and government planners, and has had considerable impact in terms of official planning.

In Papua New Guinea, the Eco-Forestry Forum (EFF) is a voice for environmentally sustainable management of forests, with strong advocacy for small-scale village forestry operations as a preferable alternative to foreign-operated and owned industrial-scale logging. The EFF has grown in stature and effectiveness, and now stands to lead the country into a new era of forest development that is sensitive to the needs of the local landowners. Needless to say, the war is not won, although some recent battles have gone EFF's way. And the depressed price of tropical hardwoods, in combination with the Asian financial crisis, tilts the table in favor of EFF.

Innovative *conservation trust funds* are being established both in Papua and Papua New Guinea. The Mama Graun ("mother earth") Trust Fund in Papua New Guinea is being established through a grant from the World Bank and will support a range of local and regional conservation efforts through a board that will award grants on a competitive basis. The Papua Conservation Fund has

been developed through the technical assistance of Conservation International, and will operate on a similar basis. Both seek to generate a steady revenue to be invested in promising programs operated by NGOs and local agencies, all with the objective of fostering nature conservation and environmentally-sustainable development. When these are fully operational, they should give the environmental movement a strong boost.

Another approach that has been highlighted in recent years in New Guinea has been the Integrated Conservation and Development Project (ICDP) approach. ICDPs are site-based, and link conservation initiatives to social and economic development. They are particularly appropriate to the needs and land-tenure realities of this island. A number of these initiatives are currently under way, the most noteworthy being situated in the 2 700-km^2 Crater Mountain Wildlife Management Area in the Highlands and in the Lakekamu Basin Project in a 1 700-km^2 tract on the border between the Gulf and Central Provinces. The Crater Mountain Project is run by the Research and Conservation Foundation of Papua New Guinea and the Wildlife Conservation Society, while the Lakekamu Basin Project is the responsibility of Conservation International and the Foundation for People and Community Development (Biodiversity Conservation Network 1999).

The Crater Mountain Project has been operating for more than 20 years, and is one of the longest-running local conservation projects in the Pacific. Although fraught with difficulties brought about by complex land tenure, diverse traditional cultures, threats of large-scale mineral development, and national economic and political exigencies, the Crater Mountain Project demonstrates that a few dedicated conservationists, working on the ground and with support from international NGOs, can effect habitat conservation on a landscape-scale in Papua New Guinea. We believe Crater Mountain is a shining example of successful Melanesian nature conservation.

The Lakekamu Project, though younger, also offers important lessons. The implementation of this ICDP has been hindered by institutional rivalries and miscommunication, major landowner disputes, and funding discontinuities, and yet the program continues and conservation appears to be succeeding in spite of the challenges. The question that faces both Lakekamu and Crater Mountain right now is: Can these programs survive in the next decades if appropriate conservation legislation is not forthcoming?

Aside from these protected areas and ICDPs, there needs to be increased attention focused on other sustainable biodiversity uses. These include much greater emphasis on non-timber forest products like fruits, nuts, and other wild plant foods, gums, resins, latex, other tree exudates, aromatic oils, tannins, rattan, orchids, sago and nipa palm products, and bamboo products, and potentially sustainable wildlife products including insects such as butterflies, crocodile skins, marine and freshwater aquarium fish, and many others. Bio-prospecting through random plant collecting in this botanically-rich country

Members of New Guinea's more than 1 100 tribal groups at the 2001 Highlands Show in Mount Hagen, Papua New Guinea.

Above, © Cristina Mittermeier; on the opposite page, © Patricia Rojo, and on pp. 162-163, © Cristina Mittermeier

and through ethnobotanical research on traditional medicines is also likely to bear fruit, as is further research on the germ plasm of globally-important crop species originating in New Guinea (e.g., sugarcane, sago palm, winged beans). Given the wonderful wood-carving traditions that exist in New Guinea, handicraft development is also likely to be productive, especially in globally-important centers of tribal art like the Sepik and New Ireland. Finally, ecotourism and cultural tourism may have the greatest potential of all. Few destinations can compare to New Guinea in terms of pristine environments, unique wildlife, and incomparable traditional cultures. Birdwatching is already significant and could increase dramatically. This combination is certain to prove appealing to tourists from around the world, and needs to be better marketed to the most appropriate target audiences. It is hindered, however, by law-and-order issues that face both Papua New Guinea and Papua, and the image that it is dangerous to travel to many parts of the island.

Most recently, Conservation International (CI) has taken the lead in developing landscape-wide conservation initiatives. Built upon the *corridor conservation* concept, these programs are operating at a scale several times larger than those of the largest ICDPs. CI's Milne Bay Marine Corridor Program is working over a marine zone of 10 million ha. In collaboration with national, provincial, and local governments, as well as with local stakeholders and landowners, the Milne Bay Program seeks to develop long-term plans for conservation and sustainable management of marine resources and habitats. The aim is to expand this program to encompass the entire Milne Bay Province, from the summit of Mt. Suckling in the west to Misima Island in the east. And the ultimate goal is to develop a management structure that will permit local implementers and managers to continue this program on their own over the long term.

CI is developing a similar program that focuses on the watershed of the Mamberamo River in northern Papua. With a forest and watershed focus, this, too, encompasses 10 million ha very rich in biodiversity and ranging from sea level to more than 4 000 m. Certainly, many challenges remain to be addressed before these two giant initiatives can be fully operational. Nonetheless, in a major tropical wilderness area like New Guinea, it is necessary to conduct conservation on this scale while the opportunity still exists. Fortunately, on much of the amazing island of New Guinea, these opportunities *do* still exist, and we very much believe that it should be possible to develop programs that both maintain the full range of biodiversity and simultaneously attend to the needs and aspirations of New Guinea's rich and diverse cultures.

BRUCE BEEHLER
GAI KULA
JATNA SUPRIATNA
RUSSELL A. MITTERMEIER
JOHN PILGRIM

THE CHACO

The Gran Chaco, or Great Thorn Forest, is South America's largest dry forest. A vast subtropical to tropical forest habitat that occurs on a Quaternary plain formed by material eroded from the Andes, it covers approximately 996 600 km². Chaco systems are spread over three countries, occupying 633 000 km² in northern Argentina (63.5%), 240 000 km² in northwestern Paraguay (24%), and 124 000 km² in southeastern Bolivia (12.5%). Approximately 70% can still be considered intact, but "extensive" ranching throughout the region is likely to have serious impacts in the long term. Our definition of the Chaco includes four WWF ecoregions: Chaco (NT0210), Arid Chaco (NT0701), Córdoba Montane Savanna (NT0706), and most of the Humid Chaco (NT0708), but excludes the Chiquitano Dry Forests (NT0212), which are often considered to be part of the Chaco (Olson et al. 2001).

The Chaco developed from a mid-latitude Tertiary flora that was adapted to a seasonally-dry climate. The uplifting of mountain ranges in the Pliocene was accompanied by extensive erosion and deposition of continental sediments to the east of the Paraná-Paraguay River Basin and the first indication of dry-adapted vegetation is recorded at this time. During the Pleistocene there were at least two periods when this basin was a cool and dry steppe. The Chaco developed during these periods over much of the area where it is found today (Solbrig 1976).

The Chaco is considered the "mother habitat" of two other major habitats in southern South America, the biome complex collectively known as the Monte Desert and the Espinal. The first is a narrow desert that begins near the Bolivian border in far-western Argentina at 27°S latitude and extends southward 2 000 km to 44°S latitude. The Espinal is considered to be an impoverished southern extension of the Chaco and is very similar to it, except for the absence of *Schinopsis* (quebracho), a Chaco dominant, and the dominance of *Prosopis* (Burkart et al. 1999; Cabrera 1976).

The Gran Chaco extends from about 16°S latitude in Bolivia through Paraguay and northern Argentina to about 34°S latitude. From east to west, it extends from 58°W longitude in eastern Argentina and Paraguay to 67°W longitude in eastern Bolivia and western Argentina. It is thus situated between the Andes and the Brazilian Plateau on the great Sub-

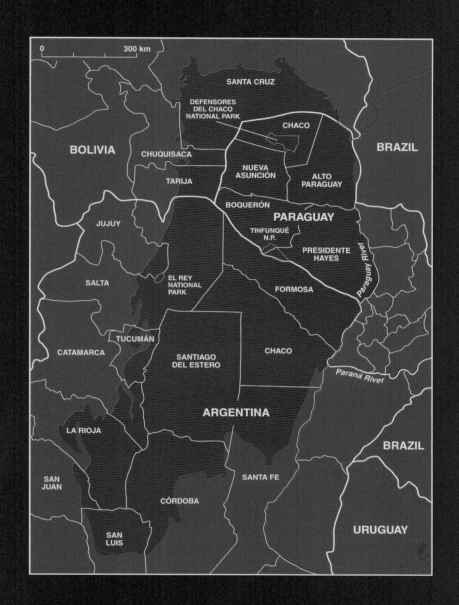

Andean Depression. To the west, it is bordered by the Yungas Forest, the Monte Desert of Mountains and Isolated Valleys, and the Monte Desert of Lagoons and Mesas; to the south by the Monte Desert of Lagoons and Mesas and the Espinal; to the northeast by the Iberá Marshes, the westernmost extension of the Atlantic forest in eastern Paraguay, and the Cerrado; and to the northwest by the Chiquitano Dry Forest and the Pantanal (Bucher 1982; Burkart et al., *op. cit.*; Cabrera, *op. cit.*; Short 1975).

The Chaco is primarily a flat plain of low elevation (100-500 m). Altitude ranges from a maximum of 2 400 m in the far west to 400 m in the east, with only a slight gradient in elevation occurring over most of the region. There are few major rivers in the Chaco (Bucher and Chani 1999). The Paraguay-Paraná river system affects the climate, vegetation,

World Heritage Area

On the opposite page, bottle tree or palo borracho (Chorisia insignis), a characteristic tree species of the region.
© **Luiz Claudio Marigo**

165

THE CAATINGA

MARANHÃO
PIAUÍ
CEARÁ
RIO GRANDE DO NORTE
PARAÍBA
SERRA DA CAPIVARA NATIONAL PARK
PERNAMBUCO
ALAGOAS
BRAZIL
SERGIPE
Rio São Francisco
CHAPADA DA DIAMANTINA NATIONAL PARK
BAHÍA
ATLANTIC OCEAN
MINAS GERAIS
0   400 km

The semiarid Caatinga of northeastern Brazil is a surprising exception to the typical pattern of landscapes in tropical South America. Across much of the continent, rainforests extend some 10° north and south of the equator; straddling this emerald band are the savannas, reaching out to 20°. Within this ancient, orderly design, the Caatinga is an anomaly —a semiarid biome unique in South America, dominating the easternmost horn of Brazil and surrounded by an array of other ecosystems. These include the semideciduous forests of eastern Amazonia, the mesic savannas of the Cerrado, and the remnants of the Atlantic forest on the coastal margin. As we define it, the Caatinga covers approximately 735 000 km², broadly equivalent to WWF's Caatinga ecoregion (NT1304) (734 400 km²) and the fourth largest biome in Brazil after Amazonia, the Cerrado, and the Atlantic forest.

Much of today's Caatinga was once a prehistoric sea floor. The terrain is dominated by Cretaceous sandstone deposits, resting on a basement of Precambrian crystalline rock. An old and weathered landscape, the sandstone in many areas has eroded to expose the basement, either as an expansive shelf of rock or a series of boulder piles and small rocky hills. This results in considerable topographic relief throughout much of the Caatinga. In several areas the sandstone deposits remain intact, creating large, contiguous plateaus reaching several hundred kilometers in length, called *chapadas* in Portuguese. These plateaus have a sandy, porous soil, very different from the surrounding plains. Along with the low mountain ranges of northeastern Brazil, these are important regions of orographic precipitation, and are wetter than the surrounding lowlands. The shallow rocky soils in the plains, coupled with the nonporous crystalline basement, result in a low capacity to retain water, generating high rates of runoff (Ab'Saber 1977). One of the largest *chapadas* is the Chapada do Araripe, on the border between the states of Pernambuco and Ceará. This extensive formation is also famous for the large deposits of fossil fish from the Cretaceous that are continually exposed in the eroding sandstone (Viana and Neumann 1999). These deposits are well known to amateur collectors as well as paleontologists, and the fossils can be found for sale throughout the open-air markets of northeast Brazil.

The limits of the Caatinga closely follow the 800-mm isohyet of precipitation. Within this overall boundary, precipitation varies from over 1 600 mm on some of the high plateaus to less than 300 mm in the most arid regions. This compares to a range of 500 to 1 000 mm per year in the semiarid Chaco, and 750 to 2 000 mm per year in the central Brazilian savanna biome. Rainfall is highly seasonal, occurring primarily between November and May; the region on average experiences a water deficit from May until December. There is great annual variation in the quantity and timing of rainfall, and the dry season can extend for as long as ten months, versus five months in the Cerrado and only three in the Chaco. Total annual precipitation may vary from extremely heavy rainfall, exceeding 600 mm in a month, to a complete lack of precipitation in very dry years. The occurrence of such arid conditions in this irregularly-shaped region has earned the Caatinga the name "The Polygon of Drought" (Nimer 1972; Markham 1972).

Wilderness Area

On the opposite page, Mandacaru cactus (Cereus jamacaru) in the Toca Velha Canyon near Canudos, Bahia. This canyon is one of only two known roosting sites of Lear's macaw (Anodorhynchus leari).
© Luiz Claudio Marigo

175

Biodiversity

The harsh and unpredictable climate of the Caatinga places a strain on the organisms that survive there. The plants in particular must be able to endure both annual and long-term droughts, and they have evolved morphological and physiological adaptations to withstand these arid conditions. The Caatinga flora includes many large-spined cacti, thorny shrubs and trees, waxy-leafed terrestrial bromeliads, and barrel-trunked trees. These structures are adaptations to conserve water and protect against damage by herbivores. Unlike desert-adapted trees, which usually have hard, waxy leaves as an adaptation to predictable drought, most Caatinga trees have soft, thin leaves that are easily shed. Botanists believe this is an adaptation not only to dry conditions, but to a dangerous unpredictability in precipitation. The widespread specializations of the Caatinga plants to drought suggest a long history of evolution under arid conditions.

Although a number of schemes exist for the classification of vegetation in the Caatinga (Sampaio and Rodal 2000), most authors agree on several broad classifications. *Agreste* is a zone of transition between the northeastern Atlantic forest and the Caatinga proper. Within the Caatinga, many authors distinguish two principal forms of Caatinga. *Caatinga Arbustiva* (or *Baixa*) is a lower-canopy, more open form of vegetation that occurs on more dry or rocky soils. Its dominant woody genera include *Aspidosperma, Astronium, Bursera, Caesalpinia, Cnidoscolus, Jatropha, Mimosa, Schinopsis,* and *Spondias,* plus the palm *Syagrus* and the cacti *Cereus* and *Pilosocereus. Caatinga Arborea* (or *Alta*) consists of tall-canopy forest dominated by the genera *Aspidosperma, Astronium, Bursera, Caesalpinia, Cavanillesia, Mimosa, Spondias,* and *Tabebuia,* as well as the cacti *Cereus* and *Pilosocereus.* Although these taxa do not differ dramatically from the scrub forms of Caatinga, the height of the canopy and overall appearance of the forests are quite different, and much more detailed subdivisions of the Caatinga vegetation are possible (e.g. Andrade Lima 1981).

The Caatinga region remains fertile ground for botanical research; neither plant associations nor diversity are well understood. One recent review of the Caatinga flora (Sampaio 1995) lists 339 woody species in 161 genera and 48 families; this modest richness is typical in harsh or unpredictable environments. Of the 437 woody species described for the Caatinga in an unpublished report, approximately 180 (41%) are endemic (D. Duarte Pereira, in litt., 1995). This same study reports 249 species of herbaceous vegetation, with no information on the level of endemism. The richness of vascular plants in the Caatinga as a whole has yet to be surveyed, but estimates range as high as 1 200 species, and overall endemism may be 30% (Andrade Lima, *op. cit.*). A report by the Associação Plantas do Nordeste (2000) lists 932 species found only in true Caatinga, excluding plants found in moist forest enclaves. This same report documents 20 endemic genera and 380 endemic species for the Caatinga proper (41%). The flora of the Caatinga includes many endemic genera, such as *Moldenhawera, Cranocarpus* (Leguminosae), *Fraunhofera* (Celastraceae), *Apterokarpos* (Anacardiaceae), *Auxemma* (Boraginaceae), and *Neoglaziovia* (Bromeliaceae). This generic-level endemism supports the definition of the Caatinga as a distinct floristic province (Lleras 1997).

The complex topography and substrate have created several important microhabitats in the Caatinga. The sandy soil has eroded throughout the region, exposing large formations of crystalline rock that vary from small outcrops or rocky hills (*serras* or *serrotes*) to extensive, exposed rock faces (*lajeiros*). *Serrotes* often serve as mesic enclaves within the Caatinga; water is trapped in fissures in the rock, and these areas often support larger trees and more diverse plant communities. *Lajeiros,* on the other hand, are often devoid of vegetation. The extensive *chapadas* that occur throughout the Caatinga also support more mesic vegetation because of the orographic precipitation they capture. Some of the larger *chapadas* support Caatinga on their leeward sides, which grades into *Cerrado* (forming a Caatinga-Cerrado complex called *carrasco* by some authors) and then into mesic forest on the windward slope. The Araripe National Forest, on the Chapada do Araripe near the city of Crato, Ceará, is an excellent example of a forest island in the Caatinga. A similar zone of orographic rainforest is located in the Serra Negra Biological Reserve in the state of Pernambuco.

Many authors have commented on the similarity of the Caatinga vegetation to that of the Chaco. However, the strongest floristic links are to dry seasonal forests in northern Argentina, eastern Paraguay, and southwestern Brazil; and also to the drier Andean valleys, from Bolivia south to Tucumán and Catamarca in Argentina (Prado and Gibbs 1993).

The faunal diversity of the Caatinga, like the vegetation that supports it, is not as rich as in surrounding biomes, and few endemic vertebrates are known. Most of the vertebrates in the Caatinga range into adjacent ecosystems, especially the Cerrado. Many vertebrates are strongly associated with mesic enclaves or more mesic microhabitats within the Caatinga. In all, 348 species of birds have been recorded from the Caatinga, of which 13% (46) are either endemic or most commonly found in the Caatinga and transitional forests (Pacheco and Bauer 2000). Their list includes 15 endemic species and 45 endemic subspecies, but preliminary assessments suggest that many of these subspecies will be ranked as full species after systematic revision. Other published lists indicate slightly fewer species (320) and only eight strict endemics (WWF, in prep.).

Mammals are represented by only two endemic species: the spiny rat, *Proechimys yonenagae* (Rocha 1995), and the recently described bat, *Micronycteris sanborni* (Simmons 1996). In an unpublished report,

Murine mouse opossum (Marmosa murina), a small marsupial found in this region.
© **Fabio Colombini**

176

Oliveira (2000) presents a list that includes 148 species of mammals, of which 10 are endemic. In any case, it is likely that future systematic research will result in the recognition of more than the currently-recognized endemics.

Rodrigues (2000) lists 96 species of reptiles (including 40 lizards, seven amphisbaenids, 45 snakes, and four turtles) as well as 44 species of amphibians (43 frogs and one caecilian). Researchers have recently discovered a complex community of reptiles in an area of relictual paleo-quaternary dunes on the Rio São Francisco in the State of Bahia. Though not representative of the Caatinga ecosystem as a whole, this community may harbor as many as 20 endemic species of reptiles (Rodrigues 1996). Endemic lizards include three species of *Calyptommatus*, two of *Procellosaurinus*, four of *Tropidurus*, and three of *Amphisbaena*, plus *Nothobachia ablephara* and *Psilophthalmus paeminosus*. Endemic snakes are *Typhlops yonenagae*, three species of *Apostolepis*, and two species of *Phimophis*. According to Rodrigues (2000), there are a total of 24 endemic reptile species in the Caatinga, including the Rio São Francisco complex, but no endemic amphibians. However, the amphibians of the Caatinga remain very poorly known, so some surprises may await us.

In contrast to the specialized flora, the animals of the Caatinga are not especially adapted either to aridity or an unpredictable climate (Mares et al. 1985). The rock cavy (*Kerodon rupestris*), a species largely restricted to the Caatinga, has an exceptionally poor urine-concentrating capacity, as do other mammals of the region. Rodents from the deserts of Africa, Asia, or the southwestern United States and Mexico are able to produce urine two or three times as concentrated.

In summary, the Caatinga is dominated by arid-adapted vegetation with high levels of endemism, while the vertebrate fauna is depauperate, with low levels of endemism and little adaptation to aridity. Nonetheless, it is important to emphasize that the flora and fauna of the Caatinga are poorly understood, and future systematic, ecological, and physiological research may alter some of these conclusions.

Flagship Species

The most important flagship species of the Caatinga are two large, Critically Endangered macaws that are endemic to the region, Lear's macaw (*Anodorhynchus leari*) and Spix's macaw (*Cyanopsitta spixii*). Lear's macaw is a spectacular blue macaw, superficially similar to the hyacinth macaw (*Anodorhynchus hyacinthinus*), but slightly smaller (70 cm long), with a larger head, and lighter in color. Only two colonies are known, both in the State of Bahia, and the species has a total population of about 150 individuals. High sandstone cliffs are vital to these macaws for roosting and nesting. The roosts are communal and birds forage in flocks.

These parrots depend primarily on the fruits of the licurí palm (*Syagrus coronata*), and an individual bird may consume 350 palm nuts per day. Lear's macaw is partly protected by the Raso da Catarina Ecological Station and is the focus of aggressive conservation and recuperation activities spearheaded by Fundação Biodiversitas, a leading Brazilian NGO (BirdLife International 2000; I.B. Santos, pers. comm.).

Spix's macaw is one of the world's most Critically Endangered birds and is now thought to be extinct in the wild. For over a decade, this species was represented by a single wild individual living in natural habitat near the town of Curaça in Bahia, but it has not been seen in the wild since October, 2000; the last wild sighting by non-Brazilians was in July, 2000 by Russell, John, and Michael Mittermeier. This strikingly beautiful bird is smaller than Lear's macaw, bluish-grey with an ashy-blue head. It is of particular importance because it is not only an endemic species, but also the only representative of a monotypic genus entirely restricted to the Caatinga. Apparently this species was originally a specialist on gallery forests of *Tabebuia caraiba*, which have been largely destroyed; wild Spix's macaws preferred the fruits of several species of the family Euphorbiaceae. A total captive population of about 60 individuals still exists, raising hopes of possible reintroduction; but they are scattered across several places —including Brazil, the Philippines, Switzerland, and the Canary Islands— and coordination of efforts has been difficult and highly-politicized (Juniper and Parr 1998; BirdLife International, *op. cit.*).

Several species of mammals and plants also merit consideration as flagship species in this region. The rock cavy, a large (700 g) rodent in the Family Caviidae, is distantly related to guinea pigs. It occupies rock outcrops where it lives in crevices and forages on foliage (Lacher 1981). With numerous adaptations to its rocky habitat, the rock cavy has many morphological, ecological, and behavioral similarities to the hyraxes and gundis of Africa (Mares and Lacher 1987). It also climbs well and often forages high in trees. When disturbed, it gives a rapid, trilling alarm call and flees deep into crevices in the boulder piles. The species is heavily hunted and its status is not known.

The Brazilian three-banded armadillo (*Tolypeutes tricinctus*) is closely related to the southern three-banded armadillo (*T. matacus*) from Bolivia. The Brazilian species was once thought to be extinct, but Silva and Oren (1993) rediscovered populations in tropical deciduous forest remnants in the State of Bahia. Like the rock cavy, the Brazilian three-banded armadillo is also heavily hunted. Although it has been observed in the Cerrado (Marinho-Filho et al. 1997), it is largely a Caatinga species. This armadillo has the ability to completely roll itself into a tight ball as a defensive posture.

Plant flagships are represented by *Cereus jamacaru*, an endemic, tree-sized, candelabra-shaped cactus considered a defining feature of the Caatinga landscape.

*Brazilian three-banded armadillo or tatu-bola (*Tolypeutes tricinctus*), a species largely restricted to the Caatinga.*
© **Fabio Colombini**

This cactus often towers over the adjacent thorn scrub, and is the only vegetation that remains green during intense droughts. It is related to other species of this genus that occur in the deserts of the southwestern United States and in the Chaco of South America. The understory euphorb shrub *Cnidoscolus urens* is also abundant throughout the region. This species has painful urticating hairs on the leaves and stems, and contact results in a blistering rash that may be life-threatening to sensitive individuals.

Human Cultures

The Caatinga region was originally inhabited by a large number of indigenous tribes (approximately 30 recognized territories; CEDI 1991) that arrived in the Northeast about 14 000 years ago. Recent archaeological evidence, still in dispute, places the arrival of humans in the Northeast thousands of years earlier. The first Portuguese colonists arrived in the 1500s, drawn by legends of silver mines to rival those of Peru. However, they soon turned to more realistic goals, exploiting the *sertão* to raise beasts of burden to drive the sugar mills of the coastal zone (Andrade 1980). The Portuguese crown had given land grants to encourage settlement —and to stave off the intrusions of the French— and by the late 1600s, colonists had entered the Caatinga in force. They introduced slave-based agriculture and large-scale cattle-raising, and swiftly developed a feudal system of large landowners (*fazendeiros*) who held their workers in effective serfdom. The expansion of this foreign society into the best growing areas of the *sertão* led to escalating conflicts with the native peoples, who resented their forcible exclusion from ancient hunting and fishing grounds. The clashes eventually drew the dreaded *bandeirantes* of São Paulo, roving freebooters whose strength of arms decided the undeclared war, annihilating the Indian resistance and relocating the survivors to the harshest pockets of the Caatinga.

By 1700, there were over a million head of cattle in the *sertão*, whose existence was dedicated to the support of the coastal sugar industry. Agriculture in the Caatinga, never optimal, remained restricted for generations to basic crops such as manioc, maize, and beans. Not until the mid-1800s did new crops become profitable for the inhabitants of the region, the *nordestinos* or *sertanejos*. First came coffee, then cotton, and finally the native wax-producing carnauba palms. Although abolition technically ended slavery in 1888, the wage laborers who worked the great *fazendas* knew little difference, ruled as they were by absentee landlords who controlled every aspect of their lives. The original system of *fazendas* retains its essentially medieval character in many parts of the Caatinga to this day. Sharecroppers and cowhands may be required to give free labor to their *fazendeiro*, but this earns no loyalty in return. They may be evicted at any time,

with or without notice or cause. Their only recourse is either to strike a deal with another *fazendeiro*, or to escape to the false promise of the coastal cities —where, despite the higher wages, workers are twice as likely to be malnourished as in the desperate conditions they left behind (Ward and Sanders 1980).

The unique climate of the Caatinga has left its mark on the human population of the region as much as on the distinctive flora. Northeast Brazil remains the poorest area in the country —by some statistics, the poorest in the Western Hemisphere—, in part because of its highly unpredictable climate. The periodic droughts have brought great hardship and poverty to the estimated 27 million people of the Caatinga, resulting in a depressed standard of living, which stands in great contrast to the wealthy states of the south. The major urban centers of northeastern Brazil —Fortaleza, Natal, Recife, and Salvador— are all on the coast, and have been placed under tremendous stress by the immigration of poor rural families fleeing recurring drought (Ward and Sanders, *op. cit.*). For this and other reasons, the Caatinga has been a source of social unrest throughout the history of Brazil.

The isolation of the Caatinga has indeed resulted in the development of a distinct culture (Vasconcelos Sobrinho, 1971), with a rich folklore, characteristic music, dances, art, and handicrafts. Indeed, many of Brazil's greatest composers are *nordestinos,* and the late author Jorge Amado wrote almost exclusively on northeastern themes. The folkways of the Caatinga exemplify the great creativity arising from populations subjected to challenges and suffering.

The most recent census data for the Caatinga show that there are more than 26 696 000 inhabitants, of which the majority live in urban areas. The rural population is 8 305 500, for an average density of 11.3 inhabitants/km^2 (Sampaio and Mazza 2000). However, large portions of the region have a much lower, wilderness-level population density. For example, the catchment basin of the Sobradinho Reservoir in the interior of the Bahian Caatinga covers some 498 425 km^2, or 68% of the entire Caatinga, and yet has a population density of 0.23 inhabitants/km^2 (International Lake Environment Committee 2002). Population growth rates vary, but have shown a steady decline in rural areas since the 1980s. What population growth does occur has been in the urban areas, especially along the coast, while the interior of the states of Ceará, Paraíba, and Pernambuco have stable or declining populations. Much of this contrast may be due to the waves of rural immigrants who have steadily sought the benefits of the wealthier coastal communities.

A recent study by Casteleti et al. (2000) estimates that about 27.5% of the Caatinga is dedicated to agricultural activities. However, the remainder, about 70%, is either not under cultivation or is subject only to other lower-intensity forms of land use, and could thus be considered relatively intact.

Above, black-chested buzzard eagle (Geranoaetus melanoleucus) *with a marmoset* (Callithrix sp.) *in its claws.*

On the opposite page, pair of Lear's macaws (Anodorhynchus leari) *at the entrance to their nest, cliffs of Toca Velha Canyon, Bahia. This Critically Endangered species is endemic to the Caatinga.*
Both photos: © **Luiz Claudio Marigo**

MIOMBO-MOPANE WOODLANDS AND GRASSLANDS

A common perception of much of Africa is that of extensive grassy plains with scattered trees and bushes, inhabited by large herds of wildlife. Whereas such landscapes exist in some popular tourist destinations in East Africa, they are atypical of tropical Africa as a whole, much of which is covered instead by various kinds of woodland and bushland. Foremost among these are the Miombo, Mopane, and other associated woodlands of southern central Africa. Together with scattered grasslands and wetlands within them, these woodlands cover about 3.7 million km² of Africa south of the equator, arguably the single largest block of more-or-less contiguous tropical dry woodlands in the world. They are characterized by the predominance of compound-leafed trees of the legume subfamily Caesalpinioideae, particularly species in the genera *Brachystegia, Julbernardia, Isoberlinia, Colophospermum, Baikiaea, Burkea,* and *Cryptosepalum.* The woodlands extend from the Angolan escarpment in the west, through Zambia, Zimbabwe, and Malawi, to Mozambique in the east, where they intersect the coastal forests and thickets of the East African coastal zone. At their northern limit in central Tanzania and the southern Democratic Republic of Congo (DRC), they border the *Acacia-Commiphora* bushlands and grasslands of the dry East African plains and the moist evergreen forests of the Congo Basin. The southern boundary is marked by transitions to the semidesert shrublands and *Acacia* woodlands of southern Angola, northern Namibia, and Botswana, and the mixed *Acacia* woodlands, highveld grasslands and subtropical bushlands of South Africa.

This large area corresponds broadly to the Zambezian Regional Center of Endemism, as described by White (1983), or the Miombo Super-Ecoregion, as defined by the World Wide Fund for Nature (Byers 2001), though it extends further south to include the Angolan Mopane Woodlands ecoregion (AT0702) (133 462 km²), and also differs marginally in the areas covered in the east and southeast. In addition to the Angolan Mopane Woodlands, this wilderness encompasses the Angolan Miombo Woodlands ecoregion (AT0701) (660 083 km²); Central Zambezian, Eastern and Southern Miombo Woodlands ecoregions (AT0704) (1 184 205 km²), (AT0706) (483 901km²) and (AT0719) (408 257 km²); Zambezian *Baikiaea* Woodlands (AT0726) (264 437 km²); *Cryptosepalum* Dry Forests (AT0203) (38 229 km²); Zambezian and Mopane Woodlands (AT0725) (473 318 km²); Itigi-Sumbu Thicket (AT0708) (7 843 km²); and Zambezian Flooded Grasslands (AT0907) (153 452 km²) (Olson et al. 2001).

Several rather different ecoregions are also encircled by the typical Miombo-Mopane Woodland habitat in this wilderness area, namely the Etosha Pan (AT0902) (7 231 km²); the Angolan Montane Forest-Grassland Mosaic (AT1001) (25 518 km²); and the mountains of eastern Zimbabwe (AT1006) (7 828 km²), southern Malawi (AT1014) (10 228 km²); and the southern Rift (AT1015) (33 497 km²). The diverse montane forests of the Eastern Arc, on the edge of this wilderness area, are highly fragmented and are treated as a hotspot (Myers et al. 2000). For the purposes of this book, the Okavango area has been treated separately, although Mopane Woodland is dominant there outside the swamps. In all, these ecoregions cover 3 891 489 km².

Almost a third (1.2 million km²) of the Miombo-Mopane Woodlands and Grasslands is relatively intact,

Biome

Intact Woodland

On the opposite page, herd of Cape buffalo (Syncerus caffer) *taking an afternoon drink, Ruaha National Park, Tanzania.*
© **Patricio Robles Gil**/*Sierra Madre*

and is the area that we treat here as wilderness, though statistics in this chapter relate to the entire biogeographic region as defined above.

Almost 60% of the region lies on the ancient Central African plateau at 1 000-1 600 m above sea level, an area of flat to gently-undulating wooded landscapes interspersed with broad ribbons of grassland marking the upland drainage of the plateau. The land is remarkably level, with little obvious variation in relief, a testimony to millions of years of weathering and erosion uninterrupted by any major geological upheavals. While grand and compelling vistas may be generally lacking, though they are found in places, the attraction of this wilderness lies in its size, and in the subtlety and intricacy of its composition and functioning.

The plateau is dissected in places by the valleys of major rivers such as the Limpopo, Zambezi, Shire, Luangwa, Rufiji, and Rovuma, as well as the upper Congo River drainage. All of them, other than the Limpopo, have their headwaters in the region. The Kalahari Basin, a huge sand-filled depression, partly bisects the plateau from the south. The valleys are generally hotter, drier, and more fertile than the plateau, and support quite different types of vegetation. Above 2 000 m, the woodlands of the plateau are replaced by grasslands and forests of the Afromontane Region, a series of isolated highlands forming the Eastern Arc Mountains of Tanzania, the Nyika Plateau and Mt. Mulanje Massif in Malawi, the Eastern Highlands of Zimbabwe, Mt. Gorongosa in Mozambique, and the Highlands of Angola. The biota of the Afromontane Region is sufficiently distinct, both ecologically and biogeographically, for the region to best be considered separately. It is not discussed further here.

More than 90% of the vegetation in the region is woodland of one type or another, interspersed with various grasslands, wetlands, and swamps. The woodlands are generally differentiated by their dominant tree species and genera, and are often referred to by the vernacular names for these. Thus, among others, we have Miombo Woodland, characterized by various species of *Brachystegia* and *Julbernardia* (the name being derived from *muombo* or *mubombo*, vernacular names in Malawi, Tanzania, and Zambia for a number of species of *Brachystegia*); Mopane Woodland, dominated by mopane (*Colophospermum mopane*); gusu, mukusi or Teak Woodland, typified by the presence of the Zambezi teak (*Baikiaea plurijuga*); and Munga Woodland, characterized by a variety of *Acacia* and *Combretum* species occurring on patches of fertile soil, often disturbed, on the plateau. Miombo is the most widespread woodland type, covering more than two thirds of the region, mostly on the weathered and leached soils of the plateau. Mopane Woodland is confined largely to alkaline, clayey soils at low altitudes in the hot, dry river valleys, while Teak Woodland is confined to the sands of the Kalahari Basin. At a regional scale, therefore, the distribution and composition of the various vegetation types is determined largely by climatic factors —principally mean

annual rainfall, rainfall variability, length of the annual dry season, and temperature regime— together with soil texture and fertility. Local variation is induced through disturbance by large herbivores and people, often interacting with fire.

Much of the region lies in the warm subhumid zone, with highly seasonal rainfall occurring mainly during the southern summer from November to April. The rest of the year is dry. More than four fifths of the region receives an annual average rainfall of 600-1 400 mm. Only 5% receives more, mostly in the east where the moisture-laden southeasterly trade winds, blowing inland off the Indian Ocean, rise up against the high inselbergs and escarpments of northern Mozambique, southern Tanzania, Malawi, and Zimbabwe. Areas receiving less than 600 mm annually are concentrated in the south, where the rainfall is highly variable and droughts are common. Mean monthly temperatures range between 19° and 24°C, the higher temperatures characterizing the major river valleys and the eastern coastal plain. Conditions for plant growth, when water is available, are generally good.

The reason for the remarkable dominance of these woodlands by a few species from a single subfamily of plants is not clear. It may be related to the ability of these trees to grow well in nutrient-poor soils in a seasonally dry environment, despite being unable to fix nitrogen, unlike many other legumes. Most of the dominant trees have compound leaves, a feature distinguishing these woodlands from similar ecosystems in South America and Australia. In part this reflects the dominance of the Caesalpinioideae, most species of which have compound leaves —efficient at dispersing heat—, but it may also reflect the advantage that trees with compound leaves have in a seasonally water-limited system. Across the Miombo-Mopane woodlands, the leaflets tend to get smaller as the environment becomes drier. Given the strongly seasonal nature of the rainfall, most trees and shrubs are deciduous, shedding their leaves sometime during the dry season. Where deep-rooted species such as *Baikiaea plurijuga*, *Brachystegia longifolia,* and *B. spiciformis* are able to reach the dry-season water table, they retain their leaves for most of the dry season, before dropping them and producing a new crop almost immediately. One particularly striking feature of Miombo Woodland is the flush of new leaves 4-8 weeks *before* the start of the rains, a quite different pattern from that seen in most other tropical deciduous woodlands. A marked pulse of nitrogen occurs in the soils immediately following the first rains, so it is advantageous to have a fully-developed canopy of leaves that can start functioning once the rains begin (Frost 1996). The new leaves, especially those of *Brachystegia spiciformis*, are various striking shades of red, due to the synthesis of anthocyanins soon after the leaves emerge. These may be important in protecting the leaves against damage by microbes and herbivores during this vulnerable stage.

Many of the dominant trees in these woodlands also

Above, white-fronted bee-eaters (Merops bullockoides).
© Heinri van den Berg/*BIOS*

On the opposite page, southern ground-hornbill (Bucorvus leadbeateri) *with lizard. This species is now mainly confined to protected areas.*
© Joe McDonald/*DRK Photo*

draught power, milk, manure for fertilizing crops, and payments for brides. And at times they also provide meat and hides, though mostly only on special occasions.

In many areas, traditional "slash-and-burn" agriculture is still practiced, though this is becoming less common as population pressures reduce the remaining amount of virgin land. The Bemba in northern Zambia practice one of the best-known forms of slash-and-burn agriculture, *chitemene*. Perhaps better thought of as "ash-fertilization" agriculture, *chitemene* involves lopping

agents, as much as they are to being dispersed by other primates and species such as elephants. The greater honeyguide (*Indicator indicator*) is attracted to the sounds of people whistling or chopping wood in the woodlands, and will actively attempt to guide them to a beehive. Local honey gatherers in turn generally leave some of the cone for the bird, which has bacteria in its digestive tract that allows it to break down and absorb the wax. People's culture —songs, dance, and art— reflect these close ties to their environment. There are rich rewards for those who visit the region to see and learn something about these diverse societies.

on what happens to the fig trees. Although they provide shade for people and livestock, they also provide the preferred fuelwood for firing brick kilns, as the wood burns slowly.

Prominent timber trees, such as the Zambezi teak, are among the few obvious flagship plant species in the region. Originally exploited largely to provide timber sleepers for the 1 400-km railway line from Bulawayo, Zimbabwe, to the Copperbelt in Zambia, Zambezi teak has become popular as a furniture wood, especially that salvaged from old railway sleepers as these have gradually been replaced by concrete and metal sleepers. The wooden sleepers have been exposed to sun, rain, and

human evolution, from the Early Stone Age *Homo habilis* and *H. erectus* to *Homo sapiens*, who emerged in the latter part of the Early Stone Age. Foremost among these is the skull of early *H. sapiens*, estimated to be about 125 000-200 000 years old, discovered in a cave at Kabwe, Zambia, in 1921. The various Middle and Late Stone Age sites provide a valuable record of the early evolution of humans and their culture, particularly the many fine examples of rock art attributable to the Late Stone Age San, most notably in the Tsodilo Hills in Botswana and Matobo Hills in Zimbabwe (Parry 2000). Evidence of the controlled use of fire by early hominids has been found at Kalambo Falls in northern Zam-

herbaceous layer, greater grass production, more frequent and intense dry-season fires, and the destruction or suppression of the growth of the remaining trees. Appropriate post-harvest management in needed to counter this, but it is seldom applied.

A further potential threat to wildlife in the region comes from the expanding trade in bushmeat, mostly small and large mammals, birds, and edible caterpillars. Together with fish, these have traditionally been important sources of protein for people who otherwise have protein-deficient diets. Initially, harvesting was a subsistence activity, with trade limited by the difficulty of accessing both productive source areas and large markets. With the increasing availability of transport, producers can now supply markets from distant source areas. Many of the markets are in urban areas where demand is substantial and people can generally afford higher prices. Having few other options to earn income, and ample time to devote to hunting, more people are being drawn to the trade. A recent report by TRAFFIC East/Southern Africa (Barnett 1997), covering both legal and illegal harvesting of wildlife in all the core countries of the region except the DRC and Angola, shows that the trade is extensive and growing. Legal game meat production, through licensed hunting, ranching, cropping, culling, or the control of problem animals, amounts to about 8 500 tons annually, with a local value of US$7.7 million. Although much of this is absorbed by domestic markets, because of veterinary restrictions on its export to more lucrative markets overseas, there are pressures to increase exports. At present, however, production is much less than the potential sustainable yield, so this is unlikely to pose a threat to wildlife in the near future. If anything, wildlife may benefit because wildlife production provides an economic incentive for landowners to conserve it rather than displace it by some other form of land use. The best example comes from Zimbabwe where, following the liberalization in the mid 1970s of regulations governing the right to exploit wildlife commercially, the area of private land devoted to some form of wildlife production (meat production, safari hunting, photographic safaris) increased from 350 km² in the 1960s to about 37 000 km² in the early 1990s.

The informal and largely illegal harvesting and trade in bushmeat is more problematic. Substantial quantities are involved (for example, more than 50 tons of bushmeat enters the urban markets of Maputo in southern Mozambique monthly) (Barnett, *op. cit.*). In some markets, bushmeat is substantially cheaper than meat from livestock, so that for the poor it represents an affordable source of protein. In others, however, it is higher, apparently because people prefer the taste of bushmeat and are prepared to pay accordingly. As in the rainforests of Central and West Africa, commercial trade is rapidly replacing the harvesting of bushmeat for purely subsistence purposes, more so as wildlife declines and people come to rely on trade to satisfy their requirements. Complex rural-to-urban trading networks have developed as

a result, rapidly transferring the incentive of urban demand through to rural supply, leading to more people becoming involved in both supply and trade. Of the wide diversity of species being harvested, more than half weigh over 5 kg –antelope, wild pigs, and even large species such as buffalo (*Syncerus caffer*) and elephant. One of the problems is that, being large-bodied, many of the antelope in the Miombo Woodlands have low reproductive rates and are therefore less able to sustain or recover from high levels of offtake. As large-bodied species decline, the trade will undoubtedly shift towards smaller-bodied animals (birds, rodents, reptiles, and edible caterpillars), and become more diffuse and harder to influence.

A relatively large international trade in live birds, reptiles, and small mammals exists in Mozambique, Tanzania, and the DRC, though this is controlled to some extent by the provisions of CITES. For example, the agreed export quotas for Mozambique for 2001 include 232 000 birds of 32 species, ranging from waterfowl to waxbills; 55 400 reptiles of 16 species, mainly tortoises, terrapins, and lizards; and 5 990 mammals of nine species, mostly small primates. The quotas for Tanzania and the DRC are less, but of similar magnitude. At present, however, these quotas are not being met, though they indicate the intention (T. Milliken, pers. comm., 2002). The problem here is not necessarily the trade itself, but whether the countries concerned have the capacity and commitment to monitor, manage, and regulate effectively both the trade and its effects on the species, and to set realistic, sustainable quotas. It remains to be seen whether the economic benefits of trade provide sufficient incentives both for the governments of the countries concerned, and for the traders and their suppliers, to invest in appropriate conservation management measures.

Whereas the trade in wildlife and wildlife products can be managed, given the right circumstances, the threat posed by alien species is more insidious and difficult to control over such a large area. Unlike some other ecoregions, the Miombo-Mopane woodlands are currently not threatened by any major invasive alien species, though some species cause concern locally. A woody South American shrub, *Mimosa pigra*, is well-established and spreading on parts of the Kafue Flats in Zambia, most notably in Lochinvar National Park. It has already proved to be a menace on floodplains of northern Australia, where control programs have been implemented. This has still to be done locally. Another South American shrub, *Lantana camara*, is much more widely-distributed and potentially threatens to crowd out understory plants on the richer soils in higher rainfall areas. It has been declared a noxious weed in some countries, with a requirement that landowners remove it from their land, but it is also well-established in communally-owned lands, where responsibility for implementing such an order is unclear. Eradicating the species is likely to be difficult; in some areas, the battle may have already been lost. Other invasive alien tree species, none

Waterbuck
(Kobus ellipsiprymnus),
Selous National Park, Tanzania.
© **Patricio Robles Gil**/*Sierra Madre*

of them necessarily posing a threat at this stage, include jacaranda (*Jacaranda mimosifolia*) and syringa (*Melia azedarach*). A number of important waterweeds also occur, particularly *Eichhornia crassipes, Pistia stratiotes,* and *Salvinia molesta*, all of which can substantially alter the functioning of waterbodies, particularly if enriched by runoff from agricultural lands.

Conservation

Almost 21% of the region as a whole —806 693 km²— is currently under some form of statutory protection or has the conservation and use of natural resources as a principal form of land use. Within the 1.2 million km² that we consider the wilderness area in this chapter, 422 000 km² (36%) is under protection. In all there are 60 national parks, botanical reserves, and wildlife sanctuaries covering 221 444 km² (6.0%) of the region; 33 game reserves, safari areas, and wildlife reserves occupying 129 236 km² (3.3%); 881 national and local forest reserves and production forests, with an area of 218 186 km² (5.6%), 10 conservancies (8 647 km², 0.2%); and more than 50 community-based natural resource management areas covering 229 180 km² (5.9%).

This does not include the numerous small areas protected by local people, primarily for spiritual reasons (Byers et al. 2001). These are frequently found across the region, but there has been no systematic attempt to survey their numbers, sizes or extent. They are widely assumed to be important sites locally for biodiversity. In addition, about 80 Important Bird Areas have been identified in the region (Barnes 1998; Fishpool 2001). These are sites of locally high diversity or which contain a significant proportion of the population of globally or nationally threatened bird species. They include the Kafue Flats, Bangweulu Swamps, Angolan escarpment, and the Matobo Hills. Whereas some of these sites are already inside the protected area network, others are outside. Initiatives are under way to ensure the integrity of these sites for the future.

The region includes some of the largest conservation areas in Africa, most notably the Selous Game Reserve (51 200 km²), which is one of the largest tropical protected areas on Earth, and Ruaha National Park-Rungwa Game Reserve (25 600 km²), both in Tanzania; Kafue National Park (22 400 km²) and North and South Luangwa National Parks (13 686 km²) in Zambia; Etosha National Park (22 270 km²) in Namibia; Hwange National Park in Zimbabwe (14 650 km²); Chobe National Park (11 000 km²) in Botswana; the Niassa Game Reserve (10 500 km²) in Mozambique; and the northern section of the 19 485-km² Kruger National Park in South Africa (see Box). Whereas most of these were established during the colonial era, the current governments have remained committed to maintaining these parks as conservation areas, despite deteriorating economic circumstances that have caused substantial reductions, in real terms, in the operating budgets of the departments concerned. Clearly, if the integrity of these areas is to be maintained, then additional support will be needed, or ways found to reduce the costs of management and increase its effectiveness.

In Africa, one person's wilderness is another person's home. Even many of the large game reserves and national parks had people living in them when they were created, with the people subsequently being evicted. Not surprisingly, this has created tension and, in some cases, led to people taking actions to reclaim the land. For example, in 1998, the Makuleke community in South Africa successfully regained title to the Pafuri section of the Kruger National Park and a small adjacent conservation area, from which they had been evicted in the 1960s. In exchange, they agreed to let the land remain as part of the national park provided that it was managed jointly, and that the community benefited in various ways (employment, building capacity and management experience, the opportunity to use certain resources sustainably, and income from ecotourism and other ventures) (de Villiers 1999). Joint management programs of one kind or the other are now being implemented in most countries in the region, particularly in the forestry sector (Wily and Mbaya 2001). Most of these initiatives should be considered experimental, as people try to find out what works, and why, and how best the interests of the different parties can be merged to produce mutually-beneficial outcomes.

Up to a point, the presence of people does not necessarily diminish the overall value of a wilderness or its prospects for conservation, though it does provide a challenge as to how conservation objectives can be achieved without undercutting people's livelihoods, and vice versa. This challenge is being met by an array of initiatives aimed at shifting the locus of conservation efforts from central government to local communities. In part, these developments have been prompted by a growing inability of governments to continue to regulate the use of natural resources and undertake the management needed for their long-term conservation. In part, they reflect the reality that unless wildlife and other natural resources make a positive contribution to development, they will eventually be lost. The underlying proposition is that if people can benefit materially from the presence of wildlife, by whatever means, they will have an incentive to protect it.

Translating this into practice is surrounded by a whole range of political, institutional, social, economic, and environmental issues, and much uncertainty (Duffy 2000; Hulme and Murphree 2001). Consequently, an incremental and adaptive approach is being adopted, with the elements being adjusted as circumstances change and new problems emerge. This has resulted in a tremendous variety of initiatives, some reasonably successful, others perhaps not, though the judgment depends largely on one's perspective and aims.

The CAMPFIRE (Communal Areas Management Programme for Indigenous Resources) in Zimbabwe is one of the pioneer programs in this initiative. In essence,

Roan antelope
(Hippotragus equinus), *Ruaha National Park, Tanzania.*
© **Patricio Robles Gil**/*Sierra Madre*

the program provides for rural communities to use the wildlife found in their areas to generate revenue to be disbursed as a dividend to households in the community or to be used for community-development projects. It is assumed that by benefiting materially from the wildlife in their area, people will be more willing to tolerate its presence and bear the occasional cost of crop or livestock loss due to wildlife. In this way, proponents of CAMPFIRE have sought to link environment and development to the advantage of both. Similar initiatives have been implemented in Botswana, Zambia, Namibia, Malawi, and Tanzania, with variations dictated by local circumstances. Much of the focus has been on the management and use of wildlife, though it is now being broadened to encompass other resources as well.

Five key principles underpin most of these initiatives (Murphree 1993). First, the benefits received by people should be tangible and measurable, otherwise the sense of benefit will not be real. Second, those who bear the costs of living with wildlife should be the primary beneficiaries —differences in inputs and costs should result in differential and proportionate benefits. Third, the quality of management and the size of the benefit should be positively related. Fourth, the decisions should be the responsibility of those who bear the costs of production and management, and who receive the benefits. Finally, the unit of proprietorship —those who make the decisions— should be as small and cohesive as is practical within given social, political, and environmental constraints. Establishing the institutional, social, and political environment in which these principles can operate, and in which governments willingly devolve the required authority to local institutions and define for themselves a new and supportive role to help these initiatives succeed, is not easy. There are many skeptics (e.g. Barrett and Arcese 1995; Logan and Mosely 2002).

Given the wide diversity of circumstances and history behind these initiatives, the different and adaptive ways in which they are developing, and the unpredictable and changing world around them, it is not difficult to find examples of apparent failure, but what long-term viable alternatives are there? The protected area networks and some of the reserves are the largest in the continent, requiring huge resources to maintain, but current funding is just not sufficient, a situation that is not likely to improve any time soon. A lot of wildlife and wildlife habitat exists outside the protected areas, in juxtaposition with people. If the wildlife and its habitats are to survive in these areas, then local people will have to be part of the solution, not the problem.

The assumption of local ownership of, and responsibility for, wildlife has also extended to privately-owned lands. Groups of landowners, particularly in Zimbabwe, Namibia, and South Africa, have come together to form conservancies in which the fences separating their properties, and land within them, have been removed. Most have been restocked with wildlife purchased from other areas or translocated from overstocked protected areas. Livestock have been greatly reduced in numbers or removed entirely, as land use has shifted to trophy hunting, ecotourism, and wildlife production. Economic analyses suggest that, in many marginal agricultural areas, this form of land use is often more lucrative than cattle ranching (Jansen et al. 1992; Price Waterhouse 1994). Most importantly, many of the conservancies have become the locus of efforts to conserve the black rhinoceros. Of the estimated 2 650 black rhinoceroses remaining in Africa, 290 (11%) live on private land in Zimbabwe, mostly in conservancies. Sadly, this initiative is threatened by the turmoil of the so-called "fast-track" land reform currently under way in the country.

Another development being pioneered in the region is the formation of Trans-Frontier Conservation Areas (TFCAs). Involving governments, the private sector, and local communities, the TFCAs would encompass a number of existing national parks, many of which are located close to national borders, game and forest reserves, community wildlife areas, conservancies, and other conservation areas. Ten TFCAs have been proposed for the region, covering about 251 200 km² (Cumming 1999). These include the 50 374-km² Gaza-Kruger-Gonarezhou Transfrontier Park (already proclaimed) in southeast Zimbabwe, northeast South Africa, and southern Mozambique; the 54 000-km² Four Corners TFCA centered on the Victoria Falls/Matetsi/Hwange region of northwest Zimbabwe; Chobe in northern Botswana; the eastern Caprivi Strip, Namibia and southern Zambia; and the 110 000-km² Niassa-Selous area of southern Tanzania and northern Mozambique. By developing the full economic potential of these regions, including tourism, and by managing the areas in an integrated and coordinated way, it is hoped to achieve economies of scale in conservation, development, management costs, and economic benefits. *Ex Africa semper aliquid novi* (Pliny).

PETER FROST
JONATHAN TIMBERLAKE
EMMANUEL CHIDUMAYO

Above, male African pygmy goose (Nettapus auritus) in breeding plumage.
© **Nigel J. Dennis**/*DENNIS AND DE LA HARPE PHOTOGRAPHY*

On the opposite page, saddle-billed stork (Ephippiorhynchus senegalensis).
© **Wayne Lynch**

204

The northern landscapes of Kruger are dominated by baobabs, another characteristic flagship species.

Human Cultures

Stone artifacts found over most of the Kruger show that people were living in the area throughout the Stone Age, between 7000 BC and AD 300 (Eloff 1990a, 1990b). The San (Bushmen), whose characteristic rock paintings are still visible in rock shelters in both the southwestern and northern areas, were associated with the latter part of this period (Cooke 1969).

During the period *ca*. AD 200 to 500, Bantu immigrants with small herds of domestic stock, ceramic traditions, and knowledge of ironworking penetrated the area (Joubert 1986). The San probably disappeared from the area at around this time through conflict with these people. From this era, Plug (1984, 1989) reported on archaeozoological remains from 12 sites in the Kruger. The dates for these sites were estimated at around AD 500.

An archaeological site known as Schroda, near the Limpopo River approximately 200 km to the west of Kruger, rendered "large quantities" of ivory and cowries, suggesting a participation in the coastal ivory trade (Plug and Voigt 1985). The ages of the remains at Schroda were estimated as originating between the eighth and ninth centuries by carbon-14 dating.

Between *ca*. AD 900 and 1220 trade in gold and ivory became established on an increasing scale between the indigenous people inhabiting the Limpopo River area and the Islamic Empire (Plug and Voigt, *op. cit.*).

Subsequent to that time, Great Zimbabwe grew in importance as a center of trade and culture (Plug and Voigt, *op. cit.*). This era lasted for approximately 100 years when, upon the decline of Great Zimbabwe in 1420, some of the people moved south and established themselves in the northern Kruger (Eloff 1966; Küsel 1992). These sites were inhabited from the fifteenth to the early nineteenth centuries.

When the first Warden of Kruger was appointed in 1903, there were still some of these people (mainly of the Shangane, Swazi, and Venda groups) living in the area. He was tasked with moving these people out of the new reserve and, since that time, there have been no people permanently resident in Kruger.

Threats

Subsistence poaching of wildlife has always been a low-level threat, but has never threatened any species with population extinction or even decline. A larger threat of commercial poaching of elephants and rhinos exists, but to date this has been kept under control through excellent proactive anti-poaching measures. Since 1999, only two elephants and five white rhinos have been poached.

Kruger's major rivers all rise far to the west of its boundaries and are subject to all the abuses imposed by modern man. Water quantity and quality are affected through excessive extraction, siltation, and pollution by agricultural and industrial chemicals.

Alien plants and animals are an ever-increasing threat. These include 370 plants, 22 insects, three fish, two birds, and one mammal (feral house cat). Some of these are innocuous, but others are aggressive and are a threat to biodiversity.

The earlier evictions of indigenous people from Kruger have given rise to successful land claims, but the areas reallocated to their traditional owners now still form part of Kruger as "contractual" national parks. Some more recent claims have not yet been finalized, but it is expected that, should they be successful, similar arrangements as contractual national parks will be negotiated.

Conservation

The National Parks Act of 1926 provides the basis for conservation in South Africa's national parks, with its primary stated objective being the maintenance of biodiversity. The Board of South African National Parks (SANParks) is mandated with the implementation of this act. Tourism is the primary funding source for SANParks, and Kruger attracts more than one million visitors each year. Kruger generates sufficient income for its own operations, but many of the other national parks do not and are dependent upon Kruger for the shortfall.

While many other national parks worldwide allow activities such as hunting and fishing, Kruger does not. Apart from certain capture and translocation programs aimed at restocking other conservation areas, Kruger's animal populations are unmanaged and its other natural resources are not exploited. Culling of a variety of species was conducted in the past for ecological reasons, but this no longer occurs, as it is now perceived as unnecessary. Elephants have remained the exception to this, as the impacts of a growing elephant population on the park's habitats are considered unsustainable. Elephant culling was practiced between 1967 and 1994, but was suspended while a new policy for elephant management was under development. This policy has not yet been implemented, and the population has since increased from 7 800 in 1994 to nearly 10 000 in 2001.

In the end, wilderness areas that enjoy substantial, strict protection, such as Kruger, are some of the places where we can best hope to preserve a full complement of ecosystem services and healthy species assemblages.

IAN WHYTE
RICK BARONGI

Above, scarlet-chested sunbird (Nectarinia senegalensis).

On the opposite page, impala (Aepyceros melampus) *herd.* *Both photos:* © **Lex Hes**

THE SERENGETI

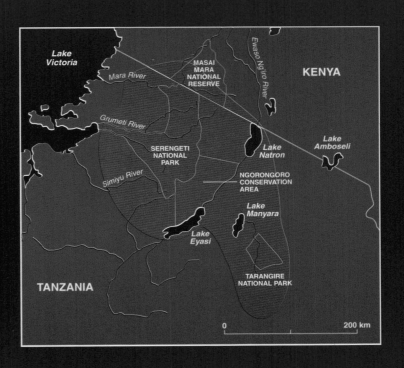

Most of us, if asked to close our eyes and visualize a scene brought to mind by the word "Africa," would conjure an image of straw-brown plains under a hot equatorial sun, the grass being grazed by herds of gazelles, zebras, and wildebeest, and a few stately giraffes browsing leaves from the tops of thorny acacia trees scattered throughout the landscape. The scene might also feature a pride of lions at rest on top of giant gray boulders, known locally as "kopjes," their gaze looking out at the plains animals and beyond, a thin heat shimmer on the horizon. The picture we have painted is perhaps more accurately described by another word, "Serengeti" which, in reality, represents the visual icon for Africa that is most commonly shared by the rest of the world.

By comparison to other wilderness areas presented in this book, the Serengeti Wilderness Area is not very large. It is essentially contained within two ecoregions defined by the World Wildlife Fund (Olson et al. 2001) including approximately 53 597 km² of the Southern Acacia-Commiphora Bushlands and Thickets Ecoregion (AT0716) (total area: 227 783 km²), and all of the Serengeti Volcanic Grasslands Ecoregion (AT0714) (18 029 km²). Thus, the Serengeti Wilderness Area totals approximately 71 626 km² that extends from northern Tanzania into southwestern Kenya and includes the protected areas of Tarangire, Manyara, Ngorongoro, and Serengeti-Mara. Of this, we estimate that 70% still remains intact —relatively free from human interference.

The Serengeti Wilderness Area landscape is largely flat to rolling and situated on what is known as the Central African Plateau. True grasslands account for only a small portion of the entire area, much more being covered by deciduous bushland and dense thicket. Montane forest patches, including Tanzania's two highest peaks, Mt. Kilimanjaro and Mt. Meru, are also scattered along the northern boundaries, but these represent a different ecoregion, have been more heavily impacted by humans, and are not considered part of this wilderness. To the southeast, the habitat includes the unique groundwater forests of Manyara at the base of the western Rift Valley wall which forms part of a biogeographical boundary resulting in some subspecies variation in the area, and finally transitions into the Lolkisale-Simanjiro grasslands and acacia woodlands that form much of the Tarangire ecosystem. The western boundary of the wilderness area is close to Lake Victoria, the world's second largest freshwater lake, exceeded in size only by North America's Lake Superior. The northernmost extension of this wilderness includes Masai Mara Game Reserve and surrounding Maasai community lands in Kenya.

The Serengeti wilderness enjoys a tropical climate, with two brief seasons of variable rainfall. Dry seasons last longer and are more predictable, and often they leave the landscape parched and susceptible to fire. There was a time when the notorious tsetse fly, which carries the dreaded sleeping sickness, kept people from this region, but its partial eradication has opened up the wilderness area to more intense human settlement and use.

Aside from its many other values, the Serengeti ecosystem has great historic value in that it was the first major site for modern nature tourism on the African continent —an activity pioneered by the great German conservationist Bernhard Grzimek in the 1960s (Grzimek and Grzimek 1959). More important still, nature tourism in East Africa and especially in the Serengeti created a great new tradition and really led the way for ecotourism and wildlife-viewing, not just for the rest of Africa but for the entire tropical world.

Wilderness Area

On the opposite page, daybreak over the savanna woodlands, Serengeti National Park, Tanzania.
© **Hans Strand**

211

Biodiversity

The bushlands and thickets that cover 90% or more of the Serengeti ecosystem are composed largely of *Acacia, Commiphora,* and *Crotalaria* shrubs and of grasses such as *Themeda triandra, Setaria incrassata, Panicum coloratum, Aristida adscensionis, Andropogon* spp., and *Eragrostis* spp. (McNaughton and Banyikwa 1995). Soils underlying grasslands are derived from rich volcanic ash. They support a number of grass species that are also characteristic of the bush, as well as *Sporobolus* spp., *Pennisetum mezianum, Eragrostis tenuifolia, Cynodon dactylon, Chloris gayana, Dactyloctenium* spp., and *Digitaria macroblephara.* It is estimated that in all there are approximately 1 200 species of vascular plants native to the Serengeti, of which 20 (1.7%) are endemic (Jon Lovett, pers. comm., 2002).

In terms of species diversity, amphibians are the least numerous of the four vertebrate classes in this arid tropical environment. They are represented by only 22 species, of which none is endemic. Serengeti reptiles are more diverse, totaling 87 species and including the Vulnerable pancake tortoise (*Malacochersus tornieri*) (Hilton-Taylor 2000; Sprawls et al., 2002). Only one of them, Grzimek's dwarf gecko (*Lygodactylus grzimeki*), is endemic.

Bird diversity is fairly impressive by comparison, with 552 species occurring in the area as defined (Zimmerman et al. 1996). The Serengeti Plains have been identified by BirdLife International as an Endemic Bird Area (EBA) and a high conservation priority for six restricted-range species (Stattersfield et al. 1998), including the gray-breasted francolin (*Francolinus rufopictus*), Fischer's lovebird (*Agapornis fischeri*), the rufous-tailed weaver (*Histurgops ruficauda*), the gray-crested helmet-shrike (*Prionops poliolophus*), and the Karamoja apalis (*Apalis karamojae*). However, only one of these, the francolin, is endemic to the Serengeti Wilderness Area.

Large mammals are by far the best-known wildlife of the East African plains, and seeing them in their natural habitat —especially those that take part in mass migrations— is certainly one of the greatest wildlife spectacles on our planet. The numbers of animals in the Serengeti-Mara migration may vary from year to year (Campbell and Borner 1995), but for two species they are easily measured in the hundreds of thousands —Thomson's gazelle (*Gazella thomsoni*) and Burchell's zebra (*Equus burchelli*)— and the wildebeest or white-bearded gnu (*Connochaetes taurinus mearnsi*) numbers over a million. As one might imagine, many of these animals, especially a large number of young wildebeest, do not survive the dangers of the migration (Matthiessen 1972). Such large herds support significant populations of predators as well, including lions (*Panthera leo*), leopard (*P. pardus*), cheetah (*Acinonyx jubatus*), spotted hyena (*Crocuta crocuta*), and the endangered African wild dog (*Lycaon pictus*). After personally viewing this spectacle of predators and prey on the Serengeti Plains, former U.S. President and conservationist Theodore Roosevelt inscribed in his diary: "A Pleistocene day!"

Numerous other smaller, less conspicuous mammals occur in the region, including primates, rodents, rabbits, hyraxes, bats, insectivores, and elephant-shrews, and bizarre creatures like the pangolins (*Manis* spp.) and the aardvark (*Orycteropus afer*), the sole living member of the Order Tubulidentata (Leakey 1969; Nowak 1991). In total, 186 mammal species inhabit the Serengeti, none of them endemic.

Flagship Species

There is no more powerful symbol of the Serengeti ecosystem than the African lion, a creature people are fond of calling "King of the Jungle" or "King of the Beasts." Wildlife biologist George Schaller (1973) summed it up well when he wrote of the lions he studied, "Man feels an emotional kinship to these predators even though he is filled with primordial apprehension by their presence." Unfortunately, lions throughout Africa are fading fast outside of the parks and reserves. Nearly half of Africa's remaining lions are found in Tanzania (C. Packer, pers. comm., 2002), with the Serengeti their primary showcase to the rest of the world. This big cat is among the largest living terrestrial predators, and its ecology and behavior has been the subject of numerous field studies (e.g., Schaller 1972; Packer and Pusey 1997). Nature tourists travel for thousands of miles and spend thousands of dollars for the opportunity to see lions in the wild.

The lion may be the king of the Serengeti, but wildebeest dominate the landscape. The annual migration, averaging 1.3 million wildebeest and hundreds of thousands of zebra and antelopes, forms the lifeline around which the heart of the Serengeti ecosystem thrives. It is this massive land migration of plains game that the Serengeti lions and other predators turn to for their sustenance. The Nile crocodile (*Crocodylus niloticus*), which reaches enormous size in this region, and is another great flagship, also preys on wildebeest, and may feed only once a year during the spectacular wildebeest crossing of the Grumeti and Mara Rivers. At its peak, from December to March, the wildebeest herds of the Serengeti, extending in many places as far as the eye can see, gather on the short grass plains to give birth to their calves in one of the world's most spectacular wildlife happenings. As they begin to move off the plains in late May and June, the rut begins, with nearly 90% of the cows becoming impregnated in just a three-week period. "The noise made by hundreds of thousands of bulls chorusing like so many giant frogs, the herding, chasing, fighting, and mating are indescribable" (Estes 1993).

The term "charismatic megavertebrate" is increasingly used by conservationists to define those large, typically warm-blooded and appealing creatures for which many people feel a special compassion and concern. These are the ultimate flagship species, and certainly there are few more charismatic and none on land more

Above, little bee-eaters (Merops pusillus), *the smallest bee-eater in the world.*
© **Art Wolfe**

On the opposite page, blue wildebeest (Connochaetes taurinus) *migrating, Maasai Mara National Park, Kenya.*

On pp. 214-215, male lions (Panthera leo) *in the early morning sun, Maasai Mara National Park, Kenya.*
Both photos: © **Günter Ziesler**

"mega" than the endangered African elephant (*Loxodonta africana*). Its presence and threatened status can be used to make powerful arguments for habitat protection and anti-poaching efforts on behalf of other wildlife (Cumming et al. 1990).

The black rhinoceros (*Diceros bicornis*) is another great flagship species group, but its history and future are far more dire than those of the elephant. Both are poached throughout their ranges, the elephant for its tusks and the rhino for its horn, but elephant populations still number in the hundreds of thousands and authorities appear to be dealing effectively with the illegal ivory trade. By contrast, black rhino numbers declined dramatically throughout Africa during the last half of the twentieth century, and current estimates put this Critically Endangered species' total population at 5 000 or less, with fewer than 20 surviving in Ngorongoro Crater —one of the last sanctuaries for black rhinos in Eastern Africa. The black rhino has already been extirpated from much of the Serengeti, a fate that has rallied wildlife conservationists in the war on poaching.

Human Cultures

The predominant indigenous culture of this region is that of the Maasai, nomadic cattle herders who are thought to have come to the Serengeti from the Sudan. The Maasai maintain goats and other domestic animals in addition to cows, but they believe their god, EnKai, has selected them to be keepers of cattle. Large numbers of well-kept cows are not only viewed as symbols of wealth and stature, but also nutritionally sustain the Maasai. Milk mixed with cow blood is a dietary mainstay, supplemented by meat from livestock versus that of game animals, as Maasai men are not hunters. They are, however, considered to be brave warriors, renowned for their ability, armed only with spears, to confront and kill adult male lions (Queeny 1954). This test of courage, in fact, was long part of the ritual transition to manhood for young Maasai men —until the practice was prohibited by national law.

More than other East African cultures, the Maasai have resisted modern Western influences. As a result, the image of a tall, lean warrior draped in a deep red cloth, holding a single spear and wearing an ostrich plume or lion-mane headdress, or that of a proud woman adorned with brightly-colored beaded necklaces, enormous hoop earrings, and copper wire armbands, is not entirely a thing of the past. Traditional Maasai villages also exist, their inhabitants protected by a perimeter fence of thornbush and living in huts constructed of branches and grass plastered with cow dung and urine. Tourism has been something of a mixed blessing, promoting both the retention of traditional practices, such as age-old beadmaking, as a means of earning income, and the introduction of foreign cultural influences. Modern-day Maasai also earn money from tourists by posing for photographs in traditional garb, by manufacturing spears and other artifacts

for sale, and by performing dances. Signs of acculturation are evident, however, in the increasing number of wooden houses and flat metal roofs.

Although the Maasai are the most evident indigenous people of the region, other smaller groups such as the traditional hunter-gatherer Wahadza (Watindinga), who likely predate the Maasai, continue to live in this area.

We estimate the current human population of the Serengeti Wilderness Area at approximately 500 000, which yields an average density of 7 inhabitants/km². While this exceeds a limit for what might be considered true wilderness, the habitat still remains largely wild and relatively well-protected, and the region as a whole is certainly regarded as a wilderness by the rest of the world.

Threats

Of the threats to the wilderness area, infectious disease is paramount. Rinderpest decimated the Serengeti ungulate population at the end of the nineteenth century, and although it has been largely controlled since the 1960s, there are still periodic outbreaks in Kenya that threaten to spread to the Serengeti. Canine distemper virus has largely exterminated the Serengeti wild dogs, and it also had devastating effects on the lions, bat-eared foxes, leopards, and hyenas in 1994 and again on lions in Ngorongoro Crater in 2001 (C. Packer, pers. comm., 2002).

Unfortunately, the very people who live off this land may represent the greatest long-term threat to its biological integrity. Although Maasai landowners traditionally have always been tolerant of wild animals, the region's pastoralist population appears to be growing at an unsustainable rate. People will either need to increase their livestock or diversify their livelihood, often with agriculture, both adding pressure on the natural habitat. The ratio of cattle to people alone can be as high as ten to one, and as cattle increase so, too, does the possibility of overgrazing and erosion (Scott 1995). Ironically, the Maasai word *siringet*, from which the name Serengeti is derived, means "endless plains," but the ever-increasing number of people threatens to someday over-extend the land's finite resources (Fisher 1972; Packer 1996). With up to 50% of wildlife migrating through or traversing land outside the boundaries of protected areas in this wilderness, the growing presence of fences and agricultural plots represents a major threat in loss of natural habitat. Among nonpastoral peoples living in the area increased need for agricultural land, particularly for coffee, tobacco, and food crops, compounds the problem. In addition to the land needed for planting, fuelwood is needed for cooking and is also used for making charcoal that is often sold in local markets. This further diminishes natural vegetation well beyond the agricultural plots themselves.

The other major threat to Serengeti wildlife is that of poaching or bushmeat hunting. The plight of the black rhinoceros has already been mentioned. Many other species are affected, however, especially now with the

Above, male Jackson's widowbird (Euplectes jacksoni)*, Maasai Mara National Park, Kenya.*
© **Fritz Pölking**

On the opposite page, giraffe (Giraffa camelopardalis)*, Serengeti National Park, Tanzania.*
© **Kevin Schafer**

historical practice of subsistence hunting having evolved into a much larger and more widespread commercial enterprise that is driven by external markets. Particularly hard hit are the antelopes, but any meat-bearing species living outside protected areas is fair game and under threat (Campbell and Hofer 1995).

Conservation

Fortunately, threats to the Serengeti's biodiversity are balanced to a great extent by relatively successful national protected area systems in both Tanzania and Kenya. Within the wilderness area as we define it, 3 087 600 ha are protected in national parks, game reserves, and the Ngorongoro Conservation Area, which collectively represent about 43% of the total area. Serengeti National Park is the oldest and largest of these units, established just over 50 years ago and covering close to 1 500 000 ha: nearly half of the region's protected habitat. The park has two dominant habitats —short and long grass plains and acacia woodlands— and is home to incredibly large wildlife populations. The immense wildebeest, gazelle, and zebra herds contribute significantly to the mammalian biomass, which has been calculated at just over 80 000 kg/km^2 (Myers 1972), but the park is also famous for its large herds of giraffe (*Giraffa camelopardalis*), as well as its lion prides and resident cheetah and hyena populations.

The Masai Mara Game Reserve (151 000 ha) is the core protected area within the Kenya portion of the Serengeti ecosystem, and is one of that country's most popular tourist destinations. It is not unusual for visitors to Masai Mara to witness lions hunting in the reserve and to spot cheetah or even leopard. Other common species include elephant, buffalo, giraffe, zebra, hippo (*Hippopotamus amphibius*), Thomson's and Grant's gazelles (*Gazella granti*), wildebeest, impala (*Aepyceros melampus*), topi (*Damaliscus lunatus*), hartebeest (*Alcelaphus buselaphus*), warthog (*Phacochoerus africanus*), bat-eared fox (*Otocyon megalotis*), side-striped jackal (*Canis adustus*), spotted hyena, and olive baboon (*Papio anubis*). A small number of black rhino still inhabit the Masai Mara, but they remain threatened by poachers and are very elusive.

The Ngorongoro Conservation Area covers approximately 830 000 ha and is part of a much larger area of interrelated plains, bush, and woodland ecosystems. Within its boundaries lies Ngorongoro Crater, the largest unflooded volcanic caldera in the world and one of Tanzania's most visited tourist attractions. Olduvai Gorge, the site made famous by Louis and Mary Leakey's historic finds of early hominid remains, also lies within the boundaries of the Conservation Area. Wildlife viewing opportunities within the crater are considered among the best Africa has to offer, and the majority of species already mentioned can be seen here. In addition, thousands of flamingos (*Phoenicopterus* spp.) feed and breed in the shallow waters of Lake Magadi at the base of the crater and Maasai tribesmen are permitted to water their cattle within Ngorongoro Crater.

At 260 000 ha, Tarangire National Park is smaller than the Serengeti and Ngorongoro, but its concentrations of wildlife are unmatched. Large mammal biomass there has been estimated at an incredible 235 000 kg/km^2 during the dry season, almost three times greater than the estimate for Serengeti National Park (Myers, *op. cit.*). This high density of wildlife, particularly elephants and zebra, is attributable to a permanent water source, the Tarangire River which, from July to October, attracts some of the largest elephant herds in all of Africa, in some cases exceeding 500 animals. With over 300 species of birds recorded in the park, Tarangire also enjoys the distinction of having the highest recorded number of breeding bird species for any habitat in the world (Snelson 1992 and 1986). Lake Manyara National Park (33 000 ha) is also part of the Tarangire ecosystem, but national park land covers less than 20% of the ecosystem as a whole. Much of the rest belongs to the Maasai community. In addition to the national park, the Tarangire Wildlife Conservation Area, covering 2 050 000 ha, has also been established —to simultaneously address local community needs while promoting wildlife conservation efforts.

The protected areas of the Serengeti wilderness are among the best known in the world and are the very essence of "wilderness" to many people. As such, they have, besides their importance for conserving the biodiversity of East Africa, great symbolic and historic value for the conservation movement as a whole. They, like other globally-known areas (e.g., the Galápagos) that have become household words over the years, are worthy of maximum protection.

COSTAS CHRIST
WILLIAM R. KONSTANT

Above, African buffalo (Syncerus caffer) *after mud bath.*
© **Günter Ziesler**

On the opposite page, Maasai man with ostrich feather headdress.
© **Art Wolfe**

CAPE YORK

The Cape York Peninsula forms the triangular north-eastern corner of Australia, pointing north to the island of New Guinea. It extends from the more humid wet tropics in the southeast and the Mitchell River flowing into the Gulf of Carpentaria north to the northernmost point of Australia at Cape York itself. The total area of the Peninsula is about 121 000 km², and it has some of the least-disturbed and lightly-populated woodland savanna systems on Earth.

The monsoonal climate is characterized by a dry season that extends from April to November with a strong gradient from the wet mountains of the north, where average rainfall is near 2 000 mm, to the drier plains of the southwest, where the more variable rainfall averages about 1 000 mm. The early wet-season storms and the paths of almost annual cyclones in the southern half of the Peninsula have a strong influence on the biological patterns of the remainder of the year. The climate is always warm, rarely falling below 15ºC, but summer means are usually lower than 35ºC.

The central metamorphic spine of the Peninsula dates from the Precambrian with Palaeozoic granite intrusions forming the higher hills, particularly the McIlwraith and Iron Ranges in the northeast (Bain and Draper 1997). Added complexity is provided by the weathered Tertiary lateritic hills in the northwest, as well as remnants of the sandstone massif in the south and east, where there are also small areas of igneous rocks. However, the landscape is much weathered with extensive erosional plains along the shores of the Gulf of Carpentaria in the west and Princess Charlotte Bay in the east. At Cape Flattery and Cape Grenville, the eroded material has been reworked as huge aeolian dunes of almost pure silica, interspersed by lakes and swamps.

For most of the last million years, the Cape York Peninsula has connected Australia to New Guinea. The Torres Strait was last inundated only 7 000 years ago, with the result that the rainforests of the northeastern Peninsula have strong affinities with those of the Fly River plains in New Guinea. Only the highest parts of the McIlwraith Range have affinities to the more Gondwanan rainforests further south in Queensland. The savannas, by contrast, have strong affiliations to the rest of northern Australia, sharing adaptability to long dry seasons and frequent fire.

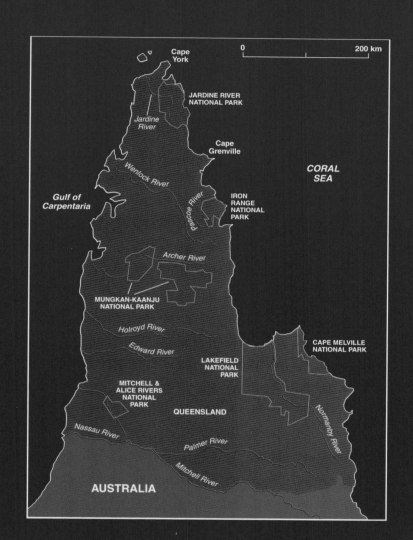

Our definition of this area corresponds very closely to that of WWF's Cape York Tropical Savanna ecoregion (AA0703) (116 300 km²).

Biodiversity

The Cape York Peninsula has a relatively diverse vertebrate fauna, but endemism is low. Birds are represented by 339 species, none of them endemic; mammals by 210 species, of which four are endemic; reptiles by 127 species, 18 of them endemic (17 lizards and one snake); and amphibians by 34 species, 5 of which are endemic (3 species of *Cophixalus*, 2 species of *Litoria*). Freshwater fish are represented by 75 species, of which 10 are endemic. The Wenlock and Jardine Rivers contain the most diverse freshwater fish faunas in the country and the Peninsula has the highest level of terrestrial bird endemism of any Australian bioregion. Most of the endemic and near endemic species, including two rock wallabies, a grassland parrot, a honeyeater, and various fossor-

Wilderness Area

*On the opposite page,
Nassau and Scrutton Rivers.
Gulf of Carpentaria,
Cape York Peninsula.*
© **Jean-Paul Ferrero**/*Auscape*

day heat. However, these termites need grassland and that grassland is threatened on two fronts. A slight rise in sea level will turn the grass to saltmarsh while, on the landward side, an army of tea trees is advancing (Neldner et al. 1997). The grassland seems to require fire late in the year to maintain it. Fires too early in the year are too cool and enhance growth of the ti-trees to a point where they can overtop the competing grass layer. If, in the few wet years, ti-tree seedlings become established, only diligent fire management stops them from becoming a dense woodland which shades the grass and eventually starves the termites.

Not far away, on the long-isolated boulder piles of Cape Melville, are stands of a highly-distinctive foxtail palm (*Wodyetia bifurcata*). Discovered less than 30 years ago from a beach-washed nut picked up by a perceptive beachcombing botanist, the foxtail palm was soon enclosed within the protective boundaries of a national park. However, this proved to be no protection from poachers who stole into the hills and exported thousands of nuts before the trade was discovered. Fortunately, many palm trees survived the onslaught, and the nursery trade has reduced reliance on wild-collected seeds. Ironically, the progeny of the stolen seeds have become amongst the most common street trees planted in several cities to the south, and a potential weed problem.

Human Cultures

When Europeans arrived in Australia, over 100 000 people may have been living on Cape York Peninsula in a way of life that had developed over 40 000 years of occupation. They had adapted to climate change and sea-level fluctuation, and the modern environment is, in large part, a product of that occupation. Most groups were concentrated along the coastal fringe but others were present in the interior, living along watercourses and among the sandstone hills.

Europeans arrived by land in 1845. Cattle were driven north some 20 years later and thus began a gradual assumption of land for pastoralism, often with much violence. Over ensuing decades the south and central spine of the Peninsula was acquired as pastoral leases, initially to supply beef to the gold-mining towns that sprang up on the rich alluvial deposits of the Palmer and Wenlock Rivers. The coastal fringes, however, remained Aboriginal land, initially under the nominal management of Christian missionaries but now fully under Aboriginal control. For a hundred years Aboriginal people were integral to the pastoral industry, and many remained on their traditional land even after it was acquired as pastoral lease. Changes in the wage structure in the 1960s, however, saw migration to the towns. There, traditional culture has struggled to survive in the face of alienation from the land on which it grew and the competing Western influence, although increasing legal recognition of native title rights and the gradual

dispersal to outstations from the socially-divisive administrative centers offers hope for the future.

Nevertheless, by far the majority of the 12 130 people now living on the Peninsula are in Aboriginal settlements, the regional center of Cooktown in the southeast, the northwestern mining town of Weipa, and the handful of small towns along the central Peninsula road. Outside of these towns, there are only 588 people, translating to an extremely low population density of 0.005 inhabitants/km². Even with the towns and other settlements, it is still only 0.1 inhabitants/km² —a density so low that it is elsewhere found only in the Polar Regions. This density increases during the tourist season in the middle of the year, but even then much of the Peninsula remains almost unoccupied by people.

Threats

Although the Peninsula's vegetation cover is still largely intact, with more than 99% still remaining and less than 0.8% cleared, clearing is not the best indication of environmental damage in the tropical woodlands. There are four major threats to the integrity of the wilderness: cattle grazing, inappropriate fire, feral animals, and weeds. The effect of the first is insidious. Surveys suggest that over much of the Peninsula little has changed in the past 30 years (Crowley and Garnett 1999). However, because there are few fences, cattle concentrate on the areas of highest nutrients and on sites where water is retained in the dry season. Thus, the stocking rate of the grassy flats and other drainage lines is far higher than in other parts of the landscape. However, because cattle remove the fuel, fires in these areas are less intense than they might be otherwise, allowing the proliferation of woody plants. In some areas, susceptible grasslands are disappearing at a rate of 10% per decade. This rate may accelerate. Improved genetic stock and animal husbandry have exacerbated the grazing pressure in the last few decades and the increasing use of dietary supplements and hormones continues the trend. Nonetheless, even taking into consideration grazing regimes, it is estimated that 80.4% of the region is still intact.

The fire regime has also changed (Crowley and Garnett 2000). In pre-European times Aboriginal burning, which appears to have occurred throughout the dry season, is thought to have produced a fine-scale mosaic of burnt areas of different fire ages and intensities, as well as many areas that were not burnt at all. The shift to burning for pastoralism in the nineteenth century led to a different pattern, with minimal deliberate burning only early in the dry season and after the first storms of the wet season. This exposed the Peninsula to accidental fires in the late dry season on a far larger scale than before. In 2001, over 85% of the Peninsula was burnt.

Another contributor to changes in fire behavior is the feral pig. For at least a century, large numbers of fer-

On the opposite page, sulphur-crested cockatoo (Cacatua galerita), a common and widespread species.
© **Patricio Robles Gil**/*Sierra Madre*

Above, great bowerbird (Chlamydera nuchalis) at its bower.
© **Cyril Ruoso**/*BIOS*

On pp. 226-227, a huge 5-m saltwater crocodile (Crocodylus porosus), one of the world's largest reptiles and still common in this region.
© **Jeff Rotman**/*Nature Picture Library*

al pigs have been rooting through the woodlands, swamps, and forests for tubers and small animals. In most years, nearly every shallow swamp on the Peninsula is completely turned over by pigs, the receding edges of drying swamps resembling rough-ploughed fields. Pig-rooting, like cattle grazing, also affects the fuel load. Although there have been quixotic attempts to reduce pig numbers by shooting and baiting, only recently has work begun to protect critical habitat with fencing. Other feral pests include feral cats (*Felis sylvestris*), possibly introduced even before the arrival of Europeans, cane toads (*Bufo marinus*), which completed their invasion of the Peninsula in the 1980s, and feral horses.

More localized, but with potential to be a far greater threat, are the weeds. Rubber vine (*Cryptostegia grandis*), introduced with nineteenth-century goldmining, smothers riparian forests along parts of the Normanby, Mitchell, and Coleman Rivers. However, a rust, combined with judicious use of fire, appears to be at least limiting its spread and may even be driving it into retreat. Unfortunately, the perennial herb sicklepod (*Senna obtusifolia*) is taking its place and has been spread in stock feed to many parts of the Peninsula over the last decade. With seeds that can persist in the soil for decades and a capacity to form 3-m-high monocultures, this plant has the potential to invade almost all parts of the Peninsula, particularly riparian areas. Deliberate introductions for pastoralism are also starting to escape into the wild. Exotic legumes are now naturalized in most systems and, in a few sites, the African perennial gamba grass (*Andropogon guyanus*) is starting to move out from where it was planted on the recommendation of agronomists. The huge fuel loads it can generate are likely to transform the vegetation in which it occurs.

Despite these broad-scale threats, the natural environment of the Peninsula has been completely alienated at only a few sites. The largest of these are the bauxite mines near the northwestern town of Weipa and the silica mines in the Cape Flattery dunefields, although both of these enterprises are making attempts to rehabilitate the mined land. Agriculture has also disturbed some areas, particularly on the volcanic soils in the south of the Peninsula. Pressures are mounting to increase the area under agriculture, either irrigated sugar or cotton. This would involve damming at least one major waterway, which would be the first in an area where currently no major stream is restricted.

Conservation

The Peninsula is well-covered by National Parks. The three largest, Lakefield, Munkun-Kaanju, and Jardine River National Parks, contain substantial areas of coastal plain and savanna, including almost the entire catchment of the Jardine River. Along with eight smaller parks and four other reserves at Iron Range, Cape Melville,

Cooktown, and the confluence of the Mitchell and Alice Rivers, they encompass some 1 557 595 ha, or 12.9% of the Peninsula, and include 80% of all ecosystems identified in the region. Negotiations are under way to increase this coverage substantially, as well as the involvement of traditional owners in park management.

Outside formal reserves, discussions are also progressing with pastoral lessees and traditional owners to manage cattle in a manner that causes minimal harm to the environment. Achievement of this aim will require fencing, which will break up the landscape, but the result will be that cattle can be at least temporarily removed to allow country to recover. In many ways the future of the Peninsula hinges on current discussions between government, Aboriginal groups, conservation NGOs, and the pastoral industry. If they fail, the current integrity of the Peninsula is likely to be eroded by increasingly intensive pastoral management, sporadic mining enterprises, and ever more ambitious attempts at agriculture as environmental degradation of the southern half of Australia forces agribusiness north. If they succeed, the status of the Peninsula as one of the most important savanna wildernesses in the world (Mackey et al. 2001) will be maintained.

STEPHEN GARNETT
GABRIEL CROWLEY

Above, remote froglet
(Crinia remota)*, Iron Range,*
Cape York.
© **C. Andrew Henley**/*Auscape*

On the opposite page, an aborigine teenager dons a mud mask in a waterhole in Cape York.
© **Sam Abell II**/*National Geographic Image Collection*

A chain of about 60 islands (the Wessel Island Group and the English Company Islands Group) extends for nearly 100 km from the mainland to the northeast of Arnhem Land. Except for occasional use by visiting Aboriginal landowners, these islands are uninhabited. They range in size from smaller than 1 ha to 210 km², and mark the ridges of a land connection to New Guinea, sundered by rising sea levels about 10 000 years ago.

Biodiversity

The pivotal environmental feature of Arnhem Land is the diversity and endemism associated with the sandstone massif of western Arnhem Land. The rugged topography of this area has provided refuge during the periods of rapid and pronounced climatic fluctuations which have buffeted and winnowed the biota of the surrounding lowlands over the last 10 000 to 100 000 years (Nix and Kalma 1972). The ruggedness has also provided some shelter from the recurrent fires of the lowlands, as well as an unusually wide microclimatic range, allowing some species typical of higher-rainfall areas to carve out an existence in deep, shaded gorges or in the spray zones of waterfalls.

Examples of such sandstone endemic vertebrates include the white-throated grasswren (*Amytornis woodwardi*), black-backed or banded fruit dove (*Ptilinopus cinctus*), chestnut-quilled rock pigeon (*Petrophassa rufipennis*), black wallaroo (*Macropus bernardus*), Arnhem Land rock rat (*Zyzomys maini*), Oenpelli python (*Morelia oenpelliensis*), geckoes (*Oedura gemmata* and *Gehyra pamela*), skinks (*Egernia arnhemensis* and *Ctenotus coggeri*), and a large freshwater turtle (*Chelodina burrungandjii*). The invertebrates are far less well known, but include many endemic species, with biogeographic oddities such as the Oenpelli whip-scorpion (*Charon oenpelli*). At least 40 species of plants are endemic to the sandstone massif (Ingwersen 1995), including the tall tree *Allosyncarpia ternata* (Myrtaceae), which dominates many of the rainforest patches on the sandstone massif (Russell-Smith et al. 1993). Many other species have their distributional stronghold on this massif, but also occur in other isolated sandstone ranges in northern Australia, and especially in the north Kimberley. In addition to individual endemic species, the sandstone massif supports distinctive vegetation types, including the *Allosyncarpia*-dominated rainforests, heathlands dominated by a diverse mixture of *Grevillea*, *Acacia*, *Calytrix*, and other small shrubs, and hummock grasslands dominated by spinifexes (*Triodia* spp.) and resurrection grasses (*Micraira* spp.).

But even the protection offered by the sandstone fortress has not been sufficient to retain all species. The extraordinary rock art of western Arnhem Land depicts several species which are no longer present, notably the large carnivorous marsupials like the thylacine (*Thylacinus cynocephalus*) and the Tasmanian devil (*Sarcophilus laniarius*), and possibly even the extinct megafaunal *Palorchestes*, a marsupial resembling a giant sloth (Murray and Chaloupka 1984). These species disappeared from northern Australia sometime between 2 000 and 20 000 years ago, possibly due to broad-scale environmental change, the introduction of the dingo (*Canis lupus dingo*), and/or hunting pressure from Aboriginal people.

Beyond the sandstone, the lowland tropical open forests and savanna woodlands support a distinctive biota well adapted to seasonality and frequent fire. The ant fauna of these environments is one of the richest in the world: typically about 100 species may be encountered within an area of less than 1 000 m² (Andersen 1992). Reptiles, frogs, and fish are also extremely diverse: the 20 000 km² of Kakadu National Park, on the western edge of Arnhem Land, contain over 130 species of reptiles, 25 species of frogs, and 55 species of freshwater fish (Press et al. 1995). Six species of marine turtles occur around the coast of Arnhem Land, and the beaches of the mainland and adjacent islands support some of the largest breeding sites for these species in Australia. Freshwater and estuarine crocodiles (*Crocodylus johnstoni* and *C. porosus,* respectively) are common, having now recovered from an intensive hunting and harvesting campaign over much of the course of the twentieth century.

Birds are numerous and diverse. The wetlands of Arnhem Land support millions of waterfowl, including the magpie goose (*Anseranas semipalmata*), the sole representative of the family Anseranatidae, most closely related to the screamers of South America. In the drying swamps of the late dry season, these congregate in vast numbers, feeding mainly by digging up with their beaks the buried corms of water chestnuts (*Eleocharis* spp., especially *E. dulcis*). Finches (with nine species), parrots (11 species), and pigeons and doves (13 species) are a distinctive feature of the savanna woodlands and open forests, and include the Endangered Gouldian finch (*Erythrura gouldiae*), widely regarded as the most beautiful bird in Australia. These woodlands also support many nectar-feeding birds (18 species of honeyeaters and two lorikeets), most of which disperse annually over tens, hundreds, or thousands of kilometers to track the continually-shifting pattern of flower availability (Woinarski et al. 2000). Two species, the dominant Darwin woollybutt (*Eucalyptus miniata*) and the small tree fern-leaf grevillea (*Grevillea pteridifolia*), which bear prolific, showy orange flowers, are especially attractive to nectarivores.

Mammals are generally a less conspicuous component of the fauna, at least partly because most are nocturnal. Twenty-eight species of bats inhabit Kakadu National Park (Press et al. 1995), and the little red flying fox (*Pteropus scapulatus*) and black flying fox (*P. alecto*) disperse across the landscape to track rich pockets of flowers and fruits in a comparable manner to the honeyeaters. They roost communally, typically in dense foliage, with some roosts containing tens of thousands of bats. The mammal fauna also includes seven species of kangaroos, ranging from the cat-sized pygmy rock

Above, yellow-spotted monitor
(Varanus panoptes).
© **Greg Harold**/*Auscape*

On the opposite page, a galah
(Eolophus roseicapillus),
a common and widespread
species at its nest in a hollow
tree. Bark is typically stripped
from around the entrance.
© **Patricio Robles Gil**/*Sierra Madre*

congregate at these missions and the new towns which   Feral cats (*Felis sylvestris*) are increasingly abundant

wallaby or nabarlek (*Petrogale concinna*) to the 50-kg antilopine wallaroo (*Macropus antilopinus*).

Overall, this wilderness area supports 293 species of

bird, with shimmering red, blue, green, black, mauve, and yellow plumage. Recent research suggests that its problem is due largely to vegetation change attributable

KIMBERLEY

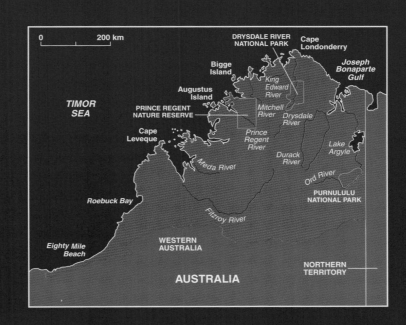

The Australian Kimberley region forms the far north of the State of Western Australia. The region is variably defined, but the most frequently-used ecological definition is that of the "Northern Botanical Province" proposed by Beard (1990), which corresponds also to the bioregions of Dampierland, North Kimberley, Central Kimberley, and the Western Australian portions of the Victoria-Bonaparte and Ord-Victoria Plains bioregions (Thackway and Cresswell 1995). This area covers 327 239 km². As recognized by the continuity of the Ord-Victoria Plains and Victoria-Bonaparte bioregions across the Northern Territory border, the Kimberley extends biogeographically to include similar environments and species assemblages in the far northwest of the Northern Territory. However, the conventional view of Kimberley is restricted to Western Australia. Many essentially Kimberley species, such as the splendid tree frog (*Litoria splendida*) the white-quilled rock pigeon (*Petrophassa albipennis*), the Ningbing antechinus (*Pseudantechinus ningbing*), and the Kimberley pebble-mound mouse (*Pseudomys laborifex*) spill across the border in similar environments and contiguous ranges to as far east as Gregory National Park in the Northern Territory.

The wilderness nature of the Kimberley is affected by a range of developments. The Kimberley region includes the towns of Kununurra, Broome, Wyndham, and Derby. Kununurra, in the northeast Kimberley, is the center of a substantial intensive horticultural project (the Ord Irrigation Scheme), supported by two major impoundments and an extensive system of irrigation canals. There are current proposals to extend this scheme from the existing 930 km² cleared for farmland and water storage to 1 570 km² and to carry out another major scheme around the Fitzroy River in the southwest. Other impacts include a large diamond mine, a major highway through the south Kimberley, a military training area, and an intricate network of secondary roads and tracks. More pervasively, much of the Kimberley is devoted to extensive (cattle) pastoralism, with this impact being especially pronounced in the south Kimberley. Setting aside the near ubiquity of pastoral enterprises, about 95% of the Kimberley can be considered to be reasonably intact.

Annual rainfall varies from about 500 mm in the south to 1 500 mm at Mitchell Plateau in the north, with more than 90% falling in the November-to-March wet season. Temperatures are warm to hot throughout the year, with average temperatures very rarely extending beyond the range of 20º-35ºC (McKenzie et al. 1991). Destructive cyclones are frequent, especially in coastal regions. Although not sharply demarcated, the southern border of the Kimberley corresponds roughly to the 500-mm isohyet and the influence of the highly-seasonal monsoon. South of this, the climate is arid and there is a substantial shift in the biota, but many arid-adapted species extend marginally into the south of the Kimberley and some species typical of higher rainfall areas extend into the deserts along drainage lines or other favorable patches.

The Kimberley is characterized by a spectacularly rugged topography, faintly reminiscent of its namesake region in southern Africa. Although there are no particularly tall peaks (maximum altitude is < 1 000 m), the many ranges are highly dissected, supporting deeply- incised gorges, tall waterfalls, and escarpments. Sandstone is the dominant substrate of these ranges, but there are also major laterite, volcanic, and limestone ranges. The complex topography is a feature found mostly in the north and central Kimberley, with lowland plains skirting this complex to the southwest, south, and southeast. However, there are some isolated ranges within the southern lowlands, most notably the spectacular Bungle Bungle Ranges in the southeast Kimberley.

The Kimberley contains a wide range of vegetation types, including tussock grasslands and open savanna woodlands in the south; *Acacia*-dominated woodlands (known locally as *pindan*) in the southwest; extensive open forests dominated by eucalypts —espe-

Wilderness Area

On the opposite page, islands in Talbot Bay, Kimberley region.
© **Jean-Paul Ferrero**/*Auscape*

cially Darwin stringybark (*Eucalyptus tetrodonta*) and Darwin woollybutt (*Eucalyptus miniata*)—; hummock grasslands and open woodlands on rugged stony substrates; floodplain grasslands and sedgelands in the far northeast; mangrove formations around much of the coast; and generally small pockets of monsoon rainforest vegetation in areas supporting year-round access to water and/or offering protection from fire.

Many uninhabited islands, typically of rugged sandstone, fringe the north and west Kimberley coast. The largest is the 180-km² Augustus Island.

Biodiversity

The Kimberley shares much of its biodiversity profile with that of Arnhem Land to the east. Many environments, species, and threat processes are common to these two regions. There are also numerous examples of sibling species, stemming from isolation and divergence between the two main sandstone massifs of northern Australia. Both areas have operated as major refugia and centers of speciation and endemism.

The biota of the Kimberley is now relatively well documented, courtesy of a series of major surveys that has included most of the areas of high diversity (Miles and Burbidge 1975; Kabay and Burbidge 1977; Burbidge and McKenzie 1978; Western Australian Museum 1981; McKenzie 1981a, 1983; McKenzie et al. 1991; Woinarski 1992). The flora comprises 1 977 native species and 108 naturalized alien species (Wheeler et al. 1992), with high richness particularly in the families Poaceae (259 spp.), Papilionaceae (164 spp.), Cyperaceae (156 spp.), Mimosaceae (103 spp.), and Myrtaceae (91 spp.). Wheeler et al. (1992) considered that this flora includes about 230 endemic species "with the status of a further 60 species uncertain."

There have been no comparable accounts of the Kimberley fauna. However, the region is known to contain about 41 freshwater fish species, of which 16 are endemic (Allen 1982); 38 frog species, of which nine are endemic; 183 reptile species (excluding sea snakes, but including 54 skink species, 35 gecko and pygopodid species, and 48 snakes, among others), of which 35 are endemic; 308 bird species (excluding seabirds), of which one is endemic; and 74 native terrestrial mammal species, of which four are endemic (unpublished data). The invertebrate fauna is generally poorly known, but sampling within a small percentage of the 1 500 rainforest patches of the Kimberley (Russell-Smith et al. 1992) revealed 115 different species of land snails (from 83 rainforest patches), 207 spider species (from eight patches), and 102 ant species (from eight patches).

The majority of the endemic species, especially the vertebrates, are mainly associated with the most rugged areas, or with highly-fragmented habitats (such as caves and rainforest patches), especially in the case of invertebrates with poor dispersal ability. In contrast, most of the fauna of the lowlands is shared widely across north-

ern Australia. Pindan vegetation (a low woodland dominated by a range of *Acacia* species, typically occurring on deep red, sandy soils) is an exception, as this lowland environment is distinctive (Kenneally et al. 1996), although it harbors relatively few endemic species.

The Kimberley contains many important wetlands and coastal areas which support some of Australia's highest populations of migratory shorebirds and waterfowl (Lane et al. 1996). Sites in the southwest Kimberley (Roebuck Bay and Plains — Eighty-Mile Beach) and the northeast Kimberley (Lakes Argyle and Kununurra, and the lower Ord-Parry Floodplain system) are included as Ramsar wetlands of international significance.

Limestone ranges and outcrops, particularly in the central Kimberley, include some of Australia's richest fossil sites, principally of Devonian marine animals.

Flagship Species

Perhaps the best flagship species in the Kimberley is the boab (*Adansonia gibbosa*), the sole Australian representative of the bottle trees or baobabs, otherwise confined mainly to Madagascar and continental Africa. Although the distribution of the boab extends marginally beyond this region, the Kimberley is its stronghold. Large individuals and groves of boab trees add a highly-conspicuous exotic element to the landscape, and the boab is celebrated with an annual festival and frequent use as a symbol in the Kimberley signage and promotions. It has also been widely used as stock fodder, as an ornamental tree, and for storage. One tree, still alive, was hollowed out and served as a gaol or jail cell more than 100 years ago. Although the boab has a wide ecological range, its current distribution may be limited by fire regimes, and it may be retreating from some areas due to changes in this regime over the last 50-100 years (Bowman 1997).

Any serious or compulsive birder visiting Australia makes a pilgrimage to the Mitchell Plateau in the most rugged north Kimberley in an attempt to encounter the highly-restricted black grasswren, perhaps the most remote and nearly mythical of a set of grasswrens confined to small isolates of hummock grasslands (also known as *spinifex*, dominated by *Triodia* spp.) scattered across the country. At nearly 30 g, this is a relative giant among grasswrens, but is otherwise similar to the mold in its ecology: most of its time is spent skulking in the prickly spinifex or feeding on invertebrates and seeds on the ground. As spinifex density, size, and occurrence is closely linked to fire, the black grasswren is also a fire-sensitive species, probably detrimentally affected by the current fire regime.

The north Kimberley is also significant for a group of medium-sized mammal species which are either endemic or characterized by widespread declines elsewhere. The most notable of these species are the scaly-tailed possum, the monjon, the golden-backed tree rat (*Mesembriomys macrurus*), and the golden bandicoot (*Isoodon*

Splendid tree frog (Litoria splendida), *Mitchell Plateau, Western Australia.*
© **Greg Harold**/*Auscape*

auratus). These species are mostly associated with rugged sandstone areas where topographic, edaphic, and microclimatic variations ensure the availability of an unusual diversity of environments compressed within a relatively small area. This terrain also offers some protection from extensive homogenizing fires, allowing the maintenance of a patchy but structurally well-developed understory (notably including the endemic tall palm *Livistona eastonii*, which codominates some eucalypt forests) rich in food resources. The ruggedness also affords some protection from predation by feral cats, and from the environmental degradation associated elsewhere with exotic livestock (cattle) and feral pigs. In parts of the Kimberley, at least some of these native mammals remain extremely abundant, offering a glimpse of how the Australian mammal fauna may have been before European settlement and its contingent broad-scale environmental degradation.

The Mitchell River Falls in the north Kimberley are one of the most spectacular natural features in Australia, a series of tall waterfalls embedded within a strikingly rugged and remote wilderness landscape. The area is also the sole known habitat of the rough-scaled python, in some ways emblematic of the wildness of the Kimberley. That this large (2-3 m long) but distinctive snake was only discovered as recently as 1981 is testament to the ongoing mysteries of the biota of this remote area. Reflecting the difficulties of access across this landscape, the species is still known from only a handful of records.

The freshwater and estuarine crocodiles (*Crocodylus johnstoni* and *C. porosus,* respectively) and barramundi (*Lates calcarifer*) are other high-profile wildlife species in the Kimberley that have major commercial importance for the tourist industry and some significance for aquaculture. High densities of large, and sometimes dangerous, estuarine crocodiles are a feature of many of the river systems and coastal areas.

Human Cultures

The Kimberley has a long history of Aboriginal occupation and land management, extending back at least 40 000 years. During the course of this history, Aboriginal use of fire has sculpted the landscape and has had profound impacts on its ecological character (Bowman 1998). From the 1890s, pastoral settlement of much of the Kimberley dispossessed Aboriginal people over very large areas and forced substantial changes in land management. As a result of the expropriation of their land and of the establishment of Christian mission stations, many Aboriginal people left their traditional living areas and aggregated in a few towns. However, the rocky and deeply-dissected north Kimberley and the more arid southern fringe remained generally unsuitable for pastoralism, and thus Aboriginal people maintained primary responsibility for much of those lands, even if this has not been recognized in land tenure. Over the last

two decades, many of the marginal cattle properties in the Kimberley have been purchased by Aboriginal groups, often with the result of some return to more traditional land management. This post-European settlement history differs markedly from that of Arnhem Land, where changes were far less disruptive, Aboriginal land ownership was recognized, and traditional management remained more intact.

A major pearling industry, centered on Broome in the southwest Kimberley, contributed to another distinctive component of the Kimberley population. In the early twentieth century, this industry was heavily dependent upon Japanese and Malaysian divers. The gradual integration of these people into the social life of the southwest Kimberley has given the area a remarkably rich and for the most part extremely tolerant multi-cultural profile.

A stark change in the relatively low-intensity but extensive land use of the Kimberley region commenced in the 1950s with the development of a major horticultural scheme in the East Kimberley. The irrigated cotton, sugar cane, and melon farms attracted a relatively high population density of primary producers, although for many years the entire government-sponsored scheme suffered through an extraordinary series of problems and downturns, largely due to the lack of understanding of the environmental constraints. "The story of the Ord River Irrigation Area is one of grandiose visions, inadequate and ill-directed research, and decisions by politicians for short-term political advantage made without reference to the experience of the thousands of years in which the region had sustained human population" (Coombs et al. 1989). However, the scheme has left a legacy of a large modern town, Kununurra, servicing much of the Kimberley.

The total population of the Kimberley region is now approximately 33 000 people, of whom about one third are Aboriginal. Excluding around 20 000 people in the major towns with populations of at least 1 000 (Kununurra, Broome, Derby, Wyndham, Halls Creek), this wilderness area has an extremely low population of 13 000, for a density of about 0.04 inhabitant/km².

Threats

Biodiversity in the Kimberley region suffers some localized intensive threats. The most fertile lowland plains (especially of the lower Ord and Fitzroy River Valleys) have been targeted for major environmental modification, with existing or proposed irrigated horticulture consuming most of these restricted and distinctive environments. Mining has disturbed relatively small areas of the southeast Kimberley, but large areas of rich bauxite deposits in the north Kimberley have attracted intermittent mining interest. Development of this resource would change the ecological fabric of the heart of this wilderness area.

However, the major threats to biodiversity are less intensive. Changed fire regimes, proliferation of exotic

Above, spiny knob-tailed gecko (Nephrurus asper).

On pp. 242-243, Purnululu National Park, Bungle-Bungle Range, Western Australia.
This sandstone range was formed 400 million years ago from layered sediments. Erosion created "beehive" formations and deep canyon-like valleys.
Both photos:
*© **Jean-Paul Ferrero**/Auscape*

weeds, feral cats, livestock, feral herbivores, and a rapidly growing track network at least partly associated with a burgeoning tourist industry are degrading almost all areas of the Kimberley. While the most accessible lowland areas have suffered the greatest impact, these threats are now almost pervasive.

In the 1890s, the first perceptive documentation of the fauna of the southwest Kimberley noted that, for the burrowing bettong (*Bettongia lesueur*), a small kangaroo, "the ground was nearly everywhere and in all directions excavated by the burrows of this little Macropod ... all the scrubs, and especially the slopes ... are inhabited by countless numbers"; that the golden bandicoot was "very numerous in the coast country around Roebuck Bay ... great numbers being brought to me"; and for the golden-backed tree rat "the houses of settlers ... are always tenanted by (this species)" (Dahl 1897). None of these species now occurs in the southwest Kimberley, although the golden-backed tree rat and golden bandicoot are still present in the rugged north Kimberley. Of 28 mammal species (other than bats) known from the southwest Kimberley before European colonization, seven have become extinct there (McKenzie 1981b). The southeast Kimberley has also suffered substantial losses of mammal fauna over this period (Kitchener 1978).

Particularly rich, accessible or spatially-limited habitats have been amongst the most affected. McKenzie et al. (1991) reported widespread damage of the highly-fragmented rainforest patch network by feral animals (principally feral cattle and feral pigs) and changed fire regimes. Riparian areas have also been especially damaged, initially by unrestrained access from livestock, and more recently by invasion of weeds, degradation by feral animals (particularly pigs, donkeys, and cattle), and manipulation of water flows. The susceptible purple-crowned fairywren (*Malurus coronatus*) and white-browed robin (*Poecilodryas superciliosa*) have been lost from much of the Ord and Fitzroy River riparian systems (Smith and Johnstone 1977), but persist in less-disturbed areas, and have made some recent recovery in riparian areas where river flows have stabilized because of impoundments.

However, even within the more widespread eucalypt forests, fire-sensitive species such as the northern cypress pine (*Callitris intratropica*) are declining over very extensive areas. Everywhere, the environment is changing, at least partly driven by the removal of fine-scale burning practiced for thousands of years by Aboriginal people and its replacement by less frequent but far more extensive and destructive wildfire.

Notwithstanding the apparent security offered by the rugged sandstone environments, components of the biodiversity (particularly the mammal fauna) may be declining even in these areas, because of the vegetation change caused by altered fire regimes, the intrusion of feral cats, and the landscape-wide impacts of other feral animals, exotic weeds, and an increase in native plants advantaged by the new burning regime.

Above, aborigine dancer painted up for a ceremony, Fitzroy Crossing.
© **Tim Acker**/*Auscape*

On the opposite page, boab tree (Adansonia gregorii), Durack River region.
© **Mike Leonard**/*Auscape*

Conservation

The Kimberley region includes some large and spectacular national parks which provide good representation of the area's most significant ecological features. It also has a range of smaller parks protecting more localized features. Purnululu National Park encompasses the extraordinary Bungle Bungle Ranges, a series of interconnected large sandstone domes, within a reserved area of 240 000 ha. Only declared in 2001, the 115 300-ha Mitchell River National Park includes much of the most spectacular and biologically-significant rugged sandstone of the north Kimberley. Several major reserves are managed primarily for conservation and are either inaccessible or very rarely visited: these include the Prince Regent River Reserve (635 000 ha), Drysdale River National Park (448 300 ha), and the recently-declared King Leopold Ranges Conservation Park (392 100 ha), all in the north Kimberley, and Coulomb Point Reserve (28 700 ha) in the southwest Kimberley. Rich gorges and significant fossil deposits are protected within the smaller Windjana Gorge (2 100 ha), Geikie Gorge (3 100 ha), Devonian Reef (41 400 ha), and Tunnel Creek (90 ha) National Parks in the central Kimberley, and an unusual meteorite crater is protected at Wolfe Creek (1 500 ha) in the southeast Kimberley. Important wetland and floodplain areas are protected within Parry Lagoons Nature Reserve (36 100 ha) and the Ord River Nature Reserve (79 800 ha) in the northeast Kimberley. The total reserved area in the Kimberley is approximately 2 150 000 ha, or almost 7% of the region's extent. This system of 27 reserves is being enhanced by a series of recent additions, and by careful assessment of the conservation values of a range of additional potential sites (Burbidge et al. 1991; Hardy 2001).

The Kimberley offers a vision of a wilder Australia, a fortress of massive cliffs, gorges, and ranges, of wild rivers and spectacular waterfalls. But the power of this landscape is beguiling: across the entire area, the biota is being chipped away by changed fire regimes, by spread of weeds, and by the impacts of livestock and feral animals. The very ruggedness which appears to protect the Kimberley environments also renders the management of these pervasive threats almost impossible.

JOHN WOINARSKI

244

THE PANTANAL

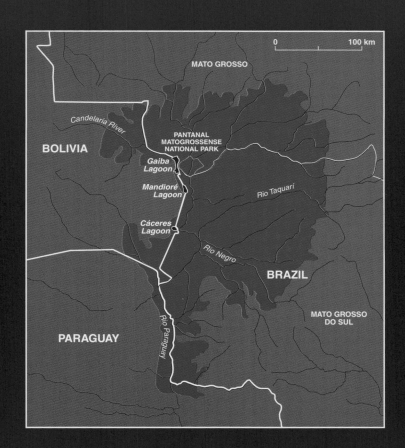

The Pantanal region of Brazil, Bolivia, and Paraguay is the world's largest contiguous wetland and is home to some of the most spectacular concentrations of wildlife on Earth. Located between 16° and 22°S and 55° and 58°W, it covers some 210 000 km², an area about half the size of California. It consists mainly of the low-altitude (average 100-110 m) floodplain of the Rio Paraguay and its tributaries, which drop off the Brazilian *planalto* or central plateau, and is a huge seasonally-flooded swampland more grandiose than any comparable region on Earth. Of the three major wetland wilderness areas described in this book, this is by far the largest, being slightly more than an order of magnitude larger than the Okavango and nearly 20% larger than the Sudd Swamp of the Sudan.

The Pantanal has an average width of 500 km and stretches in a north-south direction some 950 km along the upper Rio Paraguay Basin (Por 1995). It is bordered to the east by the savannas of the Brazilian Cerrado, extending as far as the Chapada dos Parecis; to the northwest by the semideciduous forests of the transition zone between Amazonia and the Cerrado; to the southwest by the *Chaco* formations of Paraguay and Bolivia; and to the south by low-lying mountains, the Serras da Bodoquena and Maracajú (Prance and Schaller 1982; Bertelli 1988; Mittermeier et al. 1990). To the west it transitions into the dry forests of extreme eastern Bolivia along the "Serra do Amolar." As mentioned above, the area as we define it covers some 210 000 km², of which 80% or more is still intact. Some 70% of the Pantanal lies within the Brazilian states of Mato Grosso and Mato Grosso do Sul (which account for 40% and 60%, respectively, of the Brazilian side), with the remaining 30% lying within Bolivia (20%) and Paraguay (10%).

The Pantanal floodplain has been traditionally divided into several subregions, based on history, soil type, vegetation, and the names of the main rivers in the region. These include Cáceres, Poconé, Barão de Melgaço, Paiaguás, Paraguai, Nhecolândia, Abobral, Aquidauana, Miranda, and Nabileque (Adámoli 1981).

The Pantanal gets about 1 000-1 700 mm of rainfall per year, most of it falling between November and March (Hamilton et al. 1996). This precipitation flows slowly due to the low degree of inclination –2 cm/km N/S and 25 cm/km E/W. The rain regime,

which increases from North to South, starts a flooding pulse that affects different subregions according to the amount of water received during the season. Large, permanently-flooded areas (including lakes up to 100 km² in extent) can be found mainly in the northwestern part of the region in the State of Mato Grosso (Mittermeier et al. 1990; Ravazzani et al. 1990). Much of the water of the Pantanal comes from the flooding of the Rio Paraguay itself, which flows through Brazilian territory for 1 400 km, and from its Brazilian tributaries, which run through the Pantanal for most of their length. These include the Cuiabá (647 km), the São Lourenço (672 km), the Taquari (481 km), the Aquidauana (465 km), and the Miranda (490 km), as well as several other smaller rivers such as the Nabileque, the Apa, and the Negro (Magnanini 1986). In the southern part of the Pantanal, there are a greater variety of vegetation types, and the flooding is less extensive than in the north, where immense areas are swamped during the wet season. Interestingly, not all the water in the Pantanal is fresh. In the southern part of the region, especially in the Nhecolândia subregion, there are a number of brackish lakes known as *salinas* and *baias*.

The main economic activity has traditionally been cattle ranching, which was introduced at the end of

■ *Wilderness Area*

On the opposite page, sunrise on the Rio Paraguay, Acurizal Reserve, Mato Grosso State.
© Günter Ziesler

247

the eighteenth century. However, cattle ranching in the Pantanal is far less destructive than in Amazonia. In the Pantanal, there has been relatively little felling of forest and, until 30 years ago when African grasses such as *Brachiaria* sp. were introduced into some areas, there were still enormous areas of natural grassland. Large areas are still uninhabited or are occupied by very low populations of humans and cattle. Indeed, the vast majority of the Pantanal is still in excellent condition, with incredibly rich, intact faunal assemblages of large mammals, birds, fishes, and reptiles that few other regions on Earth can match. We estimate that roughly 80% of the Pantanal is still in wilderness condition. The most damaged areas are located on the transition zones at the borders, where forests are dense and the flood is smaller or nonexistent, enabling ranchers to create more pastureland to increase cattle production.

In the earliest days of European exploration, the region was often confused with the neighboring *Chaco*. In Spanish and Portuguese maps and other references dating back as far as 1555, it was first referred to as the "Mar dos Xaraiés" or, more frequently, "Laguna de los Xarayes," probably referring to an Indian nation now extinct. In the early to mid-1800s, it was also sometimes referred to as "Melgaço," "melga" being a word used in Portugal to refer to swampy, fly-infested areas. In the nineteenth century, "Laguna de los Xarayes" evolved into "Pantanal de los Xarayes," or just the area of *pantanais* or "big swamps," which in turn finally became "the Pantanal."

Biodiversity

The Pantanal is one of the most spectacular areas on Earth for wildlife, and the only place in South America that can compete with the savannas of East and Southern Africa in terms of its amazing concentrations of large visible birds, mammals, and reptiles. In terms of overall biodiversity, it is moderately rich in species numbers but very low in endemism, the vast majority of species being shared with neighboring biomes. Brown, Jr. pointed out the importance of the Pantanal as a reservoir of generalist species, capable of resisting the dramatically-natural fluctuations of the system. As a young and evolving biome, the Pantanal wetland is a crucial breeding ground for some endangered species which are not endemic and can be used in the future to recolonize their original range (Brown 1986).

Vascular plant diversity is about 3 500 species, with no endemics (Pott and Pott 1994, 2000). However, during a recent AquaRAP Expedition carried out by Conservation International (CI), scientists working in the southern part of the Pantanal found 431 species or morphospecies of vascular plants, most of them recorded for the first time at the sites surveyed (Willink et al. 2000). In other words, relatively little appears to be known of plant distribution in the region, meaning that some endemics may yet be discovered.

Vertebrate diversity is moderately high, but again largely lacking in endemics. Mammals are represented by 124 species (Fonseca et al. 1999), reptiles by 177 species (PCBAP 1997), and amphibians by 41 species (Willink et al., *op. cit.*). The Pantanal is also home to at least 423 bird species, with 650 having been recorded (WWF, in prep.; W. Tomas, pers. comm., 2001). There are no endemic birds, although one, the white-lored spinetail (*Synallaxis albilora*), has much of its range within the Pantanal. Freshwater fish are quite diverse, with new species still being discovered on a regular basis. To date, there are an estimated 325 species in the Pantanal (Willink et al., *op. cit.*). Unlike other vertebrates, there does seem to be endemism among the fish, with at least 15 species known to be restricted to the Pantanal, the majority to the headwaters of the Rio Paraguay tributaries (H. Britski, pers. comm.).

In terms of vegetation types, there is also considerable diversity in the Pantanal, in large part dependent on the degree of flooding, soil type, topography, and elements intruding from the surrounding biomes. In the flooded areas, species from the Cerrado are prevalent; at the northern limits, more Amazonian forms are found; and in some of the drier, higher elevations there is even a xerophytic element that is reminiscent of the dry Chaco and Caatinga regions of Paraguay and northeastern Brazil. Taken as a whole, the region is a diverse mosaic of swamp, gallery forest, lake margin scrub forest, semideciduous forest, and several different kinds of savanna (Prance and Schaller 1982), which together are referred to as the "Pantanal Complex." Some authors also recognize the relationships between this biome and the surrounding inland plateaus of Brazil, referring to the entire Upper Rio Paraguay Basin as the "Greater Pantanal." If this larger region is included, then the Pantanal biome *sensu lato* increases in size to 650 000 km², an area nearly the size of the State of Texas. However, for purposes of this paper, we use a more restricted definition as indicated above, limiting our discussions to the area of 210 000 km².

Permanently-flooded areas, known locally as *baias* and *corixos,* are characterized by species like water hyacinth or *aguapé* (*Eichornia* spp.), the Pantanal species of giant Amazon water lily or *vitória-régia* (*Victoria amazonica*), and water lettuce or *erva-de-santa-luzia* (*Pistia stratiotes*), together with shallow-water species such as *Salvinia* spp. and *Nymphaea* spp. (Pott and Pott 2000). Natural open grasslands, or *campos limpos,* are also common, and are dominated by native grass species, notably those known as *capins-mimosos* (*Paratheria* spp., *Setaria* spp., *Reimaria* spp.). These tend to be in low-lying areas that are often seasonally-inundated and are known as *vazantes,* and they may have within them slightly higher islands of forest known as *capões.* These *capões* are characterized by species like *aroeira* (*Astronium* spp.), fig trees (*Ficus* spp.), *angico-vermelho* (*Anadenanthera* sp.), *piúva* or *ipê-roxo* (*Tabebuia* spp.), and *cambará* (*Vochysia divergens*). Another forest type is known as *pa-*

Above, rufous hornero (Furnarius rufus), *characteristic species of the region.*

On the opposite page, trees of the genus Tabebuia, *like this* Tabebuia heptaphylla, *are common in the Pantanal and known for their magnificent flowers.*

Both photos: © **Günter Ziesler**

ratudo, named after the thick-trunked, rough-barked *paratudo* tree (*Tabebuia aurea*), a relative of the widespread *ipê-amarelo* of the Cerrado, the name of which, "good for everything," refers to its use as a cure for diarrhea. These grasslands are also sometimes interspersed with dense patches of trees, which are named after the dominant species, e.g., *paratudais,* where *Tabebuia aurea* dominates; *carandazais,* formed by the elegant caranday wax palm or *caranda* (*Copernicia alba*), which can reach 10 m in height; or *buritizais,* after the equally spectacular, lollipop-shaped *buriti* palm, *Mauritia vinifera* (Ravazzani et al. 1990).

The edges of the many rivers and streams of the Pantanal support gallery forests. These are characterized by species like *jenipapo* (*Genipa americana*), *pau-de-novato* (*Triplaris americana*), and a number of figs (*Ficus* spp.), *embaúba* (*Cecropia* spp.), and *ingá* (*Inga* spp.). The *pau-de-novato,* or "novice tree," has an interesting name that derives from its close association with tiny, stinging ants. The inexperienced worker who cuts down this tree to clear a field or uses it to hang his hammock soon learns the origin of the name, as hundreds of these ants fall onto him. Palms are also common in these forests, notably the small *tucum* palms (*Bactris* spp.) and the *acuri* (*Scheelea phalerata*), (Ravazzani et al. 1990).

In the few higher-altitude areas of the Pantanal, Cerrado species are replaced by species like cacti, especially members of the genus *Cereus,* and bromeliads like *Dyckia* spp. These species are characteristic of drier regions like the Caatinga, and occur mainly on calcareous rock (Ravazzani et al., *op. cit.*).

Flagship Species

The Pantanal is rich in mammal, bird, and reptile flagships, and some of them are particularly spectacular. The most famous of all is the Pantanal jaguar (*Panthera onca palustris*), an enormous subspecies that reaches 200 kg in weight, or roughly double the size of the average Amazonian jaguar —making it the third largest of all the great cats after the tiger and the lion. Jaguars were once heavily hunted for sport and to protect cattle herds. However, in recent years, they have made a comeback, in part because of legal protection and in part because landowners are recognizing their great value for ecotourism. Indeed, it is far more likely to observe a jaguar in the Pantanal than anywhere else in this cat's vast range, and the fact that this subspecies is by far the largest and most impressive makes the experience all the more rewarding.

The traditional method of hunting the jaguar is also noteworthy. Instead of using guns, the traditional *pantaneiro* hunted jaguar with a huge, heavy metal-tipped spear known as the *zagaia* and a pack of dogs. Dogs would first locate a jaguar, hunters with guns would approach it and try to shoot, and once the cornered animal was wounded, the *zagaia* carrier would then

approach and try to impale the jaguar on the spear —that is, if the jaguar didn't get him first. Several *zagaieros* achieved international recognition for their prowess in this highly-risky sport, the most famous being Sasha Siemel —"the Tiger Man," who is said to have killed more than 100. In the past, almost all the ranches had a person in charge of killing jaguars and cougars, and one study covering a two-year period in the 1990s reported the killing of 42 pumas and one jaguar (Lourival and Fonseca 1997). Big cats continue to have somewhat of a bad image among cattle ranchers, and resolution of the conflict between ranching and conservation of these large predators is still a challenge. Nonetheless, given the growth in ecotourism, many ranchers are beginning to realize the value of these cats as a major attraction and some have taken proactive measures to protect these animals. This, together with the much more open habitat of the Pantanal compared to other jaguar habitats like Amazonia or Central America, makes the chance of spotting a jaguar much more likely in the Pantanal than virtually anywhere else.

Another flagship predator of major international importance is the Endangered giant otter (*Pteronura brasiliensis*), which can reach 2 m in total length and is, with the North American sea otter, one of the two largest otters on Earth. A beautiful, gregarious, territorial species, this highly-visible diurnal otter was poached to near extinction in the Amazonian part of its range during the 1960s and 1970s, but is now making a comeback in many areas. It is spottily distributed in the Pantanal, but is readily observed in several areas, most notably the Rio Negro region of Nhecolândia.

Another great flagship mammal of the Pantanal is the capybara (*Hydrochaeris hydrochaeris*), the largest rodent in the world (up to 70 kg) and a frequent prey of the jaguar and the puma. Capybaras are semiaquatic, can stay under water for up to 10 minutes, and live in large herds of several dozen individuals. They are very common and easy to see in the Pantanal, often in association with other flagship species like the Paraguayan caiman.

Still other flagship mammals include the South American tapir (*Tapirus terrestris*) and the puma (*Puma concolor*), both wide-ranging species which, like the jaguar, are more readily seen in the Pantanal than anywhere else. Two important Neotropical deer, the marsh deer (*Blastocerus dichotomus*), largest of the Neotropical deer, and the Pampas deer (*Ozotoceros bezoarticus*), count the Pantanal as one of their last major strongholds, with the former having a Pantanal population of at least 60 000 individuals (Mourão et al. 2000).

The giant anteater (*Myrmecophaga tridactyla*) and the maned wolf (*Chrysocyon brachyurus*) are more characteristic of the Cerrado, but also occur in the Pantanal, especially in habitats such as the *caronais* (*Axonopus purpusii*) and patches of scrubland or *Campo Cerrado.*

Among the many bird species of the Pantanal, two stand out above all the rest. The first is the jabiru stork

On the opposite page, Pantanal jaguar (Panthera onca palustris) *resting on a river bank, Rio Cuiaba. The Pantanal subspecies of the jaguar is by far the largest.*

Above, male black howler monkey (Alouatta caraya)*, one of the few monkey species found in the Pantanal.*

Both photos: © **Günter Ziesler**

251

(*Jabiru mycteria*), the world's largest stork and a very rare creature in most of the rest of its range. Fortunately, it is still quite common in the Pantanal, where it can often be seen high up on a tree in its enormous round nest made of thousands of twigs and branches. The other flagship bird species is the hyacinth macaw, or *arara-azul* (*Anodorhynchus hyacinthinus*), largest of the macaws (up to one meter in length) and the second heaviest member of the parrot family (after the curious, flightless, ground-dwelling kakapo *Strigops habroptilus* of New Zealand). This magnificent bird is found only in a handful of locations in the ecotone area of the Rio Xingu and Rio Araguaia in southern Amazonia, and in remote parts of the Cerrado at the boundary between the State of Bahia and the neighboring states of Tocantins, Goiás, and Maranhão. Though globally Endangered, it has a minimum population of at least 5 000 —by far the highest concentration remaining— and is still common in the Pantanal, occurring in bands of up to 15-20 individuals. It nests in hollow tree trunks and feeds principally on palm nuts such as those of the *acuri* palm (*Scheelea phalerata*), as well as the seeds of *manduvi* (*Sterculia apetala*) (A. Guedes, pers. comm.).

Herons, egrets, bitterns, and many other water birds abound in the Pantanal and reach amazing densities, the most impressive of which can be seen at the rookeries, or *ninhais*, as they are locally known. Among the many species found in the Pantanal are the roseate spoonbill (*Ajaia ajaja*), the white-necked or cocoi heron or *maguari* (*Ardea cocoi*), the wood stork (*Mycteria americana*), the great egret (*Ardea alba*), the rufescent tiger heron (*Tigrisoma lineatum*), the black-crowned night heron (*Nycticorax nycticorax*), the anhinga (*Anhinga anhinga*), the Neotropic or biguá cormorant (*Phalacrocorax brasilianus*), and the Southern screamer (*Chauna torquata*). The ostrich-like greater rhea (*Rhea americana*) and two other macaw species —*Ara ararauna* and *Ara chloroptera*— are also commonly found in the floodplain.

The most visible reptile species in the Pantanal is without a doubt the Paraguayan caiman (*Caiman yacare*). An amazingly abundant crocodilian, this animal still numbers in the millions, and can be seen almost anywhere where there's water. It arguably occurs at the highest densities of any crocodilian species, three of the authors once having counted nearly 3 000 adults in a dry-season pool some 500 m long and averaging about 20 m in width (R.A. Mittermeier, C.G. Mittermeier, and R.F.F. Lourival, pers. obs.). Although it was once heavily poached for the skin trade, with an estimated annual take of some 1 million skins in the 1980s (Gaski and Hemley 1988), hunting is now largely under control. The estimated population of non-hatchling caimans for the whole of the Pantanal is a staggering 35 million, and densities can reach 150 individuals per km² (Mourão et al. 2000). Being one of the smaller crocodilian species, the Paraguayan caiman reaches about 2.5-3 m in length and 55 kg in weight. It is basically harm-

less to humans, can be approached to a distance of less than a meter in areas where it is habituated, and is unquestionably one of the great tourism attractions of the region; night spotting can be an amazing experience.

Of comparable flagship importance but more difficult to see is the yellow anaconda or *sucuri amarela* (*Eunectes notaeus*). Even though it does not reach the length of its Amazonian relative, *Eunectes murinus*, it is nonetheless among the largest snakes on Earth.

Yet another very important reptile species is the caiman lizard (*Dracaena paraguayensis*), or *víbora-do-pantanal*, as it is known in the region. The largest member of the lizard family Teiidae, this very large, olive-brown lizard has a massive head, swims well, and eats mainly freshwater mollusks, which it crushes with its flattened teeth and powerful jaws. Its English name derives from the fact that it looks rather like a small crocodilian, while the local people call it *víbora*, or viper, because it is considered poisonous and very aggressive. It is also believed among the local folk that it can gnaw holes in canoes in an effort to sink them. In spite of its fearsome reputation, it is not venomous and is quite shy in the wild.

Other reptiles in the region include the boa constrictor (*Boa constrictor*), the green iguana (*Iguana iguana*), the tegu lizard (*Tupinambis teguixin*), and a few turtle species, at least one of which, the Pantanal swamp turtle (*Acanthochelys macrocephala*), is among the few near-endemic reptile species in the Pantanal, preferring the brackish water lakes of Nhecolândia.

In terms of plants, some of the large flowering trees are especially striking due to their explosive bloom of brilliantly-colored flowers at different times of the year. Especially noteworthy are the *cambará* and the *paratudo*, with their radiant yellow flowers and the *piúva* or *ipê-roxo*, with its spectacular pink blooms.

Human Cultures

Before cattle ranching was introduced to the Pantanal, the floodplain used to be occupied by several different indigenous communities. Some used the floodplain the entire year, moving back and forth in search of resources, while others used it only at certain times of the year, collecting mollusks and fruit and hunting for game. A number of rock paintings in different areas are a record of their presence. The Payaguá (Guató ancestors) and Guaikuru (or Guaicuru) were well-adapted to life on the floodplain, and were well-known for their canoeing and their skills with horses. Their warriors were a nightmare for the first expeditions of the *bandeirantes*, the famous Brazilian pioneers searching for El Dorado. Today only a few Guató remain, living around the Pantanal National Park in the north. The Guaicuru, on the other hand, were granted a 500 000-ha reserve in the southern Pantanal by the Portuguese, in appreciation for their help in fighting the Spanish. This land,

*Above, plumbeous ibis (*Theristicus caerulescens*), another large bird common in the Pantanal.*
© **Patricio Robles Gil**/*Sierra Madre*

*On the opposite page, giant water lilies (*Victoria cruziana*) in the Acurizal Reserve.*
© **Günter Ziesler**

*On pp. 254-255, Paraguayan or yacaré Caiman (*Caiman yacare*) fishing. This species reaches incredibly high densities in some parts of the Pantanal.*
© **Fritz Pölking**

located between the Serra da Bodoquena and Porto Murtinho in a region called Nabileque, is now occupied by Kadiwéu, descendants of the Guaicuru. The Kadiwéu still have a strong cultural identity, reflected in the top-quality pottery that they produce, some of which can be seen for sale in different parts of Brazil.

Other Indian groups occasionally entered the Pantanal, among them the Kayapó and the Terena. The Terena now live in a few small areas on the borders of the Pantanal, and survive by selling various products to neighboring towns.

The first settlers began moving into the Pantanal in the declining years of the gold rush in the Cuiabá/Poconé region in the nineteenth century. Some families established themselves on the most suitable pastureland and set up ranches. They experienced dramatic growth during the two World Wars, when jerked/corned beef industries flourished. Called *charqueadas,* the factories were strategically installed along the Rio Paraguay to facilitate shipment to Europe. Corumbá was the center of trade, and ranchers prospered. British companies also owned many properties at that time, among them the famous Miranda Estancia, later bought by the Klabin family, who later added the Refugio Ecológico Kaiman to it, one of the best-known tourist sites in the Pantanal (see below). This traditional extensive style of ranching created a balance, however unintentional, between cattle and wildlife. Together with the low human population, the large size of landholdings, difficult road access, and the low level of hunting because of the ready availability of fresh and dried beef, all of this helped to maintain the spectacular wildlife populations and the wilderness condition of the Pantanal.

Today, the human population of the Pantanal is quite small. In the Brazilian Pantanal, there are some 1 100 000 people, the vast majority of them concentrated in cities and small towns around the edges of the region (with the largest numbers in the municipalities of Corumbá, Cuiabá, Miranda, Aquidauana, Cáceres, and Coxim). The Cuiabá/Varzea Grande complex alone has about 700 000 people. Elsewhere in the Brazilian Pantanal, the human population is only about 56 000. The Paraguayan and Bolivian portions have even fewer people. Much of the land is divided into huge *fazendas,* or ranches, some of them exceeding 100 000 ha. There are less than 16 800 people in the Bolivian Pantanal and only about 8 400 in the Paraguayan Pantanal. Overall, this translates into a human population density of 0.4 inhabitant/km².

Threats

One of the first articles on threats to the Pantanal was published by Mittermeier et al. (1990), based on a trip to the region in 1986. That paper identified a series of threats to the region, some of which are still present today, whereas others have been dealt with effectively in the past 15 years. Still others, unexpected at the time,

have emerged in the interim. For example, large-scale poaching of caimans, a major issue at the time, is now no longer a threat. On the other hand, major infrastructure projects like the "Hydrovia" (see below) on the Rio Paraguay, had not yet been conceived in the 1980s, but began to emerge in the mid-1990s. What follows here is a review of the most important current threats to the region, updating what originally appeared in Mittermeier et al. (1990).

As always, habitat destruction is a major concern, and in the Pantanal it includes both deforestation and conversion of grassland habitats. This is taking place mainly to create more grazing areas for cattle, and is focused on the higher land at the edge of the floodplain and close to the Cerrado. Native grasslands such as the *caronais* (*Axonopus purpusii*) are cleared and more resistant African species such as *Brachiaria humidicola* are introduced. This highly-invasive species spreads beyond its original plantings, reducing overall diversity. These grasses also lead to more intense, uncontrolled fires. Ranchers tend not to burn these introduced grasses, increasing the fuel load. Thus, fires that begin spontaneously burn hotter and create more damage. The belief that introduced grasses increase productivity needs additional research. It may be that rotational use of natural grassland could provide comparable results, while maintaining diversity and reducing fire risk.

Although logging has not generally been seen as a major threat to the Pantanal, selective logging, which actually takes place, can have local impacts. Timber is generally cut for fences and construction of ranch buildings, with the most commonly-used species being *aroeira* (*Myracrodruon urundeuva*), *gonçalo-alves* (*Astronium fraxinifolium*), *piúva* (*Tabebuia* sp.), *cumbaru* (*Dipteryx alata*), *angico* (*Anadenanthera colubrina*), and *angelim* (*Vatairea macrocarpa*), all used to build corrals, fences, and houses. Overexploitation of some of these species has led to extinctions at a localized level.

The breakup of larger properties over the course of generations has also increased the demand for hardwood to create more fences. Replacement of fences takes place at the rate of about 10% per year, and burning also destroys fences and creates a demand for more wood to replace them. Combined with the negative effects of more intense burning, which destroys seedlings of valuable timber species, this kind of logging can have detrimental consequences.

Hunting of wildlife has always taken place in the Pantanal, but large-scale commercial exploitation did not begin until the early part of the twentieth century. Certain old references like the *Album Graphico do Estado de Mato Grosso* (1914, in Lourival and Fonseca 1997) give a good indication of the number of skins and feathers that were exported to Europe, and export of skins continued legally until 1965. After that time, when Brazilian legislation prohibited such hunting, large-scale poaching of caimans continued, with millions of skins being exported through Paraguay and Bolivia. This continued until

the 1980s, when enforcement finally became effective, thanks to the participation of ranches. However, some export for the pet trade, focused mainly on birds, continues to this day.

Traditional hunting of game species like peccary, tapir, and deer has had little impact, but the continued hunting of big cats remains an issue (Lourival and Fonseca 1997). Although it is less serious than it was in the past, it remains an issue —mainly because of the inevitable conflicts between cattle ranchers and these large predators.

Overfishing is actually more of a problem in the Pantanal than overhunting. Long a traditional activity in the region, fishing was the first tourist attraction as well. However, as the Pantanal grew in popularity among fishermen from the developed states of southern Brazil, demand for the most popular species, the "Big Five" —pintado (*Pseudoplatystoma corruscans*), *cachara* (*P. fasciatum*), *jaú* (*Paulicea lutkeni*), *dourado* (*Salminus maxillosus*), and *pacú* (*Piaractus mesopotamicus*)— grew rapidly, creating an external market, especially in the state of São Paulo. The demand stimulated illegal commercial fishing activities involving gill nets, bombing, and other unsustainable practices. The result is that some watersheds have been severely depleted, and stocks of *pacú* and *jaú* in particular have become threatened (Catella and Petrere, Jr. 2001).

Introduction of exotic species is also a cause of concern. Intentional introduction of African grasses has already been discussed above. Introduced animals include feral pigs (*monteiros*), European wild pigs (*javali*), Amazonian peacock bass (*tucanaré*), and a mussel of the genus *Limnoperna*. Dogs, cats, water buffalo, and other domestic species can also have an impact on local fauna and flora if not properly controlled. Fortunately, however, the Pantanal ecosystem is extensive and very resilient, and the large population of predators at least partly helps to control some of the introduced animals, like the pigs. All things considered, exotic species are much less of a problem in the Pantanal than in many more fragile island ecosystems.

Another major threat is runoff from agricultural and mining activities in the areas surrounding the Pantanal. The effects of agriculture in the Rio Taquari have also clearly shown the potential risk to water quality and erosion control. The fragile soils that once formed this floodplain were impacted by poor soil conservation practices and planning, with disastrous results for fish populations and the associated traditional fishing communities. Pollution is also a concern, as agricultural runoff can be very damaging to entire watersheds. Mining tailings follow the same paths as pesticides, poisoning the food chain with heavy metals and causing serious changes in water turbidity.

Industrial development in and around the Pantanal also poses a threat to the region. The new Bolivia/Brazil gas pipeline is stimulating a number of industries, including mining for iron ore and manganese near Corumbá, where a smelting facility is being created using energy from the pipeline. Both Corumbá and Bodoquena have also developed a cement industry based on the extraction of local deposits of limestone; three or four highly-polluting production facilities are already in place. These mining activities, together with soybean production in Mato Grosso and Bolivia, are among the main drivers for the Hydrovia. New energy sources are also stimulating gold extraction near Poconé, with the usual problem of mercury pollution. These industries also increase the volume of sewage and solid wastes flowing into the Pantanal.

Fortunately, the governments of the states of Mato Grosso and Mato Grosso do Sul are paying attention to these issues. The Pantanal Program, a multiyear effort funded by the Inter-American Development Bank (IDB), the Japanese Bank for International Cooperation, the Brazilian government, and the governments of the states involved, is focused on the relationships between conservation and development, especially those involving protected areas, sewage and water, and sustainable economic activities.

Ultimately, perhaps the greatest threat of all to the future of the Pantanal involves major changes in the water flow dynamics of the region —much as is the case for the Okavango in Botswana and the Sudd Swamp in Sudan. In the mid-1990s, the governments of Argentina, Bolivia, Brazil, Paraguay, and Uruguay discussed a huge project called the "Hydrovia," the intention of which was to dredge and change the course of the Rio Paraguay to allow passage of larger transport vessels and to provide a stimulus to MERCOSUR. Support for the megaproject was requested from the Inter-American Development Bank. Given that the Rio Paraguay is the major artery of the Pantanal, large-scale changes in its flow could have enormous impacts on this wilderness area.

To provide better information on potential threats caused by the Hydrovia, several Brazilian grass-roots conservation organizations, notably Coalizão Rios Vivos, together with World Wildlife Fund and Conservation International, decided to launch a series of awareness initiatives to reach key audiences and decision-makers. In August 1995, World Wildlife Fund released a televised news broadcast in London, which prompted the Brazilian government to engage in a dialogue with various environmental groups.

This was followed by the film documentary "Voices of the Pantanal," produced by Conservation International, which included interviews with more than 50 scientists, conservationists, ranchers, politicians, businesspeople, and residents. In a key segment, a leading government official promised that the Brazilian government would "leave the river as it is" to avoid environmental impacts to the Pantanal. In December of 1995, the documentary was launched in both state capitals within the region, Campo Grande and Cuiabá. This attracted huge media attention throughout the Pantanal and resulted in sev-

Above, the capybara (Hydrochaeris hydrochaeris), *the world's largest rodent and common species in the waterways of the Pantanal.*
© **Konrad Wothe**

On the opposite page, pair of hyacinth macaws (Anodorhynchus hyacinthinus), *largest of the macaws and one of the Pantanal's most important flagship species.*
© **Tui de Roy**/*Minden Pictures*

...eral full-page stories in regional newspapers, and coverage by the 10 television stations in the two capitals. CI's documentary, as well as other informational products created by Brazilian NGOs, contributed significantly to the debate over the Hydrovia. The wide distribution of the video made a withdrawal from the statement "leave the river as it is" much more difficult. This public effort was also accompanied by a number of behind-the-scenes discussions, all of which had a significant impact. In the end, the Inter-American Development Bank rejected the project and it was shelved, at least for the time being. At the same time, the private sector began to develop transport vessels that could more readily navigate the shallow waters of the region.

However, as is always the case with such large-scale infrastructure projects, the threat never disappears completely. Indeed, some of the activities originally proposed are going ahead on a smaller scale, although camouflaged by a strategy involving many minor infrastructure works throughout the basin. These tend to be less visible to the conservation community and the public at large. A political movement supported by politicians at the state level to revive the original megaproject is also becoming more evident in the press. Although the original design may no longer be attainable, new versions could well emerge —making it necessary for the conservation community to remain ever vigilant.

Finally, it is important to recognize the potential impacts of globalization on the delicate balance between rancher and nature in the Pantanal. The traditional extensive model of cattle-ranching has actually made it possible to maintain this huge wilderness —in striking contrast to Amazonia, where cattle-ranching has been extremely destructive. However, with new trends in land tenure, property size, intensification of production methods, and inability to compete with cattle production on the surrounding plateau, old relationships between ranch owner, employee, and the local environment are once again raising the age-old question of how to adapt to the modern world while at the same time maintaining the delicate balance between humans and nature in this region. Ecotourism provides one potential mechanism, as does increased investment in the enterprises of scientific research and protection. Conservation International currently has several innovative programs in progress, exploring ways in which these new alternatives for the Pantanal can be scaled up to a level that makes them competitive with other land-use activities.

Conservation

The Pantanal wilderness is truly special among Brazilian ecosystems because it is an area where the principal economic activity has not had a major impact on biodiversity. The fact that well over 80% is still intact and its animal populations are flourishing bodes well for the future. The challenge now is to address the threats discussed above, create new opportunities that will encourage continued protection, and yet also stimulate the local economy.

In order to plan for the future, in 1998 a special Priority-Setting Workshop for the Pantanal and the neighboring Cerrado was organized by Conservation International and partner organizations including the University of Brasília, FUNATURA, and Fundação Biodiversitas. Involving more than 200 scientists and carried out with the support of the Brazilian government, this workshop proposed and designed a series of corridors and core areas aimed at protecting the greatest diversity of habitats and a complete representation of species. These include both federal and state parks and reserves and also a range of private reserves — all of which are organized at a large-scale landscape level to ensure long-term ecological and evolutionary continuity. Conservation International's Pantanal Program, based in Mato Grosso do Sul, has taken responsibility for implementing this corridor vision, working with the state government and local communities to create new tools that ensure both economic sustainability and maintenance of biodiversity. Among these are easements, trust funds, ecotourism, research, and a host of small-scale enterprise projects.

This workshop had enormous impact and served as a catalyst for immediate action. Until 1999, the Pantanal only had one National Park (the Pantanal National Park, 139 000 ha) and the Taiamã Ecological Station (7 200 ha), both in Mato Grosso State and covering only 146 200 ha, or 0.6% of the region. In the past three years, the area protected has more than doubled. The State of Mato Grosso do Sul has declared five new protected areas covering 140 000 ha, including the Pantanal do Rio Negro State Park (78 300 ha), the Nascentes do Taquari State Park (35 000 ha), two scenic rivers —the Rio Formoso in Bonito and the Rio Cênico das Rotas Moncoeiras (a linear protected area along the Rio Coxim)—, and a parkway reserve along Highway MS184, and the Federal Government has created the Bodoquena National Park covering 76 481 ha, also in Mato Grosso do Sul.

At the same time, there has been a major effort to create new privately-protected areas, taking advantage of Brazil's excellent legislation that facilitates the establishment of *Reservas Particulares do Patrimônio Natural* (RPPNs). A total of 13 of these now exist in the Pantanal, and they cover 204 255 ha.

One of these has been especially noteworthy, and that is Fazenda Rio Negro. This 7 700-ha area, now run privately by Rio Negro Comércio Turismo e Serviços Ltda. in collaboration with Conservation International-Brazil, was purchased in April, 1999, with a private donation of $1.5 million dollars from Gordon Moore of Intel. This was followed by another donation of $200 000 to upgrade the infrastructure of the reserve. This site was made world famous because it was the setting of the immensely popular Brazilian soap opera entitled *Pantanal*.

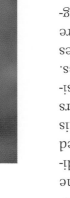

On the opposite page, marsh deer (Blastocerus dichotomus), largest of the South American deer. Above, Muscovy duck (Cairina moschata). Both photos: **© Patricio Robles Gil**/*Sierra Madre*

Before the purchase of Fazenda Rio Negro in 1999, two additional areas were proposed by local farmers, with support of CI, to be set aside as RPPNs, and together with Fazenda Rio Negro they total 24 000 ha.

This reserve complex is now the site of an ecotourism venture and field research program that currently supports 10 projects on endangered animals like the giant otter, the giant anteater, the Pantanal jaguar, and the hyacinth macaw. With support from the Ford Motor Company, CI and Earth Watch have now developed an alliance to create a Conservation Research Center that will host two Earth Watch groups of 10 people every month, and will help support an environmental education program linking local schools with schools based in the U.S. Aside from the research agenda, the program is also developing local capacity in economic enterprises such as ecotourism, bee-keeping, organic food production, and various arts and crafts.

In the northern part of the State of the Pantanal in Mato Grosso, much has happened around the Pantanal National Park. The Nature Conservancy purchased several key areas surrounding the national park and turned them over to Ecotropica, a local NGO, to manage. These include three important privately-owned areas, Acurizal, Penha, and Doroché, and almost double the size of the national park. Notably, they include a significant area of permanently-dry land that provides refuge to animals when the low-lying parts of the park flood.

More importantly, Pantanal National Park was recognized as a World Heritage Site by UNESCO in 2000, and part of the floodplain of the Pantanal has been declared a Biosphere Reserve, following a design that emerged from the Priority-Setting Workshop.

Another innovative concept that is being tried was originally conceived of in France. It is a collaborative effort with ranchers to create what is called a Natural Park, or Parc Naturelle Régional; it has no legal status, but can be used as a tool to raise ranchers' awareness about the importance of protecting their land.

Good things have also been happening on the Bolivian side of the Pantanal. In September of 2001, the Bolivian government designated three huge areas —Bañados del Izozog, Rio Parapetí, and El Palmar de las Islas-Salinas de San José— as protected sites under the RAMSAR Convention, an international treaty on wetlands created in 1971. Covering 46 000 km², these three areas represent more than 20% of the area of the Pantanal and together comprise one of the two largest wetland protection initiatives carried out under RAMSAR in its 30-year history. The decision of the Bolivian government received special recognition by the World Wide Fund for Nature (WWF), which declared the areas a Gift to the Earth —the first such gift for a freshwater system in Latin America and nearly 10% of the global goal for WWF's "Living Waters" Program.

Finally, there is the issue of appropriate ecotourism in the Pantanal. Needless to say, the region has the greatest potential for wildlife viewing of anywhere in South America, but it has to be developed in a way that has minimal impact on the environment and yields maximum return to local landowners. The creation of Hotel-Fazendas, pioneered by Refúgio Ecológico Kaimán in Mato Grosso do Sul, is especially important. This destination, based at a traditional ranch or *fazenda* owned by Roberto Klabin (who is also President of SOS Mata Atlântica, a Brazilian NGO) is a model for such an approach to ecotourism. It has now been in existence for more than a decade, and protects 5 000 ha of private land in addition to 65 000 ha of ranch land with cattle.

Indications are that ecotourism is gaining momentum in the Pantanal, and it could become a major economic force in the region. In particular, it is becoming a very important source of income for traditional ranches; especially those belonging to the Pantanal Lodge Owners' Association of Mato Grosso do Sul (APPAN), who have focused heavily on this issue. As an indication of things to come, Fazenda Rio Negro earned as much from tourism in 2000 as it did from cattle ranching, and hopefully this trend will continue in the region as a whole.

All things considered, the prospects for maintaining the Pantanal in its current wilderness state are as good as for any wilderness area discussed in this book.

RUSSELL A. MITTERMEIER
REINALDO F.F. LOURIVAL
MÔNICA HARRIS
CRISTINA G. MITTERMEIER
GUSTAVO FONSECA
HAROLDO CASTRO
JOHN PILGRIM

On the opposite page, the Rio Pimiento in the Bolivian Pantanal.
© **Staffan Widstrand**/*Nature Picture Library*

Above, Pantanal cowboy or "pantaneiro" riding his horse through the grasslands of the Pantanal.
© **Willy Kenning**

THE LLANOS

The Llanos is an extensive system of grasslands, sea-sonally-flooded plains, and forests shared by Venezuela and Colombia. It is located to the north and west of the Rio Orinoco and borders the Amazonia wilderness along its entire southern edge. In all, it covers 451 474 km², roughly corresponding to World Wildlife Fund's Llanos (NT0709) (388 998 km²) and Apure/Villavicencio Dry Forests (NT0201) (68 544 km²) ecoregions (Olson et al. 2001). Of this, about 61% (275 115 km²) lies within Venezuela and accounts for 31.2% of Venezuelan territory, and 39% (176 359 km²) lies within Colombia, where it accounts for 17.0% of that country's land area.

Located on a large downward flexure of the Earth's crust, the Llanos lies at the intersection of the Andes ridge and the Caribbean ridge in the northern part of South America. The most flooded area is the middle part, which drains into the Rio Orinoco and is transected by its tributaries from west to east. Situated over pre-Cambrian basement rocks, the Llanos is composed primarily of alluvial deposits from the Tertiary and Quaternary periods. Sediments are very recent, deposited during the upper Pleistocene uplift of the Andean ridge and deposition due to erosion from the Andes and Caribbean Cordilleras after the last glacial period. Consequently, the area as we define it here is a fairly recent ecosystem (Sarmiento 1983; Vila 1960).

There are several distinct topographic areas in the Llanos, but the general profile is flat (with a 0.02% slope to the east), with poor acidic soils, and mostly covered by grasses of low nutritional value. However, some areas with deeper and richer soils have relatively large patches of dry forest. Fires in the Llanos are natural, as evidenced by the many species of plants that have adaptations to resist or even depend on fire for their life cycle. However, human-induced fires are far more frequent. Several grasses from the genera *Trachypogon*, *Andropogon*, and *Axonopus* can regenerate very quickly after fire and constitute an important source of food for herbivores. Cattle ranchers often burn the savanna to induce regrowth of these grasses to feed their cattle. Indigenous people also burn the savannas regularly to facilitate hunting

The Llanos can be divided into four principal sub-regions: the *Alluvial Overflow Plains*, the *Aeollian Plains*, the *High Plains*, and the *Piedmont* region adjacent to the Andes (Sarmiento, *op. cit.*). The Alluvial Overflow Plains are a hyperseasonal wetland situated in a central tectonic depression in the middle of the Llanos which, due to its dramatic flooding regime, is particularly unsuited for human activities. It is very flat, with the highest elevations being less than 80 m above sea level. The dominant vegetation associated with this region is a hyperseasonal savanna with few trees or palms. Gallery (riparian) forest bordering the rivers and patches of dry forest adjacent to them interrupt the otherwise continuous plain. The entire region is subjected to two strong and contrasting seasons, a wet season with torrential rains that often cause rivers to overflow and flood most of the savanna, and a dry season with prolonged drought that causes intense fires (Berroterán 1985).

There are three distinct physiographic formations in the overflow plains: *bancos*, *bajíos*, and *esteros*. These differ in relative elevation, soil drainage, and vegetation. Bancos, which account for one third of the region, are found along riverbanks and are the most elevated areas in the riparian zone. They are 1 to 2 m higher than the surrounding areas, consist of sandy loams, are poor in organic matter, acidic, and have moderate to good drainage (López Hernández

Wildern[...]

*On the oppos[...]
forest runn[...]
Llanos, a [...]
of th[...]*
© Patricio Robl[...]

1995). The dominant vegetation is a gallery forest with several dominant tree species like palms (*Copernicia tectorum*), saman (*Pithecellobium saman*), masaguaros (*P. guachapele*), figs (*Ficus* spp.), caruta (*Genipa americana*), palo de agua (*Cordia collococa*), and camoruco (*Sterculia apetala*) (Ramia 1967; Troth 1979). Occasionally, there may also be larger trees such as *Terminalia amazonica* and *Ceiba pentandra* that can reach over 50 m (Hernández et al. 1994), and even the mighty caoba or mahogany (*Swietenia macrophylla*) is sometimes present (César Barbosa, pers. comm., 2002).

The next formation is the *bajíos*, which are lower regions found further away from the rivers and where sedimentation of finer particles takes place. They cover almost half of the total surface of the overflow plains. They have poorer drainage, their acidic soils contain a high proportion of expandable clay, and they are richer in organic matter than the *bancos* (López Hernández, *op. cit.*). During the rainy season, the *bajío* is partially covered by water, but it dries out completely in November or December. Very few trees can grow under these conditions, among them the palm *Copernicia tectorum* and the caujaro (*Cordia* sp.). Palm forests of *Mauritia flexuosa,* locally known as *morichales,* are also characteristic of the *bajíos*, and reach over 18 m in height along waterways, in the most flood-susceptible areas. This is a highly-productive association that provides food for humans and wildlife, as well as thatching material and fiber for knitting hammocks and making cloth. Scattered throughout this formation is an interesting landscape feature locally known as *surales* or *topiales*, consisting of thousands of low mounds of dirt covered with grass (predominantly *Trachypogon* spp.). In the rest of the area, it is common to find spiny shrubs, including barinas (*Cassia aculeata*), guaica (*Randia armatta*), *Mimosa pigra*, *M. dormiens*, and *Hydrolea spinosa*, and grasses such as *Paspalum* spp., *Paratheria prostata*, *Eleocharis* spp., *Leersia hexandra*, and *Hymenachne amplexicaulis* (Ramia 1967; Troth 1979).

Esteros are the third and lowest region of the overflow plains. They are characterized by poorly-drained soils with very fine texture in which the main route of water loss is evaporation. As the dry season progresses, esteros hold water longer than any other areas, and dry up only at the end of the dry season (March or April). Continued flooding throughout most of the year and clay-heavy soil inhibit most tree growth, with the exception of occasional palms. Instead, the esteros are dominated by floating vegetation of which *Eichhornia crassipes* and *E. azurea* are particularly prominent. Other common floating elements are *Salvinia* spp., *Pistia stratiotes*, and *Ludwigia* spp., while the rooted vegetation is composed of *Thalia geniculata*, *Ipomoea crassicaulis*, *I. fistulosa*, *Eleocharis* spp., and *Cyperus* spp. (Ramia, *op. cit.*; Troth, *op. cit.*).

Aeollian Plains are located to the south of the overflow plains and are large extensions of dunes indicative of arid conditions during glacial periods. This subregion is covered mostly by low-productivity grasses (e.g. *Paspalum, Trachypogon*) (Sarmiento, *op. cit.*). The gallery forests along small streams have the only trees in the area, with floristic composition being similar to that in the overflow plains. Morichales also occur along rivers, streams or pools, providing water and food for many animals, and often have the highest concentrations of species in this subregion.

The High Plains are found in two distinct areas, one in the extreme south of the Llanos and the other to the east of the overflow plains. The relief is slightly more hilly and it is possible to find eroded mesas composed of lateritic crusts that prevent root penetration and constrain tree growth. Soils are light and even coarse, acidic and rich in iron and aluminum, with the predominant vegetation cover being grasses of low nutritional value (e.g., *Trachypogon* spp.) (Sarmiento, *op. cit.*). As the great grasslands of the open savanna come closer to the waterways, woodland savannas of saladillo (*Caraipa llanorum*) start to appear. These moderately high, regionally endemic woodlands become seasonally flooded and their most prominent characteristic is their ability to inhibit the development of a shrubby understory, allowing a herbaceous one instead. There are other interesting plant associations here, such as those formed by chaparro manteco (*Byrsonima crassifolia*), a thick bark tree from which tannins are obtained for the leather industry. Its fruit is also interesting, as it is highly fatty, hence the name *manteco* ("lard"), an irresistible treat for many animals, particularly the white-tailed deer (*Odocoileus virginianus*). Other forest associations include chaparro forest dominated by *Curatella americana*, a species highly resistant to fire with large, coarse leaves that are used as sandpaper by local woodworkers. *Surales* or *topiales* may also be found scattered throughout this formation, especially in areas susceptible to flooding between riparian and chaparro forests.

Piedmont savannas are the highest part of the Llanos and are located near the Andes. Soils are deeper and richer due to alluvial deposition from the Andes, and these are the most forested areas in the Llanos. Dry tropical forest is common here and has a similar floristic composition to that of the *bancos*. Due to higher fertility and the larger areas of forest, agriculture and logging have taken a stronger toll on this subregion, and cattle ranching is slightly more intensive than elsewhere.

The average temperature in the lower Llanos is 26.6°C, the mean diurnal fluctuation is 9.5°C, and the mean seasonal fluctuation is 3.0°C. Precipitation varies from 1 000 mm on the eastern side to as much as 2 000 mm in the Guaviare River, with over 90% of the rain falling between April and November. The period between January and April is the dry season when all the water bodies shrink or disappear entirely, with the only permanent water being in the esteros and lagoons. The smaller rivers eventually stop flowing, making it necessary for aquatic wildlife to rely on the deeper portions of these waterways to survive. From July to October, there is a distinct wet season when the savanna floods and there is abundant standing water due to rain-

Orinoco goose (Neochen jubata) *in the Venezuelan Llanos.*
© **Luiz Claudio Marigo**

266

fall and overflowing of the rivers. The two months between each season are considered transitional. This extreme seasonality is less marked towards the south of the Colombian Llanos, where the dry season may be as short as two months.

Biodiversity

Plant diversity is fairly high, with 3 424 species of vascular plants recorded, while endemism, at 40 species, is low (G. Aymard and R. Duno, in litt., 2002). Among the endemics are species like *Vernonia aristeguietae, Bourreria aristeguietana, Stilpnopappus pittieri, S. apurensis, Hymenocallis venezuelensis, Eriocaulon rubescens, Limnosipanea ternifolia,* and *Gustavia acuta* (Huber and Alarcón 1988). It is important to highlight the unique plant communities that grow on the many rocky outcrops found throughout the high plains. These have a highly distinctive floristic composition which includes *Vellozia lithophila, Navia* spp. —a small bromeliad with sharp, spiny rosettes on the tips—, and a small palm of the genus *Syagrus* that is highly resistant to fire and which sheds its leaves as a survival strategy during prolonged droughts.

Many Llanos plants have special adaptations to fire, among them *Curatella americana, Byrsonima crassifolia,* and *Bowdichia virgiloides,* which have very thick bark insulating the tree. This feature reaches its extreme in the *chaparote (Palicourea rigidifolia),* which has a woody stem almost 2 cm thick, surrounded by another 2 cm of protective bark.

The fauna in the Llanos is both abundant and diverse. Birds are represented by approximately 475 species, including both residents and migrants that gather in large numbers during the dry season to feed in the drying wetlands. Important groups include herons and egrets, ibises, storks, ducks, shorebirds, and many birds of prey (Phelps and De Schauensee 1978; WWF, in prep.). Endemism, however, is low, with only the Orinoco softtail (*Thripophaga cherriei*) considered endemic, although the Orinoco piculet (*Picumnus pumilus*) can be considered a near endemic.

Mammals are represented by 198 species, including 59 species of bats (Ojasti and Boher 1986, cited in Ojasti 1990; CI unpublished data), but only three of these are endemic. Among nonvolant mammals, the most abundant is the capybara (*Hydrochaeris hydrochaeris*), a rodent adapted to a semiaquatic life-style. Following in abundance are white-tailed deer, which are commonly seen mingling with cattle, and this is one of the main causes of high mortality due to hoof-and-mouth disease (Eisenberg and Polisar 1999). Other mammals found in the savanna include edentates like the giant anteater (*Myrmecophaga tridactyla*), the southern tamandua (*Tamandua tetradactyla*), and the Llanos long-nosed armadillo (*Dasypus sabanicola*); and several carnivores such as the crab-eating fox (*Cerdocyon thous*), bush dog (*Speothos venaticus*), ocelot (*Leopardus pardalis*), puma

(*Puma concolor*), jaguar (*Panthera onca*), and giant otter (*Pteronura brasiliensis*). Only two species of monkeys, the red howler (*Alouatta seniculus*) and the weeper capuchin (*Cebus olivaceus*), occur in the Venezuelan Llanos, whereas as many as six occur in the Colombian portion of this region. The Colombian species include again the red howler, the white-fronted capuchin (*Cebus albifrons*) replacing the weeper capuchin, the widow monkey (*Callicebus torquatus*), the squirrel monkey (*Saimiri sciureus*), and two species of night monkey (*Aotus brumbacki, A. trivirgatus*), usually found in gallery forests. The only endemics are the Llanos long-nosed armadillo, Orinoco sword-nosed bat (*Lonchorhina orinocensis*), and O'Connell's spiny rat (*Proechimys oconnelli*) (WWF, in prep.).

Reptiles are very abundant in the Llanos, with a total of around 107 species (WWF, in prep.). Several of these are present in large numbers, including the giant green anaconda (*Eunectes murinus*), the spectacled caiman (*Caiman crocodilus*), the savanna side-necked turtle (*Podocnemis vogli*), the green iguana (*Iguana iguana*), and the tegu lizard (*Tupinambis teguixin*), and reptile biomass is quite high. Other reptiles found in lower numbers include the mata-mata turtle (*Chelus fimbriatus*), the scorpion mud turtle (*Kinosternon scorpioides*), the yellow-spotted Amazon river turtle (*Podocnemis unifilis*), the giant Amazon river turtle or *arrau* (*P. expansa*), and the dwarf caiman (*Paleosuchus palpebrosus*). Endemism is also low among reptiles with one endemic species, a dwarf species of rattlesnake, *Crotalus pifanorum,* and two near endemic species, the savanna side-necked turtle and the Orinoco crocodile (*Crocodylus intermedius*).

Amphibians are very abundant, and especially ubiquitous in the wet season, and are represented by around 48 species with six endemics: Kennedy's snouted tree frog (*Scinax kennedyi*), Blair's snouted tree frog (*S. blairi*), Villavicencio snouted tree frog (*S. wandae*), Mathiasson's tree frog (*Hyla mathiassoni*), *Eleutherodactylus medemi,* and *Colostethus juanii* (WWF, in prep.). The most common species include the cane toad (*Bufo marinus*), the emerald-eyed tree frog (*Hyla crepitans*), the yellow tree frog (*H. microcephala*), Rivero's tiny tree frog (*H. minuscula*), the Caracas snouted tree frog (*Scinax rostrata*), the Colombian four-eyed frog (*Pleurodema brachyops*), and the swimming frog (*Pseudis paradoxa*).

Fish diversity is also high, with 300 species of fishes in the Llanos. The level of endemism in the Llanos is not well known, but it is estimated that there are between 30 and 40 endemic species —although some of these might occasionally be found to the south of the Orinoco (C. Lasso, pers. comm., 2002). Noteworthy fish include several species of catfish (*Brachyplatystoma filamentosum, Pseudopimelodus apurensis, Phractocephalus hemiliopterus*), electric eel (*Electrophorus electricus*), freshwater rays (*Paratrygon aireba, Potamotrygon orbignyi*), and piranha (*Serrasalmus altuvei, S. elongatus, Pygocentrus notatus*). When the rivers flood the savanna, the fish invade the newly-inundated areas to forage and breed, and then return to the rivers in the dry season. Howev-

Striated heron
(Butorides striatus) *eating a frog.*
© **Tony Crocetta**/BIOS

er, large numbers often fail to find their way back, becoming isolated in temporary ponds where their density increases as the dry season progresses (Machado Allison 1993).

Flagship Species

The Llanos is noteworthy for having several flagship species that are among the largest in their taxonomic groups. Reaching between 5 and 6 m in length and with unconfirmed sightings of animals measuring 7 m, the Critically Endangered Orinoco crocodile is one of the larger crocodile species. It is also one of the most threatened species of crocodiles in the world, mainly due to its limited distribution (Thorbjarnarson 1992).

The green anaconda, the largest snake in the world, is commonly found during the dry season in the hyperseasonal savanna of the overflow plains. The arrau or giant Amazonian side-necked turtle is another giant in its group, with a carapace length that can exceed 80 cm, making it one of the largest freshwater turtles in the world. The giant otter is the longest otter in the world, and similar in weight to the North American sea otter (*Enhydra lutris*).

Finally, we have the capybara, one of the most conspicuous flagships of the Llanos, and the largest rodent in the world. The Llanos subspecies (*Hydrochaeris hydrochaeris hydrochaeris*) is the largest of all, reaching at least 79 kg and possibly as much as 90 kg. These abundant semiaquatic rodents are commonly found along the many natural channels locally known as *caños chigüireros*, and spend most of their time in the mud as a way to control their body temperature.

Human Cultures

The 2000 census showed a total of 15 719 indigenous people, belonging to several ethnic groups, living in rural communities within the Venezuelan Llanos. The largest group is the Kariña, with an estimated population of 7 253, followed by the Pumé (or Yaruro) with 5 321, the Warao with 2 485, the Guahibo with 333, the Kuiva (or Cuiba) with 325, and the Wayuu with only two individuals left. The Pumé, Guahibo, and Kuiva occupy the southwestern areas around the Capanaparo and Cinaruco Rivers, and support themselves mostly by fishing, hunting, and traditional agriculture, with yucca and produce being the principal crops. Some of the younger Pumé speak Spanish and occasionally travel to populated areas to work as crop hands or other seasonal jobs, but mostly these groups still live a traditional subsistence life-style. The Kariña and Warao occupy the Eastern high plains, the latter being the predominant ethnic group of the Orinoco Delta, and show varying degrees of acculturation.

In Colombia, there are 11 indigenous groups in the Llanos, the vast majority of which are Sikuani. Others include the Cuia, Saliba, Tunebo, Macaguan, Guahibo, Piapoco, Guayabero, Curripaco, Betoy, and Piaroa. The total population is 23 556 and they inhabit a series of Indigenous Reserves (Resguardos Indígenas) covering 2 818 182 ha (Romero et al. 1993).

Based on projections from the OCEI (2000), the estimated rural population of the Llanos in Venezuela is 714 691, yielding a human density of 2.6 inhabitants/km². In Colombia, the rural population is 351 265, for a population density of 2.0 inhabitants/km². Combining these figures, the total population for the Llanos comes to 1 065 956, or 2.4 inhabitants/km².

Threats

One of the greatest threats to the Llanos is that posed by human-induced fires. Although many plants have adaptations to fire, human use of fire is sometimes extreme. Fire is used mainly in two ways. One is as an aid in hunting, to flush animals or to utilize those killed by fire (especially by nomadic indigenous people). The other use is by ranchers, to get a "green bite" for their cattle by burning large areas at a much higher frequency than would occur naturally. This increased frequency of fires alters floristic composition and favors plants that are particularly fire-resistant.

By far the most common economic activity in the Llanos is cattle ranching. Most of the region is in the hands of a few cattle ranchers who own huge properties ranging from 10 000 to more than 100 000 ha. However, cattle exist at very low density, usually 0.2-1 per hectare, and animals range freely, feeding on natural pasture in otherwise pristine landscapes, moving from *banco* to *bajío* to *estero* as the dry season progresses, and back as the savannas flood again. As a result, it appears that the impact of cattle-ranching on wildlife is fairly low —a situation similar to areas of traditional, extensive cattle-ranching in the Pantanal.

Some ranches have engaged in water management, building dikes to manipulate the water flow in the savanna and minimize the impact of the dry season, thus increasing the area of *estero* that retains water for longer periods over the year at the expense of the *bajío*, and altering the natural processes of both ecosystems. Since the Llanos tilt to the East, pretty much every road that runs north to south has the potential to act as a dike. As a result, the lower-lying lands suffer premature drought due to the water sequestered in the upper part of the water-management areas or *módulos*. During the middle of the dry season, the gates are opened for a short period of time (one or two days) and the lower *módulos* flood again, stimulating the growth of the plants there. This draining of the upper *módulo* allows a large area to become somewhat dry, permitting grass growth to begin. This management continues throughout the dry season to provide green pasture for cattle, despite the lack of rain. When the wet season begins, the gates are opened again and the water is let out to prevent overflowing and

Above, the Orinoco crocodile (Crocodylus intermedius) *is perhaps the most important flagship species of the Llanos and one of the world's most endangered crocodilians. It is also one of the largest, reaching 5-6 m in length.*
© **Michael P. Turco**

On the opposite page, red-and-green macaws (Ara chloroptera). © **Patricio Robles Gil**/*Sierra Madre*

breaking of the dikes. Such habitat manipulation can greatly increase the production of cattle in the savanna. However, it is very expensive, and fortunately only very few ranches can afford it. Most cattle operations are quite simple and not very different from 400 years ago, with minimal impact on the ecosystem.

Fishing in the rivers has been intense near the populated areas, and the species and size-class composition of the different commercial species have changed over the last 15 years. However, this trend is less important in more remote areas.

Agriculture is even less of a threat. Soils in the Llanos are heavy in texture, acidic, and with low capacity for cationic exchange. This translates into very poor soils with practically no potential for agriculture. The only places where large-scale commercial agriculture is possible are next to dams (e.g. Calabozo and Acarigua, Venezuela), where water supply is reliable. Even in such cases, it always requires large amounts of pesticides and fertilizers, making it less profitable and more polluting. On the riverbanks, conditions are different due to regular flooding, which allows soils to be lighter and river sediments to enhance fertility. Some agriculture is possible in these areas, including cotton, corn, and other produce. However, this kind of agriculture can have a damaging impact on wildlife through fragmentation, since these riverbanks act as natural corridors for all forest-dwelling wildlife. Fortunately, such agriculture is not yet carried out on a large scale, being mostly a small-scale family activity. Lack of roads in most of the Llanos also makes all agricultural activities less profitable.

Commercial logging in forested areas is a largely uncontrolled and growing threat. It takes place mainly near the Andes, where most of the forests are located. After logging, areas tend to be replaced by pasture, and there are large areas where dry forest once existed that have now been replaced by cattle ranches.

Exotic species are also a problem. Feral domestic animals such as pigs, cats, and dogs can transmit diseases to the native wildlife, prey on smaller animals, or compete for habitat. House mice (*Mus musculus*) and rats (*Rattus rattus*) occur, and even cattle and horses sometimes go feral and live in the wild in vast areas called *cimarroneras*. The most significant impact for native ungulate species is the incidence of hoof-and-mouth disease, which has contributed to the extirpation of entire populations of white-tailed deer and peccary. Some African grasses such as *Cynodon dactylon*, *Digitaria decumbens*, *Hyparrhenia rufa*, and *Urochloa mutica* with higher nutritional value than the local species, have also been introduced for cattle. Fortunately, however, there are no reported cases of exotic species replacing native ones, and exotics are still considered a minor problem compared to many other parts of the world. Finally, as in the Pantanal, there has been —for more than a decade— a plan for a major hydrological project that would make the Apure River fit for navigation by large vessels for a longer period of the year. This would involve building dikes and damming the river, allegedly decreasing the cost for transporting produce from the Andes to the rest of Venezuela. However, as with the Hydrovia Project in Brazil, such an undertaking would dramatically alter the water regime and ecology of the western part of the Venezuelan Llanos. All species would be affected, especially those under threat such as the Orinoco crocodile and the giant Amazon river turtle, which rely on the seasonal draining of the watershed and consequent exposure of nesting beaches for reproduction. The social impact of the project would also be dramatic, since many populated areas would flood. Local conservation groups have opposed this project and hopefully will continue to be successful; nonetheless, as with the Brazilian Hydrovia, it probably will rear its ugly head from time to time in the future —making it necessary for conservationists to remain ever vigilant.

On the Colombian side, extensive oil development in the Llanos is a fairly recent threat that has brought with it construction of access roads and increased pressure on the natural resources of the area. The threat of an oil spill into a major waterway is also ever-present, exacerbated by the violent activism of radical political groups; indeed, in 2000 over 120 pipelines were bombed in different parts of Colombia. On top of this, efforts to control guerrilla groups by both government military forces and paramilitary groups sometimes involve powerful chemicals, such as defoliants, that can have disastrous impacts on the environment. Since all Llanos watersheds drain to the east, oil spills and other sources of pollution in the Colombian Llanos have the potential to affect a large area extending to the easternmost reaches of the Llanos and other biomes as well.

Conservation

There are five national parks in the Venezuelan Llanos covering a total area of 1 257 618 ha. In addition to these, there are a number of other protected areas, including forest reserves, forested areas, wildlife refuges, and protected zones, and areas of integrated development, which together add up to 6 099 274 ha (Castillo and García 2000). On the Colombian side, there is only one national park, Parque Nacional Tuparro, covering an area of 548 000 ha. Together, the protected areas in the two countries total 6 647 274 ha, representing 14.7% of the region as defined.

However, it is important to note that most of the government-protected areas have little if any management. The main reason for the largely pristine condition of the Llanos is the low human population density, combined with the land tenure system in which a few people own very large areas where low impact, low density cattle-ranching is the principal land-use activity. This is quite similar to the situation in the Pantanal region of Brazil, Bolivia, and Paraguay. These landowners enforce strict no-trespassing rules aimed to protect their cattle, but wildlife also benefits.

On the opposite page and above, green anaconda (Eunectes murinus), one of the world's two largest snakes.
© **Tony Crocetta**/*BIOS*

There are two kinds of commercial wildlife management in the Venezuelan and Colombian Llanos. The first is a traditional harvest of capybaras during Lent, following a Papal Edict permitting use of such meat in place of fish. For over 40 years, the Venezuelan government and more recently the Colombian as well, have authorized cattle ranchers to commercially exploit their capybara populations at this time of year (Ojasti 1991). This practice was considered a sustainable use of the resource and many ranches, such as Hato El Frío, practiced it on a regular basis. However, things have taken a turn for the worse in recent years, and drastic declines have resulted. In Hato El Frío, for example, a population that had once numbered between 30 000 and 45 000 had dropped to barely 4 000 individuals by 1986 (Ojasti 1978; J. Rivas, unpublished data). This dramatic crash is thought to be the result of increased poaching driven by a declining economy following the drop in oil prices in 1982. Nowadays, capybaras can still be found just about anywhere in the less-populated areas, but very few ranches have harvestable populations.

The other commercial harvest of wildlife in the Llanos involves spectacled caimans (Thorbjarnarson 1991). After the much larger Orinoco crocodile was hunted out in the 1930s and 1940s, and again in the 1970s, the spectacled caiman took over the habitat formerly occupied by the crocodile and its population numbers exploded. The harvest of wild populations for the leather trade proved to be a profitable business, and many ranches started harvesting their caimans. The harvest of over 100 000 animals per year was considered to be sustainable (Thorbjarnarson and Velasco 1999). However, there were many flaws in the implementation of the program, regulations had many loopholes, and the program has shown less than optimum results. Unfortunately, the wildlife protection agency depended on tax revenues from this program, which kept it from acting rapidly to prevent overexploitation. Skin prices dropped dramatically after 1992 because of increased availability of alligator skins from the U.S., with the result that pressures on Llanos caiman populations declined as well. Since the spectacled caiman is such a resilient species, it is still abundant all over the Llanos. However, as with the capybara, only a few ranches have populations large enough to sustain a commercial harvest.

While caiman leather revenues were booming (1986 to 1992), a large number of ranches built facilities to incubate caiman eggs collected from the wild and kept the animals long enough to grow to a commercially-profitable size (usually one year). Although many of these operations were legitimate, there were also many bogus farms that harvested animals from the wild in an unsustainable manner. The collapse of leather prices drove most of these operations out of business. Today, some of these facilities are being considered for commercial farming of the Orinoco crocodile, the skin of which is far more valuable. However, since this species is on Appendix I of CITES, only second-generation animals born in captivity can be sold, and those supporting

exploitation are increasing the pressure to downlist the Orinoco crocodile to Appendix II, so ranching and harvesting can be allowed. Currently, populations of Orinoco crocodiles have experienced only a very modest recovery after much effort and money have been invested in their conservation. Consequently, conservation groups in Venezuela strongly oppose downlisting, fearing that it might follow the slippery slope taken by the caiman ranches —with disastrous results for a far less abundant and less adaptable species than the caiman.

Overall, most of the Llanos is still in very good condition and we estimate that approximately 80% remains in wilderness state. Although most of it is being or has been used for cattle ranching, the intensity of the operation is such that the impact on the habitat is very mild. In some places where human density is higher, there have been local extinctions, but this trend disappears as one moves away from the cities. Major modifications to the environment, such as dams, dikes, and deforestation, have fortunately not yet taken a large toll on these vast plains, and the low human density over most of the area prevents other significant impacts. Overall, there is great hope for this wilderness to remain basically unchanged, at least for the time being.

JESÚS RIVAS
JOSÉ VICENTE RODRÍGUEZ
CRISTINA G. MITTERMEIER

Above, mother and juvenile capybara (Hydrochaeris hydrochaeris)*, an abundant and highly-visible flagship species of the Llanos that is also harvested for its meat in some parts of the region.*
© **Tony Crocetta**/*BIOS*

On the following page, scarlet ibises (Eudocimus ruber) *at sunset in the Venezuelan Llanos.*
© **Luiz Claudio Marigo**

BAÑADOS DEL ESTE

The Bañados del Este (or Humedales del Este) is a large area of wetlands in southeastern Uruguay, situated between latitude 33° and 35°S and between longitude 53° and 55°W, and including parts of the Departments of Rocha, Cerro Largo, Lavalleja, Maldonado, and Treinta y Tres. Some authors (e.g., Scott and Carbonell 1986) consider it a series of independent wetlands and lagoons, among them Arroyo Maldonado and Laguna del Sauce, Lagunas José Ignacio y Garzón, Laguna de Rocha, Laguna de Castillos y Arroyo Valizas, Laguna Negra y Bañados de Santa Teresa, and Laguna Merín y Bañados de San Miguel. However, for practical purposes, all individual habitats and formations occurring within this region represent a single large ecosystem, which is why we follow here the broader definition proposed by the Biodiversity Conservation and Sustainable Development Program for the Eastern Wetlands of Uruguay (PROBIDES), which recognizes the entire Bañados del Este region as a biosphere reserve covering some 3 850 000 ha (PROBIDES 2001; see also Canevari et al. 2001). Formed by a mosaic of habitats including gallery forests, palm formations, savannas, and halophytic and xerophytic formations, with about 20% of the area in permanent water bodies such as rivers, lagoons, and coastal waters, the Bañados is still 81% intact and among the most important wetland systems in South America.

Biodiversity

The main vegetation types in the Bañados del Este are: savannas, with a heterogeneous herbaceous community; native forests, including gallery forests, ravine forests, *bosque serrano*, palm forests (including the endemic *Butia capitata*), and *monte de parque*; wetlands, with a series of permanent and shallow seasonal water bodies; coastal ecosystems; and several oceanic islands. These ecosystems are highly productive and support large populations of wildlife, particularly birds and mammals, and harbor 50% of all vertebrates found in Uruguay.

In all, 311 species of birds, 79 mammals, 33 reptiles, and 31 species of amphibians have been recorded from the Bañados, but none are endemic. Plant diversity is not well documented, but it estimated at between 1 300 and 1 400 species, of which some five are thought to be endemic. (PROBIDES 1999).

Flagship Species

The Bañados del Este is world-famous for its large numbers of waterbirds, both resident and migratory. According to AZPIROZ (2001), almost all water-related species found in Uruguay are represented here, including significant populations of the Endangered marsh seedeater (*Sporophila palustris*), the yellow cardinal (*Gubernatrix cristata*), the saffron-cowled blackbird (*Agelaius flavus*), and the pampas or red-breasted meadowlark (*Sturnella defillippi*). It is also important as a stopover for migratory species that fly in from the Arctic and Patagonia, such as the American golden plover (*Pluvialis dominica*) and the white-rumped sandpiper (*Calidris fuscicollis*).

In freshwater environments, the capybara (*Hydrochaeris hydrochaeris*) and nutria or coypu (*Myocastor coypus*) are common, while the Neotropical river otter (*Lontra longicaudis*) is also present (PROBIDES 2001).

The oceanic islands near the coastline support two species of pinniped, the South American sea lion (*Otaria byronia)* and the South American fur seal (*Arctocephalus australis*), and the coastal ocean is a reproduction site for the southern right whale (*Eubalaena australis*). The area is also visited by three species of sea turtles: the olive ridley (*Lepodichelys*

Wilderness Area

On the opposite page, butia palms (Buti capitata), an unusual species endemic to this region.
© **Alejandro Olmos**

On pp. 276-277, black-necked swan (Cygnus melanocorypha) in Mangueira Lake.
© **Luiz Claudio Marigo**

THE SUNDARBANS

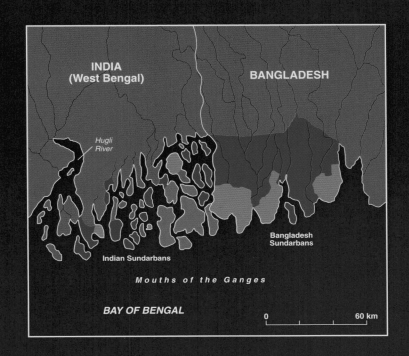

The Sundarbans, located on the border between Bangladesh and West Bengal State in India, is the world's largest tidal mangrove forest. The region treated here covers about 10 000 km², of which 62% lies in the southwest of Bangladesh (21°30'-22°30' N latitudes and 89°00'-89°55'E longitudes) and the remaining 38% in the southeast of West Bengal in India (between 21°32'-22°40'N latitudes and 88°85'-89°00'E longitudes). Roughly 80% of this region remains intact, although the size of the Sundarbans as a whole has been reduced. The total mangrove area of the world has been estimated to be around 166 700 km² (Choudhury et al. 2001), which means that this one region accounts for about 6% of all mangroves on Earth. The Bangladesh Sundarbans covers an area of about 5 770 km², of which 1 750 km² is water, in the form of rivers, canals, and creeks. It also represents about 44% of the total forested area of the country, and contributes about 50% of the revenue of the forestry sector (Tamang 1993). The Indian Sundarbans is variously estimated from 3 000 km² to 4 263 km², of which approximately 1 780 km² is water.

The Sundarbans mangrove swamp is of recent origin, formed by eroded soil from the Himalayas carried by the Ganges, Brahmaputra, Meghna, and many other river systems. These rivers deposited their silt at the apex of the Bay of Bengal and gave rise to the Sundarbans. Literally, "Sundarbans" means "beautiful forests"; the name perhaps derived from a common timber tree *sundri* (*Heritiera fomes*), which means "beauty." The word "mangrove" itself is a combination of the Portuguese *mangue* and English "grove," and can refer to an ecological group of holophytic plant communities belonging to 12 genera in eight families, or a complex of plant communities that fringe sheltered tropical shores, or more specifically, according to some authors, the vegetation formation below the high-tide mark (Seidensticker and Hai 1978). The fragile and intricate mangrove ecosystem depends on many variable components, but mainly on water salinity. The most striking adaptations of the mangrove plants are the various forms of aerial roots necessary to meet the oxygen requirements for respiration. Three ecological zones, the freshwater zone, the moderately saline water zone, and the saline water zone, can be distinguished in the Sundarbans according to salinity and species composition.

The mean annual rainfall in the Sundarbans varies from 1 600 mm to 2 790 mm. The annual temperature varies from 20°C (December-January) to 35°C (May-June). The mean annual relative humidity varies between 70%-88%.

Although there are other extensive mangrove zones within some of the major tropical wilderness areas (Amazonia, New Guinea, Congo), the Sundarbans is the only area comprised exclusively of mangroves to be profiled in this book.

Biodiversity

Unlike other mangrove forests, the Sundarbans is rich in biodiversity, especially in mangrove-oriented species. One reason for this richness is that the Sundarbans is both a tropical moist forest and a wetland with mudflats and beaches. Plant diversity in the Sundarbans is relatively well documented. A total of 334 species of vascular plants belonging to 245 genera have been recorded from the Sundarbans and adjoining forests (Prain 1903), of which at least 123 are present in the Bangladesh portion (Karim 1994a). The region is particularly rich in mangrove tree species, with about 80% of the known species found in the Bangladesh Sundarbans. *Heritiera fomes, Excoecaria agallocha,* and *Sonneratia apetala* are the most common. There are also 12 species of shrubs or scandent shrubs, 11 species of climbers, 13 species of orchids, and seven epiphytic ferns (Karim 1994a).

- ■ Sundarbans
- ■ National Park
- ■ Wildlife Sanctuary

On the opposite page, pugmarks of a tiger in the Sundarbans. Although this region has one of the world's largest remaining tiger populations, this is usually all one sees of this elusive predator.

*On pp. 282-283, chital deer (Axis axis) crossing a mangrove swamp.
Both photos:*
© **Gertrud & Helmut Denzau**

281

and many other organisms. On the Indian side, untreated sewage discharges from Calcutta also represent a considerable threat.

Natural disasters like cyclones also cause considerable damage to the Sundarbans, and are not infrequent: about one tenth of the world's tropical cyclones occur in the Bay of Bengal. Many large trees are blown down and others face major loss of branches and leaves. After the most catastrophic cyclone in 1988, approximately 260 515 m³ of timber and 164 240 m³ of firewood were collected from damaged trees in the Bangladesh Sundarbans (Karim 1994b). Many animals were also killed during this event, including eight tigers.

Conservation

Despite major human pressure on the natural resources of the Sundarbans, the area is still relatively intact and supports fairly healthy populations of plants and animals. This is mainly because of its natural inaccessibility, but fear of man-eating tigers and a growing concern for biodiversity conservation also play a role. In addition, government agencies, like the Bangladesh Forest Department, also make maximum efforts to protect this unique resource and patrol it regularly.

The entire Sundarbans was declared a forest reserve as far back as 1875-1876, and entry without permit was prohibited from that time on. In order to further conserve the biodiversity of the Bangladesh Sundarbans, the Government of Bangladesh established three wildlife sanctuaries (Sundarbans East Wildlife Sanctuary, Sundarbans South Wildlife Sanctuary, and Sundarbans West Wildlife Sanctuary) in 1977. These three sanctuaries initially covered an area of 323.8 km², but this was increased to 1 397 km² in 1996 —almost 14% of the entire region. The following year, in December 1997, UNESCO also declared these a World Heritage Site. In addition, the wildlife of the Bangladesh Sundarbans is protected under the Bangladesh Wildlife (Preservation) (Amendment) Act 1974, and thus should not be killed or captured.

These sanctuaries are primarily for the protection of wildlife, inclusive of all natural resources such as vegetation, soil, and water. The Government of Bangladesh, with other national and international partners, also runs several projects in the Bangladesh Sundarbans. These provide scientific guidelines and on-the-ground efforts on behalf of biodiversity conservation on the Bangladesh side, including the Sundarbans Wildlife Management Plan, Conservation in the Bangladesh Coastal Zone, Integrated Resource Development of the Sundarbans Reserved Forest, Development of Wildlife Conservation and Management, Project Tiger, Forest Resource Management Project, and the Biodiversity Conservation in the Sundarbans Project. In addition, there are several small-scale captive-breeding programs for spotted deer and estuarine crocodiles at Karamjal in the Bangladesh Sundarbans, as well as special measures

to protect the habitats of the estuarine crocodile in Mrigamari and several other sites.

On the Indian side, the entire Indian Sundarbans and its surrounding area (south of the Dampier-Hodges Line) has been declared a Biosphere Reserve. The total area of this reserve is 9 630 km², of which mangrove forests cover 3 000-4 263 km². This reserve has four zones: a core zone, a manipulation zone, a restoration zone, and a development zone. It supports the largest single tiger population in India, and also has populations of a number of other nationally-threatened species such as the fishing cat (*Prionailurus viverrinus*), estuarine crocodile, olive ridley turtle (*Lepidochelys olivacea*), river terrapin (*Batagur baska*), and several monitor lizards (*Varanus* spp.), with wildlife being protected under the Wildlife Protection Act 1972.

Included within this Biosphere Reserve are one national park and three wildlife sanctuaries. The national park was declared in 1989; it covers 1 330 km², and like its counterparts on the Bangladesh side, has also been recognized as a World Heritage Site. The three wildlife sanctuaries —Sajnakhali, Lothian Island, and Holiday Island— were established in 1976, and cover 406.3 km². These sanctuaries protect a number of plant communities, but were mainly established to serve as refuge for the Bengal tiger and its prey. To provide further protection, a total of 2 585 km² of the Indian Sundarbans was set aside under Project Tiger in 1973, and declared the Sundarbans Tiger Reserve. This reserve has been successful in that the tiger population there has at least remained stable or perhaps even increased.

Finally, the Government of West Bengal, under its Integrated Wasteland Project, has also initiated ecological restoration of 247.5 km² of degraded forests and 27.5 km² of cleared land and mud flats in the Indian Sundarbans and has undertaken captive-breeding and reintroduction programs for the estuarine crocodile and the olive ridley turtle (Chaudhuri and Choudhury 1994).

Looking at the region as a whole, 3 133 km² —or over 30%— is protected under either national parks or wildlife sanctuaries, with the entire Indian side receiving additional recognition as a Biosphere Reserve.

Ultimately, the future of the Sundarbans will depend on strong commitment by the governments of Bangladesh and India and active participation by the international conservation community —all of which will be needed to ensure proper management, restoration, and other critical activities. However, in spite of the many pressures, the prospects for maintaining this wilderness in one of the most densely-populated regions on Earth appear to be quite good.

M. MONIRUL H. KHAN

Above, firewood collected by local people.

On the opposite page, honey gatherers in the Sundarbans. The face mask on the back of the head of each man is intended to frighten off tigers, which often attack from behind.
*Both photos: © **Rajesh Bedi***

THE SUDD

The Sudd Swamp, Africa's most extensive swamp floodplain, is located in the southern part of Sudan, the largest country in Africa. It is one of the most extensive ecosystems of this kind in the world, considerably larger than Botswana's Okavango Delta, and second only to the huge Pantanal region of central Brazil, Bolivia, and Paraguay. The source of the Sudd is the White Nile (also known as the Albert Nile, the Victoria Nile, and the Bahr-el-Jebel). During the rainy season, the White Nile floods an area of about 30 000 km² (roughly twice that of the Okavango). Associated ecosystems extend much further, covering a total area of about 179 700 km². Although it is difficult to assess the current status of the Sudd, we estimate that more than 85% of it remains intact. The name "Sudd Swamp," which we use in this chapter, seems to be the one most frequently utilized for this amazing wetland system, but WWF's global ecoregion analysis lists it as the "Saharan Flooded Grasslands" (AT0905).

This vast wilderness is most famous for its migratory birds, its resident wetland birds, its antelopes, and for harboring some of the greatest large mammal concentrations on Earth. While there was some interest in the wildlife of the Sudd after Sudan's first civil war, both political unrest and the onset of Sudan's second conflict have made access very difficult. As a result of Sudan's two civil wars (from 1956-1972 and from 1983 to date), which have resulted in more than two million deaths, we know relatively little about what still exists in the Sudd today. However, we do know that biodiversity has suffered as a result of the conflict, as the proliferation of small arms has facilitated an increased use of wildlife for subsistence. The development of oil fields, lack of strong governance (and hence protection of resources), and the construction of the massive Jonglei Canal have also contributed to a huge loss of biodiversity in this region. Nonetheless, there is now renewed hope for conservation of this area, as local nongovernmental organizations (e.g., the New Sudan Wildlife Society), international conservation organizations, foreign donors, and governments rekindle interest in Sudan's natural resources and are once again launching initiatives to help preserve this massive wilderness area. We hope that this chapter can contribute to growing international interest in the Sudd.

Biodiversity

The Sudd Swamps are situated within the arid Sahelian region of Africa, and are thus a very important area for many species of migratory birds. Between these migratory birds and resident wetland bird populations, some 419 bird species are found here (WWF, in prep.). Although none of these are endemic, they include a number of important species like the great white pelican (*Pelecanus onocrotalus*), black crowned-crane (*Balearica pavonina*), and the largest population of the shoebill (*Balaeniceps rex*) in the world.

In terms of mammals, there are 91 species known from the Sudd, of which one is endemic (WWF, in prep.). Although the current status of herds there is not known, in the 1980s the southern Sudan was thought to hold some of the largest populations of antelope in all of Africa. One of these antelope species, the Nile lechwe (*Kobus megaceros*), is the only mammal endemic to the Sudd. Three other subspecies —the white-eared kob (*Kobus kob leucotis*), the tiang (*Damaliscus lunatus tiang*), and the Mongalla gazelle (*Gazella thomsonii albonotata*)— are known to undertake extensive migrations across the greater Sudd ecosystem following the change in the vegetation as a result of the rains. Other antelope species found in the Sudd include the sitatunga (*Tragelaphus spekii*), bushbuck (*T. scriptus*), waterbuck (*Kobus ellipsiprymnus*), roan antelope (*Hippotragus equinus*), bohar reedbuck (*Redunca redunca*), and hartebeest (*Alcelaphus buselaphus*) (Hillman and Fryxell 1988).

Wilderness Area

On the opposite page, the Nile River in the Sudd region.
© Kazuyoshi Nomachi

291

Much less is known about the reptiles and amphibians of this area, but there are at least 24 reptile species, including one endemic snake (*Chilorhinophis butleri*), and at least seven amphibian species, none of them endemic (WWF, in prep.).

The Sudd ecosystem is made up of wetlands, grasslands, and woodlands. The wetlands are composed of flowing waters, lakes, and permanent swamps. The permanent swamps are characterized as *Vossia cuspidate* swamps, *Cyperus papyrus* swamps or *Typha domingensis* swamps, depending on which species is dominant. The grasslands are either seasonally river-flooded or sea-

Tiang were among the most abundant of the wild herbivores in the Sudd. A program of reconnaissance flights during the Jonglei Canal Project provided more information on the migration routes of this species. The study revealed that while both the tiang and the white-eared kob spent the wet season in more or less the same area to the southeast, they then migrated in different directions during the dry season: the white-eared kob heading northeast to the floodplains of the Pibor River, while the tiang moved northwest to the Nile floodplains (Howell et al. 1988).

As for birds, the Sudd Swamps are one of the most

Above, the Dinka and other Nilotic tribes of the Sudd are the tallest people on Earth.
© **Ramón Llano**

On the opposite page, Dinka with Nile lechwe head.
© **Kazuyoshi Nomachi**

are representative of the entire region given that the Khartoum-Juba road, which passes along the ridge by the Jonglei Canal line, has been the scene of much military activity in the last 19 years.

Another threat to the Sudd has been the construction of the Jonglei Canal (Stuart et al. 1990), which was designed to channel water from the White Nile as it passes through the Sudd Swamp for irrigation and other purposes downstream. Construction began in 1978, but was stopped in 1984 due to the outbreak of the second civil war, and because of controversy over the benefits of the canal. The canal currently extends for 260 km of a planned 360 km, with a width of 75 m and a depth of 4-8 m. Although incomplete, it has nonetheless acted as a trap for wildlife attempting to cross it. Today the banks are eroding and the canal is filling with vegetation, but if it is ever completed, the resulting diversions would likely cause the Sudd Swamp and associated floodplains to shrink dramatically, reducing grazing areas for ungulates and threatening many other species. Siltation would also likely occur and, when combined with possible changes in climate, groundwater recharges, and water quality, could have severe impacts on local people as well as on wildlife.

In addition, there has been a growing outcry against the tactics used by the government forces in the oil fields of Western Upper Nile —the Western part of the Sudd. There are indications of a scorched earth policy, which has most likely had a severe impact on the animal as well as human inhabitants. Fighting amongst Nuer rebel groups and a recurrence of the disease Kala Azar, better known as leishmaniasis, have also caused many Nuer to flee to neighboring areas of Bahr el Ghazal. The oil companies involved have not published any environmental impact analysis. However, the oil fields are now the main battleground in the civil war and it is possible that as much as 15% of once-protected areas have been lost to the effects of war, though estimates must be treated with caution until conditions allow proper environmental surveys.

Conservation

Protected areas in the Sudd region include three Game Reserves, Zeraf Island (970 000 ha), Fanyikang (48 000 ha), and Shambe (62 000 ha), giving a total of 10 800 km², representing approximately 6% of the overall area of the Sudd. Although not directly in the Sudd, parts of Boma and Badingilo National Parks are affected by what happens in and around the Sudd, insofar as their ecosystems are adjacent and connected to the Sudd Swamp. Unfortunately, protection for these areas now exists largely in theory only, and rehabilitation of park infrastructure, both physical and administrative, will be one of the first priorities when stability returns to the region.

In the near term, one of the highest priorities for the Sudd Swamp region is to carry out further survey work to determine the status of what still exists. The Boma National Park survey mentioned above is an important step, but much more information on the Sudd's wildlife, hydrology,

and the social dynamics and structure of the human communities within the area is necessary to determine what conservation activities are feasible before a comprehensive action plan for this region can be developed.

It is important for donors and conservation organizations to begin supporting conservation activities as soon as possible. Despite the conflict, surveys can be conducted using the existing logistical infrastructure of relief operations, including the many airstrips and light aircraft. Better management outside protected areas is also possible, and here too, much can be done. For example, watering holes or points for livestock can be established outside parks, and plans can be created in consultation with local people to reduce concentrations of livestock during the dry season. In addition, tribal chiefs in areas surrounding parks can be appointed as honorary wardens to help spread the message about the importance of wildlife conservation to their communities. Conservation in the region would be a particular challenge in that convincing arguments for the benefits of conservation in the absence of any tourism in the foreseeable future would need to be demonstrated. These kinds of efforts could be conducted in parallel with ongoing conflict resolution efforts and negotiations for reductions in cattle raising.

Moreover, it would also be important to postpone development of the Jonglei Canal until there is agreement on its potential social and environmental impacts. Indeed, impact assessments are a standard feature of all large-scale infrastructure projects. For example, environmental impact studies on similar plans to make major changes in the hydrology of other great wetlands such as the Pantanal and the Okavango have indicated that they would have drastic consequences for wildlife and local communities, and so such plans have met with strong opposition from the international community as well as from local institutions.

Finally, in the longer term, sustainable conservation efforts will obviously require clearer policies and management guidelines, a stronger legal framework for the protection of wildlife, training of wildlife personnel, and adequate resources. These, in turn, will necessitate a political settlement of the causes of the civil war. It is important, however, not to neglect the potential and possibility for immediate action. Humanitarian organizations continue to maintain a presence on the ground, demonstrating that work can be conducted in this area despite the conflict. The link between human welfare and natural resources is inextricable, and therefore the efforts to conserve biodiversity in the Sudd should not only be seen as important for conservation, but also as part of a major humanitarian effort.

REBECCA HAM
JOHN PILGRIM
PHILIP WINTER
FIESTA WARINWA
CYRIL KORMOS

THE OKAVANGO

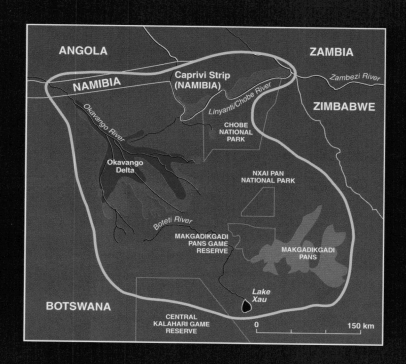

The Okavango Delta of Botswana is one of the world's great wilderness wetlands, and one of three huge inland deltas in Africa (McCarthy 1993), the other two being the Sudd in the southern Sudan and the Niger Inland Delta. It covers approximately 16 000 km² in north-central Botswana, and consists of the inland delta (or alluvial fan) of the Okavango River, a watercourse of some 1 430 km that arises in Angola. A real wetland wilderness, the Okavango Delta is still 75% or more intact. Like the Pantanal region in South America, it is a huge wetland surrounded by a series of dry forest-woodland savanna-grassland formations, in this case the Miombo-Mopane Woodlands and Grasslands. Although these woodlands and the Okavango ecosystems are ecologically intertwined, we separate them for the purposes of this book. Here we treat the Okavango wilderness to include a number of associated seasonal wetlands, including the Makgadikgadi Pans and Linyanti Swamp. WWF, in their global classification of ecoregions, includes the Okavango Delta as just one component of a much larger ecoregion that they call Zambezian Flooded Grasslands (AT 0907) (WWF 2001). However, we consider it important enough to highlight as a major wilderness in its own right.

The Delta and most of its catchment lie on fragile Kalahari sands which, given their permeability and transportability, determine much of the physical ecology of the Delta. The catchment area covers some 150 000 km², and is distributed over three countries, Angola, Botswana, and Namibia, making international collaboration critical in the conservation of the region. In all, the Delta is 175 km long and absorbs an annual sediment load of 727 000 tons. The Upper Delta, known as "the Panhandle" owing to its shape relative to the rest of the Delta, is a 90-km stretch of reed beds and river channels, and has 95% of the region's sediment deposition. The Panhandle breaks up into a variety of channels feeding into a constantly-changing mosaic of dryland islands, meandering channels, reed beds, and seasonal and permanent swamps (Ross 1988).

The average inflow to the Delta is 10 600 million cubic meters per year (McCarthy 1993), while out-

flow averages 212 million cubic meters. The lowest flow to the Delta was recorded in 1941 at 7 200 million cubic meters, while the highest was 16 200 m³ in 1963. It is estimated that 96% of the water entering the Delta is lost to evapotranspiration and 2% to infiltration, while 2% emerges from the Delta in the Boteti-Thamalakane River.

Geologically, the Delta is bounded on the south by a series of northeast-trending faults, an extension of the African Rift Valley (Ross, *op. cit.*). The wetlands of the Delta form in the low basin northwest of these faults. Shifting along these faults has created, in historic times, changing channels between the Delta and peripheral swamps such as the Savuti and Lake Ngami. Fault movement is also believed to play an important role in the channel shifting which is characteristic of the interior Delta.

The hydrology of the Delta is dominated by an annual flood, which peaks after the high rainfall months in Angola. The rains in Botswana fall mainly between November and March, and are locally important in the ecology of the Delta as well. The dominant hydrological feature is a flood tide from the peaking Okavango, which takes some five months to traverse the Delta. The flood peak reaches the upper Delta in February to March, coinciding in this area with the local rains. As the flood reaches the intricate channels and wetlands of the Delta, it moves slowly through them from northwest to southeast over the next five months (Ross, *op. cit.*). When the flood peak reaches the foot of the Delta in July-

■ Salt Pans
■ Flood Plains
■ Perennial Swamps
— Wilderness boundary

On the opposite page, a young Nile crocodile (Crocodylus niloticus) sunning on a mat of papyrus, Moremi Game Reserve, Botswana.

On pp. 300-301, herd of African elephant (Loxodonta africana) at the Chobe River, Chobe National Park, Botswana.
Both photos:
© *Patricio Robles Gil/Sierra Madre*

August, it is the dry season in Botswana. The flood brings life-giving water to a parched land. It is this juxtaposition of flood peak and dry season that makes the Delta so important to wildlife. Before the construction of

ta), the marsh mongoose (*Atilax paludinosus*), the slender mongoose (*Galerella sanguinea*), and the white-tailed mongoose (*Ichneumia albicauda*) occur in a variety of different habitats (Ross 1988). Of particular note is the

Flagship Species

The Delta is rich in flagship species. In international terms, its populations of African wild dog and cheetah are probably the most important, with elephant also being of global significance. The cheetah population in Botswana is probably the second largest in the world, after Namibia, and the Okavango is critical for the survival of this threatened cat. The African wild dog has now gone extinct through much of its former range and hangs on only in a handful of areas. The entire remaining world population has only some 3 000-5 500 individuals in perhaps 600-1 000 packs, of which some 400-600 occur within the Delta. The most important area for wild dogs is in the north of Botswana, in an area of 176 000 km² in the Ngamiland, Central, and Chobe districts. This area includes the Okavango Delta, the Chobe-Linyanti River system, the Moremi Game Reserve, Nxai Pan National Park, and the Chobe National Park. It is estimated that the population in this area is 42 packs, with about 450-500 individuals (Fanshawe et al. 1997).

In 1989, J.W. McNutt began a study of wild dogs in a 2 600-km² livestock-free area in and around the Moremi Game Reserve. This area has supported as many as 13 packs, totaling 109 yearlings and adults, although the number varies from year to year. This outstanding study, supported in part by Conservation International, is the longest running of its kind on this critically-important flagship species (Conniff 1999; McNutt and Boggs 1997).

Under the Fauna Conservation Act, dogs may not be hunted without a permit. However, such permits are not required if a farmer is defending livestock, and officials rarely investigate reported hunting very closely. Thus, wild dogs receive only partial legal protection; in practice, wild dogs straying onto farms are shot on sight (Fanshawe et al., *op. cit.*).

The elephant population is also noteworthy, with some 10 000-20 000 in the Delta and environs. In fact, during an aerial survey undertaken by Conservation International and the University of Massachusetts in 2000, the first-ever aerial survey of the Okavango Delta undertaken by an NGO, between 25 000 and 30 000 elephants were recorded (Burm and Griffin 2000). Elephant numbers have increased since their protection in 1983, resulting in what is probably the largest and least disturbed elephant population remaining in Africa.

Among the reptiles, the Nile crocodile (*Crocodylus niloticus*) is particularly important and common. Most of the Delta's crocodiles live and breed along the Panhandle, where deep water and an abundance of fish make for excellent crocodile habitat.

A creature of the night, and perhaps a symbol of all that is special about the Okavango Delta, is the magnificent Pel's fishing owl (*Scotopelia peli*). These rufous-colored owls are entirely nocturnal and superbly-adapted fishing birds. Solitary or living in breeding pairs, their preferred roosts are in the tall *mokutshumo* and fig trees that grace the banks. Pel's owl is a skillful fishing bird, catching prey up to 2 kg in weight and eating almost nothing but fish. This bird is difficult to see in the daytime, but the presence of fish skeletons on the ground is a sure sign of the feeding perch of this owl.

Human Cultures

The Okavango Delta has been inhabited for at least 100 000 years. Different San groups including the Banoka (River People) were the first to settle in the region. Today, the Delta is home to some 59 000 people, for a human population density of 3.7 inhabitants/km². They belong to five ethnic groups, each with its own identity and language and with a number of subgroups, and include the Bugakwe (Kxoe, Bugakhoe, Kwengo, Barakwena, Mbarakwena, Mbarakwengo, G/anda, /anda), the Dxeriku (Dceriku, Diriku, Gceriku, Gciriku, Vagciriku, Giriku, Mbogedo, Niriku, Vamanyo), the Hambukushu (Mbukushu, Bukushu, Bukusu, Mbukuschu, Mamakush, Mampakush, Ghuva, Haghuva, Gova, Cusso, Kusso, Hakokohu, Havamasiko), the Wayeyi (Bayei, Bayeyi, Bakoba, Bajei, Jo, Hajo, Tjaube, Yei), and the Xanekwe (Gxanekwe, //anekwe, tannekhoe, River Bushmen, Swamp Bushmen, G//ani, //ani, Banoka). The Hambukushu, Dxeriku, and Wayeyi are Bantus who survive through a mixed economic strategy of millet/sorghum agriculture, fishing, hunting, collection of wild plant foods, and pastoralism. The Bugakwe and Xanekwe are Bushmen, also called San or Basarwa, the aboriginal inhabitants of southern Africa. They live in small groups as nomadic hunter-gatherers, with the Bugakwe utilizing both forest and riverine resources and the Xanekwe mostly focused on riverine resources. Over the last 20 years, many people from all over the Okavango have migrated to Maun, and in the late 1960s and early 1970s over 4 000 Hambukushu refugees from Angola were settled in the area around Etsha in the western Panhandle. The Okavango Delta has been under the political control of the Batawana (a Tswana subtribe) for several hundred years. Most Batawana, however, have traditionally lived on the edges of the Delta, where they are customarily savanna pastoralists, and there are very few of them. Small numbers of people from other ethnic groups such as the Ovaherero and Ovambanderu also live in the Okavango Delta. There are also several other Bushmen groups represented by a handful of people. These groups were decimated last century by diseases of contact, and most of the remaining members have intermarried with the Xanekwe (Bock 1993).

During the first half of the eighteenth century, the expansion of the Balozi State north of present-day Botswana caused both BaYei and HaMbukushu to move into the Okavango Delta. While the BaYei settled along the southeastern edge of the Delta as well as the north, the HaMbukushu settled north of Gumare (Panhandle).

On the opposite page, African wild dog (Lycaon pictus). *This region is one of the last strongholds for this Critically Endangered predator.*

Above, gray go-away bird (Corythaixoides concolor). *Both photos:*
© **Patricio Robles Gil**/*Sierra Madre*

305

The BaYei brought with them the *mokoro* (dug-out canoe), which enabled them to penetrate into the Delta.

A century later, during the early 1800s, a succession dispute led to a split in the BaNgwato tribe in the east of Botswana. The group led by Kgosi Tawana eventually moved northwest to Lake Ngami and established the village of Toteng (Tlou 1985), bringing their cattle herds with them. Kgosi Tawana's group, the Batawana, expanded and incorporated all the people of the Okavango. During the early 1900s they began settling in Maun, which became and is still the area's major center.

At the beginning of the twentieth century, unhappy with German rule and land expropriation in Namibia, the Ovaherero immigrated to the southwestern side of the Okavango Delta (Campbell, *op. cit.*). Like the Batawana, they brought their large cattle herds.

Under the influence of these two groups (Batawana and Ovaherero), land use changed from being mainly hunter-gatherer and arable land agriculture to being predominantly livestock-oriented. As a result, people's settlement patterns became dependent on cattle-related issues such as the presence (or absence) of the tsetse fly, outbreaks of rinderpest, and foot and mouth diseases.

Threats

The biggest threat to the future of the Okavango Delta involves water withdrawal and flow interruption. The Delta lies at the lowest end of the river basin, with its waters rising in the highlands of southern Angola and flowing through Namibia. It is surrounded by arid and semiarid lands where water is in constant demand for livestock rearing, agriculture, potential hydropower development, and basic human use, which means the threat of water withdrawal will likely never go away. Needless to say, any reduction in water flow to any part of the Delta would alter seasonal flooding and water availability to wildlife, and would dramatically change the nature of the region (Ross 1988).

Plans to exploit the water resources of the Okavango date back nearly a century, when the first colonial administrators were drawn by the lure of larger water supplies in an arid land. A proposal made in 1918 suggested shifting the waters of the Okavango, Cunene, and Chobe Rivers to form a huge inland lake that would alter regional climate, increase rainfall, and make the area more suitable for agriculture (McCarthy and Ellery 1993). This plan was abandoned, but variations were proposed and rejected on and off until the 1940s. Small-scale water diversions and dredging have been implemented in the past 50-60 years, and a medium-scale water development plan was proposed and later withdrawn in the late 1980s.

The next biggest threat to the Okavango region is from wildlife fences. Botswana has had a long history of fence construction. Most were built to comply with strict EU disease-control regulations, which required that cattle be separated from wildlife because of possible disease infections. Since Botswana receives 60% more than the world market price for its exports to the EU, they are keen to comply. Fences have crisscrossed wilderness areas, impacting wildlife as they seek water and forage in this arid environment. Many wildlife deaths have occurred over the years, mainly impacting the central, southern, and eastern parts of the country, while the Okavango was left relatively undisturbed. However, in 1995, another cattle epidemic broke out, in Ngamiland, in the Okavango region, giving rise to a national crisis. The disease "jumped" all three fences, and threatened the national herd to the south, making it necessary to kill the entire Ngamiland herd of 320 000 head. To ensure there would be no further incursions from Namibia, the entire Namibia/Botswana border was fenced in 1996, including the extension of the Northern Buffalo Fence to the border. This isolated a large part of the Okavango ecosystem from the main Delta, and blocked important community and wildlife movement areas between the Okavango and the Caprivi Strip (Ross and Magole 2000).

In response, Conservation International-Botswana liaised with the Department of Animal Health and Production, and was instrumental in the formation of Botswana's first forum to discuss fence issues. This multisectoral group, called the Ad Hoc Committee on Fences (AHCOF), included several key government departments (Department of Animal Health and Production, Department of Wildlife, National Conservation Strategy Agency) and NGOs (CI and the Kalahari Conservation Society). As a result of the deliberations of AHCOF, and subsequent actions by Botswana's cabinet, 50 km of the Caprivi Fence were removed, thus partially opening a vital wildlife corridor between Botswana and Namibia (Conservation International 2000a). Equally significant was the Ministry of Agriculture's decision to commission a retrospective Environmental Impact Assessment (EIA) on Okavango fences, partly funded by the Department for International Development (DFID). This critical study was completed by the end of October 2000. All AHCOF members, including a larger representation of both government and NGOs, acted as the Reference Group for the study. The commissioning of this study is very much to the Government of Botswana's credit. The EIA's findings recommended that several fences in the north be realigned or moved, thus reestablishing important wildlife corridors. A major aim of CI in the future will be to assist the Government and ensure that the fences are realigned as recommended.

Other threats to the region also deserve mention. Sediment interruption is a major potential threat, given the importance of sediment in driving the formation of channels and islands in the delta. Such interruption would occur from poorly-conceived upstream waterworks, in particular the construction of dams that would trap sediment and reduce influx to the Delta. Chemical

Above, leopard (Panthera pardus).
© **Karen Ross**

On the opposite page, aerial view of wetlands and forest islands in the Okavango.
© **Konrad Wothe**

inputs, either in the form of nutrients or pesticides, could also have a major impact. Although not a current issue, upstream agricultural development could lead to problems in the future, resulting in changes in vegetation structure in the Panhandle and altering channel dynamics. Pesticide application for tsetse fly eradication may have an impact as well, although this remains largely unquantified (Ross 1988). The natural system had a welcome respite for 10 years, when odor-baited tsetse traps were scattered throughout the Delta and used as a control measure instead. Unfortunately these were not always effective, although much is blamed on the difficulty of servicing the traps in more remote parts of the Delta. In 2001, aerial spraying for tsetse commenced again. For the first time, an Environmental Impact Assessment preceded the program, and concluded that applications of pesticide were low enough so as not to be a significant threat to the natural system. In addition, and also for the first time, impacts will be monitored by the Okavango Research Center (Wildson 2001).

Aquatic weed invasion is also a serious and growing problem in the Delta, with *Salvinia* being the greatest recognized threat. This introduced weed, native to South America, first entered the Delta nearly two decades ago. Initially, rapid response on the part of the government, including draining of infested lagoons and introduction of biological controls in the form of a weevil imported from South America, kept it largely in check. Unfortunately, in recent years, this control has lapsed and major infestations of *Salvinia* have become common throughout the Santantadibe area and are spreading rapidly. The presence of hippopotamus, which move freely through the Delta and often inadvertently carry vegetation on their backs, has hastened the spread. Although the biological control using weevils has been relatively successful, there are concerns that the aerial tsetse-spraying program might also kill the weevils.

Overfishing has become an issue in the Delta over the past decade, and commercial fishing operations using powerboats and fine-mesh nets are beginning to displace traditional practices. This has led to a series of impacts, including destruction of riverine vegetation (which is cut down to dry the fish), disturbance of aquatic species by powerboats, and killing of noncommercial species in nets (Conservation International 2000b).

Hunting has been an issue as well. Poorly-controlled citizen hunting and professional hunting, combined with a license system which allows for trading of individual permits and gives permits to people from outside the Delta region, has resulted in widespread concerns about the viability of hunting in the heart of the Delta. While empirical data proving the loss of wildlife numbers is incomplete, research has indicated a threat to the lion population, which has resulted in the Government's Wildlife Department placing a moratorium on the hunting of lions.

Conservation

At this time, only one protected area of IUCN Category II or higher currently exists within the Delta, the 487 100-ha Moremi Game Reserve, which covers 30.4% of the region. This important protected area, composed of tribal land set aside by the Batawana people for conservation, is administered by the Department of Wildlife and National Parks. Almost all of the rest of the Okavango Delta is under partial protection in Wildlife Management Areas or Controlled Hunting Areas, which are cattle-free zones. In addition, the Delta was designated a Ramsar site in 1996 —it currently is the largest Ramsar site in the world.

However, given the complex dynamics of the Okavango Delta, no single park or reserve or even a series of discrete protected areas can adequately represent and maintain the biological and physical diversity of the region. Rather, as should be obvious from the preceding discussion, it is critical that the entire region, including its catchment area in the two neighboring countries, be effectively protected and maintained in a more holistic and far-reaching way. This has been the rationale for the development of a strategy that encompasses the entire Okavango River Basin (Conservation International 2000a). This strategy suggests that the entire region be recognized as a megacorridor, or a Trans-Frontier Conservation Area, and that it receive international recognition as a World Heritage Site. That said, there are certainly portions of the Delta, notably the narrow and fragile Panhandle through which all of the region's water flows before reaching the main part of the Delta, that could benefit from more intensive protection —something that could be carried out hand in hand with broader efforts for the region as a whole (Conservation International, *op. cit.*).

Ultimately, the most important conservation measure for the Okavango will be careful international planning to limit upstream water development. Dam development in the three countries of the catchment area should be assiduously avoided, and water withdrawal should be kept to an absolute minimum. Botswana, Namibia, and Angola took a major step towards coordinated planning of the Okavango in September of 1994, with the signing of the Okavango River Basin Water Commission (OKACOM). This nine-member commission is composed of three representatives from each of the three party countries, and meets at least twice a year to recommend developments and investigate impacts of surface and subsurface water use (OKACOM 1994).

Conservationists have for some time been concerned about aspects of Namibia's Master Water Plan. Scheduled for 2003, it includes the construction of a 300-km pipeline from the Okavango River to deliver water through the desert to their capital city of Windhoek. In 1996, Namibia was in the grips of a prolonged drought and the government announced emergency plans to build the pipeline. Delegates from CI-Botswana and the

On the opposite page, southern carmine bee-eater (Merops nubicoides), a strikingly beautiful species that is common in the Okavango and can be seen in large colonies nesting in holes in the riverbanks.

Above, lilac-breasted roller (Coracias caudata). Both photos:
© **Patricio Robles Gil**/*Sierra Madre*

309

Kalahari Conservation Society (KCS) traveled to Windhoek to attend the first public meeting on this pipeline, at which point it became clear that no Environmental Impact Assessment (EIA) was planned for the Delta. In response, CI and KCS founded a consortium of concerned NGOs, called the Okavango Liaison Group (OLG). Their first action was to call for an EIA. The Botswana Government carried this message forward, and Namibia's Department of Water agreed to undertake such a study. Meanwhile, CI's International Communications Department produced a 10-minute video news release, which was presented at the 1996 IUCN World Conservation Congress in Montreal and was also aired to the public on CNN and many of the world's major television stations. This video had considerable impact, but ultimately the arrival of a good rainy season in 1996, which filled Namibia's dams, was what temporarily averted the crisis.

The saga continued. With plans for the pipeline only temporarily on hold, CI continued its efforts by commissioning a study from a Namibian hydrogeologist and the International Rivers Network (IRN). This study identified ways in which Namibia could meet emergency water requirements without going to the Okavango River (Rothert 1999). At the same time, the Okavango Liaison Group continued to raise awareness and build consensus among communities in the Okavango. In October of 1999, the Paramount Chief of the Okavango communities, Chief Tawana Moremi II, traveled to Windhoek and presented the CI/IRN report to the Namibian government on behalf of his people.

This effort to raise awareness paid off, with multiple airings of the video material peaking people's concern for the Okavango. The CI/IRN report on water alternatives also caught the attention of the head of Namibia's Water Authority (NamWater), who commissioned additional studies to reexamine Windhoek's water demands and to look at deep groundwater resources. The NamWater studies were completed in June of 2000, with better results than expected. Windhoek's city water demand was found to be less than previously calculated and new deep groundwater sources were also discovered. As a result, plans for the pipeline have been shelved for at least 10 to 12 years, and a crisis for the Okavango Delta has again been temporarily averted.

Increasing community benefit from the Delta's resources is another critical conservation measure, with ecotourism being a particularly important alternative. Tourism is currently the second largest foreign exchange earner in Botswana, slightly ahead of livestock and well behind diamond production, with the Okavango and northern Botswana contributing the majority of this income. Ecotourism is a major source of employment and revenue, and should be used to create direct incentives for conservation in the region. However, until now, benefits to local communities have been relatively limited, since many of the best tourist sites are far from the local communities, which are located mainly at the periphery of the Delta. One of the best places to integrate tourism with communities is in the critically-important Panhandle, where communities and tourist resorts exist side by side.

Environmental education is also a top priority because it will help ensure that people living within the Okavango appreciate its long-term importance. Conservation International has been pioneering a program for local schoolchildren in the Delta for 10 years now, and it has had considerable success. Conservation International's Botswana Program founded the first Environmental Education Fair, in which all the region's schools and schoolchildren participate in a celebration of their environment through poetry, quizzes, plays, paintings, and other competitions. This annual event has now been embraced by the school community and is running into its eighth year. CI has also partnered with the Department of Wildlife in the development of an Education Center in Maun Park, site of a primary school outdoor education program.

All things considered, the Okavango Delta is still in remarkably intact condition and ranks as one of the most important wetland wildernesses on Earth. With vision and careful planning, there is no reason why it can't continue as it is for many generations to come.

KAREN ROSS
INNOCENT MAGOLE
RUSSELL A. MITTERMEIER
HAROLDO CASTRO

Above, basket fishing in the Okavango. The people of the region are expert basketmakers.
© **Frans Lanting**

On the opposite page, pied kingfisher (Ceryle rudis).
© **Patricio Robles Gil**/*Sierra Madre*

THE NORTH AMERICAN DESERTS

The Deserts of North America are the richest and most diverse in the world in biological terms. Together, they are home to a minimum of 5 740 vascular plant species, of which at least 3 240 are endemic, far higher than the next richest deserts, the Australian Deserts (3 000 species, 150 endemic), the Central Asian Deserts (2 500 species, 750 endemic), and the Arabian Deserts (3 300 species, 340 endemic). Vertebrate richness is also significant, with a total of 714 non-fish vertebrates, of which 136 are endemic. In this category, only the Australian Deserts, with 818 non-fish vertebrates of which 105 are endemic, can compare.

The North American Deserts also top the world list in certain categories of organisms, the most noteworthy being the Cactaceae, the majority of which occur within this region.

This diversity is also compressed into a much smaller area than the other major desert regions covered in this book, the 1 416 134 km^2 of the North American Desert wilderness areas being only 13% the size of the Sahara/Sahel, 24% the size of the Central Asian Deserts, 40% the size of the Australian Deserts, and 44% the size of the Arabian Deserts.

Given their importance, we treat each of these North American Deserts as separate chapters in this book: the Sonoran/Baja Californian Desert complex, the Chihuahuan Desert, the Mojave Desert, and the Colorado Plateau, with some of the most spectacular natural wonders on our planet.

However, in the analysis section, we lump together the biodiversity of these four regions to make them

directly comparable to the other major desert regions of Asia, Africa, and Australia.

This places them among the five biologically richest wilderness areas on Earth, in an elite category with Amazonia, the Congo Forests of Central Africa, the island of New Guinea, and the Miombo/Mopane Woodlands and Grasslands of Southern Africa.

*On the opposite page, mound cactus (*Echinocereus triglochidiatus mojavensis*) and Joshua tree (*Yucca brevifolia*) at sunset, near Kessler Peak, Mojave National Preserve, California, U.S.A.*
© **Jack Dykinga**

THE SONORAN AND BAJA CALIFORNIAN DESERTS

The Sonoran Desert is part of the large North American corridor of arid ecosystems that goes from the southeast of the State of Washington in the United States all the way into the State of Hidalgo in the Mexican Central Plateau, and from central Texas to the Pacific coast of the Peninsula of Baja California. This arid corridor, covering almost a million square kilometers, has been divided into four large deserts: the Great Basin, the Mojave, the Sonoran, and the Chihuahuan. The Greater Sonoran Desert is formed by a series of lowlands, less than 1 000 m high, that surround the Gulf of California, or Sea of Cortés. Although it is a single unit in the U.S., as it progresses into Mexico it forks into a region of continental drylands, known as the Sonoran Desert *sensu stricto*, and a strip of coastal deserts along the Peninsula of Baja California, known as the Baja California Desert.

In this chapter we will discuss these last two wild lands: the Sonoran Desert, which includes the mainland deserts of Arizona, California, and Sonora; and the Baja Californian Desert, which includes the central and southern deserts of the Peninsula —together they form a single continuum of spectacular, largely unspoiled arid ecosystems. This Sonoran-Baja Californian Desert complex, as we define it here, covers 101 291 km² of Baja Californian Desert and 223 009 km² of Sonoran Desert *sensu stricto*. Overall, 29% (93 665 km²) of this wilderness area lies in the U.S., and 71% (230 635 km²) in Mexico. We estimate that up to 80% of the whole wilderness area is still in intact condition.

Due to its unique biogeographic history and its close connections with the tropical dry forests of the southern Mexican Pacific coast, the Sonoran Desert is extremely rich in tree species and giant columnar plants, which give it the appearance of a strangely arborescent arid wilderness, with immense amounts of above-ground plant biomass when compared with other deserts of similar climate. Both the Sonoran and the Chihuahuan Deserts are dappled by a complex series of mountain ranges that emerge like

islands from an ocean of flat, dry sedimentary plains known as *bajadas* and *llanos*. Most of these mountains harbor remnants of the ancestral Madro-Tertiary flora, a set of temperate woodland plants that covered the region since the early Pliocene, some 25 million years ago. Two million years ago, when the Pleistocene brought a warmer and drier climate, desert communities gradually replaced large portions of this woodland. At the end of the last glaciation, some 15 000 years ago, the current deserts took over the plains. However, remnants of the ancestral woodland still survive, like antediluvian castaways, high up in the refuges of the cooler and moister mountains, known as the desert "sky-islands."

The evolutionary history of the Sonoran and Baja Californian Deserts is different in its mode and tem-

Baja Californian Desert

Sonoran Desert

On the opposite page, field of Mexican poppies (Eschscholtzia mexicana) *and lupines* (Lupinus sparsiflorus). *Superstition Mountains, Tonto National Forest, Arizona, U.S.A.*
© **Jack Dykinga**

315

done by Forrest Shreve (Shreve and Wiggins 1975). His classification reflects the way natural selection and evolution have adapted the predominant morphologies and life-forms to the harsh desert environments. He recognized three ecoregions in the Sonoran Desert mainland (the Arizona Uplands, the Plains of Sonora, and the Sonoran Foothills), two ecoregions in the Peninsula of Baja California (the Magdalena Plains and the Vizcaíno Desert), and two shared ecoregions (the Lower Colorado Valley that occupies both the western Sonoran mainland and the northern part of the Gulf Coast in Baja California, and the Central Gulf Coast, a narrow strip along the coasts of the mid-Sea of Cortés). Shreve's outline is still the best ecological description of the Sonoran and Baja Californian Deserts, and we will follow it in the description of this outstanding wilderness area.

The *Lower Colorado Valley* was described as a *microphyllous desert*, i.e., a region with small-leafed plants, such as the creosote bush (*Larrea tridentata*) and the burro bush (*Ambrosia dumosa*). Indeed, these plants are the desert's true xerophytes, the ones that can handle the strongest drought without wilting down. The Lower Colorado is the heart of the Sonoran Desert (Bowden and Dykinga, *op. cit.*; Hayden and Dykinga 1998), a large and extremely arid region with few mountains and large alluvial *bajadas* that form extensive dry plains, home of the Endangered Sonoran pronghorn antelope (*Antilocapra americana sonoriensis*). Here, the extensive sandy areas that border the Sea of Cortés contain several unique animals, among which the desert kangaroo rat (*Dipodomys deserti*) and the sidewinder (*Crotalus cerastes*, a rattlesnake) typify the special adaptations involved in coping with the harsh local conditions. This region has become so dramatically arid during the current interglacial period (i.e., the Holocene) that the dried-up, eastwardly wind-blown sediments of the Colorado River have formed the largest complex of continental sand dunes in the New World, the Gran Desierto de Altar. Apart from the dominant microphylls, the vegetation also includes some stunted desert trees such as ironwood (*Olneya tesota*), paloverdes (*Parkinsonia florida, P. microphylla*), and mesquites (*Prosopis pubescens, P. glandulosa* var. *torreyana*). The scarcity of woody vegetation is compensated by the large abundance of ephemeral plants that sprout after rain flushes, covering the desert with a dense bright mantle of flowers. Indeed, the abundance of seeds in this region is so high that the base of the trophic chain is formed by seed-eating species such as kangaroo rats (*Dipodomys* spp.), pack rats (*Neotoma* spp.), quail (*Callipepla* spp.), and various ants. When the Colorado and Gila Rivers flowed freely (Sykes 1937; Fradkin 1984), before being dammed in the 1930s, a dense network of riparian ecosystems, dominated by cottonwood (*Populus fremontii*), Goodding willow (*Salix gooddingii*), and large mesquites, flourished by the riverbanks, where beavers (*Castor canadensis*) were abundant.

Plants with succulent stems dominate the *Arizona Uplands*, making it a *crassicaulescent desert* (from the Greek *crassos*, succulent; and *caulon*, stem). Eastwards and higher than the Lower Colorado Valley, the uplands receive more precipitation (*ca.* 300 mm on average) and are dominated by prickly pears and chollas (subgenera *Platyopuntia* and *Cylindropuntia,* respectively, within the large genus *Opuntia*), columnar cacti such as the saguaro (*Carnegiea gigantea*), barrel cacti (*Ferocactus*), and paloverdes (mostly *Parkinsonia microphylla*). The vegetation here is more complex, the proportion of perennials increases, and the species richness is higher. The tall columnar saguaro is a flagship that not only gives this ecoregion its distinctive look, but bears an intimate relation with animals that, although not restricted to the ecoregion, represent it very well. Notable among them are the white-winged dove (*Zenaida asiatica*) and the southern long-nosed bat (*Leptonycteris curasoae*), on which many of the local pollination duties fall, and the Gila woodpecker (*Melanerpes uropygialis*), which by excavating nests in saguaros provides essential habitat for secondary cavity nesters.

The *Plains of Sonora* are found south of the Arizona Uplands, in the central lowlands of the State of Sonora. The dominant life-forms here are trees and woody shrubs, thus forming an *arbosuffrutescent desert*. Ironwoods dominate in the arboreal stratum, with the spectacular cindery-green color of the brittlebush leaves (*Encelia farinosa*) standing out from the lower woody scrub. More abundant rainfall (200-400 mm) and less frost allow the Plains to harbor four species of giant columnar cacti: the saguaro, the organ pipe (*Stenocereus thurberi*), the cina (*S. alamosensis*), and the senita (*Lophocereus schottii*). Some elements of clear tropical, southern affinity reach their northernmost range in this subdivision. Such is the case of the genera *Bursera* and *Jacquinia*, and of the striking Willard's acacia (*Acacia willardiana*), the only New World acacia that has evolutionarily lost its compound leaves and photosynthesizes with phyllodes, i.e., special structures derived from flattened petioles. Flagship species of this ecoregion are the elegant quail (*Callipepla douglasii*) and the desert tortoise (*Gopherus agassizii*).

The *Foothills of Sonora* are found eastwards of the Plains, as a series of rolling hills, small ranges, and canyons that run in a NW-SE direction, following the foothills of the magnificent Sierra Madre. The canyons, moister and more protected than the open Plains, harbor the northernmost remnants of the tropical dry deciduous forests of the Mexican Pacific. Considered an *arborescent desert*, this region is rich in woody legumes such as acacias and mesquites, and with dominance of some clearly tropical species such as the giant *cardón-barbón* cactus (*Pachycereus pecten-aboriginum*), lesser kapok tree (*Ceiba acuminata*), morning-glory tree (*Ipomoea arborescens*), tree limberbush (*Jatropha cordata*), the fragrant elephant tree (*Bursera fagaroides*), and guayacán (*Guaiacum coulteri*), among others. The northernmost regular distribution of the jaguar (*Panthera onca*) is found on these canyons, where this rare predator wanders under the cover of the tropical canopies.

On the opposite page, male desert bighorn sheep (Ovis canadensis) on Tiburón Island, Gulf of California.

Above, Xantus' hummingbird (Hylocharis xantusii), endemic to the Baja Peninsula. Both photos:
© **Patricio Robles Gil**/*Sierra Madre*

Some characteristic animals, such as the rufous-winged sparrow (*Aimophila carpalis*) and the Sonoran spiny-tailed iguana (*Ctenosaura hemilopha macrolopha*), are almost entirely endemic to this ecoregion. Some authors have disputed the classification of this region as part of the true Sonoran Desert, as it is really a complex mosaic of dry ranges with lush tropical canyons. However, the intergradation of different ecosystems and the complex fragmentation of the landscape are some of the factors that give the Sonoran Desert its great diversity.

The next subdivision is the *Central Gulf Coast*, a narrow strip of desert lands that occupies almost 800 km of coast in the Sea of Cortés in Baja California and 400 km in the Sonoran coast. Plants with gigantic, fleshy stems and smooth bark dominate it, hence its classification as a *sarcocaulescent desert* (from the Greek *sarcos*: flesh, and *caulon*: stem). Some of the most bizarre desert plants of the American Continent are found here, including the slender, 20-meter-tall boojum tree or *cirio* (*Fouquieria columnaris*) (Humphrey 1974), ocotillos (*Fouquieria splendens* and *F. diguetii*), giant-stemmed *copalquín* (*Pachycormus discolor*) with its brownish-orange smooth bark, elephant tree (*Bursera microphylla*), copal (*B. hindsiana*), lomboy (*Jatropha cinerea*), palo blanco (*Lysiloma candida*) of chalk-white stems, and the gigantic, candelabriform, cardon cactus or *sagüeso* (*Pachycereus pringlei*), together with other less-striking characteristic plants such as the brittlebush (*Encelia farinosa*) and numerous species of chollas and prickly pears. In this subdivision, the contrast between the desert and the sea creates unique microhabitats with abrupt transitions from desert communities to extremely halophytic scrubs that can prosper on pure seawater, into the northernmost mangrove swamps in the hemisphere, and down into the famous underwater sea-grass "prairies" of *Zostera marina*, traditionally harvested by the Seri people. Despite the fact that this bioregion occurs in two disjunct areas separated by the Sea of Cortés, its flagship animals are the same: the bighorn sheep (*Ovis canadensis*) and the desert iguana (*Dipsosaurus dorsalis*), both with different subspecies on each side: *O. c. mexicana* and *D. d. sonoriensis* on the Sonoran side; *O. c. weemsi* and *D. d. dorsalis* on the Baja Californian side.

Continuing on to the Pacific side of Baja California, in the *Vizcaíno Region*, many of the same fleshy-stemmed trees of the Gulf Coast are seen, growing in association with stemless plants with succulent leaves arranged in whorls or "rosettes" (Aschmann 1959). For this reason, Shreve defined this subdivision as a *sarcophyllous desert* (i.e., a desert where fleshy leaves predominate). Many of these succulent rosettes can collect and store water from the coastal fogs that arise as a result of the cold Pacific upwellings. Among them, there are a few species of *Agave*, of sword-like leaves with spiny edges, *Dudleyas*, with rounded leaves of striking white-reddish colors, tree yuccas (*Yucca valida*), and Spanish bayonets (*Y. whipplei*). The influence of the coastal fogs is noticeable in the abundant presence of the epiphytic Spanish moss (*Tillandsia recurvata*) and various lichens. In these cool-

er deserts, the gigantic, erect cardon gives way to dense formations of the smaller, prostrate sour *pitaya* (*Stenocereus gummosus*) in the coastal plains, to brushes of sweet-smelling huizapol (*Ambrosia chenopodifolia*) that covers the hillslopes with a soft, grayish-green mantle, and to the *cochal* (*Myrtillocactus cochal*), a columnar cactus of sweet, myrtle-like fruits whose closer relatives are found in southern Mexico. The lower Vizcaíno Plains, near the Ojo de Liebre coastal lagoon, harbor a low scrub of salt-tolerating plants where the Critically Endangered peninsular pronghorn (*Antilocapra americana peninsularis*) roams, in isolation from its northern Gran Desierto counterpart. Apart from the pronghorn as an obvious flagship species, this ecoregion is also represented by the gray or Baja California thrasher (*Toxostoma cinereum*), the most typically Baja Californian of all birds.

Finally, the *Magdalena Region* subdivision, located to the south of the Vizcaíno, occupies the lower Pacific coast of Baja California. The influence of the tropical dry scrubs and deciduous forests of the Cape Region, in the tip of the peninsula, is evident here. There are fewer succulent rosettes, and desert trees coexist with giant columnar cacti, forming an *arbo-crassicaulescent desert*. The *torotes*, or elephant trees (*Bursera filicifolia, B. hindsiana, B. microphylla*), mezquite (*Prosopis glandulosa*), palo Adán (*Fouquieria diguetii*), blue paloverde (*Parkinsonia florida*), the endemic ciruelo (*Cyrtocarpa edulis*), and the elegant *palo blanco* form dense thickets in some of the *arroyos*. The sour *pitaya* is abundant here, and the creeping devil, or *chirinola* (*Stenocereus eruca*) —a highly endemic and extremely rare form of columnar cactus— is found near the coast. This unique and bizarre cactus grows pressed to the ground, generating dense clusters of snake-like giant stems that seem to be creeping on the desert floor. Cardon, *sinita*, and chollas are also abundant. One of the most common sights is that of crested caracaras (*Caracara cheriway*) on top of cacti and other perching places, while a night traveler might encounter the swift fox (*Vulpes velox*) to be a typical inhabitant.

Human Cultures

The forces of evolution that have created the region's unique life-forms also molded its singular cultures (León Portilla 1989). Quite separated from the rest of Mesoamerica, the Cochimí Indians and other groups in Baja California developed one of the most incredible assemblages of cave paintings in the world, which are now one of Mexico's most prized World Heritage Sites (Crosby 2000). Later, during the Spanish colony, the Jesuit fathers founded in these deserts their own "Utopia" in a system of missions that evolved in complete independence from the hard and cruel rules of the mainland *conquistadores* (Clavijero 1789; Del Barco 1768). Alas, the Jesuit fathers also brought with them, unwittingly, the fatal germs of European diseases, and some decades after the colonization most of the highly-isolated, disease-vulnerable groups of Baja California

Above, osprey (Pandion haliaetus)*, a flagship species for the Baja and Sonoran coast.*

On the opposite page, sidewinder rattlesnake (Crotalus cerastes)*, Altar Dunes, Sonora. Both photos:*
© **Patricio Robles Gil**/*Sierra Madre*

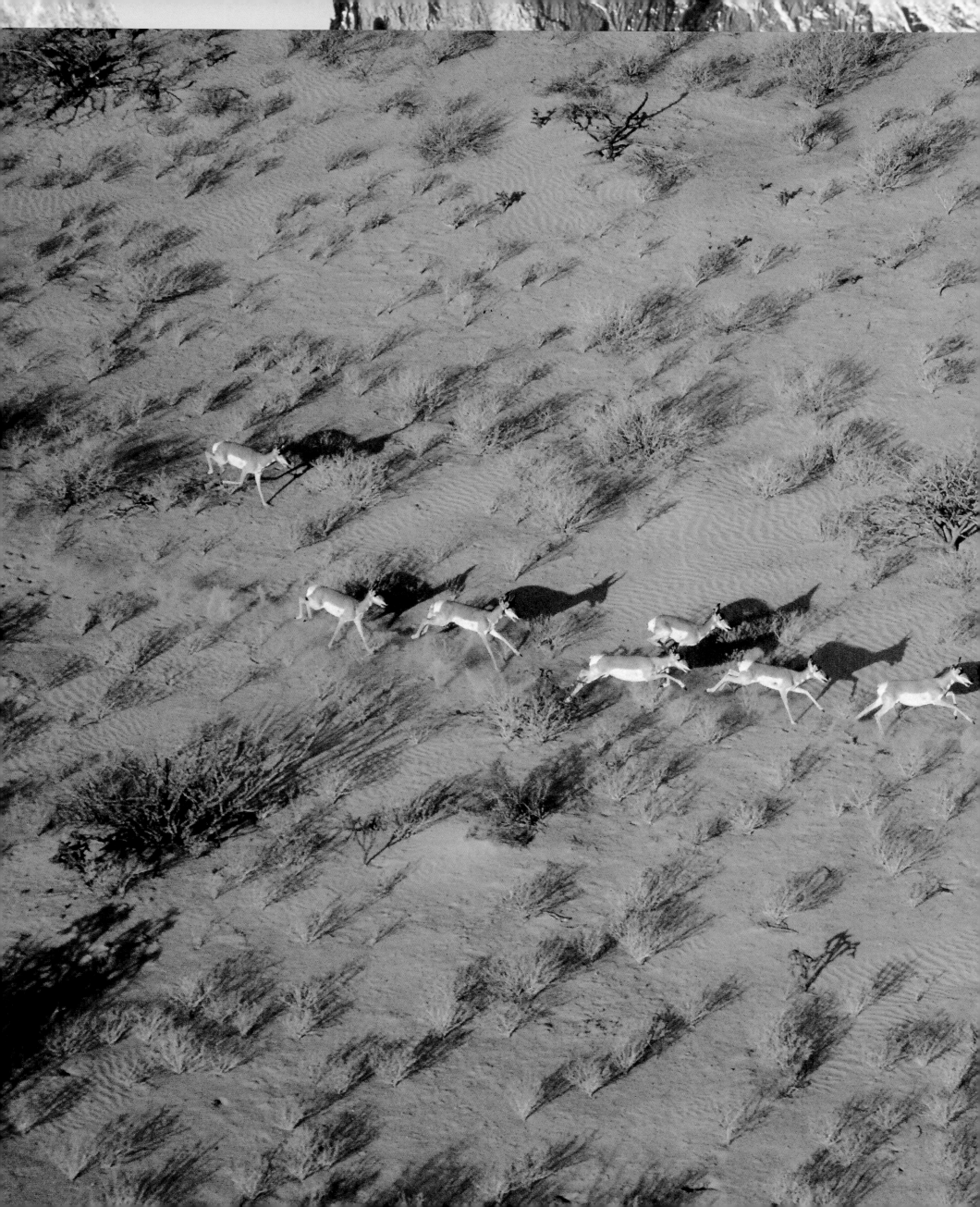

In some areas, natural vegetation is being rapidly destroyed for agricultural development and/or the planting of weedy exotic grasses –such as the African buffelgrass (*Pennisetum ciliare*)– to improve forage productivity for cattle in desert environments. Both in southern Sonora and in southern Baja California, buffelgrass does not seem to need previous land clearing to become established. Highly-adapted to the hot and dry tropical environment, it is rapidly invading the desert, especially in areas that have been cleared or are overgrazed. This fast-growing, leafy grass provides increased biomass that catches fire easily during the dry season, turning the desert into a savanna-like, fire-prone ecosystem that burns seasonally and prevents the reestablishment of the original biologically rich, but fire-sensitive, desert scrub.

Cattle grazing, a recurring problem throughout the deserts of the region, has also caused changes in the structure of the vegetation, perhaps unwittingly reestablishing some ancient ecological processes that were interrupted at the end of the Pleistocene, when the large herbivores that roamed in the desert plains, dispersing the seeds of mezquites and cacti, were driven to extinction. However, modern grazing involves removal of predators, resulting in much higher grazer densities than those found in the paleontological past.

Adventure-tourism has also had large impacts on some peninsular ecosystems. Perhaps the most destructive form of wild-land recreation is the use of off-road vehicles in the open desert and the coastal sand ridges. The vegetation in these environments has an extremely slow growth rate and a barrel cactus easily destroyed in seconds by a rash driver may have taken centuries to grow to its adult size and may take several generations to recover. Sadly, some of the international appeal of Baja California comes not from its beauty and isolation, but from its availability of off-road activities, which are advertised as an attraction in cities like Puerto Peñasco or San Felipe.

Human visitation, although potentially beneficial, has also had an impact in the island ecosystems of the Gulf of California, which are extremely fragile environments. Biological evolution in isolation has made these islands highly vulnerable to factors like exotic species, habitat deterioration, hunting, and fishing by both tourists and local fishermen. In particular, the introduction of exotic species such as rats, cats, or goats may cause true ecological catastrophes for endemic plants, marine birds, or island reptiles. Finally, the growing demand for ecotourism has generated a lot of pressure to develop the islands. Although no development has been allowed yet on any of the Gulf islands, the number of proposals has been increasing steadily over the last decade.

The estuaries and coastal lagoons of the region are also facing growing threats from industrial and tourism developments, runoff of terrestrial pollutants, habitat modification due to aquaculture developments, and disturbance by boats and jet-skis. The deterioration of the coastal lagoons affects a large number of marine organisms that spend part of their life cycle in these ecosystems, from the gray whales (*Eschrichtius robustus*) in the Pacific lagoons, to shrimp, mollusks, and fish in the Sea of Cortés. It also affects a large number of migratory birds that use these wetlands along their travel routes. The coastal lagoons provide unique ecological services that are crucial for the maintenance and survival of species that migrate yearly to other, often distant, ecosystems. These services, however, are not easily perceptible by developers, who tend to consider these environments as "wastelands" that should be used for more direct economic profit. Mangrove clearing for aquaculture or for coastal resorts is a typical example. The great value of mangroves for open-sea fisheries and marine life in general is more difficult for the average person to perceive than is the immediate benefit of clearing them for other less productive purposes.

Poaching is common in the Sonoran Desert. Big game are hunted for meat or trophies, and endemic reptiles, cacti, and other rare plants are often collected and smuggled across the international border for the pet and exotic plant markets. Many of the targeted species have small populations, often on single islands, and these often fluctuate in synchrony with environmental variations, making them particularly vulnerable.

Conservation

The Mexican and U.S. governments and environmental nongovernmental organizations (NGOs) on both sides of the border have developed actions to protect the rich and increasingly endangered ecosystems of the Sonoran and Baja Californian Deserts. There is now a wide array of protected areas, including three Biosphere Reserves in Mexico (El Vizcaíno, Alto Golfo de California y Delta del Río Colorado, and El Pinacate y Gran Desierto de Altar); three National Monuments in the U.S. (Sonoran Desert National Monument near Phoenix, Sahuaro National Monument near Tucson, and the Organ Pipe Cactus National Monument along the border which is now also a Biosphere Reserve); two coastal National Parks (Bahía de Loreto and Cabo Pulmo, both in Mexico); a State Park in California (Anza-Borrego Desert State Park); three Wildlife Refuges in Mexico (Islas del Golfo de California, the Islands of the Sea of Cortés (Bourillón et al. 1988), Cajón del Diablo, a range containing a mosaic of desert and lush tropical canyons in the central coast of Sonora, and Valle de los Cirios, in the central desert of Baja California); and a fourth refuge in the U.S. (Cabeza Prieta National Wildlife Refuge). Although not formally a protected area, the Barry M. Goldwater Military Range adjacent to Organ Pipe and Cabeza Prieta, is one of the largest unspoiled areas of the Sonoran Desert. In total, protected areas within this wilderness region cover some 18 000 km² in the U.S. and 68 000 km² in Mexico, and protect 27% of the total area.

In addition, two National Parks with temperate vegetation (Constitución de 1857 and Sierra de San Pedro

Above, flowering barrel cactus (Ferocactus cylindraeus), one of the best flagship plant species in this cactus-rich region.

On the opposite page, Gambel's quail (Callipepla gambelii) on a fruiting saguaro cactus, in the Sonoran Desert.
Both photos:
© Patricio Robles Gil/*Sierra Madre*

THE GREATER CHIHUAHUAN DESERT

The Chihuahuan Desert is a large, relatively isolated arid zone embedded in the center of the continent's subtropical latitudes. It covers most of north-central Mexico with a tongue extending northward into far west Texas and southern New Mexico (Schmidt 1979). It forms part of the much larger arid corridor discussed in the chapters on the Sonoran and Baja Californian Deserts and the Mojave and, as such, includes a mosaic of xeric plant communities as well as other biomes, such as pine-oak forests and desert oases. The core of the Chihuahuan Desert Wilderness is the area considered by some experts to be the "true desert," as defined strictly on climatic terms —using aridity data classified according to the de Martonne Index of Aridity (de Martonne 1926; Schmidt, *op. cit.*). This area spans about 11 degrees latitude (from 24.5°N to 35°N), and approximately 8 degrees longitude (101°W to 109.5°W), and covers approximately 1.5% of the North American continent (Schmidt, *op. cit.*). However, an expanded vision of the region, based upon vegetation affinities, extends 13.5° latitude (from 21.5°N to 35°N) and approximately 11° longitude (from 100.5°W to 111.5°W), an area roughly equivalent to two of the World Wildlife Fund's ecoregions (Olson et al. 2001): the Chihuahuan Desert (NA1303) (509 500 km²; 80.3%) and the Meseta Central Matorral (NA1307) (125 300 km²; 19.7%). As defined here, the area covers 634 800 km², of which approximately 70% still remains intact.

Roughly 32% of the region (205 400 km²) is in the southwestern United States, where several N-NW trending mountains, including the Mogollon Rim to the north and the Chiricahua Mountains in Arizona to the northwest, define its northern limit. These, together with other mountain ranges in northern Mexico and southeastern Arizona, make up an archipelago of "sky-islands" that eventually grade down to the west into the Sonoran Desert. From there, the desert stretches on to the east, covering the southern third of the state of New Mexico, where the increasing elevations of the two southward branches of the Rocky Mountains, one on each side of the Rio Grande Valley, as well as the Sangre de Cristo Mountains to the east, limit its extension to the north. The desert continues on across the Trans-Pecos region of Texas

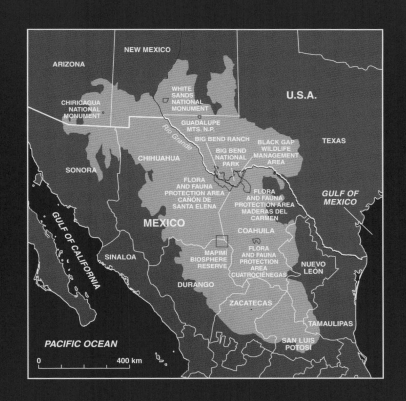

and reaches its northeasternmost limit at the Edwards Plateau.

To the south, the bulk of the Chihuahuan Desert, roughly 68% or 429 400 km², is in Mexico, and extends over large portions of the states of Chihuahua, Coahuila, Nuevo León, Durango, and Zacatecas, reaching its southernmost boundary in San Luis Potosí (Schmidt, *op. cit.*; Hernández and Bárcenas 1994). In all, it accounts for 22% of the Mexican territory. In Mexico, the Chihuahuan Desert is bordered to the west and east by the Sierra Madre Occidental and the Sierra Madre Oriental, respectively. Extensions of Chihuahuan Desert vegetation penetrate the mountain ranges along valleys and canyons in the latter, and intergrade with more mesic vegetation types. Some of these valleys, like Rayones, Aramberri, and Jaumave, are extremely important for their variety and wealth of narrowly-endemic cacti species (Hernández and Bárcenas, *op. cit.*). However, these threatened areas will not be discussed here, as they are part of an emerging biodiversity hotspot that will be covered in detail elsewhere. Further south of the main body of the Chihuahuan Desert, in the region known as the Queretaroan-Hidalgoan Arid Zone, there are other important disjunct fragments of the

░ *Wilderness Area*

On the opposite page, the Rio Grande divides Mexico's Cañón de Santa Elena Flora and Fauna Protection Area from the Big Bend National Park in the U.S.A.
© **Patricio Robles Gil**/*Sierra Madre*

Chihuahuan Desert, including Barranca de Meztitlán, Valle del Mezquital, Valle de Actopan, and Extorax River Basin. However, due to the large distance that separates them from the main body of the Chihuahuan Desert, these are not included in the wilderness area discussed in this chapter.

Climatically, the Chihuahuan Desert is what is known as a "rain shadow desert." This means that the surrounding mountains prevent most of the moisture coming from the Gulf of California, the Gulf of Mexico, and the Pacific Ocean from reaching it, which results in the uniform arid conditions typical of the region. Although almost 90% of the Chihuahuan Desert lies at an altitude between 1 100 and 1 500 m (Schmidt 1983a), one of the most interesting features in the region is the occurrence of mountain ranges, usually over 1 800 m high, separated by large valleys. This basin-and-range topography, also known as "mountain islands and desert seas" (Gehlbach 1993), is one of the reasons for the high species diversity found in the Chihuahuan Desert. Higher elevations act as biogeographical islands that harbor temperate organisms typical of more northern regions. These have evolved isolated from other populations by the surrounding "seas" of desert lowlands and Quaternary alluvium-filled valleys or *bolsones* (Schmidt 1986). By contrast, the lower elevations harbor many species that are not able to survive the cold winters of the "desert mountain islands." The result is an unusually rich biodiversity assemblage for an arid region.

The average temperature is 18.6°C, with the highest recorded temperatures reaching 50°C and the lowest -15°C (Schmidt 1979, 1983a, and 1983b). The Chihuahuan Desert is fairly cool and broadly characterized by hot summers and cold winters. Temperature in the summer is quite uniform throughout the entire region, with a range of 25°C-30°C, while winter temperatures are usually colder in the northern reaches. The annual rainfall is relatively high, with a range of 150-400 mm and an average of 235 mm, most of it falling in the summer. No portion of this region has ever registered a year without precipitation and the northern portion usually receives some snowfall during the colder months (Schmidt 1983a and 1986).

Other sources of water are the ephemeral streams, lakes, arroyos, playa lakes, and even large puddles that form during the summer monsoons but are short-lived in the hot, dry climate of this region. There also is underground water that has seeped down from the surface over centuries. The presence of this subsurface water in the Chihuahuan Desert produces interesting formations, such as oases —fertile areas of the desert usually caused by the springing up of water from below, which provide important habitats for many species that could not usually survive the arid conditions. The most famous oasis in the Chihuahuan Desert is the Bolsón de Cuatro Ciénegas, located near the eastern limits of the Chihuahuan Desert in central Coahuila. This ecosystem has a variety of aquatic features, including lagunas, playas, and associated gypsum dunes, rivers, subterranean tubes, artesian wells, *pozos,* and *ciénegas.* Steep

limestone sierras capped by conifer forests surround this astonishing setting.

There are several large rivers in the region, including the Río Grande/Río Bravo —the most significant drainage system in the region— and its tributary the Río Conchos, which have carved large canyons and riparian areas in the desert landscape. Other important bodies of water include the Río Casas Grandes, the Bolsón de Mapimí, and the Laguna de Mayrán. Canyons, like Santa Elena in Maderas del Carmen, Mexico and Big Bend in Texas, serve as biogeographic filters that produce subtle differences in the wildlife communities on different sides of the rivers and a much richer regional biota.

Biodiversity

The first scientific assessment of the biodiversity of the Chihuahuan Desert took place more than 100 years ago, when Mexico and the United States created the International Boundary Commission. Between 1892 and 1894, a party of government officials from both countries had the arduous task of locating sites for the monuments that would demarcate the new limits between the two countries. Major Edgar A. Mearns, an army surgeon for the American party, obtained permission from his government to study the plants and wildlife. He made extensive observations and recorded many species new to science (Mearns 1907). Part of his journey has been described as follows:

"Fine dust that clung to your whole body had been a problem for the last part of the long trip, particularly for those at the end of the caravan. It was the intense heat, however, sometimes as high as 43° Celsius, which had made the journey so hard. Major Edgar A. Mearns wiped the sweat from his face and was glad to see the San Luis Mountains on the horizon, in the border between New Mexico in the United States and Chihuahua and Sonora in Mexico. The scenery was surprisingly beautiful: wide plains dotted with mountains like islands; the fauna, abundant and magnificent. He decided to camp in a poplar-filled gallery forest near a seasonal stream, and stay a few days. During his work at the San Luis Mountains camp, he was able to observe mule deer, white-tailed deer, peccaries, great herds of pronghorn antelope, bighorn sheep, wolves, black and grizzly bears, beaver, and many other species of mammals. However, what surprised him the most were the immense prairie dog towns (*Cynomys ludovicianus*) stretching for hundreds of kilometers. In the foothills of the San Luis Mountains and the Las Animas Valley in New Mexico, he found a town of millions of prairie dogs, a sight he would never forget" (Ceballos et al. 1992; Ceballos and Pacheco 2000).

In all, there are five major vegetation types in the Chihuahuan Desert. The most prominent is the *desert scrub*, which accounts for up to half of the total vegetation in the Chihuahuan Desert. Species composition and dominance within this type of community vary, but it is

Above, aplomado falcon (Falco femoralis) on the dry flower of a palmito plant.

On the opposite page, group of pronghorns (Antilocapra americana mexicana), El Sueco, Chihuahua. México. Both photos:
© **Patricio Robles Gil**/*Sierra Madre*

tion to crush soft foods, and the second with a more restricted distribution and large, specialized molar-like teeth that it uses to crush the shells of the endemic snails *Mexipyrgus* on which it feeds (Minckley, *op. cit.*).

Aside from the three Cuatro Ciénegas turtles mentioned before, the Chihuahuan Desert houses a few other interesting reptiles, including the Bolsón tortoise (*Gopherus flavomarginatus*), a species endemic to the region of Mapimí and whose survival depends on the success of the protected area that harbors it. Representative snakes include the Trans-Pecos rat snake (*Bogertophis subocularis*) and the many species of rattlesnakes (*Crotalus* spp.) found here. Given that Mexico has the highest rattlesnake diversity in the world, it is not surprising that these reptiles feature so prominently in Mexican culture, most notably alongside the golden eagle on the national flag, and many of these are found in the Chihuahuan Desert.

Human Cultures

Archaeological evidence suggests that the Chihuahuan Desert has been inhabited for some 30 000 years. During that time, numerous indigenous groups have lived in the area, from nomadic groups to large and culturally-complex settlements like the Casas Grandes cultural interaction sphere, which covered portions of the southwestern U.S. and northern Mexico. The groups that inhabited the Chihuahuan Desert included the Anasazi Pueblo, the Chiricahua Apache, and the Ópata, among others. The Southern Chiricahua band, led by their famous leader Geronimo, ranged into Mexico. With the 1848 Treaty of Guadalupe Hidalgo and the 1853 Gadsden Purchase, Mexico ceded and then sold the majority of the Apache territories to the United States. Today, the Native American groups that inhabit the American portion of the Chihuahuan Desert are mostly Zuni, Navajo, Pápago, and Pima, and amount to some 32 000 people.

On the Mexican side, perhaps one of the most intact Indian cultures to depend on the Chihuahuan Desert, even though they are not settled there, is the Huichol tribe. Since long before the arrival of Europeans in the Americas, Huiricuta had been the Huichol name for the Real de Catorce region of the Chihuahuan Desert in San Luis Potosí. This landscape represents a vital space within the Huichol world and is considered an immense natural temple. In 1994, 740 km² within Huiricuta was declared a State Reserve, recognizing it as a "site of historical and cultural heritage requiring ecological conservation for the ethnic group Huixaraca (Huichol)" (WWF 2002).

The Chihuahuan Desert occupies 32 counties of three American states and portions of six states in Mexico. Although it is difficult to estimate the population density within the boundaries of the wilderness area as defined here, these political entities have a combined total population of 14.5 million people in a total area of 991 020 km², of which some 3.6 million (25%) live in rural areas. This

amounts to less than 4 inhabitants/km² (U.S. Census Bureau 2002; CONABIO 2002). Based on this information, we estimate that there are approximately 2 306 000 people in the rural parts of this wilderness area.

Threats

Habitat loss and degradation, pollution, overgrazing, hunting, habitat fragmentation, uncontrolled urban sprawl, and mining are the main threats to the Chihuahuan Desert. Since the beginning of the sixteenth century, the desert grasslands have been used to graze cattle, which has caused the direct loss of plant biomass, soil trampling, and compacting, and has resulted in massive erosion and desertification. Sadly, this is the case over most of the region, and at some point or another grazing has significantly altered even some of the relatively intact habitat areas. Common desert shrubs and, worse yet, nonnative plants, have overrun the lush grasslands of yesteryear (Ricketts et al. 1999).

Changes in the fire regime have also modified the landscape. Extensive grazing and fire-suppression practices have drastically altered the ecological function of fire in the ecosystem. As grasslands become degraded, the fuel load becomes insufficient to sustain the intensity of wildfire needed to clear invading brush. Nonnative species planted to promote erosion control or as fodder for livestock, are then able to easily outcompete native species (Ricketts et al., *op. cit.*). Perhaps the best example of such negative impacts is the extinction of wild populations of black-footed ferrets (*Mustela nigripes*), who owe their demise to the decline of grassland rodents, their favorite prey. Also, in recent years, grassland birds have shown a consistent decline, and many species are now considered threatened or of conservation concern in the U.S.A., Canada, and Mexico (Knopf 1994; Manzano et al. 1999). The decline of healthy habitats, coupled with hunting pressure, overpumping of groundwater, urban sprawl, mining, and the continuous expansion of the agricultural frontier, have all caused once abundant animal species like the pronghorn and prairie dogs to become scarce, while others, like the Mexican wolf (*Canis lupus baileyi*) and the Mexican grizzly bear (*Ursus arctos nelsoni*) have been extirpated (Bahre 1995).

Conservation

Conservation in the Chihuahuan Desert began in the U.S. in 1912, when public domain lands were set aside by Presidential Executive Order as the Jornada Range Reserve, administered by the U.S. Department of Agriculture. This became the first protected area in the region, and its name was later changed to Jornada Experimental Range, its current designation. It now covers 78 266 ha of managed arid ranges.

Two decades later, in 1933, the State of Texas established Texas Canyons State Park in the "Big Bend" of the

Above, greater roadrunner (Geococcyx californianus), *a characteristic bird of the southwestern deserts, Big Bend National Park, Texas, USA.*

On the opposite page, ocotillos (Fouquieria sp.) *and yuccas* (Yucca sp.) *in a snowstorm, Coahuila, Mexico.*
Both photos:
© **Patricio Robles Gil**/*Sierra Madre*

posed the designation of [...] ed areas as part of the U.S. contribution to the global network of biosphere reserves, including Big Bend and La Jornada. These two reserves were formally desig-

tecting this keystone area in an ecoregion of [...] tional significance is unprecedented. The El Carmen Project, as it has been called, is outstanding for several

THE MOJAVE DESERT

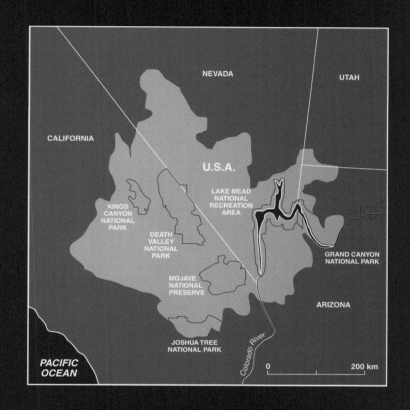

The Mojave Desert covers an area of 130 634 km² and is the smallest of the four North American deserts that form an enormous corridor of arid ecosystems in northern Mexico and the southwestern United States (Sonoran and Baja Californian Deserts, Colorado Plateau, and Chihuahuan Desert Wildernesses). Despite being surrounded by large urban areas and millions of people, vast open areas remain undeveloped. Indeed, it is still more than 75% intact. Our definition of its boundaries coincides with the one proposed by the WWF's ecoregional analysis, Mojave Desert ecoregion (NA1308) (Olson et al. 2001).

The Mojave lies entirely within the southwestern region of the United States, straddling the states of California (93 000 km² or 71%) and Nevada, and spilling over slightly into Utah and Arizona (MacMahon and Wagner 1985). It represents a distinct transition zone between the hot deserts of northern Mexico and the southwestern United States to the south and the colder, higher-elevation shrub steppes to the north (Ricketts et al. 1999). The largest portion lies within southern California (USGS-SDMT 1998).

To the southwest and northwest are the most clearly-defined edges of the Mojave Desert, given by formations like the Tehachapi and Transverse Mountain Ranges (Shreve 1925; Vasek and Barbour 1988). To the north, it transitions into Great Basin Shrub Steppe (NA1305) with increasing elevation, decreasing temperatures, and a shift in the predominant precipitation from rain to snow (USGS 1999). To the east it adjoins the Colorado Plateau Shrublands (NA1304) (Davis et al. 1998; Ricketts et al., op. cit.). The southern boundary between the Mojave and the Sonoran and Colorado Deserts is very subtle, with fully one fifth (545/2 600) of the Mojave's plants shared by the Sonoran Desert (USGS 1999).

Topography ranges from 86 meters below sea level in the Death Valley Basin —the lowest point in the United States— to 3 368 m in some mountains. However, most of this basin-and-range region lies between 610 and 1 220 m, hence the name "high desert" (Ricketts et al., op. cit.). Lower elevations are hot and dry, with daytime temperatures reaching 35°C in the summer and sometimes rising to a scorching 47°C in places like Death Valley, where in 1913, the highest temperature ever measured in the United States,

57°C, was recorded. Winter days are mild, with temperatures close to 21°C, but temperatures fall below 0°C at night and hard frost is common at higher elevations. Both spring and fall, though generally pleasant, stage strong cyclonic storms, which contribute to maximum sand transport and dune activity (Davis et al., op. cit.). Rainfall is highly variable, with 41-165 mm per year, and over 25% of this falling during the summer (Hereford and Longpré 1999).

Hydrographically, the northern Mojave is part of the Great Basin between the Rocky Mountains and the Sierra Nevada. Most streams in this area of internal drainage never reach the ocean, but instead drain into closed basins. The southern Mojave drains into the lower Colorado River, which runs through the southwestern landscape, along the border between California, Nevada, and Arizona, carving wonders like the Grand Canyon along its way and finally draining into the Gulf of California in Mexico (Grayson 1993). To the west, the main water system is the Mojave River and its associated aquifer. Unlike the Colorado, the Mojave River is an unpredictable source of water with a mostly dry streambed, except for short periods of flow after intense rains. Residents rely almost entirely on groundwater from these two river systems —in Nevada alone, some 1.3 million people depend on the Colorado for their water needs (CRWUA 2002). The ever-increasing water demand has resulted in exten-

■ *Wilderness Area*

On the opposite page, Joshua trees (Yucca brevifolia) at sunset in a summer storm, Grand Wash Cliffs.
© **Jack Dykinga**

sive damming (e.g., the Hoover Dam), and water extraction, which have significantly altered the ecology of the Colorado River, its tributaries, and the Upper Gulf of California, where the diminished flow of fresh water has had severe ecological impacts. It has also caused a region-wide lowering of the water table, changes in the quantity and spatial distribution of recharge from the Mojave River, and loss of riparian habitat throughout the region.

Other bodies of water scattered throughout the desert include isolated terminal lakes, marshes, and playas, most of which are small and only seasonally inundated, yet surprisingly numerous and important for aquatic species (Davis et al., *op. cit.*).

Biodiversity

Three vegetation communities account for 75% of the land cover within the Mojave Desert. From below sea level to 1 500 m, creosote bush scrub dominated by *Larrea tridentata* is the principal formation and covers 57% of the area. Creosote bush is a spindly, fragrant plant known from both North and South America, that reaches its northern limit in the Mojave (Vasek 1980). Woodland scrub appears at about 1 100-1 300 m and covers approximately 13% of the region. The distribution of the endemic Joshua tree (*Yucca brevifolia*) coincides well with the limits of the Mojave Desert, where it often forms an overstory and is the most visually dominant plant species in this community (Vasek and Barbour, *op. cit.*; Ricketts et al., *op. cit.*). The third major community, covering only 5% of the region, is desert saltbush scrub (*Atriplex* spp.), a well-adapted group of plants that grows in salty or alkaline sites with poor water retention, such as playas and sinks (Davis et al., *op. cit.*; Stark and Whittemore 2001). A combination of desert dunes, mixed steppe and scrub, mesquite forest, pine-oak woodland, transmontane alkali and freshwater marshes, wildflower fields, and Mojave and Modoc-Great Basin willow riparian forests covers the remaining 25% of the region. Although it is distributed over a mere 51 km², riparian vegetation makes a significant contribution to regional biodiversity, containing species such as the Fremont cottonwood (*Populus fremontii*), Goodding black willow (*Salix gooddingii*), honey mesquite (*Prosopis glandulosa*), and exotic saltcedar (*Tamarix ramosissima*) —the most common woody plant in Mojave riparian forest (Lines 1999).

Pinyon-juniper woodlands occur above 1 520 m, where annual precipitation ranges between 250-450 mm. As elevation increases, many of the ranges support scrub oak and ponderosa pine woodlands, quaking aspen forests, white fir/Douglas fir/Rocky Mountain maple woodland, and bristlecone pine woodland (Andre and Knight 1999).

Cactuses also occur in the Mojave, including ten species of the genus *Opuntia*, among them the Mojave prickly pear (*Opuntia phaeacantha*), the silver cholla (*O. echinocarpa*), and the beavertail cactus (*O. basilaris*). An interesting endemic is the charismatic barrel cactus (*Echinocactus polycephalus*), a drum-shaped, multi-headed plant

Dune evening primroses
(Oenothera deltoides)
on sand dune.
© **Patricio Robles Gil**/*Sierra Madre*

that varies in size from only 12 cm wide to giants measuring up to 1 m in width, almost 2 m in height, and weighing close to a ton (Ricketts et al., *op. cit.*). These plants produce a gorgeous ring of golden yellow to purplish-red open-faced flowers on the plant's crown.

The region also includes 22 species of bryophytes, 75 species of mosses, and five species of liverworts (Stark and Whittemore, *op. cit.*).

The Jepson Herbarium (2001) lists 1 556 vascular plant species from the Mojave Desert Floristic Province —making it one of the most diverse floristic regions in the United States. Stebbins and Major (1965) listed 138 endemic plant species, but as many as 25% (389 species) are believed to be endemic (Davis et al. 1997). One of the most interesting aspects of the Mojave's vegetation is the large number of endemic ephemeral plants, many of which are winter annuals. Of 250 taxa with this lifestyle, between 80% and 90% are endemic. Indeed, certain areas within this region support more endemic plants per square meter than any other similarly-sized areas in the United States (Ricketts et al., *op. cit.*).

The Mojave Desert is home to some 360 non-fish vertebrate species, placing it among the three richest ecoregions in North America in terms of terrestrial vertebrate diversity (Mouat et al. 1999). However, in terms of endemism, it ranks rather low with only nine endemic species among the four terrestrial vertebrate groups. Mammals are represented by 71 species, 16 of which are bats, with two species basically endemic: the Mojave ground squirrel (*Spermophilus mohavensis*) and the Inyo shrew (*Sorex tenellus*). Birds are the best-represented vertebrate group with 230 species, but none are endemic. Reptiles have 45 species, of which two are endemic (Lovich, Lovich, and Fisher, pers. comm., 2002; Stebbins 1985; Greene and Luke 1996): the Mojave fringe-toed lizard (*Uma scoparia*), found in sand dune localities throughout the Mojave, and the Panamint alligator lizard (*Elgaria panamintina*), a sky-island relict found only in portions of the Panamint Mountains (Mouat et al., *op. cit.*). There are only 14 species of amphibians in this arid region, of which five are endemic: the relict leopard frog (*Rana onca*); the Vegas Valley or Las Vegas leopard frog (*Rana fisheri*); the Inyo Mountains salamander (*Batrachoseps campi*); the Tehachapi slender salamander (*Batrachoseps stebbinsi*); and the Amargosa toad (*Bufo nelsoni*). Several of the amphibian species occur along the margins of the Mojave Desert, including both of the salamanders named above, and the Mexican arroyo toad (*Bufo californicus*) and mountain yellow-legged frog (*Rana muscosa*), both of which are federally protected. Three of the amphibian species have been extirpated, including the Yavapai or lowland leopard frog (*Rana yavapaiensis*), the Vegas Valley leopard frog (now considered Extinct by the IUCN), and the red-legged frog (*Rana aurora*).

The many isolated terminal lakes, marshes, and playas also harbor a number of unique aquatic species. Fifty-six species and 75 subspecies totaling 131 fish taxa are known historically from the Great Basin-Mojave Desert region. Of these, 10 (8%) are extinct. Of those remaining, 75 (62%) are listed or are candidates for listing under the United States Endangered Species Act, and more than 40% of the species and 90% of the subspecies are endemics (Davis et al. 1998).

Flagship Species

If a single species had to be chosen to represent the Mojave, it would have to be the Joshua tree —a tall, twisted, prominent feature of the landscape, and a plant largely unique to this desert. A noted authority on yuccas once referred to this species as "a curious looking plant, suggesting, in its oldest forms especially, another age; one would not be surprised to see a huge prehistoric monster standing by and feeding upon the fruit on its upper branches" (McKelvey 1938). It is one of about 30 members of the genus *Yucca*, all native to North America, and was apparently given its common English name by Mormon settlers, to whom this plant's upraised limbs and "bearded" appearance suggested the prophet Joshua.

Not surprisingly, most flagship species in this dry region are reptiles. One of the most charismatic and threatened is the Vulnerable desert tortoise (*Gopherus agassizii*). Reaching an average length of 15-20 cm, it can be found from the edge of the Great Basin Desert in southwestern Utah, across the Mojave Desert into the Colorado Plateau, and south into the Sonoran Desert. Despite the desert tortoise's extensive distribution, population declines have been a major concern since the 1970s. High mortality due to overgrazing, off-highway vehicle use, military training activities, illegal collection of specimens, urban sprawl, and introduced diseases have seriously diminished its numbers (Lovich 1999). Consequently, the U.S. Fish and Wildlife Service included several populations north and west of the Colorado River as Endangered under the Endangered Species Act in an emergency listing in 1989 (USFWS 1994a) and changed the listing to Threatened in 1990. After publication of the recovery plan for the species in 1994, the USFWS designated 12 areas, totaling 26 000 km², as critical habitat for the desert tortoise. Additional habitat is protected within Joshua Tree National Park and the Desert Tortoise Research Natural Area.

Among the lizards, the Mojave fringe-toed lizard is a flagship species that depends on windblown dunes and hummocks. Colored like the sand upon which it lives, this lizard and its dynamic dune habitats are under pressure from off-road vehicles, agriculture, urban sprawl, exotic plant invasions, and utility projects.

The Mojave rattlesnake (*Crotalus scutulatus*) is an appropriate flagship species, even though it is also found in the Sonoran and Chihuahuan Deserts. Some, but not all, populations of this species in the Mojave contain an extremely potent neurotoxin known as the "Mojave Toxin." The fact that some populations of the Mojave rattlesnake have a more hemotoxic venom is an indication of the diversity that exists even among populations of the same species.

The rosy boa (*Charina trivirgata*) is another flagship species that is not restricted to the Mojave Desert. This nonvenomous snake is one of only two boa species native to the United States. Its attractive coloration and gentle demeanor make it extremely popular among reptile hobbyists and collectors. Roads are a common cause of mortality for both snakes, as well as for other species of reptiles.

Of the fourteen species of amphibians found in the Mojave Desert, two can be considered flagship species. One is the Vulnerable relict leopard frog, which was previously known from southern Nevada and southwestern Utah and was thought to have gone extinct in the 1950s. It was rediscovered in 1991, when three populations were found near Lake Mead, Nevada. To this day, little is known about its ecology, behavior or distribution (Bradford and Jennings 1999; Jennings 1988).

The second amphibian flagship is the Endangered Amargosa toad, which is also considered the most imperiled amphibian in this region. It is known only from a 20-km stretch of the Amargosa River in southern Nevada, where recent surveys have found some 16 000 animals to remain. The decline of both species is likely due to competition and hybridization with introduced frog species, habitat loss and degradation from grazing, off-highway vehicle use, development, and introduced predators such as bullfrogs. Protection of riparian corridors is critical to the survival of these two species (TNC 2001).

Although a surprising number of fish species were historically found in the Great Basin and Mojave Desert, none are more emblematic of the region than pupfishes (*Cyprinodon* spp.). Of eight species, six are, or were, found in drainage systems that flowed into Death Valley's Lake, mainly during the Pleistocene. During the last 7 million years, these tiny fishes have been isolated in small springs, streams, and marshes as a result of the uplifting of mountains and changes in climate, especially the drying that accompanied the end of the last Ice Age. Some populations consist of only a few hundred individuals (Grayson 1993).

Among the mammals, the Mojave ground squirrel is restricted to desert scrub and Joshua tree forest habitat and is considered rare throughout its range. The Tehachapi or white-eared pocket mouse (*Perognathus alticola*) is named for its mountain habitat that bridges the Coast Range with the Sierra Nevada and forms a western boundary to the Mojave. Both species once occurred in San Bernardino County, California, where the encroaching urban development of the ever-expanding Los Angeles metropolitan area is believed to be responsible for the presumed disappearances of these species (Zeiner et al. 1990).

The desert bighorn sheep (*Ovis canadensis nelsoni*), best known for the head-to-head combat between males, is another candidate for listing under the Endangered Species Act. The distribution of this subspecies, distinguished by being somewhat smaller and with flatter, wider-spreading horns than other populations, once extended from northeastern California into northern

California poppies (Eschscholtzia californica) *and owl's clover* (Orthocarpus purpurascens).
© **Patricio Robles Gil**/*Sierra Madre*

areas receive less than 260 mm. Thunderstorms occur in the summer, while ordinary rains arrive in the winter. At elevations of 3 000 m to about 3 500 m, annual precipitation —falling as snow during the cooler months and as heavy rains during the summer monsoon— can be relatively high (760 to 890 mm) for this semiarid region (U.S. Forest Service 2002).

Biodiversity

There are four distinct vegetation communities represented throughout the Colorado Plateau. Desert grasslands and xeric shrublands are found in the lower areas (500-1 000 m). From 1 000 to 2 000 m, the principal vegetation is pinyon-juniper woodlands, featuring pinyon pine (*Pinus edulis*) and Utah juniper (*Juniperus osteosperma*). Slightly higher (2 000-2 400 m), these grade into pine forest, with Rocky Mountain ponderosa pine (*Pinus ponderosa* var. *scopulorum*), Gambel oak (*Quercus gambelii*), and New Mexico locust (*Robinia neomexicana*) as codominants. Above 3 600 m, it transitions into subalpine conifer forest and alpine tundra. Above 2 300 m, it is also possible to find subalpine and montane grasslands and meadows composed of perennial bunchgrasses, such as Arizona fescue (*Festuca arizonica*), needlegrasses, or wheatgrasses, as well as forbs, including yarrow, larkspur, or fleabane, and stands of the widespread quaking aspen (*Populus tremuloides*), a species of tremendous importance to wildlife.

In all, there are 2 556 vascular plant species in the Colorado Plateau, of which at least 201 are endemic. This diversity can be attributed to varied topography and geographic position —a location between the arid Great Basin to the west and the lusher Rocky Mountains to the east. The region's flora and fauna have elements of both areas, as well as a significant number of endemic species that have evolved in relative isolation atop the Plateau (WWF, in prep.).

Of the 643 species of mammals known to occur in temperate North America, 107 (17%) occur in the Colorado Plateau region, although none of them are endemic (WWF, in prep.). Birds are represented by 222 species, again none of them endemic to the region (WWF, in prep). There are 61 species of reptiles and 11 species of amphibians, again with no endemics at the species level (WWF, in prep).

Several vertebrate species have been extirpated, among them the beaver (*Castor canadensis*) and the grizzly bear (*Ursus arctos*). Others have been successfully reintroduced like the black-footed ferret (*Mustela nigripes*) and the gray wolf (*Canis lupus*).

Flagship Species

The California condor is perhaps the best example of a flagship species for wildlife conservation in this region.

Mule deer
(Odocoileus hemionus)
in the snow.
© **Patricio Robles Gil**/*Sierra Madre*

Historically widespread throughout much of western North America, this largest of the North American raptors declined rapidly throughout the twentieth century and was ultimately driven to extinction in its natural state in 1987, when the six last remaining wild birds were captured to establish a captive-breeding colony. Success in captive reproduction has allowed its reintroduction to parts of its former range, including sites in California and Vermillion Cliffs and Hurricane Cliffs in northern Arizona. However, the released birds have not yet reached reproductive maturity and still rely on food provided by the recovery program (Peregrine Fund 1998; USFWS 1996).

Among the mammals, the Kaibab squirrel (*Sciurus aberti kaibabensis*) is a notable inhabitant of the plateau's ponderosa pine forests. This beautiful black-bellied, white-tailed, and tassel-eared rodent can be found only on the Kaibab Plateau on the North Rim of the Grand Canyon, a chasm that separates it from a close relative found on the South Rim, the white-bellied and black-tailed Abert's squirrel (*S. a. aberti*). Though morphologically distinct, these two squirrels are ecologically similar, and research continues to determine if they are distinct species or not (Wallace 1972; Hoffmeister 1986).

Human Cultures

People have inhabited the Colorado Plateau for some 12 000 years. The first inhabitants were Paleoindians, followed by archaic cultures and eventually by more modern tribes, most notably the Anasazi who, over the centuries, established large and complex settlements. Today, the most remarkable of these is preserved within New Mexico's Chaco Canyon National Historic Park (Kopper 1986). The eventual collapse of Anasazi society —some 700 years ago— due perhaps to a prolonged drought, did not signify their total disappearance; at the time of Spanish arrival in the 1500s, some 100 000 Native Americans lived in about 100 Pueblo communities in northern and central New Mexico. As is the case elsewhere in the American Southwest, indigenous cultures were tragically reduced by the arrival of Europeans. Modern-day cultures include Pueblo tribes such as the Hopi and the Zuni, and those of the Pais culture, such as the Havasupai, the Hualapai, and the Paiute. Still others, like the Ute and Apache, were displaced in more recent times. The Colorado Plateau is indeed one the richest regions in North America in terms of its cultural-linguistic diversity, with at least a dozen tribes maintaining their indigenous languages (Nabhan 2002).

We estimate the total human population within this wilderness area to be approximately 2 million people (roughly one quarter of which are Native Americans), with 1 400 000 living in urban areas. This yields a rural population of close to 600 000, for a population density of 1.9 inhabitants/km^2 (USCB 2000).

Threats

This arid region has been the scene of many battles over water supply and usage, including dam construction and water-diversion schemes. Many historians, in fact, consider the Colorado Plateau as one of the birthplaces of the American environmental movement. Over the last few decades, environmental groups have steadfastly defended the Colorado Plateau's remaining large natural areas from an avalanche of development schemes, and have been slowly building support for the creation of major new protected areas in the region.

Threats to this wilderness have historically included widespread grazing, intensive logging, and water diversion for irrigation. The effects of dams and water-diversion projects on river flow are implicated in the decline of several native Colorado River fish species, such as the humpback chub (*Gila cypha*), bonytail (*G. elegans*), and squawfish (*Ptychocheilus lucius*), all of which may ultimately prove unable to adapt to the loss of swift-flowing currents and a proliferation of placid lakes and streams. Mining in some areas has permanently altered landscapes, and the recent development of coalfields for regional power generation has had an impact as well. Finally, management policies, such as the suppression of wildfires, have had an impact on the area's natural ecology. For example, fire suppression, combined with a steady increase in the elk population, is believed to have prevented the regeneration of aspen in many forests (Bennett 1974).

Conservation

The Colorado Plateau's many national parks, national monuments, and national recreation areas are testimony to America's enduring love affair with this magnificent wilderness of stone. Fortunately, the region's aridity and rugged landscape have long served as effective deterrents to settlers, and much of it has remained relatively free of human impacts (Wheeler 2002). Its spectacular beauty alone has led generations of Americans to support permanent protection for huge blocks of Colorado Plateau landscape within the national park and national wilderness preservation systems —with the result that it has within it some of the largest and most pristine protected wilderness areas within the temperate realm (Wheeler, *op. cit.*). Indeed, in 1936, Wilderness Society founder Bob Marshall determined that a 3 601 700-ha block centered upon the canyonlands of the Colorado and Green Rivers was the single largest roadless area in the lower 48 states, and this remains true today (Wheeler, *op. cit.*).

The most important and best-known protected area is unquestionably Grand Canyon National Park in Arizona. First declared a forest reserve in 1893, this 493 100-ha area was later upgraded to a game reserve, then redesignated to national monument in 1908, and finally declared a national park on February 26, 1919. In 1979, it was given international recognition through its inclusion on UNESCO's World Heritage List (WCMC 2002). Certainly one of the favorite national parks in the U.S. and indeed in the world, it attracts more than four million visitors each year (IUCN 1995). Its 2 000-m vertical drop, from the vast plateaus surrounding the canyon to the river winding its way through a maze of huge amphitheaters, spectacular tributary canyons, and isolated plateaus and mesas, all set against the backdrop of lush pine forests and rugged colored cliffs, is truly an international symbol of wilderness.

Other spectacular parks in the region include Arches, Zion, Bryce Canyon, Capitol Reef, and Canyonlands in Utah, Rocky Mountains and Mesa Verde in Colorado, and the Petrified Forest (Painted Desert) in Arizona.

We estimate that some 174 244 km² (53%) of the region is under some form of protection, with the largest area being managed by the U.S. Forest Service as National Forests (127 460 km²), including Kaibab, Coconino, Sitgreaves, and Apache National Forests. Land management in these forests includes timber and mineral extraction, so technically they are not considered strictly-protected areas. However, there is a growing trend for the U.S. Bureau of Land Management to manage these forests for their biodiversity and recreation value. Strictly-protected areas cover 47 057 km² (14.4%) —with National Parks accounting for 9 969 km², or 3% of the area, and Wilderness Areas (managed by the National Park Service, Bureau of Land Management, and Fish and Wildlife Service) accounting for 35 871 km², or 11% of the area. In addition, roughly 100 000 km² of the Colorado Plateau is protected informally under the management of Native American communities (Nabhan 2002). All things considered, and taking into account habitat alteration within national forests associated with resource extraction, it is likely that 80% or more of the Colorado Plateau remains relatively stable and intact, although only a fraction of that total is officially protected. This is indeed one of America's most-beloved "wilderness" areas, and one that we truly hope can be preserved for posterity.

CRISTINA G. MITTERMEIER
JOHN PILGRIM
RUSSELL A. MITTERMEIER
WILLIAM R. KONSTANT

Above, Kaibab squirrel (Sciurus aberti kaibabensis), found only on the north rim of the Grand Canyon, Arizona, U.S.A.
© **Tom & Pat Leeson**/*DRK Photo*

On pp. 362-363, Arches National Park, one of the many globally-renowned protected areas in this wilderness area.
© **Patricio Robles Gil**/*Sierra Madre*

COASTAL DESERTS OF PERU AND CHILE

The Coastal Deserts of Peru and Chile are among the driest in the world. Located on the west coast of South America, this system extends for more than 3 000 km along a narrow coastal strip from northern Peru (Lat. 5ºS) to northern Chile (Lat. 23ºS). Its large latitudinal extent and extreme aridity makes this coastal desert area one of the longest and certainly the most arid in the world, especially at its southern end in the Atacama Desert. These deserts owe their existence to the combined effect of a stable high-pressure system located in the western Pacific Ocean, the drying effect of the cold northward-flowing Humboldt Current, which creates a thermal inversion that obstructs the approach of warm and humid air masses from the south Pacific, and the rain shadow effect of the Andes, which impedes the penetration of moisture brought by the eastern trade winds. Although this desert is continuous from Peru to Chile, it is usually broken down into two main components, the Peruvian Coastal Desert from the area of Tumbes (*ca.* 5ºS) to Tacna (*ca.* 18ºS), and the Atacama Desert from the area of Arica in northern Chile (*ca.* 18º24'S) to Mejillones (*ca.* 23ºS) along the coast, and inland down to 25ºS. These are based mainly on differences in topography, climate, and vegetation (Rauh 1985, Arroyo et al. 1988; Marquet 1994), and correspond well with the Sechura Desert (NT1315) and Atacama Desert (NT1303) ecoregions of the World Wildlife Fund (Olson et al. 2001).

Average annual precipitation along the Peruvian portion is usually below 50 mm, and in some coastal areas within the Atacama Desert it has been below 3 mm during the last 50 years, which is among the lowest for any long-term precipitation record in the world (Dillon and Rundel 1990). Although always low, precipitation levels are highly variable due to local topographic factors and large-scale climatic phenomena. Topography comes into play through the regular formation of thick stratocumulus cloud

banks below 1 000 m which, when intercepted by isolated mountains or steep coastal slopes, give rise to a fog zone known as *garúas* in Peru and *camanchacas* in Chile. The increased moisture in the fog zone allows for the development of isolated and diverse vegetation formations called *lomas* (small hills).

The other source of climatic variability is associated with "El Niño Southern Oscillation" (ENSO) events. This oceanographic anomaly affects terrestrial ecosystems all along the western Pacific coast (Jaksic 2001) and creates brief events of heavy rainfall in the desert area of Peru and northern Chile. During the 1982-1983 ENSO event, the most intense of the century, the city of Piura in northern Peru, where normal rainfall averages 50 mm, received more than 1 200 mm between December 1982 and April 1983 (Mujica 1984). Interestingly, fog duration and intensity is increased during ENSO years which, in association with rises in precipitation levels, result in

On the opposite page, dry salt basin with Llullaillaco Volcano in the background, Atacama Desert, Chile.
© **Jean-Marc La Roque**/*Auscape*

365

flowering blooms within the *lomas* formations (Dillon and Rundel, *op. cit.*).

Temperature is remarkably homogeneous along the coastal desert area of Peru and Chile as the result of the moderating effect of the Humboldt Current. Mean January maximum temperature fluctuates between 25° and 31°C and tends to increase in a south to north latitudinal pattern (Rundel et al. 1991).

The northern part of the Peruvian Coastal Desert (5°-7°S), known as the Sechura Desert, consists of a wide coastal plain with shifting sands and extending inland some 100-150 km. Fog does not affect this region and vegetation is sparse and patchy. Further south, in the southern part of the Peruvian Coastal Desert (7°-18°S), the *lomas* formation reaches its peak (Rauh 1985; Dillon 1997). In this area, fogs are well developed, which makes possible the existence of an archipelago of discrete and diverse communities of annual and perennial plants and cacti. Following south along the coast is the Atacama Desert, located between 18°S and 23°S. Here, the landscape is essentially barren, and vegetation is restricted to a few *lomas* formations of reduced extent near the cities of Iquique and Arica, and to the Pampa del Tamarugal, an arid interior basin with several nitrate deposits or *salars*.

In all, the Atacama/Peruvian Coastal Deserts cover *ca.* 290 032 km², of which approximately 258 000 km² is rocky and sandy desert or salt flats. The area is divided roughly equally between Peru (183 519 km²) and Chile (106 513 km²). Less than 59 000 km² has been lost due to land conversion, exploitation, and degradation, leaving this wilderness 80% intact.

Biodiversity

Biodiversity along the Peruvian Coastal Desert and the Atacama Desert is restricted to small and relatively isolated areas where permanent or ephemeral water bodies develop or where moisture is enough to sustain life. Three major ecosystem types can be identified: riparian ecosystems, coastal lagoons and marshes, and *lomas* ecosystems, with the *lomas* being the most widespread and important in terms of biodiversity.

The riparian ecosystems are known in Peru as *montes ribereños* (Koepcke 1954) and develop along river courses and creeks that reach the sea. These systems are well represented in Peru, where the desert area is traversed by 52 rivers, of which 33 have permanent water (Ortega 1992). In some areas, such as near Nazca in Peru, there is extensive development of riparian forests of Chilean mesquite (*Prosopis chilensis*) and porknut (*Acacia macracantha*), along with *Salix humboldtiana, Arundo donax,* and a variety of low shrubs and herbaceous plants (Dillon 1997). In the Atacama Desert, this ecosystem type is less developed, for there are few large rivers (Lluta, Azapa, Camarones, and Loa), and water is less abundant. The Río Loa is the most important river

in the Atacama Desert, crossing it for about 130 km. Near its mouth, it is dominated by trees (*Prosopis tamarugo, P. alba,* and *Geoffroea decorticans*), shrubs in the genera *Baccharis, Atriplex, Nolana,* and *Pluchea,* and perennial herbs such as *Distichlis spicata* (Gutiérrez et al. 1998).

The fauna associated with this ecosystem type is composed of geckonid lizards in the genus *Phyllodactylus,* tropidurine lizards in the genera *Liolaemus* and *Microlophus* (e.g., *M. tarapacensis,* and the endemic *M. yanezi*), and amphibians of the genus *Bufo* (e.g., the endemic Vallenar toad, *B. atacamensis*). The birds include several threatened species, notably the endemic Chilean woodstar (*Eulidia yarrellii*) and the slender-billed finch (*Xenospingus concolor*), as well as doves, flycatchers of the genus *Muscisaxicola* (dark-faced ground tyrant, *M. macloviana;* spot-billed ground tyrant, *M. maculirostris;* rufous-naped ground tyrant, *M. rufivertex*), finches, raptors, and a number of other terrestrial and aquatic species (Marquet et al. 1998).

Coastal lagoons and marshes are usually found near the river courses and in the lower reaches of rivers and *quebradas*. Although not very common, some of them, such as the marshes near Lima (Pantanos de Villa), support more than 120 species of birds (Guillén and Barrio 1994; Pautrat and Riveros 1998). Also within this ecosystem are the so-called *aguada*s, areas where water surfacing from underground aquifers forms small saline pools that are very common in the coastal area of the Atacama Desert. These support diverse plant communities composed of mesic halophyte species, such as *Distichlis spicata, Cressa truxillensis, Baccharis juncea, Cyperus laevigatus,* and *Cotula coronopifolia* (Rundel et al. 1991).

Lomas ecosystems, sometimes referred to as the "fertile belt" (Johnston 1929) or "fog oases" (Ellenberg 1959), are primarily dependent on the moisture provided by fog and on precipitation pulses associated with ENSO events. Their distribution ranges from Lat. 7°S in Peru to 26°S in Chile. In the Peruvian Coastal Desert, where *lomas* ecosystems achieve their greatest development, there are more than 40 discrete *loma* localities covering an area of about 2 000 km² (INRENA 1996; Dillon, *op. cit.*). These ecosystems occur as discrete islands of vegetation interspersed in a hyperarid landscape and associated with areas under the influence of fogs. One of their most remarkable features is the high level of plant endemism (around 40%; Rundel et al. 1991). Cerro Reque (6°52'S), with 80 plant species, marks the northernmost extension of *lomas* ecosystems (Dillon, *op. cit.*). From this point south, *lomas* become more ubiquitous and well developed, some of the most species-rich being Cerro Campana (7°58'S), which harbors 185 plant species, Lomas de Lachay (11°21'S) with 100 species, Lomas de Atiquipa (15°48'S) in Arequipa with 120 species, and Lomas de Mollendo (16°35'S) with 122 species (see Dillon 1997 for a detailed description of *lomas* ecosystems in Peru).

Red-legged cormorant (Phalacrocorax gaimardi).
© **Patricio Robles Gil**/*Sierra Madre*

South of Lat. 18°S, in the Atacama Desert, *lomas* ecosystems are lower in species richness and plant species composition changes because of the increased aridity and the less frequent occurrence of topographic barriers to support fog oases. This area acts as a barrier for many species, differentiating the Chilean and Peruvian desert floras, which share only 68 species (*ca.* 7% of the combined total) (Rundel et al., *op. cit.*). *Lomas* ecosystems, between 18° and 23°S in Chile, usually contain only from 23 to 53 species, far less than in their Peruvian counterparts. Large portions of these are annual plants highly dependent on ENSO events (Pinto 1999, Muñoz Schick et al. 2001). *Lomas* ecosystems are mainly composed of cacti in the genera *Espostoa, Haageocereus, Melocactus, Neoraimondia, Neoporteria,* and *Eulychnia;* annuals and herbaceous perennials in the genera *Nolana, Calandrinia, Portulaca, Leucocoryne,* and *Alstroemeria;* small shrubs in the genera *Ephedra* and *Ambrosia;* and small trees in the genera *Caesalpinia, Capparis, Senna,* and *Carica.* Communities of epiphytic bromeliads in the genus *Tillandsia* represent a particular vegetation type within *lomas.* These species, which absorb fog moisture and nutrients through specialized scales on the leaf surface, are usually found forming gray bands at the lower or upper margins of typical *lomas* communities, or inland where fogs are less intense. *Tillandsia lomas* are well developed in the central and southern part of the Peruvian Coastal Desert, and rarer in the Atacama Desert. Recent botanical work carried out in the Atacama indicates the existence of pure stands of *T. marconae* near Arica (Zizka and Muñoz 1993), which adds to the previously reported *T. landbecki* (Rundel et al. 1997; Muñoz Schick et al., *op. cit.*) and *T. virescens* near Iquique (Pinto 2001), and *T. geissei* and *T. tragophoba* in Paposo (Rundel and Dillon 1998).

Current estimates of the total number of vascular plants for the *lomas* of the Peruvian Coastal Desert amount to 557 species in 72 families and 284 genera (Dillon 1997), while the Atacama Desert (between Arica and Mejillones) has 158 species in 49 families and 100 genera (Marticorena et al. 1998; Muñoz Schick et al., *op. cit.*). Considering all the ecosystem types in the area, the number of plant species for the Atacama/Peruvian Coastal Desert amounts to a grand total of nearly 1 379 species of vascular plants, of which 400 (29%) are endemic (unpublished data).

Although less studied, the fauna of the *lomas* is believed to have a large number of endemics, especially among the invertebrates. Mammal diversity for the Peruvian Coastal Desert is 42 species (39 terrestrial, three marine), of which 30 are known to occur in *lomas* (Aguilar 1985; unpublished data; Eisenberg et al. 1999). Four are endemic to Peru, including the blunt-eared bat (*Tomopeas ravus*) and three rodents, the gerbil leaf-eared mouse (*Phyllotis gerbillus*), the friendly leaf-eared mouse (*P. amicus*) and Zuniga's dark rice rat (*Melanomys zunigae*). Similarly, 85 bird and 17 reptile species are known to inhabit *lomas* ecosystems in the Peruvian

Coastal Desert (Aguilar 1985). In the Atacama Desert, the *lomas* harbor seven species of mammals, 16 species of birds, and four lizards (unpublished data).

As a whole, the region as we define it has at least 48 species of mammals, of which six are basically endemic; 184 species of birds, of which two are endemic, and a third, Markham's storm-petrel (*Oceanodroma markhami*), breeds nowhere else; 52 species of reptiles, of which an astounding 32 are endemic; and three species of amphibians, of which two are endemic (WWF, in prep.; unpublished data).

Flagship Species

This region is best known for its wonderful diversity of plants, of which several qualify as flagship species. These include the endemic tree *arrayán* (*Myrcianthes ferreyrae*) in Peru, with individuals up to 6 m tall and with a beautiful canopy and a fruit similar to a plum, and the Chilean endemic *tamarugo* (*Prosopis tamarugo*), a deciduous open-crowned tree up to 18 m tall, characterized by a dense mat of lateral roots and a deep taproot (reaching to depths of *ca.* 8 m). This species actually forms dense stands in the Pampa del Tamarugal in the Atacama Desert area, but was nearly driven to extinction during the last century as the result of intensive exploitation as a source of fuelwood for the nitrate industry (Marquet et al. 1998). Cacti are also a conspicuous element in these deserts, being represented by approximately 92 species. Among these, the gigantic columnar cacti of the genus *Neoraimondia* of Peru are especially noteworthy, with their massive stems 30 cm or more in width.

In the *lomas* formations, the genus *Nolana* (Solanaceae) stands out as one of the most conspicuous and dominant elements, being present in nearly all such ecosystems in both Peru and Chile. Species of the genera *Alstroemeria, Leucocoryne,* and *Hymenocallis* are well known for their beautiful flowers.

Although vertebrate diversity in these deserts is not particularly impressive, a few species do stand out. Perhaps the best mammal flagship is the guanaco (*Lama guanicoe*). This beautiful member of the camel family was common in the desert *lomas* and coastal areas of this region, but is now rare because of hunting. Bird flagships include the Peruvian seaside cinclodes (*Cinclodes taczanowskii*), which is endemic to the rocky coastlines of central and southern Peru and is described as the most maritime of all passerine birds; the gray gull (*Larus modestus*), which breeds in large colonies within the Atacama Desert (35 to 100 km inland); the Endangered endemic Chilean woodstar, confined to a few valleys in the northernmost Atacama Desert on the border with Peru; and the threatened Tamarugo conebill (*Conirostrum tamarugense*), an altitudinal migrant associated with *Prosopis tamarugo* stands in lowland Atacama.

Finally, the lizards of the genus *Microlophus* are an

Inca tern (Larosterna inca),
Paracas, Peru.
© **Patricio Robles Gil**/*Sierra Madre*

interesting group, which are common along the rocky coast, where they feed on insects and algae.

Human Cultures

Several human groups have occupied the Atacama and the Peruvian Coastal Deserts during the last 12 000 years. The first human groups to settle in the desert area were either specialized in the extraction of marine resources, migrating along the coast from the northern hemisphere, or Andean hunters coming from the highlands. The cultural chronology for the area identifies an early phase (*ca.* 12 000 to 8 000 B.P.) characterized by nomadic human groups with a diversified economy, which included the use of marine resources (fish, seabirds, and shellfish) and may have been complemented with camelid hunting and the gathering of edible plants obtained from the coastal *lomas*, oases, valleys, and the *quebradas* that traverse the desert (Engel 1973; Sandweiss et al. 1998; Marquet et al. 1998). By 8 000 to 4 000 B.P. they became more specialized in the exploitation of marine resources (as indicated by the development of tools such as fishhooks, harpoons, nets, and weights), marking the beginning of sedentary life in small settlements along the coast *ca.* 7 000 B.P. (Benfer 1990).

This process of settlement was favored by the nutrient-rich waters of the Humboldt Current, which provided Peru's coastal populations with a head start, allowing them to become sedentary before the development of agriculture (Moseley 1975a). During this time period, the coastal area between Ilo, in southern Peru, and Rio Loa in the northern Atacama Desert was occupied by the Chinchorro culture, famous as the first human group in the world to practice artificial mummification (Arriaza 1995; Standen 1997).

The first evidence of plant domestication in the area dates back to *ca.* 5 000 B.P., a practice that over a period of one millennium spread along the Andes and included the consumption of tubers, such as potatoes (*Solanum* spp.), achira (*Canna edulis*), sweet potatoes (*Ipomoea batata*), jíquima (*Pachyrhizus tuberosus*), peanuts (*Arachis hypogaea*), ají (*Capsicum* spp.), beans (*Phaseolus vulgaris*), and squash (*Cucurbita* spp.).

Between 4 500 and 3 500 B.P., these transformations were associated with cultural changes and particularly with the emergence of monumental architecture and increased social complexity (Lumbreras 1999). Interestingly, because of the gradual increase of desert conditions to the south, this process did not occur in southern Peru and northern Chile, where human groups were still highly dependent on marine resources complemented with some cultigens grown in small oases and *quebradas* (Núñez 1983). By 2 500 B.P. hydraulic developments, represented by a complex network of channels, allowed the expansion of agricultural land and an increase in population density in the coastal set-

tlements in north-central Peru. This process was followed by a progressive local cultural differentiation that gave way to regional cultures such as Moche or Mochica, Lima, and Nazca, and the emergence of complex societies and urban centers with a caste-like structure. One of the most important centers in the desert was the city of Chan Chan (covering near 20 km² and with a population of about 30 000 people at its peak), the capital of the conquest state of Chimor that flourished at the mouth of the Moche River near Trujillo in southern Peru after A.D. 800. Its dominion extended for more than 1 000 km along the desert coast of southernmost Ecuador to central Peru near Lima (Moseley 1975b). These regional cultures were later on dominated (*ca.* A.D. 1300) by the expansion of the Inca Empire that extended from Colombia to southern Chile. The dominance of the Inca Empire was supported by an extensive network of trails that allowed the circulation of troops, administrators, and political dignitaries, as well as a variety of goods produced by a labor tax system known as *mit'a* and imposed by the state on local communities.

Further development of this area was aborted by the Spanish invasion that began in 1532, and imposed a new social order with an economic and political system that included the introduction of all sorts of exotic cultigens and animals. Under the control of Spaniards, the fertile areas in the lowlands were colonized and the indigenous population was decimated by infectious diseases, forced to leave, or transformed into a labor force working on haciendas. However, the lack of a large population made necessary the importation of African slaves, which after the abolition of slavery were replaced by Chinese immigrants. Large cities came into existence in fertile valleys, and focused on the cultivation of olives, cotton, sugar cane, and rice, as well as cattle raising. In the latter part of the nineteenth century, guano extraction became a major economic activity in the Peruvian Coastal Desert, while in the Atacama the focus was on exploitation of nitrate deposits.

Later, the fishing industry flourished in both deserts (Chile and Peru are among the most important producers of fish flour and oil), and fishermen, clustering in small bays or *caletas*, colonized many areas along the coast. Mining also took on increasing importance on the Andean slope in central-southern Peru and northern Chile, while petroleum took on a major role in northern Peru, fostering development of large port complexes along the coast. Increased demand for fresh water soon became a limiting resource for the cities.

At present, the Peruvian Coastal Desert area is inhabited by 13.7 million people (53% of Peru's total population), while in the Atacama Desert the population is only about 750 000 (6% of Chile's population). The main population centers in the area are the city of Lima (Peru's capital) with six million people, the Peruvian cities of Chiclayo and Trujillo with more than 600 000, and several other smaller ones (ranging from 350 000 to

On the opposite page, the Andean condor (Vultur gryphus)*, a wide-ranging Andean species that also forages in the lowland desert.*
© **Wayne Lynch**

Above, male oasis hummingbird (Rhodopis vesper) *hovering over flower of* Lantana camara, *Azapa Valley, near Arica, Chile.*
© **Luiz Claudio Marigo**

On pp. 370-371, Paracas Peninsula, Peruvian Coastal Desert.
© **Patricio Robles Gil**/*Sierra Madre*

150 000) such as Piura, Chimbote, and Tacna in Peru, and Arica, Iquique, and Antofagasta in Chile. The ethnic composition of these cities is cosmopolitan, and includes the descendants of Spaniards and African slaves, British (who came because of the nitrate industry in the Atacama area), and indigenous people from the Andes who came for employment during the period of industrial growth in the second half of the twentieth century. Excluding the urban centers, the population in the region as a whole is only about 2 000 000, amounting to a human population density of 6.8 inhabitants/km². This is higher than many of the wilderness areas included in this book, but the vast unoccupied stretches of the Atacama and Peruvian Deserts justify their inclusion here.

Threats

The extreme conditions prevailing in the Atacama and Peruvian Coastal Deserts have concentrated biodiversity where limiting resources, mostly water, are sufficient to sustain life. Predictably, these areas have also attracted human groups during the last 12 000 years and presently many of them are near large urban centers. With a total human population of 13.7 million in this desert region, human encroachment on high-diversity areas is the major threat, with *lomas* being the most vulnerable. Many *lomas* sites are threatened, and some have even been eliminated, especially near cities like Lima in Peru (Dillon 1997). *Lomas* formations are further impacted by grazing by cattle, sheep, and goats, especially during favorable El Niño years, and the collection of commercially-valuable species.

These threats are also acute in riparian ecosystems, where large expanses of land have been cleared for agricultural activities and human settlements, and where trees (such as the *arrayán* near Arequipa) and cacti are collected for fuelwood or construction. Additional threats are posed by mining activities, which contaminate rivers and alter water flow patterns through water extraction.

Fortunately, human population tends to be heavily concentrated in the urban areas, meaning that there are still large expanses of wilderness that remain little impacted and should be protected.

Conservation

In terms of conservation, two areas have been identified as Centers of Plant Diversity (Site SA42: *Lomas* formations of Peru and Site SA43: *Lomas* formations of the Atacama Desert, Northern Chile; Davis et al., 1997), and two have been identified as Endemic Bird Areas by BirdLife International (EBA 052: Peru-Chile Pacific slope, from central Peru to the Rio Loa in northern Chile; EBA 045: Tumbesian region, whose southern part includes the southern Peruvian coastal desert between Piura and Lima) (Stattersfield et al. 1998).

Unfortunately, only a small fraction of the important areas for biodiversity conservation are currently protected in one reserve (La Chimba National Reserve, 30 km²) in Chile and two national reserves (Lachay, 51 km² and Paracas, 1 170 km²) in Peru. Several proposals to increase the amount of *lomas* area protected have been made in both countries, but have not yet been implemented (Muñoz Schick et al. 1996; Dillon 1997; Dillon and Hoffman 1997).

The most important coastal lagoons and marshes in Peru are protected in the Mejía National Sanctuary (7 km²) and in the Pantanos de Villa Reserved Area (4 km²), but are not yet protected in Chile. However, several sites have been proposed, notably the mouths of the Loa, Lluta, and Azapa Rivers (Muñoz Schick et al., *op. cit.*). Finally, dense stands of *Prosopis tamarugo* are protected in the Pampa del Tamarugal National Reserve (1 022 km²) in the Atacama Desert.

In total, only 2 284 km², or less than 1% of this region, is currently protected in these six parks and reserves, an extremely low percentage for an area of such importance.

The unique nature of the ecosystems in the deserts of Peru and Chile, the presence of species with astonishing morphological, physiological, and ecological adaptations, and the significant number of restricted-range endemic species of plants and animals make this region of great importance for conservation.

PABLO A. MARQUET
HÉCTOR GONZÁLEZ
RAQUEL PINTO
CALOGERO SANTORO
VIVIEN G. STANDEN
HORACIO ZEBALLOS

Above, a number of lizard species inhabit the Paracas Peninsula and the Coastal Deserts.
© **Patricio Robles Gil**/*Sierra Madre*

On the opposite page, gray gull (Larus modestus) in the Atacama Desert, Chile. Though not endemic, this species breeds mainly in this wilderness area.
© **Günter Ziesler**

THE SAHARA/SAHEL

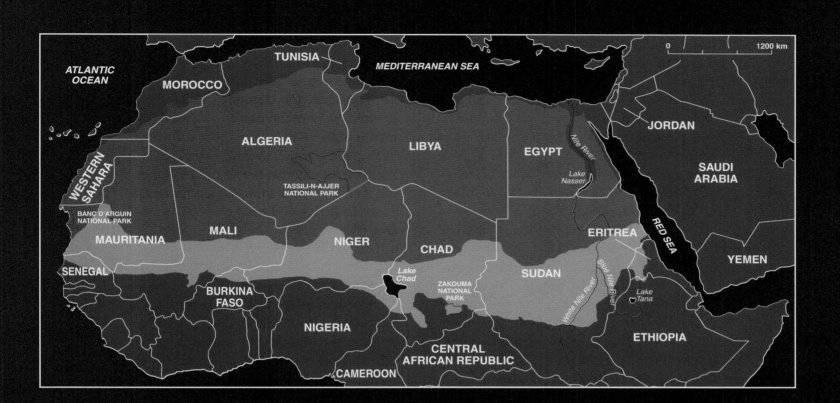

Sahara is the Arabic word for desert. To distinguish it as the largest desert in the world, the Arabs called it *Al-Sahara Al-Kubra*: the Great Desert. It covers a total area of 7 780 544 km², and stretches 4 830 km east to west from the Atlantic Ocean to the Red Sea, and 1 930 km north to south from the Atlas Mountains of Morocco and the Mediterranean Sea to the *Sahel* —a word that means "border area" in Arabic. The 5 000 km-long and 200-300 km-wide strip of steppe land of the Sahel is the transitional southern boundary of the Sahara. The Sahel covers 3 189 507.3 km² and taken together with the Sahara they measure about 10 970 051 km², an area larger than the entire continental U.S. The northern portion of the Sahara includes the nations of Algeria, Tunisia, Libya, and Egypt, while in the south it encompasses Western Sahara and the northern parts of Mauritania, Mali, Niger, Chad, and Sudan. At the Sahara's southern border, the Sahel reaches from Senegal through the southern portions of Mauritania, Mali, Burkina Faso, Niger, the northern part of Nigeria, and parts of Chad, Sudan, and Ethiopia.

As we define it, this area incorporates a total of 12 WWF ecoregions, seven in the Sahara, four in the Sahel and one, the West Saharan Montane Xeric Woodlands, shared by the two regions (PA1332) (223 096.4 km² in the Sahara; 2.9%, and 34 974.8 km² in the Sahel; 1.1%). The Saharan ecoregions are Sahara Desert (PA1327) (4 566 871.4 km²; 58.7%), North Saharan Steppe and Woodlands (PA1321) (1 659 758.3 km²; 21.3%), South

Saharan Steppe and Woodlands (PA1329) (1 101 739.8 km²; 14.2%), Tibesti-Jebel Uweinat Montane Xeric Woodlands (PA1331) (82 238 km²; 1.0%), Red Sea Coastal Desert (AT 1317) (56 323 km²; 0.7%), Saharan Halophytics (PA0905) (52 890.7 km²; 0.7%), and Atlantic Coastal Desert (PA1304) (37 626.4 km²; 0.5%). The Sahel contains Lake Chad (13 275.8 km²; 0.4%) plus the following ecoregions: Sahelian Acacia Savanna (AT0713) (3 050 432.2 km²; 95.6%), Inner Niger Delta Flooded Savanna (AT0903) (46 032.4 km²; 1.4%), East Saharan Montane Xeric Woodlands (AT1303) (27 870.6 km²; 1.0%), and Lake Chad Flooded Savanna (AT0904) (16 921.5 km²; 0.5%).

The western part of the Sahara is known as the *Maghreb*. The eastern Sahara is commonly divided into three regions: the Libyan Desert, from the Nile River west through Libya; the Nubian Desert in southern Egypt and northern Sudan; and the Eastern Desert, from the Nile Valley east to the Red Sea. To the south lies the Sudano-Sahelian zone of seasonal scrub and grassland savanna, a thin belt between the Sahara and the Sudano-Guinean dry woodland zone to the south. Oases, depressions where the water table is high or where artesian waters flow to the surface, dot this ancient trackless wilderness. These oases, which account for only 2%-3% of the Sahara's area, were used as resting and replenishment posts by the ancient caravans traveling throughout North Africa along the salt trade routes.

Sahara
Sahel

On the opposite page, Saharan landscape of dunes and rocky outcrops, northern Chad.
© George Steinmetz

The continent of Africa lies on a vast crustal block called the African Plate. The northern half of the plate continues northward and submerges beneath Europe, where its northward movement caused the rise of the Alps. Other mountain-building episodes formed the Atlas Mountains on the northwest corner as well as the lofty mountains in the center of the Sahara, attesting to great volcanic activity in the past. The surface of the Sahara and the Sahel overlie a vast sandstone base several kilometers thick, called the Nubian Sandstone. This layer is overlaid by shale layers of Cretaceous age (65-135 million years) that are topped by plateau-forming limestone of Eocene and younger epochs of the Tertiary period (2-65 million).

Stone plateaus of denuded rock (*hamada*) and plains of coarse gravel (known as *regs* in the western Sahara and *serirs* in the east) cover about 70% of the Sahara. High mountains rising in the central Sahara include the Hoggar or Ahaggar (2 918 m) and Tassili-n-Ajjer of southern Algeria (2 250 m); the Aïr Mountains of northern Niger (2 020 m); the Tibesti Massif in northern Chad (3 350 m); and the Adrar des Iforas of eastern Mali (850 m). These mountains, together with oases and transition zones, occupy about 15% of the area (Cloudsley-Thompson 1984). Sand dune fields (*ergs*) occupy the remaining 15% of the Sahara. The most prominent of these great dune systems are the Tenere of Niger, the Fezzan of Libya, and the Grand Ergs Occidental and Oriental of Algeria. The sand dune fields of the Sahara occupy topographic depressions suggesting that the sand was originally formed during wet climates in the past and carried to inland depressions by running surface water. Radar images from space reveal the ancient courses of these rivers that are now dry and covered by wind-deposited sand. The geology and climate of the Sahara gives rise to calcareous and unleached aridisol desert soils.

Archaeological evidence indicates that the Sahara has witnessed several cycles of wet and dry climate. The present dry cycle began about 5 000 years ago. From that time to 11 000 years ago, the Sahara experienced a rainy climate. Cave art depicting ostriches, giraffes, baboons, and cattle, as well as numerous human-made rock implements, bear witness to its former humid condition. Rock carvings of giraffes in the Aïr Massif of Niger provide evidence of historic local climatic variation in the region. Prior to this wet period, another dry cycle persisted.

Much of the water from the wet climate cycles appears to have seeped into the substrate where it was stored as groundwater, mostly in the Nubian Sandstone. Some oases of the Libyan Desert have water dating 25 000 to 35 000 years back. Vast ancient fossil aquifers still underlie the desert, though these are now being tapped to support urbanization and agriculture. In contrast with the Saharan landscape, the sand sheets and dune fields of the Sahel cover nearly 50% of the surface.

The only river that crosses the Sahel and the Sahara near the eastern edge is the 6 695 km-long Nile River, the longest in the world. The White Nile originates in Burundi of Central Africa and the Blue Nile in the

Ethiopian Plateau further north. It drains 2 850 000 km², or about 10% of Africa. The Nile's course clearly demonstrates the northward dip of North Africa, as it forms a vast delta from Cairo to the Mediterranean coastline. The Niger is the sole river in the western Sahel. It rises on the Fouta Djallon Plateau in southern Guinea and meanders northward toward Mali. In central Mali, it forms the vast inland Niger Delta, a maze of channels and shallow lakes covering 77 700 km².

Lake Chad is the only major body of water in the central part of North Africa, straddling the border between the Sahara and the Sahel. Three small rivers, the Komadougou, the Logone, and the Chari feed it. Satellite images from the past three decades clearly show the effects of the 4- to 11-year cycles of wet and dry climates in the Sahel, which average seven years. These alternating cycles cause major water fluctuations in the lake levels. At the present time, the northern half of the lake is essentially dry and sand dunes have replaced the elusive water.

The climate of North Africa is one of the harshest in the world. The Aridity Index of the eastern part of the Sahara is 200, meaning that the received solar radiation is capable of evaporating 200 times the amount of rainfall (Mainguet 1999; Henning and Flohn 1977). Indeed, it is common for the cloud cover over Siwa Oasis in the Libyan Desert to be zero per year. It might rain only once in 20 to 50 years and the relative humidity can be as low as 5% and rarely exceeds 30%.

The Sahara-Sahel has a classic continental climate that manifests itself in extremely wide temperature variations. In the Sahara, daily temperature variations can range from -5°C to +50°C. Daily (diurnal) ranges of 30°C are common and daytime temperatures are exceedingly high. The highest official temperature in the shade, 58°C, was measured at Al Azizyah in the Libyan Desert. However, during the December to February winter, temperatures below freezing are common.

The Sahara and Sahel are ruled by seasonal rainfall. In local lore, the constellation known as the Big Dipper or Ursa Major by Westerners is named *Rakumi* (the camel) or *Rakumi Daji* (bush camel or giraffe) by the Hausa people. In the dry season, the camel lifts its head (the dipper handle) to reach the leafy tree branches. In the rainy season, it lowers its head to eat the lush grass. This seasonal precipitation of the Sahara-Sahel is a function of the annual migration of the ITCZ or Inter-Tropical Convergence Zone, the major driving force of global weather.

During the wet season of June to August, moist air arrives from the south-southwest, while during the September to May dry season, hot, arid winds push south across the Sahara. These desert winds, known as khamsin, harmattan, scirocco, shahali, and simoom, can turn day into night within minutes as suspended dust particles block out the sun (Gautier 1935). Dust from the Sahara can at times be transported in the upper layers of the troposphere and lower stratosphere from Africa across the Atlantic to South America, and north over the

Sand cat (Felis margarita), *a typical desert species.*
© **Xavier Eichaker**/*BIOS*

Mediterranean Sea. The year-to-year variability of precipitation is great, and prolonged droughts are common. Precipitation is also locally variable. During the rainy season, a storm may inundate one area, while a few kilometers away no rain will fall. Some arid areas receive their entire annual precipitation in a few showers. In times of low food supply, droughts that cause crop failure lead to famines such as those experienced during the Great Famine of 1972 and the drought and famine of 1983-1984.

The situation in the Sahel is different because the region experiences milder weather and receives a slightly steadier 120 to 250 mm of rain per year. The Sahel region is also affected by shorter weather cycles (averaging 7 years) that are caused by variations in the extent of rain clouds from the summer monsoon. This sustains critical natural vegetation that stabilizes the dunes. A dry period of several years eliminates the vegetation, causes soil erosion, and remobilizes the sand, resulting in severe damage to farms and human settlements.

Biodiversity

The biology and ecology of the Sahara-Sahel is a function of its natural history and climate. Post-glacial eras in which glaciers retreated from mid-Europe changed the climate and contributed to the establishment of bird migration patterns. The landscapes of the Sahara and the Sahel grade from the hyperarid interior through seasonal grasslands and grassland savannas to dry woodlands. The vegetation of the Sahara includes desert shrub and desert grasslands which are rainfall-dependent, desert and salt-desert shrub, and true desert. The Sahel is generally classified as acacia-desert grass savanna. The vegetation of Africa has been described by a number of sources including Shantz and Marbut (1923), Knapp (1973), White (1983), and most recently by WWF (Olson et al. 2001).

The Sahara proper is home to some 1 600 plant species, of which over 11.8% are endemic (Quézel 1978). The flora of the Sahel includes about 1 200 species, with only 3% endemic (White, *op. cit.*). The principal plant genera include the combretums, euphorbias, and palms. However, some 80% of the woody species of the Sahel are acacias, including *Acacia ehrenbergiana, A. laeta, A. tortilis, A. scorpioides, A. senegal, A. albida,* and *A. nilotica*. The collection of acacia gum has historically been commercially important. Other woody tree species include *Balanites aegyptiaca, Boscia senegalensis, Commiphora africana,* and *Leptadenia pyrotechnica* (Walter and Gillett 1998).

Overall, the Sahara and Sahel together support at least 1 660 species of plants, 228 of which are endemic. For both the Sahara and the Sahel, many of the plants are found in isolated, hospitable pockets scattered across the hyperarid landscape. Many species like *Moringa oleifera* have both significant traditional and modern pharmaceutical value, and are therefore in need of conservation. The total number of threatened species may exceed 600, although an accurate assessment is still lacking.

Hyperarid environments tend to harbor a highly-specialized fauna capable of coping with extreme conditions. The Sahara and Sahel are no exception, and thus house a number of very charismatic desert animals, including the fennec fox (*Vulpes zerda*), the sand cat (*Felis margarita*), the horned viper (*Cerastes cerastes*), the desert monitor (*Varanus griseus*), the desert jerboa (*Jaculus* spp.), the striped hyena (*Hyaena hyaena*), the caracal or desert lynx (*Caracal caracal*), the desert hedgehog (*Hemiechinus aethiopicus*), the North African elephant shrew (*Elephantulus rozeti*), the houbara bustard (*Chlamydotis undulata*), the pharaoh eagle-owl (*Bubo ascalaphus*), and a host of scarab beetles (Family Scarabaeidae). In total, the Sahara and Sahel support 221 mammal species, of which 35 are endemic. Gerbils (*Gerbillus* spp.) are especially diverse, with 28 species, of which 15 are endemic (WWF, in prep.), and three primates occur in this dry region as well: the anubis baboon (*Papio anubis*), the tantalus monkey (*Cercopithecus aethiops tantalus*), and the patas monkey (*Erythrocebus patas*). Birds are represented by 660 species, of which five are endemic. Reptiles are moderately diverse, with 126 reptile species of which eight are endemic, but amphibians, as might be expected in such a dry region, number only 20 species, of which two are endemic.

Interspersed within the Sahara and Sahel are numerous permanent and ephemeral wetlands which, while small in size, are important fragile ecosystems supporting permanent populations of birds, freshwater fish, and invertebrates, as well as being stopovers for Palaearctic migrant birds, especially waterfowl. In a single month in 1994, some 100 000 birds representing 90 species were counted at 50 sites totaling some 17 500 ha. One 50-ha temporary lake was found to contain over 7 000 individuals of seven species of Palaearctic ducks (Brouwer and Mullié 1994). The Sahara and Sahel still maintain some remnants of recent, more favorable climatic conditions, although these have not been well documented or studied. There are also important local centers of high diversity and endemism sprinkled throughout the region, such as the Aïr Mountains of Niger.

Flagship Species

The best-known and most threatened flagship species of the region are two antelopes, the scimitar-horned oryx (*Oryx dammah*) and the addax (*Addax nasomaculatus*).

The spectacular scimitar-horned oryx, with its magnificent scimitar-shaped horns, weighs up to 220 kg. This animal is beautifully adapted to desert life and can go months without drinking water by obtaining moisture from the vegetation it eats. Its specialized survival mechanisms include important adaptations, such as kidneys that minimize the loss of water through urine and a metabolism that allows it to deal with body tempera-

The fennec (Vulpes zerda), *a small, attractive, large-eared fox of the desert.*
© **Wayne Lynch**

tures as high as 46.5°C. Although it was formerly found from Mauritania to the Red Sea, the scimitar-horned oryx has declined almost to extinction due to overhunting, land conversion, and competition from domestic animals (Newby 1978, 1980, 1984; Newby et al. 1987). As recently as 1958, there were believed to be some 10 000 scimitar-horned oryx in the wild. Sadly, by 1996 this number had decreased to only 200-500 and by 1999 it was thought to be extinct in the wild, although there was a recent unsubstantiated sighting of four animals in northern Niger. The scimitar-horned oryx will be listed by the IUCN as Extinct in the Wild until the offspring of a reintroduced population start breeding (Hilton-Taylor 2000).

The addax is also listed as Critically Endangered by the IUCN. A statuesque sand-colored antelope, this species has long, spiraled horns, a prominent brown tuft of hair, and a white chevron cross on the nose. It once ranged from Egypt to Tunisia and Morocco, but is now found only in tiny populations from Mauritania to Sudan (Newby 1984; Wilson and Reeder 1993), and is all but extinct in the wild due to illegal hunting. While there are programs to reintroduce the addax to the Sahara and Sahel, its existence depends on protection of its last remaining refuges.

The dorcas gazelle (*Gazella dorcas*), a small, horned antelope with splayed hooves, lives primarily on the perimeter of the Sahara. It can maintain a steady speed of 50 km per hour, and has been known to reach speeds as high as 95 km per hour. Although its primary predators are the golden jackal (*Canis aureus*), striped hyena, caracal, and cheetah (*Acinonyx jubatus*), its listing as a Vulnerable species is mainly attributed to hunting by humans.

Endangered species include the Nubian ibex (*Capra nubiana*), the dama gazelle or *addra* (*Gazella dama*), the slender-horned gazelle or *rhim* (*Gazella leptocerus*), the African wild ass (*Equus africanus*), and the Egyptian tortoise (*Testudo kleinmanni*). Locally-threatened species include the African elephant (*Loxodonta africana*), the cheetah, and the giraffe (*Giraffa camelopardalis*). Cheetahs now appear to be limited to only a few protected areas, and giraffes in Niger are down to just 64 animals.

Human Cultures

The Sahara has a total population of 35.2 million people. If the few, large cities such as Cairo and Nouakchott are not included, the population is only 10.3 million, meaning that population density in this vast wilderness is only 1.3 inhabitants/km². The Sahel supports some 34.4 million people, 1.5 million of whom live in large cities. The population density outside of the urban centers is about 10.3 inhabitants per km². Overall, this means that this wilderness has a mean population density of just under four inhabitants per km², with the Sahara itself having much more of a wilderness character than the densely-populated Sahel.

A tremendous diversity of languages and ethnic back-

grounds is found in the Sahara and Sahel. The influences include those of Pharaonic/Coptic Egypt and the Nubian cultures of the Sudan in the eastern part of the Sahara, as well as the Berber and Touareg (Tuareg) cultures in the west. The Touareg, renowned nomadic pastoralists, were known as the "blue people of the desert" owing to their indigo turbans that impart a blue tint to their skin. There are 750 000-1 300 000 Touareg living in the central and southern areas of the Sahara and Sahel, primarily in Algeria, Libya, Burkina Faso, and especially Niger and Mali. They are Sunni Muslims, whose language, Tamasheq, is Berber in origin. Touareg means "abandoned by God," a name given to them by their historical Arab enemies. The Touareg call themselves *Imochagh* or *Imajirhen*, a name derived from the root verb *iohargh*, meaning "it is free," "it is pure," and "it is independent." The Touareg have been spread over several states since colonization, and their traditional existence is threatened by the decline of the salt trade and, more recently, by a series of severe droughts, the expansion of permanent agriculture, and war.

To the west and south, the ancient Songhai and the Dogon culture flourished in Timbuktu. The Dogon, a tribe of some 100 000 who inhabit the Homburi Mountains near Timbuktu in Mali, have a unique, well-developed cosmology and creation mythology. First documented by the French anthropologist Marcel Griaule in 1931, the Dogon are legendary for their ancient lore regarding Sirius, the Dog Star, and their belief that it was orbited by another unseen star. This second star, a white dwarf called Sirius B, was not "discovered" until 1862 with the aid of a telescope.

Numerous other cultures and language groups are represented in the region, including the Woodabe, Hausa, Beri Beri (Kanouri), Toubou, Gourmantche, and the Peul (Fulani).

Threats

The biodiversity of the Sahara and the Sahel is under severe threat, with loss and fragmentation of natural habitat being the major cause, and introduced species playing an important role in certain areas as well. Habitats of limited extent, where much biodiversity is concentrated, are particularly vulnerable, including scattered temporary lakes and wetlands, the floodplains of rivers, tropical dry forest, and vegetation types such as tiger bush, just to mention a few. Desertification is a major driving factor for habitat change. However, it does not necessarily refer to the actual expansion of the Sahara, but rather is more an effect of land degradation in vulnerable arid, semiarid, and dry subhumid areas resulting from factors such as climatic variability and human activities. The compounding effects of drought, overgrazing, and poor irrigation practices make it difficult for the fragile Sahelian and Saharan ecosystems to survive.

Changes in land-use practices have had considerable impact. These include establishment of dry season (*con-

On the opposite page, the scimitar-horned oryx (Oryx dammah), a large, magnificent desert antelope that was once widespread throughout the region. Sadly, it is now thought to be Extinct in the Wild, but captive populations make reintroduction possible.

Above, the addax (Addax nasomaculatus), a highly-adapted desert antelope and one of the Sahara's most important flagship species. It is now Critically Endangered in the wild, but well-represented in captivity.
Both photos:
© **Zoological Society of San Diego**

On pp. 380-381, domestic camels (Camelus bactrianus) in canyon in Chad.
© **George Steinmetz**

tra-saisson) farms which upset a gentle balance between herders and farmers that had existed for hundreds if not thousands of years. In the past, nomadic pastoralists would move their herds from the wet-season grazing lands to fallow agricultural fields in the dry season, where they could both find food and fertilize the cultivated fields. The conversion to permanent irrigated cultivation taps fossil-water aquifers, depletes soil nutrients, and constrains pastoralism by removing the former dry-season food reserve of the animals. The cultivation of land to meet the demand for food for increasing populations in rural areas also impacts recuperation of soils. In the Sahel, conversion of wetlands to agriculture reduces or eliminates refuges for sedentary and migrating waterfowl. Overgrazing, especially by goats, has also upset the delicate pastoral rhythm. Programs to sink wells have resulted in the denuding of large areas by herds that congregate at these water sources. In addition, the traditional knowledge on how to find and tap hidden springs, former security in times of drought, has been lost. This impacts the ability of herders to safeguard their already scarce water resources. Human population growth and the associated increased need for water add to the depletion of fossil aquifers.

The demand for firewood has a substantial impact on soil conservation and wildlife protection, while efforts to provide more fuelwood often result in the planting of exotic species. The protein needs of the increasing human population result in more intense hunting pressure, in particular for bushmeat, and to a lesser degree waterfowl. Declining populations of addax antelopes, gazelles, primates, and other species are clear evidence of increased hunting pressure, both for meat and sport. The impact of big game hunting also requires mention.

Invasive exotic species such as *Eucalyptus* and mesquites (*Prosopis juliflora, P. chilensis*) have also been introduced in large numbers as part of reforestation programs. Mesquites now occupy most of the Nigerienne portion of what was Lake Chad.

Exploration and exploitation of petroleum and mineral resources, including uranium, continue to have a significant impact in the region, while civil strife and armed conflict have also been a cause of habitat destruction and species loss.

In spite of all the problems that this region faces, it is estimated that 85% of the Sahara can still be considered intact. Given its higher population density in a smaller area, the Sahel is much more impacted, especially by agricultural and urban expansion. Nonetheless, we estimate that it is still some 70% intact at this time. Combining the two, we believe that the Sahara/Sahel as defined here is still at least 80% intact.

Above, Tuareg nomads moving camp with camel and donkey, Azaouak Valley, Sahel region of Niger.

On the opposite page, Bororo nomad watching male beauty contest, Azaouak Valley, Sahel region of Niger.
Both photos: © **Victor Englebert**

Conservation

The Sahara and Sahel promote their own "natural protection" due to their remoteness, the low value of their natural resources, and the harsh climate and resulting low human population densities. In terms of formal protection, there are currently 11 protected areas in the Sahara and 29 in the Sahel, with two of them covering parts of both regions. In total, only a small portion of the combined region is protected, just 2.8% of the Sahara and 5.1% of the Sahel, for a total of 3.5% overall, or 380 707 km². Obviously, much more is needed in terms of protected areas.

Protected area categories include national parks, faunal and floral reserves, protected wetlands, and World Heritage Sites, which cover areas of various extent in the different countries of the region and afford differing degrees of protection. All protected areas are under threat from poaching, grazing, firewood collection, and agricultural expansion and water demands. The simple, hard fact is that areas that support plant and animal diversity in such an unforgiving climate also promote competing human demands for fuel, shelter, and sustenance.

The two largest protected areas in this wilderness area are the Aïr and Ténéré, which covers some 7 700 000 ha, and the Ouadi Rime-Ouadi Achim Faunal Reserve of Chad totaling 8 000 000 ha; they are also the two largest protected areas in all of Africa. The former is a World Heritage Site, which is classified as "in danger."

RAMSAR Wetlands of International Importance are also quite significant in this desert wilderness, and include Lac Oubeïra and Lac Tonga in Algeria, La Mare de Oursi and La Mare aux Hippopotames in Burkina Faso, Lac Fitri in Chad, Lake Bardawil and Lake Burullus in Egypt, and the Parc National du W in Niger. New RAMSAR Wetlands are the Complexe Kokorou-Namga, Lake Chad, and the Zone Humide du Moyen Niger (RAMSAR 1993, 2001). The 1.6-million-ha Partie Tchadienne du Lac Tchad (Chad portion of Lake Chad) was added as a RAMSAR wetland site in 2002.

In summary, the vast desert sea of the Sahara and its shoreline, the Sahel, are truly global treasures. The region harbors a remarkable diversity of landscapes, from the virtually lifeless Libyan Desert, to the mountain refuges of the Aïr, to the life-sustaining oases and ephemeral wetlands. That such a stark landscape and climate can provide sustenance to countless resident and migratory birds, magnificent gazelles, and small mammals and reptiles is miraculous. Their different adaptations for surviving the heat and cold, and patiently waiting for the fickle rains is testament to life on Earth. However, as adaptable as the plants and animals of the Sahara and Sahel are, their continued existence is tenuous at best in the face of land conversion and competition for resources with our own species, and much more protection will be required if they are to survive.

DOUG MUCHONEY
FAROUK EL BAZ
PETER KRISTENSEN

THE KALAHARI DESERT

The Kalahari Desert is widely regarded as one of Africa's last wilderness areas and one of the very few relatively undisturbed arid savannas in Africa, although this is rapidly changing. There are various definitions of its boundaries, with some regarding the "true" Kalahari as extending outside of the borders of Botswana due to the occurrence of Kalahari sediments extending through nine countries as far north as Gabon. The Kalahari is broadly characterized by its flatness, absence of water, and the mantles of sand that cover the solid geology of the area. As these features are widespread over much of southern Africa, the term "Kalahari" has consequently been used to describe both the "Kalahari Desert" and the "Mega-Kalahari"; some even dispute calling the Kalahari a desert at all. The term "desert" is, however, no less ambiguous than the term "Kalahari" and, while the region is in fact semiarid rather than arid, the only safe assumption about a semiarid environment is the fact that any given year can be extremely dry.

The name "Kalahari" has also been applied to a variety of ecological, climatic, and physiographic regions, as well as to a group of sediments (Thomas and Shaw 1991). "Kalahari," a corruption of the Setswana word *Kgalagadi*, means "always dry." However, it has been interpreted in different ways, such as "wilderness," "thirstland" or "salt pans" (Van Rooyen 2001). This has resulted in the word "Kalahari" being used to describe any area of desert or semidesert, and at times even being used to describe the entire Republic of Botswana.

For the purposes of this chapter, the Kalahari Desert, or the core of the Mega-Kalahari, as illustrated in the map, is the area recognized as the Kalahari Xeric Savanna (AT1309) by WWF (Olson et al. 2001). It occupies 588 100 km², has an average elevation of 950 m above sea level, and covers all of the southwestern quarter of Botswana, extending into Namibia and South Africa. Its northern boundary is at the extreme southern fringes of the Okavango-Zambezi swamp zone, extending south to the Orange River.

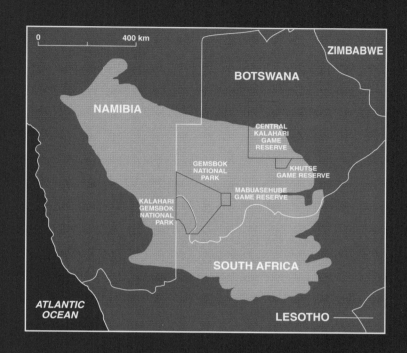

Estimates of the total area remaining intact and relatively free of human interference or any noticeable transformation differ from expert to expert, and range from 50%-80% (C. and T. Stuart, pers. comm., 2002; C. Hilton-Taylor, pers. comm., 2002).

The Kalahari landscape undulates gently and has few topographical intrusions, other than the Okavango Delta to the north, some rocky ridges on its margins, and the occasional fossil river valley (Flegg 1993). A concentration of isolated hills or inselbergs occurs near the Okavango Delta (Thomas and Shaw, *op. cit.*). A virtually dune-free, undulating landscape with abundant trees is found to the east and northeast of the Nossob River. To the west and southwest, the prevailing wind has arranged the sand in parallel dunes facing northwest, a remarkably symmetrical feature of the landscape. These dunes rise in some places to 15-30 m above the valleys between them, stretching from horizon to horizon without any real landmark and making navigation difficult (Van der Walt and Le Riche 1999; Van Rooyen, *op. cit.*). Although there are no perennial rivers in the Kalahari, seasonal rains accumulate in pans.

The Kalahari's dominant feature is its extensive sand cover —one of the largest unbroken stretches of sand on Earth. Geologists continue to disagree about the origin of this mass of sand, which appears to have been transported over great distances for long peri-

World Heritage Area

On the opposite page, meerkat (Suricata suricatta) group sunning on a cold morning in Kalahari Gemsbok National Park, South Africa.
© Nigel J. Dennis/DENNIS AND DE LA HARPE PHOTOGRAPHY

385

ods of time, with its redistribution taking place in different geological eras (Van der Walt and Le Riche, *op. cit.*). Strong winds and low rainfall have ensured that the sand was not carried away to the sea. The sand is usually a red-brown color due to the presence of iron oxide, but can fade to a pale pink or gray depending on the rainfall of the area as the water leaches out of it (Van der Walt and Le Riche, *op. cit.*). The ephemeral pans of the Makgadikgadi in the Okavango Delta are stark, salt-encrusted reminders of a vast inland lake which once covered much of the present Kalahari.

While the Kalahari Desert lies on the Tropic of Capricorn, its high elevation gives it a climate that is more temperate than tropical, characterized by hot summers and winters with warm days and cold nights. Diurnal temperatures range widely during the winter or dry season. In the southern Kalahari, the minimum temperature can go below 0ºC and there is even the occurrence of ground frost. In the southwestern corner, temperature lows of -10ºC and highs of 45.4ºC have been recorded (Thomas and Shaw, *op. cit.*; Van Rooyen, *op. cit.*).

The mean annual rainfall in the Kalahari ranges from 150 mm in the southwest to 500 mm close to the Okavango Delta (Allen and Warren 1993). Rainfall mainly occurs between October and April —the summer months of the Southern Hemisphere. High evaporation rates result in a moisture deficit in all but the very wet months (Thomas and Shaw, *op. cit.*). Although the rainfall can be considered relatively high for a desert biome, the Kalahari's organisms probably do not benefit as much as they should, given that the rain falls in localized thunderstorms of short duration, and is quickly absorbed into the deep sands (Lovegrove 1993). Nevertheless, with the arrival of significant rains, the Kalahari can be transformed almost overnight. Long-dormant seeds spout verdant pastures of new grasses, annuals bloom, and animal life proliferates in synchrony.

Biodiversity

Rutherford and Westfall (1994), in their classification of the biomes of southern Africa, included the Kalahari in their "Savanna" biome, defining it further as a portion of the "Arid Savanna." Generally arid landscapes with a sparse plant cover dominate the Kalahari, with little habitat variation. In the drier southwest, grasses and shrubs dominate the landscape, while small patches or strips of trees (particularly *Acacia* woodland and *Terminalia* sandveld) increase in a northeasterly direction. This pattern is not true for the entire area, as there are regional variations induced by sedimentary and geomorphological factors. The edge of the Okavango Delta, for example, has important swamp grassland and aquatic plant communities, with sweeping *Hyphaene* palm trees. Perennial herbaceous plants and annual plants dominate the vegetation of the Kalahari duneveld. Perennials provide the staple food supply for the

herbivores in the region, with annuals being regarded as an unreliable luxury. Annuals, however, often have showy flowers that give the desert a flash of color during favorable periods. Trees and shrubs form only 8% of the life-form spectrum, but are the visually dominant form. There are very few succulent species —possibly due to the severe night frost (Van Rooyen, *op. cit.*).

The Kalahari is poor from a floristic point of view, especially when compared to the North American deserts of comparable size, and has only some 500-700 vascular plant species and no endemics (C. Hilton-Taylor, *in litt.*, 2002). It does, however, have a variety of perennial grasses that are limited to habitats such as dune tops or under trees, represented primarily by *Eragrostis lehmanniana,* and a few genera such as *Stipagrostis* grasses appear to be dominant (Lovegrove, *op. cit.*; Van der Walt and Le Riche, *op. cit.*).

The fauna of the Kalahari is more spectacular than the flora, and has great potential to attract visitors to the area. Most of the charismatic savanna mammals such as the lion (*Panthera leo*), cheetah (*Acinonyx jubatus*), and blue wildebeest (*Connochaetes taurinus*) occur in abundance in the protected areas, and elephant (*Loxodonta africana*) are common closer to the Okavango Delta. More arid-loving animals such as the gemsbok (*Oryx gazella*) and springbok (*Antidorcas marsupialis*) and, to a lesser extent, hartebeest (*Alcelaphus buselaphus*) and eland (*Taurotragus oryx*) also occur over a widespread area. These ungulates and an abundance of rodents support many carnivores, and parts of the Kalahari have built up a deserved reputation as one of the few ecosystems in southern Africa where a variety of large predators can be maintained. In addition to lion and cheetah, leopard (*Panthera pardus*), spotted hyena (*Crocuta crocuta*), and bat-eared fox (*Otocyon megalotis*) are all well represented, with occasional sightings of the highly-endangered wild dog (*Lycaon pictus*) (Hanks 2000). In all, there are just over 101 species of mammals, but none are endemic (WWF, in prep.)

Birds are also surprisingly well represented in this semiarid region, with approximately 338 species (264 species have been recorded in the Kgalagadi Transfrontier Park alone), but there are no endemics (WWF, in prep.). However, the attractive Burchell's sandgrouse (*Pterocles burchelli*), whose distribution is centered on the sandy soils of the Kalahari Basin, is a near-endemic. The male adult, with its tightly-coiled belly feathers, has developed a unique method of transporting water to the chicks. When these feathers come into contact with water, their filaments uncoil, trapping water like blotting paper, which is then carried to the chicks, who then strip out the water (MacLean 1984).

Not surprisingly, there are only 15 amphibian species in this dry region, none of them endemic. Reptiles are better represented with 88 species and one of these, the live-bearing Gariep blind skink (*Typhlosaurus gariepensis*), is endemic to the Kalahari, with several others being near-endemics (WWF, in prep.).

Above, springbok (Antidorcas marsupialis) in Kalahari Gemsbok National Park, Botswana.

On the opposite page, male lion (Panthera leo) in the Kalahari. Both photos:
© **Patricio Robles Gil**/*Sierra Madre*

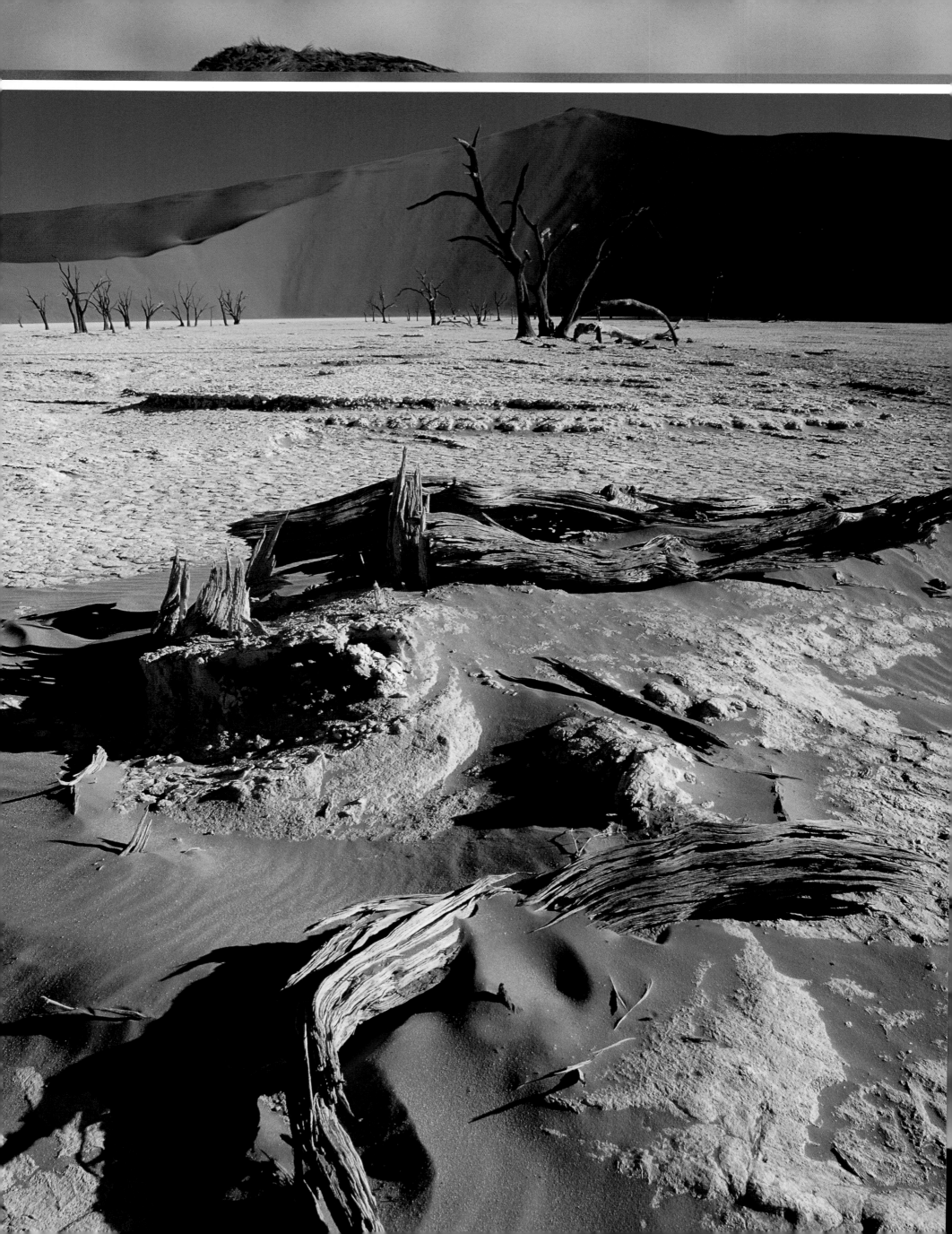

THE NAMIB DESERT

The Namib is one of the world's oldest deserts, providing an unexpected and quite extraordinary celebration of habitats and biodiversity. It stretches along the southwest coast of Africa for approximately 1 800 km from the northern edge of the Succulent Karoo Hotspot (Myers et al. 2000) at Diaz Point to the Carunjamba River in Angola, extending inland between 40-150 km and covering 126 600 km², of which an impressive 95% is still intact (J. Mendelsohn, pers. comm., 2002). This area is equivalent to the WWF Namib (AT1315) and Kaokoveld Desert (AT1310) ecoregions (Olson et al. 2001), and is split between Namibia (105 800 km², 84%) and Angola (20 800 km², 16%). Altitudinally, it reaches an elevation of 1 000 m above sea level at the Namib escarpment, and over 2 500 m at the top of the Brandberg, Namibia's highest point. Extensive marine fossil deposits are found quite far inland, indicating the shift of the present-day shoreline (Barnard 1998a; Seely 1992).

The Namib has four broad desert landforms. The southern Namib succulent zone of plains, inselbergs, and shifting sand extends northwards to about Luderitz. The spectacular sand-sea of shifting sand dunes extends largely uninterrupted for almost 400 km to the Kuiseb River and Walvis Bay. The central Namib, with gravel plains and a sea of small hummock dunes, extends to just north of the Ugab River and Brandberg. Finally, there is the northern Namib (better known as the Skeleton Coast —named after the countless shipwrecks and the many whale skeletons along its shores), with rugged mountains, deeply-incised ephemeral river valleys, and coastal hummock dunes (Barnard, 1998b; C. Brown, pers. comm., 2002). The Kunene River on the border between Namibia and Angola is the only perennial river flowing through this region, with the next nearest to the south being the Orange River on the border between Namibia and South Africa, separated by over 1 300 km of hyperarid desert. However, the Orange River is not within the Namib as we define it here, but rather within the Succulent Karoo Hotspot. Other rivers flow into the Atlantic less frequently, and many of these have a subterranean water supply, which supports the growth of large trees and the presence of other nondesert flora and fauna in some of the most arid portions of the Namib. Flash floods do

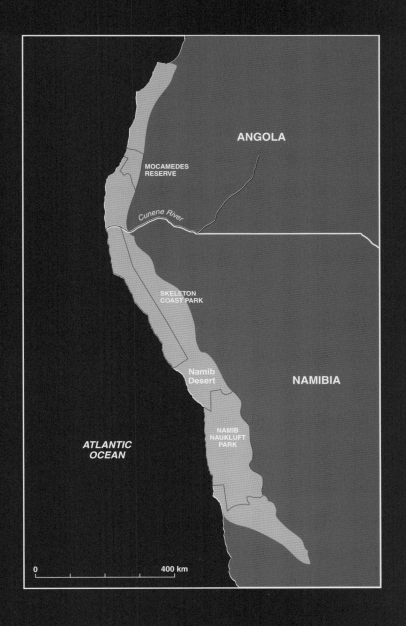

occur down the usually dry riverbeds, but the water disappears as quickly as it came (Flegg 1993; Seely, *op. cit.*).

The cold, upwelling Benguela Current that flows northwards along the Atlantic coast from Antarctica reduces the occurrence of rainfall over the land. The interaction of hot, arid desert and cold sea current is complex. The water vapor crossing the cold ocean often condenses into an early morning fog that creeps inland, the fog having a profound effect on the survival of wildlife in the area that is otherwise devoid of moisture (Allen and Warren 1993; Flegg, *op. cit.*).

Deserts are characterized by a paucity of rain, and the Namib is no exception, ranging from an annual average of 15 mm on the coast to about 100 mm on the eastern escarpment, although this is very erratic, with years of little or no rainfall at all. Most of the Namib's rain falls in the summer, with the exception

Wilderness Area

On the opposite page, dead camel thorn trees (Acacia erioloba), *Sossusvlei, Namib Desert.*
© **Hans Strand**

395

of the southern succulent Namib, which lies at the extreme northern end of the winter rainfall zone that characterizes the entire southwestern corner of Africa, and the extreme southwestern end of the summer rainfall zone. A strong southwesterly wind blows for most of the year in the Namib. The winter months often have a hot, easterly "berg" wind flowing off the escarpment, which sends temperatures into the low to mid 40°C (Barnard 1998b; Seely, *op. cit.*). Daily temperatures in the Namib are generally moderated by the fogs and sea breezes, particularly along the coast, so that the highest temperature recorded at Walvis Bay is only 35°C. The mean annual temperature on the coast is relatively low, only 14°-18°C. With the moisture supplied by fog and the relatively moderate temperatures, the Namib has one of the kindest hyperarid environments (Allen and Warren, *op. cit.*; Pickford and Senut 2000).

Biodiversity

Namibia's coastal habitats are some of the most productive in the world —the result of the complex interactions of the cold Benguela Current and the periodic intrusions of warm waters from Angola (Barnard 1998a). The perennial nature of the upwelling Benguela system ensures that the marine environment supports a high concentration of life. Some 90 species of bony fish and thirty species of cartilaginous fish have been recorded off the Namibian coast, which makes it an important commercial fisheries and recreational angling area. However, in spite of this high productivity, the Namib coast supports low diversity of species in relation to other upwelling systems, and there are no endemic fish species (Sakko 1998).

The vegetation of the Namib itself is characterized by the dominance of therophytes —annual plants that survive the droughts in the form of seed. After an effective rainfall of less than 20 mm, the barren landscape can transform overnight into a sea of grasses, mostly species of the genus *Stipagrostis*. Other interesting plant species in the Namib are the numerous geophytes and the euphorbias and commiphoras. The majority of plants in the southwest belong to the Family Mesembryanthemaceae (Lovegrove 1993; Rutherford and Westfall 1994). The way in which plants store and then release their seeds is crucially important in the unpredictable desert. The various serotinous plants in the Namib —plants that hold their seeds until a favorable time— form dense communities in which several species exist together, thereby reducing the competition for resources by the various species germinating at different times or utilizing different microhabitats (Günster 1994).

Plant diversity in the Namib as we define it is relatively low and estimated at 1 200-1 400 species, of which about 80 are endemic. This is a much lower number than the Succulent Karoo Hotspot immediately to the south (Patricia Craven, pers. comm., 2002).

As might be expected, large ungulates are restricted to species that have adapted to the harsh conditions, specifically the gemsbok (*Oryx gazella*) and springbok (*Antidorcas marsupialis*). Hartmann's zebra (*Equus zebra hartmannae*) makes occasional forays into the eastern areas. The ephemeral rivers, vegetated by large trees and shrubs, provide linear oases deep into the desert for many species that occur in the savanna systems to the east, including giraffe (*Giraffa camelopardalis*), elephant (*Loxodonta africana*), and greater kudu (*Tragelaphus strepsiceros*), as well as a host of birds and smaller mammals. The desert also provides rocky habitats ideally suited for rodents, and two of these are endemic to the Namib. The dune hairy-footed or Namib dune gerbil (*Gerbillurus tytonis*) is restricted to hot, dry sands in the central area, and the Setzer's hairy-footed or Namib bush-tailed gerbil (*G. setzeri*) is restricted to the quartz gravel plains in the Namib further north. Two other species are near endemic but extending to the south of the region, namely the Namib or Grant's golden mole (*Eremitalpa granti namibensis*) and the pygmy rock mouse (*Petromyscus collinus*), although the latter is primarily an escarpment species (Skinner and Smithers 1990). In all, 68 species of mammals inhabit the Namib Wilderness Area (WWF, in prep.).

Some 262 species of birds have been recorded in the Namib. Three of these are endemic: Gray's lark (*Ammomanes grayi*), which occurs throughout much of the Namib in the barren gravel plains, the dune lark (*Certhilauda erythrochlamys*), which is restricted to the dunes in the central area, and the recently-described Benguela lark (*C. benguelensis*) (Ryan and Bloomer 1999). Rueppell's bustard (*Eupodotis rueppellii*) is largely endemic to the Namib, but also extends inland to some of the valleys and plateaus (Fishpool and Evans 2001; Robertson et al., 1998; WWF, in prep.).

Reptiles are one of the great attractions of the Namib. There are around 74 species, 17 of which are endemic, including one snake, Peringuey's adder (*Bitis perengueyi*), and 16 lizards, six of which are geckos. Some sand specialists can "swim" deep into loose sand to avoid predators and the extreme heat (Branch 1998; WWF, in prep.).

As might be expected for such an arid environment, only 19 species of amphibians have been recorded, mainly in the east, and none are endemic (WWF, in prep.).

Last but not least, the Namib is perhaps best known for its invertebrate endemics. Most notable is an enormous family of beetles called the Tenebrionidae, containing many thousands of African species whose appearance and habits are as varied as the continent itself. The richest tenebrionid fauna is found in the Namib Desert, with the most remarkable habits and adaptations to life in one of the harshest environments. Even the apparently barren dunes support a rich fauna of these highly-specialized beetles, feeding on windborne plant and animal debris blown from distant sources into the desert. Some nocturnal species show extraordinary behavioral adaptations which enable

Above, leopard (Panthera pardus).
© **Nigel J. Dennis**/*DENNIS AND DE LA HARPE PHOTOGRAPHY*

On the opposite page, black-faced impala (Aepyceros melampus).
© **Patricio Robles Gil**/*Sierra Madre*

On pp. 398-399, gemsbok (Oryx gazella) *in the dunes on a foggy morning, Sossusvlei, Namibia.*
© **François Savigny**/*Nature Picture Library*

ARABIAN DESERTS

The Arabian Deserts lie at the center of the largest continuous arid zone on the planet, linking the Sahara and Sahel Deserts of Africa in the west to the deserts of Iran, Pakistan, and India in the east. This wilderness covers some 3 250 000 km² and spans most of the Arabian Peninsula, excluding only approximately 87 000 km² in the southwest corner, where the high mountains (above 2 000 m) capture substantial monsoonal rainfall from the Indian Ocean in the summer and are thus too highly populated and cultivated to be termed "wilderness." The region also includes the mainly mountainous Sinai Peninsula (61 000 km²) to the northwest of Arabia, and extends north to the Syrian Desert (211 000 km²) —the high desert plateau that lies between the Mediterranean Sea and the Arabian Gulf. Altogether, this enormous region extends over 12 countries, of which the Kingdom of Saudi Arabia holds the largest extent (59%), followed by the Republic of Yemen (15%), the Republic of Iraq (11%), the Sultanate of Oman (7%), and the United Arab Emirates (3%). The whole of Bahrain, Kuwait, Oman, Qatar, and the United Arab Emirates (UAE) lie within the Arabian Deserts, as does the great majority of Saudi Arabia (97%) and Yemen (93%), a substantial proportion of Iraq (80%), the Hashemite Kingdom of Jordan (74%), Israel (40%), and smaller proportions of the Syrian Arab Republic (20%) and Egypt (6%).

The Arabian Deserts, like the larger Sahara Desert to the west, are subtropical continental deserts, where constant high air pressure results in low humidity and blue, cloudless skies for much of the year. Incursions of moister air from ocean regions can only penetrate the region occasionally, as storm fronts. The outcome is an arid to hyperarid climate (the average annual precipitation is less than 100 mm throughout the region), especially in the continental areas that are farthest from the oceans, and in flat areas, where there are no mountains to force local updrafts and generate condensation. The Syrian Desert and northern Arabia can be particularly cold in winter —sub-zero night temperatures are common and snow can be widespread in some winters, though it does not lie long. Summer daytime temperatures in southern Arabia can be very high, among the highest on the planet.

The extremely arid climate that both creates this wilderness and protects it from human incursion is not a constant feature of the region. Plenty of evidence (from landscape features, ancient soils, sub-

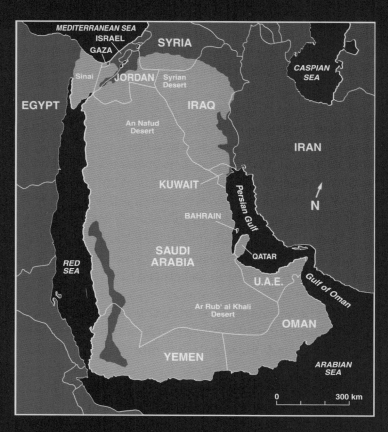

fossil bones, pollen cores, prehistoric rock art, etc.) indicates that there have been periods of wetter climate in the past, the last one ending as recently as 6 000 years ago (Mandaville 1990). Then, the Arabian Deserts were a cooler and more verdant environment of steppe and savanna, with lakes and rivers scattered across seasonally-lush grassland plains that were densely speckled with acacia trees. Hippos (*Hippopotamus amphibius*) and wild oxen occurred in the wetlands, and large herds of ungulates are thought to have roamed the plains, in a scene strikingly similar to the East African plains today.

Looking further back in time, it is clear that there have been many swings in the Arabian climate over the past one million years, between wetter and drier conditions, driven by waxing and waning in the strength of the summer monsoon winds from the Indian Ocean, that can normally (currently) only invade and bring rain to the mountains at the southern periphery of the Arabian Peninsula (Bundy et al. 1989). Therefore, it is clear that the climate over the Arabian Deserts, while tending towards aridity (as is typical of continental subtropical regions), can nevertheless be switched towards wetter conditions than it now experiences. Indeed, the opposite is true as well, in that the evidence for recent climates also indicates periods of such extreme hyperaridity that the current climate seems fairly benign!

Wilderness Areas

On the opposite page, Rub al Khali Desert, near the Shaybah, southeastern Saudi Arabia.
© **Stuart Franklin**/*Magnum Photos*

405

A number of major subregions can be distinguished within the Arabian Deserts. The most obvious are the mountains and hills that extend along the western and southern periphery of Arabia itself. The west coastal mountains, overlooking the Red Sea, are the highest in

distinctive black deserts is in northern Arabia, extending from the Golan Heights and Jabal Druze in southern Syria, across Jordan and into northern Saudi Arabia, where it is named the Harrat al-Harrah. The harrat are important natural wildlife refuges, as the rocky terrain greatly limits off-road driving and other human land

carpet the desert in spring, in places that have received a good rain. In the southern, Sudanian part of Arabia, where the climate is hotter and more arid, the rainfall is (even) more erratic and occurs mainly in the summer, brought by monsoonal storm fronts from the Indian Ocean.

On account of these same differences of climate, the Sudanian zone is characterized by the presence of thorny *Acacia* trees and bushes, which are more or less absent from the colder, northern, Saharo-Arabian zone. These tough, deep-rooted legumes can survive long droughts and are well adapted to hot climates, although over most of southern Arabia they occur at very low density, being generally restricted to wadis, ravines, and pediments. Only on the gravel plains adjacent to the rain-catching mountains of southwestern Arabia and the Hajar Range, where subsurface water is most available, do these trees occur at a density sufficient to be termed "open woodland" or savanna.

The vertebrate fauna of the Arabian Deserts is, apart from the reptiles, somewhat poor in species diversity and endemism compared to tropical ecosystems. For all groups, diversity and endemism are highest in the southwestern coastal lowlands (Tihamah and foothills), the southern highlands (Hadhramawt/Jol, Mahra, Dhofar, Jiddat al-Harasis), and the mountains of northern Oman (Hajar/Musandam ranges), these being the warmest and/or wettest and/or most mountainous parts of the Arabian Deserts. The presence of certain relict or endemic species in these regions provides strong evidence of the existence of land bridges across the mouth of the Red Sea and across the Arabian Gulf, to northeast Africa and Iran respectively, during past Ice Ages.

Reptiles are represented by 108 species, of which approximately three quarters are lizards, and the rest snakes, plus two freshwater turtles (Leviton et al. 1992). At 48% (52 species), endemism is high, reflecting the relatively-poor dispersal capabilities of these animals. Not surprisingly in such an arid region, only eight amphibian species are known to occur (five toads and three frogs), although four of them are strictly endemic to the region (Arnold 1987).

For birds, there are 213 breeding species, but only two are endemic, the Arabian waxbill (*Estrilda rufibarba*) and the Arabian golden sparrow (*Passer euchlorus*) (unpublished data). This low endemism is due to the excellent dispersal capabilities of birds, which have allowed desert-adapted species to spread easily outside the region to similar habitat elsewhere in the Saharo-Sindian Zone. About 44 bird species or subspecies that are confined to the Saharo-Sindian Zone breed within the boundary of the Arabian Deserts (Harrison 1986), with the most species-rich groups being the sandgrouse (*Pterocles* spp.), larks (Alaudidae), and wheatears (*Oenanthe* spp.).

Mammals are represented by 102 species, with 10 (9.8%) of them endemic to the region (Harrison and Bates 1991). These include one species of shrew, two of bats, four of ungulates, and three of rodents.

Desert horned viper (Cerastes cerastes gasparetti), Saudi Arabia.
© **Michel Gunther**/*BIOS*

Flagship Species

The Arabian Deserts are famous worldwide for one particular mammal: the Arabian oryx (*Oryx leucoryx*). This white antelope, the size of a small pony, once roamed in small groups across the plains and plateaus of the Arabian and Syrian Deserts, avoiding only the mountains and hills of the coastal periphery and of the Sinai Desert. Celebrated in poems and stories for its beauty, strength, and stamina, it was hunted by humans using traditional means for thousands of years but, being fleet of foot and sharp of eye, the species remained beyond serious molestation until the late 1930s, when the discovery of oil in Arabia brought increasing numbers of off-road vehicles to the region. This new mobility, combined with the advent of high-powered and accurate rifles, transformed hunting practices by allowing large, self-supporting expeditions to pursue quarry further and for longer than ever before.

Up to that point, millennia of human life in the desert had engendered ruthless hunting driven by the practicalities of daily survival and the rare chance of procuring wild protein. As a result, unbridled hunting drove populations of oryx and other game, such as gazelles, rapidly downward in the two decades following 1945. By the early 1960s, the Arabian oryx was doomed to certain extinction, unless action was taken to conserve the species. This came in 1962, when a group of wild oryx was captured from the desert in eastern Yemen to form the basis of a captive-breeding program. "Operation Oryx" captured the headlines, but did not stop the slaughter; it is believed that hunters killed the last wild Arabian oryx in 1972, in Oman.

Fortunately, captive breeding based at zoos in the U.S.A. proceeded well, and by 1982, 20 years after the program started, the first captive-bred oryx were reintroduced to the wild, to the Jiddat al-Harasis Plateau in Oman. Since then, further reintroductions to the wild have taken place at two sites in Saudi Arabia and one in Israel, and captive breeding continues apace in other Arabian countries, particularly Jordan and the Gulf States. Nonetheless, the future of the species is far from secure. The resurgence of illegal hunting from 1996 onwards has decimated the wild herd in Oman, showing how dependent the survival of this species is on the attitudes and behavior of our own species (Mallon and Kingswood 2001).

A similar tale of extinction or near-extinction due to hunting, followed by captive breeding, reintroduction or tentative recovery, applies to most of the other flagship animals of the Arabian Deserts. The five gazelles of the region —mountain gazelle or *idmi* (*Gazella gazella*; several endemic subspecies), dorcas gazelle or *afri* (*Gazella dorcas isabellina*), Saudi gazelle (*Gazella saudiya*), Queen-of-Sheba's gazelle (*Gazella bilkis*), and goitered gazelle or *reem* (*Gazella subgutturosa marica*)— are excellent flagship species, since they are well known and highly-esteemed culturally. Furthermore, the fact that they have declined greatly allows the message of conservation an entry point into society. Four of the five species are endemic to the region at the specific or subspecific level, although all evidence suggests that the two strictly endemic species (Saudi gazelle and Queen-of-Sheba's gazelle) are actually extinct in the wild, and no individuals of these two species are known to exist in private, captive collections. Captive-breeding and reintroduction programs for the remaining three species of gazelle are ongoing in most of the countries of the region.

The houbara bustard (*Chlamydotis undulata macqueenii*) is another of the famous and important wild animal species for people in the deserts, for this bird was the favored quarry of Arab falconers. Formerly, this species bred widely over the region, but after the 1950s it was swiftly wiped out by overhunting everywhere except the inaccessible and bouldery *harrat* lava fields in northern Saudi Arabia, Jordan, and Syria, and in the well-protected Negev Desert and Wadi Arava of southern Israel. Captive-breeding and reintroduction programs for this species are very active in Saudi Arabia and the United Arab Emirates. In the latter, where falconry is particularly popular, large wild falcons that are used for houbara-hunting (saker falcon, *Falco cherrug*, being the preferred species) are also used to raise conservation awareness.

The Arabian bustard (*Ardeotis arabs*), a much larger relative of the houbara, is a rare and highly-vulnerable-to-hunting inhabitant of the southern Red Sea lowlands of Yemen and Saudi Arabia that would make an ideal flagship species in support of traditional and sustainable farming systems in this area, since it is highly dependent on non-intensive land management to provide the patchwork of dry-farmed and desert habitats that it needs for breeding and feeding (Evans 1994).

Two endemic subspecies that are now extinct, but which were very characteristic of the region, were the Syrian wild ass (*Equus hemionus hemippus*, last recorded in 1928 in Syria) and the Arabian ostrich (*Struthio camelus syriacus*, last recorded in the 1940s). Attempts to captive breed the ass (using the still extant Asiatic subspecies) are ongoing in Jordan and Israel, with reintroduction to the wild being attempted in Israel, while captive breeding of the ostrich is proceeding well in Jordan and Saudi Arabia. Captive breeding is a relatively easy process with this bird, but reintroduction to the wild has not been attempted yet, in part because of a continued controversy over which of the two African subspecies should be used as a substitute (neither being as desert-adapted as was the Arabian subspecies).

The Nubian ibex (*Capra nubiana*) and the Arabian tahr (*Hemitragus jayakari*; confined to Oman and the United Arab Emirates) are two wild goats of the Arabian mountains that have also been, since 1975, major targets for conservation activities in Oman, Jordan, Israel, and Saudi Arabia, both species having being threatened by overhunting in the past. The ibex has particular resonance in southwest Arabia, where it was one of the main symbols and motifs used by the ancient Himyaritic, Sabaean, and Minean civilizations that flourished in Arabia several thousand years ago.

A number of other large and very charismatic species were driven extinct by overhunting in the Arabian Deserts during the twentienth century, including the Asiatic lion (*Panthera leo persicus*, last recorded in 1915 in Iraq); Asiatic cheetah (*Acinonyx jubatus venaticus*, last recorded in 1977 in Oman); wild goat (*Capra aegagrus*, last recorded in the late 1960s in Oman); and Asiatic mouflon (*Ovis ammon arabica*, last recorded in the late 1960s in Oman).

Human Cultures

Historically, the people of the Arabian Deserts were divided into many tribes, each paramount and fiercely independent within its tribal lands. Villages and towns were concentrated along the coasts, in the mountains, and at oases. Here, trading, date-farming, and fishing were the main occupations, with seasonal sidelines such as pearl-diving. Away from these settlements, the Arabian wilderness was the land of the *bedu* or *beduin*, the nomadic tribes of the desert. Predominantly pastoralists whose main wealth was measured in livestock, they followed the rains in a never-ending migration.

This traditional economy was totally changed in most Arabian countries by the advent of the oil industry, from the 1930s onwards, but especially since 1970. National populations expanded rapidly with improved healthcare and employment prospects, and there was large-scale immigration of foreign workers. The beduin life-style remained strong, most especially in non-oil countries such as Jordan, Egypt, and Yemen, but in all countries there was —and continues to be— a strong migration of people from the countryside into towns and cities, to settle and look for jobs and education for their children. The most recent population censuses suggest that there are almost 47 million people living within the Arabian Deserts region, with an overall population density of 14.5 inhabitants/km², but in places other than the towns and cities this density is much lower, with an estimated 15 million people living at an average density of 4.6 inhabitants/km² in the rural areas. This very low population density is one of the reasons that the Arabian Deserts may be considered a wilderness.

Threats

Superficially, much of the Arabian Deserts appears to be a wild and lonely region, totally unaffected by man's activities. Until sometime around 1900 this picture was broadly true (Thesiger 1959), but it is no longer a reality. Oil wealth has transformed many of the societies in the region, leading to very rapid population growth, increasing wealth and leisure time, abandonment of traditional and sustainable land uses, subsidized livestock fodder, cheap off-road vehicles and fuel, and easy availability of water, water trucks, and firearms. Herds of livestock have increased greatly, and their numbers are

Egyptian spiny-tailed agama (Uromastyx aegyptia) *in the desert of the high mountain region of the Sinai, Egypt.*
© Konrad Wothe

no longer kept in check by natural phenomena such as occasional droughts. Easy availability of chemicals means that perceived predators of livestock are deliberately poisoned over much of the region, and nontarget carnivore and scavenger species are thus also killed. Irrigated agriculture has been heavily subsidized and has expanded enormously, replacing much of the best traditional pastureland with vast mechanized and chemical-intensive farming systems for wheat, fruit, and vegetables. As a consequence, the remaining rangeland has come under enormous grazing pressure, and is increasingly scarred by off-road vehicle traffic. Industrialization and urbanization have also encroached to a surprising degree on the better rangelands, since cities and towns have tended to originate in such flatter and deeper-soiled areas.

Particularly in countries without oil wealth, there has been a rapidly increasing demand for fuelwood. Remaining acacia woodlands, particularly in Yemen, have come under heavy pressure from commercial wood-collectors and charcoal-burners, who rove ever more widely in order to supply the burgeoning towns and cities. Also in these countries, the pollution produced by settlements and industrial developments has been poorly controlled or mitigated, with the result that freshwater ecosystems in particular have suffered major damage in some places. Demand for water (especially for irrigated agriculture) has been high in nearly all countries in the region, and has often been satisfied by uncontrolled extraction from natural surface sources or from boreholes. These processes have degraded and destroyed some priceless natural wetlands and oases in Saudi Arabia, Yemen, Jordan, and Syria.

Despite these threats, the Arabian Deserts are still among those landscapes of the world that have been least altered by human activities. The great majority of the region, perhaps 90%, can still be considered "intact," in that these parts are not permanently settled, or regularly grazed or cultivated (Anon. 2001).

Conservation

Currently, there are about 57 areas in the Arabian Deserts region that have been formally designated by national governments for the protection and conservation of terrestrial wildlife species, vegetation, and landscapes (Evans 1994; IUCN 1997; Mallon and Kingswood 2001). Such statutory protected areas are found in seven of the 12 countries that comprise the region, the exceptions being Bahrain, Iraq, Qatar, the United Arab Emirates, and Yemen.

However, all countries in the region are known to have areas that fulfill some aspect of *in situ* wildlife conservation, such as captive-breeding stations, relatively small private reserves, areas of restricted access (e.g., military) that provide unintentional protection to fauna and flora, or traditional resource-use reserves (for sustainable grazing and beekeeping). Information on these sites is not easily available, since they do not meet the criteria for "protected areas" as defined by the global authority on such entities, the UNEP World Conservation Monitoring Center. Just as examples, in Bahrain, there is a captive-breeding center for endangered wildlife, and much of southern Bahrain (20 000 ha) is off limits to the public, while in the United Arab Emirates the federal government is currently assessing seven proposed protected areas for their possible designation. In Qatar, there are three captive-bred herds of antelope, managed by the government in fenced reserves, while in Yemen there are thought to be numerous (undocumented) traditional resource-use reserves.

The 57 "official" protected areas cover some 270 000 km^2, or about 8% of the Arabian Deserts region. Most of this estate is found in Saudi Arabia (85%), Oman (12%), and Egypt (2%), with Israel, Jordan, Kuwait, and Syria also protecting nationally significant parts of their wilderness. The types of protection afforded vary greatly, from Strict Nature Reserves where human intervention is minimized, through National Parks and Nature Reserves, where some human land uses continue, especially those considered traditional, to No-Hunting Areas, where the emphasis is on eliminating a particular threat in a defined area through ranger patrols. Protected-area designation in these seven countries is based on a systematic and scientific approach, and is an ongoing process, with more protected areas likely to be designated in the future.

As a complementary and necessary support to this process, what is needed equally urgently is a focus on conserving the wider environment, outside protected areas, where society lives and engages with the other 90% of land, habitats, and biodiversity. Here, the actions needed include: alterations in the tax and subsidy regimes that govern various important land-use sectors (agriculture, industry, energy, tourism, etc.); the introduction of comprehensive and participatory land planning and zoning; improved coordination and cooperation between different sectors of government and society; increasing public awareness of the positive values of biodiversity and public support/agreement for its conservation; allowing and encouraging the development of nongovernmental organizations; stricter requirements for rigorous environmental assessment of development programs and individual projects; improved enforcement of existing laws (especially concerning hunting and pollution); and revision of outdated or inadequate legislation.

All governments and societies on Earth are still struggling to come to terms with these "wider environment" problems, and the changes in behavior and in thinking that are required. Hopefully, this century will see progress in achieving these goals, and in ameliorating the threats that the Arabian Deserts face.

MIKE EVANS

Above, desert hedgehog (Hemiechinus aethiopicus), *Saudi Arabia.*
© **Michel Gunther**/BIOS

On the opposite page, Bedouin woman, Petra, Jordan.
© **Cristina Mittermeier**

ASIAN DESERTS

The Asian Deserts form an eastern continuation of the great Palaearctic desert belt that extends from the Atlantic coast of the Sahara Desert east across northern Africa to the Arabian Desert and then continues on into Asia. Deserts run across the Asian continent north and south of the great mountain massif of the Hindu Kush and Pamirs, from the head of the Persian Gulf through Iran and Afghanistan and from the Caspian Sea to the Tien Shan Mountains, then across northwest China to Mongolia. There are four main divisions, each with its own characteristics and endemic species: the Iranian Desert, the Central Asian Desert, the Taklimakan Desert, and the Gobi Desert, and the smaller Qaidam Basin, forming a link with the Tibetan Plateau. As a result of higher altitude or more northerly latitude, these are temperate deserts with hot summers, but where winter temperatures may drop as low as -30°C. Glaciers and permanent snow in bordering mountain ranges feed rivers that cross some of these deserts, emptying into lakes and marshy basins or just disappearing into the sand. Together these deserts total just over 5 943 000 km², an area second only to the Sahara among the desert regions of the world, and considerably larger than the Australian Deserts or the total area of the deserts of the southwestern United States and northern Mexico. With low human populations, these deserts remain between 75% and 90% intact.

The central desert basins of Iran cover much of the central plateau between the Alborz and Zagros Ranges. The Dasht-e Kavir or Great Salt Desert is a virtually rainless and uninhabited series of salt basins separated by low hills and occupying an area of 256 000 km². Much of it is covered by a salt crust over marsh and mud making travel extremely dangerous. Extending southwards is the Dasht-e Lut, a dried-out salt marsh covered with sand and stones, where some sand dunes reach 250 m in height (Wagner 1979). To the south and east is an area of largely sandy desert exceeding 250 000 km². It is centered on the Seistan Basin that sits astride the Iran-Afghanistan border, and also includes the Chagai Desert of western Pakistan and the Registan and Dasht-e Margo Deserts of southern and western Afghanistan. Rivers rising in the Hindu Kush flow westwards across this desert and empty into marshy lakes (Hamun-e-

Sabori and Hamun-e-Puzak) in eastern Iran. Deserts also occur to the south of the Zagros Mountains from eastern Iraq at the head of the Gulf along the Iranian coast into southern Pakistan. The total area of these deserts is 1 336 000 km², comprising four WWF ecoregions: South Iran Nubo-Sindian Desert and Semidesert (PA1328) (351 500 km²); Central Persian Desert Basins (PA1313) (580 900 km²); Registan-North Pakistan Sandy Desert (PA1326) (277 300 km²); and Kuhrud-Kohbanan Mountains Forest Steppe (PA1009) (126 300 km²) (Olson et al. 2001).

The Central Asian Deserts extend over approximately 2 063 000 km², from the eastern shore of the Caspian Sea across Turkmenistan, Uzbekistan, and southern Kazakhstan to the foothills of the Tien Shan and Pamir Ranges. This is equivalent to a combination of five WWF ecoregions: Central Asian Southern Desert (PA1312) (566 700 km²); Central Asian Riparian Woodlands (PA1311; 88 600 km²); Central Asian Northern Desert (PA1310) (662 400 km²); Kazakh Semi-desert (PA1318) (678 400 km²); and half (66 800 km²) of the Badkhiz-Karabil Semi-desert (PA1306) (133 600 km²). This region experiences the widest annual range of temperatures of all the Asian Deserts (Wagner, *op. cit.*).

The most extensive components are the Kara Kum (black sand) and Kyzyl Kum (red sand) Deserts. Kara

Wilderness Areas

On the opposite page, Siberian iris (Iris sibirica), Gurvansaikhan National Park, Gobi Desert, Mongolia.
© Art Wolfe

Kum stretches across most of Turkmenistan from the Caspian to the Amu Darya and Kizyl Kum lies between the Amu Darya and Syr Darya. These two great rivers, the Oxus and Jaxartes of the ancients, rise in the mountains to the south and flow into the Aral Sea. Once a vast inland sea, it is now a fraction of its original size and still shrinking as water is diverted for irrigation, especially for cotton cultivation. The rusting hulks of ships stranded in the desert far from the current shoreline mark its former extent. Smaller rivers flow into Lake Balkhash at the eastern end of the desert while the Murgab, Tejen, and Zerafshan Rivers, flowing off the highlands to the south, disappear into the desert sands. North of the Kara Kum is the desolate stone plateau of Ustyurt, while to the east lies the stony Betpak Dala Desert. There are other areas of sand as well as clay and salt desert areas.

The Taklimakan Desert occupies 796 400 km² at the center of the Tarim Basin, between the Tien Shan and Kun Lun Ranges, entirely within China, and corresponding to the Taklimakan Desert (PA1330) (741 900 km²) and the Tarim Basin Deciduous Forests and Steppe (PA0442) (54 500 km²) ecoregions. It is connected to the Central Asian Deserts through the Dzungarian Gates pass. Some parts of the Taklimakan receive less than 50 mm of rain a year and the Turfan Depression in the north less than 10 mm (Zhao et al. 1990). Sand covers around 85% of the Taklimakan, mostly shifting dunes that may reach 200 m in height. Many cities are reputed to have been swallowed by the sands. It is searingly hot in summer and bitterly cold in winter. The Swedish geographer Sven Hedin reckoned it "the worst desert in the world" (Hedin 1898). Strong winds are frequent, including the *kara-buran* or black hurricane, a fierce local tornado that whips up sand and stones, forcing all travellers to take shelter. It was rarely crossed. Two branches of the Silk Road circumvented it on its northern and southern edges, passing through oases such as Yarkand and Kashgar, where availability of glacier or snow melt on the perimeter ranges provided an opportunity for settlement and agriculture. The Tarim River flows eastwards across the northern part of the Taklimakan, into Lop Nur Lake, now dry. The Lop Nur Basin is the location of China's nuclear test site. Southeast of Lop Nur and cut off from it by the Arjin Shan and Nan Shan Mountains lies the Qaidam, an arid basin equivalent to the Qaidam Basin Semi-desert ecoregion (PA1324) (192 000 km²), at an altitude of 2 500-3 000 m, forming a transition to the high-cold desert of the Tibetan Plateau.

The Gobi Desert is a vast tract of mainly gravel desert, with some smaller areas of sand, covering around 1 556 000 km² of northern China and Mongolia, gradually merging into the arid Daurian steppes of eastern Mongolia and Manchuria. It is equivalent to five WWF ecoregions: the Alashan Plateau Semi-desert (PA1302) (673 400 km²); the Junggar Basin Semi-desert (PA1317) (304 200 km²); the Great Lakes Basin Desert Steppe (PA1316) (157 200 km²); the Gobi Lakes Valley Desert Steppe (PA1315) (139 400 km²); and the Eastern Gobi Desert Steppe (PA1314) (281 800 km²).

It extends south to the Ordos and Alashan Deserts of the great bend in the Yellow River and westwards it adjoins the Lop Desert and Taklimakan. The arid belt continues north of the Altai Mountains, through the Great Lakes Basin between the Altai and Hangai Mountains, and then northwest to the Uvs Nuur Basin, where it borders the Tannu Ola Range at the southern rim of the Siberian forests. The northern Gobi is dotted with mountains and isolated ridges. Between the Tien Shan and the Altai lies the Dzungarian (Junggar) Gobi covering 304 200 km². The Gobi is extraordinarily rich in palaeontological remains.

Biodiversity

The Asian Deserts lie entirely within the Palaearctic region. Endemic species of fauna and flora have evolved in most of these deserts. Many species of *Artemisia* are characteristically found throughout the region, as are salt-tolerant plants such as *Salsola*. Plants can only survive by being drought-resistant and need the ability to withstand searing summer temperatures and bitter winters. Saxaul trees (*Haloxylon*) are a characteristic feature of the Gobi and the Central Asian Deserts, their roots helping to bind the sand. Their tiny leaves are short-lived to minimize water loss (St. George 1974). Other plants have evolved a waxy coating, spines instead of leaves, and extremely deep roots to reach moisture. Literature on the flora of the Asian Deserts is limited and obscure, but approximately 2 200 species of vascular plants exist in the Central Asian Deserts (K. Rachkovskaya and R.V. Kamelin, in litt., 2002). Calculations of endemism in this desert range widely, and it has been estimated that 70 genera and around 25% (550 species) of all plants here are endemic (Grubov 1989). Likewise, with around 300 plant species, the Iranian desert shows 22% endemism of its psammophyte flora (23 species), the plants most adapted to desert conditions (Freitag 1986). The Gobi has low species endemism, with approximately 170 plant species confined there (Grubov, *op. cit.*). With little information on the Taklimakan or Qaidam, a minimum estimate of the combined plant diversity of the whole Asian Desert Wilderness would be at least 2 500 species, with at least 750 endemics. True figures could be much higher.

Animals also show a diversity of adaptive mechanisms to cope with the same problem of losing heat in summer but retaining it in winter when temperatures, especially in the north of the area, fall well below zero. The saiga (*Saiga tatarica*) avoids the heat by spending only the winter in the desert, migrating north to the steppes in spring. Most small mammals adopt a nocturnal life-style to reduce exposure to high levels of solar radiation, and spend the day underground. Some species block the burrow entrance to further maintain a cooler temperature. Gazelles and other large mammals deal

Above, kizil-kum or Severtzov's urial (Ovis orientalis severtzovi), *Nuratau Range, Uzbekistan.*

On the opposite page, male argali sheep (Ovis ammon collium), *Kazakhstan.*
Both photos:
© **Patricio Robles Gil**/*Sierra Madre*

with the extreme aridity by obtaining most of their water needs directly from the vegetation they eat, and can go without water for long periods. Some also pass very concentrated urine and have the ability to drink water with a high salt content. Camels have evolved the ability to withstand extreme temperatures by storing heat metabolically and radiating it at night. They also store fat in their humps for later conversion into food when needed. They have splayed hooves that allow such a heavy animal to traverse soft sand by reducing the loading on each foot. Desert hares (*Lepus* spp.) and some rodents have large ears, which are used to lose heat, while Brandt's or desert hedgehogs (*Hemiechinus hypomelas*) avoid the heat by passing the summer in a state of torpor, known as aestivation.

Around 82 species of mammals, 27 of them endemic, occur in the Asian Deserts as a whole. The greatest mammalian diversity is found among the gerbils, jirds, and jerboas, a group of largely nocturnal desert-dwelling small rodents. Few of these have been studied, some are known from only a handful of museum specimens, and many are rare. All the deserts described here have their endemic species. The Seistan Basin has at least seven species, two of which are endemic, Hotson's jerboa (*Allactaga hotsoni*) and the Baluchistan pygmy jerboa (*Salpingotus michaelis*) (WCMC 1991). The Central Asian Desert contains 11 endemic species (one shrew and ten rodents). Four of these are listed in the former Soviet Red Data Book (Neronov and Bobrov 1990). The Chinese deserts hold 11 species of jerboa and 7-8 gerbils (Zhao et al. 1990) and four more are endemic to the Gobi, including Cheng's jird (*Meriones chengi*) in the Junggar Basin. Predators on these include Ruppell's fox (*Vulpes ruppelli*), the sand cat (*Felis margarita*) and, in the Qaidam, the rare and scarcely-known Chinese desert cat (*Felis bieti*).

Birds are more mobile and can more easily colonize oases and irrigated areas, but there are few species typical of the true desert. Apart from migratory species, around 90 species occur, only six of them endemic. Four of these are ground jays of the genus *Podoces*, which is wholly endemic to the Asian Deserts, with one species each in the Iranian, Central Asian, Taklimakan, and Gobi Deserts. The saxaul sparrow (*Passer ammodendri*) is restricted to the Gobi and Central Asia, and Pallas' sandgrouse (*Syrrhaptes paradoxus*) is endemic to the Gobi, occurring in flocks of many thousands flying to water in the early morning. Several other species of sandgrouse (*Syrrhaptes*) are found in the region, even in the hottest deserts. These pigeon-sized birds spend the day exposed to the full heat of the sun or try to find some respite in the thin web of shade thrown by sparse desert trees and shrubs. They may fly many miles to water where the males wade in to soak their breast feathers and carry water back to their young. A few falcons, buzzards, eagles, and desert eagle owls prey on rodents, hares, and reptiles.

As for vertebrates, the greatest diversity in the region is found among reptiles, which are better adapted to cope with the extremes of the desert. Again, data are disparate, but there are well over 100 reptile species, including at least 20 endemics. In contrast, amphibians are represented by only six species, none of them endemic. Among the endemic reptiles is the very rare Kopet Dagh gecko (*Eublepharis turcmenicus*), which was only discovered in 1977. There are two species of tortoise, many geckoes, mainly nocturnal, and numerous species of toad-headed agamas of the genus *Phrynocephalus*. The biggest lizard is the desert monitor (*Varanus griseus*), a predator on other lizards, small mammals, and birds. Sand boas (*Eryx* spp.) are small snakes with eyes placed on the top of their head allowing them to wait in ambush, invisible just below the surface of the sand. There are at least three species of vipers and the Central Asian cobra (*Naja oxiana*) occurs in the Kara Kum and Kizyl Kum (Knystautas 1987). As examples of reptile diversity, the Seistan Basin contains 12 endemic reptile species, two snakes and ten lizards, including four species of toad-headed agama, in addition to the two endemic mammals referred to above (WCMC 1991). The Central Asian Desert has over 60 species of reptiles, including seven species of *Phrynocephalus* and ten species of racerunner lizards (*Eremias*) (Knystautas, *op. cit.*). The Gobi has the Tatar sand boa (*Eryx tataricus*) and the endemic Gobi gecko (*Cyrtopodion elongatus*).

The most numerous and most diverse, as well as the least well studied, inhabitants of the desert are the invertebrates, such as beetles, scorpions, locusts, and grasshoppers. Over 10 000 insect species have been noted in Kara Kum alone (St. George 1974).

Flagship Species

Przewalski's wild horse (*Equus przewalskii*) was once widely distributed across the Gobi, but had already become rare by the 1950s. The last wild individuals were sighted in 1966 at Takhiin Shar Nuruu on the Mongolian-Chinese border (Mallon 1985). None has been seen since, despite numerous intensive surveys. Fortunately, a few individuals had been taken into captivity and small herds now exist in several zoos worldwide. Reintroduction projects are already under way in Mongolia and a project is also planned for Gansu Province, China.

Wild camels, the ancestor of the Bactrian camel (*Camelus bactrianus*), familiar as a beast of burden throughout Central Asia, were found from the central Taklimakan across to the Transaltai Gobi of Mongolia until the middle of the nineteenth century. Now only three isolated populations remain, one consisting of a few hundred in Mongolia's Great Gobi National Park, the other two in China, in the Gashun Gobi and Lop Nur Basin (Hare 1997). Its status is Endangered and strenuous efforts are being made to save the remaining animals from extinction, including designation of a new sanctuary at Lop Nur.

The saiga is a unique species of antelope with a swollen nose and rather ungainly posture, which belies

On the opposite page, high desert, Tien Shan Mountains, China

Above, Siberian ibex (Capra sibirica), Kazakhstan.
Both photos:
© **Patricio Robles Gil**/*Sierra Madre*

its ability to cover long distances at high speed. It migrates south to the Central Asian Deserts each winter

AD 450 (Hopkirk 1980), and the trade aided the development of great centers in Central Asia such as Khiva,

AUSTRALIAN DESERTS

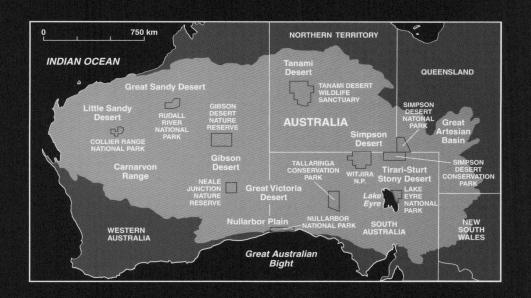

Australia is one of the world's top five megadiversity countries, and one of the most important countries on Earth for biodiversity conservation. Unlike much of the rest of the world, the greater part of Australia, aside from the most populated areas on the east coast and in the southwest, is still wilderness. With a land area of 7 682 395 km², or around 95% of the size of the continental United States, Australia has a human population of only about 19 million people —roughly equivalent to that of Mexico City or São Paulo. More than two thirds of this population lives in the major urban centers of Sydney, Melbourne, Brisbane, Perth, Adelaide, and a handful of others, with less than 7 million people in the vast remainder of the country.

Australia is also the driest continent, with more than 70% of the country in desert, shrubland, and other xeric formations, which grade into a series of savanna formations in the far north —all of them loosely defined by the popular term "Outback." Several of these savanna regions, notably Arnhem Land, Cape York, and Kimberley, also fall into our wilderness category, and are covered in separate chapters of this book. In this chapter, we include the desert and xeric formations found largely in the central and western portions of the country, where rainfall varies from 150 mm to 500 mm. Furthermore, we focus on those (the great majority) that are clearly still in the wilderness category. Although there are small human populations, and some towns of reasonable size by Australian standards (e.g., Alice Springs with 25 000 people), a very large part of this region is uninhabited and can still be considered true wilderness. This is especially true of the large deserts like the Great Sandy, the Tanami, the Great Victoria, the Gibson, and much of the Simpson, which account for the greatest portion of the area under consideration here.

The Australian Deserts can be subdivided in a variety of ways, but here we use the ecoregional classification developed by World Wildlife Fund (Olson et al. 2001), which recognizes a total of 10 ecoregions in their Deserts and Xeric Shrublands Biome. These include the following, moving clockwise from the center with the largest desert ecoregion: the Great Sandy-Tanami Desert, incorporating the Little Sandy Desert (AA1304) (823 008 km²); the Central Ranges Xeric Scrub (AA1302) (281 669 km²); the Simpson Desert (AA1308) (584 499 km²); the Tirari-Sturt Stony Desert (AA1309) (376 890 km²); the Great Victoria Desert (AA1305) (424 354 km²); the Nullarbor Plains Xeric Shrublands (AA1306) (195 200 km²); the Western Australian Mulga Shrublands (AA1310) (460 453 km²); the Carnarvon Xeric Shrublands (AA1301) (90 487 km²); the Pilbara Shrublands (AA1307) (179 779 km²); and the Gibson Desert (AA1303) (155 870 km²). Together, these regions cover an area of 3 572 209 km², or about 46.5% of the total area of Australia —and well over 90% of it is still intact. This is an area more than 10% larger than India, yet it has within it less than 400 000 people (Australian Bureau of Statistics 1996 and 2001), which translates to a human population density of 0.11 inhabitant/km². With the exception of the ice-bound polar areas, there are hardly any large tracts of land left on Earth with so few people.

Biodiversity

This vast desert region of Australia is rich in biodiversity, and especially in desert reptiles, which make a major contribution to Australia's position as number one country on Earth for reptile diversity. Lizards account for a large portion of reptile numbers, with some 271 species of which at least 74 are endemic. In all, there are some 340 species of reptiles in the Australian Desert Wilderness as we define it here, or 41% of all of Australia's reptile species. Of these, at least 83 species are completely confined to the deserts.

■ *Wilderness Area*

On the opposite page, longitudinal sand dunes in the Strzelecki Desert, South Australia.
© Jean-Paul Ferrero/Auscape

423

Amphibians are represented entirely by frogs and, as might be expected in such a dry region, are much less diverse than reptiles. Nonetheless, there is a significant frog fauna in these deserts, totaling 34 species, of which five are endemic.

The region also has an important bird fauna, with 346 species, of which three occur nowhere else. The mammals are also well-represented, with the greatest number being highly-specialized marsupials and desert-adapted rodents. In all, there are some 98 species of mammals, 14 of them endemic to the region as defined. In addition to those still extant, a number of species have been extirpated since the arrival of Europeans, and some are mentioned in the next section.

In terms of vascular plants, this region has approximately 3 000 species, of which at least 150 are endemic (A. Bowland, in litt.).

A number of different vegetation types exist but, in its simplest terms, the vegetation of this vast region can be broken down into the spinifex grasslands, chenopod shrublands, mulga woodlands, forested areas (especially in the desert ranges), and vegetation associated with desert rivers and salt lakes (Van Oosterzee 2000). Spinifex ("spear point" in Greek) grasslands are Australia's most extensive vegetation type, covering 22% of the continent (Van Oosterzee, *op. cit.*). They consist of two closely-related genera, *Plectrachne* and *Triodia*, and are the dominant vegetation over a large area of dunes and plains. Unlike other major grasslands, which have a complement of herbivorous ungulates and associated predators, the grazing animals here are the termites and the hunters are the lizards, which reach very high diversity in these grasslands. Mulga (*Acacia aneura*) is the dominant species in a large part of the deserts. In all, some 880 *Acacia* species occur in Australia, of which 118 are in the deserts —with most of these being found in the rugged ranges or tablelands. In all, *Acacia* shrublands occupy about 1.6 million km², a major portion of the arid zone, including both the deserts discussed here and the savanna areas to the north. However, only a small number of species occur on the very arid dunes and plains, with mulga being the most evident. Chenopod shrublands cover 438 000 km² and are composed of salt-tolerant xeromorphic shrubs like the saltbushes and bluebushes, and include at least 100 different genera. They occur mainly in a southern arc of inland plains and rolling lowlands less than 30 m in altitude. Characteristic genera are *Atriplex*, *Maireana*, *Sclerolaena*, *Chenopodium*, and *Rhagodia*, each with more than 30 species (Van Oosterzee, *op. cit.*). They occur on a wide variety of soils, including rocky uplands, saline drainage systems, clay soils, and calcareous sands and loams. Forested areas, especially at higher elevations in the desert ranges, are characterized by species like *Acacia* spp., *Eremophila* spp., *Eucalyptus* spp., and *Senna* spp. Gallery forests along the desert rivers, especially in the Channel Country, feature red gums and other eucalypts (Van Oosterzee, *op. cit.*).

Each of the regions defined by WWF also has its own specific vegetation and topographic features. The Great Sandy-Tanami Desert stretches over much of the northeastern part of the State of Western Australia and the central part of the Northern Territory. The Great Sandy Desert portion is characterized by high red-sand dunes that extend for hundreds of kilometers, while to the east the Tanami consists of red-sand plains broken by hills and low mountains. Vegetation is sparse and consists mainly of spinifex grasses and small saltbush shrubs, with scattered spiny acacias and desert oaks (WWF, in prep.).

The Central Ranges Xeric Scrub Ecoregion incorporates the Burt Plain, Finke, and the low mountains of central Australia, notably the MacDonnell Ranges and the Central Ranges (Thackway and Cresswell 1995). Vegetation consists of mulga scrubland, grassland, and open woodlands on sand ridges and sand plains. The higher elevations have been recognized as the Central Australian Mountain Ranges Centre of Plant Diversity (Latz and Pitts, in Davis et al. 1995). Australia's most famous natural landmark, Uluru, or Ayers Rock, and the neighboring Olgas are found in this region.

The Simpson Desert extends the furthest east of the Australian desert ecoregions and is located in eastern central Australia, in the southeastern corner of the Northern Territory and northeastern South Australia, with a small area extending into Queensland. It is drained by several large river systems and is the center of one of the largest endorheic drainage basins in the world. Within this, it includes Lake Eyre 15-16 m below sea level, Australia's largest lake, and the fifth largest terminal lake on Earth. Lake Eyre, which has only been fully filled three times in the twentieth century, is one of the world's great natural wonders. Sometimes referred to as "the sump of Australia," it is the end point of an enormous drainage system covering 1 300 000 km² (Van Oosterzee 2000).

The terrain of the Simpson Desert ecoregion ranges from below sea level to about 300 m and consists of dunefields 5-10 m in height, stony plains, low eroded ranges and mesas, ephemeral lakes and claypans, alluvial plains, and seasonal, sometimes semisaline wetlands. The floodplains and stony plains are covered mainly by ephemeral grasses and herblands. Dunefields are held together by *Zygochloa paradoxa* grassland, while sides and interdune areas are covered in *Triodia* hummock grasslands or herblands. Eucalypt woodlands are mainly found along watercourses. A key feature of the region is fairly frequent flooding, originating from rain that falls outside the region. Lakes are usually dry, but can support large bird populations when flooded. The Coongie Lakes are one of the richest wetlands in Australia (Australian Nature Conservation Agency 1996) and are listed by the RAMSAR Convention. This ecoregion includes both the Channel Country, so named because of the watercourses running through the vast floodplains, and the Simpson-Strzelecki Dunefields (Thackway and Cresswell, *op. cit.*; WWF, in prep.). The

the world. It is found on the cracked dark soil of river floodplains and in the lateritic gibber plains in eastern-central Australia on the borders between South Australia, the Northern Territory, and southwestern Queensland (Cogger 2000).

Marsupials are also amazingly diverse in the Australian Deserts, but sadly a number of these desert creatures have already gone extinct, or have been eliminated from their original habitat and now exist only on isolated offshore islands. One of the most unusual of all marsupials, and a dweller of the deserts, is the marsupial mole (*Notoryctes typhlops*). Although it superficially resembles the placental golden moles of southern Africa, an amazing case of convergent evolution, this strange, golden-furred, blind burrower is a marsupial and has no close relationships with any members of this group. Indeed, it is so distinct and such an enigma that it has been placed in its own Order, the Notoryctemorphia. It digs with two flattened claws and its burrow fills in behind it, making it look as if it were swimming through the sand. It has a large range in the central portion of Western Australia, parts of southwestern Northern Territory, and the northwestern corner of South Australia, but is rarely seen. A second species, the northwestern marsupial mole (*Notoryctes caurinus*), was described in 1920 from northwestern Western Australia, but remains very poorly known.

A number of carnivorous marsupials also inhabit the desert regions, most of them poorly known to the outside world. These include a host of unique little creatures with unlikely names, including the mulgara (*Dasycercus cristicauda*), the kowari (*D. byrnei*), the little red kaluta (*Dasykaluta rosamondae*), the fat-tailed pseudantechinus (*Pseudantechinus macdonnellensis*), Woolley's pseudantechinus (*P. woolleyae*), the red-tailed phascogale (*Phascogale calura*), the Wongai ningaui (*Ningaui ridei*), and several species of dunnarts (*Sminthopsis* spp.). The largest of the carnivorous marsupials of the desert, weighing over 2 kg, was the western quoll (*Dasyurus geoffroii*). It once occurred over the entire desert region, but following European arrival it was extirpated from the vast majority of this range, and is now found only in southwestern Australia. The amazing numbat (*Myrmecobius fasciatus*), a beautiful striped marsupial anteater the size of a large squirrel, is the only member of its family, the Myrmecobiidae. This species also once occurred over much of the southern part of the desert region, but has now gone extinct everywhere except in a few parts of southwestern Australia.

Many of the bandicoots and bilbies of the family Peramelidae are also desert animals, including the pig-footed bandicoot (*Chaeropus ecaudatus*), the golden bandicoot (*Isoodon auratus*), the western barred bandicoot (*Perameles bougainville*), the desert bandicoot (*P. eremiana*), the greater bilby (*Macrotis lagotis*), and the lesser bilby (*M. leucura*). Unfortunately, these animals were especially heavily impacted by the arrival of the Europeans and the introduction of exotic species. The golden bandicoot and

the bilby have now disappeared from much of their once-large ranges, but still occur on the mainland. The western barred bandicoot has disappeared entirely from the mainland and now occurs only on a few islands, and the desert bandicoot, the pig-footed bandicoot, and the lesser bilby are now extinct (Strahan 1995).

Much the same is true of the kangaroos and their relatives. Many of these were also desert dwellers, including the burrowing bettong (*Bettongia lesueur*), the brush-tailed bettong (*B. penicillata*), the desert rat kangaroo (*Caloprymnus campestris*), the central hare wallaby (*Lagorchestes asomatus*), the rufous hare wallaby (*L. hirsutus*), the crescent nail-tailed wallaby (*Onychogalea lunata*), the black-footed rock wallaby (*Petrogale lateralis*), Rothschild's rock wallaby (*P. rothschildi*), and the yellow-footed rock wallaby (*P. xanthopus*). As with the bandicoots and bilbies, these have suffered greatly from modification of habitat and introduction of animals like the fox, the cat, and the rabbit. The burrowing bettong and the rufous hare wallaby have now disappeared from the mainland and occur only on several offshore islands, although a captive population of about 150 animals of the latter is now in a predator-proof enclosure in Watarrka National Park in the Northern Territory. The brush-tailed bettong is now restricted to southwestern Australia, Rothschild's rock wallaby has declined on the mainland but is still abundant on several islands, the yellow-footed rock wallaby has declined over most of its range but is still locally common, and the desert rat kangaroo, the central hare wallaby, and the crescent nail-tailed wallaby have now gone extinct. Only the largest and most adaptable kangaroo species —notably the western grey kangaroo (*Macropus fuliginosus*), the red kangaroo (*M. rufus*), and the hill wallaroo (*M. robustus*)— are still widespread and abundant in these regions (Strahan, *op. cit.*).

This pattern is repeated yet again with the rodents. Of at least 19 species once found in the Australian Deserts, most appear to have declined dramatically, though the boom/bust strategies exhibited by many desert rodents make it difficult to assess trends. At least four, the lesser stick-nest rat (*Leporillus apicalis*), the short-tailed hopping mouse (*Notomys amplus*), the long-tailed hopping mouse (*N. longicaudatus*), and the big-eared hopping mouse (*N. macrotis*), are extinct or presumed extinct (Strahan, *op. cit.*). A fourth, the Central rock rat (*Zyzomys pedunculatus*), also presumed extinct, was rediscovered in 1996 and is actually locally abundant in a rather restricted range in Ormiston Gorge National Park (part of West MacDonnell National Park).

Turning to the birds, one of the most mysterious of all Australian animals is the night parrot (*Geopsittacus occidentalis*). In a similar fashion to the sandgrouse of the Arabian Deserts, this bird is largely terrestrial, sleeping there for most of the day, before flying to water at dusk. It then spends the night feeding on spinifex seeds and chenopods, living a highly-nomadic life-style in response to food availability. It was widespread over the Aus-

Above, black-footed rock wallaby (Petrogale lateralis)*, Simpson's Gap.*
© D. Parer & E. Parer-Cook/*Auscape*

On the opposite page, young male red kangaroos (Macropus rufus) *sparring. This large species is characteristic of the arid zone.*
© Jean-Paul Ferrero/*Auscape*

tralian Deserts until the beginning of the nineteenth century, when it declined considerably. It is now considered Critically Endangered and, although there have been a handful of sight records over the past few decades, the species largely eluded scientists until 1990, when a dead bird was found by the roadside in Queensland. The presence of night parrots was key to the recent establishment, by Birds Australia, of a 262 000-ha reserve at Newhaven Station, just east of the Great Sandy Desert in the Northern Territory.

The Australian Deserts are home to a number of other attractive parrots, from the familiar budgerigar (*Melopsittacus undulatus*) and cockatiel (*Nymphicus hollandicus*), to the spectacular long-tailed princess parrot (*Polytelis alexandrae*), the colorful Major Mitchell's cockatoo (*Cacatua leadbeateri*), and scarlet-chested parrot (*Neophema splendida*), all of which are characteristic species and would make good flagships for the region.

In the southeastern part of the Australian Deserts, the curious and Endangered plains-wanderer (*Pedionomus torquatus*) is as intriguing as the night parrot. While it superficially resembles the ubiquitous button quails (*Turnix* spp.), this elusive species is actually most closely related to the seed snipes (Thinocoridae) of South America and, due to its distinctiveness, is placed in a monotypic family, the Pedionomidae. Again, cultivation and introduced species threaten this unique species.

There is no shortage of other birds in the Australian Deserts that would be suitable as flagships, from the massive emu (*Dromaius novaehollandiae*) and Australian bustard (*Ardeotis australis*) to the tiny desert-endemic grasswrens (Eyrean grasswren, *Amytornis goyderi*; gray grasswren, *A. barbatus*), and including the painted firetail (*Emblema pictum*), a long list of raptors such as the letter-winged kite (*Elanus scriptus*), and a host of other attractive or interesting desert-adapted species like the spinifex pigeon (*Geophaps plumifera*) and the crimson chat (*Epthianura tricolor*).

Human Cultures

The name *Aborigine*, which means "original inhabitant," was given to the indigenous people of Australia by British colonists in the late 1700s, when the country's native population was believed to number as many as one million. And while anthropologists debate whether Australia's first humans arrived 40 000, 50 000 or 60 000 years ago, the Aborigines themselves believe that they have been there since the Dreaming: the beginning of time itself.

The ancient history of Australia's Aborigines is told in rock paintings and midden piles. At the time of colonization their tribes were already culturally diverse —with several hundred languages and dialects— and geographically widespread. They differed from the colonists in not sharing concepts of property or money nor having any heritage of farming or tending livestock.

As a result, the foreign newcomers quickly began to usurp land from the seminomadic, hunter-gatherer Aborigines under the principle of *terra nullius*, claiming that these people were now British subjects, their territories were legally unoccupied, and essentially all suitable land in Australia should be available for raising traditional European plant and animal crops.

The traditional life-style of indigenous Australians depended heavily on hunting, fishing, and gathering. Periodic burning of grasslands and woodlands was their only land management practice, as it served to encourage new plant growth and to attract kangaroos and other native game species, most of which were dispatched with weapons such as spears, clubs, boomerangs, and stone axes. The British changed the face of Australia by introducing domestic animals such as cattle, pigs, goats, donkeys, horses, cats, and dogs, as well as wild animals like rabbits, foxes, sparrows, doves, and starlings, all species that soon became serious pests. In addition, colonists essentially declared war on native predators like the dingo and the wedge-tailed eagle, dramatically reducing their numbers in many areas. The Aborigines did not take their displacement sitting down. They were tenacious in their resistance, using tactics of guerrilla warfare, battling the colonists with stolen guns, and sabotaging their economy through attacks on sheep and cattle. Ultimately, however, the Aborigines lost the battle to superior foreign technology and to the invasion of domestic animals that drove out native wildlife and altered natural plant communities.

According to the Australian Institute of Aboriginal and Torres Straits Islander Studies (1994), as many as 75 different aboriginal nations, totaling approximately 350 000 people, are found within the desert wilderness that we have defined here. This is roughly the same number of Aborigines that live in Australia as a whole but, surprisingly, more than two thirds of today's Aborigines reside in urban communities. The majority of present-day desert inhabitants, therefore, are descendants of colonists and other newcomers to this land. They are not uniformly distributed throughout the Australian "Outback," but rather tend to be concentrated in a relative handful of towns like Alice Springs in the Northern Territory, Whyalla in South Australia, Broken Hill in New South Wales, and Roebourne in Western Australia (Australian Bureau of Statistics 1996 and 2001). The overall population density of the Australian Deserts is a mere 0.11 inhabitant/km². When these towns are excluded, the wilderness population density drops to 0.08 inhabitant/km² —an amazingly low density that ranks among the lowest of any wilderness area on Earth.

Centuries-old issues of territorial rights and land ownership are still very much alive in present-day Australia, despite several landmark bodies of legislation that have been passed. The Aboriginal Lands Trust Act of 1966 ensured that titles to existing Aboriginal Reserves would be held in trust on behalf of all Aboriginal people in

On the opposite page, Mount Conner, 340 m above the plain, Northern Territory.
© **Jean-Paul Ferrero**/*Auscape*

Above, saltpan ground dragon (Ctenophorus salinarum), Lake Raeside, Western Australia.
© **Greg Harold**/*Auscape*

THE NORTHERN ROCKY MOUNTAINS

Glance at a relief map of North America and the prominence of the Rocky Mountains readily becomes apparent. The western third of the continent erupts from an endless expanse of grassy plains to form a wall of mountain peaks several thousand meters high, extending from the frozen Alaskan north all the way to Mesoamerica. The Rockies are their easternmost expression as far south as New Mexico. To the west, their peaks confront coastal ranges locked in a timeless eastern advance of plate tectonics. New and higher mountains will continue to rise between them as giant surface landmasses grind into one another, while atmospheric forces whittle away at peaks formed in bygone eras. Rocky Mountain origins reside in ancient marine limestones that were uplifted in enormous fault blocks and layered like shingles, processes that apparently reached their peak tens of millions of years ago in the mid-Cenozoic Era, but continue to this day (Clark and Stearn 1960).

For centuries, these mountains remained a mystery to the Europeans who arrived along the Atlantic coast and trekked west in search of overland routes to the Pacific. In fact, crossings of the Rockies such as those of Alexander Mackenzie in the late 1700s and Meriwether Lewis and William Clark in the early 1800s are considered among the most significant events in the early histories of Canada and the United States. To this day, large parts of the region remain uninhabited. A number of early settlements did grow to become thriving modern cities and several major transportation routes now crisscross the region, opening it to exploitation of various kinds.

Our definition of the Northern Rocky Mountains Wilderness loosely corresponds to five ecoregions recently defined by the World Wildlife Fund: South Central Rockies Forest (159 300 km²), North Central Rockies Forest (245 700 km²), Alberta Mountain Forests (39 800 km²), Central British Columbia Mountain Forests (71 700 km²), and approximately 54 000 km² of the Montana Valley and Foothill Grasslands (Olson et al. 2001). The latter grassland ecoregion differs significantly from the others both in terms of vegetation and the extent to which the overall habitat has already been altered by humans, but it is intri-

cately linked to Rocky Mountain forest ecosystems and therefore should be considered an integral part of the larger wilderness block.

The South Central Rockies are centered in the Yellowstone region, where northwestern Wyoming meets east-central Idaho and southwestern Montana, and where the Absarokas are the dominant mountain range. The North Central Rockies are more extensive, dominated by the Bitterroot Range that runs north along the Idaho-Montana border to meet the Columbia and Purcell Mountains and cross the border into Canada. Incorporating the eastern flanks of the Continental Ranges, the Alberta Mountain Forests run northwest along the provincial border with British Columbia to just beyond Jasper National Park, and from there the Central British Columbia Mountain Forests continue through the northeastern corner of that province along ranges with native American names like Missinchinka, Omineca, and Kechika. We draw the northern limit of this wilderness area here and have chosen to include the more northerly extensions of the Rockies as part of the Boreal Forest Wilderness, based on shared characteristics of ecoregions at these latitudes. We also do not include the Bighorn Mountains and Black Hills, situated near the southern boundaries of this wilder-

Wilderness Area

On the opposite page, winter sunrise over the Teton Range viewed from the Snake River, Grand Teton National Park, Wyoming, U.S.A.
© Willard Clay

439

ness area, since they are geographically distinct from it. In total then, we estimate the extent of the Northern Rocky Mountains Wilderness at about 570 500 km². Of this, we believe that as much as 70% remains intact.

Biodiversity

Coniferous forests predominate in the southern part of this wilderness. The dominant tree species are Engelmann spruce (*Picea engelmannii*), subalpine fir (*Abies lasiocarpa*), and Douglas fir (*Pseudotsuga menziesii*), with lodgepole pine (*Pinus contorta*) often the most abundant colonizing species in disturbed areas. Alpine meadows and foothill grasslands are interspersed with forests, and this region also includes the unique Yellowstone landscape with the world's largest concentration of geothermal geysers and hot springs. Wheatgrass (*Agropyron* spp.), fescue grass (*Festuca* spp.), and sagebrush (*Artemisia* spp.) carpet the valleys and foothills, but these habitats become less prominent as one heads north. Though the trees are still largely coniferous, the species composition begins to change to include some that prefer "wetter feet," such as hemlocks (*Tsuga* spp.), yews (*Taxus* spp.), larches (*Larix* spp.), and Western red cedar (*Thuja plicata*), which are more common in the Cascades and along the Pacific coast. Alpine and subalpine vegetation is characteristic of the Canadian Rockies, where heathers (Ericaceae) and sedges (*Carex* spp.) augment the forest flora at higher elevations. In all, at least 1 414 species of vascular plants are found in this wilderness area, including at least 22 endemics (Ricketts et al. 1999).

Fourteen species of amphibians are known from the Northern Rocky Mountains Wilderness, including seven frogs, four salamanders, and three toads (CI, unpublished data). Of these, two (14%) are endemics, the Idaho giant salamander (*Dicamptodon aterrimus*) and the Coeur d'Alene salamander (*Plethodon idahoensis*) (Petranka 1998). Reptiles are also only modestly represented with 14 species: one turtle, five lizards, and eight snakes, none of them endemic (CI, unpublished data).

Lewis and Clarke crossed the Rockies on their marathon trek to the Pacific. In the process, these two "amateur" naturalists wrote detailed accounts of many birds and mammals, some representing the first descriptions known to science (Burroughs 1961). Newly-described birds native to the Rocky Mountains numbered 20, including such species as the whistling or tundra swan (*Cygnus columbianus*), the great gray owl (*Strix nebulosa*), Lewis' woodpecker (*Melanerpes lewis*), and Clark's nutcracker (*Nucifraga columbiana*). A total of 264 bird species call this region home or use critical habitats within it as staging grounds, although none of them are endemic (WWF, in prep.).

Credit Lewis and Clark with original descriptions for at least seven Northern Rocky Mountain mammals as well, notable among them the pronghorn (*Antilocapra americana*) and grizzly bear (*Ursus arctos*). In all, 92 species of mammals are native to this region, represent-

ing six orders: rodents, carnivores, bats, insectivores, lagomorphs, and artiodactyls (WWF, in prep.). The only endemic mammal is the red-tailed chipmunk (*Tamias ruficaudus*), which occurs from northeastern Washington across to western Montana and into southern Canada.

For the wilderness area, then, there are at least 384 native species of terrestrial vertebrates, including only three endemic species, yielding a level of terrestrial vertebrate endemism of less than 1%.

Flagship Species

In the minds of many Americans, the Rocky Mountains and the grizzly are synonymous. This bruin's battle for survival against advancing civilization has become a rallying cry for those who seek to preserve true wilderness, and has forged the grizzly as a national symbol for wildlife conservation. Within the lower 48 states, it was extirpated in Texas and North Dakota by the late nineteenth century and eventually disappeared from California, Utah, Oregon, New Mexico, and Arizona before the middle of the twentieth century. Today, it hangs on in just four states —Idaho, Montana, Washington, and Wyoming— and the Rockies remain the heart of its range (Laycock 1997). Little was actually known of the grizzly's ecology and behavior until intensive field studies were undertaken by Frank and John Craighead in Yellowstone National Park from 1959-1971, and much of what has gone into subsequent recovery plans for this species is the result of their work (Craighead 1979). Fortunately, this bear's conservation status is considered more secure based upon larger, more viable populations in Alaska, Canada, and Russia.

What the grizzly is to the Rockies, the American bison (*Bison bison*) was to the Great Plains. Bison once roamed nearly coast to coast across the United States, reaching deep into the Canadian north, and south to just across the Mexican border (Leopold 1959). While its historic range included the mountainous west and efforts to preserve the species have been undertaken there, bison numbers on the prairies were legendary. Biologists estimate the population at the beginning of the nineteenth century at approximately 30 million animals (Haines 1970). By 1900, however, the loss of grazing land to cattle, hunting for hides and meat, and perverse military strategy (denying sustenance to Native Americans) reduced bison numbers to a low of only several hundred animals. Fortunately, a few private citizens in the United States and Canada had managed to sequester small herds that were ultimately used to reestablish populations in former range areas. President Theodore Roosevelt formed the American Bison Society in 1904 and four years later convinced Congress to create a National Bison Range in northwest Montana. Today, an additional two free-ranging herds occur within the Greater Yellowstone Ecosystem and the North American bison population has climbed to a few hundred *thousand*, managed on both public and private lands (Hodgson 1994).

Above, pronghorn (Antilocapra americana)*, National Bison Range, Montana, U.S.A.*
© **Art Wolfe**

On the opposite page, elk (Cervus elaphus)*, Banff National Park, Alberta, Canada.*
© **Patricio Robles Gil**/*Sierra Madre*

On pp. 442-443, fireweed (Epilobium angustifolium) *against a backdrop of fog-covered mountains, Glacier National Park, Montana, U.S.A.*
© **Jack Dykinga**

The gray wolf (*Canis lupus*) also roamed widely across North America and was the target of relentless persecution by hunters. As a result, when the U.S. Endangered Species Act was passed in 1973, the only wolves known to remain in the 48 contiguous states were a few hundred left in Minnesota. Some stragglers later emigrated from Canada to recolonize part of their historic range in northwestern Montana, but it wasn't until 1995 that conservationists won a symbolic victory by reintroducing Canadian wolves into Yellowstone National Park after an absence of 70 years. The reintroduction is being counted as a huge success, despite a low level of local opposition, with the present Yellowstone population estimated at over 100 and a number already having established territories well outside the boundaries of the national park.

The trumpeter swan (*Cygnus buccinator*), the largest of North America's waterfowl, is a traditional migrant through this region and perhaps the best example of a flagship species among the birds. Trumpeter numbers were severely decimated in the mid-1800s by hunters who supplied skins for European fashions, and then again in the early 1900s by collectors who took young swans for public and private zoological exhibits. Passage of the Migratory Bird Treaty Act of 1918 helped protect remaining populations in the United States, which had been reduced to the low hundreds, and in 1936 the Red Rock Lakes National Wildlife Refuge was created in Montana as a protected wintering ground for this species (Murphy 1968; Ehrlich et al. 1992).

Human Cultures

Native American habitation of the Rocky Mountains is known from 12 000-year-old remnants of the Clovis culture, peoples of the southern mountains whose descendants followed receding ice sheets north over the gradually warming millennia. These were the ancestors of the Ute and the Shoshone, the first Rocky Mountain-dwelling tribes to trade for horses with the Spanish, and then to introduce them (often in combat) to the Sioux, Blackfeet, and other tribes of the Great Plains (Josephy 1961). Actually, it is somewhat difficult to separate Native Americans (or people of the First Nation, as they are referred to in Canada) into tribes of the mountains or of the plains, since the mountains were frequently used by many plains-dwelling tribes, but perhaps only for temporary refuge from enemies or as seasonal hunting and gathering grounds.

The Blackfeet, who referred to themselves as Nitsitapii or the "Real People," spoke of the Rocky Mountains as the "backbone of the world" (Milne 1994). They, in fact, waged war in these mountains with the Absaroke (also called Crow), initially plains-dwellers who ultimately settled in the Yellowstone region, and the Shoshone, who were often referred to by others as the Snakes and were also relatively recent arrivals to the Yellowstone region, having come from traditional lands that reached much farther west (Janetski 1987). Notable among the

Shoshone were the Sheepeaters, mountain-living hunter-gatherers whose main quarry was the elusive bighorn sheep (*Ovis canadensis*). To the north of the Shoshone lived the Bannock and Nez Perce of Idaho, the Salish (also known as Flatheads) of western Montana, and the Kalispel, Coeur d'Alene, and Kutenai of the northern Idaho-southern Alberta/British Columbia border.

All Indians of the United States were the focus of a ruthless military campaign undertaken in the late 1800s. The nation's bison herds were hunted to near extinction to deny them food. Treaties were signed and broken. Many tribes were moved from their traditional lands to make way for cattle ranchers and gold miners, while others chose instead to fight. Today, the descendants of early Rocky Mountain Indians, including First Nation peoples of Canada, are working to regain their cultural identity and take control of their future.

In the wake of the Indian wars, the Rocky Mountain region was settled throughout a prolonged period of westward expansion. Most larger towns and cities were established on the plains, in the foothills, and along river valleys, while the mountainous regions themselves have remained relatively uninhabited. We estimate that today approximately 1.5 million people reside in the 570 500 km² that compose the Northern Rocky Mountains Wilderness as defined here, yielding a population density of 1.8 individuals/km². These figures exclude the major metropolitan centers of Calgary and Boise, and a number of smaller cities in Idaho (Idaho Falls), Montana (Great Falls), and Wyoming (Casper) that essentially lie outside the ecoregion borders that define this wilderness.

Threats

Threats to biodiversity in the Rocky Mountain region are varied. Historically, mining, logging, and livestock grazing have taken their toll on forest and grassland communities, as have outbreaks of large, destructive fires that may have been exacerbated by decades of fire suppression as a forestry management technique. Uncontrolled recreational use in formerly remote areas has also become a growing concern to wildlife conservationists.

In the United States, significant areas of the northern Rockies are contained within national forests such as Bridger, Shoshone, and Teton in northwestern Wyoming; Boise, Sawtooth, Challis, Salmon, Payette, Clearwater, and Idaho Panhandle in Idaho; and Beaverhead, Bitterroot, Lewis and Clark, Flathead, and Kootenai in western Montana (Schmidt and Schmidt 1995). These lands traditionally have been managed as watersheds and for timber production by the Federal Government, but have increasingly been used for recreational purposes in recent decades. Many legal battles have already been fought over land use in the northern U.S. Rockies. As of 1990, the Sierra Club Legal Defense Fund had participated in at least 15 disputes that involved issues of oil and gas leasing, clear-cutting and timber sales, wilder-

On the opposite page, bighorn sheep (Ovis canadensis), *Glacier National Park, Montana, U.S.A.*

Above, mountain goat (Oreamnos americanus), *Glacier National Park, Montana. U.S.A. Both photos:* © **Patricio Robles Gil**/*Sierra Madre*

PACIFIC NORTHWEST

The Pacific Northwest appears on the map as a thin, crescent-shaped swath that runs along the extreme western portions of the United States and Canada, covering roughly the northern two thirds of the continent's coastal temperate rainforests and adjacent inland regions. Our definition of this wilderness area corresponds roughly to all or part of five ecoregions recently identified by the World Wildlife Fund (Olson et al. 2001): Pacific Coastal Mountain Icefields and Tundra (NA1117) (106 800 km²); Northern Pacific Coastal Forests (NA0520) (60 400 km²); Queen Charlotte Islands (NA0525) (10 000 km²); much of the British Columbia Mainland Coastal Forests (NA0506) (115 000 km²); and the northernmost part of the Central Pacific Coastal Forests (NA0510) (22 600 km²). Its northern limit lies along Alaska's Kenai Peninsula and also includes the historically heavily-forested island of Afognak, only a few nautical miles east of the much more tundra-like Kodiak Island. From there, the coastal forest strip extends southward through the region where the Chugach Mountains meet the Prince William Sound and the St. Elias Mountains the Gulf of Alaska, to southeastern Alaska's Alexander Archipelago and Canada's Haida Gwaii Archipelago (Queen Charlotte Islands), on through British Columbia's Kitimat and Pacific Ranges to approach the U.S.-Canadian border, and includes approximately the northern three fourths of Vancouver Island (Ecotrust et al. 1995; Bailey 1997; Olson et al., *op. cit.*). We estimate the extent of this wilderness area at about 315 000 km², approximately 80% of which remains intact.

While its northern limit is defined entirely on biogeographical terms, the southern boundary has been drawn based more on the significant increase in human population density as one approaches the city of Vancouver and the southern reaches of Vancouver Island in British Columbia (Schoonmaker et al. 1997). The coastal forests themselves continue across the international border into well-populated and developed regions of coastal Washington, Ore-

gon, and California that today are difficult to consider wilderness, having been so heavily impacted. In fact, in southwestern Oregon and northwestern California these forests meet the California Floristic Province, a biodiversity *hotspot* that remains under significant threat from human activities (Mittermeier et al. 1999).

Westerly winds that sweep cool, moist air off the ocean heavily influence weather patterns and climate throughout the coastal temperate rainforest region. Summers are moderate and winters are both wet and mild. Rain falls most heavily on western mountain slopes, while rain shadows are created to the east. Deep fjords, rocky shores, tidal marshes, lush forests, glaciers, subalpine meadows, and muskeg wetlands dominate the landscape. A few coniferous tree species characterize the most productive low-elevation heath- and fern-laden forests —Sitka spruce (*Picea sitchensis*), western hemlock (*Tsuga heterophylla*), Douglas fir (*Pseudotsuga menziesii*), and western red cedar (*Thuja plicata*)—, while salmon, waterfowl, marine mammals, large hooved mammals, and carnivores represent faunal elements that have been of greatest importance to indigenous cultures (Alaback and Pojar 1997; Suttles 1990).

■ *Wilderness Areas*

On the opposite page, a spectacular landscape in Brotherhood Park, with fireweed (or Rose-bay willow-herb, Epilobium angustifolium) in the foreground and Mendenhall Glacier and the peaks of the Coast Range in the background, Tongass National Forest, near Juneau, Alaska, U.S.A.
© **Kim Heacox**/*DRK Photo*

Biodiversity

Plant diversity and endemism in these temperate rainforests are low by comparison to moist and dry tropical forests, and diversity also declines rapidly with higher latitude within this region. However, endemic plants are not uncommon in a handful of Pleistocene Ice Age refugia that include the Haida Gwaii Archipelago, Dall Island, and the outer coast of Glacier Bay (Alaback and Pojar 1997). Overall, the Pacific Northwest Wilderness has at least 1 088 species of vascular plants, but less than 10 are endemic, since many extend down into the fragmented Pacific coastal forests of the U.S.A. (Ricketts et al. 1999).

Vertebrate diversity in the upper Pacific Northwest, estimated at 336 species, is not on a par with that of biologically rich states such as California and Florida, but seems to be greater than that of many other regions in temperate North America (Bunnell and Chan-McLeod 1997). More than two dozen species of amphibians are inhabitants of North America's western coastal forests, but the majority of them occur only in California, Oregon, and Washington. Only 10 species —five salamanders, three frogs, and two toads— reach north into the wilderness regions of western British Columbia and Alaska, none of them endemic (CI, unpublished data). The wood frog (*Rana sylvatica*) occurs farther north along the coast than all other amphibians, being found in wetlands of the Kenai Peninsula and along the shores of Cook's Inlet, Alaska. Reptiles are even less well represented with only eight species —two turtles, two lizards, and four snakes— inhabiting these climes, none of them endemic.

Birds, with approximately 227 species, are by far the most abundant vertebrates along the coast of British Columbia and Alaska, although none are endemic to the region and many are not forest dwellers (CI, unpublished data). A total of 80 species of mammals inhabit this wilderness area, including marsupials, insectivores, bats, lagomorphs, rodents, carnivores, and artiodactyls. Only three, Canada's Vancouver Island marmot (*Marmota vancouverensis*) and Alaska's Coronation Island vole (*Microtus coronarius*) and Sitka mouse (*Peromyscus sitkensis*) from Baranof Island and environs, are endemic.

In terms of vertebrate diversity, perhaps the richest section within this ecoregion is Clayoquot Sound with more than 304 species recorded, including marine mammals (Bunnell and Chan-McLeod, *op. cit.*). Even factoring out the 17 marine mammal species that frequent these waters, there are 287 terrestrial vertebrates, or 85% of the total for the Pacific Northwest represented in a mere 1% of its land area.

Flagship Species

Marine and freshwater species represent the backbone of coastal ecosystems and thereby figure prominently as symbols for safeguarding northwestern Pacific habitats, wildlife, and indigenous cultures. Five species of Pacific salmon spawn in the rivers of this wilderness area, long representing an economic mainstay and cultural icon for its people. Pink (*Oncorhynchus gorbuscha*), chum (*O. keta*), and sockeye salmon (*O. nerka*) occur the farthest north, the pink and the chum spending much of their early life at sea and the sockeye in lakes. The more southerly species, coho (*O. kisutch*) and chinook (*O. tshawytscha*) have more prolonged residences in coastal freshwater systems (Nehlsen and Lichatowich 1997). All mature at sea and return to their native streams to spawn and die, and thus are subject to disturbances of terrestrial/aquatic habitats caused by hydroelectric projects, water-diversion schemes, logging, mining, agriculture, livestock grazing, and urbanization. All of these have combined to cause a dramatic decline in salmon numbers throughout their connected Pacific ranges. Commercial hatcheries and overfishing also impact native salmon populations. Efforts to save Pacific salmon, therefore, must emphasize restoring terrestrial habitats and maintaining ecosystem connectivity with marine environments.

A major natural predator of salmon is the bald eagle (*Haliaeetus leucocephalus*), also an historic national emblem of the United States and perhaps the most widely recognized flagship species in this country. Along with other birds of prey, the bald eagle saw its numbers plummet during the mid-twentieth century due to impacts on its reproduction by organic pesticides. Through this period, the northernmost Pacific coastal forests remained a stronghold for this species (Ehrlich et al. 1992). Fortunately, recovery efforts for this and other raptor species have been both widespread and successful.

One of the most prized trophies of North American sportsmen is the white mountain or Dall's sheep (*Ovis dalli*) of western Canada and Alaska. Others include the timber wolf (*Canis lupus*), the grizzly bear (*Ursus arctos*), the wolverine (*Gulo gulo*), the moose (*Alces alces*), the elk (*Cervus elaphus*), the mountain goat (*Oreamnos americanus*), and the golden eagle (*Aquila chrysaetos*).

Human Cultures

Descendants of post-glacial settlers along North America's northwest coast are represented today by a variety of nations, clans, bands, and kinship groups. Here we will speak of several Native American and First Nation peoples largely in terms of their cultural heritage, but we will also consider aspects of their present-day status and representation.

Historically, the Inuit, whose life-style is described in the Arctic Tundra Wilderness chapter, settled the coastal region of south-central Alaska as far south as Prince William Sound. To their south were the Eyak, apparent relatives of the Athapascans, whose original homeland was a small thin strip along the Gulf of Alaska bounded inland by the Chugach and St. Elias Mountains. The Eyak reaped the rewards of both sea and land, harpooning seals and sea otters, taking salmon by various means, clubbing molting or nesting birds, hunting bears and

Above, Townsend's chipmunks
(Tamias townsendii).
© **Günter Ziesler**

On the opposite page, mountain goat (Oreamnos americanus).
© **Craig Blacklock**/*Larry Ulrich Stock*

On pp. 452-453, Pacific Northwest coast.
© **Kevin Schafer**

mountain goats with spears and arrows, gathering mollusks and crustaceans along the shore, and collecting roots and berries in the forests (De Laguna 1990).

Still further south were the Tlingit, also fishermen and hunters who fought heroically against Russian fur traders during the late eighteenth and early nineteenth centuries (Josephy 1961). Tlingit clans belong to one of two moieties: the raven or the wolf. Their traditional lands stretch farther inland than those of the Eyak, extending to the Yukon Territory and including the glaciers, mountains, islands, and deep fjords of the Alexander Archipelago in southeastern Alaska. Today, within this wilderness area, they are represented by groups such as the Teslin and Taku River Tlingit who live along the British Columbia-Yukon Territory border.

The Haida Gwaii Archipelago is the ancestral home of the Haida, accomplished fishermen and skilled woodworkers who are known for the construction of impressive red cedar homes and their carvings of tall and elaborate totem poles (Blackman 1990). Fish, shellfish, and marine mammals were their nutritional mainstays, and plant gathering was probably of greater importance to their diet than the hunting of terrestrial mammals and birds. Today, the Council of the Haida Nation and the Haida Tribal Society represent these First Nation people.

Tsimshian villages, which ranged along the British Columbia coast opposite those of the island-dwelling Haida, were apparently distinct and autonomous settlements within a rainy, mountainous, and heavily-forested region (Halpin and Seguin 1990). Four major divisions are included within this cultural-linguistic group —the Nisga'a, Gitxsan, Coast Tsimshian, and South Tsimshian—, some of which are represented today by member bands of the Tsimshian Tribal Council.

South of Tsimshian territory along the British Columbia coast are the homelands of First Nations such as the Haisla, Heiltsuk, Oweekeno, and Homalco, members of the Kwakiutl linguistic group whose speakers refer to themselves as Kwa'k'wala. These are traditional salmon-fishing societies who also hunted, trapped, and gathered (Codere 1990). More than a dozen Kwakiutl bands also inhabit the northern regions of Vancouver Island, while a similar number of Nootka or Nuu-chah-nulth bands reside largely along the island's western coast.

Prior to the arrival of Europeans in the late 1700s, perhaps as many as 200 000 indigenous Americans inhabited the wilderness of the Pacific Northwest, but the next century saw these early cultures almost vanish, their numbers declining by more than 80% due largely to the introduction of diseases such as smallpox, malaria, measles, influenza, dysentery, whooping cough, typhus, and typhoid fever (Boyd 1990). Descendants of the surviving cultures strive today for recognition and appreciation of their heritage, as well as for self-reliance, political representation, and the successful management of natural resources in today's modern and more complex society. The routes to these goals have differed in the United States, where gains have been made largely under the U.S. Native Claims Settlement Act, and in Canada, where both federal and provincial treaties have played major roles in reestablishing indigenous rights.

The current human population of the wilderness area as defined here is approximately 770 000. This population estimate does not include Vancouver and Victoria in British Columbia or Seattle, Washington, major urban areas that essentially form the southern boundary to this 315 000-km^2 wilderness area. Omitting these areas, but including much smaller cities such as Juneau, Ketchikan, Prince Rupert, Port Hardy, and others, the population density of the northern coastal forest region is still only about 1.9 inhabitants/km^2. South of the U.S.-Canadian border, what once was coastal wilderness has been very heavily altered and fragmented by human activities to the point that the southernmost rainforests now lie within one of 25 threatened biodiversity hotspots recently identified by Conservation International (Mittermeier et al. 1999).

Threats

The greatest threat to this region continues to be natural-resource exploitation, particularly logging of primary forests —a nineteenth-century form of exploitation that amazingly still continues in two of the world's most advanced nations. Commercial logging of old-growth forests has taken place to the point that second-growth forests now predominate throughout much of the region, and logging roads have already fragmented many formerly remote expanses. Commercial exploitation of primary forests still persists in spite of strong indications that this whole process is unsustainable. The Haida Gwaii Archipelago, as an example, has sustained significant clear-cuts amidst large tracts of pristine forest. To add insult to injury, much of the timber cut in the Pacific Northwest is slated for export to Asia, not for domestic use, and the logs that are exported are "raw" or unmilled, denying the economic value of some of the planet's highest-quality lumber to local communities in this region.

Wildlife exploitation remains a problem as well. High-seas salmon fisheries reduce the numbers of fish that can return each year to spawn, while logging and other development activities in their birth rivers and streams reduce habitat suitable for spawning, a one-two punch that has several important fish species on the ropes. Even essentially nonconsumptive uses of wilderness such as tourism, are believed by many to have deleterious effects on pristine habitats in cases where they are inadequately controlled. This has led to an increased scrutiny of programs that claim lasting benefits to wilderness preservation.

Fires and insect infestations are apparently less of a threat than in boreal forests of the interior, although the spruce bark beetle (*Ips typographus*) has made its presence felt along the coast.

In the public's view, oil spills still represent the most hideous threat to wildlife of the northern coasts. On

On the opposite page, Alaskan brown bear (Ursus arctos middendorffi) hunting for salmon along a coastal river.
© **Patricio Robles Gil**/*Sierra Madre*

Above, American black bear (Ursus americanus) catching salmon, Alaska.
© **Michio Hoshino**/*Minden Pictures*

March 24, 1989 approximately 42 million liters of oil escaped the damaged Exxon Valdez and drifted landward to eventually coat the shorelines of Prince William Sound. Patches of oil reached places as far north as the Kenai Peninsula and Kodiak Island. Eleven thousand people took part in the clean-up —about one for every mile of shoreline affected— trying to save oil-soaked birds that would ultimately die by the many tens of thousands (Hodgson 1990). Images of this disaster are still vivid in the minds of many.

Canadian government and the Haida Nation (Stephenson 1997). Gwaii Haanas is both a terrestrial and marine park whose name means "Islands of Wonder" in the Haida language. It includes at least 138 islands and numerous islets that are dominated by the San Cristoval Mountains and clothed in temperate rainforest.

A more recent addition to Canada's national protected area network is the Clayoquot Sound Biosphere Reserve, a 3 500-km² tract along the western coast of Vancouver Island that harbors a very high concentra-

THE APPALACHIANS

Most people equate eastern North America with a megalopolis —Boston, New York City, Washington D.C., Atlanta, and the other sprawling concrete jungles that drive the economy of the area and of the world. Yet nature also survives and is making a comeback in the Appalachian Mountains, which run 3 200 km from northern Alabama, U.S.A., to New Brunswick, Canada, and encompass 249 000 km².

The Appalachians formed during the Palaeozoic, with major uprisings from 650-350 million years ago. By the time humans reached their slopes, they had been worn down from prehistoric peaks over 5 000 m high to 2 000 m today. Their northern biota is still recovering from repeated glaciation —the last ice age ended 10 000 years ago—, but the Southern Appalachians have never been glaciated. The chain's north-south alignment allows species to migrate easily. Had these mountains been aligned east-west, like the European Alps, they would have been a great barrier to migrations, and a trap that would have ensured mass extinctions during ice ages. On a different scale, the elevational gradients of gorges and summits allow short-range migrations to accomplish temperature changes that could only be achieved by migrations of hundreds of kilometers in the plains, and provide isolated climatic refuges for subtropical and boreal species, respectively. Perhaps this is why the Southern Appalachians are a center of endemism for slow-moving organisms, including snails, vernal herbaceous plants, and salamanders, and also hold numerous isolated populations of species more widespread to the north or south.

Biodiversity

In terms of biodiversity, the Appalachians are extremely rich given their temperate climate. The Great Smoky Mountains National Park, for example, an area of just over 2 000 km², holds over 30 species of salamanders and more tree species than in the whole of Europe. Overall, Appalachian biodiversity includes 255 species of birds, 78 mammals, 58 reptiles, and 76 amphibians. However, few are endemic, since most also range into

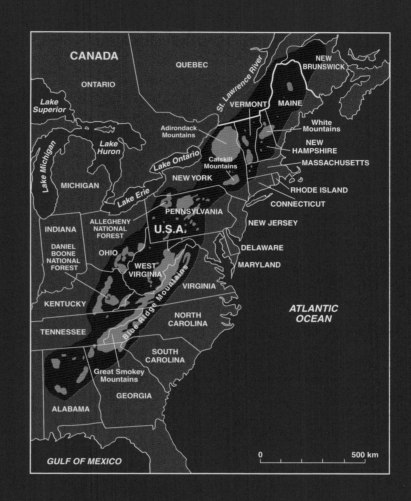

the surrounding lowlands. The exceptions are the salamanders. Of 55 salamander species recorded in the region, 21 are endemic (WWF, in prep.), and a number of the lungless salamanders (Family Pletho-dontidae) have distributions no bigger than a single mountain. This includes several members of the genus *Desmognathus*, found only in small areas of the Blue Ridge and Great Smoky Mountains, the Peaks of Otter salamander (*Plethodon hubrichti*) of Virginia, the Cheat Mountain salamander (*P. nettingi*) of West Virginia, and the Pigeon Mountain salamander (*P. petraeus*) of Georgia (Petranka 1998). Not surprisingly, some of these restricted-range endemics are considered globally threatened (Hilton-Taylor 2000).

Current knowledge of plant distribution is too coarse to tally plant species richness within the Appalachians exactly, but it is high. Kartesz and Meacham (1999) list 6 374 plant species in 10 focal states within the mapped area (AL, GA, TN, KY, WV, PA, NY, VT, NH, ME), 1 722 of which are exotic (27%) and 76 native endemics, including 6 listed as extinct; Davis et al. (1997) list 94 endemics for the southern

Wilderness Area

On the opposite page, morning fog in the southern Appalachians, Cumberland Gap National Historic Park, Kentucky, U.S.A.
© **Tom Till**/*DRK Photo*

459

Appalachians. We estimate there are some 3 000 plant species in the region. The Southern Appalachians are also a global hotspot for aquatic species, in part because they drain to the south and, unlike the major European rivers that flow northwards, allow species to escape ice-age extermination. Their fish, mussel, and crayfish richness is legendary. Tennessee has 290 fish species, for example, more than all of Europe (Stein et al. 2000).

Assemblages of contemporary vegetation in the Appalachians are strongly influenced by elevation and moisture (Whittaker 1956), but soils and history, including disturbances and pathogens, have also shaped their composition. In southern elevations below 1 500 m, chestnut oak (*Quercus montana*) and white oak (*Q. alba*) dominate the middle of the moisture gradient. These forests once had a substantial component of American chestnut (*Castanea dentata*) prior to the disastrous, introduced chestnut blight. Shortleaf pine (*Pinus echinata*), pitch pine (*P. rigida*), and other fire-dependent pines frequent dry ridges. Rich hardwood forests with tulip poplar (*Liriodendron tulipifera*), American beech (*Fagus grandifolia*), red maple (*Acer rubrum*), and black cherry (*Prunus serotina*) occupy the mesic valley flats and coves. These forests are famous for a luxuriant herbaceous growth. In a single square meter, some locations have a dozen species of spring wildflowers, such as mayapple (*Podophyllum peltatum*) and various *Trillium* species. Above 1 500 m, spruce-fir forest occurs, once dominated by red spruce (*Picea rubens*) and Fraser fir (*Abies fraseri*). Vegetation in this higher zone appears particularly vulnerable to acid rain, due to low buffering capacities of the thin soils, and to ozone pollution, which reaches high levels at these elevations. While the Southern Appalachians lack the tree line found in the north, they have scattered treeless balds, which are being invaded by heaths dominated by Catawba rhododendron (*Rhododendron catawbiense*) and mountain laurel (*Kalmia latifolia*). Higher rock outcrops have alpine tundra relicts, such as three-toothed cinquefoil (*Sibbaldiopsis tridentata*).

In the Northern Appalachians, white spruce (*Picea glauca*), black spruce (*P. mariana*), and balsam fir (*Abies balsamea*) dominate the spruce-fir forests. Red pine (*Pinus resinosa*) and white pine (*P. strobus*) are common in second-growth stands, and jack pine (*P. banksiana*), paper birch (*Betula papyrifera*), and quaking aspen (*Populus tremuloides*) establish after severe disturbances. Herbaceous understories are sparse except in openings and under deciduous trees. They often include Clinton's lily (*Clintonia borealis*) and nodding trillium (*Trillium cernuum*). The hardwood forests share many species with those of the south. American beech, sugar maple (*Acer saccharum*), and yellow birch (*Betula alleghaniensis*) dominate.

Flagship Species

White-tailed deer (*Odocoileus virginianus*), black bear (*Ursus americanus*), American beaver (*Castor canaden-*

sis), and wild turkey (*Meleagris gallopavo*) are the great survivors of the Appalachian wilderness. All four were hunted and trapped to near extinction by the early 1900s. The last-minute implementation of hunting restrictions and an ensuing campaign of reintroductions were so successful that these species are now common throughout the region. Other species were not so lucky. Appalachian history offers a stark warning: poor management leads to species extinction. Intense farming and wanton extraction of natural resources following European colonization destroyed virtually all of the region's original forest (Mowat 1994). Less than 1% of eastern deciduous forest has never been cut, the most notable being 42 900 ha in the Great Smokies and 20 000 ha in the Adirondack's Five Ponds Wilderness Area. Unregulated hunting and habitat destruction decimated populations, completely exterminating some species, such as the American bison (*Bison bison*) from the region.

Likewise, it is almost unbelievable that the most common bird in North America, the passenger pigeon (*Ectopistes migratorius*), which once numbered in the billions, crashed to extinction following hunting and habitat loss (Bucher 1992). The Carolina parakeet (*Conuropsis carolinensis*) was similarly driven to global extinction by farmers protecting their crops (Saikku 1991). Habitat destruction and senseless target shooting drove the ivory-billed woodpecker (*Campephilus principalis*) to extinction. A more purposeful onslaught of bullets, fueled by government-funded bounties, eliminated the area's top predators —gray wolf (*Canis lupus*), red wolf (*Canis rufus*), and cougar (*Puma concolor*)— although, fortunately, they survived elsewhere and are now candidates for reintroduction.

Not all of the region's charismatic flagship species were driven to extinction. In addition to the deer, bear, beaver, and turkey mentioned above, moose (*Alces alces*), elk (*Cervus canadensis*), fisher (*Martes pennanti*), and many raptor species survived the onslaught, finding refuge in remote mountain areas. With modern hunting and trapping regulations in place, and healthy forests reclaiming park and private land, these species are slowly recovering. Raptors are migrating past Hawk Mountain, Pennsylvania, in increasing numbers. Moose are spreading throughout New England and New York. Although fishers in the western U.S.A. are declining precipitously, this large relative of the weasel is now common in most northeastern wildernesses, and is even making appearances in some suburban areas.

The bog turtle (*Clemmys muhlenbergii*) is another Appalachian flagship species (T. Akre, pers. comm.), restricted to herbaceous sedge-meadows in wooded swamps, habitat that may have been historically dependent on grazing by bison and elk, and probably now reliant on beaver, white-tailed deer, and cattle (Buhlmann et al. 1997). The species is under heavy pressure from poaching for the wildlife trade, habitat loss, and suburban development (Tryon and Herman 1990), and so was list-

Above, ruffed grouse (Bonasa umbellus).
© **Wayne Lynch**

On the opposite page, moss-covered rocks in a forest stream, Great Smoky Mountains National Park.
© **Stephen J. Krasemann**/*DRK Photo*

On pp. 462-463, Great Smoky Mountains National Park, North Carolina, U.S.A.
© **Carr Clifton**/*Minden Pictures*

ed as threatened by the U.S. Fish and Wildlife Service in 1997 (U.S. Fish and Wildlife Service 2000).

Species reintroduction is an unpredictable task. In some cases, simple release of animals is sufficient. This helped the fisher and beaver spread south down the mountain chain, for example. Other species, such as the peregrine falcon (*Falco peregrinus*), require much more active involvement by biologists, and often encounter unanticipated problems. For example, a recent attempt to restore red wolves in the Great Smokies failed, largely because visitors' pet dogs transmitted a fatal virus to the wolves' cubs. Reintroductions of large predators, such as the gray wolf and the cougar, have yet to be implemented, because they are not welcomed by all members of local human communities. Less-maligned species, such as the elk, are uncontroversial and have been successfully reintroduced into Appalachian wilderness areas in the last few years.

Human Cultures

Before the arrival of Europeans, numerous Iroquoian and other Native American cultures thrived in the Appalachians. In the centuries following, these cultures suffered an onslaught as sad and as brutal as that inflicted on the region's forests and wildlife. While European "settlers" used a moniker that must be one of history's most remarkable achievements in public relations, they and their elected government devastated a continent. By today's legal standards, a case of ethnic cleansing occurred. Following President Andrew Jackson's inaugural address in 1829, for example, in which he called for eastern Indians to be relocated west of the Mississippi, Congress passed the Indian Removal Act of 1830. The Cherokee Nation's fate epitomizes the era's inhumanity. In 1838 Federal troops and state militias rounded up over 15 000 peaceful Cherokees into stockades and then started them on a 1 300-km forced march to Oklahoma. An estimated 4 000, approximately 27% of their total population, perished during this ordeal —the Cherokee Trail of Tears (National Cherokee Trail 2002).

Today, 22 million people live in this mountainous wilderness, an overall density of 88 humans per km². While human density drops to 50 inhabitants/km² in the region's 296 counties that do not include major urban areas (10 104 000 people over 201 000 km²) and to 21 inhabitants/km² in the 65 counties centered on major protected areas (2 035 000 people over 95 000 km²), over 150 million people live within 600 miles. With over half the people in North America within a day's drive of the region's 511 protected areas, millions seek outdoor recreation in the Appalachians each year. Great Smoky Mountains National Park, a jewel of the southern Appalachian wilderness, receives over 9 million visitors annually. The region's past and present conservation challenges portend those many wildernesses will face from worldwide human population growth and

encroachment likely this century. We should pay heed to the hard and expensive lessons that we have learned in these mountains.

Threats

While enlightened conservation policy and management practices have replaced those of the region's past, we must overcome new threats to restore and maintain healthy wilderness. Urban and suburban sprawl are fragmenting the region's natural areas. Private lands abound in the region, especially in the Southern Appalachians and Maine, often with few roads scarring the land (SAMAB 1996). The largest of these areas hold the potential to form the core of new wilderness areas. Smaller natural areas between them also need protection to provide corridors essential for gene exchange and recolonization. Only connected, intact ecological units can ensure long-term species survival and provide the entire region with the array of ecological benefits presently enjoyed, including air and water purification, nutrient recycling, soil renewal, and climatic stability. Existing dams and water-quality issues threaten aquatic biodiversity. Since 1936 when the Tennessee Valley Authority completed the first of its many dams, for example, the mussel fauna in the upper Tennessee River system has changed dramatically. Etnier (1999) attributes 40% of current fish imperilment in the southeast to siltation and other nonpoint source pollution, and 32% to dams and other human impacts on streamflow.

The forest of the Appalachians has recovered from historic lows 70-100 years ago, and intact forest now covers at least 60% of nearly all eastern states. Maine's forest increased from an estimated 79% in 1900 to 90% in 1990; New York's, from 39% to 62%. Unfortunately, the recovery is likely to reverse soon. Besides the predicted urbanization of millions of forested acres, many chip mills have sprung up in recent years. In 2000, 146 southern chip mills alone were being fed. Over 5 million southeastern acres were clearcut in 1998, the latest year with an available estimate. Furthermore, there is an alarming trend to switch forest production from naturally-regenerating mixed stands to planted pine monocultures. In the next 40 years, non-plantation forest acreage in the South is projected to decline at least 15% (Southern Forest Resource Assessment 2002).

Fire and recreational use are serious threats to many natural areas in the Appalachians. After 70 years of misguided fire-suppression and fuel build-up, potential wildfires threaten forests, homes, and lives. Forest managers must heed the natural cycles of burn and recovery to avoid unnatural super-fires that threaten nature and humans alike. Wilderness managers also have the power to regulate recreation, curbing trail damage from off-road vehicles, air and noise pollution from traffic jams, and poaching and overhunting. Restricting human use

Red-spotted newt (Notophthalmus viridescens) *along Middle Saluda River, Jones Gap State Park, Mt. Bridge Wilderness.*
© **Tom Blagden**/*Larry Ulrich Stock.*

of public areas is often seen as against constitutional rights, and is therefore highly political and controversial. Nevertheless, it is essential: only balanced, objective management plans will save our public lands from the tragedy of the commons.

The greatest current threat to Appalachian wilderness is biological: invasive species are wreaking havoc in the region. Around 1900, horticulturalists unwittingly introduced a blight fungus that eventually killed an estimated 3 billion chestnut trees, reducing a species that was once the largest and most dominant tree in eastern North America to insignificance. Today, American elm (*Ulmus americana*), dogwood (*Cornus florida*), butternut (*Juglans cinerea*), and beech are all battling relatively new diseases. In the last few decades, an introduced pest insect, the balsam woolly adelgid (*Adelges piceae*), has killed most Fraser fir trees. Another introduced adelgid threatens to do the same to eastern hemlock (*Tsuga canadensis*). In Virginia's Shenandoah National Park, most hemlocks are already dead. A tachinid fly that was deliberately introduced to control another exotic pest, the gypsy moth (*Lymantria dispar*), is now itself out of control, attacking over 400 species of native moths. In New England it has taken a disastrous toll on many moth populations, decimating the much-loved silk moths. Non-native species are numerous and widespread. A quarter of the 1 640 plant species inventoried in Great Smoky Mountains National Park are non-native. Finally, further external threats come from pollution and global change: the region has recorded some of the highest acid rain deposition in North America.

Conservation

Despite past failures, the Appalachian Mountains' recent history is one of hope. It shows that with proper care the region's flora and fauna is amazingly resilient. Current trends suggest that humans and nature can coexist in relatively close proximity. A century after President Theodore Roosevelt and others first advocated that conservation for future generations should be public policy, much of the region is again forested, its air cleaner, its water less polluted, its biodiversity in recovery. While much still needs to be learned and done, there is a glimmer of hope that our dominion over the planet can progress beyond extraction and slaughter to sound, sustainable stewardship.

There are caveats. Appalachian species may be generally more resilient to large-scale disturbance than biota elsewhere. In particular, island and tropical species that have not evolved under continental-scale disturbance regimes, such as glaciation, may be more susceptible to human-caused extinction than their hardy Appalachian brethren. Furthermore, much of the Appalachian biota has, or had, wide-ranging continental or subcontinental distributions. Another caveat is that ecological communities in reforested areas may differ sig-

nificantly from those that were never logged (Meier et al. 1995, 1996; Bratton and Meier 1998). Duffy and Meier (1992), for instance, report that century-old secondary forest stands have only half the number of wildflower species at small spatial scales than comparable areas that were never cut.

The Appalachians feature prominently among the conservation movements of North America. Although the land suffers many abuses, forest protection in the mountains is a tradition with more than a century of broad, bipartisan support. By 1890, forest destruction in the region was on an industrial scale, facilitated by sawmills and small-gauge railroads constructed in many watersheds, alarming visitors and residents alike. The wholesale clearing of the native forests was quickly followed by devastating wildfires and by floods, which carried away tons of the rich topsoil. In the wake of this destruction, interest in establishing a southern national forest reserve system was incubated by advocates including foresters Gifford Pinchot and Charles Sargent, and physician and hunter Chase Ambler. The first organized agitation for national legislation to set up a federal park in the mountains was led by Ambler, who arranged a meeting of businessmen, lawyers, and others in Asheville, North Carolina, in 1899, initiating a movement to persuade Congress to create the forest reserve system.

The 1899 meeting was the catalyst for a sustained campaign from Maine to Alabama that paved the way for the establishment of national forests throughout the East. Roosevelt pushed for the law that became the Weeks Act of 1911, authorizing the eastern national forest system. A year later, the first land was purchased under the Weeks Act —some 3 200 ha around Curtis Creek, now in the Pisgah National Forest.

Administrative and legislative efforts have since buttressed the Weeks Act. Under the Wilderness Act of 1964, Congress protected places such as Linville Gorge and Shining Rock, designating them Scenic Areas and Wild Areas. The 1975 Eastern Wilderness Act created wilderness areas in Georgia, Tennessee, North and South Carolina, and Virginia, along with Wilderness Study Areas (candidates for wilderness designation) in these states. In the 1980s, Congress passed Wilderness Acts for areas in North Carolina, Georgia, Tennessee, and Virginia. In 2000 and 2001, it designated national forest lands in Alabama, Virginia, and West Virginia as wilderness. Today approximately 21% (53 000 km²) of the Appalachians are protected. Nevertheless, further rounds of wilderness designations are needed to complete the process. Numerous deserving candidates include unroaded natural areas in the Bald Mountains on the border of North Carolina and Tennessee, Kelly Ridge in Georgia, and Bee Cove in South Carolina.

In the north, New York State is a model of big wilderness that should be followed by other states and provinces. Here, the state stepped in and filled a conservation role typically played by the federal govern-

Jordan's salamander (Plethodon jordani), *found in the Appalachians, representing one of the largest radiations of salamanders on Earth.*
© **William Leonard**/*DRK Photo*

ment —and they did it better. Two enormous state parks, the Adirondacks and Catskills, are protected as "Forever Wild" by the state constitution. The constitution would have to be amended to change this protection, requiring passage by two consecutive sessions of the state legislature, and then approval by voters in a statewide referendum. Thus, legally, these are among the very best-protected areas in the world (Federal wilderness areas in the U.S. could disappear with an Act of Congress). Adirondack State Park, the largest park in the lower 48 states, includes over 1 million ha of public and private land. This mix of small communities, wilderness preservation, resource extraction, and recreation has taught a number of lessons about the tradeoffs and politics of conservation. Within this matrix are 16 wilderness areas totaling 434 000 ha. Throughout the state, there are over 1.25 million ha of wilderness and wild forest lands, 9.5% of the state. Conservation opportunities for the future include the purchase of more land by the state. Challenges include fighting an unneeded interstate proposed along the northern border of the Adirondacks.

In contrast, Pennsylvania with nearly 1.8 million ha of public land, more than any state in the region, has less than 2 000 ha protected as wilderness. Nevertheless, much of the habitat between these areas remains wild, and conservationists should push for the integration of these distinct parks into a cohesive regional wilderness. Maine is another state with great potential for big wilderness, requiring state or federal protection of the extensive wild lands presently owned by logging companies in northern Maine.

Regional conservation groups, such as the Southern Appalachian Forest Coalition and the Northern Forest Alliance, have devoted years of research to identifying remaining natural areas and the means by which they can be consolidated, restored, and sustained. Their goals for long-term ecological restoration target sets of core areas that can then form a foundation for regional conservation. Their proposals, such as the Northern Forest Alliance's 1997 Wildlands Proposal identifying 10 wild areas in NY, VT, NH, and ME, highlight priorities for public-land acquisition and address how our public lands should be managed. They also document the significance of private landowners for the region's conservation and ecological integrity. Klyza (2001) gives details of current and pending wilderness in the northeast. The Maine Woods National Park and Preserve Proposal would preserve 1.3 million ha around Baxter State Park and Mt. Katahdin; the Adirondacks Headwaters Wilderness Reserve Proposal would add 3.2 million ha in northern Vermont and New Hampshire; and a 77 000-ha extension is proposed for New Hampshire and Maine's White Mountain National Forests.

Understanding and managing threats to the region's biodiversity also requires a renewed effort in ecological research. The Great Smoky Mountains National Park is a leader in this effort, and has undertaken a 15-year study to document and understand all life-forms within its borders. The magnitude of this project suggests that to extend it across the region (and indeed, worldwide) will require a network of schools, community groups, and citizen scientists, aided by scientists and technology. Without considerable help from the general public, professional scientists and conservationists can not collect enough information in time to save many species from extinction (Discover Life 2002).

Ultimately, long-term wilderness protection depends on public education and support. All members of society should gain from these areas. Outdoor recreation and education hold much promise. In Georgia, the U.S. Forest Service, in response to pressure from conservation groups, has not had a commercial timber sale in five years. It now plans to meet the needs of its rapidly-growing urban population by managing its forests for recreation and conservation education. Witness the success of efforts such as Biodiversity Days in Massachusetts, which in 2001 organized a weekend in which an estimated 20 000 children and 10 000 adults went on nature walks around the state and reported their observations. Citizens who get outdoors and learn about nature are those most likely to appreciate and support wilderness sanctuaries. "In wildness is the preservation of the world," said Henry David Thoreau. For long-term wilderness protection, we must all learn to appreciate nature as did Thoreau.

JOHN PICKERING
ROLAND KAYS
ALBERT MEIER
SUSAN ANDREW
KAY YATSKIEVYCH

Above, female black bear inside the den with cubs.
© **Wayne Lynch**

On the opposite page, red maple (Acer rubrum), Great Smoky Mountains National Park.
© **William Neill**/*Larry Ulrich Stock*

MAGELLANIC SUBPOLAR RAINFORESTS

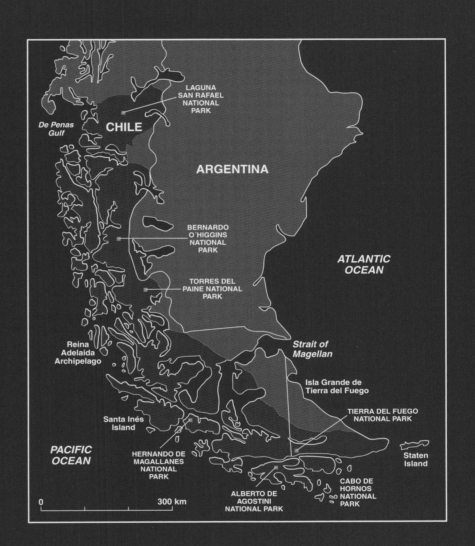

Forming a thin arch along the southern tip of the South American continent, the Magellanic Subpolar Rainforests are one of the most majestic ecosystems on Earth. Shared by Chile (86%; 125 559 km²) and Argentina (14%; 20 689 km²), this landscape is peppered with fjords, high mountains, and enormous ice fields covering some 19 500 km². Although not very rich in biodiversity, the region harbors a unique community of plants and animals. An almost entirely intact wilderness (95%), it corresponds to the ecoregion defined by the WWF as the Magellanic Subpolar Forests (NT0402) (147 200 km²) (Olson et al. 2001).

The Magellanic Subpolar Forests are bordered at their northern limit by the Valdivian temperate forests (47°S) and at their eastern edge by the grasslands and steppes of Patagonia. The Pacific Ocean marks their western and southern edges, and they reach down to Cape Horn (56°S), the southern tip of the continent. The higher peaks, towering above 3 700 m, are located to the north and include three Cordilleras, the Patagónica Insular, the Patagónica Oriental, and the Patagónica Occidental, which form the southernmost extension of the Andes (WWF, in prep.). Farther south, elevations decrease to less than 1 000 m.

An archipelago, including Tierra del Fuego (73 746 km²) —of which two thirds is Chilean and one third Argentine—, Staten Island (500.8 km²), and Wellington Island (5 555.7 km²), stretches along the coast of this wilderness area.

Several large lakes of glacial origin are found in the region, including Lake General Carrera-Buenos Aires (224 000 ha). It is located in the northernmost portion of this wilderness, is shared by Chile and Argenti-

na, and —at 590 m— is the deepest and the second largest lake in South America (after Lake Titicaca).

Climatically, the Magellanic Subpolar Forests are considered a temperate, cold rainforest. Cold oceanic currents, like the northward-flowing Humboldt and Antarctic Currents, cause this area to be cooler than other regions at similar latitudes. Precipitation with abundant snow all year round decreases from the coast to the interior and ranges between 4 000 mm to 700 mm. This high precipitation, coupled with poor drainage, low temperatures, and slow decomposition rates, makes the soils of the region generally acidic (WWF 2002). The Magellanic Rainforest develops on these thin podzols of fluvio-glacial origin (Arroyo et al. 1996).

Wilderness Areas

On the opposite page, Paso Garibaldi, Isla Grande de Tierra del Fuego, Argentina.
© **Patricio Robles Gil**/*Sierra Madre*

On pp. 470-471, Los Glaciares National Park, Argentina.
© **Willy Kenning**

469

Biodiversity

Phytogeographically, this ecoregion is part of the Sub-Antarctic Province and represents a floristically impoverished and structurally simpler version of the Valdivian forests to the north (Cabrera 1976). Two types of vegetation, varying with elevation and latitude, characterize this region of Gondwanan origin. The first, located mostly to the west, is an evergreen forest dominated by *Nothofagus betuloides.* The second, to the east and stretching into Argentina, consists of deciduous *Lenga* forests dominated by *N. pumilio* and the more arid-tolerant *N. antarctica.* Heath can be found in frost pockets, with common genera being *Empetrum* and *Bolax,* while moister parts of the forest have grasses, sedges, *Juncus,* and *Sphagnum* (WWF, in prep.). Along the southwestern margin of the continent, where precipitation often exceeds 4 000 mm, these forests give way to Magellanic moorland, dominated by cushion-forming plants. These can also be found in the higher elevations of some of the islands, particularly Chiloé Island and the Coastal Cordillera (Pisano 1977), where they have the appearance of tundra, but lack permafrost (Pisano, *op. cit*). In poorly-drained coastal zones, swamp forests of *Tepualia* and *Pilgerodendron* can be found. Also, in spite of the high latitude, six species of vines and climbing shrubs may be found in the Magellanic Rainforests, including *Campsidium valdivicum* and *Philesia magellanica* (Arroyo et al., *op. cit.*).

Arroyo et al. (1996) estimate that 450 vascular plants may be found in this region and at least 35 of those are endemic or near endemic, including *Nothofagus nitida, Crinodendron hookerianum,* and *Pilgerodendron* spp. among the trees and *Baccharis elaeoides* and *Latua pubiflora* among the shrubs. However, estimates of species richness are unavailable for the lichen and moss floras, which are poorly known but probably quite diverse in this region (Galloway 1992).

Animals tend to be neither speciose nor abundant at these latitudes. There are few endemic species, given that most inhabitants of the Magellanic Rainforests also extend north to the Andes and east to the Patagonian steppes. The uniqueness of this forest, however, is reflected in the high ratio of endemic higher taxa.

Mammals, represented by 43 species, include the widespread puma (*Puma concolor*), two foxes (*Pseudalopex griseus* and *P. culpaeus*), guanaco (*Lama guanicoe*), Chilean guemal or huemul (*Hippocamelus bisulcus*) —which has its most important populations in the area—, southern pudu (*Pudu puda*) and huillín or southern river otter (*Lontra provocax*) (Redford and Eisenberg 1992). The only endemic mammals are small rodents, such as Hershkovitz's grass mouse (*Akodon hershkovitzi*) and the woolly grass mouse (*A. lanosus*) and they number two.

Birds are represented by a total of 121 species, none of which are endemic. As might be expected, there are few reptiles in this region: only two species, of which one, *Liolaemus exploratum,* is endemic, but may already be extinct (Donoso Barros 1966; UDEC 2002). On the other hand, amphibians are represented by 11 species, two of them endemic (WWF 2002).

Flagship Species

Several species can be considered flagships for this region, with two of the most striking being the Magellanic woodpecker (*Campephilus magellanicus*) and the South Andean deer, Chilean *guemal* or *huemul* (*Hippocamelus bisulcus*). Neither is endemic, but both have important populations in the area.

The Magellanic woodpecker is the largest in South America, reaching 36-38 cm. With its black body and bright red head with long crest, the male is truly stunning, as is its loud and piercing call. This contrasting plumage is further enhanced in flight by a single white wing patch. Ranging from Ñuble to Magallanes, and from sea level to 2 000 m, this species is not considered threatened. Although it does visit disturbed forest, it is dependent on mature *Nothofagus* forest.

The *huemul* is a small deer (45-65 kg) that historically ranged all the way from the Andes to Patagonia and was even found on some of the Pacific Coast islands. However, heavy hunting, loss of habitat to erosion and fire, competition from introduced red deer (*Cervus elaphus*), and diseases transmitted from livestock have caused it to disappear from most of its range —to the point that today it remains only in protected areas.

Human Cultures

When Europeans settled in this area in the nineteenth century, the indigenous groups were mostly coastal cultures, among them the Yámana (or Yaghan) and the Alacaluf. They numbered less than 3 000 people and lived in the archipelago, where they navigated fjords and canals in bark canoes searching for shellfish, seals, whales, and birds. On the mainland and Tierra del Fuego, other cultures such as the Ona (which included the Aush and the Shelknam) survived by hunting and gathering. Many believe that it was the campfires of the Yahgan that led Ferdinand Magellan to name Tierra del Fuego ("Land of Fire") in 1520. Despite the cold and rain, the inhabitants of these latitudes wore only a single skin cape over their shoulders.

Most indigenous people fell victim to violence and diseases upon European contact and the few survivors quickly lost their ancestral customs (Martinic 1997). Today, this region is almost entirely uninhabited, with the exception of a few small cities. The total population on the Chilean side is 152 951 people, of which 89% live in the larger cities of Punta Arenas (112 661), Natales (17 250), and Por-

On the opposite page, Bosque de Lengas, Chile.
© Pablo Valenzuela

Above, Magellanic woodpecker (Campephilus magellanicus), one of the region's most important flagship species, Los Glaciares National Park, Argentina.
© Günter Ziesler

venir (5 500) (GeoHive 2002). Only 17 540 people live in smaller towns and rural areas, giving a wilderness population density of only 0.14 inhabitant/km². On the Argentinean side, 83% of the population of 100 313 is concentrated in the cities of Ushuaia (45 000) and Río Grande (38 352) (INDEC 2002; GeoHive, *op. cit.*), yielding a wilderness human density of 0.8 inhabitant/km². With a combined rural population of 34 501, this entire region has a population density of 0.2 inhabitant/km².

Threats

The arrival of Europeans brought on the first exploitation of Magellanic forests. Land was cleared for settlements and agriculture, and trees were cut for construction and fuel wood. Today, major threats include logging, afforestation, fire, and agriculture and grazing, of which logging is undoubtedly the most serious. In Tierra del Fuego, for example, where the southernmost forests of the world are found, a $200-million-dollar logging concession, the Rio Condor logging project, initiated by the U.S.-based Trillium Corp., threatens to log 360 000 ha of *Lenga* forest (*Nothofagus pumilio*) (Native Forest Network 2002). Other parties involved include a company from British Columbia and a joint Chilean-Japanese firm that have purchased several large tracts to set up logging operations for woodchip production (Gilroy 1992).

Another potential threat is oil exploitation. Currently there is a sea platform, many coastal drills, and an offshore loading area for tankers.

Fire, which at one point was the most destructive force, has been lessened considerably. Replacing it as the greatest threat is clear cutting for chip production and to make way for monoculture tree plantations. Perhaps the most serious threat to the Magellanic Rainforests is the fallacy of sustainable exploitation of native forests, which continues to turn entire stands into low-value woodchips at a totally unsustainable pace (Pickett 1996).

Introduced species are also starting to become a problem, among them the North American beaver (*Castor canadensis*), which has established itself in the southern portion of the region and caused serious ecological disturbances with its dams (Arroyo et al. 1995).

Conservation

Remoteness and harsh climate have played a critical role in the preservation of this remarkable region. However, the governments of both Chile and Argentina have recognized its importance and have declared a number of protected areas under different categories. On the Chilean side, protected areas include Laguna San

Above, Andean condor (Vultur gryphus) *in flight, Santa Cruz Lake.*

On the opposite page, bachelor group of guanacos (Lama guanicoe)*, Cuernos del Paine, Chile.*
Both photos: © **Günter Ziesler**

Rafael Biosphere Reserve (1 742 000 ha), Bernardo O'Higgins National Park (3 535 901 ha), Torres del Paine National Park (184 414 ha), Alberto de Angostini National Park (1 460 000 ha), Cabo de Hornos National Park (63 093 ha), Pali-Aike National Park (3 000 ha), Jenimeni National Reserve (158 860 ha), Alcalufes National Reserve (2 313 875 ha), Katalalixar National Reserve (674 500 ha), Lago Cochrane National Reserve (8 361 ha), Laguna Parrillar National Reserve (18 814 ha), Las Vicuñas National Reserve (209 131 ha), and Magallanes National Reserve (13 500 ha) —for a total of 10 385 449 ha or 83% of the region under some protection (WCMC/UNEP 2002). On the Argentinean side, protected areas include Perito Moreno National Park (6 700 ha), Los Glaciares National Park (161 790 ha), and Tierra del Fuego National Park (34 500 ha) for a total of 202 990 ha, or 10% of the area (WCMC/UNEP, *op. cit.*). Combined, the protected areas of these two countries cover 72% of the entire region.

Although there are many threats to the Magellanic Rainforests, this area has by far one of the highest percentages of protection in any wilderness area, an achievement that deserves international recognition and should be followed in many other fragile wildernesses around the world.

CRISTINA G. MITTERMEIER
JOHN C. MITTERMEIER

474

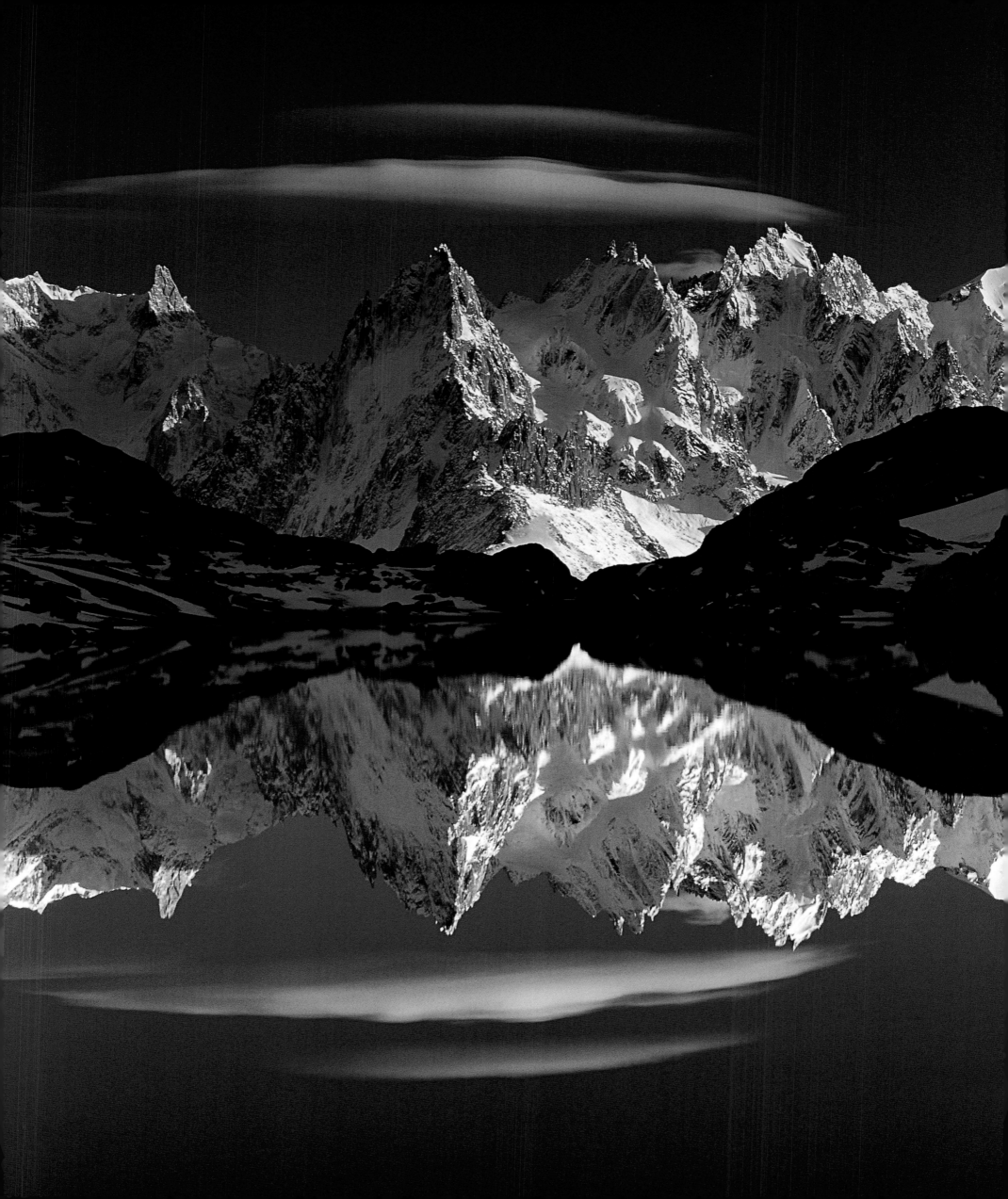

When comparing the American model of wilderness with the reality of Europe in the twenty-first century, it is hard to imagine that there are any true wilderness areas left in Europe. The European mountains have a long history of human use and settlement, meaning that areas with wilderness qualities are very limited. For many European countries, the concept of "wilderness" does not exist; indeed, in some European languages there is not even a word for it (Fritz 2001). Nevertheless, mountains are the one European biome where the idea of wilderness is understandable, even to people who do not recognize a word for it.

In this chapter we consider the five main mountain regions of Europe, covering a combined area of just over 372 000 km², the Pyrenees, the Alps, the Scottish Highlands, the Carpathians, and the Balkans. The Pyrenees mountain range extends over 400 km from the Bay of Biscay, on the Atlantic, to the Cape of Creus on the Mediterranean, an area of approximately 30 600 km², similar to the Pyrenees Conifer and Mixed Forests (PA0433) ecoregion of WWF (Olson et al. 2001). The range is split almost equally between the countries of France and Spain and entirely covers the small state of Andorra. The highest point of the range is Pico De Aneto at 3 404 m, which sits atop Palaeozoic granite, sandstone, and schist along the central ridge. On either side of this central axis lie Mesozoic limestone and chalk rocks, creating an important karstic environment. In the western and northern French slopes, a maritime climate prevails where there are mild winters and cool summers. On the central and southern Spanish slopes, a Mediterranean-continental climate dominates which provides dry summers and cold winters (Davis et al. 1994).

The Alps are the highest mountain range in Europe, covering an area of approximately 133 000 km² between Nice in southeast France and Vienna in Austria, and closely corresponding to the Alps Conifer and Mixed Forests (PA0501) ecoregion. Although landlocked, the Alps range from as low as 100 m above sea level to the highest peak, Mont Blanc at 4 807 m. Politically, the Alps cover seven countries: Italy (31% of the Alpine area), Austria (30%), France (18%), Switzerland and Liechtenstein (13%), Ger-

many (4%), and Slovenia (4%). Asymmetry exists between the mountains in the west, where sedimentary rocks prevail, and the east, where the main chain consists of crystalline rocks. An Atlantic maritime climate influences the northwest of the range, while a Mediterranean climate characterizes the southern part of the range and the northeast has a continental climate influenced by central Europe (Davis et al., *op. cit.*). The natural vegetation includes broad-leaved and coniferous forest, dwarf shrub communities, alpine grassland, and tundra (Stone 1992).

The Scottish Highlands cover 31 600 km² bordered in the west and north by the coast, and in the east by the Moray Firth and lowlands of Aberdeenshire and Angus, comprising portions of the Caledon Conifer Forests (PA0503) and North Atlantic Moist Mixed Forests (PA0429) ecoregions of WWF. Some might argue that, because the highest mountain, Ben Nevis, is only 1 344 m in height, the Highlands are not real mountains. However, their oceanic climate and northwesterly position in Europe mean that the Highlands contain ecological zones which are typical of much higher mountain regions in continental Europe.

In the Scottish Highlands, the tree line lies between 700-800 m and can be as low as 200 m in the far northwest, compared to 2 600 m in the Alps and 1 200 m in central Norway (Wightman 1996). The

Wilderness Areas

On the opposite page, the Chamonix Needles and Lake Blanc, French Alps.
© Art Wolfe

alpine zone above the tree line is composed of communities of moss and lichen heaths, snowbeds, blanket bog and dwarf shrubs. Across Scotland this zone covers 12% of the land area; and 60% of the area of Scotland falls within the submontane zone between the upper limits of cultivation and the tree line. The period of mountain building, or orogeny, occurred in the Highlands over 450 million years ago and since then the rocks have been subjected to weathering and erosion, continental drift, volcanic eruptions, and glaciation.

The climate is characterized by high precipitation (over 2 500 mm per year in the west), and strong winds of over 160 km per hour are frequently recorded (Wightman, *op. cit.*). The growing season for plants is relatively short and severely influenced by aspect, latitude, and altitude. Natural vegetation cover is dominated by heath and moor communities, native pine and birch woods, and subarctic/alpine vegetation at high elevations.

The Carpathian Mountains cover an area of over 142 600 km² in size, very similar to the Carpathian Montane Conifer Forests (PA0504) ecoregion of WWF. They span six central and eastern European countries: the Czech Republic, Hungary, Poland, Slovakia, Ukraine, and, especially, Romania. A third of Romania is dominated by these mountains, comprising over half of the extent of the Carpathians. The mountain geology is characterized by flysch formations of sediments and sedimentary rocks, interspersed with limestone and granite in places. Unlike the Alps, most of the region's valleys were formed by fluvial rather than glacial action, although the region has been glaciated three times. This has created many cirque basins and knife-edged ridges. The highest peak, Gerlach (2 665 m), lies in Slovakia, and the second highest peak lies in the Polish Tatra (2 663 m). Although much of the region is high, the lack of peaks above 3 000 m permits tree growth at high elevation and the extent of the alpine landscape is minimal (Anon. 2001b).

The Balkan Mountains, or Stara Planina, run for 530 km from eastern Serbia in the west to Vratnic Pass in the east of Bulgaria, the narrowest but highest part of the chain. In total, these mountains cover just over 34 500 km², and are similar to the area outlined by the Rodope Montane Mixed Forests (PA0435) ecoregion. Outlying ranges of the Balkan Massif, such as the Pindus, Rhodope, and Dinaric Mountains, lie to the west and the south. The main chain is divided into several submassifs surrounded by the lower elevation Fore-Balkan region.

The rocks are predominantly Cretaceous limestone, and consequently the summits are rounded and there are few peaks above 2 000 m, the highest being Mount Botev at 2 376 m. The east-west axis of the mountains separates the Central European climatic zone to the north from the more Mediterranean climate of the southern slopes. The continental climate predominates, however, and there are heavy snowfalls in winter that can last until mid-summer (Davis et al., *op. cit.*).

Above, Eurasian lynx (Lynx lynx), Bavarian Forest, Germany.
© Fritz Pölking

On the opposite page, Saalach River, near Ulrichsholz, Bavarian Alps, Germany.
© Larry Ulrich

On pp. 480-481, Ordesa National Park, Spanish Pyrenees.
© Patricio Robles Gil/*Sierra Madre*

Biodiversity

The rapid change in topography that defines mountain regions creates an environment of very high diversity, not only in the physical environment but also in its flora and fauna. Furthermore, the lack of interconnecting hills between the major mountain chains in Europe means that each has evolved unique characteristics, although geographic proximity does mean that there are a number of common threads across the region. The predominantly east-west orientation of the European chains, along with the physical barriers of the Mediterranean Sea and the Sahara Desert, have prevented interchange of species between Europe and Africa along the north-south axis. Additionally, the rapid change in geology and climate within the mountain ranges of Europe means that while a species may manage to cross a mountain ridge there may be hostile conditions on the opposing side that inhibit colonization of that species.

Overall, the European Mountains hold, very approximately, 5 000 species of plants, of which a few less than 1 000 are endemic. The region holds a total of 109 mammal species, 317 birds, 44 reptiles, and 36 amphibians (WWF, in prep.); in all, it has 9 endemic vertebrate species, including three mammals (the ibex, *Capra ibex;* the Tatra pine vole, *Microtus tatricus;* and the alpine field mouse, *Apodemus alpicola*), one bird (the Scottish crossbill, *Loxia scotia*), two reptiles, both Pyrenean species of rock lizards (*Lacerta* spp.), and three amphibians (the Pyrenees frog, *Rana pyrenaica;* the Carpathian newt, *Triturus montandoni;* and Lanza's fire salamander, *Salamandra lanzai*).

Four bioclimatic zones can be found in the Pyrenees: the meso-mediterranean (200-900 m); the montane zone (900-1 600 m); the subalpine belt (1 600-2 400 m); and the alpine zone (2 400-3 400 m). The location of the Pyrenees between two seas and between north and south climatic realms creates a region of great vegetation diversity. Within 150 km along the range, one can find all of the phytogeographical elements of Western Europe (Davis et al., *op. cit.*). Around 3 500 vascular plant species have been found in the Pyrenees, of which about 200 (6%) are considered to be endemic to the region (Davis et al., *op. cit.*). The Pyrenees are the most southwesterly of the alpine ranges in Europe and as such, many taxa reach their western limit in these mountains, for example, the edelweiss (*Leontopodium alpinum*), alpenrose (*Rhododendron ferrugineum*), and silver fir (*Abies alba*). At the same time, many Mediterranean species reach their most northerly limit, such as the Corsican pine (*Pinus nigra*). The Pyrenees hold 73 mammal species, 181 birds, 26 reptiles, and 16 amphibians (WWF, in prep.).

In total, there are between 2 000 and 3 000 species of vascular plants in the Alps and a rate of 7% endemism within the region has been proposed (Davis et al., *op. cit.*). The Alps can be divided into five main zones defined by their altitude. The colline zone is the lowest, with an altitudinal range of 700-1 300 m; here oak (*Quer-*

villages (i.e., areas exceeding 100 inhabitants/km²), the population density drops to 3.16 inhabitants/km². Over 11 000 km², some 36% of the total area, has no permanent human habitation, an important characteristic of a wilderness environment.

Within the Alps there were five distinct cultures: German, Italian, French, Slovene, and Rhaeto-Romansh, all based around a subsistence farming structure. Tourist development began in the second half of the nineteenth century, and was associated with fashionable health spas such as Davos in Switzerland and Pejo in Italy. Little changed until the rapid development of ski resorts in the 1950s, when tourism replaced agriculture as the prime economic activity. With a resident population of nearly 3.3 million people and many millions more visiting annually, the Alps are now the most populated mountain region in Europe.

Linguistically, the region contains speakers of French, Italian, German, and Slovene; there are many dialects including Bavarian German, Romani, and Ladin (Ó Donnaíle 2001). The average population density in the Alps is very high at 24.8 inhabitants/km², although the rural area covers approximately 96% of the region and has a population density of 7.8 inhabitants/km². Of this rural area, only 17 900 km² has no human population.

In the Scottish Highlands, aside from English, Gaelic is spoken by perhaps 80 000 of the population. The population is only around 102 000 people, the lowest of all the European mountain regions. The population density is on average 3.23 inhabitants/km². Removing urban areas leaves 99% of the total area classified as rural, with a population density of only 1.8 inhabitants/km². In the Highlands, 50.7% of the total area has no human inhabitants.

The Carpathians are home to numerous different nationalities and ethnic groups, and the mountains are highly populated in many areas. In the Romanian stretch of the range, there are more than five million people living in and around the mountains. In spite of the size of the Carpathian range, there was a great deal of cultural integration dating back to the fourteenth and fifteenth centuries, when inhabitants of the south and east relocated to the west of the range. The Carpathians are perhaps the most linguistically diverse mountain region in Europe. German, Romanian, Ukrainian, Polish, Slovak, and Czech are the major languages, but there are many dialects including Bavarian and Romani (Ó Donnaíle, op. cit.). This mountain chain has the highest land area and the highest human population at nearly 4.4 million people (Anon. 2001c) of all the European mountain regions. The population density is also high with on average 30.62 inhabitants/km², although in the rural areas the population density drops to 10.46 inhabitants/km². The Carpathians have the lowest proportion of area that is permanently unoccupied by people at 2.03%, only 2 899 km².

Within Bulgaria, the Balkan Mountains have traditionally been used for agriculture, including grazing of livestock on the mountain slopes. The growth in winter

Above, red deer (Cervus elaphus), *Retezat National Park, Romania.*

On the opposite page, beech forest, Vanga Preserve, Brasov Region, Romania.
Both photos: © **Gavriel Jecan AWC**

On pp. 488-489, gray wolf (Canis lupus).
© **Günter Ziesler**

tourism related industries did not begin in the Balkan region until the post-war era. The main economic activity for many people in the Balkan Mountains has now changed from a more subsistence life-style to one in the service sector. Hunting chalets and associated organized trips have grown with this increase in tourist activities. Within the Bulgarian and Serbian Balkans, the main languages are Bulgarian, Serbian, and Romani (Ó Donnaíle, op. cit.). The population in the Balkans is almost 685 000 (Anon. 2001c), with an average population density of 19.74 inhabitants/km². In rural areas, the average population density drops to 4.81 inhabitants/km². In total, 8.35% of the region holds no permanent human habitation.

Threats

Many threats are shared by all five mountain regions. Hunting has decimated populations of bear, lynx, wolf, and beaver throughout Europe and nowhere is this more severe than in the Scottish Highlands, where all of these species have been hunted to extinction. Although reintroductions have been somewhat successful, establishment is slow, and in some places hunting is still permitted. Non-sustainable forest use, both forestry and the harvesting of other forest products, threatens the biodiversity of all the mountains. The most widespread threat, however, comes from development, fueled by a rapid increase in the tourism economy. Many regions have experienced a loss of traditional economies and rural depopulation. While tourism, forestry, and road and power developments do create income and improve quality of life for mountain communities, it is vital that the natural environment is adequately protected. Areas retaining wilderness qualities can only be maintained if there is a strict zonation policy in place that prohibits road construction, power generation, and inappropriate tourism development in these regions. Finally, it is important not to underestimate the threat of global climate change. An increase in temperature and change in weather patterns will affect the extent of snowfall, in particular, with serious implications for all mountain ecosystems.

Using a technique employed by Fritz (2001) based on criteria of population, distance from roads and settlements, and degree of biophysical naturalness, it is possible to determine the intactness of the European mountain regions. It is estimated that 24% of the Pyrenees are ecologically intact, the second highest of all the ranges covered here. In the Alps, the high population, and high population density in the rural areas, results in an ecosystem intactness estimate of only 18%. In contrast, the low population density in the Scottish Highlands suggests an intactness estimate of 25%, the highest of all the European mountains. Again, high population density indicates that for the Carpathians the intactness index is very low, at only 11%. Finally, in the Balkans, where there is a relatively low population density, the

forests and changes in the socioeconomic climate have resulted in the abandonment of extensive forms of forestry and coppicing. Reduction in grazing and the neglect of fruit orchards have added to a change in the structure of the landscape and a loss of seminatur-

total, the park covers 457 km² and supports no perma- nent human habitation, although development is sup- ported in the surrounding peripheral zone provided it is compatible with the park's objectives. The eastern part of this national park and the Ordesa/Monte Perdido

TASMANIA

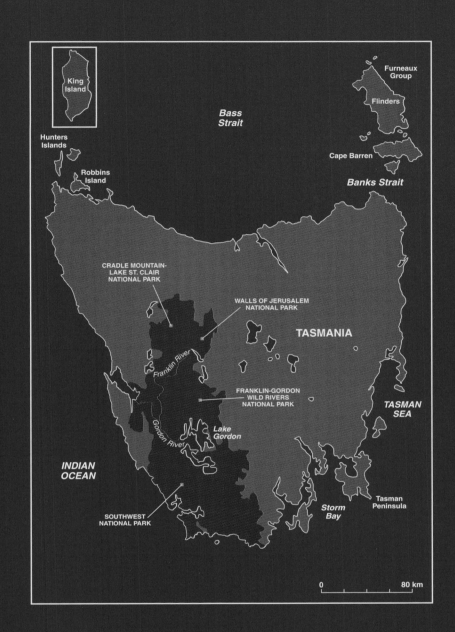

The island of Tasmania which, together with several other smaller islands, constitutes Australia's smallest state, is located to the southeast of mainland Australia, some 240 km south of Victoria across the Bass Strait. To the south lies the Southern Ocean and Antarctica, and to the east the Tasman Sea and New Zealand. With a land area of 68 049 km², Tasmania is a little larger than the American state of West Virginia. The terrain of the island is rugged, with steep hills, the only large flat area being the plains extending from Launceston to the capital of Hobart in the south. The highest mountain is Mt. Ossa, at 1 617 m, and Lake St. Clair, the largest lake, is also Australia's deepest natural freshwater lake. Both of these features are found in the Cradle Mountain-Lake St. Clair National Park in the wilderness area of the southwest.

The Tasmanian World Heritage Wilderness Area is the focal point of this chapter. It is located in the southwestern corner of the island, occupies some 13 800 km², and is composed of several contiguous national parks, including Cradle Mountain-Lake St. Clair National Park (1 610 km²), the Franklin-Gordon Wild Rivers National Park (4 400 km²), Southwest National Park (6 050 km²), Walls of Jerusalem National Park (518 km²), and Hartz Mountains National Park (71.4 km²). Of this, we estimate that more than 90% remains intact. In all, this World Heritage Area covers 20% of Tasmania's land surface and accounts for 93% of its parks and reserves. A mix of temperate rainforest, open sedgelands, moorlands, and heath, as well as high-altitude grasslands, the Tasmanian World Heritage Wilderness Area is a classic example of a smaller wilderness of significant regional value. Areas such as this one don't come close in size to major wilderness areas like Amazonia, the Congo, or the great deserts of central and western Australia, but nonetheless have enormous conservation and cultural significance in the context of the countries in which they occur and also make important contributions to maintaining global biodiversity.

The wilderness area of southwest Tasmania has also played a key role internationally because efforts to conserve this region from the 1960s to the early 1980s helped to highlight the importance of wilder-

ness everywhere. They also led to the growth of the "green" political movement within Australia which, in turn, was pivotal in stimulating the creation of "green political parties" in other parts of the world.

Biodiversity

The vegetation of the Tasmanian Wilderness Area is quite diverse, due in large part to the rugged terrain and high rainfall, which varies from 1 200-2 400 mm along the coast up to 3 000 mm or more inland; it rains 250 days of the year on average. Temperate rainforest is the predominant formation, and extends from sea level high up into the mountains. Trees in these forests can sometimes reach up to 100 m in height, making them some of the tallest forests on

World Heritage Area

On the opposite page, temperate rainforest with pandanus, Southwest National Park, Tasmanian World Heritage Wilderness Area.
© **Hans Strand**

Earth. Myrtle beech (*Nothofagus cunninghamii*) is the predominant species, with tea tree, blackwood (*Acacia melanoxylon*), sassafras (*Atherosperma moschatum*), Tasmanian horizontal scrub (*Anodopetalum biglandulosum*), and a variety of eucalypts (*Eucalyptus* spp.) also being common. Particularly noteworthy is the endemic King Billy pine (*Athrotaxis selaginoides*). Without the influence of fire, almost all of the southwest would be covered with such forest. These forests give the Tasmanian World Heritage Wilderness Area its global importance, since temperate rainforests have either disappeared or become increasingly rare in other parts of the world (Chapman 1998).

Other vegetation types include wet sedgelands, high montane moorlands, and alpine shrubberies. Wet sedgelands and moorlands grow on the extensive low-lying plains that cover about 30% of the region and are characterized by the dominant plant, thick tussocky button grass (*Gymnoschoenus sphaerocephalus*). These plains are poorly drained and often wet and muddy. Within these sedgelands, a variety of other plant species can be found in narrow, dense belts growing along the banks of creeks crossing the plains (Chapman 1998). High montane moorlands are found on the higher ranges, where a variety of very hardy plants thrive. These include orchids, pineapple grass (*Astelia alpina*), snowgrass (*Poa* spp.), and the cushion plants (*Abrotanella* spp. and *Pterygopappus* spp., among others). Alpine shrubberies consist of tough, short trees and shrubs that grow in more sheltered areas of the higher ranges. Scoparia (*Richea scoparia*) and pandani, or giant grass tree (*Richea pandanifolia*), as well as small forests of native pines, are often to be found on slopes, whereas eucalypts and scoparia are common where fire has passed through (Chapman, *op. cit.*).

In terms of species diversity, the Tasmanian World Heritage Wilderness Area has 924 of Tasmania's 1 773 species of native vascular plants, plus another 129 naturalized exotic species. Of Tasmania's 456 endemic vascular plants, the majority —256 (56%)— occur within the wilderness area, and approximately 62 are confined, or nearly confined, there (Alex Buchanan, Tasmanian Herbarium, pers. comm., 2001; Jayne Balmer, Tasmanian World Heritage Area botanist, pers. comm., 2001). Mammals are represented by 32 of Tasmania's 38 native terrestrial species, including two natural Tasmanian endemics and another three which are now extinct on the mainland (CI unpublished data, 2001; Michael Driessen, World Heritage Area zoologist, Tasmanian Department of Primary Industries, Water, and Environment, pers. comm., 2001; WWF-U.S., unpublished data). Of the 164 native bird species regularly occurring in Tasmania, 121 can be found in the wilderness area, including all but one of the 12 species endemic to Tasmania (Stattersfield et al. 1998; Michael Driessen, pers. comm., 2001). Reptiles are represented by 13 species, of which seven are endemic to Tasmania (Cogger 2000; Michael Driessen, pers. comm., 2001). Amphibians are represent-

ed by seven species, all of them frogs, and three of these are endemic to the island (CI, unpublished data, 2001; Michael Driessen, pers. comm., 2001). Finally, 16 of Tasmania's 25 native freshwater fish species, including four Tasmanian endemics, occur in the wilderness area (Michael Driessen, pers. comm., 2001).

Flagship Species

The Tasmanian Wilderness Area is home to many important flagship species, a number of them marsupials that have either disappeared on the mainland or have now become quite rare because of hunting pressure and introduced animals like the dingo and the fox. The most famous flagship species of Tasmania, the Tasmanian tiger or thylacine (*Thylacinus cynocephalus*), also known as the Tasmanian wolf, may already be extinct. A spectacular marsupial carnivore with one of the largest gapes of any mammal, this striking, striped creature was last seen in 1936, when the last known individual died in the Hobart Zoo (Guiler 1993). Although generally considered extinct, there are occasional reports of sightings and hope still persists that it might survive in remote, isolated pockets of the island. If it does indeed still survive, the most likely place would be in the sedgelands, moorlands, and forests of the Tasmanian World Heritage Wilderness Area.

This unique animal also existed on the Australian mainland until about 3 000 years ago, at which time competition from the introduced dingo resulted in its extinction there. However, it continued to thrive on Tasmania, where it was found all over the island, feeding mainly on wallabies and pademelons. Predictably, the thylacine quickly came into competition with humans and their introduced sheep. Towards the end of the century a bounty was placed on its head, which resulted in the deaths of more than 2 184 Tasmanian tigers in the period between 1888 and 1910. Clearly, heavy hunting was a major factor in its decline, but it is thought that introduced disease also had an impact on the population. Interestingly, the largest number killed at any one place (235) was at Derwent Bridge, right near the current headquarters of Crater Mountain-Lake St. Clair National Park and in the heartland of the Tasmanian Wilderness Area (Guiler, *op. cit.*).

The other great flagship species for Tasmania is the Tasmanian devil (*Sarcophilus laniarius*), which has now become famous the world over thanks to the Warner Brothers cartoon character named after it. Although it has also gone extinct on the Australian mainland, the Tasmanian devil, unlike its striped cousin, is still quite abundant on Tasmania, occurring in a wide variety of habitats, and even venturing into suburban areas. Although it is renowned for its ornery disposition and fierce demeanor, it is mainly a carrion eater and will consume any animal matter that it can find. Indeed, it is most often seen dead along the road, where it ventures forth to eat other road kills and frequently

Tasmanian devil (Sarcophilus laniarius)*, the ultimate flagship species for Tasmania.*
© **Patricio Robles Gil**/*Sierra Madre*

becomes a victim itself. It is abundant in the Tasmanian World Heritage Wilderness Area, although finding one requires a lot of patience and long nights spent driving or walking slowly along the road.

The wonderful and bizarre short-beaked echidna (*Tachyglossus aculeatus*), one of the world's three monotremes, or egg-laying mammal species, is also an important flagship for Tasmania. Although it is widespread and successful throughout Australia, it is much easier to see in Tasmania than anywhere else. A diurnal species in Tasmania, it is often seen along the road in the Wilderness Area, and is truly a delightful sight to behold.

The other Australian monotreme, the platypus (*Ornithorhynchus anatinus*), is also common in Tasmania, although generally more difficult to observe than the echidna. With its leathery ducklike bill, short, flattened beaverlike tail, and webbed feet, the echidna must rate as one of the strangest and most fascinating creatures on Earth. Fortunately, it is found in all freshwater lake and river systems in Tasmania, and is not endangered.

Quite a few other flagship marsupial species that have become very rare or extinct on the Australian mainland because of invasive species remain common in Tasmania. These include the red-bellied pademelon (*Thylogale billardierii*), the long-nosed potoroo (*Potorous tridactylus*), the Tasmanian bettong (*Bettongia gaimardi*), the eastern barred bandicoot (*Perameles gunnii*), the spotted-tailed quoll (*Dasyurus maculatus*), and the eastern quoll (*Dasyurus viverrinus*). Still others, like the red-necked wallaby (*Macropus rufogriseus*) and the common wombat (*Vombatus ursinus*), are common both in Tasmania and on the Australian mainland. Red-bellied pademelons are especially common in the Wilderness Area, and can be seen by the dozens or even hundreds on any given night.

Among the birds, one of the Wilderness Area's most important flagship species is the orange-bellied parrot (*Neophema chrysogaster*). Although it is not strictly an endemic, since it spends part of the year in Victoria, it breeds at only one site, Melaleuca, in the sedgelands at the southwestern corner of the Wilderness Area. One of the world's most endangered psittacines, it is now down to between 150 and 200 individuals in the wild, and is considered Critically Endangered (Mark Holdsworth, Orange-bellied Parrot Recovery Program, pers. comm., 2001). The swift parrot (*Lathamus discolor*), another attractive and threatened psittacine, breeds on the east coast of Tasmania, and then disperses to the Wilderness Area and the Australian mainland in winter.

Several of Tasmania's endemic birds also rate as important flagship species, including the green rosella (*Platycercus caledonicus*), the Tasmanian native hen (*Gallinula mortierii*), yellow-throated honeyeater (*Lichenostomus flavicollis*), the black-headed honeyeater (*Melithreptus affinis*), the strong-billed honeyeater (*M. validirostris*), and the yellow wattlebird (*Anthocaera paradoxa*), all of which can be found in the Wilderness Area.

Human Cultures

The first European to see Tasmania was the Dutch explorer Abel Tasman, who sighted the island in 1642 and called it Van Diemen's Land. Between 1770 and 1790, it was visited by a series of European explorers, including James Cook. When the Europeans arrived, they found a population of roughly 5 000-10 000 aborigines related to, but distinct from, the aborigines of mainland Australia. Europeans began to settle the island in 1803 and to farm the same fertile areas in which the aborigines were living. Conflict was unavoidable, many were killed on both sides, and by the 1820s fighting had become so intense that it was referred to as the Black War. Martial law was imposed in 1828, and in 1830 the Europeans put together what was called the Black Line, in which they attempted to flush all aborigines from settled areas. Although the Black Line failed to capture many aborigines, they were so upset by this action that many gave themselves up.

At about the same time, the Lieutenant Governor of Tasmania, George Arthur, gave missionary George Robinson permission to travel throughout the state, collect all the remaining aborigines on Tasmania, and move them to settlements on Flinders Island in the Furneaux Archipelago. This included even the Western aborigines, whose society was still relatively intact and who lived in an area of little interest to the Europeans. It is believed that they might have survived had Robinson not insisted on moving them as well. Many died of despair, poor food, or respiratory disease (McGaurr 1999).

In 1846, those that remained petitioned Queen Victoria to be moved back to the Tasmanian mainland. In 1847, their request was granted and they were taken to Oyster Cove south of Hobart. Unfortunately, of the 135 who were sent to Flinders Island, only 47 survived to make this move. They continued to be treated poorly, with the result that the entire population succumbed within the next 30 years; the last survivor, a woman named Truganini, died in 1876. Although she has generally been considered the last pureblood Tasmanian aborigine, it is now thought that two women that had been moved to Kangaroo Island off the coast of South Australia may have outlived her. In any case, pureblood Tasmanian aborigines had disappeared well before the beginning of the twentieth century. Even though it has generally been accepted that the Tasmanians went "extinct," there are still many mixed-blood descendants of Tasmanian aborigines living on the island today, with estimates ranging between 6 500 and 9 000. In recent years, there has been a resurgence of Tasmanian aboriginal identity (Ryan 1981).

In any case, the current population of the island is about 470 000, with the vast majority being concentrated in the Greater Hobart Area (200 000) and in Launceston (100 000). Most of the current inhabitants are of British origin, Tasmania having fewer people of non-British descent than any other Australian state. Certain

Above, platypus (Ornithorhynchus anatinus), *one of Australia's most important flagship species and one of the two monotreme species found in the Tasmanian World Heritage Wilderness Area.*
© **D. Parer & E. Parer-Cook**/*Auscape*

On pp. 498-499, Western Arthur Range, Southwest National Park, Tasmanian World Heritage Wilderness Area.
© **Dennis Harding**/*Auscape*

Court to resolve. Their 1983 ruling that the Federal government *did* have the power to prevent dam construction as part of its responsibility to implement international treaties like World Heritage was a landmark in Australian conservation history, and finally made World Heritage status for this region a reality (Chapman, in McGaurr 1999; The Wilderness Society 1999).

Of note during these trying times was the pivotal role played by photographer and conservationist Peter Dombrovskis, who dedicated his career to recording on film the beauty of Tasmania. When Premier Gray dismissed the Franklin River as "a brown leech-ridden ditch," Dombrovskis' photography drew attention to the magnificence of the region. With his evocative images of the Tasmanian wilderness, Dombrovskis was able to reach millions of people who couldn't see for themselves the beauty of what was going to be lost. It was not so much that he recorded national parks, as that national parks were created where he carried out his work. Like his mentor, photographer and conservationist Olegas Truchanas before him, Peter Dombrovskis died in the wilderness he loved.

An important by-product of these efforts by conservationists and bushwalkers was the formation of what is thought to be the first "green" political party in the world and the emergence of many "green independents." The key figure in all of this was Bob Brown, a doctor who became interested in conservation after rafting down the Franklin River in 1976. He became the Wilderness Society's first director and served in both the State Parliament and later the Federal Parliament. The Tasmanian Wilderness Society itself changed its name to The Wilderness Society in 1984, and now deals with conservation issues throughout Australia (Chapman, in McGaurr 1999; The Wilderness Society 1999).

Australia is also unique in that it is the only country in the world to have passed an Act of Parliament focused on World Heritage Sites. This act, entitled the World Heritage Properties Conservation Act of 1983, makes it possible for the Federal Government to prevent any further dam building on the Franklin and Gordon Rivers or any other World Heritage Area, and impacts how World Heritage Sites are managed throughout the country (Chapman 1998). In general, it is fair to say that Australia has made better use of and given greater recognition to the importance of the World Heritage Convention than any other nation on Earth, and this should serve as a model for others to follow.

Several sites within the Wilderness Area are of particular interest. One is Melaleuca, the above-mentioned tiny settlement in the extreme southwestern corner of the island near Port Davey. Its historical value has already been mentioned, but it has now become an important tourist site as well. A spectacular, largely pristine region of heath and sedgelands, it is quite rich in endemic and endangered birds. Indeed, Melaleuca is one of a handful of remaining breeding sites for the Critically Endangered orange-bellied parrot. This rare bird is quite easy to see from an excellent closed blind located a few hundred meters from the small gravel airstrip.

Another very interesting area is Derwent Bridge, which is the gateway to Lake St. Clair and only about 4 km from the headquarters of that national park. The entire region is very rich in wildlife, with even the parking lot of the headquarters being an excellent site for bird- and mammal-watching.

Other noteworthy sites are Frenchman's Cap, a snow-covered peak in the Franklin-Gordon Wild Rivers National Park; the Walls of Jerusalem, a striking vertical geological formation; and, of course, Lake St. Clair, Cradle Mountain, and Mt. Ossa. These are on bushwalking routes, but for those with little time, there are also scenic plane and helicopter flights available from the town of Strahan and other towns adjacent to the Wilderness Area. Boat rides are also available on Lake St. Clair and up the Gordon River from the coast.

Fortunately, after all the great effort that has gone into protecting this area and thanks to the recognition it has been given as one of the world's most important World Heritage Sites, the long-term outlook for this region is as positive and as promising as for any covered in this book.

RUSSELL A. MITTERMEIER
JOHN D. PILGRIM
CRISTINA G. MITTERMEIER
JOHN C. MITTERMEIER

Above, the orange-bellied parrot (Neophema chrysogaster), one of the world's most Critically Endangered psittacines, breeds only in a tiny area around Melaleuca in the southwestern corner of the Tasmanian World Heritage Wilderness Area. The total population is estimated at only 150-200 individuals.
© **Steven David Miller**/*Auscape*

On the opposite page, snow gum, Waterfall Valley, Cradle Mountain-Lake St. Clair National Park, Tasmanian World Heritage Wilderness Area.
© **Dennis Harding**/*Auscape*

THE BOREAL FORESTS

0   4000 km

The Boreal Forest Wilderness is a broad circumpolar belt of predominantly coniferous forest (Larsen 1980), interspersed with areas of tundra vegetation, that overlays formerly glaciated regions of the Nearctic and Palaearctic Realms. It originally covered approximately 16.2 million km², of which we consider 15.8 million km² to be wilderness in the context of this book. About 15 million km² of this was once forest, but remaining forest is now estimated at about 12 million km² (H. Shugart, pers. comm.). The region as a whole covers just under 11% of the Earth's land surface. A huge area, it is nearly double the size of the continental United States. As we define this wilderness area, it includes 30 ecoregions recently identified by the World Wildlife Fund (Olson et al. 2001): Cook Inlet Taiga (NA0603) (27 800 km²); Interior Alaska-Yukon Lowland Taiga (NA0607) (443 300 km²); Alaska-St.Elias Range Tundra (NA1101) (151 800 km²); Copper Plateau Taiga (NA0604) (17 200 km²); Interior Yukon-Alaska Alpine Tundra (NA1111) (232 600 km²); Yukon Interior Dry Forests (NA0617) (62 400 km²); Northern Cordillera Forests (NA0613) (262 800 km²); Northwest Territories Taiga (NA0614) (345 800 km²); Muskwa-Slave Lake Forests (NA0610) (262 300 km²); Mid-Continental Canadian Forests (NA0608) (367 900 km²); Northern Canadian Shield Taiga (NA0612) (613 700 km²); Midwestern Canadian Shield Forests (NA0609) (545 900 km²); Southern Hudson Bay Taiga (NA0616) (373 700 km²); Central Canadian Shield Forests (NA0602) (461 700 km²); Eastern Canadian Shield Taiga (NA0606) (753 800 km²); Eastern Canadian Forests (NA0605) (486 900 km²); Newfoundland Highland Forests (NA0611) (16 300 km²); Scandinavian and Russian Taiga (PA0608) (2 156 900 km², of which we exclude only 400 000 km² in the densely-populated southern Norway, Sweden, and Finland); Urals Mon-

tane Tundra and Taiga (PA0610) (174 600 km²); West Siberian Taiga (PA0611) (1 670 400 km²); East Siberian Taiga (PA0601) (3 899 700 km²); Trans-Baikal Conifer Forests (PA0609) (200 500 km²); Trans-Baikal Bald Mountain Tundra (PA1112) (217 600 km²); Northeast Siberian Taiga (PA0605) (1 125 700 km²); Cherskii-Kolyma Mountain Tundra (PA1103) (556 700 km²); Okhotsk-Manchurian Taiga (PA0606) (401 900 km²); Sakhalin Island Taiga (PA0607) (68 700 km²); Kamchatka-Kurile Meadows and Sparse Forests (PA0603) (146 400 km²); Kamchatka-Kurile Taiga (PA0604) (15 200 km²), and Kamchatka Mountain Tundra and Forest Tundra (PA1105) (119 300 km²). Overall, it is the largest forested region on the planet, being considerably more than twice the size of greater Amazonia. Close to 9.5 million km² of boreal forest lie within the borders of Russia, giving it the largest forested area of any nation. Canada has a total of at least 4.5 million km², ranking it third after Brazil. Russians call these northern forests *taiga*, a term that has gained global acceptance and is often used interchangeably with *boreal*. However, we consider *taiga* to be a more specific term representing the subarctic evergreen forests of Eurasia, and therefore restrict its use to that region. Most of this region is still a true wilderness and, as a whole, is still probably 80% intact.

Boreal forests are characterized by simple structure —a one-layered canopy, sparse shrub layer, and ground cover of mosses and lichens— and a relative paucity of tree species. The boreal climate is subarctic. Winters are long and frigid. An appreciable snow cover typically lasts at least half the year. Summers are short and cool. Precipitation is relatively low, but is rarely exceeded by evaporation, so boreal soils are perennially moist and often peat-covered to considerable depths. They are known collectively as *podzols*, their

▢ *Wilderness Areas*

On the opposite page, Pechora River, Pechora-Ilych Reserve, Urals, Russia.
© **Konrad Wothe**

composition and sandy texture derived from coarse-grained rock such as granite, their name derived from the Russian word for ash. Podzols are acidic and leached of key elements such as sodium, potassium, and calcium, and their original topsoil complements of iron and aluminum have migrated down to lower layers.

Treeless tundra borders boreal forests to the north, but the boundaries between these two biomes are intricately interwoven and more difficult to define as latitude decreases and altitude increases. They also fluctuate over time with climatic change. In North America, boreal forests intermingle with alpine tundra in the western interior of Alaska, then stretch eastward into Canada's Yukon and Northwest Territories, southeast into northern Alberta, Saskatchewan, and Manitoba to the shore of Hudson's Bay, through Ontario as far south as the Great Lakes, and northeastward to cover much of Quebec and Newfoundland, save for the northern extremes of these two provinces, which are considered tundra (Bailey 1997). In Eurasia, boreal forests transition with tundra along the Norwegian coast, the Boreal Forest Wilderness, as we have defined it, extending eastward through Sweden and Finland, across the northern Ural Mountains and expanding into a broad Russian swath that approaches 1 000 km in width (Larsen 1980; Olson et al., *op. cit.*). This forest belt continues eastward between the latitudes of 50°-70°N through to Siberia's Pacific rim. In northern Siberia it interdigitates with the Cherskii-Kolyma mountain tundra, to the east it includes the Kamchatka Peninsula, the Kuriles, and most of the island of Sakhalin, and to the south it reaches beyond Lake Baikal and into the Amur River Basin (Olson et al., *op. cit.*). The southern limits of the Boreal Forest Wilderness are much less obvious than the northern tree line, since they appear instead as more of an internal transition from the predominance of thin-leaved coniferous evergreens to that of deciduous hardwoods, as well as a more general change from dense forests to open woodlands and grasslands.

While some experts consider forests of North America's Pacific Northwest, the Sierra Nevada, and the central and southern Rocky Mountains to be variants of boreal forest, we do not include them within the Boreal Forest Wilderness. The temperate rain forests of the Pacific Northwest and the drier forests of the Rocky Mountains represent distinct wilderness areas covered in other chapters, while the forests of the western slopes of the Sierra Nevada are included within the California Floristic Province Hotspot (Mittermeier et al. 1999).

An appreciable part of the world's boreal regions is covered not by forests, but by water. In addition to many major river systems, North American and Eurasian biomes are peppered with expansive lakes, ponds, marshes, and other wetlands with quirky names like bogs, fens, and muskegs. These areas represent critical habitat for a variety of species that do not typically inhabit deep forests.

Above, Dall sheep (Ovis dalli), *Denali National Park, Alaska, U.S.A*

On the opposite page, moose (Alces alces)*, Denali National Park, Alaska, U.S.A. Both photos:*
© **Patricio Robles Gil**/*Sierra Madre*

On pp. 508-509, taiga forest, Penikkavaara, Finland.
© **Hans Strand**

Biodiversity

As with other northern regions, terrestrial diversity and endemism (given here for the original 16.2 million km² extent of this region) are low compared to the tropics. Vascular plants are represented by approximately 2 000 species (Derek Johnson, in litt., 2002; Luc Brouillet, in litt., 2002), of which around 150-200 are endemic (Derek Johnson, in litt., 2002). Four kinds of needle-leafed conifers predominate in northern climes —spruces (*Picea*), firs (*Abies*), pines (*Pinus*), and larches or tamaracks (*Larix*)— and these give way to deciduous hardwoods such as poplars (*Populus*), birches (*Betula*), alders (*Alnus*), and willows (*Salix*) as one progresses south. The predominant boreal tree, shrub, and low-growing plant genera are circumpolar in distribution, but their representative species tend to vary by continent.

Northern forests have a tempering effect on climate and weather, helping to create hospitable conditions for insects and other invertebrates even at harsh high latitudes. Flying insects such as midges, gnats, mosquitoes, and flies abound during the boreal spring and summer, serving as important food sources for migratory songbirds and a major blood-feasting nuisance for a host of large mammals, including humans. The presence of carnivorous pitcher plants (Sarraceniales) and sundews (*Drosera* spp.) also testifies to the prominence of insects in this biome, at least for the warmer part of the year. From autumn through winter, boreal insects remain dormant beneath tree bark, under ground, or under water.

Although slightly less stressed by living conditions in boreal regions than by those in the northern tundra, ectothermic amphibians and reptiles are still at a serious disadvantage compared to their endothermic vertebrate counterparts, the birds and mammals. Only 36 species of frogs, toads, and salamanders are boreal forest denizens. Combined, the 18 Nearctic and 18 Palaearctic species represent a mere 0.72% of global amphibian diversity (Glaw and Kohler 1998; WWF in prep.). Reptiles make even less of an inroad into northern forests. In North America, only three reptiles, the eastern painted turtle (*Chrysemys picta*), the common snapping turtle (*Chelydra serpentina*), and the common garter snake (*Thamnophis sirtalis*) reach that far into Canada. In Eurasia, nine snakes, two lizards, one turtle, and the slow worm (*Anguis fragilis*) have ranges extending into the boreal wilderness (WWF, in prep.). No boreal amphibians or reptiles are endemic.

The boreal forest-tundra ecotone serves as the northern limit for many birds, mainly insectivorous and tree-nesting species, while the boreal wetlands host large numbers of migratory waterfowl in both hemispheres. Approximately 650 species of birds inhabit this wilderness during at least part of the year, representing just under 7% of global avian diversity. Seven birds breed nowhere else, including shorebirds more widespread in winter such as the surfbird (*Aphriza virgata*) and jack snipe (*Lymnocryptes minimus*) (CI, unpublished data).

Mammals —especially the more robust carnivores and ungulates— are the terrestrial vertebrates we most readily associate with the world's northern coniferous forests. In all, 196 species occur in this wilderness area, including four bears, seven canids, 22 mustelids, 19 deer and bovids, and 77 rodents (WWF, in prep.). In size they range from the 2.5 g, 5.5 cm-long pygmy shrew (*Sorex hoyi*) to the 800 kg polar bear (*Ursus maritimus*) and moose (*Alces alces*) and the 1 000 kg American bison (*Bison bison*). None of the boreal mammals are endemic, but one mammal species, the Gaspé shrew (*Sorex gaspensis*), is almost endemic, occurring mainly on the Gaspé Peninsula in Quebec, but its range also extends to northern New Brunswick and Nova Scotia.

Flagship Species

One of the most impressive animals of the boreal forests is the brown bear (*Ursus arctos*). A large male can tip the scales at 750 kg. This species is equally at home at higher latitudes and, in fact, some of the largest individuals known are from Alaska's Kodiak Island within the Arctic Tundra Wilderness. Close rivals are found in Far Eastern Russia on the volcanically-volatile Kamchatka Peninsula. In the Amur-Ussuri region, *Ursus arctos* lives alongside the Siberian tiger (*Panthera tigris altaica*) and the Amur leopard (*P. pardus orientalis*), both Critically Endangered and the largest and most northerly populations of their respective subspecies. Brown bears and Siberian tigers are born competitors, often hunting the same prey and sometimes even one another.

The polar bear, although better identified with Arctic tundra, is also a creature of the boreal world and is commonly encountered in Canada's Hudson Bay region. Similarly, the American bison, more commonly associated with prairies and plains, has a major stronghold in the boreal forests of Canada's Wood Buffalo National Park in northern Alberta.

The moose, caribou, and gray wolf (*Canis lupus*) inhabit both tundra and boreal wilderness areas, but boreal forests represent critical habitat for each. At weights that may top 800 kg, the moose is the largest deer in the world. In Eurasia, moose are called "elk," and the animal Americans know as the elk (*Cervus elaphus*) is called the "red deer."

At 1.52 m from toe-tip to scarlet-capped crown, the whooping crane (*Grus americana*) is the tallest bird in North America. It is also one of the rarest and considered Endangered. Once distributed from the east coast to the Rocky Mountains, but never believed to be very abundant, the whooping crane was highly dependent on mid-western prairies and wetlands for its survival, and its population declined steadily as millions of hectares were drained and converted to cropland. Throughout most of the twentieth century, whooping crane numbers hovered only in the low dozens, the bulk of the individuals representing a migratory population that wintered in the Aransas National Wildlife Refuge of

Above, male willow ptarmigan (Lagopus lagopus) *in spruce tree.*
© **Kim Heacox**/*DRK Photo*

On the opposite page, gray wolves (Canis lupus) *attempting to drive a grizzly bear away from moose carcass, Teklanika River, Denali National Park, Alaska, U.S.A.*
© **Bill Watkins**

Texas and summered in the boreal muskegs and bogs of Canada's Wood Buffalo National Park (McNulty 1966). Today, approximately 180 birds migrate each year between Aransas and Wood Buffalo, and successful captive-breeding programs are now in place at the USGS Patuxent Wildlife Research Center outside of Washington, D.C., the International Crane Foundation in Baraboo, Wisconsin, and the Calgary Zoo in Alberta, Canada. In addition, eggs taken from captive cranes at Patuxent and the nests of wild birds at Wood Buffalo have helped to reintroduce a small population in the Rocky Mountains, using sandhill cranes as surrogate parents (Ellis et al. 1996; Meine and Archibald 1996; G. Gee, pers. comm., 2001).

Human Cultures

Human habitation of the boreal forests essentially began with the retreat of glaciers following the last series of ice ages. The indigenous inhabitants of North America are descendants of Asian immigrants who crossed the Bering Sea. Those that settled interior Alaska and went on to populate northwestern Canada are known as Athapaskan — People of the Deer (Van Stone 1988). Caribou was and remains their most important game animal, but other wild mammals and birds have traditionally been important sources of meat, and those populations living in river basins have relied on predictable salmon runs. Much of northern Canada remains populated by indigenous peoples today, western Athapaskan-speakers giving way to Algonquian-speakers in the forests and plains that overlay the Canadian Shield (Kopper 1986). However, settlement of this broad region has never been significant, leaving much of North America's boreal landscape only sparsely populated even today.

The fur trade, among other factors, forced civilization upon many American indigenous populations. French and English trappers, largely in search of beaver pelts, established a broad trading network with Indians across the continent, depleting large populations of beaver and other fur-bearing mammals and serving as the vanguard for eventual settlement of frontier outposts (Sandoz 1964). The expanding global market for furs, in fact, stimulated the search for a northwest passage across the continent. It was the principal quest of famed explorers such as Alexander Mackenzie, whose first journey failed in finding a route to the Pacific, but traversed western Canadian boreal forests and tundra northward to reach the Arctic Ocean (Gough 1997).

Eurasian boreal wilderness is home to various indigenous cultures, a number of which also inhabit bordering tundra regions to the north. In Norway and Sweden, the Sami retain exclusive rights to their traditional reindeer-herding economy, which they also still practice in Finland and northwestern Russia. The northern Urals to the Ob River Basin is homeland to the closely-related Khanty and Mansi peoples, nomadic hunters and fishermen who also engaged in reindeer herding, but who now represent only a tiny fraction of the current popu-

lation. By comparison, the Yakuts, whom Russian explorers first encountered farther east in the Lena River Basin, have survived in far greater numbers and are the most numerous ethnic group in Siberia. Those who inhabit forested regions remain seminomadic reindeer breeders, but also raise horses and cattle.

Buryatia, the Russian republic to the east of Lake Baikal, represents the southern limits of this wilderness area and is home to the Buryat people, close relatives of the Mongols. As is mentioned in the chapter on the Arctic Tundra Wilderness, the Amur Region may have been the staging area for migration of Asian cultures to the Americas. The region itself is ethnically diverse, being home to cultures such as the Nanal, Negidal, Oroch, Udege, and Ulcha (Fitzhugh and Crowell 1988). For all, fishing and hunting have been economic mainstays through the centuries, and their traditional life-styles have been put under pressure by the Chinese, Japanese, Koreans, and Russians. To the north of the Amur peoples are the Evenk, one of the most widely-scattered nationalities of the Russian Federation and a group that has largely been assimilated. Many who chose to retain their reindeer herding life-style moved north to live with Yakut or Even neighbors who still practice this tradition.

Both the island of Sakhalin and the Kamchatka Peninsula have dual ethnic heritages. On Sakhalin, that of the Nivkhi is rooted in the north and that of the Orok in the south, while on Kamchatka the Koryak and the Itelmen are similarly split. Itelmen peoples are also original inhabitants of the Kuriles, more than 30 islands strung between Kamchatka and Japan's island of Hokkaido. Following World War II, Japan lost control of the Kuriles to Russia and thousands of Japanese citizens were expelled (Cobb 1996).

We estimate the human populations within the boreal forest wilderness regions of Finland and Sweden at a combined 1 215 000 (essentially the northern halves of both countries, excluding the major population centers to the south), of Russia at about 18 400 000, of Canada at just under 3 million, and of Alaska at just under a half million. Therefore, the total population of the Boreal Forest Wilderness is approximately 23 million people within the area of 15.8 million km² considered in this chapter, yielding an average density of approximately 1.4 inhabitants/km².

Threats

Historically, overexploitation of wildlife has been a selective but far-reaching threat to boreal biodiversity, the fur trade perhaps being the best example. Beavers (*Castor canadensis* in the New World and *C. fiber* in the Old World) were once among the most widely-distributed of all mammals and also a prime focus of the trade on both continents. In North America, beaver trapping was indeed the backbone of westward expansion that subjected frontier habitats to a host of other destructive human activities.

At the global level, temperate regions have sustained much greater historical disturbance of natural habitats than have tropical regions, yet boreal and arctic biomes appear to be the least disturbed overall, largely because their climates are less hospitable to humans (Hannah et al. 1994). Indeed, of 76 ecoregions recognized within the continental United States, only the sparsely-inhabited boreal forest and tundra habitat types in Alaska remain relatively intact (Ricketts et al. 1999). Ongoing threats to their integrity include commercial exploitation for timber and minerals, fire, and insect damage. Commercial logging poses by far the greatest threat, especially since any net loss of biodiversity is compounded by the construction of roads that bring higher levels of human activities into former wilderness areas. Large-scale mining and petroleum exploration also pave new roads and establish settlements in remote regions.

Fire, under natural conditions, contributes to the overall health of the boreal forest and facilitates the reproduction of a number of plant species. Periodic fires are actually required for purposes of nutrient recycling. However, fires are increasing in frequency to the point that net annual losses in vegetative cover are now routinely reported for North American and European boreal regions, and predictions are that fire frequency will continue to increase due to global warming trends. Insect infestations sometimes last a decade or longer and are capable of destroying hundreds of thousands of hectares of forest each year. Major epidemics of budworm moths (*Choristoneura* spp., *Acleris gloverana*) and spruce beetles (*Dendroctonus rufipennis*) have occurred throughout northern North America during the latter part of the last century and, like forest loss attributable to fires, losses to insect infestations are expected to increase in coming years in response to warming climatic conditions.

Global warming, in fact, may be the most insidious long-term threat to the world's boreal forests. It is expected to increase over the next 30 to 50 years with continued release of human-produced greenhouse gases to the atmosphere, and possibly to have its first and most severe impacts at the higher latitudes of the northern hemisphere. Higher ambient temperatures are predicted to dry soils and to move growth zones northward at a pace beyond that which certain plant assemblages can adapt and migrate. This could result in decreases in area, biomass, and carbon sequestration capacity for boreal forests, with some experts believing that more than half of their present expanse ultimately will be lost.

Conservation

In combination, temperate and boreal forests constitute half the world's forest cover, provide ecological services of watershed protection, soil conservation, and carbon sequestration on a global scale, and are invaluable refuges for global biodiversity. They also dominate international timber markets and contribute significantly to

On the opposite page, northern hawk owl (Surnia ulula) *with rodent prey, Canada.*

Above, North American porcupine (Erethizon dorsatum), *Canada. Both photos:* © **Wayne Lynch**

national economies, most notably those of Canada and Russia. For the most part, however, these forests remain inadequately protected and are being exploited unsustainably (Smith et al. 2000). In recognition of the serious threats to the world's northern forests, IUCN-The World Conservation Union has launched a Temperate and Boreal Forest Program to provide for policy analysis and input, information gathering and sharing, and stakeholder involvement in forest management.

World Wildlife Fund's *Global 200 Ecoregions* identifies biologically outstanding regions that deserve greater attention from conservationists. Prominent among them are several areas that include significant amounts of boreal forest: Canada's Boreal Taiga and Northern Cordillera Boreal Forests; the Scandinavian Alpine Tundra and Taiga; and the Ural Mountains Boreal Forest and Taiga, Central and Eastern Siberian Boreal Forests and Taiga, and the Kamchatka Boreal Taiga and Grasslands of Russia (Olson and Dinerstein 1997). The World Resources Institute (WRI) has also homed in on boreal ecoregions in its analysis, *The Last Frontier Forests: Ecosystems and Economies on the Edge* (Bryant et al. 1997). According to the WRI report, half of the world's relatively undisturbed forest tracts —about 40% of all remaining forests— are found within the boreal forests of Canada, Russia, and Alaska. Finland and Sweden are among 11 countries that are on the verge of completely losing their frontier forests, while the greatest opportunities for preserving boreal forest frontiers lie with Russia and Canada.

The International Taiga Rescue Network has targeted more than a dozen boreal forest "hotspots" of high conservation priority. These include the last of the old-growth forests remaining in Norway, Sweden, and Finland; seven Russian forest complexes that cover more than 100 000 km² and are threatened by logging, mining, oil and gas exploration, and smelting operations; and major forest tracts in at least six Canadian provinces, all threatened by unregulated logging and many involving disputes with native American peoples who have challenged the commercial exploitation of their lands.

The extent to which the world's remaining boreal forests receive government protection varies. In the United States, approximately 194 000 km² are contained within Alaska's national parks, preserves, wildlife refuges, and wilderness areas, cooperatively managed by the U.S. Fish and Wildlife Service, Forest Service, and National Park Service, as well as in protected areas managed by the State of Alaska. Canada protects slightly less, about 176 000 km², at both the national and provincial levels, while Sweden and Finland each protect at least an order of magnitude less in terms of total area in their northern wilderness regions, about 15 500 km² and 14 000 km², respectively. The Russian Federation, with more boreal forest than any other nation, also protects a greater area of this natural treasure —at least 214 000 km²— in its extensive system of national parks and nature reserves (*zapovedniks*). This coverage is due to increase by some tens of thousands of square kilo-

meters with the addition of more than a half dozen proposed national parks and nature reserves by 2010. The current extent of Russia's protected area network, however, is difficult to reckon due to the dearth of available information regarding the number and sizes of special-purpose reserves (*zakazniks*); therefore it is likely that we have underestimated total coverage of boreal forests.

In global terms then, the authors estimate that approximately 614 000 km² —or just under 4% of the Boreal Forest Wilderness— is officially protected.

Despite this low representation, a number of the existing protected areas are true global standouts. Three Canadian national parks —Gros Morne, Wood Buffalo, and Nahanni— are included on the IUCN's list of World Heritage Sites (IUCN 1995). As its name suggests, Wood Buffalo National Park, which spans the boundary between Alberta and the Northwest Territories, was created in 1922 specifically to protect the North American bison. Today it contains the largest free-ranging herd of this species, about 5 000-6 000 animals, and also serves as the summer breeding ground for the Endangered whooping crane (McNamee 1998).

In Alaska, the 19 115-km² Denali National Park features the highest peak in all of North America and the chance for visitors to view what are commonly referred to as the "Big Four" —moose, caribou, grizzly bear, and Dall's sheep (*Ovis dalli*). Almost four times as large as Yellowstone and the largest national park in the United States, the 33 820-km² Wrangell-St. Elias National Park (most of which lies within this wilderness area) contains the largest assemblage of glaciers on the continent (National Geographic 2000).

At a depth as great as that of the Grand Canyon, Russia's Lake Baikal is said to harbor at least 1 200 endemic aquatic life-forms (Liley 1992), including the world's only freshwater seal, the Baikal seal (*Phoca sibirica*). Lake Baikal was also the site of the first *zapovednik*, Barguzinsky, created in 1916 (Center for Russian Nature Conservation 2001). Establishment of the Baikal-Lena Nature Reserve in 1969 has added to the protection given this biologically-diverse region and helped to safeguard it from further degradation wrought by commercial and industrial interests.

These are just a few examples of the world's most spectacular natural areas, ones that we have had the foresight to set aside for the benefit of future generations. Given that they represent such a small percentage of one of Earth's most extensive and productive wilderness regions, we see a great need to accelerate and expand conservation efforts in the boreal wilderness.

WILLIAM R. KONSTANT
RUSSELL A. MITTERMEIER

Above, Nenet boy coils his lasso as he stands by a reindeer corral, Yamal, Siberia.

On the opposite page, Nenet mother looking after her baby inside a reindeer-skin tent, Yamal, Siberia, Russia.
Both photos:
© Brian & Cherry Alexander

Kamchatka, one of the most spectacular wilderness areas left on Earth, is a vast, spear-shaped, volcanic peninsula that extends 1 500 km south from Russia's Siberian mainland. The peninsula covers 472 000 km², an area slightly larger than California. It is bordered on the west by the Sea of Okhotsk and on the east by the Bering Sea and North Pacific. Kamchatka's eastern shore descends rapidly into the 9 000 m-deep Kurile-Kamchatka Trench and the junction of the Pacific and Eurasian tectonic plates. The deep ocean collision of these plates fuels one of the Pacific Rim's most volcanically active regions, evident in the more than 300 volcanoes on Kamchatka, including 30 that remain active.

The middle elevations of Kamchatka's mountains and foothills are blanketed in forests of stone birch (*Betula ermanii*) and pine bush (*Pinus pumila*), while lower elevations in the north are covered with vast tundra and sphagnum wetlands, and there are "islands" of larch (*Larix dahurica*) and Yeddo spruce (*Picea ajanensis*) in the central part of the peninsula. The larger rivers are mostly alluvial and gravel-bedded with expansive, forested floodplains that support riparian communities dominated by willows (*Salix* spp.) and alders (*Alnus fruticosa kamtschatica*), and gallery forests of cottonwoods (*Populus suaveolens*), some more than two meters in diameter (Stanford et al. 2000).

Kamchatka has remained almost untouched by human development since the arrival of the Bering Expedition in the 1740s. This is due to its remote location 11 000 km east of Moscow, to the lack of connecting roads, and to the fact that the former Soviet Union designated Kamchatka as a restricted military zone. As a result, we estimate that approximately 90% of the peninsula remains ecologically intact, but that may not be the case for long. Since the 1990 breakup of the Soviet Union, Kamchatka has opened its doors to outsiders, including national and international natural resource development industries.

Biodiversity

While Kamchatka is not high in terrestrial species diversity, it does have a relatively high number of endemic plants, especially considering its latitude. About 10% of the peninsula's 1 168 plant species are endemic (Anon. 1995).

The surrounding marine environments are extremely productive, providing as much as 60% of the Russian Federation's fishery resources. Key commercial species include walleye pollock (*Theragra chalcogramma*), king crab (*Paralithodes camtschatica*), Pacific cod (*Gadus macrocephalus*), Pacific herring (*Clupea harengus pallasi*), Pacific salmon (*Oncorhynchus* spp.), and Pacific halibut (*Hippoglossus stenolepis*). Waters of the west Kamchatka shelf produce annual catches approaching 20 tons/km² (Shirkov et. al., in press). Kamchatka is also the

global center for salmonid diversity, being home to all six species of Pacific salmon —chinook (*Oncorhynchus tshawytscha*), coho (*O. kisutch*), sockeye (*O. nerka*), chum (*O. keta*), pink (*O. gorbuscha*), and masu salmon (*O. masu*)—, as well as to two species of char —Arctic char (*Salvelinus alpinus*) and white spotted char or kundzha (*S. leucomaenis*)— and one species of grayling (*Thymallus arcticus*). Kamchatka also has Russia's only populations of the Red Book-listed seagoing steelhead trout (*O. mykiss*) (Pavlov et al. 1999).

There are no reptiles on Kamchatka and only one species of amphibian, the Siberian salamander (*Salamandrella keyserlingii*), but the peninsula's bird fauna is rich in both marine and terrestrial species. Altogether, 154 bird species reside or breed in Kamchatka, including regionally-endangered species such as the gyrfalcon (*Falco rusticolus*) and peregrine falcon (*F. peregrinus*), and 50% of the global population of Aleutian terns (*Sterna aleutica*) (WWF, in prep.).

There are 28 mammal species, including mink (*Mustela lutreola*), polar wolf (*Canis lupus*), red fox (*Vulpes vulpes*), Eurasian lynx (*Lynx lynx*), sable (*Martes zibellina*), wolverine (*Gulo gulo*), caribou (*Rangifer tarandus*), brown bear (*Ursos arctos*), and snow sheep (*Ovis nivicola*) (WWF, in prep.; Smetanin 2000). Over 30 species of marine mammals occur off Kamchatka's coast, including 2 000 Steller's sea lions (*Eumetopias jubatus*), a species that has declined 80% worldwide in the last 30 years (Burkanov 2000). Kamchatka is also a global stronghold for sea otters (*Enhydra lutris*). Approximately 900 sea otters —the only population in the Eastern Pacific— float in kelp beds off the southeast coast (Anon. 2000). An additional 14 000 or more sea otters live in the waters off Russia's Kurile Islands (to the south) and the Commander Islands (to the east). The Commander Islands also supported the only known populations of Steller's sea cow (*Hydrodamalis gigas*), a species that was hunted to extinction only twenty-seven years after its discovery by the Bering Expedition in 1741.

Flagship Species

Salmon are Kamchatka's keystone species, forming the foundation of its estuarine and terrestrial food webs, and from a global perspective this is an extremely important region for their conservation. Salmon numbers have declined dramatically along most of the Pacific Rim, to the point that the peninsula's thousands of rivers, lakes, and wetlands support an estimated one fifth of the world's remaining populations (Augerot 2001). The Bolshaya River in southwest Kamchatka produces the largest runs of pink salmon on Earth, averaging 6 305 000 returning adults/year between 1995-2000, and the region's total annual production could well reach one million tons (Sinyakov et al. 2000).

Above, Apollo butterfly (Parnassius nomion), *Russia.*
© **Konrad Wothe**

On the opposite page, Karimsky Volcano erupting, Kamchatka, Russia.
© **Klaus Nigge**

PATAGONIA

"In calling up images of the past, I find the plains of Patagonia most frequently cross before my eyes," wrote Charles Darwin in retrospect of his famous voyage. Patagonia lies at the southernmost tip of South America, a land of open skies and empty spaces, remote and pristine. The Andean portion covers habitats that include much of the Chilean archipelago and the southern Andes of Chile and Argentina with its sub-Antarctic forests, fiords, high alpine environments, and permanent ice sheets and glaciers.

Non-Andean Patagonia lies mostly in Argentina. It extends from the Andes in the west to the Atlantic in the east, and from about 40ºS to the eastern tip of Tierra del Fuego, at 55ºS. This arid to semiarid region covers around 438 400 km², corresponding to the mainland portions of the Patagonian grasslands (NT0804) and steppe (NT0805) ecoregions (WWF, in prep.). Being mostly flat, the average elevation near the Andes is 500 to 1 000 m above sea level, with occasional worn hilltops reaching 2 000 m. From here the land drops gently eastward to the Atlantic, where sea cliffs 100 to 200 m high are interspersed with beaches made of highly-polished "Tehuelche" gravel, the formation of which continues to puzzle science.

The Falkland Islands (Islas Malvinas), 600 km east in the South Atlantic at 52ºS, share many features with the Patagonian mainland. Two larger islands, East Falkland and West Falkland, and around 420 smaller islands, occupy a total surface of 12 000 km². The highest elevation, Mount Usborne, rises 705 m on East Falkland. Combining the land areas of the mainland and the Falklands, the region discussed in this chapter covers 550 400 km².

Prevailing west winds, that blow unimpeded across the Southern Pacific Ocean below 40ºS, commonly exceed 40 to 50 knots. Reaching the tip of South America they discharge their moisture on the Chilean side of the Andes, before racing on across the Patagonian plains lying in the rain shadow beyond. Within the space of a few kilometers, the annual precipitation drops sharply, in places by more than an order of magnitude, to less than 250 mm. During the coldest months (June to August), average temperatures range from 0ºC to 10ºC, and during the warmest months (December to February), between 10ºC and 20ºC.

Most of the southern Andean watershed empties westward into the Pacific. East of the Andes, fresh water is limited to temporary lakes on the plains occupying wind-eroded or tectonic depressions, and small watercourses that flow briefly when it rains.

Only two permanent rivers cross the desert and reach the Atlantic, the Rio Chubut and the Rio Santa Cruz. The remaining 3 000-km coastline is broken only by the Strait of Magellan.

Except for fences and sheep, signs of habitat modification in much of Patagonia are subtle but profound and possibly irreversible. However, for now the population is sparse and land cultivation is restricted to the few irrigated valleys, and to the casual observer much of the desert appears as it must have looked to Darwin 170 years ago. Although in number, plants and animals have declined, the same array of species that existed then, still exist today, and few extinctions have been recorded. In all, we estimate that at least 70% of this region still remains relatively intact.

Biodiversity

Arid and semiarid Patagonia is 45% shrub desert, 30% shrub-grass semidesert, 20% grass steppe, and 5% meadow and water surface. Its flora is relatively rich in diversity, with 65% and 40% of all the plant families and genera of Argentina.

Out of 1 378 species of vascular plants known to exist in mainland Patagonia, 177 (13%) are introduced, which means that the total natural plant diver-

Wilderness Areas

*On the opposite page,
Golfo Nuevo, Península Valdés,
Argentina.
© Günter Ziesler*

521

sity of the region is 1 201 species (Soriano et al. 1998). However, save a few exceptions (e.g., wall barley *Hordeum murinum*), alien species have not been incorporated into the plant communities outside disturbed soils along roadsides and around settlements. A total of 283 species in 12 genera are endemic (Soriano et al., *op cit*.), most of which occur in the central and southern parts of the region. In southern Patagonia, *mata negra* (*Junellia tridens*), produces a fragrant blossom in December, which suffuses the countryside with snowy pink. On the Falkland Islands, one of the most interesting and ecologically-important plant species is tussock grass (*Poa flabellata*), now gone from many parts as a result of overgrazing by sheep. The islands have 341 species of flowering plants and vascular cryptogams, of which 177 are introduced, including at least two that have successfully invaded large amounts of natural habitat (Broughton 2001). There are 13 species of endemic plants on the Falklands, and 23 that are threatened. Combining those in the Falklands and those on the mainland, the total number of native plant species is 1 221, with 296 endemics (Soriano et al., *op cit*; Davies and McAdam 1989; Broughton 2001).

Patagonia's freshwater systems harbor 23 fish species, although only 16 of these are native (C. Gaille, in litt., 2002). Species richness of marine invertebrates in the Sub-Antarctic is 20% greater than that found in Antarctic waters, but that of subtropical and tropical waters is three times as rich in species as the former (Boltoyskoy 1981). On land, only a few families of insects in a few orders have been extensively classified. The distribution of one tribe of Tenebrionid beetle, the Nyctelini, with around one hundred species, is almost entirely restricted to Patagonia. On the Falkland Islands there are 254 species of insects in 10 orders. Information on the arachnids of Patagonia is likewise incomplete, whereas 19 species of spiders are known for the Falklands (Strange 1992).

In Patagonia, there are 47 species of reptiles belonging to 16 genera, of which 19 are endemic. The majority of the endemic reptiles are lizards in the genus *Liolaemus*. Of the 12 species of amphibians belonging to five genera, five are endemic (WWF, in prep.).

The Patagonian wilderness has 211 species of birds belonging to 52 families (unpublished data). Of these, 10 species are endemic, including the Patagonian tinamou (*Tinamotis ingoufi*), hooded grebe (*Podiceps gallardoi*) —discovered in 1974—, and Magellanic plover (*Pluvianellus socialis*). The short-billed miner (*Geositta antarctica*) is a breeding endemic, but ranges north during the austral winter. Only one migratory species, the Eskimo curlew (*Numenius borealis*), is possibly extinct; a further eight species are rare or vulnerable. Three species of birds are introduced and have become naturalized. There are 11 species of migratory shorebirds that breed in the northern hemisphere and winter in Patagonia; no shorebird does the reverse. In the Falklands there are 62 species of breeding birds, including the striated caracara or Johnny rook (*Phalcoboenus australis*), blackish cinclodes or tussock bird (*Cinclodes antarcticus*), ruddy-head-

Above, Magellanic penguin (Spheniscus magellanicus), Falkland Islands.

On the opposite page, the largest colony of black-browed albatross (Thalassarche melanophrys), Falkland Islands. Both photos:
© **Patricio Robles Gil**/*Sierra Madre*

On pp. 524-525, male guanaco (Lama guanicoe) surveys the landscape, Monumento Nacional Bosque de las Piedras, Santa Cruz, Argentina.
© **Günter Ziesler**

ed goose (*Chloephaga rubidiceps*), and the two endemics: Falkland steamerduck (*Tachyeres brachypterus*) and Cobb's wren (*Troglodytes cobbi*) (Woods and Woods 1997).

Darwin noted the proliferation of rodents in Patagonia. Of the 61 species of land mammals belonging to 15 families, 31 (over 50%) from six families are rodents, including eight species of tuco-tuco (*Ctenomys*) —small burrowing rodents that emit a loud, thudding sound underground— and the Patagonian mara (*Dolichotis patagonum*), a unique cavy-like rodent endemic to Argentina. Four species of terrestrial mammals —again, all rodents— are endemic. No mammals are known to have gone extinct within historical times, although three are currently considered Endangered and five are Vulnerable (Hilton-Taylor 2000). On the Falklands, one terrestrial mammal, the Falkland Island wolf or warrah (*Dusicyon australis*), possibly carried there accidentally from Tierra del Fuego by indigenous people, became extinct shortly after the islands were settled by Europeans in the eighteenth century.

Flagship Species

The guanaco (*Lama guanicoe*) is the largest indigenous mammal in the region and the most widely-distributed of the four South American camels, ranging from Patagonia north through western Argentina to Peru and Bolivia. Although still a common sight in many places, its distribution has shrunk by almost half, and has become uneven and patchy, with many isolated populations. Raedeke (1979) estimated that there were 30-50 million guanacos in South America at the time of the arrival of the Europeans. The total population nowadays is probably close to 600 000 (Torres 1992), barely 1% or 2% of the original figure. Introduced on the Falklands several times beginning in the nineteenth century, there were fewer than 200 in 1982 (Strange 1992).

Standing almost a meter high, the region's largest flightless bird is the lesser rhea (*Rhea pennata*). Very shy and unobtrusive, small groups of 5 to 10 birds, or a single male accompanied by anything between 20 and 100 chicks are becoming uncommon. Although still occurring throughout Patagonia, known densities have been found to be less than 0.4 birds/km² (M. Funes and R. Baldi, pers. comm.), which puts the total population at fewer than 200 000. Like the guanaco, populations are becoming severely fragmented.

Over 50 000 southern elephant seals (*Mirounga leonina*), the fourth largest world population (C. Campagna, pers. comm., 2002), breed on the coast of Península Valdés in Patagonia, and just under 2 600 southern right whales (*Eubalaena australis*), one third of the world population, breed in the sheltered waters along its shores (Best et al. 2001).

Among the 26 species of marine birds that breed in colonies on the coast of Patagonia and the Falklands, there are 1.1 million pairs of Magellanic penguins (*Spheniscus magellanicus*) (Yorio et al. 1998; Woods and

Woods 1997). In Punta Tombo alone over 200 000 pairs of Magellanic penguins breed in an area of coast barely 10 km long, making it one of the region's most valuable wildlife areas. An estimated 450 000 pairs of rockhopper penguins (*Eudyptes chrysocome*) breed in several colonies on Tierra del Fuego and the Falklands (A. Schiavini, pers. comm.; Clausen 2001); the latter are also home to 113 000 breeding pairs of gentoo penguins (*Pygoscelis papua*) and 382 000 pairs of black-browed albatrosses (*Thalassarche melanophrys*).

Human Cultures

Human occupation in Patagonia dates back 14 000 years. The Araucano and Mapuche people inhabited the mountainous northwestern part of the region. Today, few remain, living in reservations, where they retain some of their culture and language.

The most widespread indigenous people were the Tehuelche, who ranged throughout continental Patagonia, north of the Strait of Magellan and east of the Andes. Seminomadic, they relied heavily on hunting guanaco and rhea for survival. Displaced by military forces from Buenos Aires in the late nineteenth century, and ravaged by the effects of alcoholism and disease (tuberculosis, syphilis, and measles), Tehuelche populations declined. Those that remained integrated with settlers.

The indigenous people that inhabited the open and more arid parts of Tierra del Fuego were the Ona (Selk'-nam and Haush), also primarily guanaco hunters. The last Ona died during the latter part of the twentieth century. No indigenous people ever inhabited the Falkland Islands.

The current population of Patagonia is 800 000, of which 75% live in 13 towns and cities on the coast. Less than 5% of the population is rural. With the development of new industries based on oil, aluminum, fishing, manufacturing, and tourism, during the latter part of the twentieth century the population increased by immigration from other parts of Argentina and neighboring countries. Many towns grew rapidly in size. Puerto Madryn went from 7 000 inhabitants in 1970 to almost 50 000 in less than 20 years.

If one excludes the roughly 600 000 people living in urban areas, the population density for the region as a whole comes to only 0.36 inhabitant/km².

Threats

Threats to this region are many, with hunting, overgrazing, desertification, road construction for oil exploration, oil pollution, and overfishing being the principal problems. Hunting is widespread in Patagonia. Guanacos are particularly targeted because they are believed to compete with sheep, they provide meat for farm dogs, their skins sometimes fetch a price, or they are just killed for sport. Foxes (*Pseudalopex griseus* and *P. culpaeus*) and puma (*Felis concolor*) are also hunted, trapped, and poi-

soned. Between 1975 and 1985, an average of 37 000 guanaco and 500 000 fox skins were exported each year from Argentina, mostly from Patagonia (Chebez 1994).

Arid and semiarid Patagonia has been heavily overgrazed in many areas, with sheep, stocked by European settlers in the late nineteenth century, reaching densities of 20-60 animals/km². Over 30% of the region shows signs of severe erosion (Johnson 1998), and 76 species of plants, 24% of them grasses, are of conservation concern in at least part of their range (Soriano et al. 1998).

Extensive road building and clearing for oil exploration and exploitation has caused severe damage to the topsoil and vegetation, affecting over 10 000 km² in the three main oil-producing areas of Patagonia: the northwest, central coastal area, and around the Strait of Magellan.

Chronic oil pollution at sea from loading and unloading operations, accidental spills, and discharge of oily ballast and bilge were responsible for the death of 41 000 penguins each year between 1983 and 1991 on the coast of Patagonia (Gandini et al. 1994). A single spill in 1991 killed 17 000 Magellanic penguins.

On the marine end, the South Atlantic fisheries doubled in size between 1990 and 1996 to over one million metric tons. As a result of this overfishing, stocks of Argentine hake (*Merluccius hubbsi*), one of the principal target fish, collapsed in 1998. The effects on the wildlife of the South Atlantic remain uncertain.

Conservation

Over 95% of the land is privately-owned, and divided into some 10 000 sheep farms, ranging in size from 2 000 to several hundreds of thousands of hectares. Protected areas in arid and semiarid Patagonia amount to 4.7% of the total surface (Aguilera 1998), but do not include all habitats. Over 20 wildlife reserves on the coast of Patagonia provide protection for 70% of all colonies of marine birds and mammals. With 34 private reserves (6 000 ha) and 21 government-owned protected areas (1 900 ha), the Falkland Islands has 0.66% of its surface within protected areas (Strange 1992). In all, the area has 22 733 km² in protected areas of different kinds, which cover 4.13% of the total. The provinces of coastal Patagonia, together with the Wildlife Conservation Society and Fundación Patagonia Natural, began developing a Patagonian Coastal Zone Management Plan for the protection of biodiversity in 1993, and it has already led to the removal of oil tanker routes 30 miles offshore, reducing the possibility of spills. This has been a very positive development. Nonetheless, there is still a long way to go to ensure the protection of the Patagonian wilderness. Only time will tell if the magnificent coastal colonies of birds and mammals and the open desert with its rich complement of plants and unique animals will remain intact over the long term.

GUILLERMO HARRIS

Above, Patagonia cavy or mara (Dolichotis patagonum), *Chubut, Argentina*

On the opposite page, young Austral parakeets (Enicognathus ferrugineus) *in nest.*
Both photos: © **Günter Ziesler**

THE ARCTIC TUNDRA

By general definition, *tundra* is "a treeless area between the ice cap and the tree line of Arctic regions, having a permanently frozen subsoil and supporting low-growing vegetation such as lichens, mosses, and stunted shrubs." Tundra apparently originates from the Finnish word *tunturi*, which means "a barren hill." The word *arctic* characterizes the geography of northern polar regions, and can be interpreted specifically to mean those land and oceanic forms that lie north of the Arctic Circle at latitude 66°33'N. The Arctic Tundra Wilderness captures all landmasses north of the Arctic Circle, including those lacking vegetative cover and overlaid by permanent ice sheets. The Arctic Tundra Wilderness stretches below the Arctic Circle, well into more southerly latitudes, where it meets a meandering tree line and forms an ecotone with the Boreal Forests Wilderness (Flegg 1990). The two wilderness areas roughly form concentric, circumpolar rings that span the northern hemisphere, melding into one another in terms of both their floral and faunal assemblages. Isolated landscapes of high-altitude, treeless terrain known as *alpine tundra* are also found well into more southerly ecoregions. In North America some actually occur close to the United States' southwestern border with Mexico (Zwinger and Willard 1986), but these are not considered part of the Arctic Tundra Wilderness. A number of these are incorporated in the Boreal Forests, Northern Rocky Mountains, and Pacific Northwest wilderness areas.

Geographically, our definition of the Arctic Tundra Wilderness includes the following 28 ecoregions as identified in a biogeographical analysis conducted by the World Wildlife Fund (Olson et al. 2001): Arctic Desert (PA1101) (161 400 km²); Aleutian Islands Tundra (NA1102) (5 500 km²); Beringia Lowland Tundra (NA1106) (150 900 km²); Beringia Upland Tundra (NA1107) (97 300 km²); Alaska Peninsula Montane Taiga (NA0601) (47 800 km²); Ogilvie-MacKenzie Alpine Tundra (NA1116) (208 400 km²); Brooks-British Range Tundra (NA1108) (159 500 km²); Arctic Foothills Tundra (NA1104) (129 100 km²); Arctic Coastal Tundra (NA1103) (98 200 km²); Low Arctic Tundra (NA1114) (796 500 km²); Middle Arctic Tundra (NA1115) (1 032 800 km²); High Arctic Tundra (NA1110) (463 700 km²); Davis Highlands Tundra (NA1109) (87 900 km²); Torngat Mountain Tundra (NA1118) (32 300 km²); Baffin Coastal Tundra (NA1105) (9 100 km²); Kalaallit Nunaat Low Arctic Tundra (NA1113) (171 000 km²); Kalaallit Nunaat High Arctic Tundra (NA1112) (303 600 km²); Iceland Boreal Birch Forests and Alpine Tundra (PA0602) (91 500 km²); Scandinavian Montane Birch Forest and Grasslands (PA1110) (243 200 km²); Kola Peninsula Tundra (PA1106) (58 800 km²); Northwest Russian-Novaya Zemlya Tundra (PA1108) (284 200 km²); Yamalagydanskaja Tundra (PA1114) (412 100 km²); Taimyr-Central Siberian Tundra (PA1111) (954 700 km²); Novosibirsk Islands Arctic Desert (PA1109) (36 900 km²); Northeast Siberian Coastal Tundra (PA1107) (222 600 km²); Chukchi Peninsula Tundra (PA1104) (298 400 km²); Bering Tundra (PA1102) (474 200 km²); and Wrangel Island Arctic Desert (PA1113) (7 500 km²). To these we add the ice caps that cover much of Greenland (1 701 000 km²), high mountain regions of Iceland (11 500 km²), and about a third of three northern Canadian islands (98 400 km²), which were not included in the biogeographical analysis above. Arctic polar ice falls within the realm of this wilderness and serves as marginal wildlife habitat, but is not true land. Therefore, we estimate the terrestrial extent of the Arctic Tundra Wilderness at about 8.85 million km², just under 6% of the planet's surface, an area larger than the United States minus Alaska, or the entire country of Brazil. Overall, we estimate that at least 90% remains largely intact.

Wilderness Areas

On the opposite page, fjord landscape, Cape Hooper, Baffin Island, Nunavut.
© Hans Strand

The most northerly terrestrial expression of the polar realm is commonly referred to as *arctic desert* and is composed of island groups that are icebound for much of the year. In the Old World, these include Norway's Svalbard and Russia's Franz Joseph Land, the northern half of Novaya Zemlya, Severnaya Zemlya, the Novosibirsk (New Siberian) Islands, and Wrangel Island. Where arctic desert ends and arctic tundra begins is largely a matter of semantics, but tundra ecoregions are generally less barren in terms of vegetation and wildlife. High and low arctic tundra known as Kalaallit Nunaat cover close to half-a-million square kilometers of coastal Greenland and a bit more than 90 000 km² in Iceland. Tundra ecosystems also predominate along the Barents Sea coast in northern Fennscandia and northwestern Russia, in the southern half of Novaya Zemlya, throughout the Yamal, Gydan, and Taimyr Peninsulas south of the Kara and Laptev Seas, and in northeastern Siberia, including the Chukchi (Chukotka) Peninsula and lands that border the Bering Sea, reaching to the peninsula of Kamchatka. Arctic tundra in North America begins at the western tip of the Aleutian Island chain and stretches northeastward along the Bering Sea and Chukchi Sea coasts of Alaska, incorporating the Brooks Range, meeting the Arctic Ocean and entering the Canadian Yukon. There, it crosses the British Range and begins its expansion well up into the high arctic regions of Canada's Northwest and Nunavut Territories, including the Queen Elizabeth Islands and the large islands of Banks, Victoria, Southampton, Baffin, Devon, and Ellesmere.

Biodiversity

The tundra climate offers only a very short, cool summer of perhaps six to ten weeks and a long, cold, dark winter of six to ten months that, together with poor soil derived largely from the mechanical breakup of rock through cycles of freezing and thawing, can only support a vegetative cover of grasses, sedges, lichens, heaths and dwarf willows, birches and conifers underlaid by permafrost that is 300 m thick or more throughout the region (Bailey 1995; Knystautas 1987). It is the proximity of the permafrost to the soil surface that inhibits tree growth, not necessarily low temperatures. Parts of the tundra world receive meager precipitation that may average only 130 to 300 mm/year. Much of what does fall, however, tends to remain as snow, an almost perennial insulating blanket that protects a variety of lifeforms from chronic subfreezing temperatures. Other parts of the tundra are water-laden swamps for months on end because the little rain that does fall can not penetrate the permafrost.

Lichens are numerous in the tundra and an integral part of the ecology, the crustose forms being the most common. They occur farther north than any other "plant," as well as at higher altitudes, some being found at or above 6 000 m, and as many as 500 species of lichen can be observed on the Russian island of Nova

Zemlya alone (Knystautas, *op. cit.*). Most are very slow-growing, adding perhaps only a millimeter of new tissue per year, and some are believed to be several thousands of years old (Flegg 1990). Lichens represent an important dietary item for some of this region's prominent hooved mammals.

The number of vascular plants found within the Arctic Tundra Wilderness is at least 1 125 species, of which approximately 100 are endemic (Takhtajan 1986; CAFF 1999). Most tundra plants grow low to the ground as tussocks, cushions, carpets, and rosettes, the vegetation manifesting itself largely as low heath, willow, and birch scrub. Unlike the situation found in moister regions, the mass of living vegetation below ground is greater than that above ground. Genera that produce tall trees in more temperate climates are represented in the Arctic by stunted shrub-like forms. At northern latitudes their leaves develop thick, waxy skins with reduced numbers of stomata, rendering them highly impervious to cold winds and desiccation. These cold-climate denizens are either wind-pollinated, self-pollinating, or reproduce by vegetative propagation, as they can not rely on insect pollinators. Many kinds produce berries that provide food for both wildlife and humans, and some species routinely carry out the process of photosynthesis at subfreezing temperatures.

While south of the tree line as many as 10 000 species of insects are able to endure, north of it the number drops to as few as 500 (Hummel 1984). Flies, gnats, mosquitoes, and midges are the most successful Arctic insects, while common temperate species such as dragonflies, grasshoppers, and crickets are conspicuously absent. Spiders, mites, and centipedes are among the other invertebrates that can survive at higher latitudes, most of which overwinter in the soil as larvae, not as eggs or pupae.

Amphibians and reptiles are largely absent from Arctic regions. Only three North American frog species —the wood frog (*Rana sylvatica*), the leopard frog (*Rana pipiens*), and the western chorus frog (*Pseudacris triseriata*)— enter the southern margins of the tundra, and none are endemic to this biome (Duellman and Sweet 1999). Seven more amphibians occur in the Eurasian tundra (WWF-U.S., unpublished data). The three widespread Eurasian reptiles that edge into the Arctic are the common viper (*Vipera berus*), the common viviparous lizard (*Lacerta vivipara*) and, marginally, the slow worm (*Anguis fragilis*).

A total of 379 bird species are found in the Arctic Tundra Wilderness (CI, unpublished data). This represents a mere 4% of the world total in approximately 6% of Earth's land area, significantly less than expected from the size of the region. McKay's bunting (*Plectrophenax hyperboreus*) is the only bird wholly endemic to this region, breeding on St. Lawrence Island and wintering on the Alaskan coast. Only a few other hardy birds are year-round residents, the snowy owl (*Nyctea scandiaca*) and ptarmigans (*Lagopus lagopus* and *L. mutus*) among them. The stunted trees of the tundra-boreal forest eco-

Above, walrus (Odobenus rosmarus) *on an ice floe.*

On the opposite page, polar bear (Ursus maritimus). *Both photos:*
© **Patricio Robles Gil**/*Sierra Madre*

tone represent a northern limit to the ranges of most woodland-nesting bird species, while the expansive meadows and wetlands are critical breeding areas for many migratory ground-nesting shorebirds and waterfowl, whose numbers frequently reach into the hundreds of thousands and even into the millions. In fact, approximately 48 species, commonly winter inhabitants of many other parts of the world, breed only in tundra regions, among them the black-bellied plover (*Pluvialis squatarola*) and brant (*Branta bernicla*). The Arctic tern (*Sterna paradisaea*) is famous for the longest migration of any bird, traveling from pole to pole about 20 000 km in each direction and nesting every summer along the fringes of the Arctic Ocean (Burton 1992). This species experiences very little darkness during the course of its life, arriving at both polar destinations in time to enjoy seemingly endless days of midnight sun.

The Arctic Tundra Wilderness is home to 115 mammals —just over 2% of the world total and, again, less than might be expected in a land area of this size. Ten of the mammals are endemic, including the walrus (*Odobenus rosmarus*), the Alaskan hare (*Lepus othus*), Pribilof Island shrew (*Sorex hydrodromus*), insular vole (*Microtus abbreviatus*), and six lemmings (*Dicrostonyx* spp.). Although lemmings may not be among the most prominent Arctic mammals in terms of size, their numbers are vast and they represent a critical food resource for many of the region's mammalian and avian predators. Female lemmings reach maturity at less than a month of age and their gestation period is a mere 20 days. At that rate, a single mother can produce six to seven litters a year, with each brood containing up to a dozen young —plentiful food for resident snowy owls, ermine (*Mustela erminea*), and Arctic foxes (*Alopex lagopus*) (Flegg 1990).

Flagship Species

As a group, the marine mammals that inhabit coastal Arctic waters, and especially those whose reproductive biology ties them to the land, are excellent flagships for the preservation of northern biodiversity, pristine landscapes, and indigenous human cultures. Indeed, parts of this region attract incredible concentrations of marine mammals, numbering easily in the thousands and sometimes in the tens of thousands. The walrus, one of the largest living pinnipeds, inhabits only circumpolar waters near the polar pack ice (Riedman 1990). Its Latin name translates as "tooth-walking seahorse" and very likely originates from its habit of hauling out onto the ice by use of its enormously enlarged upper canines. At least two subspecies are recognized, representing Atlantic and Pacific populations. The walrus is polygamous. During the breeding season, large aggregations form on pack ice and rocky coasts, adult males competing for choice sites and the dominant bulls attracting potentially receptive females. Killer whales (*Orcinus orca*) and polar bears (*Ursus maritimus*) are the natural

predators of walruses, who have also been hunted by the Inuit and other native northern coastal peoples for thousands of years. Such subsistence hunting had little appreciable effect on walrus populations through the ages, and it was not until commercial exploitation of walrus ivory, oil, and hides began that the species' future became uncertain. Throughout the past two centuries, annual harvests have often exceeded 10 000 animals, causing the extirpation of some populations and dramatic declines in others, and calling into question the global management of this species (Fay et al. 1989; Nowak 1991). Today, walruses are largely protected throughout their range by national laws and international agreements (USFWS 1994b). The total population is believed to consist of approximately 22 500 Atlantic walruses (6 000 in Norway and Russia, 12 000 in Canada, and 4 500 in Greenland) and a minimum of 200 000 Pacific walruses in eastern Russia and the United States (Seal Conservation Society 2001).

Waters off the Aleutian Islands and the Alaska Peninsula represent the core range of the sea otter (*Enhydra lutris*), a once highly-threatened marine carnivore whose population began its drastic decline in the mid-1700s at the hands of Asian, American, and European fur traders. Sea otter fur is the densest and the most precious of all the mammals, the pelt of a single individual capable of fetching as much as US $1 000 on the European market at the turn of the twentieth century. Numbers in Alaskan waters probably sank to their lowest level —the low thousands— at that time, but have since rebounded to between 100 000 and 150 000 thanks to international protection (Nowak 1991).

The world's two largest bears —the polar bear and the grizzly or brown bear (*Ursus arctos*)— are denizens of the world's arctic regions. While brown bears also occur in far more temperate latitudes, the frigid north is the polar bear's uncontested realm. Head-body lengths approaching 2.5 m and weights of up to 800 kg have been known to be recorded for large male polar bears, but typical adults are only slightly more than half that mass (DeMaster and Stirling 1981; Nowak, *op. cit.*). This species is unique among bears, spending so much time at or about the sea that it is commonly considered a marine mammal. It still occupies much of its original distribution and is protected by the 1973 International Agreement on the Conservation of Polar Bears and Their Habitat, signed by the five nations with polar bear populations: Canada, Denmark (which represents Greenland), Norway, the former Soviet Union, and the United States (Brown 1993). Biologists estimate the total population between 22 000 and 27 000, of which 15 000 are in Canada.

Size in brown bears is governed by diet, and the world's largest are those of Alaska's Kodiak Island, where springtime salmon runs and the occasional marine mammal carcass supplement a basic fare of sedges and berries, providing much greater amounts of protein and energy. Approximately 3 000 bears inhabit the 9 376-km^2 island, perhaps the highest density of *Ursus*

arctos on the planet (Eliot 1993). Opportunities to view the spectacular Kodiak bears fishing for salmon are strictly regulated. Only a limited number of permits are distributed each year as part of a state-run tourist lottery.

Caribou (*Rangifer tarandus*) are also circumpolar in their distribution and highly migratory as well, dependent in part on both tundra and boreal forest habitat. Known more commonly as reindeer in Scandinavia and Russia, many of Eurasia's originally wild herds have been domesticated over the centuries. By contrast, attempts at domestication have consistently failed in North America, where as many as 14 major herds remain, spreading from Alaska in the west to Baffin Island in the east (Calef 1981; Gurvich 1988). Each spring many thousands migrate from woodlands to barren tundras where the females calve (Calef, *op. cit.*).

Of all the hooved mammals, it is the massive-horned, shaggy-coated musk ox (*Ovibos moschatus*) that best exemplifies the Arctic realm. These animals travel in herds and are famous for their characteristic defensive posture, in which adults stand shoulder-to-shoulder to face potential predators, while the younger, weaker animals stay to the rear, protected by this living shield. Humans have traditionally exploited them for their meat, hides, and horns, and although the point at which Palaearctic populations were ultimately extirpated is debated (Nowak, *op. cit.*), we know they disappeared from Alaska by the early twentieth century, and were also nearly wiped out by that time in mainland Canada. Fortunately, a series of reintroduction efforts have succeeded in Alaska, Canada, Norway, and Russia, and today the world population probably stands at about 150 000, including herds that have survived in Greenland (CAFF 2001).

Survival of the Siberian crane (*Grus leucogeranus*), a tall and stately bird listed as Critically Endangered by IUCN, rests in part with the protection of its breeding grounds in the Russian Far East. Three migrating populations remain, but the west and central groups are very close to being extirpated. Fortunately, the eastern population remains at least 2 300 strong. Cranes that winter as far south as China's Poyang Lake travel several thousand kilometers north each spring to nest in northeastern Siberia's coastal tundra (BirdLife International 2000).

Human Cultures

Greek explorer Pytheas launched the earliest known expedition to Arctic regions, around 325 years before the birth of Christ, searching for a land known as Thule and a source of tin to make bronze swords and armor (Flegg 1990; Roots 1995). He did not reach his goal. Humans had, however, already been part of the tundra landscape for many millennia, their movements into northeastern Siberia from more temperate regions of eastern Asia believed to have begun about 16 000 years ago with the passing of the last Ice Age (Fitzhugh and

Crowell 1988). Russia's Lower Amur Basin and the Maritime Provinces of the Russian Far East were likely the staging ground for this migration, and became home to native cultures known as Nanai, Negidal, Nivkhi, Oroch, Orok, and Udehe, predominantly fishermen of salmon and sturgeon and hunters of both land and marine mammals (Black 1988). The Negidal and Orok also included reindeer herding in their subsistence economy, as did the Koryak who inhabited the northern part of Kamchatka (Arutiunov 1988a). Eastern Siberia's Lamut, today known as the Even, were more a tribe of the interior and far more dependent on the reindeer, both as hunters and herders (Arutiunov 1988b). Their neighbors farther east, the Chukchi, again with greater access to coastal regions, combined reindeer, fishing, and trading economies (Arutiunov 1988c).

The Eskimo or Inuit are descendants of those adventurous Siberians who first crossed the Bering land bridge to reach North America and who settled in Alaska and Canada's Northwest and Nunavut Territories. In Greenland, descendants of the trans-Beringian crossing are called Kalaadlit, the easternmost representatives of the most widespread aboriginal people in the world (Fitzhugh 1988). Alaska remains the stronghold of the Inuit culture, marine mammal hunters along the coasts and caribou hunters in the interior. For centuries they have relied on their prey not only for food, but also for clothing, utensils, cooking and heating fuel, hunting and fishing tools, and basic building materials. Yet contact with Europeans compromised the Inuit's traditional life-style. They quickly learned to barter skins and hides for guns, metal tools, cooking pots, and fishnets. The animals on which they depended for their livelihood, such as the bowhead whale (*Balaena mysticetus*), walrus, and musk ox, were hunted to near extinction by the newcomers, who also brought with them diseases like tuberculosis and smallpox, to which the indigenous Inuit were highly susceptible. As a result, already small populations of Inuit were further reduced, in some cases drastically (Hummel 1984). Only the Aleut who live along the 2 000-km Aleutian Archipelago, a barren landscape of volcanic origin and devoid of large terrestrial mammals, are more dependent on the sea than the Inuit (Black and Liapunova 1988).

The population of Iceland, about 266 000, is mostly descended from Scandinavian and Celtic settlers (Swaney 1997). The indigenous Sami people of Scandinavia are also known as Laplanders, traditional herders of reindeer. To their east across northern Russia they are replaced by such tribes as the Izhor, Kamchadal, Komi, Samoyed, Vep, Yakut, and Yukagir, eventually reaching the far eastern cultures described earlier (Magga 1995; Rasmussen 1995).

Due to the broad expanse of this remote wilderness, it is difficult to obtain accurate population figures for the entire area. However, we estimate that between two and three million people reside in its 8.85 million square kilometers, which would yield a maximum population density of less than 0.4 inhabitant/km^2.

On the opposite page, caribou (Rangifer tarandus)*, Northwest Territories, Canada.*

Above, Arctic ground squirrel (Spermophilus parryii)*. Northern Canada. Both photos:*
© **Patricio Robles Gil**/*Sierra Madre*

Threats

The most serious historical threat to the biodiversity of Arctic regions has been the wholesale slaughter of vulnerable wildlife that has led, in some cases, to the extinction of once-prominent species. Steller's sea cow (*Hydrodamalis stelleri*), an incredible marine animal that reached lengths of eight meters, is the best known. This species was discovered in 1741 by George Wilhelm Steller, a German naturalist on the Russian expedition commanded by Vitus Bering, who found the animal while shipwrecked on what is now known as Bering Island. Unfortunately, news of this amazing discovery only brought Russian traders and hunters who easily dispatched this animal with harpoons. Its extinction may have occurred less than a quarter-century later, although unconfirmed reports of its survival continued through to the early 1800s (Allen 1942).

The sea cow's sad saga is matched among the birds by that of the great auk (*Alca impennis*), a species that entered the Arctic realm along the coasts of Greenland, Iceland, and northern Scandinavia. It was much more widespread than the sea cow and survived far longer after its discovery: from the beginning of the sixteenth century to 1844. Unfortunately, it too ultimately succumbed to the uncontrolled slaughter for its flesh, eggs, and feathers (Day 1989; Greenway 1958).

A similar fate might well already have befallen the Eskimo curlew (*Numenius borealis*), once relatively abundant and commonly referred to as the "doughbird" because of its fat-laden meat prior to migration. The last confirmed sighting of this species was in 1962 (Ehrlich et al. 1992). Today, Arctic birds are at much less risk from hunting than they are from the serious depletion of major prey species due to overfishing and pollution.

It is fortunate that centuries of exploration have not produced more significant settlement of Arctic regions. Despite low human population densities, however, a variety of our commercial activities have become serious threats to the health of tundra ecosystems and their wildlife. The most serious and widespread threats are mining and the production of fossil fuels. While the days of the gold rush may be long gone, large-scale mining of coal, lead, zinc, and nickel continues. Smelting operations, such as those that render nickel into platinum, also contribute heavily to air and water pollution, which has become a severe problem in places like the Taimyr-Central Siberian Tundra. Oil extraction and sea-transport operations pose the constant threat of spills that can have devastating long-term effects on coastal environments. In addition, the transport of oil over land is not without its risks to tundra ecology, a major concern during construction of the Trans-Alaska pipeline in the 1970s (Ellis and Kristof 1971; Hodgson 1976). Chemical pollutants and by-products of energy production have also been released in Arctic regions. Biologists are concerned about excessive levels of polychlorinated biphenyls (PCBs) that now routinely turn up in tissues of top predators such as polar bear and walrus, and

nuclear waste and fallout have become serious concerns in the Aleutian Islands, on Russia's Kola Peninsula, and on the island of Nova Zemlya, where the evacuation of indigenous populations was required (Magga 1995). By comparison, poaching, the introduction of alien species, and uncontrolled ecotourism might be regarded as less severe threats to Arctic biodiversity.

Over the long term, it is likely that the effects of global warming overshadow all other threats to the world's northern biomes. Since the Industrial Revolution, the atmospheric content of carbon dioxide has increased approximately 20%, largely due to the burning of fossil fuels, and this has been a major contributor to the greenhouse effect. Early predictions were that continued increases could raise temperatures in Arctic regions by as much as 4°-6°C before the end of the twenty-first century, almost twice the level of change predicted for more southerly climes. However, recent research points to a 1°C rise per decade over the past 30 years —well above the predicted rate— and the effects of higher ambient temperatures are already becoming apparent. According to a Bering Sea Impact Study, significant permafrost thawing has been documented both in Alaska and Siberia, glaciers are receding, and the extent of Bering Sea ice has declined by 5% over the past quarter-century (Weller and Anderson 1998). These temperature-induced changes are beginning to cause physical damage to roads and other elements of human infrastructure in the Arctic, and also appear to be implicated in the more erratic regional weather patterns (presumably caused by a reduction of sea ice and its climate-mediating effects) and the increased frequency of forest fires and greater insect infestations enhanced by warmer conditions that the region is experiencing. Ecologists also point to global effects of higher sea levels and to an overall loss of tundra habitats as boreal forests expand north with increasing temperatures.

Conservation

Of the 8.85 million km² included within the Arctic Tundra Wilderness, at least 1 732 500 km² (approximately 20%) are within officially-protected areas. The North East Greenland National Park may be the only protected area in the country but, at 970 000 km², it is the largest one in the world and represents more than half the total area of the Arctic tundra that is under protection (Swaney 1997). Much of the park, as well as most of Greenland, lies buried under a massive ice cap. In its entirety, it contains more than 4 million km³ of ice, it has grown to three thousand meters in thickness, and its weight has essentially driven the land surface in the central part of the island to a depth of 360 m below sea level.

The United States has set aside the next largest portion of this wilderness area in Alaska, where close to 477 000 km² are protected in a national system of monuments, parks, preserves, wildlife refuges, and wildernesses. Canada is third with 129 740 km² in national park-

Greenland is the largest true island in the world, measuring 2 656 km long and 1 045 km wide and covering 2 175 600 km^2, more than two-and-a-half times the size of New Guinea, which is the next largest island on the list. It is closer to the North Pole than any other landmass and expeditions by Robert E. Peary and other North Pole explorers were launched from North Greenland. About 85% of its area is ice-covered, containing about 9% of the world's fresh water. The massive central ice cap rises more than 3 300 m in elevation at the highest point and extends to the sea in many locations, accommodating large numbers of icebergs, particularly in central West and East Greenland. The most active iceberg-producing glacier moves at a rate of 18-30 m each day. All of Greenland is usually considered to be Arctic although its southern tip, Cape Farewell, is about the latitude of Anchorage, Alaska, or Oslo, Norway, which are Subarctic.

Biodiversity

The size of Greenland, its varied climatic conditions, and different types of soil all contribute to a diverse flora, represented largely by algae, fungi, lichens, and mosses (about 3 500 species). At least 497 species of vascular plants also have been documented, of which 15 are endemic (Davis et al. 1997). The first plant species list was published in 1770 and since then there has been a rich history of botanical investigations.

In terms of birds, Boertmann (1994) lists 235 species. Of these, he considers 58 as "well-established breeders," about 17 as "regular visitors," and the remainder as "more or less rare vagrants." Some species are numerous. For example, in North Greenland the estimated population of dovekies or little auks (*Alle alle*) is between 30 and 60 million birds.

Terrestrial mammals number nine species including the Arctic or northern collared lemming (*Dicrostonyx groenlandicus*), Arctic hare (*Lepus arcticus*), gray wolf (*Canis lupus*), Arctic fox (*Alopex lagopus*), polar bear (*Ursus maritimus*), ermine (*Mustela erminea*), caribou (*Rangifer tarandus*), muskox (*Ovibos moschatus*), and wolverine (*Gulo gulo*), although any sightings of wolverine would be considered extremely unusual (Muus et al. 1982). Lemming and ermine only occur in northeast Greenland and are absent elsewhere on the island. Marine mammals are more numerous, totaling 24 species and include the walrus (*Odobaenus rosmarus*), five species of seals, and 18 species of cetaceans (Muus et al., *op. cit.*).

Fish species number about 216 (Nielsen and Bertelsen

1992). There are also about 70 species of spiders and 700 species of insects in Greenland, including two species of bumblebees and 35 beetles (Böcher 2001). There are 52 species of butterflies, of which 15% have colonized Greenland from Europe, 46% derive from North America, and the remainder are circumpolarly distributed.

Flagship Species

Greenland is a truly spectacular corner of our planet, a vast and incredibly scenic land of seemingly endless ice, meandering fjords intersected by plummeting glacier-filled valleys capped by hanging glaciers, windswept and ice-fractured rock peaks with shear vertical faces a kilometer tall, and nature-sculpted icebergs rising a hundred meters above plankton-rich seas which narwhal (*Monodon monoceros*) regularly frequent. A single valley can contain more than two million breeding dovekies and have muskoxen grazing the green carpets of dense grass below the bird colonies.

Several species stand out as real flagships. Once called the "Greenland falcon," the gyrfalcon (*Falco rusticolus*) is one of these. With plumage from white to dark gray, this largest and most powerful of all falcon species occurs throughout most of Greenland. During the Renaissance, expeditions were sent from Europe to capture these gyrfalcons for falconry and they were paid as ransom for the return of captured royalty during the Crusades. Other species synonymous with Greenland and the Arctic are the polar bear, narwhal, and muskox. The ecology of the polar bear is strongly influenced by ringed seals (*Phoca hispida*), which form a large part of their diet. Sharing the remote icy environment with the bear and seal is the narwhal, a small cetacean species in which the males grow a protruding living tooth that may reach 2.4 m long. These long, twisted tusks were once thought to be from mythical unicorns. The muskoxen were lost throughout large portions of their range in North and West Greenland and reintroductions occurred from a population in East Greenland in the 1960s. In a large ice-free area near the Arctic Circle (Angujaartorfiup Nunaa), 27 released founders had resulted in a population of about 4 000 animals by 1990.

Human Cultures

Greenland has a population of about 56 000 people (88% born on the island), about 90% of whom live along the

On the opposite page, muskox (Ovibos moschatus).
© **Staffan Widstrand**/*Nature Picture Library*

Above, gyrfalcon (Falco rusticolus).
© **Tom & Pat Leeson**/*DRK Photo*

island's west coast, south of 71°N latitude. Over 45 000 live in towns, including 13 000 inhabiting the capital city, Nuuk (Kalallit Nunanni Naatsorsueqqissaartarfik 2001). Almost all of the remainder live in about 80 villages of 100 to 600 people. Although the official language is Kalaallisut, there are several local dialects. Danish is widely spoken and many Greenlanders are of Inuit and Scandinavian descent. Greenland was granted home rule by Denmark in 1979, but remains part of the Kingdom of Denmark. Two members of the Danish Parliament come from Greenland. Greenland Home Rule is a parliamentary democracy headed by a premier. Denmark maintains control over foreign policy, defense, and certain other functions, but otherwise Greenland rules itself, although financially it is still heavily subsidized by Denmark.

Greenland is sparsely populated and if the 90% of the people who live in towns and villages along the coast of only one third of Greenland are excluded, the population density is only about 0.003 inhabitant/km^2 (one person per 400 km^2), making Greenland one of the world's last great wildernesses.

Threats

Although the total human population is small compared to the landmass, some fish and wildlife populations have been importantly affected and even extirpated in areas where humans are concentrated. Avian species of special concern are the common eider (*Somateria mollissima*) and thick-billed murre or Brünnich's guillemot (*Uria lomvia*). One former murre colony had at least 100 000 pairs. Declines are believed to be the result of heavy hunting of breeding birds. Other colonial breeding seabirds are also being importantly affected, e.g., black-legged kittiwake (*Rissa tridactyla*) and Arctic tern (*Sterna paradisaea*). In addition to birds, some marine mammal populations appear to be threatened and are being monitored. While many local runs of anadromous fish —that is, fish that spend most of their lives in the ocean, but migrate to fresh water to spawn and complete their life cycle— have been greatly reduced or even eliminated in areas easily accessible to communities, the commercially-important fishing industry is currently fairly well managed, although data is still inadequate for some species to provide optimal harvest guidelines. Fortunately, Pinngortitaleriffik, the Greenland Institute of Natural Resources, was established in 1994 to advise the government on sustainable consumption of fish and wildlife resources.

Exploitation of natural resources and ecotourism are believed to have the greatest financial potential for Greenland. Fisheries provide 95% of Greenland's total export, and over the last decade the most important species have been shrimp (*Rimicaris borealis*; 59%), Greenland halibut (*Reinhardtius hippoglossoides*; 17%), and snow crab (*Chionoecetes opilio*; 11%). Atlantic cod (*Gadus morhua*) was the most important species until around 1990, but has now virtually disappeared due to changes in the marine environment along West Greenland. About 20% of the human population is directly or indirectly dependent on hunting and fishing activities. Marine mammals are important for local consumption, and export of sealskins for coats and outer garments occurs, but the financial benefit is limited because of importation prohibitions by the United States and other countries. Although Greenland is rich in minerals, presently there is very limited mineral extraction. Ecotourism, on the other hand, has increased rapidly as support facilities have improved. Most visitors are European as transportation from the United States and Canada is very difficult. External threats include bioaccumulation of chemical pollutants such as PCB and DDT.

Conservation

The Nature Conservation Act of 1980 and following parliamentary regulations (1988) provide the basis for protection of the environment in Greenland, and a completely revised and modern Conservation Act is in the pipeline for 2002. In 2001, a new Bird Protection Executive Order was passed, considerably shortening the open season in late winter and spring for most species. Commercial fisheries are regulated by annual quotas set by the Home Rule in line with biological advice, and subsistence whaling quotas are negotiated through the International Whaling Commission (IWC) and the North Atlantic Marine Mammal Commission (NAMMCO).

The Northeast Greenland National Park was established by a Danish Act of Parliament in 1974 and expanded in 1988 by the Home Rule Government Act. This is the largest park in the world, totaling 972 000 km^2, an area larger than Great Britain and France together. Eleven RAMSAR protected wetland areas covering 15 385 km^2 have also been designated (RAMSAR 2002). These protected areas represent 45% of the island as a whole. With so few people, and such a large area under protection, Greenland remains about 98-99% intact.

KURT BURNHAM
BILL BURNHAM
KNUD FALK

Above, king eider
(Somateria spectabilis).
© **Wayne Lynch**

On the opposite page, The Icefjord,
Ilulissat, Greenland.
© **Hans Strand**

ANTARCTICA

Antarctica is the fifth largest of the seven continents; covering some 13.9 million km² or 10% of the Earth's surface, an area nearly double the size of Australia, 1.5 times the size of the U.S.A., and 50 times that of Great Britain. It is actually divided into two geologically distinct sections, East Antarctica (also called Greater Antarctica), which covers some 10.4 million km², and West Antarctica (or Lesser Antarctica), which is about 2 million km² in extent. The Antarctic Peninsula adds another 520 000 km².

It is the highest and the lowest continent, with both designations caused by ice, the defining feature of this region. In striking contrast to all other continents, Antarctica is covered in over 98% of its extent by an enormous ice cap that averages 1 800 m in thickness, and at its highest point (Dome Argus) rises to over 4 000 m. Although the tallest mountain, Vinson Massif, is only 5 140 m, the mean surface elevation of this continent is more than 2 000 m, much more than Asia which, at 960 m, is the next highest. However, much of this altitude is caused by the continental ice dome rising up from the land. The same ice that gives Antarctica this tremendous altitude also lowers the continent with its unimaginable weight. Most of the land surface of Antarctica is actually depressed below sea level. If the ice were to be removed, the land, relieved of the weight, would rise above sea level. In all, Antarctica holds about 30 million km³ of ice, or about 90% of the ice on Earth (Stonehouse 2000). If it were to melt, the world's oceans would rise 60-65 m.

Antarctica plays an important role in the Earth's climate and weather patterns, and is of vital interest to science, since it provides clues about our planet's evolution and atmosphere. Layers of ice, compacted over millions of years, provide a history of Earth's climate. By studying cores drilled out of the ice, scientists can detect temperature changes over the centuries. Trapped air bubbles, like tiny gas chambers, record variations in the concentration of carbon dioxide in the atmosphere, essential to our understanding of global warming.

As we define it, Antarctica covers the continent and offshore islands lying within the Antarctic Circle, and also those cold temperate Sub-Antarctic islands lying within the Antarctic Convergence. These include Crozet Island, Prince Edward Island, Marion Island, Kerguelen Island, South Georgia, the South Orkney Islands, the South Shetland Islands, the South Sand-

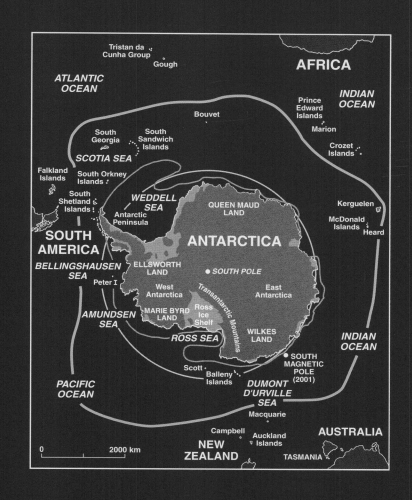

wich Islands, Peter Island, Signy Island, Scott Island, Bouvet Island, the Balleny Islands, Macquarie Island, and the McDonald and Heard Islands. The Antarctic Convergence (or Polar Front) is that area in which the cold, northward-spreading surface current reaches the warmer, saltier waters of the temperate latitudes; at this point, the cold, denser water disappears under the warmer. This convergence line is also the limit of the pack ice, and is generally taken to be the boundary of both the Southern Ocean and the Antarctic region. These sinking cold waters are a major force in the global ocean current system and take on the name "Antarctic Bottom Water." The dense Antarctic bottom water forms an underwater stream, falling to the seafloor and flowing north, helping to drive the interlocking conveyor belts of ocean currents and eventually warming and rising back to the surface some 1 000 years later. The Southern Ocean surrounding Antarctica covers some 35 million km² and is the fourth largest ocean on Earth.

Taken as a whole, more than 99% of Antarctica is still wilderness and has by far the lowest human population of any continent. The principal human

■ *Ice shelves*
— *Antarctic Convergence*
— *Antarctic Circle*
— *Summer Limit of Pack Ice (March)*

On the opposite page, arched tabular iceberg 40 m high, Gerlache Strait along the Danco Coast, Antarctic Peninsula.
© Kim Heacox/*DRK Photo*

inhabitants on the continent itself are researchers at various stations, while the Sub-Antarctic Islands have very small human populations dating back no more than 100-150 years.

Although remote and hostile, this huge continent is rich in wildlife, breathtaking scenery, and natural resources. The most obvious and abundant areas of biodiversity are along the coast, including both the terrestrial and adjacent marine areas. Most of Antarctica's true coastline is under the edges of the ice sheet, with 96% of what one sees from the ocean being ice cliffs. There are only a few thousand kilometers of rocky shore on the continent and the Southern Ocean islands, and these are where most of the life-forms fully or partly dependent on land are to be found (Stonehouse 2000). They are also the areas where human impact has been the greatest.

Biodiversity

The terrestrial and freshwater biodiversity of Antarctica is by far the lowest of any continent. Nonetheless, the region is very important because it represents one of the extreme environments on Earth where animals and plants are cold-adapted, and many are endemic or near endemic. Marine biodiversity is much richer, but will only be touched upon briefly here. In terms of plant diversity, Antarctica has mainly a cryptogamic flora, that is, mosses, lichens, and their relatives. At present, there are over 250 species of lichens, 250 mosses, 70 macrofungi, and 85 hepatics, but only 60 angiosperms (Convey 2001), with the most extensive stands of vegetation and the greatest diversity being found in Maritime Antarctica, i.e., the Antarctic Peninsula (especially the west coast), its off-lying islands, and other Southern Ocean islands, with much less being found in Continental Antarctica. This low diversity is in part attributable to geographic isolation, very cold temperatures, and lack of fresh water, with Continental Antarctica having mean monthly temperatures below 0°C in summer, -25°C in winter, and infrequent summer precipitation, almost all of it snow, meaning there is very little liquid water available. Maritime Antarctica has more precipitation (250-1 000 mm), some of it falling as summer rain, and mean monthly temperatures are somewhat higher, those in summer being between 0°C and 2°C and those in winter rarely falling below -15°C. In addition, soils are immature and low in certain mineral nutrients, especially available nitrogen, and there is little accumulation of organic matter (Longton 1985).

Several different vegetation types exist in Maritime Antarctica, including Antarctic herb tundra formation (with the two native flowering plants, *Deschampsia antarctica* and *Colobanthus quitensis*), and at least eight Antarctic cryptogamic tundra formations (crustaceous lichen subformation, fruticose and foliose lichen subformation, short moss turf and cushion subformation, tall moss subformation, bryophyte carpet and mat subformation, moss hummock subformation, algae subformation, and

snow algae subformation). Continental Antarctica has far fewer, and only locally does cryptogamic vegetation comprise a prominent feature of the landscape. Those that do exist can be classified as lichen subformations (which tend to be more widespread and variable than those of mosses), short moss turf and cushion subformation, algae subformation, and microphytic vegetation.

In terms of animal life, the terrestrial fauna is dominated by invertebrates. These include, in the whole region, at least 83 established protozoans, about 70 species of nematodes, at least 29 species of tardigrades, at least 21 rotifers, several enchytraeids (small white worms related to earthworms), over 167 arachnids, and more than 210 species of insects, including flies, beetles, aphids, thrips, and parasitoid wasps. A few of these insect species are free-living, the remainder being parasites on warm-blooded animals. The only free-living insects of the 49 in Continental Antarctica are the Collembola or springtails: primitive, wingless species up to 1 or 2 mm in length. In the Maritime Zone, there are also two free-living species of midges (Somme 1985; Australian Antarctic Division 1995; Convey 2001). In addition, there are about 70 species of mites in the Continental and Maritime zones (Gressitt 1967), and over 140 on the Sub-Antarctic Islands (Convey 2001). There are at least 20 spiders on the Sub-Antarctic Islands, including three on Macquarie Island which are the most southerly-occurring spiders on Earth (Forster 1962).

Looking briefly at the marine realm, there is no place on Earth where the contrast between ecosystems of the sea and those of land is greater than in Antarctica. Terrestrial ecosystems are mainly restricted to the few rock exposures and coasts and are very low in diversity. Marine systems, on the other hand, are extremely rich and productive, and support diverse assemblages of plants and animals during the brief but explosive growing season each austral summer, when 24 hours of continuous daylight produce phytoplankton blooms that feed the Antarctic krill, the basis of the marine food chain. The Antarctic krill is channeled to higher predators such as seals, birds, and whales (Bonner and Walton 1985). There are no freshwater fish within the Antarctic Convergence, but about 200 deep-sea and shallow-water bottom-dwelling and pelagic fish species are known from within the Antarctic Convergence. These include 126 species of coastal fish in 15 families and 54 genera. About 85% of the coastal species are endemic, while only about 25% of the deep-sea species are restricted to the region (Kock 1985).

As for birds, there are some 49 breeding species in Antarctica. Nearly all of these are seabirds, with the exception of an endemic pipit, three native species of ducks, and two sheathbills that feed along the shore and scavenge on penguin colonies. The seabirds include six species of albatrosses, 17 typical petrels, prions, and shearwaters, three storm-petrels, two diving-petrels, one gull species, two terns, two skuas, three shags and, of course, the seven species and eight taxa of penguins (Harrison 1983; BirdLife International 2000; Clements

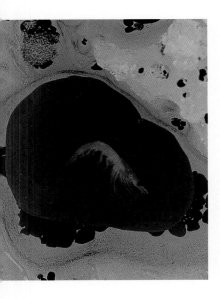

Above, Antarctic krill (Euphausia superba), the basis of the Antarctic food chain.

On the opposite page, Gentoo penguin (Pygoscelis papua), Antarctic Peninsula.
Both photos:
© **Patricio Robles Gil**/*Sierra Madre*

2000). The diversity of birds may not be very impressive, but the number found in the region during the breeding season is staggering, with as many as 100 million individuals competing for nesting sites.

All mammal species in Antarctica, which number 18, are either entirely marine (whales, dolphins) or mainly marine (seals), hauling out onto land only to breed. These include six species of seals and 10 species of whales. Of the toothed or odontocete whales, the killer whale, Arnoux's beaked whale, and southern bottlenose whale can routinely be found in Antarctic waters. There may also be a new species or subspecies of killer whale in Antarctica, but that remains to be confirmed with further molecular biology and morphological studies. If confirmed, this may be an endemic species that stays in Antarctic waters year round, while the common killer whale, also found in Antarctica, is more migratory. The smaller dolphins and porpoises are much rarer, but dusky dolphins and Commerson's dolphins may occasionally be found south of the Antarctic Convergence.

Eight mammal species have also been introduced to the Sub-Antarctic Islands, including the Norway rat (*Rattus norvegicus*), the black rat (*Rattus rattus*), the house mouse (*Mus musculus*), the rabbit (*Oryctolagus cuniculus*), the sheep (*Ovies aries*), the mouflon (*Ovis ammon*), the reindeer (*Rangifer tarandus*), and the domestic cat (*Felis catus*) (Leader-Williams 1985). Domestic cattle and pigs are also present on these islands.

Flagship Species

The most obvious and important flagship species of Antarctica are the seven species (and eight taxa) of penguins, the six seal species, and the 10 species of whales. Of the world's six genera and 17 species of penguin, three genera, seven species and eight taxa are found in Antarctica. The two most spectacular penguin species are unquestionably the emperor penguin (*Aptenodytes forsteri*), at 30 kg and 1.15 m the largest penguin species in the world, and the King penguin (*A. patagonica*), the next largest. Others include the Adelie (*Pygoscelis adeliae*), the chinstrap (*P. antarctica*), the southern gentoo (*P. papua papua*), the northern gentoo (*P. papua ellsworthii*), the macaroni (*Eudyptes chrysolophus*), and the rockhopper (*E. crestatus*) (Stonehouse 2000). Penguins are not only appealing because of their delightful appearance; their colonies are among the world's most amazing wildlife phenomena, sometimes numbering in the hundreds of thousands or even millions.

Of the six seal species of Antarctica, five are true seals (family Phocidae), while one, the Antarctic fur seal (*Arctocephalus gazella*), is a member of the eared seal family, Otariidae. The crabeater seal (*Lobodon carcinophagus*) is an amazingly abundant animal numbering between 15 and 40 million individuals, making it one of the most prolific large mammals on Earth. Indeed, its biomass is about four times that of all other pinnipeds put together and one in every two seals in the world is a crabeater.

The leopard seal (*Hydrurga leptonyx*) is well known as a predator of penguins, and can often be seen in the vicinity of penguin colonies. The Ross seal (*Ommatophoca rossii*) is the least abundant, the most poorly known, and the smallest of the Antarctic seals, and appears to be an inhabitant of heavy pack ice. The Weddell seal (*Leptonychotes weddelli*) is the most southerly-occurring mammal in the world and, in contrast to its relatives, is found in the near-shore region and is the species most often seen by visitors. The southern elephant seal (*Mirounga leonina*) is the largest pinniped and one of the largest non-cetacean mammals, with some males weighing about 4 000 kg. Finally, the Antarctic fur seal, which is a very different animal and much more agile on land than the five other species. All of these species may be seen outside Antarctic waters, but the Ross seal and the Weddell seal seem to be most closely tied to Antarctica, the latter actually living permanently under the ice during the winter months and using sonar to locate its food and find its way back to its breathing holes (Bonner 1985).

The 10 whales living in Antarctic waters include six baleen whales [blue whale (*Balaenoptera musculus*), fin whale (*B. physalus*), humpback whale (*Megaptera novaeangliae*), sei whale (*B. borealis schlegellii*), minke whale (*B. acutorostrata*), and southern right whale (*Eubalaena australis*)]; two toothed whales [sperm whale (*Physeter macrocephalus*) and killer whale (*Orcinus orca*)]; and two smaller whale species, the southern bottlenose whale (*Hyperoodon planifrons*), and Arnoux's beaked whale (*Berardius arnuxii*) (Gambell 1985).

Human Cultures

Indigenous people did not inhabit Antarctica. The current human population is international and consists of people associated with the several dozen research stations distributed around the continent; it varies between approximately one thousand people in the austral winter and perhaps 10 000 in the austral summer. Needless to say, the human population density, which ranges from 0.00007 to 0.0003 people/km², is the lowest on Earth.

Threats

The first of Antarctica's resources to be exploited were fur seals. Captain Cook noted that the beaches of South Georgia were swarming with fur seals, and the sealers followed soon after. By 1822, it was calculated that 1 200 000 skins had been taken from South Georgia and the species was nearly extinct there. When fur seals declined, the sealers switched to elephant seals.

The last catch of fur seals was in 1907, and none were seen again until 1919. In the 1930s, a small colony was found again at South Georgia, and since then they have recovered dramatically there and have spread to other breeding sites in the South Shetlands, the South Orkneys, and the South Sandwich Islands as well. A bio-

On the opposite page, Antarctic fur seal (Arctocephalus gazella), male, female, and cub, South Georgia, U.K.

Above, Adelie penguin with two chicks (Pygoscelis adeliae), Antarctic Peninsula. Both photos:
© **Patricio Robles Gil**/*Sierra Madre*

On pp. 550-551, Troll Castle (2 806 m), Filchner Mountains, Queen Maud Land, Antarctica
© **Gordon Wiltsie**/*National Geographic Image Collection*

logically-based plan to exploit elephant seals was introduced in the 1950s, and it resulted in one of the best examples of sustainable management to date. Nonetheless, it too collapsed in 1964, not because of a shortage of seals, but because the whaling industry, of which seal-

400 000 tons. Over half the krill harvest is for nonhuman consumption —usually ending up as fish meal or animal feed. If it is for human consumption, krill must be processed within three hours of being caught. Otherwise, following the death of the animal, its enzymes begin to

BIBLIOGRAPHY

ADÁMOLI, J. 1981. O Pantanal e suas relações fitogeográficas com os cerrados. Discussão sobre o conceito de "Complexo do Pantanal". In: Anais do XXXII Congresso Nacional de Botânica. *Congresso Nacional de Botânica 32,* Teresina, pp. 109-119.

ADIS, J. 2001. Arthropods (terrestrial), Amazonian. In: *Encyclopaedia of Biodiversity,* Vol. 1, Academic Press, London. pp. 249-260.

ADIS, J., A.Y. HARADA, C.R.V. da FONSECA, W. PAARMANN, and J.A. RAFAEL. 1989. Arthropods obtained from the Amazonian tree species "cupiuba" (*Goupia glabra*) by repeated canopy fogging with natural pyrethrum. *Acta Amazonica* 28:273-283.

ADIS, J. and M.S. HARVEY. 2000. How many Arachnida and Myriapoda are there worldwide and in Amazonia? *Studies in Neotropical Fauna and Environment* 35:139-141.

AGNAGNA, M. 1983. Results of the first Congolese Mokele-Mbembe Expedition. *Cryptozoology* 2:103-112.

AGUILAR, P.G. 1985. Fauna de las lomas costeras del Perú. *Boletín de Lima* 41:17-28.

AGUILERA, M.O. 1998. Sustainable use and livestock production: A viable alternative for grazing rangelands. In: M. OESTERHELD, M.R. AGUIAR, and J.M. PARUELO (Eds.). *Ecosistemas patagónicos. Ecología Austral* 8:75-84.

ALABACK, P. and J. POJAR. 1997. Vegetation from ridgetop to seashore. In: P.K. SCHOONMAKER, B. von HAGEN, and E.C. WOLF (Eds.). *The Rain Forests of Home: Profile of a North American Region.* Island Press, Washington, D.C., pp. 69-87.

ALCORN, J. 1993. *Papua New Guinea Conservation Needs Assessment.* Two volumes. Biodiversity Support Program, Washington, D.C.

ALEGRETTI, M.H. 1990. Extractive reserves: An alternative for reconciling development and environmental conservation in Amazonia. In: A.B. ANDERSON (Ed.). *Alternatives to Deforestation: Steps Toward Sustainable Use of the Amazon Rain Forest.* Columbia University Press, New York, pp. 252-264.

ALLEN, G.M. 1942. *Extinct and Vanishing Mammals of the Western Hemisphere.* American Committee for International Wildlife Protection, Washington, D.C. and The Intelligence Printing Company, Lancaster, Pennsylvania.

ALLEN, G.R. 1982. *A Field Guide to Inland Fishes of Western Australia.* Western Australian Museum, Perth.

ALLEN, T. and A. WARREN (Eds). 1993. *Deserts: The Encroaching Wilderness.* A World Conservation Atlas. Mitchell Beazley International Ltd., London.

ALVAREZ, B.B., M.E. TEDESCO, A.B. HERNANDO, J.A. CÉSPEDES, and R.H. AGUIRRE. 2001. Diversidad de anfibios y reptiles de Corrientes, Chaco y Formosa, Argentina. Situación actual. Comunicaciones Científicas y Tecnológicas, Ciencia y Técnica, Universidad Nacional del Nordeste.

ANDERSEN, A.N. 1992. Regulation of "momentary" diversity by dominant species in exceptionally rich ant communities of the Australian seasonal tropics. *American Naturalist* 140:401-420.

ANDERSON, A.B. 1990. Deforestation in Amazonia: Dynamics, causes, and alternatives. In: A.B. ANDERSON (Ed.), *Alternatives to Deforestation: Steps Toward Sustainable Use of the Amazon Rain Forest.* Columbia University Press, New York, pp. 3-23.

ANDRADE, M.C.O. 1980. *The Land and People of Northeast Brazil.* University of New Mexico Press, Albuquerque.

ANDRADE-LIMA, D. 1981. The Caatinga dominium. *Revista Brasileira de Botânica* 4:149-153.

ANDRE, J.M. and T.A. KNIGHT. 1999. An overview of special status plants in the Mojave Desert. *Presentation Minutes of the Mojave Desert Science Symposium,* February 25-27, 1999. USGS Western Ecological Research Center.

ANONYMOUS. 1992. *Estudio ambiental nacional. Organización de los Estados Americanos.* Washington, D.C.

ANONYMOUS. 1995. *The Volcanoes of Kamchatka World Heritage Nomination.* Prepared by the Ministry of Environmental Protection and Natural Resources of Russia.

ANONYMOUS. 1999a. *Europe's Carnivores: A Conservation Challenge for the 21st Century.* WWF-U.K. Report.

ANONYMOUS. 1999b. *Propuesta de Estrategia Nacional para la Conservación y Uso Sostenible de la Diversidad Biológica del Uruguay. Proyecto Biodiversidad, Uruguay.* MVOTMA, PNUD, GEF, Montevideo.

ANONYMOUS. 2000. *Project Brief: Demonstrating Sustainable Conservation of Biological Diversity in Four Protected Areas in Russia's Kamchatka Oblast.* United Nations Development Programme, New York.

ANONYMOUS. 2001. *The CIA Factbook.* www.cia.gov/cia/publications/factbook

ANONYMOUS. 2001a. The Carpathian Ecoregion Initiative, World Wildlife Fund for Nature (WWF). www.carpathians.org/hm_info.htm

ANONYMOUS. 2001b. The Carpathian Mountains, Carpathian Heritage Society. www.carpathians.pl/carpathians.html

ANONYMOUS. 2001c. LandScan 2000, 1 km Resolution Global Population Database. Socioeconomic Data and Applications Center, Center for International Earth Science Information Network. http://sedac.ciesin.org/snews/seda-news_aug2001.txt or www.ornl.gov/gist/projects/LandScan/landscan_doc.htm

ARAMBURÚ, C.E. 1984. Expansion of the agrarian and demographic frontier in the Peruvian selva. In: M. SCHMINK and C.H. WOOD (Eds.). *Frontier Expansion in Amazonia.* University of Florida Press, Gainesville, pp. 153-179.

ARAÚJO-LIMA, C.A.R.M., M.T. PIEDADE, and F.A.R. BARBOSA. 1998. Water as a major resource of the Amazon. In: M. de L.D. de FREITAS (Ed.). *Amazonia: Heaven of a New World.* Editora Campus, Rio de Janeiro, pp. 55-70.

ARNOLD, E.N. 1987. Zoogeography of the reptiles and amphibians of Arabia. In: F. KRUPP, W. SCHNEIDER, and R. KINZELBACH (Eds.). *Proceedings of the Symposium on the Fauna and Zoogeography of the Middle East.* Wiesbaden, Germany. Dr. Ludwig Reichert Verlag, pp. 245-256.

ARRIAZA, B. 1995. *Beyond Death, the Chinchorro Mummies of Ancient Chile.* Smithsonian Institution Press, Washington, D.C.

ARROYO, M.T.K., F. SQUEO, J.J. ARMESTO, and C. VILLAGRÁN. 1988. Effects of aridity on plant diversity on the northern Chilean Andes: Results of a natural experiment. Annals of the Missouri Botanical Garden 75:55-78.

ARUTIUNOV, S.A. 1988a. Koryak and Itelmen: Dwellers of the Smoking Coast. In: W.W. FITZHUGH and A. CROWELL (Eds.). *Crossroads of Continents: Cultures of Siberia and Alaska.* Smithsonian Institution Press, Washington, D.C., pp. 31-35.

ARUTIUNOV, S.A. 1988b. Even: Reindeer herders of eastern Siberia. In: W.W. FITZHUGH and A. CROWELL (Eds.). *Crossroads of Continents: Cultures of Siberia and Alaska.* Smithsonian Institution Press, Washington, D.C., pp. 35-38.

ARUTIUNOV, S.A. 1988c. Chukchi: Warriors and traders of Chukotka. In: W.W. FITZHUGH and A. CROWELL (Eds.). *Crossroads of Continents: Cultures of Siberia and Alaska.* Smithsonian Institution Press, Washington, D.C., pp. 39-42.

ASCHMANN, H. 1959. *The Central Desert of Baja California: Demography and Ecology.* University of California Press, Berkeley.

ASSOCIACÃO PLANTAS DO NORDESTE. 2000. Diagnóstico da vegetação nativa do bioma caatinga. Relatório Técnico, Projeto "Avaliação e Ações Prioritárias para a Conservação da Biodiversidade do Bioma Caatinga". www.biodiversitas.org/caatinga

AUGEROT, X. 2001. Unpublished data. Wild Salmon Center, Portland, Oregon.

AUSTRALIA. 1997. *Introduction of Disease into Antarctic Birds.* Information Paper 51, XXI Antarctic Treaty Consultative Meeting, Christchurch, New Zealand.

AUSTRALIAN ANTARCTIC DIVISION. 1995. *Heard Island Wilderness Reserve Management Plan.* Australian Antarctic Division, Kingston, Tasmania.

AUSTRALIAN BUREAU OF STATISTICS. 2002. Census information. www.abs.gov.au

AUSTRALIAN INSTITUTE OF ABORIGINAL AND TORRES STRAITS ISLANDER STUDIES. 1994. *Aboriginal Australia,* AIATSIS, Canberra.

AUSTRALIAN NATURE CONSERVATION AGENCY. 1996. *Application of IUCN Protected Area Management Categories: Draft Australian Handbook.* Australian Nature Conservation Agency, Canberra.

AYRES, D.L., E. MOURA, and J.M. AYRES. 1995. Mamirauá: Ribeirinhos e a preservação da biodiversidade da várzea amazonica. In: G.A.B. da FONSECA, M. SCHMINK, L.P. de S. PINTO, and F. BRITO (Eds.). *Abordagens Interdisciplinares para a Conservação da Biodiversidade e Dinâmica do Uso da Terra no Novo Mundo.* Conservation International do Brasil, Universidade Federal de Minas Gerais, Belo Horizonte and Universidade de Florida, Gainesville, pp. 169-182.

AYRES, J.M. and C. AYRES. 1979. Aspectos da caça no alto Rio Aripuanã. *Acta Amazonica* 9:287-298.

AYRES, J.M., D. de MAGALHAES LIMA, E. de SOUZA MARTINS, and J.L.K. BARREIROS. 1991. On the track of the road: Changes in subsistence hunting in a Brazilian Amazonian village. In: J.G. ROBINSON and K.H. REDFORD (Eds.). *Neotropical Wildlife Use and Conservation,* University of Chicago Press, Chicago, pp. 81-92.

AYRES, J.M. and T.H. CLUTTON-BROCK. 1992. River boundaries and species range size in Amazonian primates. *American Naturalist* 140:531-537.

AYRES, J.M., G.A.B. da FONSECA, A.B. RYLANDS, H.L. QUIROZ, L.P. de S. PINTO, D. MASTERSON, and R.B. CAVALCANTI. 1997. *Abordagens Inovadoras para Conservação da Biodiversidade do Brasil: Os Corredores Ecológicos das Florestas Neotropicais do Brasil.* Volume 1: *Amazônia,* Versão 3.0. PP/G7 - Programa Piloto para a Proteção das Florestas Neotropicais: Projeto Parques e Reservas. Ministério do Meio Ambiente, Recursos Hídricos e da Amazônia Legal (MMA), Instituto Brasileiro do Meio Ambiente e dos Recursos Naturais Renováveis (IBAMA), Brasília.

BADEN, J.A. and D. LEAL (Eds.). 1990. *The Yellowstone Primer: Land and Resource Management in the Greater Yellowstone Ecosystem.* Pacific Research Institute for Public Policy, San Francisco.

BAHRE, C.J. 1995. Human impacts on the grasslands of southeastern Arizona. In: M. McCLARAN and T.R. van DEVENDER (Eds.). *The Desert Grassland.* Tucson, University of Arizona Press, pp. 230-264.

BAILEY, R.G. 1995. *Description of the Ecoregions of the United States.* U.S. Department of Agriculture, Forest Service, Washington, D.C.

BAILEY, R.G. 1997. *Ecoregions of North America.* U.S. Department of Agriculture, Forest Service, Washington, D.C.

BAIN, J.H.C. and J.J. DRAPER. (Eds.). 1997. *North Queensland Geology.* Australian Geological Survey Organization and Geological Survey of Queensland.

BARNARD, P. 1998a. Biological diversity in Namibia: A clash of sea and land, fog and dust. Guest Editorial in: *Biodiversity and Conservation* 7(4):415-417.

BARNARD, P. (Ed.). 1998b. *Biological Diversity in Namibia -A Country Study.* National Namibian Biodiversity Task Force, Directorate of Environmental Affairs, Windhoek.

BARNES, F.A. 1988. Canyonlands National Park: Early history and first descriptions. Canyon Country Publications. Moab, Utah.

BARNES, K.N. (Ed.). 1998. *The Important Bird Areas of Southern Africa.* BirdLife South Africa, Johannesburg, and Avian Demography Unit, University of Cape Town.

BARNES, R.F.W., G.C. CRAIG, H.T. DUBLIN, G. OVERTON, W. SIMONS, and C.R. THOULESS. 1998. *African Elephant Database 1998.* Occasional Paper of the IUCN Species Survival Commission No. 22. IUCN, Gland, Switzerland.

BARNETT, R. (Ed.). 1997. *Food for Thought: The Utilization of Wild Meat in Eastern and Southern Africa.* Traffic East/Southern Africa, Nairobi.

BARQUEZ, R.M. 1997. Viajes de Emilio Budin: la expedición al Chaco, 1906-1907. *Mastozoología Neotropical.* Publicaciones Especiales 1:1-82.

BARRETT, C.B. and P. ARCESE. 1995. Are Integrated Conservation and Development Projects (ICDPs) sustainable? On the conservation of large mammals in Sub-Saharan Africa. *World Development* 23:1073-1085.

BARTHEM, R.B., H. GUERRA, and M. VALDERRAMA. 1995. *Diagnóstico de los recursos hidrobiológicos de Amazonia.* Tratado de Cooperación Amazónica, Secretaria ProTempore, Quito.

BARTHEM, R.B. and M. GOULDING. 1997. *The Catfish Connection.* Columbia University Press, New York.

BATES, H.W. 1864. *The Naturalist on the River Amazons.* Everyman's Library, London.

BAYLEY, P.B. and M. PETRERE Jr. 1989. Amazon fisheries: Assessment methods, current status, and management options. *Proceedings of the International Large River Symposium.* Canadian Special Publications of Fisheries and Aquatic Sciences 106:385-398.

BEARD, J.S. 1990. *Plant Life of Western Australia.* Kangaroo Press, Kenthurst, New South Wales.

BEEHLER, B. and J.P. DUMBACHER. 1996. More examples of fruit trees visited predominantly by birds of paradise. *Emu* 96:81-88.

BEKENOV, A.B., D.A. BLANK, Y.A. GRACHEV, and K.N. PLAKHOV. 2001. Kazakhstan. In: D.P. MALLON and S.C. KINGSWOOD (Compilers), *Antelopes. Part 4: North Africa, the Middle East, and Asia. Global Survey and Regional Action Plans.* SSC Antelope Specialist Group. IUCN, Gland, pp. 134-140.

BELL, R.H.V. 1982. The effect of soil nutrient availability on community structure in African ecosystems. In: B.J. HUNTLEY and B.H. WALKER (Eds.). *Ecology of Tropical Savannas.* Springer-Verlag, Berlin, pp. 193-216.

BENFER, R.A. 1990. The preceramic period site of Paloma, Peru: Bioindications of improving adaptation to sedentism. *Latin American Antiquity* 1:284-318.

BENNETT, P.S. 1974. The ecological role of fire in North Rim forests, Grand Canyon National Park. *Plateau* 46:168-181.

BENSON, C.W. and M.P.S. IRWIN. 1966. The *Brachystegia* avifauna. *Ostrich,* Supplement 6:297-321.

BERGER, B. 1998. *Almost an Island: Travels in Baja California.* University of Arizona Press, Tucson.

BERNALT, O.M. 2001. *Karakú del Chaco: territorio humano del milenio.* Cromos, Asunción.

BERROTERÁN, J.L. 1985. Geomorfología del área de llanos bajos centrales venezolanos. *Sociedad Venezolana de Ciencias Naturales* 143:31-77.

BERTELLI, A. de P. 1988. *O Pantanal -Mar dos Xaraes.* Edições Sicilano, Sao Paulo.

BERTONATTI, C. and J. CORCUERA. 2000. *Situación ambiental Argentina 2000.* Fundación Vida Silvestre.

BEST, P.B., R.L. BROWNELL Jr., and G.P. DONOVAN (Eds.). 2001 Proceedings of the Research and Management Workshop. In: *Report of the Workshop on the Comprehensive Assessment of Right Whales IWC.* Cambridge Sp. Issue 2, 1:60.

BIERREGAARD Jr., R.O., C. GASCON, T.E. LOVEJOY, and R. MESQUITA (Eds.). 2001. *Lessons from Amazonia: The Ecology and Conservation of a Fragmented Forest.* Yale University Press, New Haven.

BIODIVERSITAS. 2000. Biodiversidade do Bioma Caatinga. Seminário realizado no periodo de 21 a 26 de maio de 2000. www.biodiversitas.org/caatinga

BIODIVERSITY CONSERVATION NETWORK. 1999. *Evaluating Linkages Between Business, the Environment, and Local Communities -Final Stories From the Field.* Biodiversity Support Program, Washington, D.C.

BIODIVERSITY SUPPORT PROGRAM. 1995. *A Regional Analysis of Geographic Priorities for Biodiversity Conservation in Latin America and the Caribbean.* Biodiversity Support Program, Conservation International, The Nature Conservancy, Wildlife Conservation Society, World Resources Institute, and World Wildlife Fund. Washington, D.C.

BIRDLIFE INTERNATIONAL. 2000. *Threatened Birds of the World.* Lynx Ediciones, Barcelona and BirdLife International, Cambridge, U.K.

BLACK, L.T. 1988. Peoples of the Amur and Maritime regions. In: W.W. FITZHUGH and A. CROWELL (Eds.). *Crossroads of Continents: Cultures of Siberia and Alaska.* Smithsonian Institution Press, Washington, D.C., pp. 24-31.

BLACK, L.T. and R.G. LIAPUNOVA, 1988. Aleut: Islanders of the North Pacific. In: W.W. FITZHUGH and A. CROWELL (Eds.). *Crossroads of Continents: Cultures of Siberia and Alaska.* Smithsonian Institution Press, Washington, D.C., pp. 52-57.

BLACKMAN, M. 1990. Haida: Traditional culture. In: W. SUTTLES (Ed.). *Northwest Coast,* Volume 7: *Handbook of North American Indians.* Smithsonian Institution, Washington, D.C., pp. 240-260.

BLANCO, D.E., and M. CARBONELL (Eds.). 2001. *The Neotropical Waterbird Census. The First 10 years: 1990-1999.* Wetlands International, Buenos Aires, Argentina and Ducks Unlimited, Inc., Memphis.

BÖCHER, J. 2001. Insekter og andre smådyr - I Grønlands fjeld og ferskvand. Atuagkat, Nuuk.

BOCK, J. 1993. *Okavango Delta Peoples of Botswana.* In: M.S. MILLER (Ed.). *State of the Peoples: A Global Report on Human Rights.* Beacon Press and Cultural Survival, Boston, pp. 174-175.

BODMER, R.E., J.F. EISENBERG, and K.H. REDFORD. 1997. Hunting and the likelihood of extinction of Amazonian mammals. *Conservation Biology* 11:460-466.

BOERTMANN, D. 1994. *An Annotated Checklist to Birds of Greenland.* Bioscience 38. Meddelelser om Grønland.

BOLTOYSKOY, D. 1981. *Atlas de zooplankton del Atlántico sudoccidental.* INIDEP. Mar del Plata.

BONACCORSO, F.J. 1998. *Bats of Papua New Guinea.* Conservation International, Washington, D.C.

BONNER, W.N. 1985. Birds and mammals -Antarctic seals. In: W.N. BONNER and D.W.H. WALTON (Eds.). *Key Environments -Antarctica.* Pergamon Press, Oxford, pp. 202-222.

BONNER, W.N. and D.W.H. WALTON. 1985. Marine habitats –Introduction. In: W.N. BONNER and D.W.H. Walton (Eds.). *Key Environments –Antarctica*. Pergamon Press, Oxford, pp. 133-134.

BORKIN, L.J. 1999. Distribution of amphibians in North Africa, Europe, Western Asia, and the former Soviet Union. In: W.E. DUELLMAN (Ed.). *Patterns of Distribution of Amphibians: A Global Perspective*. The Johns Hopkins University Press, Baltimore, pp. 329-420.

BOURILLÓN, L., A. CANTÚ, F. ECCARDI, E. LIRA, J. RAMÍREZ, E. VELARDE, and A. ZAVALA. 1988. *Islas del Golfo de California*. Secretaría de Gobernación–Universidad Nacional Autónoma de México, Mexico City.

BOWDEN, C. and J.W. DYKINGA. 1993. *The Sonoran Desert*. Harry N. Abrahms, New York.

BOWEN, T. 2000. *Unknown Island: Seri Indians, Europeans, and San Esteban Island in the Gulf of California*. University of New Mexico Press, Albuquerque.

BOWMAN, D.M.J.S. 1997. Observations on the demography of the Australian boab (*Adansonia gibbosa*) in the northwest of the Northern Territory, Australia. *Australian Journal of Botany* 45:893-904.

BOWMAN, D.M.J.S. 1998. The impact of Aboriginal landscape burning on the Australian biota. *New Phytologist* 140:385-410.

BOYD, R.T. 1990. Demographic history, 1774-1874. In: W. SUTTLES (Ed.). *Northwest Coast*, Volume 7: *Handbook of North American Indians*. Smithsonian Institution, Washington, D.C.

BRAACK, L.E.O. 1997. Policy proposals regarding issues relating to biodiversity maintenance, maintenance of wilderness qualities, and provision of human benefits. Volume VIII: Supplement to Kruger National Park Management Plan. Kruger National Park Scientific Services Section. South African National Parks, Skukuza.

BRADFORD, D.F., and R.D. JENNINGS. 1999. Populations status of the relict leopard frog (*Rana onca*) (abstract). *Proceedings of the Desert Fishes Council* 29:3.

BRANCH, B. 1998. *Field Guide. Snakes and Other Reptiles of Southern Africa*. Struik, Cape Town.

BRATTON, S.P. and A.J. MEIER. 1998. Restoring wildflowers and salamanders in southeastern deciduous forest. *Restoration Notes* 16:158-165.

BRAUNSTEIN, J. and E.S. MILLER. 1999. Ethnohistorical Introduction. In: E.S. MILLER (Ed.), *Peoples of the Gran Chaco*. Bergin and Garvey, London, pp. 1-220.

BROADLEY, D.G. 2000. The herpetofauna of the Zambezi Basin wetlands. In: J.R. TIMBERLAKE (Ed.), *Biodiversity of the Zambezi Basin Wetlands*, Vol. II. Consultancy Report for IUCN ROSA. Biodiversity Foundation for Africa, Bulawayo, and Zambezi Society, Harare, pp. 279-361.

BROOKS, R.R. and F. MALAISSE. 1985. *The Heavy Metal –Tolerant Flora of Southcentral Africa*. A.A. Balkema, Rotterdam.

BROUGHTON. D. 2001. Falkland Islands flora –Establishing status and distribution. *Falklands Conservation* 1:11-13.

BROUWER, J. and W.C. MULLIÉ. 1994. Conservation of the white stork in its winter quarters. International Symposium on the White Stork, 1994, Basel, pp. 296-297.

BROWN, G. 1993. *The Great Bear Almanac*. Lyons and Burford, Publishers, New York.

BROWN Jr., K.S. 1975. Geographical patterns of evolution in neotropical Lepidoptera. Systematics and derivation of known and new Heliconiini (Nymphalidae: Nymphalinae). *Journal of Entomology* (B) 44(3):210-242

BROWN Jr., K.S. 1986. Zoogeografia da Região do Pantanal Mato-Grossense. In: Anais do I Simpósio sobre Recursos Naturais e Sócio-Econômicos do Pantanal. EMBRAPA, Corumá, pp. 137-138.

BROWN Jr., K.S. 1987. Biogeography and evolution of neotropical butterflies. In: C. WHITMORE and G.T. PRANCE (Eds.). *Biogeography and Quaternary History in Tropical America*. Clarendon Press, Oxford, pp. 66-104.

BRYANT, D., D. NIELSEN, and L. TANGLEY (Eds.). 1997. *The Last Frontier Forests: Ecosystems and Economies on the Edge*. World Resources Institute, Washington, D.C. and New York.

BUCHER, E.H. 1982. Chaco and Caatinga –South American arid savannas, woodlands, and thickets. In: B.J. HUNTLEY and B.H. WALKER (Eds.), Ecology of Tropical Savannas. Springer-Verlag, Berlin, pp. 48-79.

BUCHER, E.H. 1992. The causes of extinction of the passenger pigeon. *Current Ornithology* 9:1-36.

BUCHER, E.H. 1995. Indicators of biophysical sustainability: Case study of the Chaco savannas of South America. In: M. MUNASINGHE and W. SHEARER (Eds.). *Defining and Measuring Sustainability: The Biogeophysical Foundations*. Washington, D.C., United Nations University and World Bank, pp. 147-152.

BUCHER, E. and J. CHANI. 1999. Región 2. Chaco. In: P. CANEVARAI, D. BLANCO, E. BUCHER, G. CASTRO, and I. DAVIDSON (Eds.), *Los humedales de la Argentina: clasificación, situación actual, conservación y legislación*. Wetlands International Publ., No. 46, Buenos Aires, pp. 74-96.

BUHLMANN, K.A., J.C. MITCHELL, and M.G. ROLLINS. 1997. New approaches for the conservation of bog turtles (*Clemmys muhlenbergii*) in Virginia. In: J. van ABBABA and M.W. KLEMENS (Eds.). Proceedings: Conservation, Restoration, and Management of Tortoises and Turtles –An International Conference. New York Turtle and Tortoise Society, New York, pp. 359-363.

BULMER, S. 1982. Human ecology and cultural variation in prehistoric New Guinea. In: J. GRESSITT (Ed.). *Biogeography and Ecology of New Guinea*. Vol. I. W. Junk, The Hague.

BUNDY, G., R.J. CONNOR, and C.J.O. HARRISON. 1989. *Birds of the Eastern Province of Saudi Arabia*. London: Witherby (in association with Saudi Aramco, Dhahran).

BUNNELL, F.L. and A.C. CHAN-McLEOD. 1997. Terrestrial vertebrates. In: P.K. SCHOONMAKER, B. von HAGEN, and E.C. WOLF (Eds.). *The Rain Forests of Home: Profile of a North American Region*. Island Press, Washington, D.C., pp. 103-130.

BURBIDGE, A.A., and N.L. McKENZIE (Eds.). 1978. *The Islands of the Northwest Kimberley, Western Australia*. Wildlife Research Bulletin No. 7. Department of Fisheries and Wildlife, Perth.

BURBIDGE, A.A., N.L. McKENZIE, and K.F. KENNEALLY. 1991. *Nature Conservation Reserves in the Kimberley, Western Australia*. Department of Conservation and Land Management, Perth.

BURKANOV, V.N. 2000. Steller's sea lion population status and dynamics in Russian waters in 1989-1999. *Marine Mammals of the Holarctic Regions*. Materials from International Conference, Archangelsk, Russia, 21-23 September, pp. 56-65 (in Russian).

BURKART, R., N.O. BÁRBARO, R.O. SÁNCHEZ, and D.A. GÓMEZ. 1999. Ecorregiones de la Argentina. Administración de Parques Nacionales. Programa Desarrollo Institucional Ambiental, Buenos Aires.

BURM, J. and C.R. GRIFFIN. 2000. *The Seasonal Abundance and Distribution of Wildlife Population in Northern Botswana*. Final Report. Botswana Aerial Wildlife Inventory. University of Massachusetts and Conservation International.

BURNHAM, R.J. and A. GRAHAM. 1999. The history of neotropical vegetation: New developments and status. *Annals of the Missouri Botanical Garden* 86:546-589.

BURROUGHS, E.D. 1961. *The Natural History of the Lewis and Clark Expedition*. Michigan State University Press, East Lansing.

BURTON, R. 1992. *Bird Migration*. Aurum Press, London.

BYERS, B.A., R.N. CUNLIFFE, and A.T. HUDAK. 2001. Linking the conservation of culture and nature: A case study of sacred forests in Zimbabwe. *Human Ecology* 29:187-218.

CABIDO, M., A. ACOSTA, and S. DÍAZ. 1990. The vascular flora and vegetation of granitic outcrops in the upper Córdoba mountains, Argentina. *Phytocoenologia* 19: 267-281.

CABRERA, A. 1976. Regiones fitogeográficas argentinas. *Enciclopedia Argentina de Agricultura y Jardinería*. ACME, Buenos Aires.

CABRERA, A. and J. YEPES. 1940. *Mamíferos sudamericanos*. Vol. 1. Historia Natural Ediar, Buenos Aires.

CABRERA, A.L. and A. WILLINK. 1973. *Biogeografía de América Latina*. OEA, Serie de Biología, Monografía 13, Washington, D.C.

CABRERA, M.R. 1998. *Las tortugas continentales de Sudamérica austral*. BR Copias, Córdoba.

CAFF (Conservation of Arctic Flora and Fauna). 1999. *Atlas of Rare Endemic Vascular Plants of the Arctic*. Technical Report No. 3. CAFF, Akureyri, Iceland.

CAFF (Conservation of Arctic Flora and Fauna). 2001. *Arctic Flora and Fauna: Status and Conservation*. Edita, Helsinki.

CAFF (Conservation of Arctic Flora and Fauna). 2002. http://grida.no/caff/index.html

CALEF, G. 1981. *Caribou and the Barren-lands*. Canadian Arctic Resources Committee, Ottawa. Firefly Books Limited, Toronto.

CALIFORNIA STATE PARKS. 1995. *Official Guide to California State Parks*. Sacramento.

CALLICOTT, J.B. and M.P. NELSON (Eds.). 1988. *The Great New Wilderness Debate*. The University of Georgia, Atlanta.

CAMPBELL, K. and M. BORNER. 1995. Population trends and distribution of Serengeti herbivores: Implications for management. In: A.R.E. SINCLAIR and P. ARCESE (Eds.). *Serengeti II: Dynamics, Management, and Conservation of an Ecosystem*. University of Chicago Press, Illinois, pp. 117-145.

CAMPBELL, K. and H. HOFER. 1995. People and wildlife: Spatial dynamics and zones of interactions. In: A.R.E. SINCLAIR and P. ARCESE (Eds.). *Serengeti II: Dynamics, Management, and Conservation of an Ecosystem*. University of Chicago Press, Illinois, pp. 534-570.

CANEVARI, P., I. DAVIDSON, D.E. BLANCO, G. CASTRO, and E.H. BUCHER. 2001. *Los humedales de América del Sur: una agenda para la conservación de la biodiversidad y las políticas de desarrollo*. Wetlands International, Wageningen.

CARPE (Central African Regional Program for the Environment). 2001. *Congo Basin Information Series: Taking Action to Manage and Conserve Forest Resources in the Congo Basin. Results and Lessons Learned from the First Phase (1996-2000)*. College Park, Maryland.

CASE, T.J. and M.L. CODY (Eds.). 1983. *Island Biogeography in the Sea of Cortés*. University of California Press, Berkeley.

CASTELETI, C.H.M., J.M. CARDOSO da SILVA, M. TABARELLI, and A.M. MELO SANTOS. 2000. Quanto ainda resta da Caatinga? Uma estimativa preliminar. Relatório Técnico, Projeto "Avaliação e Ações Prioritárias para a Conservação da Biodiversidade do Bioma Caatinga". www.biodiversitas.org/caatinga

CASTILLO, A.O. and V.A. GARCÍA. 2000. *Áreas bajo régimen de administración especial por figura. Dirección General de Planificación y Ordenación del Ambiente*. Dirección de Ordenación del Territorio, Ministerio del Ambiente y de los Recursos Naturales Renovables, Venezuela.

CASTLEMAN, D. and D. PITCHER. 1997. *Alaska-Yukon Handbook*. Moon Publications, Inc., Chico, California.

CASTRILLÓN-MÁRQUEZ, Z. 2000. *Colombia: los daños a la biodiversidad por los cultivos ilícitos y fumigaciones*. Diario El Occidente, Cali, Colombia. http://usembassy.state.gov/posts/col/wwwhandl.html

CASTRO, D. and A. ARBOLEDA. 1988. A lista preliminar de peces del Río Caquetá. *Boletín Biología Mariña* 8:7-14. Universidad Jorge T. Lozano.

CATELLA, A.C. and M. PETRERE Jr. 1996. Feeding patterns in a fish community of Baía da Onça, a floodplain lake of the Aquidauana River, Pantanal, Brazil. *Fisheries Management and Ecology* 3:229-237.

CEBALLOS, G., E. MELLINK, and L. HANEBURY. 1992. Distribution and conservation status of prairie dogs *Cynomys mexicanus* and *C. ludovicianus* in Mexico. *Biological Conservation* 63:105-112.

CEBALLOS, G. and L. MÁRQUEZ. 2000. *Las aves de México en peligro de extinción*. Conabio-UNAM-Fondo de Cultura Económica, Mexico City.

CEBALLOS, G. and J. PACHECO. 2000. The prairie dogs of Chihuahua and their long-term conservation. *Voices of Mexico* (UNAM) 54:106-109.

CEDI (Centro Ecumênico de Documentação e Informação). 1991. *Povos Indígenas no Brasil 1987/88/89/90*. Centro Ecumênico de Documentação e Informação, São Paulo.

CEI, J.M. 1980. Amphibians of Argentina. Monitore zoologico italiano. *Italian Journal of Zoology*. Publicato dalla Università degli studi di Firenze con il contributo del Consiglio Nazionale delle Ricerche.

CEI, J.M. 1986. Reptiles del centro, centro-oeste y sur de la Argentina. *Herpetofauna de las zonas áridas y semiáridas*. Museo Regionale di Scienze Naturali, Torino.

CEMEX. 2000. *El Carmen. Cemex en la conservación de la biodiversidad*. CEMEX, Monterrey.

CENTER FOR RUSSIAN NATURE CONSERVATION. 2001. Wild Russia. www.wild-russia.org

CESSFORD, G. (Ed.). 2001. *The State of Wilderness in New Zealand*. Department of Conservation, Wellington, New Zealand.

CHADWICK, D.H. 1996. Sanctuary: U.S. National Wildlife Refuges. *National Geographic* 190(4):2-35.

CHALLENGER, A. 1998. *Utilización y conservación de los ecosistemas terrestres de México*. CONABIO, Mexico City.

CHAO, N.L. 1993. Conservation of Rio Negro's ornamental fishes. *Tropical Fish Hobbyist*. January, pp. 99-114.

CHAPMAN, J. 1998. *South West Tasmania*. Melbourne.

CHAPMAN, J. 1999. In: L. McGAURR. *Lonely Planet –Tasmania*. Lonely Planet Publications, Melbourne.

CHEBEZ, J.C. 1994. *Los que se van. Especies Argentinas en peligro*. Editorial Albatros, Buenos Aires.

CHERNOFF, B. and P.W. WILLINK (Eds.). 1999. A biological assessment of the aquatic ecosystems of the upper Río Orthon basin, Pando, Bolivia. *RAP Bulletin of Biological Assessment* 15:1-145. Conservation International, Washington, D.C.

CHIN, H.E. AND H. BUDDING 1987. *Surinam: Politics, Economics and Society*. Francis Pinter, London.

CIESIN (Center for International Earth Science Information Network), IFPRI (International Food Policy Research Institute), and WRI (World Resources Institute). 1995. *Gridded Population of the World (GPW) Version 2*. CIESIN, Columbia University, New York. http://sedac.ciesin.org/plue/gpw

CINCOTTA, R.P. and R. ENGELMAN. 2000. *Nature's Place. Human Population and the Future of Biological Diversity*. Population Action International, Washington, D.C.

CLARK, P. and S. MAGEE (Eds.). 2001. *The Iraqi Marshlands. A Human and Environmental Study*. Unpublished report available from the AMAR International Charitable Foundation. www.amarappeal.com

CLARK, T.H. and C.W. STEARN. 1960. *The Geological Evolution of North America: A Regional Approach to Historical Geology*. The Ronald Press Company, New York.

CLAUSEN, A. 2001. Seabird Conservation –Monitoring & Ecological Studies. *Falklands Conservation* 1:11-13.

CLAVIJERO, F.X. 1789. *Historia de la Antigua o Baja California* (published by Imprenta del Museo Nacional de Arqueología, Historia y Etnografía, 1933, México City). In: H.W. CROSBY. 1994. *Antigua California: Mission and Colony on the Peninsula Frontier, 1697-1768*. University of New Mexico Press, Albuquerque.

CLEMENTS, J.F. 2000. *Birds of the World: A Checklist*. Pica Press, Robertsbridge, East Sussex, U.K., and subsequent updates at www.ibispub.com/updates.html

CLOUDSLEY-THOMPSON, J.L. (Ed.). 1984. *Sahara Desert*. IUCN/Pergamon Press, Oxford.

COBB, C.E. 1996. Storm watch over the Kurils. *National Geographic* 190(4): 48-67.

CODERE, H. 1990. Kwakiutl: Traditional culture. In: W. SUTTLES (Ed.). *Northwest Coast*, Volume 7: *Handbook of North American Indians*. Smithsonian Institution, Washington, D.C., pp. 359-377.

COGGER, H. 2000. *Reptiles and Amphibians of Australia*, sixth edition. Ralph Curtis Publishing, Sanibel Island, Florida.

COLLAR, N.J. 1990. The Amazon as ark. *World Birdwatch* 12(1-2):10-12.

COLLAR, N.J., M.J. CROSBY, and A.J. STATTERSFIELD. 1994. *Birds to Watch 2. The World List of Threatened Birds*. BirdLife Conservation Series No. 4. BirdLife International, Cambridge, U.K.

COLORADO RIVER WATER USERS ASSOCIATION. 2002. http://crwua.mwd.dst.ca.us/nv/crwua_nv.htm

COLYN, M., A. GAUTIER-HION, and W. VERHEYEN. 1991. A re-appraisal of palaeoenvironmental history in Central Africa: Evidence for a major fluvial refuge in the Zaire Basin. *Journal of Biogeography* 18:403-407.

COMBÈS, I. 1999. Arakae: Historia de las comunidades Izoceñas. Santa Cruz, Bolivia: Kaa-Iya Project, Capitanía del Alto y Bajo Izozog/Wildlife Conservation Society-Bolivia.

CONABIO. 2002. *Regiones terrestres prioritarias de México*. www.conabio.gob.mx/rtp/regiones_terrestres_prioritarias.html

CONNIFF, R. 1999. Africa's wild dogs. *National Geographic* 195:36-63.

CONSERVATION INTERNATIONAL. 1990a. *The Rain Forest Imperative*. Conservation International, Washington, D.C.

CONSERVATION INTERNATIONAL. 1990b. *Biodiversity at Risk*. Map produced by Conservation International, Washington, D.C.

CONSERVATION INTERNATIONAL. 1991. *Workshop-90, Biological Priorities for Conservation in Amazonia*. Map, scale 1:5.000.000. Legend by A.B. RYLANDS, O. HUBER, and K.S. BROWN Jr. Instituto Brasileiro do Meio-Ambiente e dos Recursos Naturais Renováveis (IBAMA), Brasília; Instituto Nacional de Pesquisas da Amazônia (INPA), Manaus; and Conservation International, Washington, D.C.

CONSERVATION INTERNATIONAL. 1998. Botswana rolls back fences for wildlife. *CI News from the Front* 3:3.

CONSERVATION INTERNATIONAL. 2000a. *The Okavango River Basin: A Biological Corridor Strategy*. March, 2000. Typescript prepared by the CI Okavango Program staff and the CI/DC Monitoring and Evaluation Team.

CONSERVATION INTERNATIONAL. 2000b. *A Rapid Aquatic Biological Program (AQUARAP) for the Okavango Delta*. Conservation International-Botswana Program.

CONSERVATION INTERNATIONAL 2000c. *Designing Sustainable Landscapes. The Brazilian Atlantic Forest*. Center for Applied Biodiversity Science (CABS/CI) and Institute for Social and Environmental Studies of Southern Bahia (IESB), Washington, D.C.

CONSERVATION INTERNATIONAL. 2002. *Zero Biodiversity Loss*. Conservation International, Washington, D.C.

CONVEY, P. 2001. Antarctic ecosystems. In: S.A. LEVIN (Ed.). *Encyclopedia of Biodiversity*, Vol. 1. Academic Press, London, pp. 171-184.

COOKE, C.K. 1969. *Rock Art of Southern Africa*. Books of Africa, Cape Town.

COOPER, T.G. (Ed.). 1996. *Proceedings of the Wilderness Management Symposium, Waterberg Plateau, Namibia*. Hosted by the Ministry of Environment and Tourism.

COSTA, M. de F. 1999. *Historia de um Pais Inexistente. O Pantanal entre os Seculos XXVI e XXIII*. Editora Kosmos, Rio de Janeiro.

COTTERILL, F.P.D. 2000. Reduncine antelope of the Zambezi Basin. In: J.R. TIMBERLAKE (Ed.). *Biodiversity of the Zambezi Basin Wetlands*, Vol. II. Consultancy Report for IUCN ROSA. Biodiversity Foundation for Africa, Bulawayo, and Zambezi Society, Harare, pp. 145-199.

COVENEY, J. 1993. *Australia's Conservation Reserves*. Cambridge University Press, Cambridge, U.K.

CRAIGHEAD Jr., F.C. 1979. *Track of the Grizzly*. Sierra Club Books, San Francisco.

CROSBY, H.W. 2000. *The Cave Paintings of Baja California: Discovering the Great Murals of an Unknown People*. Sunbelt Natural History Books, Sunbelt Publications, San Diego.

CROWLEY, G.M. and S.T. GARNETT. 1999. Vegetation change in the grasslands and grassy woodlands of east-central Cape York Peninsula. *Pacific Conservation Biology* 4:132-148.

CROWLEY, G.M. and S.T. GARNETT. 2000. Changing fire management in the pastoral lands of Cape York Peninsula of northeast Australia, 1623-1996. *Australian Geographical Studies* 38:10-26.

CRUZ, F.B., M.G. PEROTTI, and L.A. FITZGERALD. 1992. Lista de anfibios y reptiles colectados en una localidad del Chaco salteño. *Acta Zoológica Lilloana* 42(1):101-107.

CUMMING, D.H.M. 1999. *Study on the Development of Transboundary Natural Resource Management Areas in Southern Africa -Environmental Context.* Biodiversity Support Program, Washington, D.C.

CUMMING, D.H.M., R.F. du TOIT, and S.N. STUART. 1990. *African Elephants and Rhinos: Status Survey and Conservation Action Plan.* International Union for the Conservation of Nature and Natural Resources, Gland, Switzerland.

DA FONSECA, G.A.B., G. HERRMANN, and Y.L.R. LEITE. 1999. Macrogeography of Brazilian mammals. In: J.F. EISENBERG and K.H. REDFORD (Eds.). *Mammals of the Neotropics: The Central Neotropics.* Volume 3: *Ecuador, Peru, Bolivia, Brazil.* University of Chicago Press, Chicago, pp. 549-581.

DAHL, K. 1897. Biological notes on north Australian mammalia. *Zoologist,* Series 4(1):189-216.

DARLINGTON, D. 1996. *The Mojave: Portrait of the Definitive American Desert.* Henry Holt and Company, New York.

DA SILVA, M.N.F., A.B. RYLANDS, and J.L. PATTON. 2001. Biogeografia e conservação da mastofauna na floresta amazônica brasileira. In: A. VERÍSSIMO, A. MOREIRA, D. SAWYER, I. dos SANTOS, L.P. PINTO, and J.P.R. CAPOBIANCO (Eds.). *Biodiversidade na Amazônia Brasileira: Avaliação e Ações Prioritárias para a Conservação, Uso Sustentável e Repartição de Benefícios.* Instituto Socioambiental, Estação Liberdade, São Paulo, pp. 110-131.

DAVIES, T.H. and J.H. McADAM. 1989. *Wildflowers of the Falkland Islands.* Falkland Island Trust.

DAVIS, F.W., D.M. STOMS, A.D. HOLLANDER, K.A. THOMAS, P.A. STINE, D. ODION, M.I. BORCHERT, J.H. THORNE, M.V. GRAY, R.E. WALKER, K. WARNER, and J. GRAAE. 1998. *The California Gap Analysis Project -Final Report.* University of California, Santa Barbara. www.biogeog.ucsb.edu/projects/gap/gap_rep.html

DAVIS, S.D., V.H. HEYWOOD, and A.C. HAMILTON (Eds.). 1994. *Centres of Plant Diversity. A Guide and Strategy for Their Conservation.* Volume 1: *Europe, Africa, South West Asia and the Middle East.* WWF-UK and IUCN, Gland, Switzerland.

DAVIS, S.D., V.H. HEYWOOD, and A.C. HAMILTON (Eds.). 1995. *Centres of Plant Diversity. A Guide and Strategy for Their Conservation.* Volume 2: *Asia, Australasia and the Pacific.* IUCN Publications Unit, Cambridge, U.K.

DAVIS, S.D., V.H. HEYWOOD, O. HERRERA-MACBRYDE, J. VILLA-LOBOS, and A.C. HAMILTON (Eds.). 1997. *Centres of Plant Diversity: A Guide and Strategy for Their Conservation,* Volume 3: *The Americas.* WWF (World Wildlife Fund for Nature) and IUCN (The World Conservation Union). IUCN Publications Unit, Cambridge, U.K.

DAVIS, W. 2002. *Light at the Edge of the World: A Journey through the Realm of Vanishing Cultures.* National Geographic Books, Washington, D.C.

DAY, D. 1989. *Vanishing Species.* Gallery Books, New York.

DAY, L. and F. ODENDAAL. 1998. *Last Edens of Africa.* Southern Book Publishers, Halfway House.

DE LAGUNA, F. 1990. Eyak. In: W. SUTTLES (Ed.). *Northwest Coast,* Volume 7: *Handbook of North American Indians.* Smithsonian Institution, Washington, D.C., pp. 189-196.

DE MARET, P. 1995. Pits, pots, and the far-west streams. In: J.E.G. SUTTON (Ed.). *The Growth of Farming Communities in Africa from the Equator Southwards,* Vol. Azania XXIX-XXX. London, The British Institute in Eastern Africa, pp. 318-323.

DE MARTONNE, E. 1926. Areisme et indice d'aridite. *Computes Rendus l'Academie des Sciences Paris* 182:1395-1398. In English: Regions of Interior Basin Drainage. *Geographical Review* 17:397-414 (1927).

DE VILLIERS, B. 1999. *Land Claims and National Parks -The Makuleke Experience.* HSRC Publishers, Pretoria, South Africa.

DEDINA, S. 2000. *Saving the Gray Whale. People, Politics, and Conservation in Baja California.* University of Arizona Press, Tucson.

DEFENDERS OF WILDLIFE. 2002. Arctic National Wildlife Refuge. www.defenders.org/wildlife/arctic/arissue.html

DEGEN, R. and F. MERELES. 1996. *Check-list de las plantas colectadas en el Chaco Boreal, Paraguay. Rojasiana* 3:1-176.

DEL BARCO, M. 1768. *Correcciones y adiciones a la historia o noticia de la California en su primera edición de Madrid, año de 1757* (edited by M. León-Portilla under the title, *Historia natural y crónica de la antigua California.* Universidad Nacional Autónoma de México, Instituto de Investigaciones Históricas, 1988, Mexico City).

DELOACH, C.J., R.I. CARRUTHERS, J.E. LOVICH, T.L. DUDLEY, and S.D. SMITH. 2000. Ecological interactions in the biological control of saltcedar (*Tamarix* spp.) in the United States: Toward a new understanding. In: N.R. SPENCER (Ed.). *Proceedings of the X International Symposium on Biological Control of Weeds.* July, 1999, Montana State University, Bozeman, pp. 819-873.

DEMASTER, D.P. and I. STIRLING. 1981. *Ursus maritimus* (Polar bear). *Mammalian Species* No. 145:1-7.

DENNY, P. 1991. Africa. In: M. FINLAYSON and M. MOSER (Eds.). *Wetlands.* International Waterfowl and Wetlands Research Bureau. Facts on File, Oxford, U.K., pp. 115-148.

DESPAIN, D., D. HOUSTON, M. MAEGHER, and P. SCHULLERY. 1986. *Wildlife in Transition: Man and Nature on Yellowstone's Northern Range.* Roberts Rinehart, Inc., Boulder, Colorado.

DILLON, M.O. 1997. Lomas Formations-Peru. In: S.D. DAVIS, V.H. HEYWOOD, O. HERRERA-MacBRYDE, J. VILLA-LOBOS, and A.C. HAMILTON (Eds.). *Centres of Plant Diversity. A Guide and Strategy for their Conservation.* WWF, Information Press, Oxford, U.K., pp. 519-527.

DILLON, M.O. and A.E. HOFFMANN Jr. 1997. *Lomas Formations of the Atacama Desert, Northern Chile.* In: S.D. DAVIS, V.H. HEYWOOD, O. HERRERA-MacBRYDE, J. VILLA-LOBOS and A.C. HAMILTON (Eds.). *Centres of Plant Diversity. A Guide and Strategy for their Conservation.* WWF, Information Press, Oxford, U.K., pp. 528-535.

DILLON, M.O. and P.W. RUNDEL. 1990. The botanical response of the Atacama and Peruvian Desert flora to the 1982-1983 El Niño Event. In: P.W. GLYNN (Ed.). *Global Ecological Consequences of the 1982-1983 El Niño-Southern Oscillation,* Elsevier, Amsterdam and New York, pp. 487-504.

DINERSTEIN, E., D.M. OLSON, D.J. GRAHAM, A.L. WEBSTER, S.A. PRIMM, M.P. BOOKBINDER, and G. LEDEC. 1995. *A Conservation Assessment of the Terrestrial Ecoregions of Latin America and the Carribbean.* World Wildlife Fund-U.S., The World Bank, Washington, D.C.

DIRECTION REGIONALE DE L'ENVIRONNEMENT. 2000. *Schema de Service Collectifs des Espaces Naturels et Ruraux, Contribution de la Guyane, Premier Document.* Republique Française, Prefecture de la Region Guyane.

DISCOVER LIFE. 2002. www.discoverlife.org

DOS SANTOS, B.A.1983. *Amazônia: Potencial Mineral e Perspectivas de Desenvolvimento.* T.A. Queiroz, Editor, Ltda., São Paulo.

DOWSETT-LEMAIRE, F. 1995. *Contribution à L'étude de la Végétation Forestière du Parc National d'Odzala (Congo).* Agreco-CTFT.

DPNVS. 1999. *1065 motivos iniciales para proteger el Parque Nacional Defensores del Chaco: evaluación ecológica rápida.* Asunción, Dirección de Parques Nacionales y Vida Silvestre, DeSdelChaco, The Nature Conservancy, and the United States Agency for International Development.

DUCKE, A. and G.A. BLACK. 1953. Phytogeographical notes on the Brazilian Amazon. *Anais da Academia Brasileira de Ciências* 25(1):1-46.

DUDLEY, C.J. 2000. Freshwater molluscs of the Zambezi River Basin. In: J.R. TIMBERLAKE (Ed.). *Biodiversity of the Zambezi Basin Wetlands,* Vol. II. Consultancy Report for IUCN ROSA. Biodiversity Foundation for Africa, Bulawayo, and Zambezi Society, Harare, pp. 487-526.

DUELLMAN, W.E. 1982. Quaternary climatic ecological fluctuations in the lowland tropics: Frogs and forests. In: G.T. PRANCE (Ed.). *Biological Diversification in the Tropics.* Columbia University Press, New York, pp. 389-402.

DUELLMAN, W.E. (Ed.). 1999. *Patterns of Distribution of Amphibians: A Global Perspective.* The Johns Hopkins University Press, Baltimore.

DUELLMAN, W.E. and S.S. SWEET. 1999. Distribution patterns of amphibians in the Nearctic region of North America. In: W.E. DUELLMAN (Ed.). *Patterns of Distribution of Amphibians: A Global Perspective.* Johns Hopkins University Press, Baltimore, pp. 31-109.

DUFFY, D.C. and A.J. MEIER. 1992. Do Appalachian herbaceous understories ever recover from clearcutting? *Conservation Biology* 6:196-201.

DUFFY, R. 2000. *Killing for Conservation. Wildlife Policy in Zimbabwe.* James Currey, Oxford, U.K.

ECOTRUST, PACIFIC GIS, and CONSERVATION INTERNATIONAL. 1995. *The Rain Forests of Home: An Atlas of People and Places,* Part 1: *Natural Forests and Native Languages of the Coastal Temperate Rain Forest.* Portland, Oregon.

EHRLICH, P.R., D.S. DOBKIN, and D. WHEYE. 1992. *Birds in Jeopardy: The Imperiled and Extinct Birds of the United States and Canada.* Stanford University Press, California.

EISENBERG, J.F. 1989. *Mammals of the Neotropics: The Northern Neotropics.* Volume 1: *Panama, Colombia, Venezuela, Guyana, Suriname, French Guiana.* University of Chicago Press, Chicago.

EISENBERG, J.F. and J.R. POLISAR. 1999. The mammals of North-Central Venezuela. *Bulletin of the Florida Museum of Natural History* 42:115-160.

EISENBERG, J.F. and K.H. REDFORD. 1999. *Mammals of the Neotropics.* Volume 3: *The Central Neotropics: Ecuador, Peru, Bolivia, Brazil.* University of Chicago Press, Chicago.

ELIOT, J.L. 1993. Kodiak: Alaska's island refuge. *National Geographic* 184(5):34-59.

ELLENBERG, H. 1959. Über den Wasserhaushalt tropischer nebeloasen an der Küstenwüste Perus. *Berichte Geobotanische Forschung des Institut Rübel* 1958:47-74.

ELLIOT, A. 1992. Family Balaenicipitidae (shoebill). In: J. del HOYO, A. ELLIOT, and J. SARGATAL (Eds.). *Handbook of Birds of the World,* Vol. 1. Lynx Edicions, Barcelona, pp. 466-471.

ELLIS, D.H., G.F. GEE, and C.M. MIRANDE (Eds.). 1996. *Cranes: Their Biology, Husbandry, and Conservation.* U.S. Department of the Interior, National Biological Service, Washington, D.C., and International Crane Foundation, Baraboo, Wisconsin.

ELLIS, W.S. and E. KRISTOF. 1971. North Slope: Will Alaska's oil and tundra mix? *National Geographic* 140(4):485-517.

ELOFF, J.H. 1966. *Verslag van werk by Makahane, noord van Punda Milia.* Unpublished report. University of Pretoria.

ELOFF, J.H. 1990a. Toe die Laeveld nog woes en leeg was. In: U. de V. PIENAAR (Ed.). *Neem uit die verlede.* South African National Parks, Pretoria.

ELOFF, J.H. 1990b. Swart indringing en kolonisasie in die Laeveld. In: U. de V. PIENAAR (Ed.). *Neem uit die verlede.* South African National Parks, Pretoria.

ENGEL, F. 1973. New facts about Pre-Columbian life in the Andean Lomas. *Current Anthropology* 14:271-280.

ENRIGHT, N.J. 1982. The Araucaria forests of New Guinea. In: J. GRESSITT (Ed.). *Biogeography and Ecology of New Guinea,* Vol. I. W. Junk, The Hague.

ENVIRONMENT AUSTRALIA. 2002a. Collaborative Australian Protected Area Database 1999. www.ea.gov.au/parks/nrs/protarea

ENVIRONMENT AUSTRALIA. 2002b. Indigenous Protected Areas. www.ea.gov.au/indigenous/fact-sheets

ERWIN, T.L. 1983. Beetles and other insects of tropical forest canopies at Manaus, Brazil, sampled by insecticidal fogging. In: S.L. SUTTON, T.C. WHITMORE, and A.C. CHADWICK (Eds.). *Tropical Rain Forest: Ecology and Management.* Blackwell Scientific Publications, Oxford, pp. 59-75.

ERWIN, T.L. 1988. The tropical forest canopy: The heart of biotic diversity. In: E.O. WILSON and F.M. PETER (Eds.). *Biodiversity.* National Academy Press, Washington, D.C., pp. 123-129.

ERWIN, T.L. and J. ADIS. 1982. Amazonian inundation forests: Their role as short-term refuges and generators of species richness and taxon pulses. In: G.T. PRANCE (Ed.). *Biological Diversification in the Tropics.* Columbia University Press, New York, pp. 358-371.

ESTES, R.D. 1991. *The Behavior Guide to African Mammals.* University of California Press, Berkeley.

ESTES, R.D. 1993. *The Safari Companion: A Guide to Watching African Mammals.* Chelsea Green, White River Junction, Vermont.

ETHNIES. 1985. La question amerindienne en Guyana Française. *Ethnies* (Survival International France) 1 (1-2).

ETNIER, D.L. 1999. Jeopardized southeastern freshwater fishes: A search for causes. In: G. BENZ and D. COLLINS (Eds.). *Aquatic Fauna in Peril: The Southeastern Perspective.* Southeast Aquatic Research Institute Special Publication I, Cohutta, Georgia.

EVANS, M.I. (Ed.). 1994. *Important Bird Areas in the Middle East.* BirdLife International, Cambridge, U.K.

EVRARD, C. 1968. *Recherches écologiques sur le peuplement forestier des sols hydromorphes de la Cuvette Centrale congolaise, ONRD.* Institut National pour l'Etude Agronomique du Congo Belge, Brussels.

EZCURRA, E. 1984. Planning a system of Biosphere Reserves in Mexico. In: *Proceedings of the First International Biosphere Reserve Congress, Minsk, Byelorussia, U.R.S.S.* UNESCO-UNEP, Vol. I, Part One, pp. 85-92.

EZCURRA, E. and C. MONTAÑA. 1990. Los recursos naturales renovables en el norte árido de México. In: E. LEFF (Ed.). *Medio ambiente y desarrollo en México.* Miguel Ángel Porrúa Editores, Mexico. Vol. 1, pp. 297-327.

FANSHAWE, J.H., J.R. GINSBERG, C. SILLERO-ZUBIRI, and R. WOODROFFE. 1997. The status and distribution of remaining wild dog populations. In: R. WOODROFFE, J.R. GINSBERG, D.W. MacDONALD, and IUCN/SSC CANID SPECIALIST GROUP (Eds.) *The African Wild Dog: Status Survey and Action Plan.* IUCN, Gland, Switzerland, pp. 11-57.

FANY, R. 2001. Terras Indigenas na Amazonia Legal. In: A. VERÍSSIMO, A. MOREIRA, D. SAWYER, I. dos SANTOS, L.P. PINTO, and J.P.R. CAPOBIANCO (Eds.). *Biodiversidade na Amazônia Brasileira: Avaliação e Ações Prioritárias para a Conservação, Uso Sustentável e Repartição de Benefícios.* Instituto Socioambiental, Estação Liberdade, São Paulo, pp. 251-258.

FAO and UNEP. 1985. *Un sistema de áreas silvestres protegidas para el Gran Chaco. Proyecto FAO y PNUMA FP 6105-85-01, Documento Técnico No. 1.* FAO, Santiago, Chile.

FAY, F.H., B.P. KELLY, and J.L. SEASE. 1989. Managing the exploitation of Pacific walruses: A tragedy of delayed response and poor communication. *Marine Mammal Science* 5:1-16.

FAY, J.M. 1997. The ecology, social organization, populations, habitat, and history of the western lowland gorilla (*Gorilla gorilla gorilla;* Savage and Wyman, 1847). Ph.D. Thesis,

Washington University, St. Louis, Missouri, Univ. Microfilms.

FEARNSIDE, P.M. 1985. Environmental change and deforestation in the Brazilian Amazon. In: J. HEMMING (Ed.). *Change in the Amazon Basin: Man's Impact on Forests and Rivers.* Manchester University Press, Manchester, U.K., pp. 70-89.

FEARNSIDE, P.M. 1989. Brazil's Balbina Dam: Environment versus the legacy of the pharaohs in Amazonia. *Environmental Management* 13:401-423.

FEARNSIDE, P.M. 1990. Predominant land uses in Brazilian Amazonia. In: A.B. ANDERSON (Ed.), *Alternatives to Deforestation: Steps Toward Sustainable Use of the Amazon Rain Forest.* Columbia University Press, New York, pp. 233-251.

FEARNSIDE, P.M. 1995. Hydroelectric dams in the Brazilian Amazon as sources of "greenhouse" gases. *Environmental Conservation* 22:7-19.

FEARNSIDE, P.M. 2001. Soybean cultivation as a threat to the environment in Brazil. *Environmental Conservation* 28:23-38.

FELGER, R.S. 2000. *Flora of the Gran Desierto and Rio Colorado Delta.* Southwest Center Series, University of Arizona Press, Tucson.

FERNANDES, A. and P. BEZERRA. 1990. *Estudo Fitogeográfico do Brasil.* Stylus Comunicações, Fortaleza.

FERREIRA, L.V., R.M. LEMOS de SÁ, R. BUSCHBACHER, G. BATMANIAN, J.M.C. da SILVA, M.B. ARRUDA, E. MORETTI, L.F.S.N. de SÁ, J. FALCOMER, and M.I. BAMPI. 2001. Identificação de áreas prioritárias para a conservação da biodiversidade por meio da representatividade das unidades de conservação e tipos de vegetação nas ecorregiões da Amazônia brasileira. In: A. VERÍSSIMO, A. MOREIRA, D. SAWYER, I. dos SANTOS, L.P. PINTO, and J.P.R. CAPOBIANCO (Eds.). *Biodiversidade na Amazônia Brasileira: Avaliação e Ações Prioritárias para a Conservação, Uso Sustentável e Repartição de Benefícios.* Instituto Socioambiental, Estação Liberdade, São Paulo, pp. 268-286.

FISHER Jr., A.C. 1972. African wildlife: Man's threatened legacy. *National Geographic* 141(2):147-186.

FISHPOOL, L.D.C. and M.I. EVANS (Eds.). 2001. *Important Bird Areas in Africa and Associated Islands: Priority Sites for Conservation.* Pisces Publications and BirdLife International (BirdLife Conservation Series No. 11), Newbury and Cambridge.

FITTKAU, E.J. 1971. Ökologische Gliederung des Amazonasgebietes auf geochechemischer Grundlage. *Münster Forschungsbericht Geologisch-Paläontologisches* 20-21:35-50.

FITTKAU, E.J. 1974. Zur ökologischen Gliederung Amazoniens. I. Die erdgeschichtliche Entwicklung Amazoniens. *Amazoniana* 5:77-134.

FITZGERALD, L.A., J.M. CHANI, and O.E. DONADIO. 1991. *Tupinambis* lizards in Argentina: Implementing management of a traditionally exploited resource. In: J.G. ROBINSON and K.H. REDFORD (Eds.). *Neotropical Wildlife Use and Conservation.* University of Chicago Press, Chicago, pp. 303-316.

FITZGERALD, L.A., F.B. CRUZ, and G. PEROTTI. 1999. Phenology of a lizard assemblage in the dry Chaco of Argentina. *Journal of Herpetology* 33(4):526-535.

FITZHUGH, W.W. 1988. Eskimos: Hunters of the frozen coasts. In: W.W. FITZHUGH and A. CROWELL (Eds.). *Crossroads of Continents: Cultures of Siberia and Alaska.* Smithsonian Institution Press, Washington, D.C., pp. 42-51.

FITZHUGH, W.W. and A. CROWELL. 1988a. *Crossroads of Continents: Cultures of Siberia and Alaska.* Smithsonian Institution Press, Washington, D.C.

FITZHUGH, W.W. and A. CROWELL. 1988b. *Crossroads of continents: Beringian oecumene.* In: W.W. FITZHUGH and A. CROWELL (Eds.). *Crossroads of Continents: Cultures of Siberia and Alaska.* Smithsonian Institution Press, Washington, D.C., pp. 9-16.

FITZPATRICK, M. 2000. Review of Odonata associated with the wetlands of the Zambezi Basin. In: J.R. TIMBERLAKE (Ed.). *Biodiversity of the Zambezi Basin Wetlands,* Vol. II. Consultancy Report for IUCN ROSA. Biodiversity Foundation for Africa, Bulawayo, and Zambezi Society, Harare, pp. 527-564.

FLANNERY, T.F., R. MARTIN, and A. SZALAY. 1996. *Tree Kangaroos: A Curious Natural History.* Reed, Port Melbourne, Victoria.

FLEAGLE, J.G. and R.A MITTERMEIER. 1980. Locomotor behavior, body size, and comparative ecology of seven Suriname monkeys. *American Journal of Physical Anthropology* 52:301-314.

FLEGG, J. 1990. *Poles Apart: The Natural Worlds of the Arctic and Antarctic.* Pelham Books, London.

FLEGG, J. 1993. *Deserts: A Miracle of Life.* Blandford, London.

FLEMING, L.V., A.C. NEWTON, J.A. VICKERY, and M.B. USHER (Eds.). 1997. *Biodiversity in Scotland: Status Trends and Initiatives.* The Stationary Office, Edinburgh, U.K.

FLORES VILLELA, O. 1995. Herpetofauna mexicana. *Special Publications, Carnegie Museum of Natural History* 17:1-73.

FOREST ACTION NETWORK. 2002. Great Bear Rainforest Campaign Overview. www.fanweb.org/overview.htm

FORSTER, R.R. 1962. Insects in Macquarie Island. Araneida (spiders). *Pacific Insects* 4(4):917-929.

FOSTER, R.B., T.A. PARKER III, A.H. GENTRY, L.H. EMMONS, A. CHICCHÓN, T. SCHULENBERG, L. RODRÍGUEZ, G. LAMAS, H. ORTEGA, O. ICOCHEA, W. WEST, M. ROMO, J.A. CASTILLO, O. PHILLIPS, C. REYNOL, A. KRATTER, P.K. DONAHUE, and L.J. BARKLEY. 1994. *The Tambopata-Candamo-Río Heath Region of Southeastern Peru: A Biological Assessment*. Conservation International.

FRADKIN, P.L. 1984. *A River No More: The Colorado River and the West*. University of Arizona Press, Tucson.

FRANKLIN, W.L. 1982. Biology, ecology, and relationship of man to the South American camelids. In: M.A. MARES and H.H. GENOWAYS (Eds.). *Mammalian Biology in South America,* Volume 6. Special Publication Series, Pymatuning Laboratory of Ecology. University of Pittsburgh, Pittsburgh, pp. 457-489.

FREITAG, H. 1986. Notes on the distribution, climate, and flora of the sand deserts of Iran and Afghanistan. *Proceedings of the Royal Society of Edinburgh B (Biological Sciences)* 89:135-146.

FRITZ, S.M. 2001. *Mapping and Modelling of Wild Land Areas in Europe and Great Britain: A Multi-scale Approach.* Ph.D. Thesis, School of Geography, University of Leeds, U.K.

FROST, P.G.H. 1996. The ecology of Miombo woodlands. In: B. CAMPBELL (Ed.). *The Miombo in Transition: Woodlands and Welfare in Africa*. CIFOR, Bogor, pp. 11-57.

FRYXELL, J.M. and A.R.E. SINCLAIR. 1988. Seasonal migration by white-eared kob in relation to resources. *African Journal of Ecology* 26:17-32.

FUNDACIÓN PUERTO RASTROJO. 2001. *Atlas de la Amazonia Colombiana*. CD-ROM Database. Bogotá.

GALLARDO, J.M. 1979. Composición, distribución y origen de la herpetofauna chaqueña. In: W.E. DUELLMAN (Ed.). *The South American Herpetofauna: Its Origin, Evolution, and Dispersal.* Monograph No. 7, Museum of Natural History, University of Kansas, pp. 299-307.

GAMBELL, R. 1985. Birds and mammals -Antarctic whales. In: W.N. BONNER and D.W.H. WALTON (Eds.). *Key Environments -Antarctic.* Pergamon Press, Oxford, pp. 223-241.

GANDINI, P., P.D. BOERSMA, E. FRERE, M. GANDINI, T. HOLIK, and V. LICHTSCHEIN. 1994. Magellanic penguins (*Spheniscus magellanicus*) affected by chronic petroleum pollution along coast of Chubut, Argentina. *Auk* 111(1): 20-27.

GARDINER, A. 2000. Review of wetland Lepidoptera of the Zambezi Basin. In: J.R. TIMBERLAKE (Ed.). *Biodiversity of the Zambezi Basin Wetlands*, Vol. II. Consultancy Report for IUCN ROSA. Biodiversity Foundation for Africa, Bulawayo, and Zambezi Society, Harare, pp. 565-612.

GARGETT, V. 1990. *The Black Eagle.* Acorn Books and Russel Friedman Books, Randburg and Halfway House, South Africa.

GARNETT, S.T. and G.M. CROWLEY. 1999. *Golden-shouldered Parrot Recovery Plan 1999-2000.* Environment Australia, Canberra.

GASKI, A.L. and G. HEMLEY. 1988. The ups and downs of the crocodilian skin trade. *Traffic (U.S.A.)* 8(1):5-16.

GAUTIER, E.F. 1935. *Sahara: The Great Desert*. Columbia University Press, New York.

GEHLBACH, F.R. 1993. *Mountain Islands and Desert Seas.* Texas A&M University Press, College Station, Texas.

GENTRY, A.H. 1986. Endemism in tropical versus temperate plant communities. In: M.E. SOULÉ (Ed.). *Conservation Biology*. Sinauer Press, Sunderland, Massachusetts, pp. 153-181.

GENTRY, A.H. 1988. Tree species richness of Upper Amazonian forests. *Proceedings of the National Academy of Sciences* 85:156.

GENTRY, H.S. 1982. *Agaves of Continental North America.* The University of Arizona Press, Tucson.

GEORGES, A. and M. ROSE. 1993. Conservation biology of the pig-nosed turtle. *Chelonian Conservation and Biology* 1:3-12.

GERTENBACH, W.P.D. 1983. Landscapes of the Kruger National Park. *Koedoe* 26:9-122.

GÉRY, J. 1984. The fishes of Amazonia. In: H. SIOLI (Ed.). *The Amazon. Limnology and Landscape Ecology of a Mighty Tropical River and Its Basin.* Dr. W. Junk Publishers, Dordrecht, pp. 353-370.

GLAW, F. and J. KÖHLER. 1998. Amphibian species diversity exceeds that of mammals. *Herpetological Review* 29(1):11-12.

GOETTSCH, B. 2001. Diversidad beta e índices de similitud entre comunidades de cactáceas en el Desierto Chihuahuense. Tesis de Licenciatura. Facultad de Ciencias, Universidad Nacional Autónoma de México. Mexico City.

GOLDAMMER, J.G. 1999. Forests on fire. *Science* 284:1782-1783.

GÓMEZ-HINOSTROSA, C. and H.M. HERNÁNDEZ. 2000. Diversity, geographical distribution, and conservation of Cactaceae in the Mier y Noriega region, Mexico. *Biodiversity and Conservation* 9:403-418.

GOODLAND, R.J.A. and H.S. IRWIN. 1975. *Amazon Jungle: Green Hell to Red Desert.* Elsevier Scientific Publishing Co., Amsterdam.

GOODWIN, W. 2001. 2000 Black eagle survey. *Honeyguide* 47:107-108.

GOPAL, B. 2001. Holy Ganga and the mighty Amazon. *Amazoniana* 16:337-348.

GOUGH, B. 1997. *First Across the Continent: Sir Alexander MacKenzie*. University of Oklahoma Press, Norman.

GOULDING, M. 1980. *The Fishes and the Forest: Explorations in Amazonian Natural History*. University of California Press, Berkeley.

GOULDING, M., M. LEAL CARVALHO, and E.G. FERREIRA. 1988. *Rio Negro: Rich Life in Poor Water*. SPB Academic Publishing, The Hague.

GRALL, G. 1995. Cuatro Ciénagas. Mexico's Desert Aquarium. *National Geographic Magazine* 188(4):84-97.

GRAY, B. 1975. Size-composition and regeneration of Araucaria stands in New Guinea. *Journal of Ecology* 63:273-289.

GRAYSON, D.K. 1993. *The Desert's Past: A Natural Prehistory of the Great Basin*. Smithsonian Institution Press, Washington, D.C.

GREENE, H.W. and C.A. LUKE. 1996b. Reptile and amphibian diversity. In: C. LUKE, J. ANDRÉ, and M. HERRING (Eds.). *Proceedings of the East Mojave Desert Symposium, 7-8 November 1992, University of California, Riverside.* Technical Reports, Natural History Museum of Los Angeles County, 10, pp. 53-58.

GREENWAY Jr., J.C. 1958. *Extinct and Vanishing Birds of the World.* American Committee for International Wildlife Protection, NewYork.

GRENAND, P. and F. GRENAND 2001. Les groupes humains. In: J. BARRET, *Atlas Illustré de la Guyane.* Centre d´Impression, Limoges, France, pp. 30-33.

GRESSITT, J.L. 1967. Entomology of Antarctica, Introduction. *Antarctic Research Series* 10:1-13.

GRESSITT, J.L. 1970. Subantarctic entomology and biogeography. *Pacific Insects Monographs* 23:295-374.

GRESSITT, J.L. (Ed.). 1982. *Biogeography and Ecology of New Guinea.* W. Junk Publishers, The Hague. 2 vols.

GRIFFIN, M. 1998a. The species diversity, distribution, and conservation of Namibian mammals. *Biodiversity and Conservation* 7(4):483-494.

GRIFFIN, R.E. 1998. Species richness and biogeography of non-acarine arachnids in Namibia. *Biodiversity and Conservation* 7(4):467-482.

GROOMBRIDGE, B. and M. JENKINS. 1998. *Freshwater Biodiversity: A Preliminary Global Assessment*. World Conservation Press, Cambridge, U.K.

GRUBOV, V.I. 1989. Endemismus in der Flora der Mongolei. *Erforschung biologischer Ressourcen der Mongolischen Volksrepublik* (Scientific reports of the Martin Luther University, Halle-Wittenberg) 6:87-90.

GRZIMEK, B. and M. 1959. *Serengeti Shall Not Die.* Collins, London, U.K.

GUERRERO, A.J. and A. ARAMBIZA. 2001. *Lista preliminar de las aves del P.N. Kaa-Iya del Gran Chaco e Izozog.* Santa Cruz, Bolivia: Kaa-Iya Project, Capitanía del Alto y Bajo Izozog/Wildlife Conservation Society-Bolivia.

GUILER, E. 1993. *The Tasmanian Tiger in Pictures.* St. David's Park Publishing, Hobart.

GUILLÉN, C. and J. BARRIO. 1994. Los pantanos de Villa y sus aves. *Boletín de Lima* 91-96:53-58.

GULLISON, T., M. MELNYK, and C. WONG. 2001. *Logging Off: Mechanisms to Stop or Prevent Industrial Logging in Forests of High Conservation Value.* Union of Concerned Scientists, Centre for Tropical Forest Science, Smithsonian Institution, Washington, D.C.

GÜNSTER, A. 1994. Retaining seeds. A winning or losing battle? *Veld and Flora* 80(4):113.

GURVICH, I.S. 1988. Ethnic connections across the Bering Strait. In: W.W. FITZHUGH and A. CROWELL (Eds.). *Crossroads of Continents: Cultures of Siberia and Alaska.* Smithsonian Institution Press, Washington, D.C., pp. 309-319.

GUTIÉRREZ, J.R., F. LÓPEZ-CORTÉS, and P.A. MARQUET. 1998. Vegetation in an altitudinal gradient along the Río Loa in the Atacama Desert of northern Chile. *Journal of Arid Environments* 40:383-399.

HAFFER, J. 1969. Speciation in Amazonian forest birds. *Science* 165:131-137.

HAFFER, J. 1987. Biogeography of Neotropical birds. In: T.C. WHITMORE and G.T. PRANCE (Eds.). *Biogeography and Quaternary History in Tropical America.* Clarendon Press, Oxford, pp. 105-150.

HAFFER, J. and G.T. PRANCE. 2001. Climatic forcing of evolution in Amazonia during the Cenozoic: On the refuge theory of biotic differentiation. *Amazoniana* 16(3/4): 579-607.

HAINES, F. 1970. *The Buffalo*. Thomas Y. Crowell Co., New York.

HALFFTER, G., P. REYES-CASTILLO, M.E. MAURY, S. GALLINA, and E. EZCURRA. 1981. La conservación del germoplasma: soluciones en México. *Folia Entomológica Mexicana* 46:29-64.

HALPIN, M.M. and M. SEGUIN. 1990. Tsimshian peoples: Southern Tsimshian, Coast Tsimshian, Nishga, and Gitksan. In: W. SUTTLES (Ed.). *Northwest Coast,* Volume 7: *Handbook of North American Indians*. Smithsonian Institution, Washington, D.C., pp. 267-284.

HAMILTON, S.K., S.J. SIPPEL, and J.M. MELACK. 1996. Inundation patterns in the Pantanal wetland of South America determined from passive microwave remote sensing. *Archiv fur Hydrobiologie* 137(1):1-23.

HANKS, J. 2000. The role of Transfrontier Conservation Areas in southern Africa in the conservation of mammalian biodiversity. In: A. ENTWISTLE and N. DUNSTONE (Eds.). *Priorities for the Conservation of Mammalian Biodiversity: Has the Panda Had Its Day?* Conservation Biology 3, Cambridge University Press, pp. 239-256.

HANKS, J. 2002. Transfrontier Conservation Areas (TFCAs) in southern Africa: Their role in conserving biodiversity, socioeconomic development, and promoting a culture of peace. *Journal of Sustainable Forestry* (in press).

HANNAH, L., D. LOHSE, C. HUTCHINSON, J.L. CARR, and A. LANKERANI. 1994. A preliminary inventory of human disturbance of world ecosystems. *Ambio* 23:246-250.

HANNAH, L., R.A. MITTERMEIER, K. ROSS, F. CASTRO, H. CASTRO, G. DODGE, R.B. MAST, and D.B. LEE. 1997. New threats to the Okavango Delta of Botswana. *Oryx* 31(2):86-89.

HANSEN, B. 2002. Colombia's environment, a casualty in U.S. war on drugs. *Environment News Service.* http://ens.lycos.com/ens/nov2000/2000L-11-20-15.html

HARDNER, J. and R. RICE. 2002. Rethinking green consumerism. *Scientific American,* May 2002, pp. 89-95.

HARDY, A.M. (Ed.). 2001. Terrestrial Protected Areas in Australia. *2000 Summary Statistics from the Collaborative Australian Protected Areas Database (CAPAD).* Environment Australia, Canberra.

HARE, J. 1997. The wild Bactrian camel *Camelus bactrianus ferus* in China: The need for action. *Oryx* 31:45-48.

HARRISON, C.J.O. 1986. The Saharo-Sindian arid zone birds. *Sandgrouse* 7:64-69.

HARRISON, D.L. and P.J.J. BATES. 1991. *The Mammals of Arabia.* Harrison Zoological Museum, Sevenoaks, U.K.

HARRISON, M.J.S. 1988. A new species of guenon (genus *Cercopithecus*) from Gabon. *Journal of Zoology* 215:561-575.

HARRISON, P. 1983. *Seabirds: An Identification Guide.* Croom Helm Ltd., Beckenham, U.K.

HART, J. and C. SIKUBWABO. 1994. *Exploration of the Maiko National Park of Zaire: 1989-1992. History, Environment, and the Distribution Status of Large Mammals.* Working Paper No. 2, Wildlife Conservation Society, New York.

HART, J. and J. HALL. 1996. Status of eastern Zaire's forest parks and reserves. *Conservation Biology* 10:316-327.

HART, J.A., R. HART, M. DECHAMPS, M. FOURNIER, and M. ATAHOLO. 1996. Changes in forest composition over the last 400 years in the Ituri Basin, Zaire. In: L.J.G. van der MASEN, X.M. van der BURGT, and J.M. van MEDENBACH DE ROOY (Eds.). The Biodiversity of African Plants. Proceedings XIVth AETFAT Congress, Wageningen, The Netherlands, Kluwer Academic Press, Dordrecht.

HART, J.A. and A. UPOKI. 1997. Distribution and conservation status of Congo peafowl *(Afropavo congensis)* in eastern Zaire. *Bird Conservation International* 7:295-316.

HARVEY, M.B., L. GONZÁLES, and G.J. SCROCCHI. 2001. New species of *Apostolepis* (Squamata: Columbridae) from the Gran Chaco of southern Bolivia. *Copeia* 2:501-507.

HAWTHORNE, W.D. and M. ABU JUAM. 1995. *Forest Protection in Ghana.* IUCN, Gland, Switzerland and Cambridge, U.K.

HAYDEN, J.D. and J.W. DYKINGA. 1998. *The Sierra Pinacate.* Southwest Center Series, University of Arizona Press, Tucson.

HAYES, F.E. 1995. *Status, Distribution, and Biogeography of the Birds of Paraguay.* American Birding Association, New York.

HECHT, S.B. 1982. Cattle ranching in the Amazon: Analysis of a development strategy. Ph.D. Dissertation, University of California, Berkley.

HEDIN, S. 1898. *Through Asia.* 2 vols. Methuen, London.

HEMAMI, M.R. and C.P. GROVES. 2001. Iran. In: D.P. MALLON and S.C. KINGSWOOD (Compilers). *Antelopes,* Part 4: *North Africa, the Middle East, and Asia. Global Survey and Regional Action Plans.* SSC Antelope Specialist Group. IUCN, Gland, Switzerland, pp. 114-118.

HENNING, D. and H. FLOHN. 1977. *Climate Aridity Index Map.* UN Conference on Desertification, UNEP, Nairobi, Kenya.

HENRICKSON, J. and M.C. JOHNSTON. 1986. Vegetation and community types of Chihuahuan Desert. In: C. BARLOW, A.M. POWELL, and B.N. TIMMERMANN (Eds.). *Second Symposium on Resources of the Chihuahuan Desert Region.* Allen Press, Lawrence, Kansas.

HEREFORD, R. and C. LONGPRÉ. 1999. Climate history of the Mojave Desert Region, 1892-1996, including data from 48 long-term weather stations and an overview of regional climate variation. www-wmc.wr.usgs.gov/mojave/climate-history/statimage.html

HERNÁNDEZ, C.J.I., M.E. ROMERO, H. SÁNCHEZ, and G. SARMIENTO. 1994. *Sabanas naturales de Colombia*. Banco de Occidente, Bogotá.

HERNÁNDEZ, H.M. and R.T. BÁRCENAS. 1994. Endangered cacti in the Chihuahuan Desert: I. Distribution patterns. *Conservation Biology* 9(5):1176-1188.

HERNÁNDEZ, H.M. and R.T. BÁRCENAS. 1995. Endangered cacti in the Chihuahuan Desert: II. Distribution patterns. *Conservation Biology* 10(4):1200-1209.

HERNÁNDEZ, H.M., C. GÓMEZ-HINOSTROSA, and R.T. BÁRCENAS. 2001. Diversity, spatial arrangement, and endemism of Cactaceae in the Huizache area, a hotspot in the Chihuahuan Desert. *Biodiversity and Conservation* 10:1097-1112.

HERSHKOVITZ, P. 1977. *Living New World Monkeys (Platyrrhini) with an Introduction to Primates,* Vol. 1. The University of Chicago Press, Chicago.

HERSHKOVITZ, P. 1983. Two new species of night monkeys, genus *Aotus* (Cebidae, Platyrrhini): A preliminary report on *Aotus* taxonomy. *American Journal of Primatology* 4:209-243.

HIDES, J.G. 1936. *Papuan Wonderland.* Blackie and Son Limited, London.

HIGGINS, G., L. CRONIN, and J. McDONALD. 1988. *Presenting Australia's National Parks.* Child and Associates, New South Wales, Australia.

HILLMAN, J.C. and J.M. FRYXELL. 1988. Sudan. In: *Antelopes Global Survey and Regional Action Plans,* Part 1: *East and Northeast Africa.* IUCN/SSC Antelope Specialist Group. Gland, Switzerland.

HILTON TAYLOR, C. (Compiler). 2000. *2000 IUCN Red List of Threatened Species.* IUCN/The World Conservation Union, Cambridge, U.K. (and CD-ROM).

HINRICHSEN, D. 1998. Wolves around the world. *Defenders of Wildlife* 73(4):6-13.

HOCHSCHILD, A. 1999. *King Leopold's Ghost: A Story of Greed, Terror, and Heroism in Colonial Africa.* Houghton Mifflin Company, Boston and New York.

HODGSON, B. 1976. The pipeline: Alaska's troubled colossus. *National Geographic* 150(5):684-717.

HODGSON, B. 1990. Alaska's big spill: Can the wilderness heal? *National Geographic* 177(1):5-43.

HODGSON, B. 1994. Buffalo: Back home on the range. *National Geographic* 186(5):64-89.

HODGSON, W.C. 2000. *Food Plants of the Sonoran Desert.* University of Arizona Press, Tucson.

HOFFMEISTER, D.F. 1986. *The Mammals of Arizona.* University of Arizona Press, Tucson.

HÖFT, R. 1992. *Plants of New Guinea and the Solomon Islands: Dictionary of the Genera and Families.* Wau Ecology Handbook No. 12. Wau Ecology Institute, Wau, Papua New Guinea.

HÖGBERG, P. and G.D. PIEARCE. 1986. Mycorrhizas of Zambian trees in relation to host taxonomy, vegetation communities, and successional patterns. *Journal of Ecology* 74:775-785.

HOOGHIEMSTRA, H. and T. van der HAMMEN. 1998. Neogen and Quaternary development of the Neotropical rain forest: The forest refugia hypothesis and a literature review. *Earth Science Reviews* 44:147-183.

HOOGMOED, M.S. 1969. Notes on the herpetofauna of Suriname III –A new species of *Dendrobates* (Amphibian Salientia, Dendrobatidae) from Suriname. *Zoologische Mededelingen* 44(9):133-141.

HOPKIRK, P. 1980. *Foreign Devils on the Silk Road.* John Murray, London.

HORNADAY, W.T. 1908. *Campfires on Desert and Lava.* Published again in 1985 by University of Arizona Press, Tucson.

HOWELL, P., M. LOCK, and S. COBB. 1988. *The Jongeli Canal: Impact and Opportunity.* Cambridge University Press.

HSUMD (Historical Society of the Upper Mojave Desert). 1996. www.maturango.org/Hist.html

HUBER, O. 1989. Shrublands of the Venezuelan Guayana. In: L.B. HOLM-NIELSEN, I.C. NIELSEN, and H. BASLEV (Eds.). *Tropical Forests: Botanical Dynamics, Speciation, and Diversity.* Academic Press, London, pp. 271-285.

HUBER, O. and C. ALARCÓN. 1988. *Mapa de vegetación de Venezuela,* 1:2,000,000. Ministerio del Ambiente y de los Recursos Naturales Renovables, Caracas, Venezuela.

HUECK, K. 1966. Die Walder Sudamerikas. Ökologie, Zussamensetzung und Wirtschaftliche Bedeutung. *Vegetationsmongraphien* Bd. II. Stuttgart.

HUECK, K. 1972. *As Florestas da América do Sul.* Polígono, São Paulo. (Translation of Hueck, 1966).

HUGHES, R. 1987. *The Fatal Shore: The Epic of Australia's Founding.* Alfred A. Knopf, New York.

HUGHES, R.H. and J.S. HUGHES. 1992. *A Directory of African Wetlands.* IUCN, Gland, Switzerland, and Cambridge, U.K.

HULME, D. and M. MURPHREE. 2001. *African Wildlife and Livelihoods. The Promise and Performance of Community Conservation.* James Currey, Oxford, U.K.

HUMBOLDT, A. von and A. BONPLAND (Eds.). 1811-1812. *Recueil d'observations de zoologie et d'anatomie comparée,*

faites dans l'Ocean Atlantique dans l'interieur du nouveau continent et dans la Mer du Sud pendant les années 1799, 1800, 1801, 1802 et 1803. Paris.
HUMMEL, M. 1984. *Arctic Wildlife.* Chartwell Books, Inc., Secaucus, New Jersey.
HUMPHREY, R.R. 1974. *The Boojum and Its Home.* University of Arizona Press, Tucson.
HUNTLEY, B.J. 1982. Southern African savannas. In: B.J. HUNTLEY and B.H. WALKER (Eds.). *Ecology of Tropical Savannas.* Springer-Verlag, Berlin, pp. 101-119.
HUYBREGTS, B., P. de WACHTER, L.S. NDONG-OBIANG, and M. AKOU. 2000. Forte baisse des populations de grands singes dans le massif forestier de Minkebe, au nord-est du Gabon. *Canopee* 8:12-15.
ICBP. 1992. *Putting Biodiversity on the Map.* International Council for Bird Preservation, Cambridge, U.K.
INDERENA (Instituto Nacional de los Recursos Naturales Renovables y del Medio Ambiente). 1989. *A Guide to the National Natural Parks System of Colombia*, Bogotá.
INEI (Instituto Nacional de Estadística e Informática). 1996. Proyecciones departamentales de la población 1995-2025. www.inei.gob.pe
INGWERSEN, F. 1995. Kakadu –Alligator Rivers Region, Northern Territory, Australia– CPD Site Au4. In: S.D. DAVIS, V.H. HEYWOOD, and A.C. HAMILTON (Eds.). *Centres of Plant Diversity. A Guide and Strategy for their Conservation.* Volume 2: *Asia, Australasia and the Pacific.* IUCN Publications Unit, Cambridge, U.K., pp. 471-475.
INPE (Instituto Nacional de Pesquisas Espaciais). 1996. *The Large-scale Biosphere-Atmosphere Experiment in Amazonia.* São Jose dos Campos, Brazil.
INPE. 2000. Monitoramento da floresta amazônica brasileira por satelite 1998-1999. FUNCATE, Instituto Nacional de Pesquisas Espaciais (INPE), São José dos Campos, Brazil.
INRENA. 1996. *Guía explicativa del mapa forestal 1995.* Ministerio de Agricultura, Lima.
INTRODUCED SPECIES SUMMARY PROJECT: Little fire ant (*Wasmannia auropunctata*) 2002. www.columbia.edu~jd363/JDB/invasion_bio/inv_spp_summ/Wasmannia_auropunctata.htm
IPCC (Inter-Governmental Panel on Climate Change). 2000. *IPCC Special Report on Land Use, Land Use Change, and Forestry.* Cambridge University Press, Cambridge, U.K.
IRVINE, J.R. and N.E. WEST. 1979. Riparian tree species distribution and succession along the lower Escalante River, Utah. *Southwestern Naturalist* 24:331-346.
IUCN/THE WORLD CONSERVATION UNION. 1992. *Protected Areas of the World:* Vol. 3: *Afrotropical.* IUCN, Gland, Switzerland, and Cambridge, U.K.
IUCN. 1995. *Paradise on Earth: The Natural World Heritage List.* JIDD Publishers and Harper McCrae Publishing, Patonga, Australia.
IUCN. 1997. *1997 United Nations List of Protected Areas.* IUCN, Gland, Switzerland.
JACHMANN, H. 1989. Food selection by elephants in the "miombo" biome, in relation to leaf chemistry. *Biochemical Systematics and Ecology* 17:15-24.
JACKSON, J. 1996. *Natural Wonders of Tasmania's World Heritage Area.* Tasmanian Parks and Wildlife Service.
JACOBSOHN, M. 1990. *Himba: Nomads of Namibia.* Struik, Cape Town.
JAKSIC, F.M. 2001. Ecological effects of El Niño in terrestrial ecosystems of western South America. *Ecography* 24:241-250.
JANETSKI, J.C. 1987. *Indians of Yellowstone Park.* University of Utah Press, Salt Lake City.
JANSEN, D., I. BOND, and B. CHILD. 1992. *Cattle, Wildlife, Both or Neither. Results of a Financial and Economic Survey of Commercial Ranches in Southern Zimbabwe.* Report No. 27, WWF Multispecies Project, Harare, Zimbabwe.
JANZEN, D.H. 1974. Tropical blackwater rivers, animals, and mass-fruiting by the Dipterocarpaceae. *Biotropica* 6:69-103.
JANZEN, D.H. 1988. Tropical dry forests: The most endangered major tropical ecosystem. In: E.O. WILSON (Ed.). *Biodiversity.* National Academy Press, Washington, D.C., pp. 130-137.
JENNINGS, M.R. 1988. Rana onca. *Catalogue of American Amphibians and Reptiles.* 417:1-2.
JEPSON HERBARIUM OF THE UNIVERSITY OF CALIFORNIA AT BERKELEY. 2001. *Jepson Flora Project. List of Taxa Grouped by Bioregion.* http://ucjeps.herb.berkeley.edu/region_page.html
JESSOP, J. 1981. *Flora of Central Australia.* A.H. & A.W. Reed Pty Ltd., Sydney.
JOHNS, R.J. 1982. Plant zonation. In: J. GRESSITT (Ed.). *Biogeography and Ecology of New Guinea.* Vol. I. W. Junk, The Hague.
JOHNS, R.J. 1986. The instability of the tropical ecosystem in Papuasia. *Blumea* 31:341-371.
JOHNS, R.J. 1995. Malesia –An introduction. *Curtis's Botanical Magazine* 12(2):52-62.
JOHNSON, A.D. 1998. Possible germoplasm evaluation procedures for water-limited, overgrazed environments in Patagonia. In: M. OESTERHELD, M.R. AGUIAR, and J.M. PARUELO (Eds.). *Ecosistemas Patagónicos. Ecología Austral.* 8:75-84.
JOHNSON, W.W. 1972. *Baja California.* Time-Life Books, New York.
JOHNSTON, I.M. 1929. Papers on the flora of northern Chile. *Contributions to the Gray Herbarium* 85:1-17.
JOHNSTON, M.C., D.H. RISKIND, M. BUTTERWICK, J. LAMB, and S. OSBURN. 1976. *A Botanical Survey of the Lower Canyons of the Rio Grande.* Division of Natural Resources and Environment, University of Texas at Austin.
JORDÁN, F. 1951. *El otro México: biografía de Baja California.* Biografías Gandesa, Mexico City.
JOSEPHY Jr., A.M. (Ed.). 1961. *The American Heritage Book of Indians.* Simon and Schuster, Inc., New York.
JOUBERT, S.C.J. 1986. *Masterplan for the Management of the Kruger National Park.* Unpublished internal memorandum. Skukuza, South African National Parks.
JUNIPER, T. and M. PARR. 1998. *Parrots: A Guide to Parrots of the World.* New Haven: Yale University Press.
JUNK, W.J. 1980. Areas inundáveis –um desafio para limnologia. *Acta Amazonica* 10:775-795.
JUNK, W.J. 1983. Aquatic habitats in Amazonia. *The Environmentalist* 3(Suppl.):24-34.
JUNK, W.J. 1984. Ecology of the várzea, floodplain of Amazonian white-water rivers. In: H. SIOLI (Ed.). *The Amazon. Limnology and Landscape Ecology of a Mighty Tropical River and Its Basin.* Dr. W. Junk Publishers, Dordrecht, pp. 215-243.
JUNK, W. J. and K. FURCH. 1985. The physical and chemical properties of Amazonian waters and their relationships with the biota. In: G.T. PRANCE and T.E. LOVEJOY (Eds.). *Amazonia.* Pergamon Press, New York, pp. 3-17.
JUNK, W.J, P.B. BAYLEY, and R.E. SPARKS. 1989. The flood pulse concept in river-floodplain systems. *Proceedings of the International Large River Symposium. Canadian Special Publication of Fisheries and Aquatic Sciences* 106:110-127.
KAA-LYA PROJECT/SERNAP. 2001. *Plan de Manejo: Parque Nacional y Área Natural de Manejo Integrado Kaa-Iya del Gran Chaco.* Servicio Nacional de Áreas Protegidas, Capitanía del Alto y Bajo Izozog, and Wildlife Conservation Society-Bolivia, Santa Cruz, Bolivia.
KABAY, E.D. and A.A. BURBIDGE (Eds.). 1977. *A Biological Survey of the Drysdale River National Park, North Kimberley, Western Australia.* Wildlife Research Bulletin No. 6. Department of Fisheries and Wildlife, Perth.
KALALLIT NUNANNI NAATSORSUEQQISSAARTARFIK GRØNLANDS STATISTIK. 2001. Homepage updated Nov. 1st., 2001. www.statgreen.gl
KAMCHATRYBVOD. 2001. Unpublished data. Petropavlovsk, Kamchatka.
KARTESZ, J.T. and C.A. MEACHAM. 1999. *Synthesis of the North American Flora.* CD Version 1.0. North Carolina Botanical Garden.
KEEGAN, R.A. and J.M. KEEGAN. 1993. *Atlas de la República Argentina.* Agrupación de Diarios del Interior, S.A., Buenos Aires. Editorial Antártica, Chile.
KEITER, R.B. and M.S. BOYCE. 1991. *The Greater Yellowstone Ecosystem: Redefining America's Wilderness Heritage.* Yale University Press, New London, Connecticut.
KENNEALLY, K.F., D.C. EDINGER, and T. WILLING. 1996. *Broome and Beyond. Plants and People of the Dampier Peninsula, Kimberley, Western Australia.* Department of Conservation and Land Management, Perth.
KENNEDY, D.I.D. and R.T. BOUCHARD. 1990. Bella Coola. In: W. SUTTLES (Ed.). *Northwest Coast,* Volume 7: *Handbook of North American Indians.* Smithsonian Institution, Washington, D.C., pp. 323-339.
KENYON, K.W. 1971. Return of the sea otter. *National Geographic* 140(4):520-539.
KERASOTE, T. (Ed.). 2001. *Return of the Wild, The Future of Our Natural Land.* The Pew Wilderness Center, New York.
KIKKAWA, J., G.B. MONTEITH, and G. INGRAM. 1981. Cape York Peninsula. Major region of faunal interchange. In: A. KEAST (Ed.). *Ecological Biogeography in Australia.* Junk, The Hague, pp. 1695-1742.
KINGDON, J. 1997. *The Kingdon Field Guide to African Mammals.* Academic Press Ltd., London.
KITCHENER, D.J. 1978. Mammals of the Ord River area, Kimberley, Western Australia. *Records of the Western Australian Museum* 6:189-219.
KLAMMER, G. 1984. The relief of the extra-Andean Amazon Basin. In: H. SIOLI (Ed.). *The Amazon. Limnology and Landscape Ecology of a Mighty Tropical River and Its Basin.* Dr. W. Junk Publishers, Dordrecht, pp. 47-83.
KLYZA, C.M. 2001. Public lands and wildlands in the Northeast. In: C.M. KLYZA (Ed.). *Wilderness Comes Home: Rewilding the Northeast.* Middlebury College Press, Hanover, New Hampshire, pp. 75-103.
KNAPP, R. 1973. *Die vegetation von Afrika.* Gustav Fischer Verlag, Stuttgart.
KNOPF, F. 1994. Avian assemblages on altered grasslands. *Studies in Avian Biology* 15:247-257.
KNYSTAUTAS, A. 1987. *The Natural History of the U.S.S.R.* Century Hutchinson, London and McGraw-Hill Book Co., New York.
KOCK, K.H. 1985. Marine habitats –Antarctic fish. In: W.N. BONNER and D.W.H. WALTON (Eds.). *Key Environments –Antarctica.* Pergamon Press, Oxford, pp. 173-192.
KOEPCKE, M. 1954. Corte ecológico transversal en los Andes del Perú central con especial consideración de las aves. *Memorias del Museo de Historia Natural Javier Prado* 3:1-119.
KOHLHEPP, G. 2001. 2000: An evaluation of three decades of regional planning and development programs in the Brazilian Amazon region. *Amazoniana* 16:363-395.
KOPPER, P. 1986. *North American Indians: Before the Coming of the Europeans.* Smithsonian Books, Washington, D.C.
KRUTCH, J.W. and E. PORTER. 1957. *Baja California and the Geography of Hope.* Sierra Club Books, San Francisco.
KRUTCH, J.W. 1961. *The Forgotten Peninsula: A Naturalist in Baja California.* W. Sloane Associates, San Francisco. (Published by A.H. Zwinger, 1986, University of Arizona Press, Tucson).
KÜSEL, M.M. 1992. A preliminary report on settlement layout and gold melting at Thula Mela, a late Iron Age site in the Kruger National Park. *Koedoe* 35(1): 55-64.
LACHER Jr., T.E. 1981. The comparative social behavior of *Kerodon rupestris* and *Galea spixii* and the evolution of behavior in the Caviidae. *Bulletin of the Carnegie Museum* 17:1-71.
LANE, J., R. JAENSCH, and R. LYNCH. 1996. Western Australia. In: *A Directory of Important Wetlands in Australia.* Australian Nature Conservation Agency, Canberra, pp. 759-943.
LARSEN, J.A. 1980. *The Boreal Ecosystem.* Academic Press, New York.
LASSO, C., D. LEW, F. PROVENZANO, O. LASSO-ALCALÁ, D. TAPHORN, and A. MACHADO-ALLISON. 2002. Biodiversidad ictiológica continental de Venezuela: lista actualizada de especies y distribución por cuencas. Memorias de la Fundación La Salle de Ciencias Naturales (in press).
LAYCOCK, G. 1997. *The Grizzly: Wilderness Legend.* Northwood Press, Minocqua, Wisconsin.
LEADER-WILLIAMS, N. 1985. The sub-Antarctic islands –Introduced mammals. In: W.N. BONNER and D.W.H. WALTON (Eds.). *Key Environments –Antarctica.* Pergamon Press, Oxford, pp. 318-328.
LEAKEY, L.B. 1969. *Animals of East Africa.* National Geographic Society, Washington, D.C.
LEGGETT, K.E.A, J.T. FENNESSY, and S. SCHNEIDER. 2002. Seasonal distributions and social dynamics of elephants in the Hoanib River catchment, northwestern Namibia. *Journal of African Zoology* (in press).
LEÓN-PORTILLA, M. 1989. *Cartografía y crónicas de la antigua California.* Universidad Nacional Autónoma de México, Mexico City.
LEOPOLD, A.S. 1959. *Wildlife of Mexico.* University of California Press, Berkeley.
LEVITON, A.E., S.C. ANDERSON, K. ADLER, and S.A. MINTON. 1992. *Handbook to Middle East Amphibians and Reptiles.* Society for the Study of Amphibians and Reptiles, Oxford, Ohio.
LEYNAUD, G.C. and E.H. BUCHER. 1999. *La fauna de serpientes del Chaco sudamericano: diversidad, distribución geográfica y estado de conservación.* Miscelanea No. 98. Academia Nacional de Ciencias, Córdoba, Argentina.
LILEY, C. 1992. *Baikal: Sacred Sea of Siberia.* Sierra Club Books, San Francisco.
LINDEN, E. 1999. *The Future in Plain Sight.* Simon and Schuster, New York.
LINES, G.C. 1999. Riparian vegetation along the Mojave River. In: *Presentation Minutes of the Mojave Desert Science Symposium, February 25-27, 1999.* USGS Western Ecological Research Center. www.werc.usgs.gov/mojave-symposium/presentations.html
LLERAS, E. 1997. Caatinga of northeastern Brazil: CPD site SA19. In: S.D. DAVIS, V.H. HEYWOOD, O. HERRERA-MacBRYDE, J. VILLA-LOBOS, and A.C. HAMILTON (Eds.). *Centres of Plant Diversity. A Guide and Strategy for Their Conservation,* Volume 3: *The Americas.* IUCN Publications Unit, Cambridge, U.K., pp. 393-396. www.nmnh.si.edu/botany/projects/cpd/sa/sa19.htm
LOEB, V., V. SIEGEL, O. HOLM-HANSEN, R. HEWITT, W. FRASER, W. TRIVELPIECE, and S. TRIVELPIECE. 1997. Effects of sea-ice extent and krill or salp dominance on the Antarctic food web. *Nature* 387 (6636):897-900.
LÖFFLER, E. 1977. *Geomorphology of Papua New Guinea.* CSIRO in Association with Australian National University Press, Canberra.
LÖFFLER, E. 1982. Pleistocene and present-day glaciations. In: J. GRESSITT (Ed.). *Biogeography and Ecology of New Guinea.* Vol. I. W. Junk, The Hague.
LOGAN, B.I. and W.G. MOSELEY. 2002. The political ecology of poverty alleviation in Zimbabwe's Communal Areas Management Programme for Indigenous Resources (CAMPFIRE). *Geoforum* 33:1-14.
LONGTON, R.E. 1985. Terrestrial habitats –Vegetation. In: W.N. BONNER and D.W.H. WALTON (Eds.). *Key Environments –Antarctica.* Pergamon Press, Oxford, pp. 71-105.
LÓPEZ-HERNÁNDEZ, D. 1995. Balance de elementos en una savana inundada. Mantecal, Estado Apure, Venezuela. *Acta Biológica Venezuélica* 15:55-88.
LOURIVAL, R.F.F. and G.A.B. FONSECA. 1997. Análise de sustentabilidade do modelo de caça tradicional, no Pantanal da Nhecolândia, Corumbá, MS. In: C. VALLADARES-PÁDUA and R.E. BODMER (Eds.). *Manejo e Conservação de Vida Silvestre no Brasil.* MCT-CNPq, Brasilia, pp.123-172.
LOURIVAL, R.F.F., M.B. HARRIS, and J.R. MONTAMBAUD. 2000. Introduction to the Pantanal. In: *Biological Assessment of the Aquatic Ecosystems of the Pantanal – Mato Grosso do Sul – Brazil.* University of Chicago Press, Chicago.
LOURIVAL, R.F.F, C.J. da SILVA, D.F. CALHEIROS, M.A. BEZERRA, L.M.R. BORGES, Z. CAMPOS, A.C. CATELLA, G.A.D. DAMASCENO Jr., E.L. HARDOIM, S.K. HAMILTON, F. de ARRUDA MACHADO, G.M. MOURÃO, F.K. NASCIMENTO, F.M. de BARROS NOGUEIRA, M.D. OLIVEIRA, A. POTT, M. SILVA, V. PINTO-SILVA, C. STRUSSMANN, A.M. TAKEDA, and W.M. THOMAS. 1999. Os impactos da Hidrovia Paraguai/Paraná sobre a biodiversidade do Pantanal – Uma discussão multidisciplinar. In: *II Simpósio de Recursos Naturais e Sócio-econômicos do Pantanal – Manejo e Conservação.* EMBRAPA, Brazil.
LOVEGROVE, B. 1993. *The Living Deserts of Southern Africa.* Fernwood Press, Vlaeberg.
LOVICH, J. 1999. *Synopsis of Conservation of the Desert Tortoise.* USGS Western Ecological Research Center. Sacramento, California. www.werc.usgs.gov/cc/synopsis.htm
LOVICH, J. 2001. *Ecology of the Western Pond Turtle in the Mojave River.* USGS Western Ecological Research Center. Sacramento, California. www.werc.usgs.gov/cc/pond-turtle.htm
LOVICH, J.E. and R.C. DE GOUVENAIN. 1998. Saltcedar invasion in desert wetlands of the southwestern United States: Ecological and political implications. In: S.K. MAJUMDAR, E.W. MILLER, and F.J. BRENNER (Eds.). *Ecology of Wetlands and Associated Systems.* Pennsylvania Academy of Science, Easton, Pennsylvania, pp. 447-467.
LOVICH, J.E. and D. BAINBRIDGE. 1999. Anthropogenic degradation of the southern California desert ecosystem and prospects for natural recovery and restoration. *Environmental Management* 24:309-326.
LUMBRERAS, L.G. (Ed.). 1999. *Historia de América Andina,* Volumen 1: Las Sociedades Aborígenes. Universidad Andina Simón Bolivar, Quito, Ecuador.
LUMHOLTZ, C. 1990. *New Trails in Mexico: An Account of One Year's Exploration in Northwestern Sonora, Mexico, and Southwestern Arizona.* University of Arizona Press, Tucson.
MACKAL, R., J.R. GREENWELL, and M.J. WILKINSON. 1982. The search for evidence of Mokele-Mbembe in the People's Republic of Congo. *Cryptozoology* 1:62-72.
MACKEY, B.G., H. NIX, and P. HITCHCOCK. 2001. *The Natural Heritage Significance of Cape York Peninsula.* ANUTECH Pty. Ltd., Canberra.
MacLEAN, G.L. 1984. Avian adaptaions to the Kalahari environment: A typical continental semidesert. In: G. de GRAAF and D.J. van RENSBURG (Eds.). *Proceedings of the Symposium on the Kalahari Ecosystem, 11-12 October 1983. Koedoe.* Supplement 27:187-194.
MacMAHON, J.A. and F.H. WAGNER. 1985. The Mojave, Sonoran, and Chihuahuan Deserts of North America. In: M. EVENARI, I. NOY-MEIR, and D.W. GOODALL (Eds.). *Hot Deserts and Arid Shrublands. Ecosystems of the World,* Vol. 12A. Elsevier, Amsterdam, pp. 105-202.
MacQUARRIE, K. 2001. *Where the Andes meet the Amazon –Peru and Bolivia's Bahuaja-Sonene and Madidi National Park.* Jordi Blassi, Barcelona.
MAGGA, O.H. 1995. Indigenous peoples of the north. In: V. G. MARTIN and N. TYLER (Eds.). *Arctic Wilderness: The 5th World Congress.* North American Press, Golden, Colorado, pp. 27-31.
MAGGS, G.L., P. CRAVEN, and H.H. KOLBERG. 1998. Plant species richness, endemism, and genetic resources in Namibia. *Biodiversity and Conservation* 7(4):435-446.
MAGNANINI, A. 1986. *Pantanal.* Edições Siciliano, São Paulo.
MAHAR, D.J. 1989. *Government Policies and Deforestation in Brazil's Amazon Region.* The World Bank, World Wildlife Fund, Conservation International, Washington, D.C.
MAINGUET, M. 1999. *Aridity: Droughts and Human Development.* Springer, New York.
MALAISSE, F. 1997. *Se Nourir en Forêt Claire Africaine.* CTA. Wageningen.
MALEY, J. 1996. The African rain forest –Main characteristics of changes in vegetation and climate from the Upper Cretaceous to the Quaternary. *The Royal Society of Edinburgh Proceedings Section B (Biological Sciences)* 104:31-74.
MALLON, D.P. 1985. The mammals of the Mongolian People's Republic. *Mammal Review* 15:71-102.
MALLON, D.P. and S.C. KINGSWOOD (Eds.). 2001. *Antelopes.* Part 4: *North Africa, the Middle East and Asia. Global Survey and Regional Action Plans.* IUCN-SSC Ante-

lope Specialist Group, Gland, Switzerland, and Cambridge, U.K.

MANZANO, P., R. LIST, and G. CEBALLOS. 1999. Grassland birds in prairie dog towns in northwestern Mexico. *Studies in Avian Biology* 19:263-271.

MANDAVILLE, J.P. 1990. *Flora of Eastern Saudi Arabia*. Kegan Paul International, London.

MARAJAN, M.D., I.M. HASHIM and H. EL FAKI. 1995. Economic aspects of wildlife in Sudan. *Wildlife and Nature*. International Journal on Nature Conservation in Africa.

MARES, M.A. and R.A. OJEDA. 1984. Faunal commercialization and conservation in South America. *BioScience* 34:580-584.

MARES, M.A., M.R. WILLIG, and T.E. LACHER Jr. 1985. The Brazilian Caatinga in South American zoogeography: Tropical mammals in a dry region. *Journal of Biogeography* 12:57-69.

MARES, M.A. and T.E. LACHER Jr. 1987. Ecological, morphological and behavioral convergence in rock-dwelling mammals. In: H.H. GENOWAYS (Ed.). *Current Mammalogy*. Vol 1. Plenum Press, New York, pp. 307-348.

MARES, M.A., J.K. BRAIN, R.M. BARQUEZ, and M.M. DIAZ. 2000. Two new genera and species of halophytic desert mammals from isolated salt flats in Argentina. *Occasional Papers, Museum of Texas Tech University* 203:1-27.

MARINHO-FILHO, J., M.M. GUIMARÃES, M.L. REIS, F.H. GUIMARÃES RODRIGUES, O. TORRES, and G. de ALMEIDA. 1997. The discovery of the Brazilian three-banded armadillo in the Cerrado of Central Brazil. *Edentata* 3:11-13.

MARKER, L., D. KRAUS, D. BARNETT, and S. HURLBERT. 1999. *Cheetah Survival on Namibian Farmlands*. Cheetah Conservation Fund, Windhoek.

MARKHAM, C.G. 1972. *Aspectos climatológicos da seca no Brasil-Nordeste*. SUDENE Assessoria Técnica, Divisão de Documentação, Recife.

MARQUET, P.A. 1994. Small mammals in the Atacama Desert and in the adjacent Andean area: Biogeography and community structure. *Australian Journal of Zoology* 42:527-542.

MARQUET, P.A., F. BOZINOVIC, G.A. BRADSHAW, C.C. CORNELIUS, H. GONZÁLEZ, J.R. GUTIERREZ, E.R. HAJEK, J.A. LAGOS, F. LÓPEZ-CORTÉS, L. NÚÑEZ, E.F. ROSELLO, C. SANTORO, H. SAMANIEGO, V.G. STANDEN, J.C. TORRES-MURA, and F.M. JAKSIC. 1998. Los ecosistemas del desierto de Atacama y área andina adyacente. *Revista Chilena de Historia Natural* 71:593-617.

MARSH, B.A. 1990. The microenvironment associated with *Welwitschia mirabilis* in the Namib Desert. In: M.K. SEELY (Ed.). *Namib Ecology: 25 Years of Namib Research*. Transvaal Museum, Pretoria, pp. 149-154.

MARSHALL, B. 2000. Freshwater fishes of the Zambezi Basin. In: J.R. TIMBERLAKE (Ed.). *Biodiversity of the Zambezi Basin Wetlands*, Vol. II. Consultancy Report for IUCN ROSA. Biodiversity Foundation for Africa, Bulawayo, and Zambezi Society, Harare, pp. 393-459.

MARSHALL, N.T., D. MULOLANI, and L. SANGALAKULA. 2000. *A Preliminary Assessment of Malawi's Woodcarving Industry*. TRAFFIC East/Southern Africa Report, c/o WWF SARPO, Harare, Zimbabwe.

MARTICORENA, C., O. MATTHEI, R. RODRÍGUEZ, M.T.K. ARROYO, M. MUÑOZ, F.A. SQUEO, and G. ARANCIO. 1998. Catálogo florístico de la región de Antofagasta. *Gayana (Botánica)* 55:23-83.

MARTIN, P.S., D.A. YETMAN, M.E. FISHBEIN, P.D. JENKINS, T.R. van DEVENDER, and R. WILSON (Eds.). 1999. *Gentry's Rio Mayo Plants: The Tropical Deciduous Forest and Environs of Northwest Mexico*. Southwest Center Series, University of Arizona Press, Tucson.

MARTIN, V.G. 1995. Wilderness designation: A global trend. In: V.G. MARTIN and N. TYLER (Eds.). *Arctic Wilderness: The 5th World Congress*. North American Press, Golden, Colorado, pp. 8-19.

MARTIN, V.G. and A. WATSON. 1990. International Wilderness and Other Protected Areas. In: J.C. Hendee, G.H. Stankey, and R.C. Lucas, *Wilderness Management*, 2nd ed. Fulcrum Publishing, Golden, Colorado.

MARTÍNEZ, M. 1947. *Baja California: reseña histórica del territorio y su flora*. Ediciones Botas, Mexico City.

MATTHIESSEN, P. 1972. *The Tree Where Man was Born*. E.P. Dutton & Co., Inc., New York.

MAYAUX, P., T. RICHARDS, and E. JANODET. 1999. A vegetation map of Central Africa derived from satellite imagery. *Journal of Biogeography* 26:353-366.

MBIDA, M.C. 1996. *L'émergence de communautés villageoises au Cameroun meridional: Etude archéologique des sites de Nkang et de Ndindan*. Université Libre de Bruxelles, Brussels.

McALLISTER, D.E., A.L. HAMILTON, and B. HARVEY. 1997. Global freshwater biodiversity: Striving for the integrity of freshwater ecosystems. *Sea Wind* 11(3):1-140.

McCARTHY, J. 1998. *Wild Scotland*. Luath Press, Edinburgh, U.K.

McCARTHY, T.S. 1993. The great inland deltas of Africa. *Journal of Africa Earth Sciences* 17(3):275-291.

McCARTHY, T.S. and W.N. ELLERY. 1993. The Okavango Delta. *Geobulletin* 36(2):5-8.

McCOY, C.J. 1983. Ecological and zoogeographic relationships of amphibians and reptiles of the Cuatro Ciénagas Basin. Desert Fishes Council Symposium on Cuatro Cienegas. Arizona State University, Tempe, 18-20 November, 1983. *Journal of the Arizona-Nevada Academy of Science*. 1984. Volume 19, Number 1. www.utexas.edu/depts/tnhc/.www/fish/dfc/cuatroc

McFARLAND, D. 1992. *Fauna of the Channel Country Biogeographic Region, Southwest Queensland*. Unpublished report to Department of Environment and Heritage.

McGAURR, L. 1999. *Lonely Planet –Tasmania*. Lonely Planet Publications, Melbourne.

McKELVEY, S.S. 1938. *Yuccas of the Southwestern United States*. Arnhold Arboretum of Harvard University, Massachusetts.

McKENNA, S.A., G.R. ALLEN, and S. SURYADI (Eds.). In press. *A Rapid Marine Biodiversity Assessment of the Raja Ampat Islands, Papua Province, Indonesia*. RAP Bulletin of Biological Assessment 22. Conservation International, Washington, D.C.

McKENZIE, N.L. (Ed.). 1981a. *Wildlife of the Edgar Ranges Area, Southwest Kimberley, Western Australia*. Wildlife Research Bulletin No. 10. Department of Fisheries and Wildlife, Perth.

McKENZIE, N.L. (Ed.). 1981b. Mammals of the Phanerozoic southwest Kimberley, Western Australia: Biogeography and recent changes. *Journal of Biogeography* 8:263-280.

McKENZIE, N.L. (Ed.). 1983. *Wildlife of the Dampier Peninsula, Southwest Kimberley, Western Australia*. Wildlife Research Bulletin No. 11. Department of Fisheries and Wildlife, Perth.

McKENZIE, N.L., R.B. JOHNSTON, and P.G. KENDRICK (Eds.). 1991. *Kimberley Rainforests of Australia*. Surrey Beatty & Sons, Sydney.

McNAMEE, K. 1998. *The National Parks of Canada*. Key Porter Books, Toronto, Ontario.

McNAUGHTON, S.J. and F.F. BANYIKWA. 1995. Plant communities and herbivory. In: A.R.E. SINCLAIR and P. ARCESE (Eds.). *Serengeti II: Dynamics, Management, and Conservation of An Ecosystem*. University of Chicago Press, Chicago, pp. 49-70.

McNULTY, F. 1966. *The Whooping Crane: The Bird That Defies Extinction*. E.P. Dutton & Co., Inc., New York.

McNUTT, J., and L. BOGGS. 1997. *Running Wild: Dispelling the Myths of the African Wild Dog*. Smithsonian Institution Press, Washington, D.C.

MEADE, R.H., C.F. NORDIN, W.F. CURTIS, F.M.C. COSTARODRIGUES, and C.M. DOVALE. 1979. Sediment loads in the Amazon River. *Nature* 278:161-163.

MEARNS, E.A. 1907. *Mammals of the Mexican Boundary of the United States*. U.S. Department of Agriculture, Division of Biological Survey Bulletin 10, Washington, D.C.

MEDEM, F. 1955. A new subspecies of *Caiman sclerops* from Colombia. *Fieldiana: Zoology* 37:339-344.

MEGGERS, B.J. 1971. *Amazonia: Man and Culture in a Counterfeit Paradise*. Aldine Press, Chicago.

MEGGERS, B.J. 1973. Some problems in cultural adaptation in Amazonia, with emphasis on the pre-European period. In: B.J. MEGGERS, E.S. AYENSU, and W.D. DUCKWORTH (Eds.). *Tropical Forest Ecosystems in Africa and South America: A Comparative Review*. Smithsonian Institution Press, Washington, D.C., pp. 311-320.

MEGGERS, B.J. 1988a. Archeological and ethnographic evidence compatible with the model of forest fragmentation. In: G.T. PRANCE (Ed.). *Biological Diversification in the Tropics*. Columbia University Press, New York, pp. 483-496.

MEGGERS, B.J. 1988b. Implications of archeological distributions in Amazonia. In: P.E. VANZOLINI and W.R. HEYER (Eds.). *Proceedings of a Workshop on Neotropical Distribution Patterns*. Academia Brasileira de Ciências, Rio de Janeiro, pp. 275-294.

MEIER, A.J., S.P. BRATTON, and D.C. DUFFY. 1995. Possible ecological mechanisms for loss of vernal herb diversity in logged eastern deciduous forests. *Ecological Applications* 5:935-946.

MEIER, A.J., S.P. BRATTON, and D.C. DUFFY. 1996. Biodiversity in the herbaceous layer and salamanders in Appalachian primary forests. In: M.B. DAVIS (Ed.). *Eastern Old Growth Forests: Prospects for Rediscovery and Recovery*. Island Press, Washington, D.C.

MEINE, C.D. and G.A. ARCHIBALD. 1996. *The Cranes: Status Survey and Conservation Action Plan*. IUCN-The World Conservation Union, Gland, Switzerland and Cambridge, U.K.

MENEZES, N.A. 1996. Methods for assessing freshwater fish biodiversity. In: M. BICUDO and N.A. MENEZES (Eds.). *Biodiversity in Brasil: A First Approach. Proceedings of the Workshop "Methods for the Biodiversity in Plants and Animals"* Campos do Jordão, Brazil, May 26-30, 1996, pp. 11-16.

MERRON, G.S. (1989). A checklist of the fishes of the Kwando River, Selinda Spillway, Lake Liambezi, and Chobe River systems. *Botswana Notes and Records* 21:135-150.

MIHOVA, B. 2000. *Comprehensive Inventory of the Biodiversity of the Central Balkan National Park*. Wilderness Fund, Sofia, Bulgaria.

MILES, J.M. and A.A. BURBIDGE (Eds.). 1975. *A Biological Survey of the Prince Regent River Reserve, Northwest Kimberley, Western Australia*. Wildlife Research Bulletin No. 3. Department of Fisheries and Wildlife, Perth.

MILLIKEN, W. and J.A. RATTER. (Eds.). 1998. *Maracá: The Biodiversity and Environment of An Amazonian Rain Forest*. John Wiley and Sons, Chichester, U.K.

MILLIMAN, J.D. and R.H. MEADE. 1983. World-wide delivery of river sediment to the oceans. *Journal of Geology* 91(1):73-84.

MILNE, C. 1994. *Sacred Places in North America: A Journey into the Medicine Wheel*. Stewart, Tabori, and Chang. New York.

MILNER-GULLAND, E.J., M.V. KHOLODOVA, A. BEKENOV, O.M. BUKREEVA, I.A. GRACHEV, L. AMGALAN, and A.A. LUSHCHEKINA. 2001. Dramatic declines in saiga antelope populations. *Oryx* 35:340-345.

MINCKLEY, W.L. 1983. Cuatro Ciénegas fishes: Research review and a local test of diversity versus habitat size. Desert Fishes Council Symposium on Cuatro Ciénegas. Arizona State University, Tempe, November 18-20, 1983. *Journal of the Arizona-Nevada Academy of Science*. 1984. 19(1). www.utexas.edu/depts/tnhc/.www/fish/dfc/cuatroc

MINNICH, R.A. and E. FRANCO VIZCAÍNO. 1998. *Land of Chamise and Pines. Historical Accounts and Current Status of Northern Baja California's Vegetation*. UC Publications in Botany No. 80, University of California Press, Berkeley.

MITCHELL, J.G. 1997. In the line of fire: Our national forests. *National Geographic* 191(3):58-87.

MITTERMEIER, R.A. 1973. Recommendations for the creation of national parks and biological reserves in the Amazonian region of Brazil, based on a four month primate survey in the Upper Amazon, Rio Negro, and Rio Tapajós. Unpublished report to World Wildlife Fund-U.S.

MITTERMEIER, R.A. 1975. A turtle in every pot. *Animal Kingdom* 78(2):9-14.

MITTERMEIER, R.A. 1977. Distribution, synecology, and conservation of Suriname monkeys. Doctoral dissertation, Harvard University, Cambridge, Massachusetts.

MITTERMEIER, R.A. 1978. South America's river turtles: Saving them by use. *Oryx* 14(3):222-230.

MITTERMEIER, R.A. 1988. Primate diversity and the tropical forest: Case studies from Brazil and Madagascar and the importance of megadiversity countries. In: E.O. WILSON and F.M. PETER (Eds.). *Biodiversity*. National Academy Press, Washington, D.C., pp. 145-154.

MITTERMEIER, R.A. 1991. Hunting and its effect on wild primate populations in Suriname. In: J.G. ROBINSON and K.H. REDFORD (Eds.). *Neotropical Wildlife Use and Conservation*. University of Chicago Press, Chicago, pp. 93-107.

MITTERMEIER, R.A. and A.F. COIMBRA-FILHO. 1977. Primate conservation in Brazilian Amazonia. In: H.R.H. PRINCE RAINIER III OF MONACO and G.H. BOURNE (Eds.). *Primate Conservation*. Academic Press, New York, pp. 117-166.

MITTERMEIER, R.A. and M.G.M. van ROOSMALEN. 1981. Preliminary observations on habitat utilization and diet in eight Suriname monkeys. *Folia primatológica* 36:1-39.

MITTERMEIER, R.A, and M.G.M. van ROOSMALEN. 1982. Conservation of primates in Surinam. *International Zoo Yearbook* 22:59-68.

MITTERMEIER, R.A., I. de GUSMÃO CÂMARA, M.T. JORGE PADUA, and J. BLANCK. 1990. Conservation in the Pantanal of Brazil. *Oryx* 24(2):103-112.

MITTERMEIER, R.A., M. SCHWARZ, J.M. AYRES. 1992. A new species of marmoset, genus *Callithrix* Erxleben 1777 (Callitrichidae, primates), from the Rio Maués region, state of Amazonas, Central Brazilian Amazonia. *Goeldiana Zoologia* (14):1-17.

MITTERMEIER, R.A., P. ROBLES GIL, and C.G. MITTERMEIER (Eds.). 1997. *Megadiversity: Earth's Biologically Wealthiest Nations*. CEMEX, Mexico.

MITTERMEIER, R.A., N. MYERS, P. ROBLES GIL, and C.G. MITTERMEIER. 1999. *Hotspots: Earth's Biologically Richest and Most Endangered Terrestrial Ecoregions*. CEMEX, Mexico.

MOLION, L.C.B. 1975. A climatonomic study of the energy and moisture fluxes of the Amazonas Basin with considerations of deforestation effects. Ph.D. Dissertation, University of Wisconsin, Madison.

MORELLO, J. 1983. El Gran Chaco: el proceso de expansión de la frontera agrícola desde el punto de vista ecológicoambiental. In: *Expansión de la frontera agropecuaria y medio ambiente en América Latina*. United Nations and CIFCA, Madrid, pp. 341-396.

MORELLO, J. and J. ADÁMOLI. 1968. La vegetación de la República Argentina. Las grandes unidades de vegetación y de ambientes del Chaco argentino. Primera parte: Objetivos y metodología. INTA, Buenos Aires. *Serie Fitogeográfica* 10:1-125.

MORELLO, J. and G. HORTT. 1985. Changes in the areal extent of arable farming, stock raising, and forestry in the South American Chaco. *Applied Geography and Development* 25:109-127.

MOSELEY, M.E. 1975a. *The Maritime Foundations of Andean Civilization*. Cummings, Menlo Park, California.

MOSELEY, M.E. 1975b. Chan-Chan: Andean alternative of the preindustrial city. *Science* 187(4173):219-225.

MOUAT, D.A., A.L. KIESTER, R. FISHER, M. MEYERS, and J.S. HEATON. 1999. Mojave Desert Biodiversity Project, "Analysis and Assessment of Impacts on Biodiversity: A Framework for Environmental Management on DoD Lands within the California Mojave Desert." Department of Defense's Strategic Environmental Research and Development Project (SERDP), Desert Research Institute, USDA Forest Service, Utah State University, and Oregon State University.
http://bufo.geo.orst.edu/mojave/biodiv.html

MOURÃO, G., M. COUTINHO, R. MAURO, Z. CAMPOS, W. TOMÁS, and W. MAGNUSSON. 2000. Aerial surveys of caiman, marsh deer, and pampas deer in the Pantanal wetland of Brazil. *Biological Conservation* 92(2):175-183.

MOWAT, F. 1996. *Sea of Slaughter*. Chapters Publishing Ltd., Shelburne, Vermont.

MUJICA, R. 1984. Departamento de Piura rainfall in 1983. *Tropical Ocean-Atmosphere Newsletter* 28.

MULLER, K. 1997. *New Guinea: Journey into the Stone Age*. Passport Books, Lincolnwood, Illinois.

MUNDY, P.J. 2000. Wetland birds of the Zambezi Basin. In: J.R. TIMBERLAKE (Ed.). *Biodiversity of the Zambezi Basin Wetlands*, Vol. II. Consultancy Report for IUCN ROSA. Biodiversity Foundation for Africa, Bulawayo, and Zambezi Society, Harare, pp. 213-234.

MUNDY, P.J., F. MAOZEKA, and J.T. COUTO. 2001. An update on the status of wattled cranes in Zimbabwe. *Honeyguide* 47:129-134.

MUÑOZ-SCHICK, M., H.C. NÚÑEZ, J.V. YÁÑEZ (Eds.). 1996. *Libro rojo de los sitios prioritarios para la conservación de la diversidad biológica en Chile*. Ministerio de Agricultura, Santiago, Chile.

MUÑOZ-SCHICK, M., R. PINTO, A. MESA, and A. MOREIRA. 2001. Oasis de neblina en los cerros costeros del sur de Iquique, región de Tarapacá, durante el evento El Niño 1997-1998. *Revista Chilena de Historia Natural* 74:389-405.

MURASHKO, O.A. 2000. *Recommendations for Preservation and Maintenance of Indigenous Peoples' Experience and Practices as a Component of Salmon Biodiversity Conservation and Indigenous Peoples' Potential Development Program within the Framework of UNDP/GEF "The Conservation and Sustainable Use of Wild Salmonid Diversity in Kamchatka."* United Nations Development Programme, Petropavlovsk, Kamchatka, Russia.

MURPHREE, M. 1993. *Communities as Resource Management Institutions*. Gatekeeper Series No. 36, Sustainable Agriculture Programme. International Institute of Environment and Development, London.

MURPHY, R. 1968. *Wild Sanctuaries: Our National Wildlife Sanctuaries – A Heritage Restored*. E.P. Dutton and Co., Inc., New York.

MURRAY, P. and G. CHALOUPKA. 1984. The dreamtime animals: Extinct megafauna in Arnhem Land rock art. *Archaeology in Oceania* 19:105-116.

MUUS, B., S. SALOMONSEN, and C. VIBE. 1990. *Grønlands Fauna, Fisk, Fugle, Pattedyr*. Glydendalske Boghendel, Nordisk Forlag, København.

MYERS, N. 1972. *The Long African Day*. The MacMillan Company, New York.

MYERS, N. 1990.The Biodiversity challenge: Expanded hotspots analysis *The Environmentalist* 10 (4): 243-256.

MYERS, N. 1988. Tropical forests and their species: Going, going...? In: E.O. WILSON and F.M. PETER (Eds.). *Biodiversity*. National Academy Press, Washington, D.C., pp. 28-35.

MYERS, N. 1996. The rich diversity of biodiversity issues. In: M.L. REAKA-KUDLA, D.W. WILSON, and E.O. WILSON (Eds.). *Biodiversity II: Understanding and Protecting our Natural Resources*. National Academy Press, Washington, D.C., pp. 125-138.

MYERS, N., R.A. MITTERMEIER, C.G. MITTERMEIER, G.A.B. da FONSECA, and J. KENT. 2000. Biodiversity hotspots for conservation priorities. *Nature* 403:853-858.

MYERS, P. and R.M. WETZEL. 1983. Systematics and zoogeography of the bats of the Chaco Boreal. *Miscellaneous Publications, Museum of Zoology, University of Michigan* 165:1-59.

NABHAN, G.P. 2002. Linking cultural diversity and biodiversity conservation on the Colorado Plateau. Society for Conservation Biology.
www.conbio.net/SCB/Publications

NAIPAUL, S. 1980. *North of South: An African Journey*. Penguin Books, Harmondsworth, U.K.

NASH, R.F. 2001. *Wilderness and the American Mind*. 4th ed. Yale University Press (1st ed. 1967).

NATIONAL CHEROKEE TRAIL. 2002. The Trail of Tears.
http://rosecity.net/tears/trail/tearsnht.html

NATIONAL GEOGRAPHIC. 2000. *National Geographic Atlas of Natural America.* National Geographic Society, Washington, D.C.
NATIONAL GEOGRAPHIC. 2001. Explorers pinpoint source of the Amazon. http://news.nationalgeographic.com/news/2000/12/1221amazon.html
NATIONAL PARKS CONSERVATION ASSOCIATION. 2002. Eagle Mountain landfill: A threat to Joshua Tree National Park. www.npca.org/flash.html
NAVARRO, G. 1997. *Izozogia nellii* (Fam.: Zygophyllaceae). *Novon* 7(1):1-5.
NAVARRO, G., J. GUERRERO, L. GONZÁLES, J.C. HURTADO, J.L. SANTIBÁÑEZ, E. CUÉLLAR, J.M. ROJAS, and A. FUENTES. 1998. *Tipificación y caracterización de los ecosistemas del Parque Nacional Kaa-Iya del Gran Chaco (Departamento de Santa Cruz, Bolivia).* Technical Report No. 36. Santa Cruz, Bolivia: Kaa-Iya Project, Capitania del Alto y Bajo Izozog/Wildlife Conservation Society-Bolivia.
NAVARRO, G. and A. FUENTES. 1999. Geobotánica y sistemas ecológicos de paisaje en el Gran Chaco de Bolivia. *Revista Boliviana de Ecología y Conservación Ambiental* 5:25-50.
NAVARRO, G. and M. MALDONADO. In press. *Biogeografía y sistemas ecológicos de Bolivia.* Fundación Simón I. Patiño, Cochabamba.
NEHLSEN, W. and J.A. LICHATOWICH. 1997. Pacific salmon: Life histories, diversity and productivity. In: P.K. SCHOONMAKER, B. von HAGEN, and E.C. WOLF (Eds.). *The Rain Forests of Home: Profile of a North American Region.* Island Press, Washington, D.C., pp. 213-226.
NELDNER, V.J. and J.R. CLARKSON. 1995. *Vegetation Survey and Mapping of Cape York Peninsula.* Cape York Peninsula Land Use Strategy –Queensland Commonwealth Government.
NELDNER, V.J., R.J. FENSHAM, J.R. CLARKSON, and J.P. STANTON. 1997. The natural grasslands of Cape York Peninsula, Australia: Description, distribution and conservation status. *Biological Conservation* 81:121-136.
NEPSTAD, D.C., A. VERÍSSIMO, A. ALENCAR, C. NOBRE, E. LIMA, P. LEFEBVRE, P. SCHLESINGER, C. POTTER, P. MOUTINHO, E. MENDOZA, M. COCHRANE, and V. BROOKS. 1999. Large-scale impoverishment of Amazonian forests by logging and fire. *Nature* 398(403):505-508.
NEPSTAD, D.C., D. McGRATH, A. ALENCAR, A.C. BARROS, G. CARVALHO, M. SANTILLI, and M. del C. VERA DÍAZ. 2002. Frontier governance in Amazonia. *Science* 295: 629-631.
NERONOV, V.M. and V.V. BOBROV. 1991. In: J.A. McNEELY and V.M. NERONOV (Eds.). *Mammals in the Palaearctic Desert: Status and Trends in the Sahara-Gobian Region.* Russian MAB Committee for the UNESCO Programme on Man and the Biosphere, Moscow, pp. 232-242.
NEWBY, J.E. 1978. Scimitar-horned oryx: The end of the line? *Oryx* 14:219.
NEWBY, J.E. 1980. Can addax and oryx be saved in the Sahel? *Oryx* 15:262.
NEWBY, J.E. 1984. Large mammals. In: J.L. CLOUDSLEY-THOMPSON (Ed.). *Sahara Desert.* Key Environments Series. Pergamon Press, Oxford, pp. 277-290.
NEWBY, J.E., P. VINCKE and G. SOURNIA. 1987. Addax et Oryx : l'heure de la decision. In: P.P. VINCKE, G. SOURNIA, and E. WANGARI (Eds.). *Pour une gestion de la faune du Sahel ; vers une politique de concertation et de coopération régionale internationale. Actes du séminaire de Nouk-chott - mars 1986.* Environnement Africain, Serie Etudes et Recherches. MAB/ENDA/UICN, pp. 41-47.
NGATOUA, U. 2002. *Conservation of Biodiversity in the Central African Republic.* www.yale.edu/forestry/bulletin/102pdfs/102Ngatoua.pdf
NIELSEN, J.G. and E. BERTELSEN. 1992. *Fish in Greenlandic Waters.* Atuakkiorfik, Nuuk.
NIMER, E. 1972. Climatologia da região Nordeste do Brasil: introdução à climatologia dinâmica. *Revista Brasileira de Geografia* 34:3-51.
NISHIMURA, A., K. IZAWA, and K. KIMIRA. 1995. Long-term studies of primates at La Macarena, Colombia. *Primate Conservation* (16):7-14.
NIX, H.A. and J.D. KALMA. 1972. Climate as a dominant control in the biogeography of northern Australia and New Guinea. In: D. WALKER (Ed.). *Bridge and Barrier: A Natural and Cultural History of Torres Strait.* ANU Press, Canberra, pp. 61-91.
NOGUEIRA NETO, P. 1991. *Ecological Stations: A Saga of Ecology and Environmental Policy.* Empresa das Artes, São Paulo.
NOGUEIRA NETO, P. and J.C. de M. CARVALHO. 1979. A programme of ecological stations for Brazil. *Environmental Conservation* 6(2):95-104.
NORMAN, D.R. and L. NAYLOR. 1994. *Los anfibios y reptiles del Chaco paraguayo.* San José, Costa Rica.
NOSS, A.J. 2001. Conservation, development, and the forest people: The Aka of the Central African Republic. In: L. NAUGHTON-TREVES, A. VEDDER, W. WEBER, and L.J.T. WHITE (Eds.). *African Rainforest Ecology and Conservation.* Yale University Press, New Haven and London, pp. 313-333.
NOWAK, R.M. 1991. *Walker's Mammals of the World* (5th edition). Volume II. The Johns Hopkins University Press, Baltimore.
NOWAK, R.M. and J.L. PARADISO. 1983. *Walker's Mammals of the World.* 4th edition. John Hopkins University Press, Baltimore.
NÚÑEZ, L. 1983. Paleoindian and archaic cultural periods in the arid and semiarid regions of northern Chile. *Advances in World Archaeology* 2:161-222.
OATES, J.F. 1996. *African Primates: Status Survey and Conservation Action Plan* (rev. ed.). IUCN/SSC, Gland, Switzerland.
O'BYRNE, D., R. MOON, V. MOON, H. FINLAY, and J. WILLIAMS. 1998. *Outback Australia.* Lonely Planet Publications, Hawthorn, Victoria.
OCEI (Oficina Central de Estadística e Informática). 2000. Venezuela. www.ocei.gov.ve
Ó DONNAÍLE, C.P. 2001. European minority languages. www.smo.uhi.ac.uk/saoghal/mion-chanain/Failte_en.html
OJASTI, J. 1978. The relation between population and production of the capybara. Unpublished Ph.D. Dissertation, University of Georgia, Athens.
OJASTI, J. 1990. Las comunidades de mamíferos en sabanas neotropicales. 3. In: G. SARMIENTO (Ed.). *Las sabanas americanas: aspectos de su biogeografía y utilización.* Fondo Editorial Acta Científica de Venezuela, Caracas, pp. 259-293.
OJASTI, J. 1991. Human exploitaition of capybaras. In: J.G. ROBINSON and K.H. REDFORD (Eds.). *Tropical Wildlife Use and Conservation.* University of Chicago Press, Chicago, pp. 236-252.
OJASTI, J. and S. BOHER. 1986. *Bases para el diseño de medidas de mitigación y control de las cuencas hidrográficas de los ríos Caris y Pao,* Edo. de Anzoategui. Vol. V: *Fauna.* Universidad Central de Venezuela, MENEVEN, Caracas.
OKACOM. 1994. *Agreement between the Governments of the Republic of Angola, the Republic of Botswana, and the Republic of Namibia on the Establishment of a Permanent Okavango River Basin Water Commission (OKACOM).* Department of Water Affairs, Windhoek, Namibia, and Department of Water Affairs, Gaborone, Botswana.
OLDFIELD, S., C. LUSTY, and A. McKINVEN. 1998. *The World List of Threatened Trees.* World Conservation Press, Cambridge, U.K.
OLIVEIRA, J.A. 2000. Diversidade de Mamíferos e o Establecimento de Áreas Prioritárias para a Conservação do Bioma Caatinga. Relatório Técnico, Projeto "Avaliação e Ações Prioritárias para a Conservação da Biodiversidade do Bioma Caatinga". www.biodiversitas.org/caatinga
OLMOS, F. 1992. Serra da Capivara National Park and the conservation of northeastern Brazil's Caatinga. *Oryx* 26(3):142-146.
OLROG, C.C., R.A. OJEDA, and R.M. BÁRQUEZ. 1976. *Catagonus wagneri* (Rusconi) en el noroeste argentino. *Neotrópica* 22:53-56.
OLSON, D. and E. DINERSTEIN. 1997. *The Global 200: Conserving the World's Distinctive Ecoregions.* Conservation Science Program, World Wildlife Fund–U.S., Washington, D.C.
OLSON, D.M., E. DINERSTEIN, P. CANEVARI, I. DAVIDSON, G. CASTRO, V. MORRISET, R. ABELL, and E. TOLEDO (Eds.). 1998. *Freshwater Biodiversity of Latin America and the Caribbean: A Conservation Assessment.* Biodiversity Support Program, World Wildlife Fund, Washington, D.C.
OLSON, D.M., E. DINERSTEIN, E.D. WIKRAMANYAKE, N.D. BURGESS, G.V.N. POWELL, E.C. UNDERWOOD, J.A. D'AMICO, I. ITOUA, H.E. STRAND, J.C. MORRISON, C.J. LOUCKS, T.F. ALNUTT, T.H. RICKETTS, Y. KURA, J.F. LAMOREUX, W.W. WETTENGEL, P. HEDAO, and K. KASSEM. 2001. Terrestrial ecoregions of the world: A new map of life on Earth. *BioScience* 51(11):933-938.
OREN, D.C. and F.C. NOVAES. 1986. *Prioridades para a conservação da natureza nas florestas do Estado do Maranhão. Estudo baseado em pesquisas ornitológicas.* Report, Departamento de Zoologia, Museu Paraense Emílio Goeldi, Belém, Pará.
ORTEGA, H. 1992. Biogeografía de los peces continentales del Perú, con especial referencia a especies registradas a altitudes superiores a los 1 000 m. In: K.R. YOUNG and N. VALENCIA (Eds.). *Biogeografía, ecología y conservación del bosque montano del Perú. Memorias del Museo de Historia Natural-UNMSM* 21:39-45.
ORTEGA, H. and R.P. VARI. 1986. Annotated checklist of the freshwater fishes of Peru. *Smithsonian Contributions to Zoology* (437): 1-250.
ORTIZ, S. 1984. Colonization in the Colombian Amazon. In: S. SCHMINK and C.H. WOOD (Eds.). *Frontier Expansion in Amazonia,* University of Florida Press, Gainesville, pp. 204-230.
OSLISLY, R. 1996. The middle Ogooué Valley, Gabon: Cultural changes and palaeoclimatic implications of the last four millennia. In: J.E.G. SUTTON (Ed.). *The Growth of Farming Communities in Africa from the Equator Southwards,* Vol. 29-30 *Azania:* Journal of the British Institute in Eastern Africa, London, pp. 324-331.
OSLISLY, R. 1998. The history of human settlement in the Middle Ogooué Valley (Gabon): Implications for the environment. In: W. WEBER, A. VEDDER, H. SIMONS MORLAND, L.J.T. WHITE, and T. HART (Eds.). African Rain Forest Ecology and Conservation. Yale University Press, New Haven.
OSLISLY, R. and B. PEYROT. 1992. Un gisement du paléolithique inférieur: La haute terrasse d'Elarmekora (Moyenne vallée de l'Ogooué) Gabon. Problèmes chronologiques et paléogéographiques. *Comptes Rendus Academie des Sciences, Paris* 314:309-312.
OVERAL, W.L. 2001. O peso dos invertebrados na balança de conservação biológica da Amazônia. In: A. VERÍSSIMO, A. MOREIRA, D. SAWYER, I. dos SANTOS, L.P. PINTO, and J.P.R. CAPOBIANCO (Eds.). *Biodiversidade na Amazônia Brasileira: Avaliação e Ações Prioritárias para a Conservação, Uso Sustentável e Repartição de Benefícios.* Instituto Socioambiental, Estação Liberdade, São Paulo, pp. 50-59.
PACHECO, J., G. CEBALLOS, and R. LIST. 2000. Los mamíferos de la región de Janos-Casas Grandes, Chihuahua, México. *Revista Mexicana de Mastozoología* 4:71-85.
PACHECO, J.F. and C. BAUER. 2000. As aves da Caatinga. Relatório Técnico, Projeto "Avaliação e Ações Prioritárias para a Conservação da Biodiversidade do Bioma Caatinga". www.biodiversitas.org/caatinga
PACKER, C. 1996. Who rules the park? *Wildlife Conservation* 99:36-39.
PACKER, C. and A.E. PUSEY. 1997. Divided we fall: Cooperation among lions. *Scientific American* 276(5):52-59.
PAIJMANS, K. 1976. *Vegetation of New Guinea.* Elsevier, Amsterdam.
PARMENTIER, I. and J. MALEY. 2001. L'arbre et le pigeon ou le pigeon et l'arbre? *Canopée* 19:12-14.
PARRY, E. 2000. *Legacy on the Rocks.* Oxbow Books, Oxford, U.K.
PARSONS, M. 1998. *The Butterflies of Papua New Guinea. Their Systematics and Biology.* Academic Press, London.
PATTEN, D.T. 1991. Defining the Greater Yellowstone Ecosystem. In: R.B. KEITER and M.S. BOYCE (Eds.). *The Greater Yellowstone Ecosystem: Redefining America's Wilderness Heritage.* Yale University Press, New London, Connecticut, pp. 19-26.
PAUTRAT, L. and J.C. RIVEROS. 1998. Evaluación de la avifauna de los Pantanos de Villa. In: A. CANO and K.R. YOUNG (Eds.). *Los Pantanos de Villa. Biología y conservación.* Universidad Nacional Mayor de San Marcos, Museo de Historia Natural, Serie de Divulgación No. 11, pp. 85-103.
PAVLOV, D.S., K.A. SAVVAITOVA, and K.V. KUZISHCHIN. 1999. To the problem of forming of the epigenetic variations of life history strategy in red data book species –Kamchatkan mykizha *Parasalmo mykiss* (Salmonidae, Salmoniformes). *Reports of Russian Academy of Science, Biological Series* 367(5):709-713.
PCBAP. 1997. Aspectos ecológicos dos vertebrados terrestres e semiaquáticos no Pantanal. In: PCBAP. *Plano de Conservação da Bacia do Alto Paraguai, Diagnóstico dos Meios Físico e Biótico –Meio Biótico,* Volume II, Tomo III. Empresa Brasileira de Pesquisa Agropecuária, Projeto Pantanal, Programa Nacional de Meio Ambiente, Brasilia, pp. 197-433.
PÉFAUR, J.E. and J.A. RIVERO. 2000. Distribution, species-richness, endemism, and conservation of Venezuelan amphibians and reptiles. *Amphibian and Reptile Conservation* 2:42-70.
PEREGRINE FUND. 1998. *Peregrine Fund Annual Report 1998.* Peregrine Fund, Boise, Idaho.
PERES, C.A. 1990. Effects of hunting on western Amazonian primate communities. *Biological Conservation* 54:47-59.
PERES, C.A. 2000a. Evaluating the impact and sustainability of subsistence hunting at multiple Amazonian forest sites. In: J.G. ROBINSON and E.L. BENNETT (Eds.). *Hunting for Sustainability in Tropical Forests.* Columbia University Press, New York, pp. 31-56.
PERES, C.A. 2000b. Effects of subsistence hunting on vertebrate community structure in Amazonian forests. *Conservation Biology* 14:240-253.
PERES, C.A. and J.W. TERBORGH. 1994. *Amazonian Nature Reserves: An Analysis of the Defensibility Status of Existing Conservation Units and Design Criteria for the Future.* Center for Tropical Conservation, Duke University, Durham, North Carolina.
PETERS, J.A. and R. DONOSO-BARROS. 1986. Lizards and amphisbaenians, with new material by P.E. Vanzolini. In: *Catalogue of the Neotropical Squamata,* Part II. Smithsonian Institution Press, Washington, D.C. and London, pp. 1-293.
PETRANKA, J.W. 1998. *Salamanders of the United States and Canada.* Smithsonian Institution Press, Washington, D.C.
PETTERSON, D. 1999. *Inside Sudan. Political Islam, Conflict, and Catastrophe.* Westview Press.
PHELPS, Jr., W.H. and M. de SCHAUENSEE. 1978. *A Guide to the Birds of Venezuela.* Princeton University Press, Princeton, New Jersey.
PICCOLO, A. 1993. *Aborígenes de la Argentina.* Editorial Betina, Buenos Aires.
PICKFORD, M. and B. SENUT. 2000. *Geology and Palaeobiology of the Namib Desert, Southwestern Africa.* Volume I: *Geology and History of the Study.* Ministry of Mines and Energy, Windhoek.
PIENAAR, U. de V. 1978. Freshwater fishes of the Kruger National Park. National Parks Board, Pretoria.
PIENAAR, U. de V., N.I. PASSMORE, and V.C. CARUTHERS. 1976. Frogs of the Kruger National Park. National Parks Board, Pretoria.
PIENAAR, U. de V., W.D. HAACKE, and N.H.G. JACOBSEN. 1978. Reptiles of the Kruger National Park. National Parks Board, Pretoria.
PIENAAR, U. de V., S.C.J. JOUBERT, A. HALL-MARTIN, G. DE GRAAFF, and I.L. RAUTENBACH. 1987. Field guide to the mammals of the Kruger National Park. Struik Publishers, Cape Town.
PIETERS, P.E. 1982. Geology of New Guinea. In: J. GRESSITT (Ed.). *Biogeography and Ecology of New Guinea.* Vol. I. W. Junk, The Hague.
PIGRAM, C.J. and H.L. DAVIES. 1987. Terranes and the accretion history of the New Guinea orogen. *BMR Journal of Australian Geology and Geophysics* 10:193-211.
PINKAVA, D.J. 1978. Vegetation and flora of the Cuatro Ciénegas Basin, Coahuila, Mexico. In: R.H. WAUER and D. RISKIND (Eds.). *Transactions of the Symposium on the Biological Resources of the Chihuahuan Desert Region, United States and Mexico.* U.S. National Park Service Transactions and Proceedings Series 3 (1977). Government Printing Office, Washington, D.C.
PINTO, R. 1999. *Oasis de niebla, El Niño 1997. Una expedición botánica a los cerros costeros de Iquique, norte de Chile.* Imprenta Ograma S.A., Santiago, Chile.
PINTO, R. 2001. Presencia de *Tillandsia virescens* en el sistema de tillandsiales de la cordillera de la costa de Iquique, norte de Chile. XIII Reunión anual Sociedad Botánica de Chile. *Gayana Botánica* 58(1):90.
PIRES, J.M. 1974. Tipos de vegetação da Amazônia. *Brasil Florestal* 5(17):48-58.
PIRES, J.M. and G.T. PRANCE. 1985. The vegetation types of the Brazilian Amazon. In: G.T. PRANCE and T.E. LOVEJOY (Eds.). *Amazonia.* Pergamon Press, New York, pp. 109-145.
PLUG, I. 1984. Man, animals, and subsistence patterns during the early Iron Age in the Kruger National Park. In: M. HALL, G. AVERY, D.M. AVERY, M.L. WILSON, and A.J.B. HUMPHREYS (Eds.). *Frontiers: Southern Africa Archaeology Today.* Cambridge Monographs in Africa Archaeology 10. BAR International Series 207. B.A.R., Oxford, U.K.
PLUG, I. 1989. Aspects of life in the Kruger National Park during the early Iron Age. *South African Archaeological Society Goodwin Series* 6:62-68.
PLUG, I. and E.A. VOIGT. 1985. Archaeozoological studies of Iron Age communities in Southern Africa. *Advances in World Archaeology* 4:189-238.
POR, F.D. 1995. *The Pantanal of Mato Grosso (Brazil).* Kluwer Academic Publishers, The Netherlands.
POSEY, D.A. 1983. Indigenous ecological knowledge and the development of the Amazon. In: E. MORAN (Ed.). *The Dilemma of Amazonian Development.* Westview Press, Inc., Boulder, Colorado, pp. 225-257.
POTT, A. and V.J. POTT. 1994. *Plantas do Pantanal.* EMBRAPA, Brasília.
POTT, A. and V.J. POTT. 2000. *Plantas Aquáticas do Pantanal.* EMBRAPA, Brasília.
POWELL, A.M. 1994. *Grasses of the Trans-Pecos and Adjacent Areas.* University of Texas Press, Austin.
POWELL, A.M. 1998. *Trees and Shrubs of Trans-Pecos Texas.* Big Bend Natural History Association, Austin.
PRADO, D.E. 1993. What is the Gran Chaco vegetation in South America? I. A review. Contribution to the study of flora and vegetation of the Chaco, V. *Candollea* 48(1): 145-172.
PRADO, D.E. and P.E. GIBBS. 1993. Patterns of species distributions in the dry seasonal forests of South America. *Annals of the Missouri Botanical Gardens* 80:902-927.
PRANCE, G.T. 1973. Phytogeographic support for the theory of Pleistocene forest refuges in the Amazon Basin, based on evidence from distribution patterns in Caryocaraceae, Chrysobalanaceae, Dichapetalaceae, and Lecythidiceae. *Acta Amazonica* 3(3):5-28.
PRANCE, G.T. 1977. The phytogeographic subdivisions of Amazonia and their influence on the selection of biological reserves. In: G.T. PRANCE and T.S. ELIAS (Eds.). *Extinction is Forever.* New York Botanical Garden, New York, pp. 195-212.
PRANCE, G.T. 1979. Notes on the vegetation of Amazonia III.

The terminology of Amazonian forest types subject to inundation. *Brittonia* 31:26-38.
PRANCE, G.T. 1987a. Vegetation. In: T.C. WHITMORE and G.T. PRANCE (Eds.). *Biogeography and Quaternary History in Tropical America.* Clarendon Press, Oxford, pp. 28-45.
PRANCE, G.T. 1987b. Biogeography of Neotropical plants. In: T.C. WHITMORE and G.T. PRANCE (Eds.). *Biogeography and Quaternary History in Tropical America.* Clarendon Press, Oxford, pp. 46-65.
PRANCE, G.T. 2001. Amazon ecosystems. In: S.A. LEVIN, (Ed.). *Encyclopaedia of Biodiversity,* Vol. 1. Academic Press, London, pp. 145-157.
PRANCE, G.T. and G. SCHALLER. 1982. Preliminary observations on woody vegetation types on the Pantanal of Mato Grosso, Brazil. *Brittonia* 34:228-251.
PRANCE, G.T., H. BEENTJE, J. DRANSFIELD, and R. JOHNS. 2000. The tropical flora remains undercollected. *Annals of the Missouri Botanical Garden* 87(1):67-71.
PRESS, T., D. LEA, A. WEBB, and A. GRAHAM. 1995. *Kakadu: Natural and Cultural Heritage and Management.* Australian Nature Conservation Agency and North Australia Research Unit, Darwin.
PRICE WATERHOUSE. 1994. *The Lowveld Conservancies: New Opportunities for Productive and Sustainable Land-Use.* Savé Valley, Bubiana and Chiredzi River Conservancies, Price Waterhouse Wildlife, Tourism and Environmental Consulting, Harare, Zimbabwe.
PROBIDES. 1999. *Plan Director. Reserva de Biosfera Bañados del Este, Uruguay.* Rocha.
PROBIDES. 2001. *Information Document.* Rocha.
PROKOSCH, P. 1995. A protected area system for the Arctic. In: V.G. MARTIN and N. TYLER (Eds.). *Arctic Wilderness: The 5th World Congress.* North American Press, Golden, Colorado, pp. 174-180.
PUJALTE, J.C. and A.R. RECA. 1985. Vicuñas y guanacos. Distribución y ambientes. In: J.L. CAJAL and J.N. AMAYA (Eds.). *Estado actual de las investigaciones sobre camélidos en la República Argentina.* Ministerio de Educación y Justicia, Secretaría de Ciencia y Técnica, Programa Nacional de Recursos Naturales Renovables, Buenos Aires, pp. 21-49.
QUEENY, E.M. 1954. Spearing lions with Africa's Masai. *National Geographic* 56(4):487-517.
QUÉZEL, P. 1978. An analysis of the flora of Mediterranean and Saharan Africa. *Annals of the Missouri Botanical Gardens* 65:479-534.
RAEDERAEKE, K.J. 1979. Population dynamics and socioecology of the guanaco (*Lama guanicoe*) of Magallanes, Chile. Ph.D. Dissertation. University of Washington, Seattle.
RAHR, G.R. 1999. Kamchatka at the crossroads. *International Journal of Salmon Conservation* 3:1-7. Wild Salmon Center, Portland, Oregon.
RAMIA, M. 1967. Tipos de savana en los llanos de Venezuela. *Boletín de la Sociedad Venezolana de Ciencias Naturales* 28:264-288.
RAMIA, M. 1972. Cambios en la vegetacion del Hato El Frio (Alto Apure) causados por diques. *Boletín de la Sociedad Venezolana de Ciencias Naturales* 30:57-90.
RAMSAR. 1993. *A Directory of Wetlands of International Importance,* Volume 1: *Africa.* http://www.ramsar.org
RAMSAR. 2001. *The List of Wetlands of International Importance.* www.ramsar.org
RAMSAR. 2002. *The List of Wetlands of International Importance.* http://ramsar.org/sitelist.doc
RANDALL, R. and M. HERREMANS. 1994. Breeding of the slaty egret *Egretta vinaceigula* along the Boro River in the central Okavango Delta (Botswana). *Ostrich* 65:39-43.
RASMUSSEN, H. 1995. The indigenous peoples of the Arctic: Survival demands. In: V.G. MARTIN and N. TYLER (Eds.). *Arctic Wilderness: The 5th World Congress.* North American Press, Golden, Colorado, pp. 41-45.
RAUH, W. 1985. The Peruvian-Chilean deserts. In: M. EVENARY, I. NOY-MEIR and D.W. GOODALL (Eds.). *Hot Deserts and Arid Shrublands.* Elsevier, Amsterdam, pp. 239-266.
RAVAZZANI, C., H. WIEDERKEHR FILHO, J.P. FAGNANI, and S. da COSTA. 1990. *Pantanal.* Editora Brasil Natureza, Paraná.
REDFORD, K.H. 1993. Hunting in neotropical forests: A subsidy from nature. In: C. HLADIK, M.A. HLADIK, O.F. LINARES, H. PAGEZY, A. SEMPLE, and M. HEDLEY (Eds.). *Tropical Forests, People, and Foods: Biocultural Interactions and Applications to Development.* UNESCO, Paris, pp. 227-247.
REICHENBACHER, F.W. 1984. Ecology and evolution of southwestern riparian plant communities. *Desert Plants* 6:15-22.
REITSMA, J.M., A.M. LOUIS, and J.J. FLORET. 1992. Flore et végétation des inselbergs et dalles rocheuses : première etude au Gabon. *Bulletin du Muséeum du Histoire Naturelle du Paris,* 4me ser. 14. 1992 section B, Adansonia 1:73-97.
REVENGA, C., S. MURRAY, J. ABRAMOVITZ, and A. HAMMOND. 1998. *Watersheds of the World: Ecological Value and Vulnerability.* World Resources Institute, Washington, D.C.
RICARDO, F. 2001a. Terras Indígenas na Amazônia Legal. In: A. VERÍSSIMO, A. MOREIRA, D. SAWYER, I. dos SANTOS, L.P. PINTO, and J.P.R. CAPOBIANCO (Eds.). *Biodiversidade na Amazônia Brasileira: Avaliação e Ações Prioritárias para a Conservação, Uso Sustentável e Repartição de Benefícios.* Instituto Socioambiental, Estação Liberdade, São Paulo, pp. 251-258.
RICARDO, F. 2001b. Sobreposições entre Unidades de Conservação (UCs) federais, estaduias, terras indígenas, terras militares e reservas garimpeiras na Amazônia Legal. In: A. VERÍSSIMO, A. MOREIRA, D. SAWYER, I. dos SANTOS, L.P. PINTO, and J.P.R. CAPOBIANCO (Eds.). *Biodiversidade na Amazônia Brasileira: Avaliação e Ações Prioritárias para a Conservação, Uso Sustentável e Repartição de Benefícios.* Instituto Socioambiental, Estação Liberdade, São Paulo, pp. 259-262.
RICARDO, F. and J.P.R. CAPOBIANCO. 2001. Unidades de Conservação na Amazônia Legal. In: A. VERÍSSIMO, A. MOREIRA, D. SAWYER, I. dos SANTOS, L.P. PINTO, and J.P.R. CAPOBIANCO (Eds.). *Biodiversidade na Amazônia Brasileira: Avaliação e Ações Prioritárias para a Conservação, Uso Sustentável e Repartição de Benefícios.* Instituto Socioambiental, Estação Liberdade, São Paulo, pp. 246-250.
RICHARD, E. 1999. *Tortugas de las regiones áridas de Argentina.* Monografía especial, Literature of Latin America No. 10, Buenos Aires.
RICHARDS, S., D.T. ISKANDAR, and A. ALLISON. 2000. In: A.L. MACK and L.E. ALONSO (Eds.). *A Biological Assessment of the Wapoga River Area of Northwestern Irian Jaya, Indonesia.* RAP Working Papers 14. Conservation International, Washington, D.C., pp. 54-57.
RICKETTS, T.H., E. DINERSTEIN, D.M. OLSON, C.J. LOUCKS, W. EICHBAUM, D. DELLSAIA, K. KAVANAGH, P. HEDAO, P.T. HURLEY, K.M. CARNEY, R. ABELL, and S. WALTERS. 1999. *Terrestrial Ecoregions of North America: A Conservation Assessment.* Island Press. Washington, D.C.
RIEDMAN, M. 1990. *The Pinnipeds: Seals, Sea Lions, and Walruses.* University of California Press, Berkeley.
RILLA, F. 1992. Humedales del sureste del Uruguay: situación actual y perspectivas. *Vida Silvestre* (Madrid) 72:44-49.
RILLA, F. 1998. *Bañados del Este, Eastern Wetlands of Uruguay. Wetlands Conservation In Summary* (Poster). 2nd International Conference on Wetlands and Development, Dakar, Senegal.
RIZZINI, C.T., A.F. COIMBRA-FILHO, and A. HOUAISS. 1988. *Ecossistemas Brasileiros/Brazilian Ecoystems.* Editora Index, Rio de Janeiro.
ROBERTSON, A., A.M. JARVIS, C.J. BROWN, and R.E. SIMMONS. 1998. Avian diversity and endemism in Namibia: Patterns from the Southern African Bird Atlas Project. *Biodiversity and Conservation* 7(4):495-512.
ROBERTSON, M., K. VANG, and A.J. BROWN. 1992. *Wilderness in Australia, Issues and Options.* Written for the Minister of Arts, Sport, the Environment and Territories. Australian Heritage Commission, Canberra.
ROBICHAUX, R.H. (Ed.). 1999. *Ecology of Sonoran Desert Plants and Plant Communities.* University of Arizona Press, Tucson.
ROBICHAUX, R.H. and D.A. YETMAN (Eds.). 2000. *The Tropical Deciduous Forest of Alamos. Biodiversity of a Threatened Ecosystem in Mexico.* University of Arizona Press, Tucson.
ROBINSON, J.G. and K.H. REDFORD. 1991a. *Neotropical Wildlife Use and Conservation.* University of Chicago Press, Chicago.
ROBINSON, J.G. and K.H. REDFORD. 1991b. Sustainable harvest of neotropical forest mammals. In: J.G. ROBINSON and K.H. REDFORD (Eds.). *Neotropical Wildlife Use and Conservation.* University of Chicago Press, Chicago, pp. 415-429.
ROBLES GIL, P., G. CEBALLOS, and F. ECCARDI. 1993. *Diversidad de fauna mexicana.* Cemex and Agrupación Sierra Madre, Mexico City.
ROBLES GIL, P., E. EZCURRA, and E. MELLINK (Eds.). 2001. *The Gulf of California. A World Apart.* Agrupación Sierra Madre, Mexico City.
ROCHA, P.L.B. 1995. *Proechimys yonenagae,* a new species of spiny rat (Rodentia: Echimyidae) from fossil sand dunes in the Brazilian Caatinga. *Mammalia* 59:537-549.
RODGERS, W.A. 1996. The miombo woodlands. In: T.R. McCLANAHAN and T.P. YOUNG (Eds.). *East African Ecosystems and their Conservation,* OUP, Oxford, pp. 299-326.
RODRIGUES, M.T. 1996. Lizards, snakes, and amphisbaenians from the Quaternary sand dunes of the middle Rio São Francisco, Bahia, Brazil. *Journal of Herpetology* 30:513-523.
RODRIGUES, M.T. 2000. Fauna de Répteis e Anfíbios das Caatingas. Relatório Técnico, Projeto "Avaliação e Ações Prioritárias para a Conservação da Biodiversidade do Bioma Caatinga". www.biodiversitas.org/caatinga
RODRIGUES FERREIRA, A. 1972. *Viagem Filosófica pelas Capitanias do Grão Pará, Rio Negro, Mato Grosso e Cuiabá. Memórias. Zoologia, Botânica.* Conselho Federal de Cultura, Departamento da Imprensa Nacional, Rio de Janeiro.
ROMERO, M.E., L.M. CASTRO, and A. MURIEL. 1993. *Geografía humana de Colombia. Región de la Orinoquía,* Vol. 1. Instituto Colombiano de Cultura Hispánica, Bogota.
RON, T. 2001. Conservation and study of the great apes and other fauna and flora in the Maiombe Forest, Cabinda Enclave, Angola: A preliminary project proposal. Unpublished report.
ROOTS, F. 1995. Polar wilderness: What does it contribute and to whom? In: V.G. MARTIN and N. TYLER (Eds.). *Arctic Wilderness: The 5th World Congress.* North American Press, Golden, Colorado, pp. 118-127.
ROSS, K. 1988. *Okavango: Jewel of the Kalahari.* Macmillan, New York.
ROSS, K. 1991. *Status and Distribution of Sitatunga in the Okavango Delta, Botswana.* Typescript report for the Department of Land Use Planning, Maun, Botswana.
ROSS, K. 2002. *Jewel of the Kalahari, Revisited.* Struik Publishers, Cape Town.
ROSS, K. and I. MAGOLE (2000). *Looking at the Big Picture: Ecosystem Management in Mountains, Watersheds, and River Basins: Experiences in the Okavango Delta and River Basin.* IUCN World Congress, Amman, Jordan, October 2000.
ROTHERT, S. 1999. *Meeting Namibia's Water Needs while Sparing the Okavango.* Okavango Program Publication Series, Maun, Botswana. Jointly produced by CI and International Rivers Network.
RUDOLF, J.C., G. BARDIER, D. QUEIROLO, and F. LAGOMARSINO. 1993. Uruguay: situación actual de los Humedales del Este en relación al desarrollo agropecuario y la conservación. In: F. RILLA (Ed.). *Memorias, II taller regional de humedales.* IUCN, Paraty, Brazil, Sept. 14-18, 1992, pp. 33-40.
RUNDEL P., B. PALMA, M.O. DILLON, M.R. SHARIFI, and K. BOONPRAGOB. 1997. *Tillandsia landbeckii* in the coastal Atacama Desert of northern Chile. *Revista Chilena de Historia Natural* 70:341-349.
RUSSELL-SMITH, J. and D.M.J.S. BOWMAN. 1992. Conservation of monsoon rainforest isolates in the Northern Territory, Australia. *Biological Conservation* 59:51-63.
RUSSELL-SMITH, J., N.L. MCKENZIE, and J.C.Z. WOINARSKI. 1992. Conserving vulnerable habitat in northern and northwestern Australia: The rainforest archipelago. In: I. MOFFATT and A.WEBB (Eds.). *Conservation and Development Issues in Northern Australia.* North Australia Research Unit, Darwin, pp. 63-68.
RUSSELL-SMITH, J., D.E. LUCAS, J. BROCK, and D.M.J.S. BOWMAN. 1993. *Allosyncarpia*-dominated rain forest in monsoonal northern Australia. *Journal of Vegetation Science* 4:67-82.
RUTHERFORD, M.C. and R.H. WESTFALL. 1994. *Biomes of Southern Africa: An Objective Categorization.* (2nd edition). National Botanical Institute, Pretoria.
RYAN, L. 1981. *The Aboriginal Tasmanians.* Allen & Unwin, St. Leonards, New South Wales.
RYAN, P.G. and P. BLOOMER. 1999. Long-billed lark complex, a species mosaic in southwestern Africa. *Auk* 116(1): 194-208.
RYLANDS, A.B. 1987. Primate communities in Amazonian forests: Their habitats and food resources. *Experientia* 43(3):265-279.
RYLANDS, A.B. 1990a. *Evaluation of the Current Status of Federal Conservation Areas in the Tropical Rain Forest of the Brazilian Amazon.* Vol. 1: *Review of Conservation Units System.* Vol. 2: *National Parks.* Vol. 3: *Biological Reserves.* Vol. 4: *Ecological Stations and Reserves.* Vol. 5: *Appendices.* Final Report, Project No. 6083, World Wildlife Fund-U.S., Washington, D.C.
RYLANDS, A.B. 1990b. Priority areas for conservation in Amazonia. *Trends in Ecology and Evolution* 5(8):240-241.
RYLANDS, A.B. 1991. *The Status of Conservation Areas in the Brazilian Amazon.* World Wildlife Fund Publications, Washington, D.C.
RYLANDS, A.B. and L.P. de S. PINTO. 1998. Conservação da biodiversidade na Amazônia Brasileira: Uma análise do sistema de unidades de conservação. *Cadernos FBDS,* No. 1. Fundação Brasileira para o Desenvolvimento Sustentável (FBDS), Rio de Janeiro.
RYLANDS, A.B., H. SCHNEIDER, A. LANGGUTH, R.A. MITTERMEIER, C.P. GROVES, and E. RODRÍGUEZ-LUNA. 2000. An assessment of the diversity of New World primates. *Neotropical Primates* 8(2):61-93.
RYLANDS, A.B., R.A. MITTERMEIER, and W.R. KONSTANT. 2001. Species and subspecies of primates described since 1990. *Neotropical Primates* 9(2):75-78.
SAGE, B. 1985. Conservation and exploitation. In: W.N. BONNER and D.W.H. WALTON (Eds.). *Key Environments -Antarctica.* Pergamon Press, Oxford, pp. 351-369.
SAIKKU, M. 1991. The extinction of the Carolina parakeet. *Environmental History Review* 14:1-18.
SAKKO, A.L. 1998. The influence of the Benguela upwelling system on Namibia's marine biodiversity. *Biodiversity and Conservation* 7(4):419-434.
SALATI, E. 1985. The climatology and hydrology of Amazonia. In: G. PRANCE and T. E. LOVEJOY (Eds.). *Amazonia.* Pergamon Press, Oxford, pp. 18-48.
SALATI, E., A. DAL'OLIO, E. MATUSI, and J.R. GAT. 1979. Recycling of water in the Brazilian Amazon Basin: An isotopic study. *Water Resources Research* 15:1250-1258.
SALATI, E., P.B. VOSE, and T.E. LOVEJOY. 1986. Amazon rainfall, potential effects of deforestation, and plans for future research. In: G.T. PRANCE (Ed.). *Tropical Rain Forests and the World Atmosphere,* Westview Press, Boulder, Colorado, pp. 61-74.
SALO, J.S., R.J. KALLIOLA, I. HÄKKINEN, Y. MÄKINEN, P. NIEMELÄ, M. PUHAKKA, and P.D. COLEY. 1986. River dynamics and the diversity of Amazon lowland forest. *Nature* 322:254-258.
SAMAB (Southern Appalachian Man and Biosphere program). 1996. The Southern Appalachian Assessment. www.samab.org/saa/saa_intro.html
SAMPAIO, E. and M. de JESÚS RODAL. 2000. Fitofisionomias de Caatinga. Relatório Técnico, Projeto "Avaliação e Ações Prioritárias para a Conservação da Biodiversidade do Bioma Caatinga". www.biodiversitas.org/caatinga
SAMPAIO, E.V.S.B. 1995. Overview of the Brazilian Caatinga. In: S.H. BULLOCK, H.A. MOONEY, and E. MEDINA (Eds.). *Seasonally Dry Tropical Forests.* Cambridge University Press, Cambridge, U.K., pp. 35-63.
SAMPAIO, Y. and J.E. MAZZA. 2000. Diversidade sócio econômica e pressão antrópica na çaatinga Nordestina. Relatório Técnico, Projeto "Avaliação e Ações Prioritárias para a Conservação da Biodiversidade do Bioma Caatinga". www.biodiversitas.org/caatinga
SANDOZ, M. 1964. *The Beaver Men: Spearheads of Empire.* Hastings House, Publishers, New York.
SANDWEISS, D.H., H. McINNIS, R.L. BURGER, A. CANO, B. OJEDA, R. PAREDES, M. de C. SANDWEISS, and M.D. GLASCOCK. 1998. Quebrada Jaguay: Early South American maritime adaptations. *Science* 18:1830-1832.
SARAVIA TOLEDO, C. 1982. Chaco semiárido. In: *Conservación de la vegetación natural en la República Argentina.* Serie Conservación de la Naturaleza. Simposio XVIII Jornadas Argentinas de Botánica 2, pp. 29-34.
SARMIENTO, G. 1983. The savannas of tropical America. In: F. BOURLIERE (Ed.). *Ecosystems of the World.* Vol 13. *Tropical Savannas.* Elsevier Scientific Publishing Co., New York, pp. 245-288.
SAYER, J., C. HARCOURT, and N. COLLINS (Eds.). 1992. *The Conservation Atlas of Tropical Forests. Africa.* The World Conservation Union, U.K.
SCBS (Society for the Conservation of Bighorn Sheep). 2000. http://desertbighorn.cjb.net
SCHALLER, G.B. 1972. *The Serengeti Lion: A Study of Predator-Prey Relations.* University of Chicago Press, Illinois.
SCHALLER, G.B. 1973. *Golden Shadows, Flying Hooves.* Alfred A. Knopf, New York.
SCHMIDT, J. and T. SCHMIDT. 1995. *The Smithsonian Guides to Natural America: The Northern Rockies.* Smithsonian Books, Washington, D.C.
SCHMIDT Jr., R.H. 1979. A climatic delineation of the "real" Chihuahuan Desert. *Journal of Arid Environments* 2: 243-250.
SCHMIDT Jr., R.H. 1983a. Climate and the Chihuahuan Desert. In: E. CAMPOS and R.J. ANDERSON (Eds.). *Natural Resources and Renewable Resources and Development in Arid Regions.* Westview Press, Boulder, Colorado, pp. 35-52.
SCHMIDT Jr., R.H. 1983b. *Clima y desierto chihuahuense.* Desierto y Ciencia. Centro de Investigacion en Química Applicada (CIQA), Saltillo, Coahuila.
SCHMIDT Jr., R.H. 1986. Chihuahuan climate. In: J.C. BARLOW, A.M. POWELL, and B.N. TIMMERMANN (Eds.). *Second Symposium on Resources of the Chihuahuan Desert.* Chihuahuan Desert Research Institute, Alpine, Texas, pp. 40-63.
SCHMIDT Jr., R.H. 1989. The arid zones of Mexico: Climatic extremes and conceptualization of the Sonoran Desert. *Journal of Arid Environments* 16:241-256.
SCHNEIDER, J.S. 1996. The desert tortoise and early peoples of the western deserts. Special report to the Desert Tortoise Preserve Committee, Inc. www.tortoise-tracks.org/publications/schneider.html
SCHOEMAN, A. 1996. *Skeleton Coast.* Southern Book Publishers, Halfway House, South Africa.
SCHOONMAKER, P.K., B. von HAGEN, and E.C. WOLF. 1997. *The Rain Forests of Home: Profile of a North American Region.* Island Press, Washington, D.C.
SCHUBERT, C. and O. HUBER. *The Gran Sabana: Panorama of a Region.* Lagoven Booklets, Caracas.
SCHULLERY, P. 1997. *Searching for Yellowstone.* Houghton Mifflin Company, Boston.
SCM, CNPq/MCT, and IPAAM. 1996. *Mamirauá: Plano de Manejo (Síntese).* Sociedade Civil Mamirauá (SCM), Conselho Nacional de Desenvolvimento Científico (CNPq), Ministério de Ciências e Tecnologia (MCT), Instituto de Proteção Ambiental do Estado do Amazonas (IPAAM), Brasília and Manaus.
SCOTLAND'S BIRD CLUB. 2002. www.the-soc.fsnet.co.uk

SCOTT, D.A. and M. CARBONELL (Compilers). 1986. *Inventario de Humedales de la Región Neotropical.* IWRB, Slimbridge, and IUCN, Cambridge.
SCOTT, J. 1995. *Kingdom of Lions.* Kyle Cathie Ltd., London.
SEAL CONSERVATION SOCIETY. 2001. Walrus (*Odobenus rosmarus*). www.pinnipeds.fsnet.co.uk/species/walrus
SEELY, M.K. 1989. Is there anything special about the Namib Desert? *South African Journal of Science* 85(4):215.
SEELY, M.K. 1992. *The Namib: Natural History of an Ancient Desert.* (2nd edition). Shell, Namibia, Windhoek.
SEKHRAN, N. and S. MILLER (Eds.). 1994. *Papua New Guinea Country Study on Biological Diversity.* Report of United Nations Development Programme, Department of Environment and Conservation, and the Africa Centre for Resources and Environment, Waigani, Papua New Guinea.
SHANTZ, H.L. and C.F. MARBUT. 1923. *The Vegetation and Soils of Africa.* American Geographical Society, Research Series No. 13, New York.
SHIRKOV, E.I., A.S. AVDEYEV, A.M. TOKRANOV, L.V. YEGINA, and E.E. SHIRKOVA. In press. *Comparative Economic Evaluation of Aquatic Biological and Hydro-Carbon Resources and Mineral Resources at Western Kamchatka in Relation to the Problems of Energy Supply and Development in the Region.* The Wild Salmon Center, Petropavlovsk, Kamchatka, and Portland, Oregon.
SHORT, L.L. 1975. A zoogeographic analysis of the South American Chaco avifauna. *Bulletin of the American Museum of Natural History* 154(3):163-352.
SHREVE, F. 1925. Ecological aspects of the deserts of California. *Ecology* 6:93-103.
SHREVE, F. 1942. The desert vegetation of North America. *Botanical Review* 8:195-246.
SHREVE, F. and I.L. WIGGINS. 1975. *Vegetation and Flora of the Sonoran Desert.* Stanford University Press, Stanford.
SIEGFRIED, W.R. 1985. Birds and mammals: Oceanic birds of the Antarctic. In: W.N. BONNER and D.W.H. WALTON (Eds.). *Key Environments -Antarctica.*, Pergamon Press, Oxford, pp. 242-265.
SILVA, J.M. and D.C. OREN. 1993. Observations on the habitat and distribution of the Brazilian three-banded armadillo (*Tolypeutes tricinctus*), a threatened Caatinga endemic. *Mammalia* 57:149-152.
SIMMONS, N.B. 1996. A new species of *Micronycteris* (Chiroptera: Phyllostomidae) from northeastern Brazil, with comments on phylogenetic relationships. *American Museum Novitates* 3158:1-34.
SINCLAIR, I. and I.J. WHYTE. 1991. *Field Guide to the Birds of the Kruger National Park.* Struik Publishers, Cape Town.
SINYAKOV, S.A., N.B. MARKEVICH, V.Y. UPRYAMOV, A.G. OSTROUMOV, N.V. VARNAVSKAYA, A.V. MASLOV, V.P. URNYSHEVA, Y.L. MUZUROV, P.N. GORDEICHUK, M.R. KOROLYOV, D.S. PAVLOV, K.A. SAVVAITOVA, K.V. KUZISCHIN, S.V. MAKSIMOV, and G.R. RAHR. 2000. *Site Selection and Analysis of River Systems.* A report prepared for the UNDP/GEF Project "Conservation of Salmonid Biodiversity and Their Sustainable Use." UNDP, Petropavlovsk, Kamchatka, Russia.
SIOLI, H. 1967. Studies in Amazonian waters. In: *Atas do Simpósio sobre a Biota Amazónica,* Vol. 3, *Limnologia.* Fundação Brasileira para a Proteção da Natureza, Rio de Janeiro, pp. 9-50.
SIOLI, H. 1984. The Amazon and its main affluents: Hydrography, morphology of the river courses, and river types. In: A. SIOLI (Ed.). *The Amazon. Limnology and Landscape Ecology of a Mighty Tropical River and Its Basin.* Dr. W. Junk Publishers, Dordrecht, pp. 127-165.
SIZER, N. and R. RICE. 1995. *Backs to the Wall in Suriname: Forest Policy in a Country in Crisis.* World Resources Institute, Washington, D.C.
SKAIFE, S.H. 1979. *African Insect Life.* New edition revised by John Ledger. Struik Publishers, Cape Town.
SKINNER, J.D. and R.H.N. SMITHERS. 1990. *The Mammals of the Southern African Subregion.* University of Pretoria, Pretoria.
SMETANIN, M.M. 2000. *Catalog of Vertebrates of Kamchatka and Adjacent Waters, Petropavlovsk-Kamchatsky.* Kamchatskiy, Pechatniy Dvor.
SMITH, H.S. 1995. *Handbook of Lizards: Lizards of the United States and Canada.* Comstock Publishing Associates, Ithaca, New York.
SMITH, L.A. and R.E. JOHNSTONE. 1977. Status of the purple-crowned wren (*Malurus coronatus*) and buff-sided robin (*Poecilodryas superciliosa*) in Western Australia. *Western Australian Naturalist* 13:185-188.
SMITH, N.H., E.A. SERRAO, P.T. ALVIM, and I.C. FALESI. 1995. *Amazonia: Resiliency and Dynamism of the Land and Its People.* United Nations University Press, New York.
SMITH, W., B. EVANS, T. WILSON, A. NIKIFORUK, K. BALTGAILIS, A. BRADY, L. BREWSTER, T. GRAY, W. HORTER, P. LEE, R. LIVERNASH, C. McGLYNN, S. MINNEMEYER, A. O'CARROLL, A. PENN, G. QUALIE, M. SAWYER, E. SELING, and D. BRYANT. 2000. *Canada's Forests at a Crossroads: An Assessment in the Year 2000.* A Global Forest Watch Canada Report. World Resources Institute, Washington, D.C.
SMITHERS, R.H.N. 1971. *The Mammals of Botswana.* Museum Memoir No. 4. The Trustees of the National Museums of Rhodesia. Salisbury, Rhodesia.
SNELSON, D. (Ed.). 1986. *Lake Manyara National Park.* Tanzania National Parks/African Wildlife Foundation, Arusha, Tanzania.
SNELSON, D. (Ed.). 1992. *Tarangire National Park.* Tanzania National Parks/African Wildlife Foundation, Arusha, Tanzania.
SOLBRIG, O.T. 1976. The origin and floristic affinities of the South American temperate desert and semidesert regions. In: D.W. GOODALL (Eds.). *Evolution of Desert Biota.* University of Texas Press, Austin and London, pp. 7-49.
SOMME, L. 1985. Terrestrial habitats: Invertebrates. In: W.N. BONNER and D.W.H. WALTON (Eds.), *Key Environments -Antarctica.* Pergamon Press, Oxford, pp. 106-117.
SORIANO, A., M. NOGUÉS LOZA, and S. BURKART. 1998. Plant biodiversity in the extra-Andean Patagonia: Comparisons with neighbouring and related vegetation units. In: M. OESTERHELD, M.R. AGUIAR, and J.M. PARUELO (Eds.). *Ecosistemas Patagónicos. Ecología Austral* 36-45.
SOUTHERN FOREST RESOURCE ASSESSMENT. 2002. www.srs.fs.fed.us/sustain
SOUTHGATE, R., C. PALMER, M. ADAMS, P. MASTERS, B. TRIGGS, and J. WOINARSKI. 1996. Population and habitat characteristics of the golden bandicoot (*Isoodon auratus*) on Marchinbar Island, Northern Territory. *Wildlife Research* 23:647-664.
SPARKS, J. 1992. *Realms of the Russian Bear.* Little, Brown and Company, Boston.
SPRAWLS, S., K. HOWELL, R. DREWES, and J. ASHE. 2002. *A Field Guide to the Reptiles of East Africa.* Academic Press, London.
SPECIAL SUPPORT SERVICES. 1999. *Aerial Census of Wildlife in Northern Namibia.* Report of the Ministry of Environment and Tourism, Namibia.
STANDEN, V.G. 1997. Temprana complejidad funeraria de la cultura chinchorro (norte de Chile). *Latin American Antiquity* 8:134-156.
STANFORD, J.A., N.J. GAYESKI, D.S. PAVLOV, K.A. SAVVAITOVA, and K.V. KUZISHCHIN. 2000. *Biophysical Complexity of the Krutogorova River (Kamchatka, Russia).* Flathead Lake Biological Station, Montana.
STARK, L.R. and A.T. WHITTEMORE. 2001. Noteworthy bryophyte records from the Mojave Desert. *Southwestern Naturalist* 45:226-232.
STATTERSFIELD, A.J., M.J. CROSBY, A.J. LONG, and D.C. WEGE. 1998. *Endemic Bird Areas of the World: Priorities for Biodiversity Conservation.* BirdLife Conservation Series No. 7, BirdLife International, Cambridge, U.K.
STEBBINS, G.L. and J. MAJOR. 1965. Endemism and speciation in the California flora. *Ecological Monographs* 35:1-35.
STEBBINS, R.C. 1985. *A Field Guide to Western Reptiles and Amphibians.* (2nd edition, revised). Houghton Mifflin Company, Boston.
STEIN, B.A., L.S. KUTNER, and J.S. ADAMS (Eds.). 2000. *Precious Heritage: The Status of Biodiversity in the United States.* Oxford University Press.
STEPHENSON, M. 1997. *Canada's National Parks: A Visitor's Guide.* Prentice Hall Canada, Inc., Scarborough, Ontario.
STEVENSON, M.R., R.E. TOTH, T.C. EDWARDS Jr., L. HUNTER, R.J. LILIEHOLM, K.S. KARISH, J. DENORMANDIE, M. GONZÁLEZ, and M. CABLK. 2002. *What If? Alternative Futures for the California Mojave Desert.* www.esri.com/library/userconf/proc00/professional/papers/PAP192/p192.htm
STEWART, D.J., R. BARRIGA, and M. IBARRA. 1987. Ictiofauna de la cuenca del río Napo, Ecuador oriental: lista anotada das especies. *Revista del Politécnica* 12:9-63.
ST. GEORGE, G. 1974. *Soviet Deserts and Mountains.* Time-Life International, Amsterdam.
STONE, P.B. (Ed.). 1992. *State of the World's Mountains: A Global Report.* Zed Books Ltd., London.
STONEHOUSE, B. 1985. Birds and mammals: Penguins. In: W.N. BONNER and D.W.H. WALTON (Eds.). *Key Environments -Antarctica.* Pergamon Press, Oxford, pp. 266- 292.
STONEHOUSE, B. 2000. *The Last Continent -Discovering Antarctica.* SCF Books, Norfolk, U.K.
STRAHAN, R. 1995. *The Mammals of Australia.* Imago Productions, Singapore.
STRANGE, I.J. 1992. *A Field Guide to the Wildlife of the Falkland Islands and South Georgia.* Harper Collins.
STRUHSAKER, T.T. 1987. Forestry issues and conservation in Uganda. *Biological Conservation* 39:209-234.
STUART, S.N., R.J. ADAMS, and M.D. JENKINS. 1990. *Biodiversity in Sub-Saharan Africa and Its Islands: Conservation, Management, and Sustainable Use.* Occasional Paper 6. IUCN/SSC, Gland, Switzerland.
SUPRIATNA, J. 1999. *The Irian Jaya Biodiversity Conservation Priority-Setting Workshop Final Report.* Conservation International, Washington, D.C.
SUTTLES, W. 1990. Environment. In: W. SUTTLES (Ed.). *Northwest Coast,* Volume 7: *Handbook of North American Indians.* Smithsonian Institution, Washington, D.C., pp. 16-29.
SWANEY, D. 1997. *Iceland, Greenland, and the Faroe Islands.* Lonely Planet Publications, Victoria, Australia.
SZARO, R.C. 1991. Wildlife communities of southwestern riparian ecosystems. In: J.E. RODIEK and E.G. BOLEN (Eds.). *Wildlife and Habitats in Managed Landscapes.* Island Press, Washington, D.C.
TABER, A.B. 1991. The status and conservation of the Chacoan peccary in Paraguay. *Oryx* 25(3):147-55.
TABER, A.B., G. NAVARRO, and M.A. ARRIBAS. 1997. A new park in the Bolivian Gran Chaco: An advance in tropical dry forest conservation and community-based management. *Oryx* 31(3):189-198.
TAKHTAJAN, A. 1986. *Floristic Regions of the World.* University of California Press, Berkeley.
TARDIN, A.T., D.C.L. LEE, R.J.R. SANTOS, O.R. de ASSIS, M.P. dos S. BARBOSA, M. de L. MOREIRA, M.T. PEREIRA, D. SILVA, and C.P. dos SANTOS FILHO. 1980. *Subprojeto Desmatamento. Convênio IBDF/CNPq-INPE, 1979.* Instituto Nacional de Pesquisas Espaciais, Relatório INPE-1649-RPE/103. São José dos Campos, São Paulo.
TER STEEGE H. 2000. *Plant Diversity in Guyana.* Tropenbos Series 18. Tropenbos Foundation, Waginigen, The Netherlands.
TEUGELS, G.G. and J.F. GUÉGAN. 1994. Diversité biologique des poissons d'eaux douces de la Basse-Guinée et de l'Afrique Centrale. *Annals du Musée Afrique Central Zoologique* 275:67-85.
THACKWAY, R. and I.D. CRESSWELL (Eds.). 1995. *An Interim Biogeographic Regionalisation for Australia: A Framework for Establishing the National System of Reserves, Version 4.0.* Australian Nature Conservation Agency, Canberra.
THE NATURE CONSERVANCY. 2001. Landmark conservation agreement marks success of broad community partnership.
http://nature.org/wherewewor.ica/states/nevada/news/news455.html
THE NATURE CONSERVANCY and ASSOCIACÃO CAATINGA. 2000. Estratégias para Conservação. Relatório Técnico, Projeto "Avaliação e Ações Prioritárias para a Conservação da Biodiversidade do Bioma Caatinga".
www.biodiversitas.org/caatinga
THESIGER, W. 1959. *Arabian Sands.* Penguin Books, Harmondsworth, U.K.
THE WORLD GAZETEER. 2002. www.gazetteer.de/home.htm
THOMAS, D.S.G. and P.A. SHAW. 1991. *The Kalahari Environment.* Cambridge University Press, Cambridge.
THOMPSON, L.G., E. MOSLEY-THOMPSON, M.E. DAVIS, P.N. LIN, K.A. HENDERSON, J. COLE-DAI, J.F. BOLZAN, and K.B. LIU. 1995. Late glacial stage and Holocene tropical ice-core records from Huascarán, Peru. *Science* 269:46-50.
THORBJARNARSON, J.B. 1991. An analysis of the spectacled caiman (*Caiman crocodilus*) harvest program in Venezuela. In: J.G. ROBINSON and K.H. REDFORD (Eds.). *Tropical Wildlife Use and Conservation.* University of Chicago Press, Chicago, pp. 217-235.
THORBJARNARSON, J.B. (Compiler), H. MESSEL, F.W. KING, and J.P. ROSS (Eds.). 1992. *Crocodiles: An Action Plan for Their Conservation.* IUCN, Gland, Switzerland.
THORBJARNARSON, J.B. and A. VELASCO. 1999. Economic incentives for management of Venezuelan caiman. *Conservation Biology* 13:397-406.
TIMBERLAKE, J.R. 1998. *Biodiversity of the Zambezi Basin Wetlands: Review and Preliminary Assessment of Available Information.* Biodiversity Foundation for Africa, Bulawayo, and Zambezi Society, Harare, Zimbabwe.
TIMBERLAKE, J.R. (Ed.). 2000. *Biodiversity of the Zambezi Basin Wetlands.* Consultancy Report for IUCN ROSA. 4 volumes. Biodiversity Foundation for Africa, Bulawayo, and Zambezi Society, Harare, Zimbabwe.
TIMBERLAKE, J.R., R.B. DRUMMOND, P. SMITH, and M.J. BINGHAM. 2000. Wetland plants of the Zambezi Basin. In: J.R. TIMBERLAKE (Ed.). *Biodiversity of the Zambezi Basin Wetlands,* Vol. II. Consultancy Report for IUCN ROSA. Biodiversity Foundation for Africa, Bulawayo, and Zambezi Society, Harare, Zimbabwe, pp. 31-81.
TJIN, R. and E. SCHELLEKENS. 1999. *The Guide to Suriname.* Brasa Publishers, Amsterdam.
TLOU, T. 1985. *A History of Ngamiland 1750-1906: The Formation of an African State.* Macmillan, Gaborone, Botswana.
TOHAM, A.K. 2001. *Addressing Threats Affecting Biodiversity in Central Africa.* WWF Central Africa Regional Office (CARPO). Draft, unpublished.
TOLEDO, V.M. 1988. La diversidad biológica de México. *Ciencia y Desarrollo* XIV(81):17-30.
TORRES, H. (Ed.). 1992. *South American Camelids: An Action Plan for Their Conservation.* IUCN, Gland, Switzerland.
TROTH, R.G. 1979. Vegetational types on a ranch in the central Llanos of Venezuela. In: J.F. EISENBERG (Ed.). *Vertebrate Ecology in the Northern Neotropics.* Smithsonian Institution, Washington, D.C., pp. 17-30.
TRYON, B.W. and D.W. HERMAN. 1990. Status, conservation, and management of the bog turtle (*Clemmys muhlenbergii*) in the southeastern United States. In: K. BEAMAN, F. CAPRASO, S. McKEOWN, and M. GRAFF (Eds.). *Proceedings of the First International Symposium on Turtles and Tortoises: Conservation and Captive Husbandry.* Chapman University, Orange, California, August 9-12, pp. 36-53.
TURKALO, A.Z. and J.M. FAY. 2001. Forest elephant behavior and ecology-observations from the Dzanga Saline. In: L. NAUGHTON-TREVES, A. VEDDER, W. WEBER, and L.J.T. WHITE (Eds.). *African Rainforest Ecology and Conservation.* Yale University Press, New Haven and London, pp. 207-213.
TURNBULL, C. 1961. *The Forest People.* Simon and Schuster, New York.
TURNER, T. 1990. *Wild by Law: The Sierra Club Legal Defense Fund and the Places It Has Saved.* Sierra Club Books, San Francisco.
TYLER, M.J. 1999. Distribution patterns of amphibians in the Australo-Papuan Region. In: W.E. DUELLMAN (Ed.). *Patterns of Distribution of Amphibians: A Global Perspective.* Johns Hopkins University Press, London, pp. 541-563.
TYLER, S.J. and D.R. BISHOP. 2001. Botswana. In: L.D.C. FISHPOOL and M.I. EVANS (Eds.). *Important Bird Areas in Africa and Associated Islands: Priority Sites for Conservation.* BirdLife Conservation Series No. 11. Pisces Publications and BirdLife International, Newbury and Cambridge, U.K., pp. 99-112.
UETZ, P. 2001 and 2002. *The EMBL Reptile Database.* 5th Anniversary edition.
www.embl-heidelberg.de/~uetz/LivingReptiles.html
UNDP (United Nations Development Programme). 1998. *Final Report: Consultation of Local Communities as Part of Sub-contract No. 4, "Stakeholders Consultations for Enhancing the Capacity of Suriname to Conserve Biodiversity."* United Nations Development Programme, Pre-Investment Facility (PRIF) of the Global Environment Facility, NGO Services Bureau, Paramaribo, Suriname.
UNEP/WCMC. 2002. The World Conservation Monitoring Centre. www.unep-wcmc.org/cgi-bin/padb.p
USCB (United States Census Bureau). 2000.
http://factfinder.census.gov.htm
USCB (United States Census Bureau). 2002.
www.census.gov
United States Embassy in Colombia. 2002.
http://usembassy.state.gov/colombia
USFWS (United States Fish and Wildlife Service). 1994a. *Desert Tortoise (Mojave Population) Recovery Plan.* U.S. Fish and Wildlife Service, Portland, Oregon.
USFWS (United States Fish and Wildlife Service). 1994b. *Conservation Plan for the Pacific Walrus in Alaska.*
USFWS (United States Fish and Wildlife Service). 1996. *California Condor Recovery Plan.* Portland, Oregon.
USFWS (United States Fish and Wildlife Service). 2000. *Bog Turtle* (Clemmys muhlenbergii), *Northern Population, Recovery Plan.* Technical Draft. Hadley, Massachusetts.
UNITED STATES FOREST SERVICE 2002.
http://www.fs.fed.us
USGS (United States Geological Survey). 1999. *Status and Trends of the Nation's Biological Resources.* USGS-Biological Resources Division, National Status and Trends Reports Series. Washington, D.C.
USGS/LUHNACP (United States Geological Survey/Land Use History of North America-Colorado Plateau). 2002.
http://biology.usgs.gov/luhna/index.html
USGS-SDMT (United States Geological Survey-Science Data Management Team). 1998. Report on the Mohveg Project: Map of the existing plant communities of the 23 million acres of the California portion of the Mojave. Inventory of major ongoing scientific activities in the California or Mojave Desert.
http://wrgis.wr.usgs.gov/MojaveEco/SDMT/sd3.html
UQUILLAS, J. 1984. Colonization and spontaneous settlement in the Ecuadorean Amazon. In: M. SCHMINK and C.H. WOOD (Eds.). *Frontier Expansion in Amazonia.* University of Florida Press, Gainesville, pp. 261-284.
USHER, M.B. and D. BALHARRY. 1996. *Biogeographical Zonation of Scotland.* Scottish Natural Heritage, U.K.
VAISMAN, A. 2001. *Trawling in the Mist: Industrial Fisheries in the Russian Part of the Bering Sea.* TRAFFIC International, Cambridge, U.K.
VAN DER WALT, P. and E. le RICHE. 1999. *The Kalahari and Its Plants.* Published by the authors, Pretoria.
VAN OOSTERZEE, P. 2000 *The Centre: The Natural History of Australia's Desert Regions.* J.B. Books Pty. Ltd., Marleston, South Australia.
VAN ROOSMALEN, M.G.M., T. van ROOSMALEN, R.A. MITTERMEIER, and G.A.B. da FONSECA. 1998. A new and distinctive species of marmoset (Callitrichidae, Primates) from the lower Rio Aripuanã, state of Amazonas, central Brazilian Amazonia. *Goeldiana Zoologia* (22):1-27.

VAN ROOSMALEN, M.G.M., T. van ROOSMALEN, R.A. MITTERMEIER, and A.B. RYLANDS. 2000. Two new species of marmoset, genus *Callithrix* Erxleben, 1777 (Callitrichidae, Primates), from the Tapajós/Madeira interfluvium, south central Amazonia. *Neotropical Primates* 8(1):2-18.

VAN ROOSMALEN, M.G.M., T. van ROOSMALEN, and R.A. MITTERMEIER. 2002. A taxonomic review of titi monkeys, genus *Callicebus* Thomas, 1903, with the description of two new species, *Callicebus bernhardi* and *Callicebus stephennashi*, from Amazonia. *Neotropical Primates* 10(suppl.): In press.

VAN ROOYEN, N. 2001. *Flowering Plants of the Kalahari Dunes*. Ekotrust CC., Lynwood, Pretoria.

VANSINA, J. 1990. *Paths in the Rainforests: Toward a History of Political Tradition in Equatorial Africa*. James Currey, London.

VANSTONE, J.W. 1988. Northern Athapaskans: People of the deer. In: W.W. Fitzhugh and A. Crowell (Eds.), *Crossroads of Continents: Cultures of Siberia and Alaska*. Smithsonian Institution Press, Washington, D.C., pp. 64-68.

VASCONCELOS SOBRINHO, J. 1971. *As Regiões Naturais do Nordeste, o Meio e a Civilização*. Conselho do Desenvolvimento de Pernambuco, Recife.

VASEK, F.C. 1980. Creosote bush: Long-lived clones in the Mojave Desert. *American Journal of Botany* 67(2):246-255.

VASEK, F.C. and M.G. BARBOUR. 1988. Mojave Desert scrub vegetation. In: M.G. BARBOUR and J. MAJOR (Eds.). *Terrestrial Vegetation of California*. California Native Plant Society, Special Publication No. 9. Sacramento, pp. 835-867.

VELLARD, J. 1948. Batracios del Chaco argentino. *Acta Zoológica Lilloana del Instituto "Miguel Lillo"* 5:137-174.

INPARQUES (Instituto Nacional de Parques), Venezuela. 1982. *Guía de los Parques Nacionales y Monumentos Naturales de Venezuela*. Instituto Nacional de Parques, Ediciones Fundación de Educación Ambiental, Caracas.

VERÍSSIMO, A., A. MOREIRA, D. SAWYER, I. dos SANTOS, L.P. PINTO and J.P.R. CAPOBIANCO (Eds.). 2001. *Biodiversidade na Amazônia Brasileira: Avaliação e Ações Prioritárias para a Conservação, Uso Sustentável e Repartição de Benefícios*. Instituto Socioambiental, Estação Liberdade, São Paulo. www.socioambiental.org/website/bio/index.htm

VERON, J.E.N. 1998. Corals of the Milne Bay region of Papua New Guinea. In: T.B. WERNER and G.R. ALLEN (Eds.). *A Rapid Biodiversity Assessment of the Coral Reefs of Milne Bay Province, Papua New Guinea*. RAP Working Papers 11. Conservation International, Washington, D.C., pp. 26-34.

VIANA, M.S. and V.H.L NEUMANN. 1999. The Crato member of the Santana formation, Ceará State, Brazil. In: C. SCHOBBENHAUS, D.A. CAMPOS, E.T. QUEIROZ, M. WINGE, and M. BERBERT-BORN (Eds.), *Sítios Geológicos e Paleontológicos do Brasil*. www.unb.br/ig/sigep/sitio005/sitio005english.htm

VILA, P. 1960. *Geografía de Venezuela. 1. El territorio nacional y su ambiente físico*. Ministerio de Educación. Dirección de Cultura y Bellas Artes, Caracas.

WAGNER, F.H. 1979. *Wildlife of the Deserts*. Chanticleer Press, New York.

WALL, D. 1996. *Western National Wildlife Refuges*. Museum of New Mexico Press, Santa Fe.

WALLACE, A.R. 1853a. *Narrative of Travels on the Amazon and Rio Negro*. Reeve and Co., London.

WALLACE, A.R. 1853b. *The Geographical Distribution of Animals*. Vols. 1 and 2. Macmillan, London.

WALLACE, R. (Ed.). 1972. *The Grand Canyon*. Time-Life Books, New York.

WALLS, J.G. 1994. *Jewels of the Rainforest: The Poison Frogs of the Family Dendrobatidae*. T.F.H. Publications, Neptune City, New Jersey.

WALTER, H., D.S. PAVAHAN, and J.B. FROKE. 1991. Terrestrial vertebrates of the U.S.-Mexico borderlands: Results of a preliminary zoogeographical transect. In: P. GANSTER and H. WALTER (Eds.). *Environmental Hazard and Bioresource Management in the United States-Mexico Borderlands*. Latin American Center, UCLA, Los Angeles, pp. 407-432.

WALTER, K.S. and H.J. GILLETT (Eds.). 1998. *1997 IUCN Red List of Threatened Plants*. Compiled by the World Conservation Monitoring Center. IUCN–The World Conservation Union, Gland, Switzerland, and Cambridge, U.K.

WARD, J.O. and J.H. SANDERS. 1980. Nutritional determinants and migration in the Brazilian northeast: A case study of rural and urban Ceará. *Economic Development and Cultural Change* 29(1):141-163.

WARINWA, A.F. 2001. The impact of conflict on wildlife and food security in south Sudan: Report on wildlife component. Unpublished report to USAID.

WATSON, A.E., G. APLET, and J.C. HENDEE. 2000. *Personal, Societal, and Ecological Values of Wilderness: Sixth World Wilderness Congress Proceedings on Research, Management and Allocation*. Volumes I and II. United States Department of Agriculture, Forest Service.

WCMC (World Conservation Monitoring Centre). 1991. *Biodiversity Guide to Pakistan*. World Conservation Monitoring Centre, Cambridge.

WCMC (World Conservation Monitoring Centre). 2002a. www.wcmc.org.uk/data/database/un_combo.html

WCMC (World Conservation Monitoring Centre), 2002b. www.unep-wcmc.org/sites/wh/grandcan.html

WEBB, K. 1974. *The Changing Face of Northeast Brazil*. Columbia University Press, New York.

WEINER, D.A. 1999. *A Little Corner of Freedom: Russian Nature Protection from Stalin to Gorbachev*. University of California Press, Berkeley.

WELLER, G. and P. ANDERSON (Eds.). 1998. *Assessing the Consequences of Climate Change for Alaska and the Bering Sea Region*. Workshop on the Consequences of Global Change for Alaska and the Bering Sea Region. Center for Global Change and Arctic System Research. University of Alaska, Fairbanks.

WENDEL DE MAGALHÃES, N. 1992. *Conheça O Pantanal*. Terragraph, S/C, São Paulo.

WERGER, M.J.A. and B.J. COETZEE. 1978. The Sudano-Zambezian Region. In: M.J.A. WERGER (Ed.). *Biogeography and Ecology of Southern Africa*. W. Junk, The Hague, pp. 301-462.

WESTERN AUSTRALIAN MUSEUM. 1981. *Biological Survey of Mitchell Plateau and Admiralty Gulf, Kimberley, Western Australia*. Western Australian Museum, Perth.

WETTERBERG, G.B., M.T.J. PÁDUA, C.S. de CASTRO, and J.M.C. VASCONCELLOS. 1976. Uma análise de prioridades em conservação da natureza na Amazônia. *Projeto de Desenvolvimento e Pesquisa Florestal (PRODEPEF) PNUD/FAO/IBDF/BRA-45, Série Técnica* (8):1-63.

WETZEL, R.W., R.E. DUBOS, R.L. MARTIN, and P. MYERS. 1975. *Catagonus*, an "Extinct" peccary, alive in Paraguay. *Science* 189:379-381.

WHEELER, J.R. (Ed.). 1992. *Flora of the Kimberley Region*. Department of Conservation and Land Management, Perth.

WHEELER, R. 1990. The Colorado Plateau region. In: *Wilderness at the Edge: A Citizen Proposal to Protect Utah's Canyons and Deserts*. Utah Wilderness Coalition, Salt Lake City, pp. 97-104.

WHITE, F. 1976. The underground forests of Africa: A preliminary review. *Gardens' Bulletin (Singapore)* 24:57-71.

WHITE, F. 1983a. *The Vegetation of Africa*. Natural Resources Research No. 20. UNESCO, Paris.

WHITE, F. 1983b. *UNESCO/AETFAT/UNSO Vegetation Map of Africa*. Scale 1:5 000 000 (in colour). UNESCO, Paris.

WHITE, F. 1983c. *The Vegetation of Africa: A Descriptive Memoir to Accompany the UNESCO/AEFTAT/UNSO Vegetation Map of Africa*. UNESCO, Paris.

WHITE, L. 1995. *Etude de la végétation de la Lopé*. Projet ECOFAC, AGRECO, CTFT. Libreville, Gabon.

WHITE, L. and K. ABERNETHY. 1997. *A Guide to the Vegetation of the Lopé Reserve, Gabon*. Wildlife Conservation Society. ECOFAC, Libreville, Gabon.

WHITE, L. 2001. The African Rain Forest: Climate and Vegetation. In: L. NAUGHTON-TREVES, A. VEDDER, W. WEBER, and L.J.T. WHITE (Eds.). *African Rainforest Ecology and Conservation*. Yale University Press, New Haven and London, pp. 3-29.

WHITE, L., A. VEDDER, and L. NAUGHTON-TREVES. 2001. *African Rain Forest Ecology and Conservation*. Wildlife Conservation Society, Yale University Press, New Haven.

WHITTAKER, R.H. 1956. Vegetation of the Great Smoky Mountains. *Ecological Monographs* 26:1-80.

WIGGINS, I.L. 1980. *Flora of Baja California*. Stanford University Press, Stanford.

WIGHTMAN, A., 1996. *Scotland's Mountains: An Agenda for Sustainable Development*. Scottish Wildlife and Countryside Link, U.K.

WILD, H. 1965. The flora of the Great Dyke of southern Rhodesia with special reference to the serpentine soils. *Kirkia* 5:49-86.

WILD, H. and L.A.G. BARBOSA. 1967. *Vegetation Map of the Flora Zambesiaca Area*. M.O. Collins, Salisbury (Harare), Zimabwe.

WILD RUSSIA. 2002. Center for Russian Nature Conservation. www.wild-russia.org

WILDSON, S. 2001. *Environmental Impact Assessment of Tsetse Eradication Programme in Ngamiland*. Final Report. Government of Botswana and Department for International Development, Maun, Botswana.

WILLIAMS, J.H. 1982. Paraguay's unchanging Chaco. *Américas* 34(4):14-19.

WILLIG, M.R., S.J. PRESLEY, R.D. OWEN, and C. LÓPEZ-GONZÁLEZ. 2000. Composition and structure of bat assemblages in Paraguay: A subtropical-temperate interface. *Journal of Mammalogy* 81(2):386-401.

WILLINK, P.W., B. CHERNOFF, L.E. ALONSO, J.R. MONTAMBAULT, and R. LOURIVAL (Eds.). 2000. *A Biological Assessment of the Aquatic Ecosystems of the Pantanal, Mato Grosso do Sul, Brasil*. RAP Bulletin of Biological Assessment 18. Conservation International, Washington, D.C.

WILSON, D.E. and D.M. REEDER (Eds.). 1993. *American Society of Mammalogists Mammal Species of the World: A Taxonomic and Geographic Reference*. 2nd edition. Smithsonian Institution Press, Washington, D.C.

WILY, L.A. and S. MBAYA. 2001. *Land, People, and Forests in Eastern and Southern Africa at the Beginning of the 21st Century. The Impact of Land Relations on the Role of Communities in Forest Future*. IUCN-EARO, Nairobi, Kenya.

WOINARSKI, J.C.Z. 1990. Effects of fire on bird communities of tropical woodlands and open forests in northern Australia. *Australian Journal of Ecology* 15:1-22.

WOINARSKI, J.C.Z. (Ed.). 1992. *The Wildlife and Vegetation of Purnululu (Bungle Bungle) National Park and Adjacent Area*. Wildlife Research Bulletin No. 6. Department of Conservation and Land Management, Perth.

WOINARSKI, J.C.Z., D. FRANKLIN, and G. CONNORS. 2000. Thinking honeyeater: Nectar maps for the Northern Territory, Australia, showing spatial and temporal variation in nectar availability. *Pacific Conservation Biology* 6:61-80.

WOINARSKI, J.C.Z., D.J. MILNE, and G. WANGANEEN. 2001. Changes in mammal populations in relatively intact landscapes of Kakadu National Park, Northern Territory, Australia. *Austral Ecology* 26:360-370.

WOOD, G.A. 1984. Tool use by the palm cockatoo (*Probosciger aterrimus*) during display. *Corella* 8:94-95.

WOODS, R. and A. WOODS. 1997. *Atlas of Breeding Birds of the Falkland Islands*. WWF-U.K./F.C., A. Nelson, U.K.

WORLD RESOURCES INSTITUTE. 1994. *World Resources 1994-1995: A Guide to the Global Environment*. World Resources Institute, Washington, D.C.

WRIGHT, D.D., J.H. JESSEN, P. BURKE, and H.G.S. GARZA. 1997. Tree and liane enumeration and diversity on a one-hectare plot in Papua New Guinea. *Biotropica* 29:250-260.

WWF (World Wildlife Fund). 1999. *Map of Terrestrial Ecoregions of Africa*. Revised edition. Conservation Science Program, WWF-U.S., Washington, D.C.

WWF (World Wildlife Fund). 2002. Indigenous peoples and conservation. www.panda.org/resources/publications/sustainability/indigenous.htm

WWF (World Wildlife Fund). In prep. WWF Ecoregion –Species Database. Washington, D.C. www.worldwildlife.org/science

WWF-SARPO. 2001. *Miombo Ecoregion Report*. WWF-SARPO, Harare, Zimbabwe.

YEAR BOOK AUSTRALIA. 1997. Aboriginal lands in South Australia. www.abs.gov.au/ausstats/abs@nsf

YIBARBUK, D., P.J. WHITEHEAD, J. RUSSELL-SMITH, D. JACKSON, C. GOHUWA, A. FISHER, P. COOKE, D. CHOQUENOT, and D.M.J.S. BOWMAN. 2001. Fire ecology and Aboriginal land management in central Arnhem Land, northern Australia: A tradition of ecosystem management. *Journal of Biogeography* 28:325-343.

YORIO P., E. FRERE, P. GANDINI, and G. HARRIS (Eds.). 1998. *Atlas de la distribución reproductiva de aves marinas en el litoral patagónico argentino*. Fundación Patagonia Natural, Puerto Madryn.

YOUNG, J.V. 1989. *State Parks of Utah: A Guide and History*. University of Utah Press, Salt Lake City.

ZEINER, D.C., W.F. LAUDENSLAYER, J.R., K.E. MAYER, and M. WHITE. 1990. *California's Wildlife*, Volume III: *Mammals*. State of California Department of Fish and Game, Sacramento.

ZHAO J., Z. GUANGMEI, W. HUADONG, and X. JIALIN. 1990. *The Natural History of China*. Collins, London.

ZIMMERMAN, B.L., C.A. PERES, J.R. MALCOLM, and T. TURNER. 2001. Conservation and development alliances with the Kayapó of southeastern Amazonia, a tropical forest indigenous people. *Environmental Conservation* 28:1-22.

ZIMMERMAN, D.A., D.A. TURNER, and D.J. PEARSON. 1996. *Birds of Kenya and Northern Tanzania*. Christopher Helm, London.

ZIZKA, G. and M. MUÑOZ-SCHICK. 1993. *Tillandsia marconae* Till & Vitec, a bromeliad species new to Chile. *Boletín del Museo Nacional de Historia Natural de Chile* 44:11-17.

ZWINGER, A.H. 1983. *A Desert Country Near the Sea: A Natural History of the Cape Region of Baja California*. Harper and Row, New York.

ZWINGER, A.H. and B.E. WILLARD. 1986. *Land Above the Trees: A Guide to American Alpine Tundra*. Harper and Row, New York.

Authors

John Aguiar
Department of Wildlife and Fisheries Sciences
2258 TAMU
Texas A&M University
College Station, TX 77843-2258, U.S.A.
steelshard@tamu.edu

Thomas S.B. Akre
Doctoral Student
MS3E1 Dept. of Biology
George Mason University
Fairfax, VA 22030, U.S.A.
takre@earthlink.net

Susan Andrew
Southern Appalachian Forest Coalition
46 Haywood St., Suite 323
Ashville, NC 28801, U.S.A.
susan@safc.org

Fabio Arjona
Conservation International-Colombia
Carrera 13 No. 71-41
Bogotá, COLOMBIA
F.Arjona@tutopia.com

Patricio Arrata
Conservation International-Ecuador
Coruña 17-54 y Noboa Camaño
Quito, ECUADOR
p.arrata@conservation.org

Conrad Aveling
Coordinator ECOFAC
Program-Conservation et Utilisation
Rationnelle des Ecosystemes-
Forestiers en AfriqueCentrale
BP 15115 Libreville, GABON
ecofac.cord@internetgabon.com
caveling@solsi.ga

José Márcio Ayres
NYZS The Wildlife Conservation Society
185th Street and Southern Boulevard
Bronx, New York 10460-1099, U.S.A.
and
Projeto Mamirauá
Departamento de Antropologia
Universidade Federal do Pará
Campus do Guamá
Caixa Postal 531
Belém 66073-250
Pará, BRAZIL
ayreswcs.bel@zaz.com.br

Mohammed I. Bakarr
Senior Technical Director
Center for Applied Biodiversity Science
Conservation International
Washington, DC, U.S.A.
m.bakarr@conservation.org

Rick Barongi
Director
Houston Zoological Gardens
1513 N. MacGregor
Houston, TX 77030, U.S.A.
rbarongi@aol.com

Bruce Beehler
Melanesia Program Director
Conservation International
Washington, DC, U.S.A.
b.beehler@conservation.org

Anthony E. Bowland
Parks and Wildlife Commission
of the Northern Territory,
PO Box 1046, Alice Springs, NT0871,
AUSTRALIA
Tony.Bowland@plmbay.pwcnt.nt.gov.au

Ian A. Bowles
Senior Research Fellow
Kennedy School of Government
Harvard University
79 JFK Street
Cambridge, MA 02138, U.S.A.
ian_bowles@harvard.edu
www.ksg.harvard.edu/bcsia
and
Senior Advisor
The Gordon and Betty Moore Foundation
Building 386, The Presidio
San Francisco, CA 94129, U.S.A.
www.moore.org

Nicholas H. Brooks
BMT Cordah
Kettock Lodge
Aberdeen Science and Technology Park
Bridge of Don
Aberdeen, AB22 8GU, UNITED KINGDOM
n.brooks@cordah.com

Thomas M. Brooks
Director
Biodiversity Analysis
Center for Applied Biodiversity Science
Conservation International
Washington, DC, U.S.A.
t.brooks@conservation.org

Bill Burnham
The Peregrine Fund
5668 W. Flying Hawk Lane
Boise, ID 83709, U.S.A.
bburnham@peregrinefund.org

Kurt Burnham
The Peregrine Fund
High Arctic Institute
5668 W. Flying Hawk Lane
Boise, ID 83709, U.S.A.
kurt@peregrinefund.org

Alberto Búrquez
Instituto de Ecología, UNAM
Estación Regional Noroeste
Apdo. Postal 1354
83000 Hermosillo, Sonora, MEXICO
montijo@servidor.unam.mx

Jim Cannon
Senior Director
Resource Economics Department
Conservation International
Washington, DC, U.S.A.
j.cannon@conservation.org

Jose Maria Cardoso da Silva
Diretor para a Amazônia
Conservation International-Brasil
Av. Nazaré 541/Sala 310
66035-170
Belém, PA, BRAZIL
jmc.silva@uol.com.br
j.silva@conservation.org.br

Haroldo F. Castro
Vice President
International Communications
Conservation International
Washington, DC, U.S.A.
h.castro@conservation.org

Gonzalo Castro
The World Bank
1818 H Street, NW
Washington, DC 20433, U.S.A.
GCastro@worldbank.org

Roberto Cavalcanti
Instituto de Ciencias Biológicas
Universidade de Brasilia, DF, BRAZIL
rbrandão@cic.unb.br

Gerardo Ceballos
Instituto de Ecología, UNAM
Apdo. Postal 70-275
04510 Mexico City, MEXICO
Gceballo@toluca.podernet.com.mx

Emmanuel Chindumayo
Department of Biological Sciences
The University of Zambia
PO Box 32379, Lusaka, ZAMBIA
echindumayo@natsci.unza.zm

Costas Christ
Senior Director-Ecotourism
Conservation International
Washington, DC, U.S.A.
c.christ@Conservation.org

Jenny Chun
Conservation International
Washington, DC, U.S.A.
j.chun@conservation.org

Gabriel Crowley
Queensland Parks and Wildlife Service
and School of Tropical Biology
James Cook University
PO Box 2066
Cairns, Queensland 4870, AUSTRALIA
Gabriel.Crowley@env.qld.gov.au

Luis Dávalos
Coordinador HCI
Conservation International-Peru
Ave. Pezet 1970
Magdalena del Mar, Lima 17, PERU
l.davalos@conservation.org

Monica Díaz
Noble Oklahoma Museum of Natural History
University of Oklahoma
Norman, OK 73072, U.S.A.
mdiaz@ou.edu

Crewenna I. Dymond
School of Geography and Centre
for Biodiversity and Conservation
University of Leeds
Leeds, LS2 9JT, UNITED KINGDOM
pgcd@geography.leeds.ac.uk.edu

Farouk El-Baz
Director
Center for Remote Sensing
Boston University
725 Commonwealth Avenue
Boston, MA 02215, U.S.A.
farouk@bu.edu

Mike Evans
BirdLife International
Wellbrook Court
Girton Road
Cambridge CB3 0NA, UNITED KINGDOM
mike.evans@birdlife.org.uk

Exequiel Ezcurra
Instituto Nacional de Ecología, Semarnat
Ave. Periférico Sur 5000
Col. Insurgentes Cuicuilco
Delegación Coyoacán
04530 Mexico City, MEXICO
eezcurra@ine.gob.mx

Knud Falk
Danish Polar Center
Strandgade 100 H, DK-1401
Copenhagen, DENMARK
kf@dpc.dk

Lisa Famolare
Guianas Regional Program
Conservation International
Washington, DC, U.S.A.
l.famolare@conservation.org

J. Michael Fay
Expeditions Council
The National Geographic Society
1145 17th St. NW, 4th floor
Washington, DC 20036, U.S.A.
MFay@ngs.org
www.savethecongo.org

Ana Liz Flores
Conservation International Venezuela
Avenida las Acacias, Edif. Torre La Previsora
Piso 15, Oficina 15-1
Los Caobos
Caracas 1040, VENEZUELA
analizflores@hotmail.com

Adrian Forsyth
Director of Biodiversity Science
Gordon and Betty Moore Foundation
adrian.forsyth@moore.org
www.moore.org
and
Amazon Conservation Association
President
1834 Jefferson Place NW
Washington, DC 20036, U.S.A.
adrianforsyth@email.msn.com

Steffen M. Fritz
GIS specialist
Global Vegetation Monitoring Unit
Joint Research Centre of the European
Commission
TP 440, I-21020 Ispra (VA), ITALY
steffen.fritz@jrc.it

Peter Frost
Institute of Environmental Studies
University of Zimbabwe
PO Box MP 167, Mount Pleasant
Harare, ZIMBABWE
pfrost@science.uz.ac.zw

Stephen Garnett
Queensland Parks and Wildlife Service
and School of Tropical Biology
James Cook University
PO Box 2066
Cairns, Queensland 4870, AUSTRALIA
Stephen.Garnett@env.qld.gov.au

Claude Gascon
Senior Vice President
Field Support Division
Conservation International
Washington, DC, U.S.A.
c.gascon@conservation.org

Bárbara Goettsch
Departamento de Botánica
Laboratorio de Cactología
Instituto de Biología
Instituto de Ecología, UNAM
04510 Mexico City, MEXICO
bgoettsch@yahoo.com

Héctor González
Departamento de Arqueología y Museología
Universidad de Tarapacá, casilla 6-D
Arica, CHILE
hgonzale@uta.cl

Marianne Guerin-McManus
Vice President
Global Conservation Fund
Conservation International
Washington, DC, U.S.A.
m.guerin-mcmanus@conservation.org

Rebecca Ham
Research Fellow
Center for Applied Biodiversity Science
Conservation International
Washington, DC, U.S.A.
r.ham@conservation.org

John Hanks
Conservation International
Cape Town Regional Support Office
Kirstenbosch National Botanical Garden
Private Bag X7,
Claremont 7735, SOUTH AFRICA
hanksppt@iafrica.com

Guillermo Harris
Wildlife Conservation Society
Southern Cone
J.A. Roca 1882 (C.C. 119), Puerto Madryn
Chubut 9120, ARGENTINA
gharris@satlink.com.ar

Mónica Harris
Coordinator for the Pantanal Corridor
Rua Eduardo Santos Pereira, 1550 - Sala 16
79020-170 Campo Grande, MS, BRAZIL
m.harris@conservation.org.br

John A. Hart
Senior Scientist
International Programs
Wildlife Conservation Society
Bronx, NY 10460, U.S.A.
johnhartwcs@aol.com

Héctor M. Hernández
Director
Instituto de Biología, UNAM
3er circuito exterior s/n a un costado del
Jardín Botánico. Ciudad Universitaria
Apartado Postal 70-233
04510 Mexico City, MEXICO
hmhm@servidor.unam.mx

Charles Hutchinson
Conservation International-Suriname
Kromme Elleboogstraat 20
Paramaribo, SURINAME
c.hutchinson@conservation.org

Víctor Hugo Inchausty
Director Técnico
Conservation International-Bolivia
Calle Pinilla 291
La Paz, BOLIVIA
vinchausty@conservation.org.bo

Roland Kays
Curator of Mammals
New York State Museum
CEC 3140
Albany, NY 12230, U.S.A.
www.nysm.nysed.gov/WildSci

M. Monirul H. Khan
Wildlife Research Group
Dept. of Anatomy
University of Cambridge
Downing Street, Cambridge
CB2 3DY, UNITED KINGDOM
tiger_monirul@yahoo.com
and
109 West Akurtakur
Tangail 1900, BANGLADESH

William R. Konstant
Special Projects Director
Conservation International
Washington, DC, U.S.A.
b.konstant@conservation.org

Cyril Kormos
Senior Director
Program Management
Conservation International
Washington DC, U.S.A.
c.kormos@conservation.org

Peter J. Kristensen
Senior Director of Operations
Asia-Pacific Division
Conservation International
Washington, DC, U.S.A.
p.kristensen@conservation.org

Gaikovina R. Kula
Executive Director
Melanesia Program
Conservation International
PO Box 106,
Waigani, PAPUA NEW GUINEA
g.kula@conservation.org

Thomas E. Lacher, Jr.
Department of Wildlife and Fisheries Sciences
2258 TAMU
Texas A&M University
College Station, TX 77843-2258, U.S.A.
tlacher@tamu.edu
and
Center for Applied Biodiversity Science
Conservation International
Washington, DC, U.S.A.

Olivier Langrand
Vice President
Conservation International
Africa and Madagascar Division
Washington, DC, U.S.A.
o.langrand@conservation.org

Nicholas P. Lapham
Field Support Division
Conservation International
Washington, DC, U.S.A.
n.lapham@conservation.org

Fausto López
Conservation International-Ecuador
Coruña 17-54 y Noboa Camaño
Quito, ECUADOR
f.lopez@conservation.org

Reinaldo Francisco Ferreira Lourival
Regional Director for the Pantanal
Rua Eduardo Santos Pereira, 1550-Sala 16
79020-170 Campo Grande, MS, BRAZIL
r.lourival@conservation.org.br

Jeffrey E. Lovich
Research Manager
USGS, Western Ecological Research Center
7801 Folsom Blvd., Suite 101
Sacramento, CA 95826, U.S.A.
www.werc.usgs.gov/cc/lovich.htm

Robert Lovich
Wildlife Biologist
AC/S Environmental Security
Box 555008
Marine Corps Base
Camp Pendleton, CA 92055-5008, U.S.A.
lovichre@pendleton.usmc.mil

Innocent L. Magole
Country Director
Conservation International-Botswana
Private Bag 132, Maun, Botswana
i.magole@conservation.org
ci.okavango@info.bw

David Mallon
3 Acre Street
Glossop
Derbyshire SK13 8JS, United Kingdom
d.mallon@zoo.co.uk

Stanley A.J. Malone
Director
Conservation International-Suriname
Kromme Elleboogstraat 20
Paramaribo, SURINAME
CIMalone@sr.net

Dr. Michael A. Mares
Sam Noble Oklahoma Museum of Natural
History and Department of Zoology
University of Oklahoma
Norman, OK 73072, U.S.A.
mamares@ou.edu

Pablo Marquet
Centro de Estudios Avanzados
en Ecología y Biodiversidad
and Departamento de Ecología Pontificia
Universidad Católica de Chile
Casilla 114-D
Santiago CP 6513677 CHILE
pmarquet@genes.bio.puc.cl
www.bio.puc.cl/pmarque1.htm
www.bio.puc.cl/caseb

Vance G. Martin
President
The WILD Foundation
PO Box 1380, Ojai, CA 93024, U.S.A.
vance@wild.org

Roderic B. Mast
Vice President
Conservation International
Washington, DC, U.S.A.
r.mast@conservation.org

Albert J. Meier
Department of Biology
Western Kentucky University
Bowling Green, KY 42101, U.S.A.
albert.meier@wku.edu

Adam Mekler
Curator Amazonian Art
Houston Museum
Locksley Dr.
Pasadena, CA, 91107 U.S.A.

Eric Mellink
CICESE, Departamento de Ecología, km 107
Carr. Tijuana-Ensenada
22800 Ensenada, B.C., MEXICO
emellink@cicese.mx

Freddy Miranda
Responsable SIG
Conservation International-Bolivia
Calle Pinilla 291
La Paz, BOLIVIA
fmiranda@conservation.org.bo

Cristina G. Mittermeier
432 Walker Rd.
Great Falls, VA 22066, U.S.A.
cgmittermeier@aol.com

John C. Mittermeier
Phillips Exeter Academy
20 Main
Exeter, New Hampshire, 03833 U.S.A.
jmittermeier@exeter.edu

Russell A. Mittermeier
President
Conservation International
Washington, DC, U.S.A.
r.mittermeier@conservation.org

Douglas M. Muchoney
Center for Applied Biodiversity Science
Conservation International
Washington, DC 20036, U.S.A.
d.muchoney@conservation.org

Stephen D. Nash
Scientific Illustrator
Conservation International
Department of Anatomical Sciences
Academic Tower A, T-8, Room 045
Health Sciences Center
SUNY at Stony Brook, NY 11794-8081, U.S.A.
snash@mail.som.sunysb.edu

Reggy Nelson
Conservation International-Suriname
Kromme Elleboogstraat 20
Paramaribo, SURINAME
r.nelson@conservation.org

Andrew J. Noss
Associate Conservation Zoologist
Wildlife Conservation Society-Bolivia
Casilla 6272
Santa Cruz, BOLIVIA
anoss@infonet.com.bo

Erwin Palacios
Carrera 13 No. 71-41
Bogotá, COLOMBIA
palacioserwin@hotmail.com

Sonal Pandya
Carbon Offsets Program Manager
Center for Environmental Leadership
in Business
Conservation International
Washington DC, U.S.A.
s.pandya@conservation.org

Eduardo Peters
Instituto Nacional de Ecología, Semarnat
Ave. Periférico Sur 5000
Col. Insurgentes Cuicuilco
Delegación Coyoacán
04530 Mexico City, MEXICO
edpeters@ine.gob.mx

John Pickering
711 Biological Sciences Building
University of Georgia
Athens, GA 30602-2602, U.S.A.
pick@discoverlife.org
www.discoverlife.org/who/Pickering,_John.hml

John Pilgrim
Center for Applied Biodiversity Science
Conservation International
Washington DC, U.S.A.
j.pilgrim@conservation.org

Raquel Pinto
Equipo de Estudios de Ecosistemas de Niebla
Dalmacia 3251
Iquique, CHILE
raquelpinto@entelchile.net

Carlos F. Ponce del Prado
Vicepresidente Residente
Conservation International-Peru
Ave. Pezet 1970
Magdalena del Mar
Lima 17, PERU
c.ponce@conservation.org

Glenn T. Prickett
Senior Vice President and Executive Director
Center for Environmental Leadership
in Business
Conservation International
Washington DC, U.S.A.
g.prickett@conservation.org

Guido R. Rahr III
President
The Wild Salmon Center
721 NW 9th, Portland, Oregon 97209, U.S.A.
grahr@wildsalmoncenter.org

Richard Rice
Chief Economist
Center for Applied Biodiversity Science
Conservation International
Washington, DC, U.S.A.
d.rice@conservation.org

Jesus A. Rivas
5105 Trenton Lane
Knoxville TN 37920, U.S.A.
anaconda@prodigy.net
http://pages.prodigy.net/anaconda

Patricio Robles Gil
Agrupación Sierra Madre, S.C.
Ave. Primero de Mayo 249
San Pedro de los Pinos
03800 Mexico City, MEXICO
asumpc@infosel.net.mx

Roberto Roca
Vice President
Executive Director, Andean Regional Program
Conservation International
Washington, DC, U.S.A.
r.roca@conservation.org

José Vicente Rodríguez
Conservation International-Colombia
Carrera 13 No. 71-41
Bogotá, COLOMBIA
jvrm@tutopia.com

Karen Ross
Conservation International
Southern Africa Program
c/o Kirstenbosch Botanical Gardens
P. Bag X7,
Claremont 7735, SOUTH AFRICA
k.ross@conservation.org

José Vicente Rueda Almonacid
Coordinador
Evaluaciones Ecológicas Rápidas
Conservation International-Colombia
Carrera 13 No. 71-41
Bogotá, COLOMBIA
jvrueda@yahoo.com

Anthony B. Rylands
Senior Director, Conservation Biology
Center for Applied Biodiversity Science
Conservation International
Washington, DC, U.S.A.
a.rylands@conservation.org

Calogero Santoro
Departamento de Arqueología y Museología
Universidad de Tarapacá, Casilla 6-D
Arica, CHILE
csantoro@uta.cl

Robert Schmidt
Dept. of Geological Sciences
University of Texas, El Paso
El Paso, TX 79968, U.S.A.
schmidt@geo.utep.edu

Major General Joseph G. Singh
Executive Director
Conservation International-Guyana
266 Forshaw Street, Queenstown
Georgetown, GUYANA
j.singh@conservation.org

Vivien G. Standen
Departamento de Arqueología y Museología
Universidad de Tarapacá, Casilla 6-D
Arica, CHILE
vstanden@uta.cl

Gregory S. Stone
Vice President
Global Marine Programs
New England Aquarium
Central Wharf
Boston, MA 02110, U.S.A.
Gstone@neaq.org

Simon Stuart
Senior Director
SSC/CABS Biodiversity Assessment Unit
Center for Applied Biodiversity Science
Conservation International
Washington, DC, U.S.A.
s.stuart@conservation.org

Cheri Sugal
1735 Corcoran Street, NW
Washington, DC 20009, U.S.A.
cheri_sugal@yahoo.com

Jatna Supriatna
Executive Director
Conservation International-Indonesia
Jl. Taman Margasatwa 61
Jakarta 12540, INDONESIA
j.supriatna@conservation.org

Jorgen B. Thomsen
Senior Vice President and Executive Director
Critical Ecosystem Partnership Fund
Conservation International
Washington, DC, U.S.A.
j.thomsen@conservation.org

Jonathan Timberlake
Biodiversity Foundation for Africa
PO Box FM730
Famona, Bulawayo, ZIMBABWE.
timber@telconet.co.zw
timberj@mweb.co.zw

Annette Tjon Sie Fat
Conservation International-Suriname
Kromme Elleboog Straat No. 20
Paramaribo, SURINAME
CISgravn@sr.net

Michael Totten
Senior Director of Climate
and Water Programs
Center for Environmental Leadership
in Business
Conservation International
Washington, DC, U.S.A.
m.totten@conservation.org

Ambassador Willem Udenhout
Executive Director
Conservation International-Suriname
Kromme Elleboogstraat 20
Paramaribo, SURINAME
CISgravn@sr.net

Marc van Roosmalen
Pesquisador Titular
Departamento de Botânica
Instituto Nacional de Pesquisas
da Amazônia (INPA)
Caixa Postal 478
69083-000 Manaus
Amazonas, BRAZIL
roosmalen@internext.com.br

Neville A. Waldron
Director
Conservation International-Guyana
266 Forshaw Street, Queenstown
Georgetown, GUYANA
n.waldron@conservation.org

Robert Waller
GIS Specialist
Center for Applied Biodiversity Science
Conservation International
Washington DC, U.S.A.
r.waller@conservation.org

Fiesta Warinwa
New Sudan Wildlife Society
PO Box 8874-00100
Nairobi, KENYA
fwarinwa2002@yahoo.com

Lee J.T. White
Wildlife Conservation Society
Conservation Scientist
SEGC BP 7847 Libreville, GABON
wcs@compuserve.com
wcsgabon@assala.net

Ian Whyte
Specialist Scientist: Large Herbivores
Kruger National Park
IanW@parks-sa.co.za

Philip Winter
PO Box 47796
Nairobi, KENYA
qmmpew@botsnet.bw

John Woinarski
Parks and Wildlife Commission
of the Northern Territory
PO Box 496 Palmerston,
Northern Territory, 0831, AUSTRALIA
john.woinarski@nt.gov.au

Kay Yatskievych
Coordinating Editor
Flora of the Venezuelan Guayana
Missouri Botanical Garden
4344 Shaw Blvd.
St. Louis, MO 63110, U.S.A.
Kay.Yatskievych@mobot.org

Horacio Zeballos
Asociación Naturaleza y Desarrollo
Jorge Polar 308, Miraflores
Arequipa, PERU
hzeballo@genes.bio.puc.cl

ACKNOWLEDGEMENTS

First and foremost, the authors would like to thank CEMEX for supporting the production of this book, and for their interest in biodiversity conservation in Mexico and around the world. The books they have produced in collaboration with Agrupación Sierra Madre over the past decade have been of the highest quality and have done a great deal to further interest in conservation both in Mexico and internationally. Without their continued support and concern, this book would never have been possible.

Thanks also to the Board of Directors of Conservation International (CI) for their incredible involvement in and support for CI's global activities. Special thanks to Gordon Moore, Chairman of CI's Executive Committee, for writing the Foreword to this book, and to Peter Seligmann, Chairman and CEO of CI, for his Prologue.

The authors and contributors to this book wish to acknowledge the following people and institutions, who provided information essential to the writing of these chapters. Without their critical inputs, preparation of this book would not have been possible. They include: Robert G. Bailey (USDA Forest Service), Spencer Beebe (Ecotrust), Art Bogan, Vernon Booth, David Boufford (Harvard University Herbaria), Don Broadley, Luc Brouillet (Université de Montréal), Cristina Cabello, Shannon Carlton (CI-South Africa), Steven Chown (University of Stellenbosch), Don Church, Isabelle Combès, Dave Connell (Australian Antarctic Data Centre), David Cumming, Jen D'Amico (WWF-U.S.), Brian da Silva (USAID), David Evans (Mala Mala Private Game Reserve), Patrick Fisher (Sam Noble Oklahoma Museum of Natural History), Robert Fisher (U.S. Geological Survey), Lee Fitzgerald (Texas A&M University), Kathleen A. Galvin (Colorado State University), Alan Gardiner, George F. Gee (U.S. Geological Survey), Ian Gill (Ecotrust-Canada), Andrea Grill, Jesús Guerrero, Art Harris (University of Texas at El Paso), Chris Hill, Cathryn A. Hoyt (Chihuahuan Desert Research Institute), Natalie Jackson (University of Tasmania), Mohsen Jalali, Derek Johnson (Canadian Northern Forest Research Centre), Harrison Kojwang (WWF-SARPO), John Lamoreux (WWF-U.S.), Greg Leach (Parks and Wildlife Commission of the Northern Territory), Daniela Maestro (CI-DC), Brian Marshall, Terence S. McCarthy, Ray Méndez, Fátima Mereles, Tom Millicken (TRAFFIC), John Morrison (WWF-U.S.), Peter Mundy, National Geographic Society, National Science Foundation, Gonzalo Navarro, John Neldner (Queensland Herbarium), Craig Packer (University of Minnesota), Helen Peat (British Antarctic Survey), Hugo Pimentel, Norm Platnick (American Museum of Natural History), Lee Poston (WWF-U.S.), Ekatherina Rachkovskaya (Kazakhstan Botanical Institute), Peter Raven (Missouri Botanic Garden), Sam Noble Oklahoma Museum of Natural History, Jan Schipper (WWF-U.S.), Herman H. Shugart Jr. (University of Virginia), Line Sørensen (ZMUC), Ali Stattersfield (BirdLife International), Holly Strand (WWF-U.S.), Miguel Treffault Rodrigues (Universidad de São Paulo), Peter Uetz (Research Center Karlsruhe), Kristen Walker (CI-DC), Margaret Williams (WWF-U.S.), and Edward C. Wolf (Ecotrust).

Special thanks to Antonio Bolívar and all the staff at Redacta for their valuable collaboration in the editorial preparation of this series, as well as to Martín Jon García-Urtiaga in the original design of these books.

Thanks also to Joaquín Ardura, Juan Ignacio Bremer, Bill Broyles, Carlos Castillo, Comunidad Seri Conca'ac, Miguel Ángel Díaz Castorena, Diana Doan-Crider, Jack Dykinga, Margaret Dykinga, Billy Finan, Nelly Finan, Steve Freligh, Rafael García Zuazua, David Garza Lagüera, Vico Gutiérrez, Fernando Holschneider, Sandy Lanham, Raymond Lee, Rurik List, Jesús López García, Carlos Manterola, Billy Pat McKinney, Bonnie McKinney, Dolores Mestre de Robles Gil, Doris Osuna, Sandra Osuna, Rosa Osuna de Llano, Guillermo Osuna Sáenz, Guillermo Osuna Villar, Raúl Pérez Madero, Javier Robles Gil Mestre, Patricia Rojo, Elvira Rojo de López, Víctor Sánchez, Rodolfo de los Santos, Sonoran Park Friends, Texas Park and Wildlife, and Jonás Villalobos.

Last but not least, special thanks to Shawn Concannon for helping to support the research behind this analysis, to Ella Outlaw and Jill Lucena for their work in compiling the massive Literature Cited list, and to Stephen Nash and Álvaro Couttolenc for preparing the maps that illustrate each chapter.

Finally, we would like to dedicate this book to the memory of Dolores Martínez viuda de Cabello, Cristina's Grandmother, who lived her entire 101-year-long life in Saltillo, Coahuila, the heart of the Chihuahuan Desert Wilderness, and who died during the editing of this book. May the desert she so loved remain wild.

PRODUCTION
Agrupación Sierra Madre, S.C.

EDITORIAL COORDINATION
María Luisa Madrazo Bolívar

GRAPHIC DESIGN, PHOTO EDITING, AND PRINTING SUPERVISION
Patricio Robles Gil   Juan Carlos Burgoa

COMPILATION OF MANUSCRIPTS
Cristina Goettsch Mittermeier

EDITORIAL REVISION AND CORRECTION
María Luisa Madrazo Bolívar   Susan Beth Kapilian

EDITORIAL ASSISTANCE
Roxana Vega
Mina Salinas

TECHNICAL SUPPORT
Oswaldo Barrera
Eugenia Pallares
Elena León

MAPS
Stephen Nash
Álvaro Couttolenc

On page 558, Chimpanzee (Pan troglodytes), *Gabon.* © **Cyril Ruoso**/*BIOS*
On page 569, Noel Kempff Mercado National Park, Bolivia. © **Willy Kenning**
On page 570, Huli man, Papua New Guinea. © **Patricia Rojo**
On page, 576, Maasai warriors, Kenya. © **Tom Brakefield**/*DRK Photo*